TRANSLATING Coaching
Codes of Practice

Other books in the Series:

Much Ado About COACHING (Rydwairay)

Insights from the Leading Edges of Everyday Practitioners

Reviews

5 star review in Coaching at Work, *"Having been in coaching and mentoring for three decades, it takes a unique text to stop me in my tracks and go 'wow!' This book does that. It is written with heart and passion by 20 coaches who share their insights in the form of poetry and prose in of various lengths and styles. This diversity is unsurprising as these are mini autoethnographies drawn from blogs posted over a two-year period on the good coach. Put simply these coaches talk about what they really do, offer opinions on the field and discuss what they care deeply about. Their intention is to reflect upon their practice, share this with peers and to validate their work. The desire is to push back the boundaries of the coaching frontier, with integrity, they do just that.*

It is a true collaborative and multi-vocal work. It is creative, bold and courageous and should be the 'go to' title (and blog) for any aspiring practitioner who is about to embark on coach training. IT may also inspire experienced practitioners to step-forward and write about their own experiences of life in the field for the blog. In doing so this will help to build a much richer picture of what is happening beyond the plethora of text books that often tell us what to do rather than capture the lived experience of what, day-to-day, it means to coach and be coached."

"Translating Coaching Codes of Practice is a grown-up, mature book that puts the finger on the pulse on what coaching is, in all its diversity and richness."

"I found this book to be very accessible. As a Health Professional, it made me appreciate how much I use coaching in my client relationships. I have never seen it this way before. It's stimulated me to reflect more coherently on what I do, with some ideas and tips I've taken away."

"I found this book very impressive and richly affirming; stimulating and thought provoking, with plenty of practical tips and original insights for review. ... I do not feel it's a one-off read through book. Rather it is something that I can see myself coming back to frequently as a regular reference point because of the very rich and diverse menu of material on offer in this book."

"This book is lucid and serves as a good primer to the world of executive coaching and its intricacies. The content is approachable and jargon-free. Given that the contributors come with experience in different industries, the book gives a good bird-eye's view of how executive coaching gets rendered across both work as well as life. Other writers have brought in real – life examples from their work which makes their ideas even more relatable. One might at times get tempted to experiment some of those thought processes at work or at home."

"What a roller coaster - I found myself violently agreeing and disagreeing in equal measure, challenged by the various theories and sharing in the apparent frustrations of the authors as they try to define and capture this thing called 'coaching'. But that's exactly the way it should be. Every coach knows what works - for them - and that's the point of the book. Practitioners putting their practices out there for all to agree/disagree with based on personal preference or experience. I loved the lack of conclusions that sense that there is so much more to learn and share."

TRANSLATING Coaching Codes of Practice

Leading the way into the personal knowledge bases of everyday practitioners

EDITED BY

Yvonne Thackray

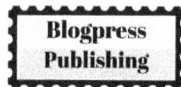

Blogpress
Publishing

Most of the material in this book first appeared on the World Wide Web in 2016-2017 on www.the-goodcoach.com

First Printing: 2017

ISBN: 978-0-9954895-5-4

Published by Blogpress Publishing: London. Hong Kong.

Special discounts are available on quantity purchases by corporations, associations, educators, and others. For details, contact the publisher at www.blogpresspublishing.org

CONTENTS

CHAPTER 2: MAKING SENSE OF COACHING EXPERIENCES WITH EXTERNAL REFERENCES

CHAPTER 3: MAKING SENSE OF COACHING PRACTICE FROM PROFESSIONAL, AND PERSONAL, EXPERIENCES

PART 2: CUTTING EDGE: INVESTIGATING PATTERNS FROM PRACTITIONER EXPERIENCES

CHAPTER 4: LEADERSHIP

CHAPTER 5: TAKING A COACHING APPROACH IN ORGANISATIONS

CHAPTER 6: BOUNDARIES, CONTRACTS AND CONTRACTING

CHAPTER 7: INTUITION

CHAPTER 8: QUALITIES OF ATTENTION

PART 3: OPPORTUNITIES AT THE COMPETITIVE EDGE: BRANDING, PROFESSIONAL DEVELOPMENT AND SOCIETAL NEEDS

CHAPTER 9: BRANDING AND PROFESSIONAL DEVELOPMENT

CHAPTER 10: CONNECTING COACHING TO SOCIETAL NEEDS

PART 4: MOVING FORWARD, WHAT NEXT?

CHAPTER 11: PRACTITIONER RESEARCH

PREFACE

THE GOOD COACH IS GROWING AND DEVELOPING TOWARDS BECOMING A PRACTITIONER RESEARCH INSTITUTION WHOSE CORE PROPOSITION IS TO UNDERSTAND WHAT IS COACHING.

Having the opportunity to year-on-year publish a new book as part of the 'Translating Coaching Codes of Practice' series gives the good coach community both validation and confidence that the good coach approach is making positive headway in delivering a sustainable and robust approach that is slowly reaching its vision; to touch 1 percent of the global population with inspiring, and effective, coaching conversations.

We believe it is only through the rich and diverse contributions from each and every coaching practitioner's to willingly engage in and share their personal experiences of professional practice that makes this project possible. Altogether we make up the good coach community. A space for experienced, as well as mature, practitioners to individually benefit from the principles underpinning the good coach, and a place where we are all collectively contributing through the good coach to a practitioner knowledge base that serves the broader community.

Representing the community, we bring together these individual reports and accounts from the front line of every day coaching practitioners - whether as narratives, stories, cases, and other ways of professional reporting. Collectively, they begin to provide evidence that more fairly represents the diversity of approaches that exist. Each coaching practitioner is unique, with their own patterns of behaviour that they recognise as demonstrating their codes of practice from their personal knowledge base formed from all of their experiences.

POSITIONING THE GOOD COACH ALONGSIDE TRADITIONAL INSTITUTES KNOWN FOR KNOWLEDGE CREATION

In Book 2, *Insights from the leading edges of every day practitioners*, we shared an example of technological ingenuity from the field of biosciences the Human Genome Project (HGP): an ambitious international effort to sequence the three billion nucleotides within thirteen years that would revolutionize health and welfare benefits. As the research progressed, less than 3 percent of the DNA of a human genome was sequenced whilst the remaining 97 percent was labelled 'junk', unfortunately, by no less a molecular luminary than Francis

Crick, co-discover of DNA's double-helical structure. The term initially suggested that there was a lot of non-relevant material, however as later studies progressed they turned out to be a long way from junk and morphed into the ENCODE project!

For the field of coaching this is a useful example of a cautionary tale. In traditional science, particularly natural science (which HGP belongs to), strict laboratory conditions and methodologies are fundamental in how they describe, predict and understand natural 'stable' phenomena. Their disciplines are typically supported by a knowledge base that incorporates mechanisms such as peer review and repeatability of findings to ensure the validity of scientific advances. This has reached a level of efficiency after thousands of years of debate and consensus-building. And yet, any scientist, or expert in the field, who attempts to suggest that they've fully understood the phenomena and that knowledge is now complete are quickly exposed.

In coaching, we're still in the very early stages of articulating, identifying, understanding and appreciating which knowledge is more relevant, and directly contributes to, enabling our practice. There is still more to learn, explore and be curious about. Setting arbitrary boundaries (or what scientists unfortunately referred to as 'junk') of what is considered to be the real knowledge base for coaching in this multidimensional and multifaceted world dominates coaching. This is why the good coach continues to choose to adopt an approach to ownership that is in-line with best practice for achieving real independence (similar to those traditional institutions that values independent knowledge creation). Furthermore, there are big implications for an approach that aims to respect the diversity of codes of practice of each practitioner, across a very diverse range of circumstances

Coaching is, by nature, dynamic from each moment to moment. Attempting to apply a traditional scientific approach that starts with isolating factors that can then be tested to get to some acceptable results, is ambitious. It creates a 'superficial' understanding of coaching, which is actually complex and messy. Instead a more open and inclusive approach is required that allows more opportunities to connect those words with (patterns of) behaviours that more accurately captures how each practitioner makes coaching work for them in their context. With time, and as recognizable patterns begin to emerge, it provides us with opportunities to start exploring, debating and building consensus as a community from a common framework.

TAKING A MORE OPEN APPROACH TO PRACTITIONER RESEARCH, THIS HAS LED US TO OUR THIRD BOOK IN OUR SERIES:

Translating Coaching Codes of Practice - Leading the way into the personal knowledge bases of everyday practitioners.

An edited volume from a series of blogs first published on the good coach.

Over thirty established practitioners (both new and regular contributors) share their insights, experiences and patterns of how they are making a difference through their coaching approach. They may be working from within an organisation - as a manager, leader, internal coach (individual, group and/or team) - or from a portfolio of service contracts with professionals (individual, group and/or team) in various organisations.

Together with our current practitioner-authors, it has led the good coach to its most important insight, even confirmation, to date, as we can show in this publication: the leading edge in practice comes from every day practitioners who draw on their experiences and skills, whilst adapting relevant theories where appropriate, that constitutes their personal knowledge base.

Each coaching practitioner speaks from:

- **A diversity of contexts:** They work in a different context and in different locations around the world. They have developed their credibility and reputation for delivering a professionally tailored learning space that meets the objectives of other stakeholders involved in their market.

- **Their unique Practice:** They share how they are leading the way in "making it work". Their practices are typically hard for another individual to fully replicate because they have their own words infused with their own personal meaning to talk about what they are doing.

- **Setting their standards of practice:** They demonstrate how they are leading the way in being "fit-for-practice". This involves, in various degrees, comfortably engaging in the words used by their clients, diagnosing the individual and the situation to appropriately engage at the client's level of readiness, a willingness to provide alternative and independent perspectives, and to ask the right questions, all whilst continuously creating and maintaining the conditions for coaching.

- **Connecting their knowledge to others:** They readily draw from their personal knowledge base that connects their living experiences with, and where appropriate, to a broad array of currently available knowledge from the wider context. The breadth of their personal knowledge base is also compelling because it suggests that the current resources for finding relevant coaching knowledge is still too simple for the realities which practitioners operate in.

LEADING THE PROCESS OF FORMING PRACTITIONER KNOWLEDGE. EVOLVING THE BENEFITS OF SELF-REPORTING TO SELF, COMMUNITY AND THE MARKET THROUGH BLOGS.

We continue to be interested in finding those patterns that may eventually lead to similarities from the realities of the diverse practice that already exist. We're not interested in rushing to 'a final solution'. We're still in those early stages of learning and appreciating the unique differences between each other's practice that's covered sweepingly under this broad term 'coaching'. The level of detail required to begin reaching consensus particularly around definitions amongst a small group, let alone the 1 percent of coaching practitioners the good coach is looking to engage with, makes this a long-term project.

All the practitioners that choose to engage with the good coach are contracting to engage in a meaningful and rigorous process that helps them to continue to make sense of how they practice as they write up and report on it through the medium of a blog/blog-article.

The idea of Blog remains essential as a form of personal written expression; to talk about their practice, to increasingly want to write about their practice in the wider context of the field, and other coaching practice as they know it.

The various parts of Practice can be reported in different ways,

- Key events that have been important experiences that have influenced how they apply their coaching approach,

- Immediate situations or challenges they are facing in their current assignments,

- Reviewing past situations in order to improve their current and future practice,

- Patterns of behaviours as a result of an accumulation of learning experiences over a period of time (a month, six months, a year, even a life time).

Importantly, it is how they describe these events-patterns through their use of 'I'. Each practitioner-author has a different starting point as they engage in their reporting yet what is consistent, and becomes apparent for all, is acknowledging who the real audience is for their piece.

Themselves!

Writing has important advantages. For example it creates a mechanism of expression that has proven to be have important advantages for sharing;

as well as an important basis for proposing and agreeing meaning for others; and to begin engaging in broader conversations that could eventually lead to building consensus.

This process of writing is also evolving in the material our community is collecting:

- **The initial focus:** Our authors value practitioner knowledge as a means of progressing their understanding and use of coaching. That is why the first draft is for the author.

- **The second draft is for the good coach community**: Here, our central, core group of blogatorial members help to represent the good coach community and provide important editorial (blogitorial) support

- **The published version, through the good coach web site distribution, is for the much wider audiences of readers**: Feedback from wider audiences again illustrates the wide range of interests in the wider community for what catches their attention.

We have also directly received positive feedbacks from the practitioners themselves that the benefits of writing about their practice has helped them to deepen their awareness, confidence and reflection around their client work. A greater authority over their practice. A usable resource that becomes part of their portfolio and branding in client development, and most importantly it has added to their development as a practitioner.

Moreover, it's through the process of writing that we begin to learn more about the contexts in which coaching takes place, which is more important than the content itself. For eventually, context will be what allows practitioners to more openly compare their practices with others. the good coach encourages practitioner-authors to write about their practice and asks them to more thoroughly consider, explain and ground how their practice is formed from their experiences (some might even call this coaching coaches). And importantly, it incorporates the discipline of providing definitions, as well as revealing all those subtle and significant reciprocating behaviours that are as much as part of the conversation as the words spoken themselves.

DEFINITE PATTERNS IN THE MATERIAL OUR AUTHORS PRODUCE ABOUT THE FIELD OF COACHING OVERALL: SUMMARIZED IN FOUR THEMES AND 8 KEY TRENDS

Curating this 'growing' collection of writings straight from the front lines and those published through the good coach that affords us to share some key trends from applying the good coach approach.

Book 2 referred to '*Insights from the Leading Edges of Everyday Practitioners*'. We consider there is a growing confidence in the way that Coaching practitioners are finding more coherence in their Practices. Albeit while still covering a very broad range of circumstances.

Book 3 refers to '*Leading the way into the personal knowledge bases of everyday practitioners*'. We consider the continued learning, collected from a range of materials, starts with coaching practitioners being the first to acknowledge that this is part of their Practice (and review of their 'fitness-to-practice'). How they are making the most of their experiences in Coaching, as well as progress in establishing the territory where coaching can contribute.

We have grouped the current material into four themes:

1. *Leading Edge: Influences on Practitioner's Learning and Development*
   Part 1 brings together material broadly around the subject of how Practitioners live on their own edges of continually making sense of their coaching circumstances – continually learning and developing their Practice.

2. *Cutting Edge: Investigating patterns from Practitioner Experiences*
   Part 2 focuses more on the challenges of the external conditions that have to be appreciated, and how Practitioners have to marshall their experience of these immediate circumstances.

3. *Opportunities at the Competitive edge: Branding, professional development, societal needs*
   Part 3 talks about how Practitioners also work to link what they are doing to a wider context.

4. *What's next: Practitioner research*
   Finally, Part 4 is a collection of material where Practitioners are thinking forwards, both for themselves, as well as wider ways of connecting, researching further how to make the most of what they bring.

And we share the 8 key trends that has emerged from evolving the good coach process:

1. **Emphasis on actual practice descriptions**. There is a trend towards coaching practitioners using individual examples and cases as representative of their overall approach to practice, and even the shape and identity of their practice.

2. **Detail about the actual context** in a specific case as well as the wider field, with an acceptable level of **disclosure** to the extent that the descriptions are personal rather than over generalized.

3. **Diversity factor** of how authors are increasingly unashamed in expressing their own focus rather than feeling they must conform to some approved focus in how they talk about their practice.

4. **Extraordinary diversity of material**. No two coaches write about the same things because of the lens they are looking through, however, some themes are beginning to show themselves.

5. **Trend towards writing a series on their practice**. They are seeing the personal benefit that far exceeds the simple marketing benefit.

6. **Coaching in an organisational context offers more support**, and gets to a level of coherence that practitioners are interested in, due to the very nature of an organisation's focus on process and output which makes process and output easier to talk about (compared to coaching individuals on a wider basis).

7. **Length**. Practitioners are writing longer pieces because they are beginning to look at their practice, their practice in comparison with others, and giving more attention to some of the wider field.

8. **References** are used as a more overt inclusion of connection to the wider field that's typically used in the traditional sense of reference to available publications in which knowledge basis is formed and some measurement of knowledge formation is possible i.e. by the no. of references to any material across the field.

Importantly, this informs us that there is a growing awareness and deepening of confidence about how much there is still to do in making the most of each coaching practice.

WHERE NEXT:
the good coach aims to continue developing the concept of practitioner research and make it a more accessible approach for everyday practitioners. Broadly speaking the three areas we want to carry on investigating are:

- **The real researchers are the practitioners, themselves.**
  The emphasis being on the practitioners themselves learning to report on their own research - their real-life experiences of applying their coaching approach in their own words - using best practices of reporting from traditional institutions where more formal research is typically carried out. Sharing those experiences through a blog or blog-article emphasizes the expression of a personal view that also consider the audience. It enables practitioners to feel freer to talk about their personal experiences from their practice, and it gives them

the opportunity to write about how they view what they are doing with some depth and understanding.

- **Practitioner research is about exploring the wide range of factors, data, and contexts that better represents the complex reality that each individual lives and works in.**
  It's moving out of the laboratories where isolating factors in stable and simplified conditions dominates. It's all about having the confidence and capacity to describe, predict and understand how each practitioner's personality has learnt to connect with others, particularly those individuals who they work better with, in their situation and context to do good coaching.

- **Validity of practice can thus be measured through those behavioural patterns.**
  They can typically be predicted once the practitioner is aware of how and why they are using them (cause-effect) and shown to produce fairly similar results when those same behaviours are applied across a range of contexts and individuals. Writing about practitioner experiences and observing where similar behavioural patterns emerge across them is where practitioner research really begins to inform and give shape to a practitioner's practice, and how it compares with another coaching practitioner's practice and the wider field of practice.

Each practitioner continues to build their personal knowledge base, and in parallel contributes to building up a quality body of practitioner knowledge that truly represents the diversity of unique practices and leading edges of everyday practitioners. This is where we continue to believe the real knowledge lives. We just have to continue finding ways to get to it that eventually becomes reproducible by others.

ACKNOWLEDGEMENTS

"Never doubt that a small group of thoughtful, committed people can change the world. Indeed, it is the only thing that ever has."

– Anon

I would like to thank everyone who has supported and participated in our third book, in particular Jeremy Ridge and Sue Young (tgc's rock - the blogitorial team), Light Hurley (our formidable proofreader), James Thackray (my husband) and all our contributors - Alan Robertson, Aubrey Rebello, Aurora Aritao, Chris Paterson, Claire Sheldon, Dino Laudato, Doug Montgomery, Geoffrey Ahern, Ian Flanders, Isobel Gray, Jeremy Ridge, Julian Danobetia, Katy Tuncer, K.C. Char, Laci Ritas, Larissa Conte, Laurent Terseur, Lilian Abrams, Lisa W Haydon, Liz Hill-Smith, Lucille Maddalena, Luis San Martin, Lynne Hindmarch, Margaret Chapman-Clarke, Peter Young, Petra Macdougald, R Ramamurthy Krishna, Robbie Swale Rosemary Harper, Sally East, Simon Darnton, Simon Dennis and Sue Young from all over the world. Thank you for entrusting us with their words to continue delivering the good coach's vision.

For me, personally it continues to be a humbling experience to be part of this project. Knowing that each day, in every encounter I have with someone from the good coach community, I learn something new about them, and from them. I'm constantly in awe; how we each show up - always full of vigor and attention - and continue choosing to invest your time to help the good coach deliver its potential, alongside your busy lives. It's because of your genuine attitude that the good coach can maintain its independence and be progressive in its approach. Finally, just as we are about to go to press, it was a huge compliment to hear that we look like a 'professional' community. To hear this level of commendation, from someone I hugely respect and I know doesn't use the word 'professional' lightly - is a real testament to the work carried out voluntary by the operational team and to all the members of the good coach who contribute to the community. My sincerest gratitude and thanks to you all! And of course, they deserve none of the blame for any deficiencies in this final version.

PART 1

Leading Edges: Influences on Practitioner's Learning and Development

CHAPTER 1

MAKING SENSE OF COACHING
EXPERIENCES THROUGH CASES/EVENTS

Appreciating how diagnosis in coaching is best as a collaborative exercise

Jeremy Ridge

want to explore how diagnosis is a central part in coaching, and consider how it operates in my coaching practice. Diagnosis, as a concept, helps to emphasise the need for a careful approach to ensure that large amounts of information are carefully considered. This important information can also best come from multiple sources – hence a collaborative approach. This is applicable not just between coach and coachee, but even in a wider 'peer' process.

I am aware of the considerable focus on coaching 'tools and techniques' but it is useful to review which of these work for me, including the how and the why. From my perspective, coaching tools and techniques still appear to put the emphasis on how the coach should set about seeing things and organising agendas.

Given that the coachee owns and sets the agenda, and arguably holds most of the data about their readiness and capabilities with regard to their agenda, their role in any coaching process or diagnosis is critical.

The inclusion of the term 'diagnosis' is attractive to me due to the care and rigour that can be taken when arriving at a process and outcome in a coaching process.

I also consider that the best approach to collaborative diagnosis between coach and coachee is still the perspectives initiated by Malcolm Knowles' principles of andragogy. Knowles' approach to andragogy or 'adult learning' places the clearest emphasis on the need to focus on the other person's insights about themselves.

1. WHY DIAGNOSIS – SOME OF THE IMPORTANT THEMES IN THE IDEA

DEFINING DIAGNOSIS AS A TERM

The word 'diagnosis' increasingly carries important meaning. It is typically at the centre of established professions, not just the 'people' professions, where the application of knowledge to a particular set of circumstances may need some investigation of:

- What is happening

- What is causing the situation

- What actions there are to take

This suggests an important focus for coaching dialogue.

The origins of the term refer to this idea of knowledge and understanding. The word has come some distance from its origins origins in the English language. Authorities describe it as a combination of 'Gnosis' and 'dia'.

Gnosis refers to

- Gnostic: supposedly revealed knowledge of various spiritual truths, especially that said to have been possessed by ancient Gnostics [ultimately from Greek: knowledge, from gignōskein to know]

  and

- Dia: meaning separating or apart[1]

So the modern meaning is... The identification of the nature and cause of something. This often refers to collecting and sifting through a range of information for its relevance, according to available understanding, toward what action may also be relevant. Coaching may start with an interest in some particular desired outcome (itself often expressed in general terms).

Diagnosis can also be used as either a verb or a noun – both a process for getting to an end; or the end point itself. My interest is in the process of diagnosis involved in coaching and its need to be collaborative.

2. TYPICAL DIAGNOSTIC INFORMATION USED IN EXECUTIVE COACHING

The information that is available for diagnosis in coaching can be huge. This can be true of either broader life matters or of a particular focus in 'executive coaching' – i.e. where a person is making a particular contribution (e.g. in a 'role') in a wider collective effort.

---

[1] Collins English Dictionary – Complete and Unabridged. 2014. 12th Edition. HarperCollins.

My practice often works with people in some form of organisational context. (This can be wider than 'business' organisations; e.g. public or voluntary sector.) An organisational context may make information more available (e.g. a 'role' is typically a description of behaviour). However, broader life matters for a coachee are always a factor as well.

Some typical sources of information:

1. **The boss has spoken!** Many times, such as in executive coaching, the diagnosis is provided by 'the boss'. There are a number of typical ethical dilemmas for coaches in these circumstances.

2. **Wider 'organisational' data performance appraisal/HR policies about current priority development themes.**

3. **360-degree feedback**: Either using a structured questionnaire, or using and including qualitative data from stakeholders, in their own terms (which I prefer).

4. **Other structured data/questionnaires e.g. 'psychometrics[2]'.** Again, the terminology, let alone interpretation carry risks.

5. **The first formal session**: The initial contract may be based on a 'symptom'/output in general terms required. The coaching conversation itself is then a long process of gathering data relevant to understanding.

6. **Working with someone as they perform/behave, through direct observation**. This is more the original basis for coaching, e.g. in sports coaching.

I typically find coaching can involve a mix of each of the above. It often depends on the coachee and their organisation's practices, effective readiness and appreciation of how such sources of data may add value.

3. IMPORTANT THEMES FOR DIAGNOSIS IN COACHING

Many definitions of 'coaching' exist. However, in broad terms coaching is generally seen as how a coach can form a dialogue that adds to the ability of a coachee. The coaching can help the coachee make some changes to their personal and professional circumstances toward benefit.

There are some immediate implications for any diagnosis process.

- **How to start**: Diagnosis raises the key question of where to start as well as where to get to. The coachee may already themselves have a

---

[2] See Lynne Hindmarch in *the good coach* March and May 2016.

PART 1: Leading edge: Influences on Practitioner's Learning and Development

very wide ranging and even confusing amount of information relevant, but it may not be so straight forward as to know where to start.

- **Continuing diagnosis**: There are challenges with the coaching diagnosis process in that it is often a very dynamic process. It does not all get done in the first few moments, or even the first session. Factors relevant to the matter may continue to emerge throughout the dialogue. Factors such as the coachee's own concentration and comfort in the process may be vital to sourcing important information.

- **Directive or non-directive**: There is an important balance to be found here. Coaching in its common social and original practice was someone who knows how things should be done and can be very directive in dictating the approach. This is not the case in all circumstances however. Some direction in organising data around established key factors may be helpful.

  For example, in sports coaching the need to diagnose a person's muscular capabilities, dietary needs, resting patterns, observation of the field and competitors, skills and techniques borrowed from adjacent/diametrically opposite/even unknown fields, strong discipline developed to routinely check everything, working to continually optimise different facets of themselves that has incremental improvements etc.

- **Challenges of Collaborative Diagnosis**: And of course, the big item is that the coachee must have control both of the agenda as well as the information that will be the basis for any agenda – as it concerns their world. The coachee makes their own choices.

- **Availability of relevant data is another key item**: People are not in the habit of keeping a full portfolio of data on their organisational life and the learning that has gone into it so far. Hence the diagnosis process in coaching can be a continuous exploratory process.

Coaching can thus be about sharing leadership in a joint collaborative manner. There is still opportunity for confusion in how this may happen. Starting clearly with the sort of principles and processes proposed initially by Knowles, and andragogy, can be of considerable help in clarifying expectations.

4. TAKING THE APPROACH INTRODUCED BY ANDRAGOGY, OR ADULT LEARNING

My practice is based on approaches and data which emphasise the 'learning' processes reported by the person themselves. Andragogy has been a term used to focus on this study of how normal adults learn. The core principles are already summarised in Sue Young and Lucille Maddelena[3] recent publications on *the good coach*.

Another excellent summary of this perspective of Andragogy (including Knowles' work) is provided by Clardy[4].

AS A REMINDER OF THE CORE PRINCIPLES

1. Self-concept of autonomy and self-direction.

2. A higher level of life background and experience.

3. The need to understand the reasons for learning something.

4. A learning motivation based upon personal need.

5. A pragmatic orientation.

6. An internally driven motivation to learn.

These are important, yet very general principles of how individuals learn. And people are all different. Studying human perception though quickly emphasises how different peoples' perception can be – such as how witness's reports of the same event can vary.

Knowles (see Clardy[5]) also lays out a next level of more practical detail. For me this outlines a more practical picture of how I see myself using this as a diagnostic process in the overall way practice works.

PRACTICAL PROCESSES FOR ACHIEVING THESE PRINCIPLES

1. Learners should be prepared for the learning program.

2. A climate conducive to learning should be created.

3. A mutual planning procedure should be used that involves the learner in planning what the learning will cover.

4. Diagnosing learning needs. First, desired outcomes are identified, and second, discrepancies between those desired outcomes and the learner's current abilities are noted. The result is a self-assessment of what the learner wants to learn.

5. Specifying learning objectives: identifying practical stages involved.

---

[3] Young, Sue. 2015. "Adult Learning – The Real Leading Edge of Coaching." *the good coach*. http://the-goodcoach.com/tgcblog/2015/7/21/adult-learning-the-real-leading-edge-of-coaching-by-sue-youn.html. Accessed September 9. And Maddalena, Lucille. 2015. "Critical Assumptions in Coaching." *the good coach*. http://the-goodcoach.com/tgcblog/2016/3/7/critical-assumptions-in-coaching-by-lucille-maddalena-edd-guest. Accessed September 4.

[4] Clardy, Alan. 2005. "Andragogy: Adult Learning and Education at its Best?" *ERIC*. http://eric.ed.gov/?id=ED492132. Accessed September 4.

[5] ditto

6. Designing the learning program.

7. Operating the program: Here, the teacher acts more in the capacity of a facilitator,

8. Resource person and mutual student than as independent expert.

9. Program evaluation.

There is still a great deal more specification needed than is outlined here. For example, what exactly is meant by 'climate conducive to learning'? The other missing element is how exactly 'facilitation' works.

Nonetheless, this practical process is an outline for a contract. This particular contract captures learner goals and shows how those goals will be pursued and evaluated. This begins a description that is similar to the growing practice of formal coaching contracts, where the contract is a formal specification of expectations.

5. CONSIDERING MY OWN PATTERNS OF PRACTICE – AND EXTENDING THE IDEA OF COLLABORATION TO PEER GROUPS

The pattern of practice that I am particularly interested in sharing is where collaboration is geared up even further than just between a coach and a single coachee. I have increasingly found that the process of collaboration often works most powerfully when undertaken in a group, with other 'peers'.

This provides a really essential range of perspectives for all concerned, as when there is both a consensus about matters worth anyone's attention. It is not just the coach or even the coachee by themselves just trying to make sense.

The language of peers is also often more relevant because they can more easily recall evidence and examples that can be/are more relevant.

THE WORKSHOP APPROACH

I have found in practice that getting a 'joint' diagnosis can be considerably enhanced by applying some key principles:

1. Including peers in the process directly.

2. Enabling the peer group to lead the agenda and exploration.

3. Selecting expert input according to their direction and focus.

Formally, I find this takes place in a workshop or development centre approach.

Importantly this also includes a one to one (i.e. 'currently typical' coaching) with each participant also on a personal and confidential basis before and after (and until the peers themselves can take this over!)

In my practice experience, coaching works best when it involves multiple sources of data, live and direct, and not just on paper. It's the combination of one-to-one coaching, expert perspectives, as well as living realities of perspectives by people with more intimate knowledge of the circumstances.

Working in peer groups, or teams, can be more demanding for the coach. It requires attention to a wider range of dialogue, as well as ensuring that you keep pace with how the dialogue is developing through a number of stages.

A practical example/coaching approach to workshops

Initial contracting: This is started by a person with the wherewithal to call people together. Typically, in organisations, this will involve a person in a position of authority to make this happen.

Preparation: Any event starts as soon as people hear about it; not when they arrive for the formal session. It is important to ensure the right atmosphere/conditions are set from the start. For example, the person in authority communicates clearly their own readiness to learn as part of the event!

Duration: A workshop may be a two-hour session over lunch or last for several days. It may be a set of events separated over time, rather than one single event. However, it does typically involve people being in the same room. Current technology is also creating more effective options for physical distance not to be a barrier.

The theme: There is usually a theme on the table to be able to start the exploration… such as 'leadership' or 'strategic futures'. The key is to get the participants to share their thoughts on the theme (A real organisational matter is best rather than an abstract issue).

Participants views first: Whatever the starting point for the activity, say 'leadership' or any other organisational theme, a workshop approach gets the participants to express, share and discuss where they come from on the starting theme, first.

This may need some coaching/facilitation and structuring. Participants may need confidence building about expressing what they really believe, as well as paying attention to their peers' views.

Perspectives that add to participants' views: After the views of the group have been expressed, shared and discussed, it may well serve to bring in something appropriate from the background of wider learning on the theme. E.g. Appropriate theories/research to the subject concerned, to add/confirm the sense the group already has formed for itself.

Participants form an agenda: Usually the participants have already expressed a great deal of what is involved in their own language and terms.

PART 1: Leading edge: Influences on Practitioner's Learning and Development

This builds their confidence in further setting the agenda for them as a group in a powerful atmosphere of collective collaboration.

Continue the dialogue/exercises: Which may be designed to enable dialogue about real circumstances.

1. I find this is often a powerful means by which individuals can review their own behaviour – getting perspectives from colleagues – not just 'experts' or coaches, and exactly what could make a valuable difference.

2. Participants may also bring in matters arising from the dialogues on a one-to-one basis. The language and experience of peers is really important 'diagnostic' data for any of the individuals.

Normally, people are then well motivated to search for the actions and outcomes from this exploration. I find there is also a natural tolerance and comfort with this process. It makes sense to people on an intuitive basis.

6. CONCLUSIONS/NEXT STEPS...

- Personally, I have found it useful to consider how the idea of diagnosis can be a useful lens for making sense of what can be a complex process in coaching.

- This complexity is especially in evident when needing to ensure coaching is a collaborative process; between the coach and coachee and when the added value of involving others in a more collective and collaborative process as peers.

- The reality of how fragile information is and how it can only ever be a 'perception' – and thus always subject to being a partial, rather than total understanding of what is happening, makes this wider testing of collaborative diagnosis especially important.

- The short summary here of these perspectives, is for me, a good basis on how to build this insight further into my practice.

- It would also be valuable to get a similar experience of practice such as what has been mentioned here, in order to share, compare and build our collective understanding.

Self-disclosure: Powerful material from which to construct a safe space

Ian Flanders - Dispatch from the [Internal Coaching] Front

I've started two new coaching relationships in the last couple of months. As is usual with my coaching clients, I was aware of both men, but not involved with either of them on a day-to-day basis. Both are managers. One in a very specialised technical services leadership role and the other in a much more commercial role. The 'public' agenda both men, separately, brought to coaching was stakeholder management.

Robert is technically well qualified, by profession, and a spreadsheet man by inclination. His coaching agenda was to improve his stakeholder management skills; for him this meant addressing a deficit in his 'soft skills'. I suspect that based upon his 'coaching objectives' Robert expected a discussion about tools and techniques for managing stakeholders, hopefully involving a spreadsheet! But, at our first coaching session he put on the table an emotional intelligence self-audit that he had recently completed. That was the rabbit hole down which we disappeared. Though clearly not a surprise to him, he had scored particularly low on 'empathy' and this was causing him some distress. I felt that he was looking at me, imploringly, to make him empathic! I told him that it was beyond my powers as a coach to make him empathic. Then I surprised him by questioning whether it was necessary for him to be empathic. But the surprise that changed the nature of our relationship came when I used a personal experience to back up my questioning position.

Eighteen months previously, I had been absent from the organisation for four months. Robert was aware that this had been the case, but didn't know why. I now shared with him that my absence was triggered by the serious illness of my partner and used the behaviour of my line manager to discuss with Robert what role, if any, empathy played in what had happened. I experienced the attitude of my boss as practical, helpful, but not empathetic. He had only joined the company quite recently at that time. I felt anxiety that an extended absence might damage the relationship I was trying to build with him, and ultimately my job. He recognised this anxiety and took it off the table; no fuss, no warm words, just a simple statement. But, I experienced his attitude as hugely supportive and very helpful.

The effect of my disclosure was dramatic. It enabled Robert to re-evaluate his assumptions about the need to feel empathy. It led onto a discussion about a member of his team who was coping with a similarly challenging personal situation. I watched Robert decide to change the way he approached this colleague; to stop trying to make himself empathise, and instead to focus on practical ways to support his colleague. Reflecting back on this conversation I realise that Robert experienced no difficulty in 'doing the right thing' for his colleague, but needed permission to separate the practical from the emotional.

The other impact my disclosure had was upon our relationship. Robert later admitted that he had been surprised that I had shared such a personal and difficult experience. He described experiencing my disclosure as being trusted, and found trusting me an easier decision as a result.

Phillip was nervous at our first meeting. This surprised me a little, as my impression was of a confident, almost brash young man. As we got acquainted I asked a question which accidentally opened a box of emotions. In answering my question, about a recent job change, he told me that his young child had recently been diagnosed with a very rare condition and that this had been a factor in his decision. Rather than stepping back from this clearly difficult topic I chose to share with him my partners ongoing health challenge. He admitted later that he had been surprised that I had shared such a personal story, but was grateful, as, in doing so I had removed the stigma he feared might attach to him if he were to become emotional during our sessions.

I regard myself, after De Haan, as a relational coach. The relationship that I seek to build with my client is central to my approach. My goal is to create a 'safe space' within which my client can explore their situation. Reflecting upon the two relationships I have written about here I realise that my aim, in disclosing something so personal to me, was to construct a strong, secure safe space for my clients. I am also clear that, in part, my success in building the safe space was a result of the surprise that my clients felt at the personal nature of the building materials I employed; that the contrast with my work persona was significant.

Another way of looking at my approach could be in terms of 'risk' and 'reward'. It might be argued that I took the risk and that my clients gained the reward; but this is not the way I see it. In disclosing information personal to me it is true that I took a risk, but, I did this with a purpose, intentionally, and was rewarded by the relationship that was the result. I ask clients to trust me every time we have a conversation; for me, reciprocating their trust is part of the deal.

As an internal coach, I have a persona within my organisation that is for everyone, except those that I have coached, made up of images from my day-job. Looking back, it becomes clear that almost every new coachee I have worked with has assumed that my work persona is the whole me. This assumption must, for some, raise power/hierarchy concerns, a barrier to the formation of our relationship. Being able, and willing, to use personal disclosure to jump this barrier is, for me, a risk worth taking.

Embracing the current reality - the crucial step to explore the way forward

Petra Macdougald

One particular aspect of the coaching process holds immense benefit for me. But only if I have fully explored and brought to full realisation that crucial step when the coachee completely accepts their current reality without any reservations.

By this I mean the coachee, being enabled through the coaching process, to consciously come to terms with and seeing eye-to-eye with sometimes highly uncomfortable or unloved truths.

The coachees' clear view on 'what is' and accepting this current reality is absolutely necessary as a stable launch pad to explore future options. If the 'what is' is not fully accepted and still generates background noise for the client, some possible solutions to their problems might go unexplored, or may never even enter their consciousness.

So there is great value of seeking acceptance of the current situation and how one ended up there.

WHAT MAY GET IN THE WAY

All coaches use some sort of coaching model, such as the TGROW model, to provide a framework to explore five key elements in the coaching conversation: the topic, the goal, the reality, the options and the will.

It may be tempting to expect that acceptance of 'what is' comes as a natural product of the reality exploration in our coaching conversations.

Yet in practice it is not always as simple as that.

- For the coachee it is uncomfortable being made aware of possible blind spots or being invited back maybe numerous times by their coach to investigate aspects of their life that they would rather not see or take full ownership for.

- The coach will draw on their relationship with the coachee, their coaching style as well as their experience, to 'endure' staying for as long as necessary for a useful outcome in this more challenging part of the coaching process.

- As owner of the process, the coach will also need to identify the appropriate moment and actions to exit this difficult space once the coachee has gained the insights that were important for the way forward.

I believe that supporting their clients in this 'coming to terms' with the current reality can represent a dilemma for the coach: on the one hand, we are highly empathic human beings and want to be supportive to the coachee, which could imply thoughts of being gentle and always by their side. On the other hand, we are also aware that this part alone can often not be usefully explored without serious challenging, probing and insisting. This may indeed bear risk for a particular part of the conversation we are leading the coachee to, and we know it.

This requires the coach to strike a balance between safeguarding the relationship with the coachee while staying sufficiently long enough or deeply engaged with a challenging matter.

CHALLENGING AND PAUSING TO BECOME FULLY AWARE OF THE CURRENT REALITY

Bringing a coachee into a situation where we support them to see those difficult aspects and help him/her to embrace them is something that needs to be done in the right circumstances. If we are to support the client in building a stable platform they can explore a wide variety of options from there.

I personally will only do it when I believe that my relationship with the client is sufficiently established and strong, so certainly not in the first and maybe not even in the second session.

This is mainly for two reasons:

- I first want to build rapport. I want to understand the coachee's personal preferred communication style before I may bring them to a more difficult spot. This is to ensure that they will not take a more challenging approach from me as an affront, but will sufficiently trust me that anything I do in the coaching intervention is in their best interest.

- I need to collect and fully understand the information they perceive in their reality.

In a situation where I am comfortable with the above two elements and I have identified possible contradictions or inconsistencies in the information they discuss, I have taken to very openly challenging my coachee to confront their reality.

The purpose of this is to make them aware of a blind spot or make them realise that they are talking about themselves into some rosier kind of reality. I will ask some very direct questions about the information they have provided. I will highlight where it does not add up for me. I obviously do this in a non-judgmental way and only with the information received. This often then leads to a deep reflection with the client. I have learned about the value of staying and pausing in this uncomfortable spot with the coachee for a while. I will be gentle in my approach, but bring them back to the subject repeatedly if I have the impression that they have arranged their thought patterns in such a way that some important element is being avoided.

Having a client really accepting where they are today may be upsetting for the client as admitting to themselves that they have may not have achieved certain things they meant to achieve by now. Or that they are not as performing as well as the target they had set for themselves.

In essence, this acceptance of all facets of 'what is now' can mean the end of a long-harboured dream.

Obviously, I am looking in my coaching practice always for the best result for my client. I have noticed that at the end of this usually more uncomfortable and emotional part of the coaching process the client is more resourceful in exploring options. I believe that this is due to the fact that they have made inner peace by allowing something into their consciousness that behind the scenes held them back.

A PRACTICAL ILLUSTRATION

Recently I worked with a client who is very experienced in their job and was looking for their next challenge. Their initial belief was that this challenge was to come from a complete change of career. However, as we explored the reality of their situation it became apparent that there were important aspects of their job that they actually enjoyed very much. Furthermore, and to illustrate what I have been outlining on acceptance, I asked them if they were not using the idea of a complete career change to run away from some less attractive aspect of their job. I had also sensed that the coachee had some certain fears relating to the inherent risk of taking on a completely new position that I brought out in the open for them to face.

This led to a long reflection and coming to terms with the fact that indeed the idea of 'running away' from the situation was attractive, but it would never happen as they were not in a position to take certain risks linked to a complete change. Once the coachee understood this, they had the freedom of mind to explore other options than the unrealistic complete change of position. In the end, the coachee took action with their management to change their current role in such a way that the aspects of the job they were really good at (and enjoyed) were increased. The client had also accepted that leaving the current position was not an option, which made them make a conscious decision to stay, and which felt much better for them at an emotional level.

IN CONCLUSION

Accepting difficult aspects of their current reality and closing a chapter can set our clients free. It channels the energy that was used on the unaccepted situation onto something new and maybe previously unexplored.

This is fantastic news for the client. It is also rewarding for me as a coach who has faced the challenge of sufficiently challenging my client.

For it to work well for me the following elements need to be present:

- A strong, trusting relationship with the client, where challenging or confrontation is not perceived as personal attack.

- The coach's willingness to go into this less comfortable space (giving themselves permission to become maybe more directive than they would otherwise be).

- The stamina of coach and coachee to stay there for the time it takes to ensure the best outcome for the client.

- The coach as guardian of the process, needs to identify the opportune moment to move on.

- The work on the inconsistencies in the client's reality being strictly non-judgmental and only conducted on the information provided by the client.

What do you do when inquiry doesn't work?

Alan Robertson

We've come to take it as axiomatic that coaching should be based on Inquiry. The coach poses thought-provoking questions, enabling the coachee to think again and come up with his own answers. But where do you go, when the coachee won't engage with this reflective process?

This is a case in two parts. The first presents my thoughts on it now. The second part is what I wrote to tackle this problem at the time, a couple of years ago.

LOOKING BACK

Socratic questioning was not D's cup of tea. He was eager to have a coach, or more precisely he had been agitating to get this particular indicator of his executive status, and he was more than ready to talk. He didn't hold back. But he wouldn't stick to the question asked. If he did start to address it, he would very quickly veer away onto other points that he wanted to make. As often as not, he challenged or argued about the original question. He was pent-up with things to say.

Our initial get-to-know-you session was sprawling and shapeless. "*May I give you some feedback?*" I said, as we ran out of time. I proceeded without, on this occasion, waiting for an answer. "*You talk too much. And you don't listen enough. You seem to be oblivious to the effect this has on the person who is trying to talk with you.*" I tried to explain how these tendencies would limit what he could expect to get out of coaching.

Despite my best efforts to steer it, our next session rapidly went in the same direction. 'D' was a rolling barrage of indignation and self-justification. It was clear that this case needed a different approach. I put my preference to one side, abandoned Inquiry and switched to a radically different voice. I went into Challenge.

It would be good to be able to say that I did this because it was D's own dominant voice, and because I was carefully selecting the mode of expression most likely to resonate for him. I certainly knew it was his dominant voice, but I joined him in using it for the much simpler (and very common) reason that our interaction had already turned into a conversational wrestling match.

So I chose to interrupt. He talked over me and I talked over him. I pointed it out as soon as he went off issue. I dragged him back to the objectives that the coaching had been set up to address. I accused him of dodging my questions. I told him that he was too stuck in his own thinking. I even told him that I didn't feel as if he was treating me with much respect as a person. I was abrupt. I was severe. I was blunt.

Of course, I can be all these things, but I like to think that it's generally sparingly, more like a punctuation mark than a slab of text. On this occasion, I was giving my coachee a verbal battering, a taste of his own tendency. It was hard, tiring work and almost certainly more uncomfortable for me than for 'D' who had a well-armoured skin when it came to verbal jousting. If he'd been surprised by my sudden and then protracted directness, he showed it in the most useful of ways: he started to pause, to focus and to reflect.

By the end of that session we'd had what can only be described as a robust exchange on a variety of points. But were we getting anywhere? What had 'D' taken out of the discussion?

So I did something else that I don't ordinarily do: I followed up our meeting by sending him a set of written reflections. I don't like to do this for several reasons. It's as far away as you can get from a coachee-led approach. It feels like giving too much weight to my interpretations, especially early in the coaching relationship when my perspective is still provisional and emerging. It risks taking the responsibility for sense-making and action away from the coachee, the one who needs to own it.

But it felt necessary on this occasion, both for his benefit and for mine. And it required another voice which was not Inquiry. It needed Articulation, a summarising and clarifying of what we had discussed, partly as a point of reference but also to provide a fresh platform so that we could move on and not keep going round in circles.

I reproduce (with D's agreement) what I wrote at that time in the final part of this blog. In retrospect it still feels too one-sided and, like anything set down in black and white, potentially too sure of itself. I had no idea at the time whether it would work, but it served a purpose. While D and I never went systematically through it together, he referred back to specific comments that I had made in it from time to time during our subsequent sessions. In that sense it had clearly given him pause for thought. More importantly, it marked a turning point in the quality and productiveness of our work together.

D's case ended quite well. He wasn't dramatically transformed by the process, but he declared himself pleased with it and so, for the most part, did his sponsor. I felt we'd achieved less than I'd hoped and more than I'd expected.

LOOKING BACK ON THIS CASE NOW, I THINK IT HIGHLIGHTS THREE IMPORTANT POINTS ABOUT COACHING

1. While the received wisdom might have it that Inquiry is the basis of good coaching, this presupposes that the coachee will play his part in making Inquiry work. If he won't, then the process of developing the individual needs – unapologetically – to shift to an altogether different basis. If you can't explore, then it seems to me you have to turn either to controlling or towards taking a position.

2. We talk of coaching processes and techniques, and this rather leads us to expect them to have a greater regularity, predictability and efficacy than they actually have. In practice we spend much of our time having to improvise, and having to do it in real time, in the moment. We need a broad repertoire, a light touch and a ready ear for what's going on, more like jazz musicians than technical experts.

3. We probably all have habitual patterns in our personal approaches to coaching. It might not feel it at the time, but it probably does us - or at least the development of our own adaptability - good to be shaken by a coachee from time to time. I was jolted by my encounter with D. During our initial bouts, I felt as if I were regressing into the Industrial Relations Manager that I had been once upon a time. But it was still coaching.

So thank you, 'D', even if you were hard going at the time.

———————————————————

Appendix:

Written At the Time

Dear D,

I've had a week to reflect on our first coaching session. Let me share my reflections with you.

We signed up to three objectives:-

- To develop your awareness of your personal impact in interactions with others and your ability to create and maintain positive and productive working relationships with others;

- To develop the range, repertoire and sensitivity of your communication skills;

- Assuming the achievement of these fundamental requirements, to strengthen your capability to provide contextually relevant and developmental leadership for your own team.

We then began to pursue these objectives by examining your recent 360-degree feedback report and also your VoicePrint self-perception profile. One provides a portrait of how you are seen by your colleagues, the other gives us insights into how you see yourself. My sense is that both documents, and especially our discussion of them, have given us important clues about what you will have to tackle to achieve your objectives.

You described yourself at one point in our discussion as feeling as if, "Everything I do is within a prison cell." I'm going to put it to you that this cell is at least partly of your own construction. More importantly, the only person who can remove its barriers is, ultimately, yourself. Here's my sense of what came out in that first session and how it relates to this proposition.

I observed your reactions to your 360 become progressively stronger and more exasperated, as you read through it. "*All the things they've marked me down for,*" you commented, "*are things I can't control or things I've raised in the past. I set out visions for my team and they are ignored!*"

It's not unusual to find 360-degree feedback frustrating. Few, if any, of us consciously set out to impede our own progress. Yet, unconsciously most of us do. As you verbalised your frustrations, three things in particular struck me about how you may be unconsciously getting in your own way. The first lay in your comments, "*People don't want to hear what I have to say*" and "*You can only speak what you know.*" These remarks both suggest to me that you may be focusing too much on the content of what you want to say and too little on the manner of how you talk.

Secondly, you exclaimed at one point, "*What do other people who have been promoted have that I don't have?*" I think this is an important question for you to ponder and I would suggest that you frame it more broadly. "*What do other people have (or do) that I don't have (or do)?*" The reason I say this is because you seem to place a very great, and probably excessive, weight of expectation on yourself alone. We should return to this in our next session.

In the meantime, my third observation is related to this. Your frustrations often seem to be to do with your sense of control or the lack of it. "*I can't control the number of people I have, I can't control the increase in workload I have.*" "*I don't have access to the information I need.*" "*If a third party comes to assess my design or decision, am I going to get burned?*" The issue of being in control is clearly much on your mind. I wonder if you are investing too much of your energy in that direction.

This possibility is certainly reflected in your VoicePrint profile, which is your own estimation of how you use talk. (And remember that we talk to ourselves as well as to others, so this profile can also be an indication of how you tend to think.) The centre of gravity in your case is currently located in the three 'controlling' voices: Critique, Challenge and Admonish. These are therefore highly likely to colour your other relatively strong voice, which is Advocacy, the position you adopt for or against particular issues.

The upside of the controlling voices, provided they are used in a skilful and timely way, is essentially their contribution to quality and conformity to standards. An effective Challenge interrupts to improve. An effective Critique ensures rigorous, balanced, objective judgement. Effective Admonishment calls attention to specific responsibilities.

You will recall that we discussed the potential downside of over-using these voices. You recognised that they could have a constraining effect: 'Reducing free thinking and the opportunity to back-test your decision.' But you were not alert to the adverse effect that they can have on working relationships, when perceived by others as attack, personal criticism or punishment.

When you talk, I think you speak to your own concerns. You do not tune in to the needs and concerns of the other person(s) in the conversation. I pointed this out to you when we first met, as I experienced it myself in our introductory meeting. In your profile of voices, the two which are most likely to discover others' needs and concerns, and therefore most likely to engage them – Inquire and Probe – are ones which, relative to most people, you under-use. Consequently, the overall pattern in how you talk, and its impact, is too heavily on the 'already decided' voices and too light on the 'exploring with others' voices.

I understand where you're coming from because you told me. "*I feel I have to explain myself all the time.*" "*You have to justify your own thinking to take people with you,*" you said.

Actually, that's not the only way to take people with you. It is one way, but it's loaded with social and inter-personal risk, because it drags people rather than involving them or treating them as respected partners in the conversation.

You see yourself as 'a problem solver,' a 'voice of reason' in a world where there are not enough people who understand the nuts and bolts'as you do. "*I'm trying to build a function that can work at one hundred miles an hour across any terrain. My frustration is I'm not being allowed to do it.*"

You are seriously overestimating, I suggest, your ability (indeed the ability of any individual in a complex organization) to make things happen without the involvement, co-operation and support of others. You discount the contribution that others can make. (And if you habitually discount others, they in turn will discount you.) There were two fascinating, but disturbing glimpses of this during our session last week.

The first was when you were reading your 360-degree feedback. You came to the end of the numerical analysis and laid the document aside. It was only when prompted by me that you took the trouble to read the inputs that your colleagues had provided for you in the open-ended Qualitative Questions section.

The second was your response, when I asked you whether you regarded people as a commodity. It was a deliberately provocative question. A socially sensitive person would almost certainly have answered, "*No.*" You, interestingly, replied, "*It depends.*" "*They're people,*" you said, "*if they share my values of integrity, hard work, thinking, bettering yourself and encouraging innovation. If not, you simply learn how to get the best out of them.*"

Here, I think, are the roots of your tendency to over-use the Challenging, Critiquing, Admonishing and Advocating voices. Here is an inter-personal narrowness and inflexibility. Here may be the basis of an answer to your question, "*What do other people that have been promoted have that I don't have?*"

I'm not saying that changing this pattern of thinking and behaving will necessarily get you promoted. I am saying that the way in which you use talk, the principal medium of exchange in organisational life, is entirely within your own control. How you currently use it, and the effects that has on your impact and reputation, are important insights that have come out of your first coaching session. You will need to decide how you are going to make use of those insights to achieve your coaching and career objectives.

I look forward to our next session, when perhaps we can focus on the particular people and interactions that you find most problematic.

With best wishes

Alan

How coaching can inform all professional advisors about improving relationships

Julian Danobetia

The early nineties: phones like bricks; a hairstyle like a children's pop-up book; legal loves everyone and they are in hire mode... Somehow I managed to find my way into a serious London law firm. On the first day of my articles I found myself to be alongside twenty Oxbridge graduates who had a whole set of attributes I thought I could never compete with. Not surprisingly, I made some assumptions such as...

> *"I know how this works for someone like me; I work harder than anybody else and know more law than the rest of them put together, and that's how I communicate my value."*

And that's precisely what I set out to try and do. At one point, it was going so well that I was actually able to build up such a huge pile of files on my desk that nobody could see me behind it. Brilliant. People just left me alone to get on with my work without bothering me. I saw myself as a 'work-doer', and, funnily enough, so did others around me. As a consequence, I was given more work to do. I thought that was what success looked like. Yet I suspect those around me saw things differently.

HOW I STARTED TO APPRECIATE THE IMPORTANCE OF RELATIONSHIPS

After a few years of private practice, I decided to give in-house a try. When I got there I knew what I had to do. In transitioning from private practice to in-house, I managed to shift my attitude towards work and stayed employed as an in-house lawyer for a number of years.

Around 2004-5, I was lucky enough to be asked to become involved with something called the Addleshaw Goddard Client Development Centre (CDC). This CDC was the first consultancy started by a law firm to help lawyers communicate their value as effectively as possible, and at Downthecorridor we are pleased to continue to work closely with lawyers and other professional advisers today.

WHAT WAS THE DIFFERENCE?

After working in the CDC, I quickly started to notice that professional advisers fell broadly into two categories.

- 'Service': We might call the first category "service". Service teams see their role as being one of responding to requests from the business to mitigate risk.

- 'Experience': On the other side of the spectrum, I saw what we might call "experience" teams. Experience teams are involved at the early stages; are high on the radar of the key decision makers and are seen as an essential part of the business.

The fundamental difference between them is this: Their focus on relationships... 'Service' teams are not focused on relationships, so they create relationships with their clients by accident. 'Experience' teams on the other hand, think hard about the experience they want to create for their clients, along with how they want their clients to feel. They do this by creating relationships on purpose.

TO START WITH, IT HAS TO BE A DELIBERATE CHOICE

In my view, all professional advisers have a choice about the kind of relationships they want to build with their clients. This includes whether they want those relationships to happen by accident or on purpose.

I think lawyers and other professionals that actively engage with this question are likely to experience a very different level of fulfilment.

HOW COACHING CAN MAKE A REAL DIFFERENCE

Recently, I have seen how coaching can make a real added value difference to appreciating what is involved. More often this may include what could be called a Coaching Approach as well as formal one-to-one sessions, as in the most talked about way of doing coaching.

Helping professionals think about the experience they want to create for their clients can take many forms – itself depending on the circumstances. For those in professional services, the relationship with the client is the value they deliver above the service itself. It's how they differentiate themselves. Good coaching creates unique and enduring relationships. If a professional services person wants to coach their client and develop their own coaching skills, the best way to do it is to get a good coach. Good coaches are coach able.

DEVELOPING EFFECTIVE RELATIONSHIPS ARE AN ACCEPTED 'BUSINESS SKILL'

Likewise, after years of coaching professionals at all levels, I also believe that looking at relationships is a matter of leadership.

By leadership, I simply mean doing what others in the same space haven't done yet.

The ability to foster and develop effective relationships has long been recognised in the wider business community as an essential part of the personal development of any corporate leader.

If we don't receive relationship management training during our professional formation, then private practice can be a difficult environment where we simply put relationship development in the 'just-a-bit-too-difficult box' – especially with the chargeable hour issue lurking at the end of every day.

It does take work, but a focus on relationships can mean a lot more fun.

So, how do you see client relationships in your business?

Do what you say and say what you do

Aubrey Rebello

In my four years of coaching practice I have found improving Time Management is a common goal across clients.

Most CEOs and Business Leaders work long hours. Yet they are still not able to complete all what they had planned to do and this typically leads to frustration, health issues and disturbed family ties.

Prioritising and planning are obvious areas the client needs to work on and this can give good results.

In India where I do most of my coaching, I have found that practicing one simple work ethic can bring positive results. I call this,

"Do What You Say And Say What You Do"

SOUNDS VERY SIMPLE BUT WHAT IS THE REALITY?

- When someone is late for a meeting you get a call, "I will be there in two minutes." How precise? In reality, it could mean anything from ten minutes to even thirty minutes.

- Tasks with specific due dates are rarely completed by the due date. When delayed, there is rarely given a delay indication with reasons and a new completion date.

- Sometimes completed tasks may not actually be fully completed. For example, only five out of seven items in the task are fully complete. Rarely will someone say "Only five out of the seven items have been completed whilst the remaining two will be completed in the next three days.

In India (and some other Cultures) our habit for most of these times is to,

"Not Do What We Say And Not Say (precisely) What We Do."

With that sort of work ethic, to get anything done requires lots of follow-up. We can never be sure of committed dates and the start of the next tasks to be done!

The end result is non-value follow-up work, delays, longer reviews and meetings, lots of phone calls, mails and clutter.

IMAGINE HOW IT WILL BE IF EVERYONE IN A TEAM FOLLOWS "DO WHAT YOU SAY AND SAY WHAT YOU DO"

This work ethic will require that commitments are given after all aspects and dependencies of task completion are factored, and every effort is made to meet committed dates. Start with simple things like being on time for a meeting.

If committed dates cannot be met it should be conveyed before the due date with reasons and a new date given. Gradually with better analysis of all the factors that are impacting the outcome, slippage from committed dates should reduce. Any slippage, then, can only be due to dependencies on which you have no control or cannot be factored in accurately.

A few benefits that will happen with this work ethic are:

- Follow-up (non value added) activity will drop to zero.
- Future tasks based on completion of previous tasks can be planned and scheduled better and projects completed earlier.
- Meetings and reviews will be shorter and crisper.
- Increase in productivity and customer (internal & external) satisfaction.

EMBEDDING "DO WHAT YOU SAY AND SAY WHAT YOU DO" WITH MY CLIENTS

Most of my clients have been able to achieve improvements in excess of 50 percent where customer satisfaction, productivity and response time are concerned. They do this by ensuring that they and their teams adhere to this work ethic.

This work ethic does not require anyone to work beyond his or her level of capability and improves a team or a group's dynamic because it only requires commitment to completion dates, timeliness and preciseness in communication. It can therefore be practiced by everybody: by the Expert, by the non-Expert, by the "A" graded Team members as well as the" C" graded Team members.

Old habits die hard, and a Team Leader should explain the work ethic to his Team and regularly review whether the new work ethic is followed or not. The approach has to be top down with Leaders applying the work ethic first for everyone else to follow.

Sometimes there is intense pressure from Customers or from the Boss to commit delivery in a short time span. As a way out of the pressure situation some people commit to a time which they are unsure about. This should be avoided. It is better to bear the unpleasantness now and meet your committed dates. While Customers are not always expected to listen, Management should listen and give in where the explanation for more time is reasonable. After all just like no baby can be delivered before 9 months some tasks may require more time than demanded.

Several Managing Directors whom I coached have made placards and pasted them on each work desk so that their Team members keep in mind and practice this work ethic everyday.

With regular persuasion it will take 3 to 6 months for the Work Ethic to be part of a Team's DNA.

I believe that this is one of the 'Lowest Hanging Fruit' for improving Personal Effectiveness that's worthwhile leveraging.

Besides productivity, response time and customer satisfaction improvements, the biggest takeaway would be '**dependability**'. Everything that's committed is delivered and occasional delays are communicated well in time. For any organization, particularly in Indian culture, this would be a breakthrough step.

It would be interesting to know how Coaches in similar situations or other work cultures might be doing this.

Acknowledging disempowerment when you're a bullet-proof person

Katy Tuncer

've often observed a paradox in very senior leaders:

A. They are working too hard, feel disempowered, and are struggling to escape a victim mindset but,

B. They are definitely 'not a weak person'... so they must deny/ignore A!

They try to be and show everyone how bullet proof they are. Ironically, this feeds the very circumstances which lead to their disempowerment. When we become disempowered we feel that we have limited personal control over events. The impact can be more stress, unnecessarily hard work, inefficiency and distance in key relationships...

Typically, my clients come to me for coaching that focuses on hard business performance rather than "the soft stuff". This might be skewing my sample of course, but I wonder how many other coaches help clients deal with this paradox again and again?

I often notice that clients first communicate a feeling of disempowerment when they talk about a persistent complaint, for example:

- The work is piled on me, I have to do it myself
- Someone is being overbearing
- My position doesn't allow me to show what I'm really capable of
- Someone else is cheating, it's not fair

- I'm being exploited and unappreciated

- Etc

What I've observed is that conflating vulnerability with weakness shuts the door firmly on taking action to address disempowerment. If we are deeply committed to never showing weakness, and we think this means never showing vulnerability, we are stuck with the need to show that we are powerful all the time. We truly end up believing that disempowerment doesn't apply to us and we simply cannot address something we do not know exists.

As we know, the first step is acknowledgement. Only then can we get to practical actions (and I've shared a few of these at the end).

HOW DO WE HELP A 'BULLET-PROOF' SENIOR LEADER IDENTIFY WHAT THEY'RE PUTTING THEMSELVES THROUGH?

I've tried a few approaches. Here is what I have found has worked, but I'm looking forward to hearing other ideas too.

1. SHARE AND TALK FROM PERSONAL EXPERIENCE

I can think of countless occasions in my own leadership journey when I'm acting the tough, senior leader, playing the bullet-proof part whilst feeling dreadfully sorry for myself when people (predictably) try out their bullets on me!

> *"Two members of a team I am running have a major fall out and accuse each other of bullying and incompetence. I wade in, I try to help each one to see the other's point of view and both respond with aggression towards me. I work harder and harder to deliver the outputs of the team myself while the pair battle it out with zero productivity. I'm resentful; how don't they realise I'm the one suffering here? The lesson is that until I acknowledge that I'm not bullet proof and that there is an impact on me, the pair will remain oblivious."*

My own insight is that if you act bullet proof you attract bullets.

2. I INVITE CLIENTS TO LOOK AT THEIR OWN UNDERLYING MINDSETS

I talk about other great leaders who have made a shift to overcome disempowerment and see if this triggers ideas for my clients.

> *"We like to tell stories of great leaders overcoming adversity. But imagine working twice as hard and being half as effective because you created the extra struggle yourself? Person X played the hero and worked himself into the ground with insufficient recognition, while spinning out a narrative about how he just had to do everything himself. Then he identified an unconscious commitment he had: that he must struggle to make himself valuable and important. And he realised (after some*

uncomfortable struggling!) that he was routinely creating conditions for himself that required a heroic struggle." "Is this you?" I ask.

3. I DO A DEAL WITH MY CLIENTS TO JUST TRUST ME AND TRY IT OUT!

One high-performing client who I was working with to increase his satisfaction at work and avoid burnout, pushed back really hard on how necessary everything he did was. At one point, I even stood up and said, "Ok keep it how it is, you don't need me." Eventually though, he agreed to try out a first step. He chose a small task (in this case giving a member of staff some direction on a major website development programme) and promised to make it effortless. In practice, he avoided revisiting decisions, he saved the time he might have spent ranting about the problem to others and he kept the conversation short. He was then able to use this success to identify where he was adding unnecessary effort around other bigger areas of work. For him, the breakthrough in overcoming disempowerment was to see things as effortless.

However we get there, I often find a breakthrough moment is when clients stop confusing impact with effort. Impact is what we make happen in reality. Effort is how hard we try. Following this acknowledgement, then they can start to address disempowerment...

SEVEN TRIED AND TESTED ACTIONS

Please note that I'm coming at this from a very practical perspective. Let me share seven actions that I've seen clients take that very quickly give them power to lead and make a difference once they acknowledge disempowerment. For some, a number of these actions can work like switches, the insight leads to action and change happens overnight. For others, even the same actions may need a lot of practice and repeated commitment when it doesn't go right first time. Maybe this is for further discussion in another article!

3. Stand for something. What do you want to achieve? What kind of person do you want to be? Drop the complaints and create a vision for yourself and your workplace.

4. Take action. What can you do, right now, that will get you moving? Can you make a bold offer or a bold request? Then acknowledge and celebrate what you did (whatever the outcome).

5. Be honest about what you are scared of. What happens if you fail? Yes, that word sounds bad, but how bad is it really? Remember the expression "better to have tried and failed than to have never tried at all"? It's true. Failure doesn't mean a thing (expect that now you know more than you did before). Can you accept that?

6. Know that in (almost) every situation you have a choice. Yes, you do. You choose your job. You choose where you live. You choose who you work with. You choose what you say "no" to. You choose who you delegate to. Don't fight me on this one. Things works better when you accept that you have a choice in everything and then you can be powerful in your choosing. (Although I recognise that many of us are very deeply committed to things being tough, as it helps us to feel valuable.)

7. Listen and relate to the people around you. Consider them as being good people. Be generous in your opinions. Everyone around you is human (believe it or not!). They have their own issues, dreams, fears... We can waste a lot of time fighting, disliking and moaning. Just give it up.

8. Say "No" to some things. Nicely. Acknowledge the request and the impact of your "No". Be clear why you are saying "No" (for example, what can you say, "Yes" to instead?). And don't say that you are sorry if you don't mean it.

9. Be honest about what you are pretending. See how freeing and empowering it is to stop pretending that you are 100 percent committed/brilliant/honest or whatever. See how much energy you get back.

Our relationship with uncertainty and how it can facilitate active learning processes and personal inquiry: good coaching still has a lot to learn about learning

Simon Darnton

C haos is probably an appropriate word to describe what has been unfolding since the Brexit vote of June 23. The world, and especially the United Kingdom, has found itself dealing with considerably more uncertainty.

Both chaos and uncertainty are thus terms which are being bandied around a lot at the moment, not only in the media, but also with my clients in business and organisational contexts. I have noticed that there can be a tendency to use them interchangeably.

My Definitions:

Chaos as I refer to it here is that of complete disorder and confusion.

Uncertainty is where:

- There is a lack of (or missing) information and/or knowledge.
- The consequences or outcomes of events, actions and/or decision are unpredictable.

In differentiating these meanings, I intend to focus on the uncertainty we face in a complex and dynamic world.

FOR THE SAKE OF FALSE CERTAINTY

One could surmise following recent media coverage that uncertainty is a bad thing and that the logical resolution lies in (re)creating perceived certainty. This response is, of course, one of the natural reactions people have toward uncertainty, so it isn't entirely surprising.

Uncertainty is generally considered to be an aversive state in psychology due to its association with uncomfortable and unpleasant emotions, most notably that of anxiety. As a result, we tend to seek ways of avoiding or reducing the associated discomfort.

To me the question lies in how we might do this, or not.

Uncertainty and how we function in relation to it is a real fascination for me, mostly because of the profiles of clients that I work with who live, work and compete in contexts that are steeped in uncertainty and danger. In this world, uncertainty is a fact of life. Rather than being avoided, it is embraced. It is part of the allure. This is what motivated me to write this piece; to provide some balance around uncertainty.

How we relate to uncertainty is in my experience critical to effective learning, development and growth, as well as performance improvement. In this post, I wanted to begin exploring how we might approach intentionally developing our relationship with it. Most importantly, I'll be viewing it in a more positive light; one which not only enables learning and performance enhancement, but also how it can act as a powerful ally in psychological adventure and deep personal growth.

AN INTRODUCTION TO MY APPROACH AND HOW IT RELATES TO UNCERTAINTY

Whilst I have significant organisational experience, my approach to coaching, as it is today, has been heavily influenced by years of dedicated coaching research into the psychology of elite motorcycle racers and athletes in extreme sports. Take for example, downhill mountain biking. Alongside my business and organisation services, I run a specialist performance coaching practice where I work with world-class athletes.

My interest in this area stems from my own experience riding and racing motorcycles. When I sought to understand psychological difficulties that I was experiencing during competition, I found the available body of psychology woefully inadequate for me. It didn't match my experiences. I was drawn to conduct my own phenomenological[1] inquiry with elite motorcycle racers.

One of the common themes that I found, unfolded out of my research[2]. It continues to consistently feature in the racers' descriptions of their experiences when competing at their best and revolves around an acceptance of stepping

---

[1] A phenomenological study is one where the researcher seeks to understand the conscious experience of participants and how they construct their meaning of the experience without trying to provide causal explanation or attempting to objectify the experience.

[2] Darnton, Simon. 2001-2016. Inside the Minds of Motorcycle Racers. Simon Darnton. http://www.simondarnton.com/inside-the-minds-of-motorcycle-racers

into the unknown and the uncertainty inherent in racing. This uncertainty is not just about the outcome of the race. It is an uncertainty which extends all the way to riders entering corners at such speeds that they don't know if they're going to make it through the corner or whether they'll crash. Within this theme, it appeared to me that the most successful ones were those that dealt best with this uncertainty. Those that didn't quite make it, or found themselves struggling to improve their performance, would instead hold more onto a notion of certainty.

A simple example of holding onto a notion of certainty is something most of us do on a daily basis: in both the repetition of movements and especially learning new movements. The commonly held, yet false, belief is that we learn by repeating the same movement over and over again, whereas we are really learning because every repeated movement is different (and infinitely so). So we learn mastery through the experience of difference and variation[3].

The concept of uncertainty and how we relate to it therefore forms a central part of my approach in almost all the work that I do. It also helps to inform my approach to learning in the coaching relationship where I consistently find it important in breaking performance barriers with my clients.

LET ME SHARE AN EXAMPLE FROM MOTORCYCLE RACING:

I was approached by a motorcycle racer who had been knocking on the door to a podium finish for some time. He had discussed this glass ceiling at length with fellow racers and had already undergone training to develop his riding technique. Another racer I had previously worked with recommended that he talk to me because there weren't any apparent technical or capability limitations to his performances.

The contract we agreed mutually was to enable him to break through and finish on the podium. Once this had been achieved, we would explore how to develop consistency in his performance. We agreed an initial block of six-hour-long sessions.

Within three sessions he achieved his first race win. Following which, he fed back to me that his most important realisation during the process was accepting that he was always in unknown territory and that everything in racing was uncertain. This, he felt, opened the door to winning. He has since gone on to win multiple championships and continues to dominate his class.

This client was also a successful businessman and entrepreneur. At the end of our engagement he fed back that he had been approaching his business decisions in a similar way and had found more freedom and consistency as a result of being uncertain in the way he operated. He had found himself better

---

[3] Bernstein, Nicholai. 1996. *Dexterity and Its Development (Resources for Ecological Psychology)*. Edited by Turvey. Mahwah, NJ: Lawrence Erlbaum Associates, Inc.

able to explore and get a better feel for his operating environment which was becoming much more competitive.

HOW IS THIS ACHIEVED? FLIPPING THE PSYCHOLOGICAL SIDE

The most successful elite racers I studied all described a quality of reaching out of themselves as essential to their performance. This way of working developed from an important, notable theme which also emerged out of my research. For example, finding the grip or traction, finding good lines and finding good rhythm. All these qualities came from a process of letting the circuit come to them, which depended on their connection with it. Combined with this, elite racers in my research tended to concur with each other that they did not believe they would ever know their environment. This is a frame of mind which keeps them exploring.

It was notable in my research that this tendency to keep exploring related to how those performing at the pinnacle of their context literally saw the world differently, which enabled them to perform in remarkable ways within those contexts.

The themes relating to:

• embracing uncertainty, and;

• reaching outside themselves;

are inextricably linked. In order to explore them effectively in my work, I had to find a different psychological approach.

APPLYING A MORE PRACTICAL AND RELEVANT PSYCHOLOGICAL APPROACH

I do not view learning and development, or subsequent performance enhancement for that matter, as processes which arise out of the development or refinement of a client's mental processes (which is generally the dominant approach in psychology today, one which was derived from cognitive approaches).

Instead, I engage with clients in a mutual and co-operative journey to explore their perspectives and relationship with the world. This is done by employing a process of seeking further information and developing deeper knowledge about the characteristics of the environment within which my clients operate. (Another important related quality which I won't go into detail about here is that at the both the executive/entrepreneur and elite athlete levels, my clients are already sophisticated and aware thinkers within their context, so this is rarely the issue in my experience).

This aspect of my approach is grounded in the branch of Ecological Psychology derived from the work of JJ Gibson and others[4] . I have used the principles (and

---

[4] See for example: Gibson, James. 1979. *The Ecological Approach to Visual Perception*. Boston: Houghton Mifflin. Heft, Harry. 2001. *Ecological Psychology in Context: James Gibson, Roger Barker, and the Legacy of William James's Radical Empiricism (Resources for Ecological Psychology)*. Mahwah, NJ: Lawrence Erlbaum Associates, Inc. Reed, Edward. 1996. *Encountering*

a generous sprinkle of the underlying philosophical foundations) of Ecological Psychology to inform my work. One of the key aspects of my work and how I employ Ecological Psychology is in working with what Gibson introduced as 'affordances'. The complete meaning of affordance is still under debate but I view them as qualities of the environment and how these qualities afford context based actions in relation to the perceiver[5].

For example, take an elite skier. Put her at the top of a world cup ski run. The nature of that environment will afford her a certain relationship with it, followed by appropriate and highly skilled actions. Put me at the top of the same slope and the outcome will be entirely different, probably quite disastrous. I would not have much idea how to tackle that particular environment as a skier.

This view of psychology, learning and development, applies just as well to any context because it applies to understanding the underlying principles of how we function as active participants in our world and specific contexts.

In my work, I employ this psychological approach through continuous cycles of exploring the characteristics of our environment. I do this in relation to ourselves as if they are and always will be new, novel and unknown. This, I think, requires a special appreciation of things.

WE DON'T KNOW AND WE NEVER WILL...

The paradox of uncertainty here is that my clients, business and extreme sports ones, tend to report that when they begin to embrace uncertainty from a perspective of continuously developing and refining their relationship with the world/environment, they can more readily accept it.

For example:

- There seems to be a qualitative shift in how they act which encompasses an acceptance of the unknown realities of a complex world.

- They also feel more connected to themselves as a whole and, as a result, less uncertain in themselves.

- The process changes their relationship with fear and anxiety about the outcome of their actions which also yields a much better, purer and natural engagement with it.

My clients tell me that our work helps them to get out of their heads more. In finding themselves out there more by connecting more directly with their environment, they become more inquisitive, more searching of the qualities

the World. New York: Oxford University Press.
[5]Chemero, Anthony. 2010. "An Outline of a Theory of Affordances." In *Ecological Psychology* 15 (2): 181-195.

of both what is going on around them and how they are doing themselves, with their feelings, emotions, thinking and the relationships between these characteristics of their experiences.

THE OUTCOME MEASURES

Due to the nature of my client engagements, both my clients and I assign most value in the outcome of my clients' experiences and the changes in their experiences that emerge from the process.

In business contexts, it is harder to provide consistent and specific concrete measures to back up self-reporting (because of the inherent complexity, ambiguity and difficulties in determining reliable causality in such contexts). In the elite sports context however, things are measured to the nth degree. There tends to be a greater emphasis on environmental controls where formal competition is involved (e.g. a race course associated with highly specific rules and regulations). Therefore, results from this approach have been measured by my clients through lap times and both race and championship results.

CONCLUSIONS AND WHERE NEXT

As you may have noticed, this is an area of passion and fascination for me. It's a journey I feel I'm only beginning. Writing this article has been a valuable process of re-engaging with some of the underlying principles of my work, attempting to explicate these in what I hope is a meaningful and helpful way for others.

As the next step, my mind is wondering towards something which is more akin to exploring and describing some of the phenomenological qualities of my clients' experiences of developing their relationships with uncertainty.

How do moods encroach on our coaching relationships, and help us to become a good coach?

Simon Dennis

I remember years ago, I used to travel to coaching sessions. During the traveling, I could kind of get myself in the right frame of mind, in the right mood. More often than not now, I find that my coaching occurs in amongst my day-to-day role to the point where I can literally go from one meeting into a coaching session without breaks. For example, there might be a finance discussion about budgets and forecasts and then suddenly I have to switch into coaching. I began exploring this shift with colleagues, and started to ask questions around moods and mindsets,

- Can you coach if you're in a bad mood?
- Can you coach only if you're in a good mood?
- Can you only coach if you're in a kind of coaching mood?

MANAGING MOODS 'ON THE RUN'

I connected moods with a phrase that's prevalent in our field that is typically about,

a) Do you bring your stuff into coaching,

and

b) when in a coaching conversation is it your stuff versus their stuff?

And for me, the mood I bring as the coach is clearly my stuff.

I then began asking and reflecting on, how much do you or should you then hold that back if the other person is here to talk about their stuff? Then, how much is not being dealt with genuinely?

For example, If I'm in a bad place because I've just had a heated conversation with my wife or my children, and I then go into a coaching conversation, is it right that I share that information with the coachee and say, "*Just to let you know, I'm in a bit of a bad mood at the moment because I've just had a row with my wife/children.*" Are they going to turn around and say, "*Well, do I care?*" or are they going to respond and say, "*Well, if you are in a bad mood, maybe you need to go and fix that first before you try and fix me?*"

A mood is not that kind of technical issue that can be resolved by a singular technical response, rather it's something more to do with recognising the imbalance or, better still, finding ways to regain balance.

For me, it's back to trying to be good at what I do in the moment. So if I want to be a good coach, then my mood can't come into it even though you might come away from the session and have that kind of epiphany that says, "*I'm going to scream now because I've got to go back to what I was doing before the coaching.*" But there is a balance issue in terms of, how do you hold that inside without it becoming a barrier to success in the coaching session?

It's not happened to me often, to be fair, but there are times when I just thought, "*You know, I'm not in a great place. How am I going to do the best I can as a coach?*" Sometimes literally having that thought walking from one meeting to another and thinking, "*How am I going to do that without it...?*" It becomes a valuable conversation. I guess I have learnt some tricks of the trade.

- Compartmentalize a little bit.

- Try and deflect it e.g. some people might say, "Hang on a minute. I need to make a quick phone call. I'm going to do a two-minute walk around the block to clear my head."

- Sometimes it's a physical thing where they have to physically remove themselves.

For me, it's a combination of things, I don't sit and meditate or such, but I might just take two minutes just to get myself focused on the individual by reviewing any notes that were taken from the last meeting. Sometimes I give myself a bit of a talking to and say, "*Hang on a minute that is my stuff. That's not what this next meeting's about. This next meeting's about their stuff.*" Even when I'm with my team, I can have a tricky meeting at work and afterwards I think, "*Well, this is about their stuff now and why has this just happened? I need to park that.*"

Likewise, moods can be a positive thing too. You can arrive in a really good frame of mind and then shift the individual that's in front of you who isn't in a great place.

MOODS IS ABOUT MANAGING BOUNDARIES

Many people will say and give the model response, "*Oh, yeah. I can put that to one side and I can compartmentalize that. And then I can then be the coach for you in the room.*" For some it might be as easy as that, just breathe and then just put the nice mask on and then take that step into the coaching thing.

From my experience it's not something I think you can necessarily train, but it's something that I think you have to learn to do to an extent.

The reality, I think, and almost in nature of *the good coach*, is that you are who you are, and you bring yourself to the coaching and that's what makes you a good coach.

That's what makes you a different coach to the next coach and therefore the individual whose being coached by you, I think, almost has a right to get you, the coach, in the room. And if that means you're coming with baggage, you know, where does the level come where the baggage starts to encroach and you recognize that as a coach and say, "*Hang on a minute. My stuff's now getting in the way. I need to either compose myself or I need to take a break. Or we need to go down a different avenue.*"

The worst-case scenario, I could imagine, is if you're in a coaching relationship and the thing that comes up in the coaching conversation is the very thing that's causing you the pain as well. For example,

- You're moving into a new house and home, with all the stresses that involves. You step away from that to coach somebody and they then start saying, "*We're leaving the house and we're going through all this stress. And it's putting stress on my home life and my work life.*" At that point as a coach, where do you go with that? Because suddenly it's like, "*Well, hang on a minute. I really do empathize with what you're going through but you don't want to hear about my pains of moving house. And I really don't want to hear about your pains from moving house either because all that's going to bring it back home to me.*"

- Or as one of the organisational coaches working on a transformation program, if you're a senior person in the company, you might know more than the coachee knows. Not only bringing your own stuff, they will be talking about their perception of it and you might be tempted to begin responding with, "*A*ctually, you've got it wrong. That's not what's really going on.*"

These are real dangers. Where do you tread that path as a coach?

Someone once said to me, "*You can't not know what you know. It's just how much of it do you then share in a bid to help the coachee.*" If we keep our intent clean, there's juggling going on inside the coach which says, "*I know stuff. I'm in a similar place to them but I've got to be careful I don't step over the line and start pushing myself onto them because I need to get them to recognize where they are and how they can help themselves.*"

This is the challenge. Coaches are human beings. They're going to experience those same challenges. And there is a possibility that their coachee will be bringing exactly that challenge to the table. This is because what we're doing works at quite an intimate level, and as a compromise it's worthwhile to check out the assumptions you're making about the way you're looking at things.

LET ME SHARE SOME EXAMPLES

Quite often I find myself in internal situations where people will talk about team changes or structural changes, where they'll say, "*You know, I understand this is going to happen.*" Depending on whom made the comment, I might say, "*What makes you think that?*" or "*How valid is your information source?*"

As the conversation continues, I've learnt how to respond and acknowledge where they're coming from because in their mind, it's going to happen (probable) and so I subtly shift the conversation by adding the idea of 'possible' as I engage with them. I'll start saying, "*But if that did happen, what would be your course of action? What would be your options?*" Trying to use a language of possibility rather than probability in a bid to help them see that maybe what they're firmly believing is maybe not so firm after all. I've found sometimes I use language that closes down a conversation that ends up with them responding and saying, "*So what do you know that I don't know? And what aren't you telling me?*" These are quite subtle and indirect ways to test assumptions, and maybe there's a point where you just have to say to them, "*Look, I do know some things about that. What I can tell you is your assumptions aren't correct. But let's just leave it there.*" And sometimes I have to be formal and say, "*I'm not at liberty to tell you what's happening.*"

I had a situation many years ago where people were asking for me to be their coach because they knew I would know other details. They knew that I was in a position of leadership in this particular area so they were - I'm thinking of one case in particular - they actually admitted and said, "*Well, the reason I chose you as my coach is because you know an awful lot more about the strategy and where this is going.*"

I said, "*I can't say that's true, but that shouldn't affect your choice of me as a coach and it certainly shouldn't affect the way I coach you. If you actually want me to divulge strategy and future plans, that's a different conversation. And you need to approach me as a professional and say, 'What is happening?' because that's not part of the coaching contract.*" I was very clear upfront, but sometimes your coachee isn't clear about their motives. Unless you're particularly perceptive as a coach and know where their motives come in, it might take some time to say, "*I get the sense that, actually, you want me to divulge information rather than coach you.*"

Another time, very early on when I was attending coach training, I was paired with a guy as part of observed coaching. He began to discuss a project that he was really struggling with and with people on the project, and we had a really good twenty-minute dialogue that was being fully observed by the other attendees.

What was interesting was at the end of the conversation, after he achieved what he was looking for, as we were getting the feedback, a number of the observers said, "*Oh, that was a really good clean coaching session.*" When I was chatting to them all over coffee and mentioned that I'd been working on the same project for the last two years, and so almost everything he'd said, I knew already. In effect, he hadn't told me anything I wasn't already aware of and yet no one in the room had noticed. The facilitator who was leading the training said, "*Were you that aware of what you did?*" The guy I was coaching said, "*You hid it very well.*" And I responded that, "*I wasn't consciously hiding it but in my head, I didn't think it would add anything to the coaching for me to share that. I didn't feel the need.*"

For me, as I reflected on this thought, "*If I said to you right now, actually, I've been on the project for two years so I kind of know what's going on. I think it would just shut down the whole conversation. And so I said, 'It was more about the intent. The intent was to help the individual. You need to let them air their perspective.'*" And that's the decision I made in those initial few minutes to give this guy the space to work through his challenges and lift his mood.

For me, there are different ways to air the elephant in the room at that point and respond appropriately to those moods in those moments. Where are those boundaries? How do you recognize those boundaries? And what do you offer rather than what do you hold back and how does that effect the relationship?

CONTINUALLY REDISCOVERING BALANCE

All the time as coaches, I think we're walking that line between what's genuine and real and what people want to present to you. It's being able to quickly assess and diagnose whose mood is impacting the quality of the relationship in those moments. And I guess the whole nub of coaching is to get underneath that and get to what's really driving it. What's really going to improve? What's really going to make a difference?

There is value in sometimes sharing that and saying, *"You know what, whatever you're saying isn't hitting home."* And I think the careful bit is knowing when it is your stuff, because I can say to somebody, *"You know what, I'm hearing what you're saying but it's just not registering with me."* And they may reply, *"Well, that's your problem. That clearly has something to do with you."* With that response comes the jolt of reality and you might say, *"Actually, you're right. I need to switch and just be more in tune with what's going on."* Whereas at other times, they may respond, *"No, actually, you're right. I'm just talking for the sake of it."* So it's trying to get that.

It's about at what point would you say, *"I'm afraid I can't continue this dialogue."* At what point do you step over the boundary and say, *"I'm afraid I don't subscribe to that point of view."*

For me, I guess it's about walking that tightrope, maintaining rapport, maintaining integrity, maintaining authenticity. It's recognizing that the person in front of me may have different views, may have different cultures, may have different beliefs and what I can do is work with the individual in the room and what they bring to the table. And importantly, noticing how and when I'm bringing my stuff, my moods, into our coaching conversations and that when I do it's used with the right intention.

Question: How do you recognise, and then use moods to keep appropriate boundaries?

Shifting the negative to positive in judgement-blame cycles

Rosemary Harper

was recently asked by a peer colleague, Katy Tuncer, a question over email, amongst others,

> *"I've observed a cycle of behaviour when coaching senior teams in conflict recently – where judgment and blame reinforce each other. I see people enter conversations/interpret emails/make points in meetings from a defensive and judgmental perspective. Identifying common goals, making commitments together, making/accepting requests about behaviours etc. have helped break the cycle to some extent for my clients. I was wondering if there is an established model or someone has written something in the literature about this judgement-blame cycle?"*

Broadly speaking, the description shared by Katy in what she described as the judgement-blame cycle is something I have frequently worked with in senior teams. I have also found it within functions (e.g. the marketing team blames the sales team, who blames the production team etc.). Each of us responded from our experiences.

I shared from my experiences that unfortunately I have not found a single model that works for all occasions. It also offered me an opportunity to quickly review and reflect on my own practice, and I shared what I believed to be my top eleven ways of working with the 'judgement-blame' cycle over the years particularly in team coaching.

All of these are simply entry points into getting the team to name their issues and then find an appropriate way of responding to them.

MY TOP ELEVEN WAYS OF WORKING WITH THE 'JUDGEMENT-BLAME' CYCLE

1. AT THE CONTRACTING STAGE, I SPEND A LOT OF TIME UNDERSTANDING THE CIRCUMSTANCES, THE TEAM'S PURPOSE AND OBJECTIVES, WHAT THEY DO WELL, LESS WELL ETC. WHAT HAS LED THEM TO TEAM COACHING? (OFTEN THIS IS AN ISSUE)

Ideally, I will meet each team member prior to working with the team, and use a structured format to understand:

- Their individual role and key objectives, and who else needs to be involved in order to achieve their goals.
- The purpose of the team from their viewpoint.
- How the team as a whole adds value.
- What it does best?
- What it does least well?
- What one or two things, if changed, would make the most difference to the team?

If there are blame-judgement cycles, this will normally become apparent at this stage. This will give me a clue about how best to proceed with the whole team. I may often feed back anonymised team results at relevant times during team coaching.

If I cannot meet everyone individually in advance, I may start a team coaching intervention asking them to gain more clarity by answering some of the above questions. It is surprising how often there is disagreement about the team's shared purpose. Without that agreed purpose, they are likely to become frustrated at team interactions.

2. SOMETIMES IT IS ABOUT UNCLEAR ACCOUNTABILITIES

At a team session, I will ask people to share their accountabilities, together with who else in the team needs to be involved and how (I will sometimes use a simple matrix - joint decision/consult/ inform). They will need to prepare in advance, but this often throws up interesting (and judgemental) discussions.

3. IN MY CONTRACTING WITH THE WHOLE TEAM, I WILL TALK ABOUT TEAM PROCESSES AND HOW THEY WORK TOGETHER

We might explore the difference between conversation, discussion, debate and dialogue. I will ask them what mode they usually operate in and how successful it is. I will ask for permission to call a time out if I feel something is happening in the team process that needs further exploration. Quite often, they will take over for themselves, with team members calling for a time out before I do.

4. I OFTEN ASK TEAMS IF THEY WOULD ALLOW ME TO OBSERVE THEM IN NORMAL WORKING MODE, ASKING THEM TO PICK A DIFFICULT/ CONTENTIOUS ISSUE

I will explain that I will be observing key moments, 'air time', body language, language used. I will keep a rough record of air time for each person. I keep a record of the amount of time spent in positive ways – e.g questioning, encouraging, exploring options etc. versus negative time spent defending, blocking, disagreeing etc.

My normal rule of thumb is a three-to-one ratio of positive to negative in an effective team.

I will then provide feedback. The key here is to get them to take over the feedback session. They normally will be a bit defensive at first but questions like, 'What went particularly well? What were the less successful parts? What was happening then?' I keep very detailed notes and timings which allows me to give specific feedback if necessary. During this time, the coach must remain very open and calm, even if the team is at first a bit defensive or angry. Building the trust of the team first is key.

5. SOMETIMES IT IS A PERSONALITY ISSUE

I know many see it as 'old hat', but I have found MBTI a helpful tool to start non-judgemental discussion about why people see things differently and sources of conflict. I have also found Belbin useful. Both have given teams and individuals "aha" moments. It also gives them a language they can use to surface issues.

6. TRUST WITHIN THE TEAM IS ALWAYS KEY

Different people, and certainly, different nationalities, will often differ in what they need in order to trust others. I have used a questionnaire called ITTI (International Trust in Teams) with both multi- national teams and national teams. It will start a discussion about what is going on in the team and why people may feel a lack of trust.

7. WORKING WITH CLEAR DISAGREEMENTS

If there is a clear disagreement about particular decisions or courses of action, I will often ask the team to select two or three potential actions, and then work with all three. I make it clear that their job at this point is not to make a decision on which one. Every person in turn, including the proposer, can only give the advantages of each option. Any negative comments will not be allowed.

After two or three rounds, everyone has then to go through all the negatives of each option. Very often, a way forward becomes clear. If they decide one option looks best, I will then ask them to look at the advantages of the other two options and try find a way of incorporating them into their preferred option.

This stops early polarising of views, makes everyone look at the advantages and disadvantages of each option, and hopefully ensures that something from each option is included in the final solution. A variation on this is to take the most diametrically opposed choices and work with those. Often, a third way spontaneously occurs.

8. IF THE TEAM IS FEELING SPIKY

I might ask them to do a sort of negative Ishikawa. Whatever the question/issue, I ask them to find the worst possible solution/outcome and then highlight all the awful things within that. They normally have a bit of fun with this. It allows them to think what needs to change to turn all the negatives to positives.

9. IF I CAN, I LIKE TO HAVE A MIX OF TEAM INTERVENTIONS AND INDIVIDUAL COACHING

I make it clear that all the individual coaching is confidential - but that during this confidential coaching, we will be covering team issues, and how the individual feels within the team. Here, I can offer feedback from what I have observed, and we can discuss that. Where there is a clear dislike/power struggle, this can be explored.

I have found that for some people, perceptual positions have helped at this point. If it is a clear power struggle, we can discuss the implications. If they decide to change their approach, I can offer to observe at the next team session and give them feedback.

10. WHEN THE TEAM COACHING IS A LITTLE MORE ADVANCED, I MAY ASK INDIVIDUALS TO GIVE EACH OTHER FEEDBACK

This may start along the lines of, 'What I really value about you as a team member, and what one or two things you might change to make an even greater contribution?'

I will sometimes do this in a circle (in which case I keep out of the circle), and sometimes gallery style, with a flip chart for each person. Before we look at the results, I talk about the value of feedback. I also make it clear that the recipients cannot challenge the feedback, but only respond with what pleases me, what surprises me, and what I intend to work with.

I have also used a variation where the team gives feedback in pairs (which rotate). This can be quite powerful and may well expose some of the judgemental aspects. I only do it when I feel the team is ready.

11. PICTURE AND METAPHORS CAN BE VERY HELPFUL

I sometimes ask team members to produce banners, which include pictures on their values, how they see themselves and how they think others may see them. I will also ask them to draw an image that represents the team. We then share and talk about the images.

REFLECTING ON MY APPROACHES

My approaches may all sound very process driven, but the key with each and every one of them is in building the quality of relationship between team and coach. This is so you can ask the difficult questions and get them to trust you enough to take them to challenging places. All these tools are vehicles to allow you to do that.

This can also be uncomfortable for the coach too, because there are no easy answers. Often your role is to hold the tension until they feel brave enough to name what is going on.

Question: How have you managed to hold similar tensions within team and individual coaching?

A systematic approach to turning around a slump in self confidence

Katy Tuncer

L ike many coaches, I often have clients report increased self-confidence following a particularly high-impact series of one-to-one coaching sessions, or after they attend a leadership-development programme.

A quick poll of a few of my recent clients and fellow coaches suggested that guiding leaders through the steps for turning around a slump in self-confidence could be one of the most valuable tools in our coaching box of tricks.

We are all aware that high self-confidence can be the platform for conviction, determination, resilience, inspiration, rapid learning and many other helpful leadership traits. My aim in this blog is to provide a framework and ideas for both coaches and leaders themselves dealing with a confidence slump. I also observe that committing to a systematic process and being in action can be a major step forward in itself on the road to building self-confidence.

So, here is a simple five-step process that I have seen work wonders, when applied patiently and diligently.

1. LABEL THE SLUMP IN SELF-CONFIDENCE AND CHOOSE TO DO SOMETHING ABOUT IT

I very rarely hear 'I want to invest in building my self-confidence' before a client engages me as a coach or participates in one of my leadership training programmes. (And that's despite the raft of testimonials after working with me emphasising the boost they've achieved in self-confidence as a result). I have observed that as long as we are fighting to prove we are confident, able, resilient people, it can be hard to consider that we may lack self-confidence.

In my experience, an irony exists: the harder people resist acknowledging a self-confidence slump, the more they convince themselves that they actually do have something to hide and that they are not good enough.

One way to have a breakthrough with this step, is to consider the difference between social confidence and inner self-confidence. Try asking: Are you articulate, poised, able to converse naturally with a range of people, well-presented and armed with a 'track record of achievement'? If so, the bad news is that step 1 will be tough because high social confidence can stand in the way!

Sometimes, as a coach, I've also found it helps to ask, "*What would it be like if you had more inner self-confidence?*" The answers I've received range from, "*I'd believe I'm the right person for my job*" to "*I'd stop saying yes to everything*" to "*my pitches would be so much more compelling*".

By achieving step 1, you have a case for action, more freedom and more options.

2. DESCRIBE YOUR GREATNESS, WHAT DO YOU STAND FOR?

A simple but very powerful technique for re-programming the brain is simply through positive self-description. The question could be: 'What are you great at?' or 'What impact do you have in the world?' or even 'What are the best things you make happen?' It just needs to be empowering, and allow the individual to start freely describing their own greatness.

When I ask clients to do this exercise, the rule I usually apply is 'no talking about weaknesses, what you can't do, mistakes, or caveats'. After all Einstein said a person who has never made a mistake has never tried something new. I'm ruthless in bringing clients back to the question and only talking about their greatness, by which I mean their personal impact and strengths. As they start slowing down I ask them to consider what others have said they value most. I ask them to be specific about exactly what they have done and I encourage them to think bigger.

This can be done individually with a piece of paper or it can be done with a coach, a peer, a mentor or a friend. The fundamental requirement is to avoid distractions and modesty. The listener (or the piece of paper!) captures what they hear and starts grouping together consistent themes.

Creating space for the brain to puzzle out and acknowledge what's really going on and what really matters in this way can be very powerful. One of my clients described this as "*digging down into your intuition, defining your own values and coming back to your real self.*"

This exercise can create content for many useful personal marketing channels – LinkedIn profile, biographies, job applications, introductions to speeches and presentations – and it will be iterated on many times. The key is to get started.

3. MOBILISE YOUR SUPPORT NETWORK

Loss of self-confidence can have an unfortunate side effect of underestimating the strengths and value of the support networks people have around them. I advise clients to be unreasonable with themselves with how much effort, time and financial investment they put into surrounding themselves with positive influences.

I recommend first explaining to a selection of trusted mentors/advisors that you are committed to getting your mojo back and building confidence. I suggest asking them what they think you are great at and listening carefully to their advice. It's important to be authentic, to explain what you are working on and ask for specific help. There are various techniques for identifying the ideal go-to personal team members (such as network mapping) but I find it's best not to waste time considering who to talk to first. Just do it.

Simultaneously, I say, get out there! Go on courses, go to events, go to parties. Expand your inspiration and connections. Show deep interest in other people's passions, ask questions and learn. Building perspective is vital. It's also helpful to use books, blogs, YouTube etc. to get ideas and build your repertoire of skills and styles out there in the world.

4. STOP FIGHTING WRONG-DOERS

Surrounding ourselves with positive influences is vital, but it can take us only so far. We also need to deal with the people who are just there in our lives and who it would be impractical to avoid.

The first breakthrough is to accept and believe that 'I get to choose whether others make me feel bad'. Unless physical force is involved, no one can make us feel bad unless we choose to let them.

The most effective technique I know of for living by this belief is to stay focused on goals and never ever get sucked into 'teaching them a lesson'.

Next, if my client can get to the point of letting things go and focussing on goals, I then recommend taking on another challenge. It's well documented that human beings are influenced, make assumptions and draw information from others in a far more complex way than simply via listening to the words being said. As a result, we can learn techniques for handling our body language, for using cleverly positioned language, for perfecting eye contact and the right amount of tactility... But what about making it all natural? If we genuinely consider someone as a collaborative partner, one who we trust and value, all of our subtle behaviours toward that person will naturally align with that. The other person will pick up on it and hey presto; they're acting like a collaborative partner right back.

I ask client to simply try 'seeing the gold' in people who they might otherwise judge to be dominating/incapable/aggressive/manipulative/powerful – or any other adjectives that induce negative emotions. It doesn't have to mean denying any true dysfunctions. However, countless clients (and I myself countless times) have found that by focusing the mind on the good points about the other person typically leads to a more productive and effective interaction with them.

5. TAKE CARE OF THE ONLY BODY YOU HAVE

How many people think 'I have a body' vs. 'I am my body'?

There is sadly still a common workplace culture that drives us to push our bodies to the limit. We hear the mantras: 'I eat rubbish', 'I don't have time to exercise', 'I don't need sleep'. (Interestingly McKinsey recently found that many senior executives think other people's performance suffer through lack of sleep, but not their own, and there is evidence that impaired judgement through lack of sleep is comparable with that through alcohol consumption!). Beyond depriving ourselves of the fuel and rest we need physically, there are the psychological stresses we impose on our bodies by not prioritising thinking space, relaxation and social connections. 'I never relax', whilst often said as a badge of heroism, can be a red flag for me as a coach.

I often hit a brick wall with clients when I try the 'you should look after yourself' line. For many people, caring for mind and body is not seen as an essential life skill to be learned and practised. Instead, I encourage them to start considering why they need to be on their A-game. For example: to perform better in a key meeting; to be present with other people and so more influential; to stay calm under pressure etc. I find this makes the case for self-care stronger.

Then, once someone is committed to take care of the only body they have, the issue is often not designing the perfect combination of sleep, exercise, meditation etc. (although that may be the subject of another article!), but how to stick at it...

Here, my role as a coach here is often helping them put mechanisms in place to keep to their commitment. Declarations work well, in particular when shared with a loved one: "*I will go to bed by *11pm every week night.*" This increases a feeling of accountability. Scheduling activities (such as gym visits) into work diaries can also be helpful, especially when coupled with effective task management systems.

SUMMARY AND CONCLUSION

- Self-confidence is vital for human beings to perform optimally in life and work.

- A drop in self-confidence can often go un-recognised by the individual experiencing it.

- Acknowledging the slump and taking concerted and systematic action can lead to a turnaround over a period of days, weeks or months.

- The five steps outlined here are best done with support, be that from a professional coach or another trusted person.

In researching and writing this article I have become even more aware of how widespread self-confidence slumps are. Thank you to all the people who have contributed input and helped shape the piece. There is a certain stigma attached to low self-confidence, which I think is a real shame. I hope this article will unstick a few more people, ones who are either experiencing their own slump or coaching someone out of theirs.

Hammers, nails and mindfulness: The dangers of coaching when you have a favourite intervention 'If the only tool you have is a hammer...'

Peter Young

I'm curious about something that is cropping up more and more in my coaching at present. I'm noticing a growing frequency with which I'm introducing mindfulness to clients; whether this is in the form of a theoretical introduction to the field, or a short practice within the coaching session, or suggestions of exercises to undertake between sessions. It's not that I am doing this 'mindlessly'. It's deliberate and supposedly well justified. Yet it is also raising questions for me.

My curiosity is piqued, probably because there is a little concern gnawing at the back of my mind that this pattern may have more to do with me (and my interests and enthusiasms) than it has to do with the client. In the past I have noticed a similar thing at work, where new frameworks, or specific techniques that have been recently introduced to me (for example in books or on courses), suddenly start cropping up in my coaching. And at the time they feel like the exact thing that the client needs! (Yet perhaps a month or a year earlier, these techniques would not have been on my radar.)

This raises a number of important questions including the following, 'How do I as a coach decide in the moment what is the most appropriate intervention for the client?' We know from research that the precise technique or approach is a less significant predictor of success than the appetite of the client and the quality of the partnership. But what is the importance of 'technique' or approach? I would consider that if the only tool you have is a hammer, then you'll treat everything as if it was a nail. It is also important to remember that every coach's toolbox is limited – even those coaches who are inveterate learners and addicted to attending courses! So the hammer–nail thing must surely always be just a matter of degree?

HOW DO YOU DECIDE IN THE MOMENT WHAT IS THE MOST APPROPRIATE INTERVENTION FOR THE CLIENT?

I'm going to consider how I decide in the moment what the most appropriate intervention is for the client. The 'official' answer, and the one that I would most likely give at an interview where my coaching style was being questioned, would be to make reference to my coaching model. (NB: my personal 'coaching model' was first articulated as part of a programme of professional coach development. Interestingly it has lain dormant in a folder on my computer for a number of years. This observation is a reminder to dust it off and to explore its continued relevance. Challenge to self: do I really only produce a coaching model in order to gain a qualification?)

Referencing my model then, I might talk about how I enhance the client's levels of self-awareness; how I help her discern her habitual patterns of thoughts, feelings and behaviours, etc. How her resourcefulness and resilience is strengthened as she recognises and begins to integrate those less obvious or even pushed-aside aspects of her experience. So interventions that encourage such awareness-raising might fit well with my model.

Reflecting on the question of appropriateness further, other issues come to mind. Issues which challenge my practice more than what might be seen as the intellectualising of the previous paragraph. There is surely something to be asked about,

- How I assess the readiness of the client for a particular intervention?
- What else have they tried already, and to what degree has it worked?
- What else do they really need, given what they already know and have tried?
- What is their degree of appetite in this particular area?
- How much are they willing to invest in bringing about change in this space?

As I write these questions, I'm aware that I may not always conduct such due diligence with the client. That I run the risk of making assumptions about need, readiness and appropriateness. Perhaps this is in part driven by my own appetite to share my latest enthusiasm, perhaps driven by a hurry towards solutions, and maybe driven by other, as yet hidden, motivations!

CREATING A PATH TO GREATER FREEDOM AND CHOICE

This then raises a number of important areas for further learning and experimentation.

First and foremost, can I bring a quality of mindful awareness to those moments in coaching when I feel 'drawn to action'? Whether that is grabbing the pad of paper and explaining a model, introducing a tool or suggesting an exercise. Can I press pause in those moments and connect with my own intention and energy in that moment? Can I especially pay attention to any movement towards 'teaching' or 'sharing my passions'?

Second. In that pause, there needs to be a process of checking that the client and I are moving in sync. That I've not got ahead of things, that we've done the groundwork together to establish why we're doing this and that the client is fully ready. That we've clearly contracted for where we are in the process and the intervention is meeting the real articulated need, not one that has just been heard in my own mind.

Third. Am I in a position where I can actively choose an intervention from a range of options, rather than to automatically default to my current favourite? Perhaps if I only have one method in mind, I should start to challenge myself more actively. What else could I use here? What other approaches might serve the client as well or even better?

There is a delicious irony here: just as I'm challenging myself around my ability to deploy interventions appropriately, in the current case mindfulness, the solution that I'm diagnosing for myself is... greater mindfulness. Well, what a surprise!

'Is this my stuff or the client's stuff?' Putting frustration on the table for discussion

Doug Montgomery

Coaching, in the way I practice, is not a social conversation. It is a specific non-judgemental, contracted conversation in which a coach and a client have very specific roles and responsibilities. I want to share a recent experience of how I addressed the frustration I felt during a coaching conversation that resulted in me being totally honest and direct with a coaching client.

I have been working with this particular client for a little while, and we have built up a good rapport, established their coaching goals and got input from some colleagues and their manager. I realised that my main feeling was of intense frustration in the way that each of the sessions were being eaten up by my client's long monologues.

THE FEELING SURFACES

At one of our sessions, this client started by telling me their plans to work better with one of their senior colleagues. They had worked out a way of building trust with this very difficult colleague and was describing the plan, how it would help and why this would be useful and valuable to both the client and to the colleague. The explanation included a detailed description with lots of logic and reasons to believe it would work.

I noticed that a feeling of frustration began to arise in me.

It started as a distraction. Then I noticed that I was tapping one of my feet on the floor. I felt I wanted to ask questions but there was no space to insert them. When I paused to step back and ask myself what was going on – the feeling of frustration came to the surface.

THE CURIOUS PLUNGE

So I interrupted the flow, asking permission to share an observation with my client. This felt risky – both the interruption and what I was about to share.

"I am noticing that I am feeling very frustrated just now. What is going on for you?"

They responded saying that they too were feeling frustrated and that they often felt that way with this colleague and with others that it is a struggle to work with. The client started to give me examples and war stories which I listened to for a few moments.

I felt under a deluge of information and my frustration rising again. So I interrupted again. I was even more direct.

"I notice that you are giving me a lot of detail, a lot of which I don't need, and some of which sounds like justification of your actions, and some which sound like explanations of why its ok for them to act the way they do with you. Are you aware of this?"

"No I am not!" they responded slightly taken aback.

"Is this typical for you?" probing a little further, having now received their attention.

After a pause to think... *"Yes it is, mainly with the difficult colleagues..."* And again the explanations came forth.

So I interrupted again, *"What is going on just now?"*

"I'm doing it again, aren't I?" And I replied, *"Yes, you are doing it again. What might others be experiencing talking with you?"* They answered without hesitation, *"I don't get to the point, or when I do, I confuse the message with lots of other information and asides. I try to justify myself and I feel I need to keep them happy or they won't work with me. They don't know what I really want or need from them. And I let them off the hook and don't hold them to account."*

To shift the atmosphere, I straightened up in my seat and with a twinkle in my eyes, I asked *"Are you up for some fun with this?"* *"What do you mean?"* they asked. And I shared more of what I was seeking permission to do, *"Would you be willing to try to answer in a maximum of two short sentences? And I can interrupt if they a very long or if you start a third sentence?"*

They agreed, and so I then asked, *"What message do you want the colleague you started the session with to hear loud and clear?"* Without hesitation they replied with, *"I need them to commit to their actions. I need them to deliver on their commitments."*

RE-CONTRACTING

From this point on, we re-contracted for the real work that they wanted to address in their behaviour and included the permission for me to interrupt, when I was getting information and especially justification I don't need, and for them to seek to be brief and to the point.

THE LEARNING

What I learned from this example, is that being aware of my whole self – thinking, feelings and energy levels – that allowed me to leverage all my senses in service of the client. Sharing what I am experiencing, in an open, honest, direct manner, enables my client to connect with their own feelings. In this case, there was a parallel process of frustration present that we surfaced and then used. We were able to use what was in the room to explore what was going on outside in the client's world. This can be a very powerful exploration because it is 'real and now' rather than a recollection of a different time and place.

MULTIPLE PARALLELS

When I reflected back on the previous sessions the same pattern of long descriptions and justifications were there. So was my unease. A sense of time being wasted and not getting on with the work. So perhaps there was a second parallel process – of pleasing others – holding me back from this direct intervention being made earlier in the work and holding my client back from being direct with her colleagues?

AND SO...

My social discomfort in being very direct, of interrupting and pointing out that I was frustrated, is just that – a social discomfort. In a coaching conversation, one responsibility of the coach is to be open and direct with their observations and feedback, and to use these observations to raise awareness in the client. If not shared, these feelings may become distractions for the coach. Of course, they need to be held lightly, as they may be the coach's own stuff and have no meaning for the client. The light hold allows the coach to let them go easily if they are not useful to the client. By not sharing our own experiences and feelings with our clients we risk being a witness to their thinking rather than a supportive and challenging thinking partner.

Question: How have you dealt with this feeling of frustration that's emerged through a coaching conversation?

Feeling for the edges and finding insights in unexpected places

Alan Robertson

I'm making myself revisit old coaching assignments in the belief that this will improve my current and future practice. It's an interesting form of self-discipline because it doesn't have any rules other than to articulate something in writing about each case. Other than that, it's simply a matter of:

- Revisit an assignment which is formally over;

- Re-read the notes that I made at the time and notice how I now think and feel about the case with the benefit of distance, hindsight and whatever I've taken from experience since;

- Err on the side of self-criticism rather than self-congratulation.

It's certainly a form of reflective learning because the passage of time offers fresh perspectives to open-mindedness. I also think it's a form of action learning, especially when the product is presented as a blog and opened up to additional observations and feedback from independent peers.

I'm sure the architect of action-learning, the late Reg Revans, would have approved of it as a way in which we "*can suddenly begin to see, with the help of such comrades, the immense, unused – indeed unknown – assets that are our own lived experiences[1].*" It is a form of self-supervision or even self-coaching, if there is such a thing.

OBJECTIVELY LEARNING FROM A COMPLETED ASSIGNMENT

The coaching that I did with 'O' seemed to have gone well. She had been pleased with it. So had her sponsoring manager. On the face of it the case was

---

[1] Revans, Reginald. 1984. *Action Learning: Back to Square One, in The Sequence of Managerial Achievement*. Bradford: MCB University Press.

straightforward. However, returning to it after a gap of eighteen months, I am left wondering whether it's actually telling me that it's good practice to look for learning where you least expect to find it.

THE COACHING CONTRACT

O was a subject matter expert in a large commercial organisation. Her coaching was at the instigation of her manager, not because O was regarded as difficult, problematic or in need of remedial work (as so often seems to be the case when people are put forward for coaching), but because she was well-regarded. Her boss felt O had further potential and wanted her to get professional help to be able to achieve it.

Three objectives were agreed for her coaching (Three seems to be a good number when setting objectives. Is that because it prompts you to think more broadly rather than too narrowly about the purpose of the coaching?).

1. To use the challenges that she would face in her work over the next twelve months as opportunities to develop her personal brand, resilience and confidence;

2. To develop and extend the quality of her relationships with her stakeholders;

3. To clarify her career ambitions and develop the awareness and capabilities to take the next steps in pursuing them.

DIAGNOSING AND ASSESSING THE READINESS OF THE CLIENT

In one respect O was very easy to coach. She was attentive, eager to learn and prompt at trying things out in practice between coaching sessions. In another respect O was very difficult to coach, if you take the view – as I do – that coaching is not so much about advising people how to do things as about encouraging them to think for themselves and extending their capability to do so. O was very open-minded and actively sought advice. She found it more difficult either to articulate her own thinking processes or to stretch them in new and unfamiliar ways.

In retrospect, there was a clue that this might turn out to be a difficulty. O completed a number of psychometrics when we began to work together. We both agreed that this would be a useful way of obtaining some initial insights about her styles, interests, motivations and self-awareness. And so it was. O was a team player. She was optimistic about people in general, liked working with others and was sensitive to their feelings. She was inclined to be flexible rather than rigid, at least in the sense that she was energetic and willing to put herself out to do what she understood needed to be done. She was hard-working and conscientious. Crucially, and this was the clue, she was grounded and task-focused rather than idea-oriented, unorthodox or imaginative[2].

MY APPROACH TO COACHING

When I coach, I'm always looking for the edge of the individual's comfort zone. I see my role as being to encourage and enable the coachee to put at least one foot outside that comfort zone, to test their footing in that unfamiliar space and to learn to step beyond their previous limits.

When I use psychometrics to assist this process, I regard a personality profile as a picture of the individual's personal resourcefulness. I'm looking for a knot among the patterns which might constrain that resourcefulness, if only in particular situations.

In O's case the 'knot' was her belief that she ought already to have the answers, literally that she should have the answers 'all ready.' Her VoicePrint profile revealed a strong tendency to admonish, especially when she felt under pressure. Our exploration of this result quickly confirmed that this directive voice took the form of self-talk, aimed at herself rather than others.

- "I should know that. I should be responding to that question."
- "I should have the answers. After all, I'm supposed to be the subject matter expert."
- "I can let go, when I have 100 percent confidence in the other person to do the job."
- "I'm worried that I'm going to sound like a muppet, when I don't know what I'm talking about."
- "I don't do well in conversations, when I'm suddenly put on the spot."

This self-limiting belief (and the internal monologue that kept it alive) was compromising the quality of O's performance in a number of areas:

- Delegation of tasks to her team;
- Handling disagreements and potential conflicts;
- Contributing to more open-ended discussions about strategy;
- Feeling confident and speaking up in the presence of senior management.

---

[2] Blanchard, Ken. 2007. *Situational Leadership II: The Integrating Concept in Leadership at a Higher Level.* FT Prentice Hall.)

PART 1: Leading edge: Influences on Practitioner's Learning and Development

EXTRACTING MY LEARNINGS: REFLECTING ON THE EXPECTATIONS AND REALITIES OF DELIVERING COACHING

So how did we tackle these issues? By introducing 'O' to a variety of models and frameworks which she had not previously encountered. Specifically, these were Hersey and Blanchard's 'Situational Leadership[3]', Thomas and Kilmann's 'Conflict Handling Styles[4]' – both of which are widely used – and Robert Keidel's much less well-known 'Triarchic Theory[5]' , which I admire very much for its powerful insight into the deep forces perpetually at work (and in tension) in organisational life.

What I was hoping was that O would learn to use these frameworks as organisers for her own thinking. I wanted them to give her criteria and dimensions to think about as she tackled specific challenges. What I always say to my coaches is not to expect these models to give them answers, but to explore them, play with them, not treat them with too much respect but test them out, 'test them to destruction' so that you can learn when and to what extent they are and are not useful.

What actually happened is that O used them more like algorithms than heuristics. She used them very carefully and very diligently, as someone with her sense of responsibility and concern for others is always likely to do. She never, at least during the time that we were coaching together, became comfortable with using them in a looser or more creative way to provoke her own thinking or develop the independent-mindedness that is such an important ingredient in more senior roles.

The extent of how far we got with my 'frameworks-for-thinking' strategy was exposed by the limited progress that we made on the third coaching objective. O came into coaching unclear about her future career ambitions and, I regret to say, she left in the same state. Neither my inviting her to 'have any career wish you like – what would it be?', nor our exploration of her earlier life interests, nor my observations about the sorts of careers that tended to be pursued by others with similar personality profiles took us any closer to defining where she wanted to go with her own career. She, I and her sponsoring manager alike, although all satisfied that O had made visible progress on coaching objectives 1 and 2, were all equally agreed that we hadn't made any progress on number 3.

---

[3] Kilmann, Thomas. 2007. *Conflict Mode Instrument*. Mountain View, CA: CPP, Inc.

[4] Keidel, Robert. 1995. *Seeing Organizational Patterns: A New Theory & Language of Organizational Design*. San Francisco: Berrett-Koehler.

[5] The psychometrics used were the LaunchPad assessment battery, Percept Resource Management Ltd, http://www.launchpadpsychometrics.com/ and VoicePrint https://letstalk.voiceprint.global

And yet, in retrospect, I now think that we had got somewhere without realising it. We certainly had not defined her future career ambitions or how to reach them, but we had established that she was someone who found it very difficult to think about the question. And I think also we had uncovered something about why. O was someone, at least at that stage in her development, who needed problems and opportunities to be presented to her. Given a challenge, she would assiduously get stuck into tackling it, but she needed the challenges to be supplied.

FINDING INSIGHTS IN UNEXPECTED PLACES

Having reflected on this case, I'm left with two final wonderings. They both expand my sense that 'feeling for the edges' is an important part of what a coach should be doing.

My first wondering is about where we set our level of expectation upon ourselves as coaches and upon our coachees. We're an idealistic lot, we people developers. I wonder whether it would be more realistic to expect that most of our coaching assignments are going to be only partially successful. As 'transitional objects' ourselves, accompanying our coachees through a relatively short period in their working lives, we should perhaps take the leaf about 'good enough parenting' out of Donald Winnicott's book[6]. Perhaps *the good coach* is actually the good-enough coach.

The second thought is, as so often, related to the first. I wonder if one of the coach's goals, or even responsibilities, in any assignment should be to find out – and comment explicitly on – where the boundary of the coachee's readiness for further development currently appears to be. (And now I'm nodding an acknowledgement in the direction of Lev Vygotsky and his concept of the 'zone of proximal development[7]'). Certainly in the past I have hesitated to voice my sense of where that boundary might be for fear of limiting or damaging a coachee's prospects, fuelling self-doubt or even setting up a self-fulfilling label. I'm now asking myself whether it might better serve coachees and their sponsors, as well as illuminating the coaching task in hand, if I were to contract to offer a considered opinion about the individual's current level of readiness for further development at the point at which my own involvement as that person's coach comes to an end.

With special thanks to Sue Young for a very stimulating, thought-provoking and enriching discussion, when I first outlined my thoughts about this case to her.

---

[6] Winnicott, D.W., 1960. "The Theory of the Parent-Infant Relationship." In *The International Journal of Psychodynamics* 41: 585-595

[7] Vygotsky, Lev. 1978. "Readings on the Development of Children." In *Mind in Society: The Development of Higher Psychological Processes*, 79-91. Harvard Cambridge, MA: University Press.

CHAPTER 2

MAKING SENSE OF COACHING EXPERIENCES WITH EXTERNAL REFERENCES

Your motivation in coaching: what is your *Ikagi*?

Laurent Terseur

My observation is that motivation in coaching is a much explored field, as long as it refers to the coachee's work on motivation - a little less so on the coach's side.

Having recently read Jeremy Ridge's thought provoking contribution on "Attention in Coaching[1]", I realised how fundamental the role of motivation is in securing quality attention, and I would like to share my thoughts on this matter here.

WHAT IS MOTIVATION AND WHY DOES IT MATTER?

A simple definition of motivation (Merriam-Webster's Learner Dictionary) points at three dimensions:

- The act or process (giving someone a reason for doing something).
- A condition (being eager to act or work).
- A force or influence that causes someone to do something.

Coaching requires an excellent quality of attention. Building on this, I think that giving excellent attention requires an intense motivation on the coach's side. What it takes for the coach to go out, and sit in front of unknown individuals and/or teams, consciously open up and dedicate to that team or that person an absolute, full, pure and supportive attention, then sustain that attention while interpreting a massive amount of signals, and decipher and probe those signals against their specific context so that the clients can dramatically enhance their thinking. Furthermore, and at the same time, a coach must keep

---

[1] Ridge, Jeremy. 2016. "Attention! What Really Makes Coaching Work." *the good coach*. https://the-goodcoach.com/tgcblog/2016/2/19/attention-what-really-makes-coaching-work-or-not-by-jeremy-ridge#sthash.kMIE3Dat.dpuf Accessed September 9.

their attention on the coaching process so the clients translate their insights into tangible and sustainable change.

Just as in other performance arts or in sports at a high level, I believe this quality of attention can only happen when it is supported by an intense driving force: a profound desire, a genuine and compelling reason for being in this space. It makes me think of the *Ikigai*, a Japanese concept meaning 'a reason for being, or a reason to wake up each day[2]'.

WHY (SELF) MOTIVATION IS IMPORTANT TO ME

Motivation has been quite defining in my own journey to become an Executive Coach.

Even though I had been coaching individuals and teams for a long time in my executive career, it took me some time to become conscious of it and allow myself to be a coach in my own mind. I remember when I finally gave myself that permission. What happened, literally overnight, was the immediate shift in the degree and quality of attention that I was able to dedicate to my coachees. It was measured both by the coachees' sudden, impressive feedback and by my inner experience of feeling deeply, perfectly present and in the moment - for the first time in years.

At the time, I reflected on this as I was curious to understand what had enabled this change. I realised that by letting go of those self-limiting thoughts that had been holding me back from fully embracing my role as a coach, it had freed up that space where I could simply be focused on the why I was coaching: I wanted my coachees to flourish. I wanted them to create a better future for themselves, and I deeply enjoyed seeing them doing so.

That was my Ikigai. The one important thing that truly did matter to me. My reason to sit in front of these people and to dedicate them this quality of attention. Ever since then I have been going from surprise to surprise, finding out that I could make that level of presence progress over the years. The more it progressed the more it regenerated me and furthered my motivation.

HOW DOES IT HAPPEN, AND WHAT DOES IT CHANGE?

As I observe my relationship to my Ikigai, I can see that it plays at different levels:

1. In general: Being mindful of my motivation is clearly enlightening my days and supporting my overall morale. I feel privileged because I am doing what is important to me in life.

2. Before starting a coaching relationship with a new individual or team: When approaching a chemistry conversation or the exploration phase in view of team coaching, I can feel a flow of positive energy invading

---

[2] Buettner, Dan. 2008. "What is your Ikigai? How to Live to be 100+." *TED Talks*. https://www.ted.com/talks/dan_buettner_how_to_live_to_be_100 Accessed September 9.

me and opening all my sensors as I think of the prize: cracking that code. Making it happen. The magic of turning up in front of complete strangers without any prejudice. Building together that incredible amount of trust that will enable the creation of an environment in which they'll be able to explore and find ways to change their future, no less.

3. During the coaching conversation and as the coaching process unfolds: from what I have observed, part of what I use is a set of strengths I have been using for a long time, including in my previous career. Listening and attention skills. Multi-lateral thinking, patience, creativity and tenacity which are all ignited and powered by the same engine: a strong drive. I am relaxed as my motivation is what will underpin the quality of attention my clients deserve. Therefore I am able to pick the right approaches to best support them as they go along with their coaching journey.

Being conscious of my motivation changes the level, quality and sustainability of attention. It creates a space where I am both entirely focused and confident so I can monitor in real-time both my clients and my own levels of energy, attunement and engagement.

WHAT ARE THE POSSIBLE DILEMMAS/QUESTIONS FOR SUPERVISION - AND EVEN SELF-SUPERVISION?

From my observations and what I could explore in supervision, I see at least three potential dilemmas or risk areas:

1. **Paying attention to our own motivation as a coach** is, I believe, an essential part of the awareness required to understand our own practice. This self-awareness should not end up competing for or with the coach's quality of attention given to the coachee. Rather, I think it needs to be part of the awareness of the overall coaching interaction. This would include noticing how much it serves and nurtures the process, and mitigating the risk of the coach bringing their biases into the process.

   - For example, if part of the motivation is the reward of seeing the client achieve positive changes, how will the right distance be maintained with that motivation? Without distance, that motivation might influence the process towards looking for immediately visible outcomes, instead of leaving a more ample amount of time for the insights to percolate.

   - Another example is the coach's fundamental motivation about being willing to be helpful or being useful. What changes in the nature of the resulting attention (for instance the focus on needs or on expectations...)? How can it impact the process?

2. **Other situations potentially testing the coach's relationship to their own motivation**. For instance, when working with clients who change their objectives as the process unfolds. Such adjustments or changes can make perfect sense: whether as a function of the evolution of the client's context, the occurrence of major events or important insights. There also might be cases where changing objectives might be an escape or avoidance strategy.

   This poses the question of how to strike the right balance between respecting the client's autonomy versus keeping them accountable for their initial objectives. This is yet another reminder of the importance of the clarity of the mandate and the contracting work done upstream. I find it an interesting area for the coach to pause and reflect on: what might be the influence of their own motivation whilst reviewing the situation.

3. **And what if motivation drops?** I feel fortunate that I haven't experienced this feeling, but I accept the idea that this situation can happen. For me, that would be the signal that the situation needs to be confronted and explored immediately and with honesty. I see such a link between the coach's motivation and his/her ability to be present and authentic, that I doubt the expected professional standards in coaching can be met if the coach's motivation isn't there. The implication being that, in case the motivation couldn't be restored, I would consider this legitimate and in the interests of the client to end the coaching relationship.

IMPLICATIONS WITH CONTINUED PROFESSIONAL DEVELOPMENT

In light of the above, I consider that observing and noticing my motivation and what fuels it is vital in gauging my practice. By doing so, I have so far come to the conclusion that my motivation is being nurtured at the same time my client's learning journey is progressing.

That learning and the associated wonder comes from both because of:

- The discovery journey about the person as well as their environment.

- The developmental journey and the resulting enhanced future.

- The increase in awareness, through feedback and growth from learning and attention capabilities.

As I am more and more aware of the importance of being conscious of my motivation, the result is:

- I exercise myself regularly to notice my levels of motivation, both in general and in the moment when I coach, in a sort of a real-time self-supervision process.

- I regularly reflect on related clients' situations, and bring to external supervision those for which I would wonder if my judgement could be affected.

- I use my relationship to my motivation more and more to prepare my conversations, and to be in the right mindset.

AND WHAT ABOUT YOU?

- What is your "*Ikigai*"?

- How often do you revisit it?

- What do you observe about it, and how does that inform/influence your practice?

- How do you nurture it?

Engaging with energy - an exploration of energy in coaching, facilitation, business and life

Liz Hill-Smith

"GOING WITH THE ENERGY"

have recently been finding myself being more drawn to the theme of "Energy" as being central to my coaching and facilitation work, in particular:

- How I use my awareness of both my own and other people's energy in coaching, facilitation, business and life. Exploring new approaches to help my clients tap into, find and use this energy for themselves.

I have been exploring this concept, noticing my energy, the energy of others and the energy of "the field". This has been stimulated by my work with systemic constellations[1] over the last few years, and through attending training with some of the key proponents of working with the body, such as Simon Cavacchio[2] and others. In this blog, I am going to explore the difference I am noticing between being in formal work within an organisation, where one's time is more stiffly dictated, with being self-employed. I will look at tuning into energy and emotion in the coaching and facilitation work I do. I will also make further links between my experience and other emerging schools of thought, such as Otto Scharmer's U-lab[3] and his work with Presencing, the increased use of mindfulness, and ongoing work I have been doing around developing emotional intelligence in leaders. I hope to open a discussion about how others use this, both in coaching and facilitation, and in a practical day to day way of guiding their life and choices.

---

[1] Systemic Constellations as taught by Jenny Mackewn and based on the work of Bert Hellinger, Virginia Satir, and native indigenous tradition
[2] Simon Cavacchio – Working with the Body in Mind
[3] Otto Scharmer – Theory U – Leading from the Emerging Future. MIT led MOOC course here: https://www.edx.org/course/u-lab-leading-emerging-future-mitx-15-671-1x

PART 1: Leading edge: Influences on Practitioner's Learning and Development

NOTICING DIFFERENCES IN MY ENERGY PATTERNS BETWEEN BEING EMPLOYED AND SELF EMPLOYED

I shall start by exploring the difference between being in paid work and being my own boss. I was in paid work for about eight years, running programmes that I was passionate about and doing some excellent coaching work with people I was interested to work with. I was also charged with developing business. This was a balance of creating materials, making calls, attending meetings, creating thought leadership and writing proposals. In addition, there was internal work to be done. Building relationships with colleagues, managing projects, reviewing materials, attending to the office systems such as finance and quality systems. I had a desk in an open plan space and, in one organisation, strict rules about when I had to be at that desk and in that office.

I often find I am at my most creative in the mornings or when a spark hits me. Often I found it hard to find the right space at the right moment to make use of a particular energy. I found myself thinking I will do this when I have attended to various fiddly tasks that just needed doing. Fair to say, the moment for the burst was too often lost or hidden. By contrast, after a busy morning I was often ready for a snooze in the early hours of the afternoon and found myself feeling fogged, sleepy and unable to think as clearly. While it was perfectly permissible to go for fresh air and a stroll to attend to these moments, that would only result in the need to nap an hour later.

Despite being in places where there was a lot of thinking about how we best use our energy to be productive, I found myself being ironically unable to really make use of my energies. I attribute this to the physical and social constraints of the space around me.

By contrast, now working from home in a home office, I can check in with myself more easily. I can go with what activity feels right for that moment. I can pursue the people I have energy to pursue and pay attention to what sort of energy I notice coming back. I am much more in tune with what is happening in myself physically – so my energy radar feels better tuned. I can go for a walk or a nap whenever I need to (so long as I am not on a call or heading out somewhere).

I find that I can easily create my list of goals at the start of each day – and deal with these as the energy for each hits me. Some get left behind, but only for good reason. Some get greater attention. Some days I feel like sleeping for longer in the mornings. This might not be a good energy signal for me to give in to – but maybe on some days I should. I haven't tried that yet, as I do like to be around to have breakfast with my family. That experiment is yet to come.

With not forcing myself into the office shaped task box, I am more tuned into my energy generally as I have less need to suppress it. It is an interesting discovery. The challenge now is to find ways to help myself and others access their energy as the valuable guide that it is, even in a restrained environment.

HOW I USE DIFFERENT KINDS OF ENERGY THINKING IN COACHING

In coaching, I find many uses for energy thinking. When I am in a one-on-one coaching conversation, I really listen out for where the client's energy is and reflect that back when it seems relevant. This is usually experienced as being very validating or as a useful challenge to thinking. It is generally of great value either way.

The longer-term impact seems to be that it encourages the client to start to use this as a way of accessing their own energy and motivation more readily. On the occasions when I use constellations-based techniques with clients, the impact of energy and, what in constellations work we call 'emotional' 'intuitive' or 'embodied' knowing, is really important. It proves a valuable counter-balance to the cognitive knowing that is typically more readily accessible. For some clients, in particular those who think a lot and are very in their heads, accessing their internal emotional knowing can be quite tricky. Yet it always seems to prove a worthwhile journey to take.

For example, I was working with a client whose organisational role was expected to morph at some point. That point was approaching. The client was starting to recognise this, and needed to make plans for himself and his team. He also needed to create a strategy for the new way of working for the organisation. Together we identified options for this next phase of his career. We created quite a wide-ranging set and explored his energy for each. Interestingly, the morphed state of his existing role drew a strong repulse reaction. It was very clear that held little attraction. Other ideas created great excitement and sparked a bounce of energy. While this client clearly felt strongly about all these things, he hadn't really discovered, until that coaching, how to use his physical responses to consciously aid his decision making. He now uses it a lot to great effect.

Sometimes I have coached while taking a walk or being outdoors. In this more physical situation, revelations of energy have been more physical. For example, a client breaking into a skip when telling me about a new opportunity, or walking faster as energy was greater, and slowing down as it diminished. All these were unconscious ways of revealing the energy and emotion behind the ideas. It was of great value to each when I shared those observations back with the clients.

Another way I explore energy with coaching clients is to ask questions around, 'What energy is coming back to you in response to this?' So, for example, 'What is the world out there – be it potential clients, interested parties, whoever – what is it saying about what you are communicating?' 'What are you learning about where that energy is?' A client was looking for ways to extend the reach of some ideas he had shared. He had had a fantastic response from those he had shared them with in a face-to-face forum, but very little response when he had offered them for the first time in a written offer or proposal. This gave him strong clues as to how to proceed in building his reach.

REFLECTIONS ON TRACKING ENERGY IN FACILITATING GROUPS

Using my energy gauge in facilitating groups is incredibly valuable, but not always totally reliable. I know that reliability drops off if I am very tired. I cannot tell the difference between my own exhaustion and that of the group. That said, being able to measure the mood in the room is of great value. Sometimes the group doesn't see so clearly when energy needs to shift to make progress. I do believe that as facilitator, sometimes you need to give a group a bit of a shove.

For example, groups often need that shove to go from a plenary discussion to break into smaller groups to do group work or to come back again. This can be because they don't believe the group work will be of value or it is poorly spelt out. That is fair enough. Sometimes, it is because the work is harder to do in small groups, and will require more thinking and more 'real work'. The group needs to trust the process and to trust the facilitator. The facilitator needs to really trust that this is the right switch for the group.

I facilitated a workshop where we had simultaneous translation and group working happening in a language I did not speak. I was having to judge what was happening in the groups by the body language of those involved. This was most interesting. Sometimes, I could see that the group was making real progress, that there was a real energy and intensity about their work and dialogue.

Other times, a group would seem disconnected and I could sense a stuck-ness, or boredom, among participants. I found that paying attention to these body signals and taking care to intervene appropriately, despite having no idea what they were talking about, was really important to the quality of my facilitation of the process.

THEORETICAL PERSPECTIVES AND FRAMEWORKS THAT ADD TO MY UNDERSTANDING OF USING ENERGY THEMES IN COACHING AND FACILITATION

Working with Otto Scharmer's Theory U, 'Leading from the Emerging Future', process has given me further cause for reflection on the role of energy use and sensing in leading groups and self. Central to the Theory U process is a period of presencing. This takes place once the intention for the work has been set, and after a process of deep sensing and exploration of the stakeholder's perspectives has been made.

The presencing demands a mindfulness and presence both to one's own emotional and energy fields, and to one's own impact on the situation in hand. It also requires an awareness of what 'everything out there that isn't me' is saying in response.

Similarly, working with emotional intelligence and embodiment work, where the behaviours, emotions and sensations arising in the body are paid significant attention to, is being increasingly recognised as valid and relevant in the coaching and development worlds. A past colleague, a respected thinker in the field of embodiment, said "*Too many of us treat our bodies as merely a taxi that takes our brain to meetings*". I am increasingly finding how true this is, as I help people reconnect their bodies to their brains.

I have had the opportunity to work extensively with the JCA Emotional Intelligence Profile in running EQ based leadership development programmes. This invites clients to build an increasing awareness of the emotion and energy they have in response to situations, and the emotion and energy they experience in others.

Giving this some attention has proved transformational for many clients, particularly those who had developed highly effective ways of blocking these signals from conscious awareness. For example, people who just kept going and going and going, without stopping to replenish and look after themselves and then ended up in a medically critical condition. Others who were immune to the signals they were or weren't getting back from others found that by just putting more effort into being aware of this had an amazing impact on their relationships and effectiveness.

IN CONCLUSION...

In sharing these thoughts, I hope I have stimulated some insights. I would love to hear others' reflections on: How you use your awareness of both your own and others' energy in coaching, facilitation, business and life. How do you explore new approaches to help our clients tap into, find and use this energy for themselves?

Feedback in the blink of an eye: From sled dogs on a snow covered mountain to a corporate office meeting, feedback is always there if you look for it

Lucille Maddalena, Ed.D.

I n his book *BLINK*, Malcolm Gladwell describes thinking that happens at a bit faster rate, as a gut feeling or snap judgment—or the message I send my husband with a certain look across the room. There is a bit of mystery about how we reach these conclusions and impressions: are our reactions inspired by the words or actions of others, or is it some deeper instinct and understanding that we tap into?

Perhaps we can explore the topic of feedback by looking at how we read and react to others. Why are we able to interpret body movement as small as the wink of an eye to elicit a response? Considering perception-action responses, why did renowned management expert Peter Drucker describe us as "poorly designed machine tool[s][1]"?

In my article "ON BY[2]", I relate an incident that occurred during my first sled dog race. In that story I described how, when at the crucial moment to pass the first team we had caught up to on the trail, I failed to call a command to the dogs to "on by."

We had just come out of a wooded area into sparkling white snow. The dogs' tails went up and all ears pointed forward: on the trail before us, about a quarter mile ahead just climbing a small hill, was another team. We had caught up the three minutes between each team's start.

---

[1] Stein, Guido. 2010. *Managing People and Organisations: Peter Drucker's Legacy*. Emerald Group Publishing Limited.
[2] Maddalena, Lucille. 2013. "On By – Taking the Risk." *Mtm Coach*. http://www.mtmcoach.com/on-by-taking-the-risk/ Accessed September 9.

Surprised, pleased and amazed, time seemed to stop[3]. Realizing I must act, I found myself calling out to the driver of the other team with the question "May I pass you"? The startled driver looked at me as though I didn't have a brain in my head by asking his permission to pass. An embarrassing moment, it was also a learning point. While I was working like a dog, I later realized that my thoughts then were of habits formed in another environment, far away from that snow covered hill. I was not mentally part of the team.

My body continued to work while my brain took its cue from a different world. I had one foot on a sled runner while the other was pushing that sled up the hill, taking the weight of the sled off the dogs to maximize speed. What brought me to my senses, was my lead dog. It occurred in a blink of an eye. We had practiced this: she knew what was needed from me. After my witless question to the other driver, mid-stride, she turned her head for just a moment to catch my eye. We exchanged a glance. Inspired, I called "On By". She lowered her head and haunches, reaching out for even greater speed, moving forward leading her pack smoothly around the other team to regain the trail.

The moment required only one specific command to take the required action that would benefit the team. On my part, I initially pulled from the wrong well of information: the lead dog required different data. Basic communication occurs when the receiver accepts the message with the meaning intended by the sender. The observation of the receiver's response is called feedback[4]. A connection occurred on that snow-covered trail between a dog and a person: it was feedback.

The work of Dr Gerd Gigerenzer[5], may shed some understanding on this experience. A supporter of Gladwell's who has been able to show how aspects of intuition work and how ordinary people successfully use it in modern life.

Dr Gigerenzer describes gut reactions as a fast judgment "that comes quickly into a person's consciousness. The person doesn't know why they have this feeling. Yet, this is strong enough to make an individual act on it. What a gut instinct is not is a calculation. You do not fully know where it comes from."

---

[3] Perception-action as referred to by Drucker is a psychological theory that people perceive their environment and events within it in terms of their ability to act. For example, softball players who are hitting better see the ball as bigger. Tennis players see the ball as moving slower when they successfully return the ball. Furthermore, the perceiver's intention to act is also critical; while the perceiver's ability to perform the intended action influences perception, the perceiver's abilities for unintended actions have little or no effect on perception.

[4] In other words, the part of the receiver's response communicated back to the sender is called feedback. Actually it is the amount of response of the receiver that reaches to the sender. It enables the sender to evaluate the effectiveness of the message. Bizcom_coach. 2015. "What is Feedback?" *Business Communication*. http://bizcommunicationcoach.com/what-is-feedback-definition-of-feedback-in-communication/ Accessed September 9.

[5] Dr Gigerenzer is director of the Max Planck Institute for Human Development in Berlin known in social science circles for his breakthrough studies on the nature of intuitive thinking.

My research indicates that gut feelings are based on simple rules of thumb, what we psychologists term 'heuristics.' These take advantage of certain capacities of the brain that have come down to us through time, experience, and evolution. Gut instincts often rely on simple cues in the environment. In most situations, when people use their instincts, they are heeding these cues and ignoring other unnecessary information[6].

Dr Gigerenzer defines intuition as a neurologically based behavior that evolved to ensure that we humans respond quickly when faced with a dilemma[7]. Our reactions, applications of cues from the past, will most likely lead us to make decisions that support our productive and healthy futures.

Offering a clue as to when we are able to acknowledge gut feelings, it is interesting to consider Peter Drucker's description of the importance of mind and body coordination: "The human being is a very poorly designed machine tool. The human being excels in coordination. He excels in relating perception to action. He works best if the entire human being, muscles, senses, and mind, is engaged in the work." Drucker addresses the need to be in the moment, to employ all of our faculties, to embrace the task with enthusiasm and commitment.

When I think back to how we became involved in dog sledding, I am aware that it was one of several life-changing decisions made very quickly, on-the-spot. I had been offered the use of a fully-trained team of Alaskan Sled dogs from a nationally respected ranch for one season by promising to keep the dogs in good condition. When I had the opportunity to work with this team for a year I immediately said "yes." No deliberation, no second thoughts: a true gut reaction.

As an Executive Coach I warned against quick decisions, offering methods to research and form collaborative decisions. Discussion of these topics often addressed personal relationships, both at work and at home, as well as stress factors. The solution to most issues evolve around issues of communications, feedback, messaging, trust, rapport, and empathy. Gladwell and Gigerenzer add a new dimension to my understanding of the decision making process, entertaining the value of personal contribution to achieve leadership goals.

It wasn't until much later after I had accepted the loaned team that what Dr Gigerenzer describes as 'reflection and reason' were considered. It is not surprising that the primary issues confirming the decision were business related:

1. I was able to assume a leadership role with my own team that worked in my comfort range and preferred running style: somewhat like quarter horses, this breed of sled dogs preferred speed for shorter

---

[6] Dreifus, Claudia. 2007. "Through Analysis, Gut Reaction Gains Credibility." In The New York Times. http://www.nytimes.com/2007/08/28/science/28conv.html?_r=0 Accessed on September 9.
[7] Gigerenzer, Gerd. 2008. Gut Feelings: The Intelligence of the Unconscious. Penguin Books.

distances. These could easily be reasons someone would choose a new job.

2. Dogsledding provided a balance to offset the non-physical activity of a typical corporate work day. The activity was conducted in a natural setting, with a familiar breed of dog I had experience training.

Which brings us to Malcom Gladwell's collection of stories in his book What the Dog Saw. Intuition, feedback, perception, and action all come to mind when reading Gladwell's description of the inventors of automatic vegetable choppers and hair dye (or of Cesar Millan, the American "Dog Whisperer" behind the title piece).

From the very small cues sent through the movements we interpret as information in a dog's behavior, to the major impact of individual and group actions leading to man-made global catastrophes, we respond to the flow of messages we accept with the same vigor as those dogs on a snow covered trail. That is the mystery of a gut reaction, of a response that occurs in the blink of an eye, a look between spouses.

Gladwell's common theme is his desire to show us the world through the eyes of others – even if the other happens to be a dog. It is up to us to embrace and connect with the information surrounding us, seeking the feedback that has a value to all of us, reminding us that we are more than cogs in a machine, that we have history, evolution, and spontaneity on our side. The key is to listen, to observe, and to be receptive.

Self-efficacy and coaching

Lynne Hindmarch

There may be a number of reasons why a client does not progress as well as expected on a coaching programme. For example, they may lack motivation, or commitment to the goal, or application through overwork or disorganisation. They may not receive much support from their manager or have other preoccupations in their lives which demand their attention. In the open, empathic and supportive relationship that ideally develops between the coach and the client, these issues can often be identified early in a coaching programme, discussed and successfully addressed.

I am not suggesting that tackling any of the above is easy, but in my experience an even more difficult situation can arise in coaching if the client lacks belief in their own self-efficacy.

Self-efficacy, for my working practice, is defined as a person's belief in their capacity to achieve a desired outcome. The psychologist most widely associated with the concept is Albert Bandura, who describes the role of self-efficacy in human functioning: that "people's level of motivation, affective states and actions are based more on what they believe than what is objectively true[1]."

A high level of self-efficacy will help a motivated client attain their goals. Another client may be equally committed and motivated to the coaching programme and the agreed goals, but little progress is made because they do not believe they have the capacity to achieve the desired outcome.

---

[1] Bandura, Albert. 1997. "Self-efficacy: Toward a Unifying Theory of Behavioural Change." In *Psychological Review* 84: 191-215.

ASSESSING SELF-EFFICACY

One of the difficulties for a coach is identifying that lack of self-efficacy is an issue. Bandura states that self-efficacy is situational, so assessment immediately becomes problematic. The anxiety scales in a general personality assessment are unlikely to highlight low self-belief that is so domain specific.

This is the essence of self-efficacy; it is specific to a particular situation[2].

A client may have a high level of confidence in their abilities across most situations, but in one particular aspect (for example, speaking out in meetings) they lack the confidence and belief in their ability to do anything about it. This means that despite being highly motivated to address the problem, they may struggle because they do not believe they are capable of doing anything about it.

Bandura has in fact developed a number of different scales for measuring self-efficacy in different domains, including exercising, eating habits, teaching and problem-solving, and in 2001 wrote a monograph that provides general guidance for people wanting to develop their own domain specific scales.

In coaching, this form of measurement is likely to be unrealistic or inappropriate so other methods of identifying the client's self-efficacy may need to be considered.

These may range from using carefully structured questioning, to elicit the client's level of self-belief in achieving a specific goal, to the use of a simple question, such as suggested by Whitmore who proposes that the coach asks the client to rate on a scale of one-to-ten the degree of certainty that the client will carry out the actions agreed[3]. Whitmore points out that this is not to rate the certainty of the outcome actually being achieved, but to rate the client's intention to carry out their part of the job. If the rating is less than ten it is reasonable for the coach to ask what needs to happen to make the rating higher.

In my experience, this simple technique can identify issues around the client's belief in their capability to achieve the goal so that these can be addressed during the coaching session.

DEVELOPING SELF-EFFICACY

Bandura described what he called the sources of self-efficacy as:

"mastery experiences, vicarious experiences, social persuasion and physical and emotional states[4]."

I have used this as a framework to briefly explore different approaches to increasing self-efficacy in coaching.

---

[2] Ditto
[3] Whitmore, John. 2001. *Coaching for Performance*. London: Nicholas Brealey.
[4] See [1]

PART 1: Leading edge: Influences on Practitioner's Learning and Development

Mastery experiences

Bandura believes that resilient self-efficacy develops from mastery experiences in which goals are achieved through perseverance and overcoming obstacles.

This is likely to be an approach which will be used by most coaches.

One of the most widely used methods of developing efficacy is setting appropriate goals and breaking them down into sub-goals while the coach supports the client through the process. This is so the client feels the goals are attainable but still provide a certain amount of 'stretch' with the support of the coach. I have used this approach in a career coaching context, for example, when the client's goal is a career change. The goal may be highly desirable, but the client may not believe that they have the capacity to achieve it. By working with the client to break the goal down into a number of small steps, starting with a sub-goal which is within the client's capability but slightly outside their comfort zone, a pathway can be created to help them achieve their ultimate goal.

One client I worked with was a senior manager in a large media organisation. His coaching goal was to become Managing Director of a particular part of the business. He believed in his capability to do the role, but despite enthusiasm during the session he failed to take agreed actions. Discussion during the following session led him to admit how daunting he found the process. This was linked to his belief that he didn't have the social clout to be considered for the role or the ability to do anything about it. As part of the plan to address this, we mapped out his network, qualifying individuals by how well he knew them, how important they were to help him progress towards his goal, and the extent to which they were gatekeepers for more senior people. I helped him develop an approach which he used with the most familiar people first, to help him master it. As he began to believe in his ability to build relationships, he felt able to connect with more influential people. A few months later he had the role he aspired to.

Vicarious experience

An example of this source of self-efficacy is modelling. This involves identifying proficient models who exhibit the competencies the client aspires to develop and who can transmit the knowledge to the client.

This may be used less in the coaching sessions, but may be identified as a possible source of developing self-efficacy outside the sessions – for instance mentors can be a good source for developing self-efficacy. In certain forms of coaching (such as developing emotional intelligence competencies), inevitably the coach will need to exhibit the behaviours in which they are coaching, so an element of modelling will come into play during the sessions. This can be reinforced by suggesting that the client identifies a colleague who is particularly emotionally intelligent, encouraging them to observe how that person behaves and what changes they may incorporate into their own behaviour.

SOCIAL PERSUASION

The third method of developing self-efficacy that Bandura suggests is persuading a client verbally that they possess the capabilities to master a given activity. Then giving them manageable challenges to confirm the coach's belief.

This might include challenging a client's limiting self-belief ('What is the evidence for your view of your capability in this area? What alternative perspectives are there on this situation?'). It might also involve an aspect of Appreciative Inquiry – using questions to call up strengths that have helped the client in the past and lessons learned that may apply to the present challenge.

These approaches are widely used in coaching already.

Indeed, as I write about the different methods that Bandura suggests, I think it is important to emphasise that all of them can be used concurrently. Persuading a client that there is an alternative way of looking at his or her capability is an approach I use often in coaching. Where self-efficacy may be an issue, I would use this alongside the other methods outlined above.

PHYSICAL AND EMOTIONAL STATES

Bandura also points out that reducing a person's stress reactions and altering their negative mood can enhance self-efficacy. One would hope that taking the actions identified above might help the client feel more in control of events, lower stress and help develop a more positive outlook.

However, Bandura also indicates that when people are asked to judge how much they expect to benefit from a given procedure[5], they may relate it to external sources (for example, the expertise of the coach) rather than from their own resources. In these cases the coach needs to reinforce the client's own capability; to emphasise that it is their own actions which have brought about a successful outcome.

FINALLY...

> "Successful efficacy builders do more than convey positive appraisals. In addition to raising people's beliefs in their capabilities, they structure situations for them in ways that bring success and avoid placing people in situations prematurely where they are likely to fail often[6]." Bandura

---

[5] Bandura, Albert. 1994. "Self-Efficacy." In *Encyclopaedia of Human Behaviour* 4: 71-81. New York: Academic Press.
[6] ditto

This would seem to indicate that as coaches we need to pay attention to being 'efficacy builders', and that this approach needs to underpin how the coach works with the client. If self-efficacy is ignored or overlooked, the client may fail to achieve the goal and opportunities to enhance their self-efficacy beliefs may be missed.

Pacing for clarity and alignment to minimize the 'tragedy of hierarchy': how to get better at getting things right the first time

Dino Laudato

I n my day job as an internal coach, and somebody who manages the operations of the coaching group in GSK, and in my previous roles where I've been managing and leading business-critical services, being able to just slow down a bit is valuable *because there is time to think and aim to do things right the first time rather than doing the work and then spending so much time just thinking about why it went wrong*. Hence it's about being proactive to opportunities versus reacting to problems after the event.

As human beings, because we're working under the cause so much, we tend to just run at a hundred miles an hour and not think of the direction we're running. A useful phrase that many people here use from time to time is 'go slower to go faster'.

People come in from the corporate energy wheel and it is sometimes quite difficult to slow them down. Many of my clients are business executives who are busily trying to get a million and one things done. They will say, "*I haven't had the time to do things, or I've had a number of issues*". **It's only when they come into coaching and create that calm environment to be able to do some thinking that they start to get some clarity.**

They've already been 'running at a hundred miles an hour.' Not fully present in a team, not paying attention to what's going on around them. They have six different things to complete. They also have to contribute right away to the conversation in the room! Then, because they haven't paid full attention to what was going on in the room, haven't expressed their views, haven't contributed to the decisions, it results in that same argument resurfacing a week, even a month, later. All those present, may not have all been fully present. Finally, after someone's actually started to do something or pay attention, everyone has to regroup. Everyone has to refocus without making another series of wrong decisions. This creates more work for each other, and back on the wheel they go.

Helping my clients to pace, to be able to just slow down and think, is one of the key learnings for me when it comes to my coaching practice and to what I see with my clients.

'TRAGEDY OF HIERARCHY'

Working and sustaining such high speeds, without space to really think of the consequences, reminds me of the Tenerife Airport disaster. The deadliest accident in aviation history.

When Pan Am 1736 and KLM 4825 came together at full take-off speed on the runway of Tenerife North Airport 583 people were killed. There were a number of reasons that this tragedy happened. Ultimately it comes down to human error and one of the indicators was the hierarchy in the cockpit.

The main Gran Canaria Airport in the Canary Islands was closed due to a bomb threat. All the flights were redirected to the North Airport, which was not equipped to deal with jumbos and high traffic. Planes were parked everywhere. The runway was being used for taxiway and take offs. The whole situation was made worse with fog descending onto the airport (600 meters above sea level) reducing visibility to less than a hundred meters.

The KLM flight was lined up to take off. Neither the controller in the tower nor the KLM captain could see the Pan Am flight taxiing on the runway. The combination of miscommunication and radio interference meant that the KLM captain, who in a rush to avoid the newly introduced limitation of flight duty time, misunderstood the supposed take-off instructions for permission to take off. He disregarded the second officers questioning of the instructions. "Take off" was then liberally used and the rest is history; the two came together with a loss of life.

A lot was learned. Hence the aviation industry was made much safer under the same token. It resulted in an immediate response where standard phrases were properly defined, to be used in very specific situations. And then finally, a change of emphasis in team decision-making: to remove the hierarchy in the cockpit. It resulted in what they call "crew resource management", which has been adopted by NASA and all other airlines. The focus of it, interestingly enough, is on interpersonal communication, leadership and decision-making:

- Understanding leadership and what is positional leadership,
- How we communicate amongst ourselves, and
- Most importantly, how is it when we go and make decisions.

PART 1: Leading edge: Influences on Practitioner's Learning and Development

The lessons I learnt which can directly be linked to organisations are:

1. The importance of clarity and alignment,

2. The importance of haste not hurrying and constantly rushing.

And when it comes to the team, be it a small team, be it a corporation, if we're all not pulling in the same direction, then we're not working together. From an organisation standpoint, it would be a question of survival.

ALL PULLING IN THE SAME DIRECTION!

Pulling in the same direction asks:

- How are we organised?
- How are we working together to deliver?
- What is it that we certainly want to deliver?
- How will we know we're on the right track?

Having that level of clarity, naturally leads to who sets the direction, and that invites challenge in different perspectives. The direct response would be the chairperson at the top, once they have set the direction with a team they've invited different perspectives from.

Achieving not only the picture, the final destination, and how to get there creates a continuous feedback loop for clarity and alignment because of the many different routes to be able to get there. There's always haste in organisations. We need to create more space for 'pausing and acting' as opposed to merely 'reacting'.

A lot of my clients are high achievers and looking for longevity. All are asking the question, so can I maintain this pace in ten years' time, fifteen years' time? Is that the work-life balance that I want? Certainly. By stepping into a coaching space. Actually talking about the situation, what they have learned from it and what they could have done differently. They raise an awareness of pace, a slower pace where help is possible. They also realize that a fast pace is unsustainable and damaging for a human being.

MAKING SURE YOU HAVE A HEALTHY WORKFORCE, MENTALLY AS WELL AS PHYSICALLY, SO THAT ALTOGETHER WE CAN DO WHAT WE NEED TO DO

As a leader there's an element of complete transparency with your team. There's balance to be had. And importantly for me: "*If I look after you, then you would look after me.*" This requires, and I encourage, that you retain some kind of control and that you take as well as give.

I often find in my coaching practice getting people to look at the whole is when we start seeing some new scenarios. It would be interesting, to ask things like, "What would your wife say?" "What would your mother say?" And that helps with raising awareness, as well as considering the effect it's having on those around them outside of work.

This is an early pioneering of what's going to become inevitable. Of what's going to make for much better planning in many ways. You will be able to hear, *"Gosh. I never realized how a little bit of space can create such an impact!"*

This approach is just as important when working with teams, where we continue with the coaching beyond the initial workshop. We contract with each team about what is it that they're trying to achieve, ensuring that the pace is right for them to achieve their goals.

Again, with coaching as well, if that's what the coachee is bringing to the table and that's what they want to work on its setting a pace that helps them to slow down. And if that's what they want to work on, then we'll ask how you're doing with this pacing.

MY LEARNINGS SO FAR

As coaches we do not ask our clients to do anything, we make them aware of the fact that they're calling to our parameters whilst they're running a hundred miles an hour.

Coaching often picks up on the things that are falling off the edge of the table.

Yet how sustainable and how long does the client really want to work in the way they are doing before they make changes? I hear it and I see it at all levels within an organisation; some people are better than others and should be rewarded as much as those who make alternative choices.

I also wonder, in general, how long it will take to get our leaders to bring this issue forward and say, "Work slower to get more done". That would be quite an interesting conversation. In my coaching practice I'm consciously looking out for it because I'm aware of it and always working towards getting things done right the first time.

On irrationality, defense mechanisms and change

Aurora Aritao

PUZZLING LIMITATIONS OF OUR MIND

As a keen observer of the intricacies of human behaviour, I am as inspired by the human capacity for greatness as I am fascinated by our irrationality. Through my own life experiences, I've come to terms with the fact that a large part of my views, opinions, and decisions are influenced by unconscious processes. My day-to-day decisions are influenced by my gut feelings, intuitions as well as snap judgments and biases, whether I realize it or not.

Taking a closer look also reveals that in denying negative emotions, the mind may project whatever is unwanted onto others as a defense mechanism. In others, I may see what I reject in myself. To protect myself from negative feelings such as anxiety, I might attribute what does not fit with my view of myself to someone else, or keep them hidden away, ignored and denied for as long as possible. Not a sunny picture at all.

EXAMPLES OF IRRATIONAL BEHAVIOUR

INSEAD's Prof Manfred Kets de Vries teaches and writes about the hidden undercurrents that affect human behavior. In an article on organisational leadership Kets de Vries, Florent-Treacy and Korotov (2013) posit that only by accepting the fact that leaders, like the rest of us, are not paragons of rationality can we begin to understand why many well-laid plans and strategies derail, or conversely, why great leaders sometimes come from very unexpected places.

One of the premises of this psychodynamic paradigm supports that:

> "a great deal of mental life – feelings, fears, motives – lies outside of conscious awareness, but still affects our conscious reality and even

physical wellbeing. We all have blind spots. People aren't always aware of what they are doing – much less why they are doing it...[1]"

Politics and business offer a rich repository of stories on failures of leadership through irrational actions of those with access to power and critical information.

Alexis Stenfors, for one, was a fixed income derivatives professional turned rogue trader after mismarking his trading books resulting in more than a USD$100 million error back in 2009. In March this year, he gave an interview with author and coach Peter Bregman. They discuss the fallout of this mistake and Alexis' journey to rebuild his life. At one point in the interview, Alexis reflected:

> *"I should have acted differently. Of course I should have told my boss. I should have told everybody. I should have informed. I should have done something else, but instead, I sort of just continued, until I had a chance to go away, and realized, hang on a minute, this is completely, completely wrong[2]."*

Interestingly, recent news on grievous lack of diversity, bullying and sexual harassment in technology firms call into question the legitimacy of the industry and its role as the most powerful mover in the global economy and in wider society[3].

Uber lost its CEO after numerous scandals such as alleged systemic sexism and the company's interference in the investigation of a rape by a driver in India. One of its women employees reported to have received a string of chat messages from her male manager on her first official day there. He was apparently looking for women to have sex with. What was also worrying was how HR responded when this was reported to them: they asked her to either move to a different team or risk getting a poor performance review from that manager.

Daniel Kahneman in his book *Thinking Fast and Slow*, writes about the two modes of thinking, System 1 and System 2 and their link to errors of judgement and choice. He addresses a puzzling limitation of our mind: our excessive confidence in what we believe we know, and our apparent inability to acknowledge the full extent of our ignorance and the uncertainty of the world we live in. He also believes that we are prone to overestimate how much we understand about the world and to underestimate the role of chance in events[4].

---

[1] Kets de Vries, M. F. R., Florent-Treacy, E., and Korotov, K. 2013." Psychodynamic Issues in Organizational Leadership". *The Wiley-Blackwell Handbook of the Psychology of Leadership, Change and Organizational Development*, New Jersey

[2] Bregman, P. 2017. Podcasts. http://peterbregman.com/podcast/alexis-stenfors-a-barometer-of-fear/#.WZj2ExQ057Y

[3] Hefferman, M. 2017. "Silicon Valley is developing a trust deficit" In *Financial Times* .

[4] Kahneman, D. 2011 . *Thinking Fast and Slow*, Farrar, Straus and Giroux, New York

DEFENSE MECHANISMS KEEP ANXIETIES AT BAY

Meanwhile, social psychologists have continued to (re)discover the existence of processes by which humans deceive themselves, enhance self-esteem, and foster unrealistic self-illusions[5].

Many of us know that particularly in challenging, uncertain and distressing situations, a part of our brain evolutionarily functions to automatically protect us against perceived threat, and nudges us to fight, flee or freeze. These days, as we no longer live in the stone age, fighting or fleeing literally may not be an option. In the workplace, unless we are ready to quit our job, we may just soldier on and mask our true feelings.

This act of 'self-defense' can also manifest by blaming others, denying the truth, rejecting kindness from others, living in the past, holding grudges, lashing out, obsessing, self-sacrificing, procrastinating, daydreaming distancing, self-idealizing, being indecisive etc[6].

In the organisational context, employees often rely on systems and structures to 'contain' such anxiety. When these offer insufficient 'containment', people may engage in regressive social defenses such as splitting (seeing everything as black or white); projection (seeing one's own short-comings in others); displacement (expressing negative emotions by focusing on a less threatening target); denial (refusal to accept facts), and other defensive routines[7].

The cognitive processes involved in the defense of projection, also known as attribution or the false consensus effect[8] might show up when, for example, executives in a department deny or reject an uncomfortable experience by imagining that it belongs to another group of executives or another team. This other group—the recipient of the projection— is subtly inducted to think, feel, and act in congruence with the projection received from the first group[9].

Repression is another type of defense mechanism, first described by Sigmund Freud, as a way that people keep unpleasant memories out of their conscious mind. It is a compensatory style that deals with threat and stress by blocking unpleasant emotional experiences that might bring up anxiety, distress and vulnerability[10].

---

[5] Cramer, P. 2000. "Defense mechanisms in psychology today: Further processes for adaptation". In *American Psychologist*, 55 6 : 637-646.
[6] Anatomy of Defense Mechanisms according to DSM-III-R
[7] See [1]
[8] See [6].
[9] See [1]
[10] Namka, Lynne. 2008. *"Defense Mechanisms That Affect Relationships."* https://byregion.byregion.net/articles-healers/Defense_Mechanisms.html. Accessed September 9.

CASE EXAMPLE

ROLE CONFUSION

Lea, a highly skilled and well-educated senior communications executive was ecstatic to join a private consulting firm. With her experience and credentials, she expected to be part of the decision-making strategy team.

A year later, Lea was deflated, demotivated and ready to quit the job. She was assigned to do too much implementation work, which was giving her a lot of stress. Her work was split between two departments, each with different expectations of her role. The role in her mind was not at all aligned with that of the two teams. Out of frustration, she became resigned to the fact that they did not appreciate her true potential nor did they value her worth.

CONSUMED BY EMOTIONS

On our first meeting, Lea was emotionally triggered. She declared that nobody understands her, that people only use her, and that she must be difficult to get along with. She said she could not trust anybody in the office. She was making assumptions about what her colleagues might be thinking of her.

I began to work with Lea on a strategy to break the negative downward spiral she was in, while creating space for her to reflect on the possible forces at play, the explicit and observable forces, as well as what may be lurking under the surface. It turns out that even though Lea felt very strongly about the seemingly unfair and ambiguous environment she was 'stuck with' at work, she had not been able to address it fully and directly with her boss. Her internal struggle comes from a very high degree of perfectionism - which she realized was unhelpful - coupled with a great dislike for confrontation. Suppression was not a great sustainable strategy.

SPACE FOR REFLECTION

Having the space for reflection in coaching allowed her to become more aware of her intense reactions, within a safe environment. Sometimes looking at the situation from a distance (on the balcony instead of the dance-floor) can make us realize the disparity of the intensity of our reactions against the true size and weight of the issue at hand. It may even help us to realize that the issue is not what it appears to be. Once we find some respite we can better see the positive side to the circumstance, i.e. Lea as she later recounted was otherwise successful in delivering high quality work to two critical functions of the organisation, which was helping her start to build a positive reputation and trust from colleagues.

Once Lea found stability and managed to cut the negative spiral in her head, she realized she needed to objectively and assertively make her views and intentions clearly known to her manager. She was committed to the role and they needed to know how she was feeling and what she was thinking about the workload issue. She stayed, found common ground, and thrives at the company to this day.

CHANGE AND TRANSFORMATION

Change begins with the self. Without deep self-awareness and self-management, there can't be sustainable change. It would make good sense to always challenge our thinking and to create space for reflection before we react to any kind of stimuli, especially stress-inducing stimuli.

Hence, what might an interpersonal model for change that takes into account our irrationality, look like? How can we discard what is no longer relevant and unhelpful in our belief systems? How can we regularly pause, go inward and reflect?

I have found these steps useful in this process of deep transformation, and I'd be interested to hear what has worked for you:

- **Illuminate unconscious thinking** – discover more deeply the concealed and hidden dynamics in relationships with others and even with our self (snap judgements, biases, generalizations, automatic thoughts). Acknowledge that they affect you as much if not more than conscious thinking.

- **De-energize maladaptive thoughts and feelings** – take the focus and energy away from negativity, and be present. When the mind starts to ruminate and get hooked on negative thoughts, acknowledge it, take a breath and notice what is new in your environment. This immediately brings you back to the present moment.

- **Modulate anxiety** – regulate emotions through healthy mind and body habits. Exercise regularly, take time to breathe more deeply and mindfully and learn to reframe situations to get a fresh perspective.

- **Reflect and learn** – find the time and space to go inward and reflect on the day, the week and the year. Write down your thoughts on a journal. See if you can detect any patterns in behaviour that is serving you well or serving you badly. Enhance what is working and discard toxic habits.

- **Re-wire the brain through new experiences** – Create new wiring and new habits. The brain is plastic – it can change if you make new connections stronger than the old wiring. Approach new experiences with openness and creativity. Practice and repeat.

This work is like building new muscle – of becoming a reflective leader of change, starting from the self.

How we can balance individual freedom with ecology and planetary sustainability in coaching

Geoffrey Ahern

We take it for granted that individual liberty will accompany the growing Zeitgeist of ecology and planetary sustainability. Originally the science of the distribution and abundance of organisms and their interactions and transformations, by now ecology has also become a worldwide movement and climate of thought.

But there's a question mark over the liberty of the individual because ecology, the inspirer of environmentalism, has a whole-population approach that includes humans, the opposite end of the spectrum from starting with the civil rights of each person. Ecology's field-wide mentality fits well with the collective approach of Asian economies which have been rapidly ascending while becoming more environmentally attuned; but not with Western individualised freedoms.

My practice having coincided with coaching's expansion, I believe that it is well-placed as a person-centred art to contribute to a forward-looking balance between individual freedoms and the whole-population approach of ecology. Coaching's process seems to me to be complementary because it raises the importance of individual life from within the whole.

Thus innovation is required to make individual liberty an indispensable complement to our global era of ecology. Though from about 1980 social justice for all has been grafted onto ecology to form 'sustainability' and 'sustainable development', this development has tended to leave out freedom under the law.

I identify some innovatory developments which are related to business and so to the practices of 'people developers' like professional coaches:

- Increasing transparency.

- Redefining individual rights.

- Promoting representative participation within multinational and other companies.

- Clarifying when we should and should not prioritise beyond our species.

New social boundaries like these are increasingly required for trust, including the trust of clients in the processes professionals contract for with their employers.

This is within the overall context of envisaging the planet as a humanly influenced living whole: the signature of today's geological era, the Anthropocene. The word means 'qualitatively new and man-made' and is so-named because humans have a significant influence on the Earth.

In implementing sustainability, its 'people' and 'planet' aspects tend to be divided into the separate practitioner, NGO and academic silos. However, this blog-article looks at how the people and planet aspects interact. It follows on from my introductory one (January 11, 2017) on having an Anthropocene mindset and a further one (March 20, 2017) on the planet, environmental science and ethical consequences for coaching.

ECOLOGY PRIORITISES WHOLE POPULATIONS, WHETHER YOURS OR MINE OR BOTH, OR HUMAN OR NOT

Ecology as a social movement has at its core a whole-population perspective.

Ecology's whole-population thinking recently developed into social justice, more than individual liberty, for all humans.'

Ecology is a post-industrial social movement with mainly European and North American origins. Originating in the era of late nineteenth century imperialism, it was sadly associated with ethnically exclusive thinking. A glimpse at this serves as a warning which, as we shall see, we need to remember in the novel circumstances of today:

- Its founder Ernst Haeckel (1834-1919) formulated a kind of social Darwinism stating *"usually it is the more perfect and ennobled human being who gains the victory over others[1]"*.

- Ecology became associated with eugenics and the idea that capitalism and urbanisation weaken people.

- Up to the end of the Second World War it was linked, though not exclusively, with soft right wing politics, for example: rustic self-sufficiency in support of the Norwegian National Socialist Party; 'Blood and Soil' sensibility (though its organic farming was not endorsed by Hitler);

---

[1] Quoted in Kleeberg, Bernhard. 2007. "God-nature Progressing: Natural Theology in German monism." In *Science in Context* 20 3: 547.

British enthusiasts for healthy soil and food who tended to be pro-German at the time of National Socialism[2].

After the Second World War, ecology as a social movement developed a soft left global environmentalism which advocated social justice for all humans (i.e. non-discriminatory universalism)[3]. The turning point was in 1980, when environmental issues were pulled together with people development through the paradoxical concept of sustainable development[4]. Change agents for this included third world governments and NGO lobbies.

This recent emphasis has been more on equity and community than on individual liberty.

- Oxfam, for example, focuses on resources, livelihood and social capital.

- The Paris Climate Agreement, ratified at the end of last year, refers to equity and reducing poverty; similarly the UN's influential 17 Sustainable Development Goals emphasise removing poverty and hunger and promoting equality and community.

- Non-discriminatory universalism more than individual liberty is the spirit of transnational sustainability movements like the African Ubuntu and Latin American Buen Vivir (also of the growing metropolitan managerial mindset?).

As in Maslow's hierarchy of needs, survival comes first. Compassion and self-interest rightly give prominence to the needs of the poverty struck and stuck global bottom billion, but an outcome is that championing individual freedoms tends to be postponed to later, to sustainability's endgame.

Many of us, whether coaches or not, use phrases like 'this day and age' or 'now we are in 2017' because we assume there's an inevitable global progress towards egalité, gender-inclusive fraternité and liberté. But this is not somehow natural or historically inevitable: it's a particular recent cultural context, that of the post-war peak of North Atlantic democracy, which has shaped the recent human rights version of ecology.

THE DANGER THAT ECOLOGY MAY DISCRIMINATE IN NEW WAYS BY CHOOSING ONE HUMAN POPULATION OVER ANOTHER

The hard-won legitimacy of ecology's recent non-discriminatory universalism could come unstuck. There are signs, in the name of ecology, of possible new

---

[2] For this paragraph see Bramwell, Anna. 1989. *Ecology in the 20th Century. A History*. New Haven, Yale: 115-122, 150-151, 173, 207.
[3] Banerjee, Subhabrata. 2007. *Corporate Social Responsibility - The Good, the Bad and the Ugly*. Cheltenham: Elgar Press.
[4] Mebratu, Desta. 1998. "Sustainability and Sustainable Development: Historical and Conceptual Review." In *Environmental Impact Assessment Review* 18 6: 493-520.

types of discrimination against geographical, ethnic, religious and national groups, for example through:

- Unilateral geoengineering, as with polluters releasing sulphur into the atmosphere to cool it without reducing CO_2 to help seaboard nations and others affected by continuing ocean acidification.

- Mass migrations though climate-change causing water shortages, for example in Northern India.

- Climate wars, for example one of Gwynne Dyer's military scenarios is of a Lifeboat Britain and Ireland just about managing to feed their inhabitants through not letting too many people aboard[5].

The potential for geographical exclusivism could be legitimated through unscrupulous PR distorting visions like Thomas Berry's proposed regionally-based biocracy and Chandran Nair's much more pragmatic case that Asia should put an end to under-priced resources. On the fringe a few have even advocated reducing the human population through famine[6].

SAFEGUARDING INDIVIDUAL LIBERTY WHERE ECOLOGY PRIORITISE NON-HUMAN POPULATIONS

In going on to embed individual liberty, clarity is needed about circumstances in which all rights for humans come to be seen as merely a part of the biocentric whole. Environmentalists' whole-population perspective can prioritise animals, habitats and the biosphere above humans; and for many it is the benchmark of genuineness that it should happen at least occasionally.

Some deep greens have been accused of misanthropy because they prioritise other species, or the ecology of the whole, over humans. They range from sentiments like 'naïve, non-contributing and non-consenting non-humans [are] caught up in massive change imposed on them by humans', to 'sooner shoot a man than a snake'[7].

Deep greens may believe:

- Human beings are moral agents but without ethical privilege.

- Arranging matters so that humans cannot lose is not ecocentric[8].

[5] Dyer, Gwynne. 2010. *Climate Wars: The Fight for Survival as the World Overheats*. Oxford: Oneworld: 183.
[6] See Berry, Thomas. 1988. *The Dream of the Earth*. San Francisco, CA: Sierra Club Books. and Nair, Chandran. 2011. *Consumptionics. Asia's Role in Reshaping Capitalism and Saving the Planet*. Oxford: Infinite Ideas. For a discussion of famine see Smith, K. 2008. "How Immigration May Affect Environmental Stability." In *Scientific American*.
[7] For the first quote see Albrecht et al. 2013. "The Ethics of Assisted Colonization in the Age of Anthropogenic Climate Change." In *Journal of Agricultural and Environmental Ethics* 26: 831. The second quote is from Lo, Y. 2001. "The Land Ethic and Callicot's Ethical System (1980-2001: An Overview and Critique." *Inquiry* 44 3: 334.
[8] See Sylvan, Richard., and David Bennett. 1994. *The Greening of Ethics. From Human Chauvinism*

This ecocentricity contrasts with the Abrahamic Genesis tradition giving man dominion over nature. This traditional animal/man divide is no longer absolute: post-Darwinists today perceive animals as having culture, creativity and intelligence while human reason is not so independent as once thought.

ECOLOGY'S WHOLE-POPULATION APPROACH HAS MORE IN COMMON WITH NEO-CONFUCIANISM THAN WITH WESTERN INDIVIDUALISM

As stated in the introduction, the emerging Asian century reinforces the challenge of ecology to individual freedom.

The most powerful collective cultures today include Islam as well as neo-Confucianism. Islam's community (Umma) is in tune with the whole-population approach of ecology, but there's a big difference in the authority given to science. Ecology is science-based whereas, given Islam's transcendental revelation fixing Sharia (God's way), the struggle within Islam over the authority of science is thought to be more fundamental than its struggle against the West[9].

China and its massive diaspora, as in Indonesia, have in neo-Confucianism a collective tradition which resonates more completely with ecology. It is compatible with science. Unlike Western thinking in terms of the rights of the individual, it emphasises virtues such as benevolence (ren). Confucianism has a ground independent of humans for valuing the non-human world, and a role-based ethics in which humans are part of a larger community dependent on the non-living environment (though it would be a projection backwards in time to call traditional Confucianism ecological[10]).

to Deep-green Theory. Cambridge: White Horse Press: 91,137. and Curry, Patrick. 2011. Ecological Ethics. An Introduction. Cambridge: Polity Press: 59.

[9] Drees, Willem. 2013. "Islam and Biomedical Ethics". In Zygon, 48 3: 733-744; Davary, Bahar. 2012. "Islam and Ecology: Southeast Asia, Adat and the Essence of Keramat." In ASIA Network Exchange, 20 1: 12-22; Haq, S. Nomanul. 2001. "Islam and Ecology: Toward Retrieval and Reconstruction." In Daedalus 130 4: 141-177.

[10] Chan, Gary. 2008. "The Relevance and Values of Confucianism in Contemporary Business Ethics." In Journal of Business Ethics 77: 347-360; Wong, Pak-Hang. 2015. "Confucian Environmental Ethics, Climate Engineering, and the 'Playing God' Argument." In Zygon 50 1: 28-41; Nuyen, Anh. 2008. "Ecological Education: What Resources are there in Confucian Ethics?" In Environmental Education Research 14(2): 187-197; Jung, Hwa. 2013. "A Prolegomenon to Transversal Geophilosophy." In Environmental Philosophy 10 1: 83-112; Chan, Benedict. 2015. "Animal Ethics, International Animal Protection and Confucianism." In Global Policy 692: 172-175; Pfister, Lauren. 2007. "Environmental Ethics and Some Probing Questions for Traditional Chinese Philosophy." In Journal of Chinese Philosophy 34: 101-123.

THE STRUGGLE FOR INDIVIDUAL LIBERTY IN THE SUSTAINABILITY ENDGAME

The contrast between ecology and individual liberty displays tensions within sustainability and suggests future struggles in an endgame. This needs to start now, assuming sustainability becomes orthodox, to prevent it setting in an unnecessarily authoritarian and manipulative form. Continuing to have an unchallenged safe space in which to work with clients is the nub of the matter for coaching and other people-development professionalism.

Some promising, business-related developments to uphold individual liberty:

Increasing transparency. Transparency to guard against the compromise of individual liberty by corruption is a liberal-democratic cultural export. Transparency International defines corruption, whether grand, petty or political as the abuse of entrusted power for private gain .

Transparency's chipping away effect will need to be profound:

- To replace the machismo and charisma of the systemic, embedded corruption of many cultures.

- To have the wisdom to discern where traditional systems of influence, notably Arab wasta and Chinese guanxi, are questionably being post-industrially redefined as corrupt.

- To create multi-cultural platforms so that transparency and anti-bribery legislation are not widely perceived as a new form of imperialism.

Redefining individual rights. Preserving civil rights through redefining them may become necessary if surveillance becomes increasingly accepted. This could arise because technological developments (e.g. nanotechnology threatening the planet itself) exponentially increase the asymmetric power of those minded to use force to express political or other ends[11]. Redefining civil rights might include:

- New institutions to counter erosion through redefining online privacy rights. Alongside this there may be a generational shift towards greater openness and tolerance in some areas of shame and guilt.

- Judicial safeguards accompanying increased state surveillance against terrorism.

Companies could extend and strengthen their fiduciary legal duties[12]. Currently there are UN guiding principles covering individual rights like freedom of association, which controversial companies like Nestlé can state they opt in to.

---

[11] See Rees, Martin. 2003. *Our Final Century. Will Civilisation Survive the Twenty-First Century?* London: Random House.

[12] Banerjee, Subhabrata. (See 4 above) p.144.

Promoting representative participation within multinational and other companies. Representative participation in the supply chain is critical for sustainability. But business-as-usual culture is based on profits, not on being good:

- For example in the garment industry in Tirapur, India, buyer-driven voluntary codes broke down; factories did anything to meet exacting delivery and quality targets and the tensions led to the production of false documents.

Sustainability-as-usual is different:

- In the same industry in Sri Lanka, suppliers to Marks and Spencer's sustainability plan (Plan A) treated low status female employees as ends in themselves giving them well designed working conditions and emancipating them to open bank accounts and have career prospects[13].

Identifying when we should and should not prioritise beyond our species. To which entities should rights be given? The question may seem silly: there should be non-discriminatory universalism for humans and that's all. But the situation is dynamic not static. Even in the West women only got the vote quite recently, and eco-feminism since then, in combatting the essentialist view of women as mainly mothers and nurturers, has also eroded taken-for-granted humanism. For example, Ecuador's constitution recently granted rights to nature. Drawing an anthropocentric line in the sand is problematic in our increasingly socio-ecological age:

- There's discussion today over whether animals and indeed the planet itself should have rights. Business is closely affected because animals are in the supply chain, are directly sold in the food and clothing industries, are experimented on by big pharma and have their habitats destroyed by the extractive and construction industries.

- Technologies for merging human intelligence with technology are predicted. Blueprints for life itself can in effect be owned by large corporations through the law of intellectual property.

Freedom as the absence of external obstacles

Business developments such as the above can help safeguard human freedoms from intrusions, like improper surveillance, because they emphasise the individual, not the ecological collective (negative not positive freedom). However, such individualism may well not be extendable to possibilities of action enabled by high-tech advances, like the claimed 'right' to have designer children.

---

13 Soundararajan, Vivek., and Brown, Jill. 2016. "Voluntary Governance Mechanisms in Global Supply Chains: Beyond CSR to a Stakeholder Utility Perspective."In *Journal of Business Ethics* 134: 95-96; and Lowcarbonworks, Bath. 2009. *Centre for Action Research in Professional Practice (CARRP), Insider Voices, Human Dimensions of Low Carbon Technology*. University of Bath conference 14/7/09.

THE LIBERTY OF THE INDIVIDUAL COMPLEMENTS ECOLOGY

It has been held in this blog-article that individual liberty complementing ecology is a hopeful possibility but should not be taken for granted. This is as, to survive, the need for an ecological-whole-system thinking becomes increasingly recognised. Especially given its affinity with the social solidarity of emerging and greening Asian economies.

Upholding individual liberty is not a process which is inherent in ecology as a social movement, but it has the potential to be seen as a necessary component and meaning, even as ecology's ultimate purpose. When combined with ecological thinking it forms a highly complicated and complex whole. Not a neat unity or monism. Its differentiation of individuals is in contrast with eco-mythologies like Ray Kurzweil's singularity, which ends with the planet itself radiating intelligence.

Coaching, unlike ecology, is centred on consciousness; also having board members, CEOs and other employees as its clients put it close to what is probably the most significant driving seat of planetary change. Thus it is well-placed to understand corporate aspects of the tensions between the liberty of the individual on the one hand and collective approaches to ecology on the other, and to raise awareness of the need for a new, creative balance.

A question for us all, given the pressures of the here-and-now, is how we raise this awareness.

A model for discussing power when coaching leaders

Lynne Hindmarch

Power and politics are an inevitable part of organisational life. Most of my clients are interested in power, though they may not explicitly state it. I work as an executive coach, and many of my clients are in senior positions in organisations. Working with them over the years, it's clear to me that the desire to be in a position of power has been a strong driver in taking them to the top.

Leaders need power to influence others to do things they might not otherwise choose to do. But I have noticed that leaders are not necessarily aware of how they influence others, or that they may have some alternatives which they haven't considered. This is important because at times the inappropriate or counterproductive use of power has been a trigger for coaching. Using French and Raven's Five Bases of Interpersonal Power[1] (1959) as a model or framework can be useful in helping clients (particularly those who rely heavily on one approach) consider that they have options in how they influence, and what those options look like.

Firstly, I would like to position the model in the context of leadership. Leadership is a massive topic, which I will touch on lightly, simply to indicate two perspectives on the subject which I think are relevant to this blog- article:

- The first is what is known as **the contingent style of leadership**[2] , which suggests that there is **no one best way to lead**; the effective leader stays mindful of the interactions and factors that are affecting the ability to lead effectively.

[1] French, John., and Bertram Raven. 1959. The Bases of Social Power. In D. Cartwright and A. Zander. *Group dynamics*. New York: Harper & Row.
[2] Fiedler, F. 1978. "The Contingency Model and the Dynamics of the Leadership Process." In *Advances in Experimental Social Psychology* 11: 59-112.

- The other perspective was presented in an article in the *Harvard Review*. This takes the view that you can have too much of a good thing (overuse of strengths), and that **the most effective leader is versatile, flexible and agile**[3].

Both these perspectives have a common theme: effective leaders are able to adapt their leadership style to what is appropriate at the time. In coaching leaders, therefore, helping them understand their prevailing style of influencing others can be illuminating and assist them in considering other options. This can be an important part of developing their flexibility, and thus effectiveness, as a leader.

FRENCH AND RAVEN'S FIVE BASES OF INTERPERSONAL POWER

French and Raven's Five Bases of Interpersonal Power provides a useful framework for starting a conversation about the leader's power base and how they use it. Of course, the conversation has to be appropriate to the coaching goals. However, it is a way of reviewing the leader's influencing style in a manner which generally they haven't come across before.

The model is shown below, but when I'm with a client I usually sketch it out on a pad while I'm talking it through. I feel this draws the client into the discussion much more readily than just presenting them with the model already printed on a piece of paper. The five bases of power refer to what the power-holder controls that allows them to influence the behaviour of another (known as the 'target' for the purposes of the model).

POSITIONAL POWER

In the model, the first three of the power bases I describe are 'positional'; that is, they relate to the leader's role in the organisation.

Coercive power

This form of power draws on punishment and the threat of punishment to influence. All organisations have forms of negative outcomes that a powerholder can use.

- *At the extreme*, this can mean threatening dismissal, or a disciplinary process, docking of pay or loss of privileges.

- *If coercive power is overused*, there will be increased compliance on the people who it is targeted at, but the powerholder is likely to be disliked and surveillance is needed to ensure that people remain compliant.

Using coercive power will cause resentment and dissatisfaction among people it's applied to. It is also likely to be hard to maintain as the target is likely to engage in

---

[3] Kaplan, Robert., and Robert Kaiser 2003. "Developing Versatile Leadership." In *MITS Loan Management Review* 44 4: 19-26.

avoidance behaviour where possible. It can lead to bullying behaviour, which may result in people leaving – possibly the best people who can easily get jobs elsewhere.

I have seen this behaviour used in a team led by a boss who was very driven by making money. His overbearing style was matched by shouting and intimidating people who did not perform as he wished. People become very distressed and many left. The problem spread as his behaviour became accepted in his department as the norm for leadership. In this particular case he refused to acknowledge that his behaviour needed to change and his contract was eventually terminated. Ironically he became the recipient of the ultimate use of coercive power!

Reward power

This is power based on the ability to reward people for compliance. If people expect that you will reward them for something they are more likely to do it. Reward is any benefit that is attractive to the target. It may be a pay rise, or promotion or other job benefits.

- *Reward power* is likely to lead to desired behaviour change lasting longer than that achieved through coercion. It also leads to liking of the power-holder.

- *It has its limitations* as it depends on the degree that a leader has control over benefits such as pay and promotion. However, there are less tangible forms of reward that a leader can use that are often overlooked such as positive feedback, gratitude, admiration and recognition. This can be very effective.

Example: One client recalled taking part in a major IT project, which involved working over the weekend. Late on the Saturday night the MD of the company appeared, carrying pizzas and cans of lager for the IT team, to show his appreciation for what they were doing. Later that week the IT team bumped into the MD in the staff restaurant. He stopped and spoke to them, remembering the name of every member of the team.

Years later my client described him as the best boss he had ever had. Reward does not have to be difficult. At the very least it can be something as small as bothering to remember someone's name. Not as strong as first seems – how much control does a leader have over pay and promotion? When you use up rewards, power base weakens.

Legitimate power

This is power based on the authority that comes with the position or job. So it belongs to the role rather than the individual.

- It is based on the belief that *a person has a formal right* to make demands and expect others to obey.

- It can be *limiting to use this as the sole basis of power*, as people can be very creative at avoiding carrying out orders if they wish. It is unpredictable and unstable because if the person loses their position their legitimate power is lost as well.

Example: A client who was not particularly assertive was amazed when he joined a company where legitimate power was respected. His position as a senior manager meant that his demands were carried out without him experiencing the discomfort of asserting himself very much. However, when he moved to another position in a matrix organisation, where roles were less clear cut, with more 'dotted line' responsibilities and less acknowledgement and respect for legitimate authority, the limitations of this power base became clear.

PERSONAL POWER

The final two of the power bases are personal: that is they are part of the leader's style and are therefore not dependent on a formal role in the organisation. Because they are personal they are also transportable as they travel with the leader to whatever organisation they are in.

Expert power

This is based on a person's high level of knowledge and skills. Many professionals rely on this as a power base to influence others and get work done.

- *Having expertise* means that others are more likely to listen to opinions, trust judgement and acknowledge leadership.

- However, the basis of *this power is reduced* if the expertise becomes more widely available or is no longer appropriate.

This is an important point that leaders sometimes miss. At times becoming a leader means leaving behind their area of expertise. Other aspects of leadership become important. This happens frequently when people who are experts in their field are promoted into leadership positions where that expertise is not part of the requirements of leadership.

Referent power

This power base comes from the identification of the target with the aims, goals, values, attitudes or needs of the power-holder.

- It is a *deeper, more effective and longer-lasting* basis of influence as the target agrees in many respects with the power-holder and is therefore more inclined to engage in the behaviour willingly. Liking increases identification.

- Indeed, *anyone in the organisation* can have referent power, regardless of their formal position.

The advantage of referent power is that there is no need for close supervision as the target can generally be relied upon to agree with the instruction or request. I have seen this power exercised in a small business, when the dynamic and highly regarded MD was involved in a business that was ground-breaking in an area that was highly competitive yet adding value to human well-being. The degree of motivation amongst the team was compelling.

HOW I MAKE BEST USE OF THE MODEL

There are a number of occasions when I might introduce the model. I coach on an emerging leaders programme. It can help my clients, in the early stages of leadership, reflect on the different styles of influencing, where they might most naturally gravitate and the advantages of developing other approaches. In coaching more experienced leaders, the conversation about their style might be part of the reason they came for coaching. Their style might emerge as part of the feedback session on a personality assessment. In all cases, it can lead to a discussion about their developmental needs and how they can improve their ability to lead effectively.

When I'm talking through this model with a client, I emphasise that there is no power base that is intrinsically better or worse than others. I ask them to reflect on their leadership style and how aware they are of the power bases they use most often.

- Do they mainly use just one or two?
- What consequences have they noticed, both expected and unexpected?
- Can they think of a time when they have used it effectively?
- When hasn't it worked?
- What are the advantages and disadvantages?
- What other power bases might they use to increase their effectiveness as a leader?
- What kind of followers do the different power bases produce?
- What sources of power do the people who influence them draw on?
- To what extent is there a prevalent power base in their organisation and how has this affected its culture?

These are examples of questions that I have used to help leaders deeply consider their leadership style, the effect it has on those around them and the extent it helps or hinders them in achieving their objectives as a leader.

WHERE NEXT?

Leaders use power as a means of attaining team and organisational goals. It is a means of facilitating their achievements and what is desired as being an effective leader. Through the model and shared examples, I hope I have demonstrated in this blog-article that leadership and power are closely intertwined. Here I focus on helping leaders quickly understand, through a simple framework, the different bases of power that co-exist with each other. I help them reflect on how they might develop further their ability to influence others by increasing their flexibility.

The way a leader behaves towards others, and how effectively they get the best from those others, can depend on the source and use of power. That power might not come from official status or title. In my experience, helping clients understand the power they use, aiding them to learn alternative methods and flex their style enhances their success as a leader.

Question: How have you talked about power in a constructive way with clients working in leadership roles?

CHAPTER 3

MAKING SENSE OF COACHING PRACTICE FROM PROFESSIONAL, AND PERSONAL, EXPERIENCES

Being genuinely interested in you: my pathway into coaching

Simon Dennis

LEARNING TO STEP BACK FROM THE SOLUTION

It **begins with** understanding the individual in the room. The individual that's present in the room. Not the individual you might have read about. Not the individual that you might have seen the last time. Not even the individual that you may have read up on in your notes before you go into the room.

In my coaching conversations it's very easy to be prepared for a coaching conversation. By prepared I mean, having an understanding of what happened the last time you met and the actions taken and a little bit about the background. The danger is if you are too prepared for the moment. If you're not open as a coach, because I think we're less ready and available. The idea of being a coach is to be present for them, not necessarily prepared for them. And I love that surprising element.

I like to be surprised by coaching.

To me it's great. That's why when you coach people where you have little or no understanding of their world, you're more inquisitive. I think one of the great skills of coaching, if you like, is to be genuinely inquisitive because it matters. If it matters to the client, it will always matter to me. I find myself saying things when clients say to me, *"Oh, do you want me to tell you more about that?"* my response is, *"Well, do you want to tell me more about that? Because actually, if you don't want to tell me more, that is equally fine. But if you believe that I need to know more, if you want to share more, my job is to be there in the moment."*

I think that element gives you real insight into what people are. It allows you to understand the context that you work with. The intent. It's a genuine desire to know the answer rather than just to make conversation. As adults, we learn this wonderful ability to feign interest in order to make conversation.

BEING GENUINELY INTERESTED AND DISARMING: THE EARLY DAYS

I try and be - both in my body language and in my approach-disarming. This is something which cannot easily be captured in written words because of the way in which words express things, such as emphasis and tone.

I learned that very early on in my radio career because it came genuinely from the heart. I was working with people whose job I'd never do or, even after trying, didn't do as well and wouldn't be pursuing. Yet it was literally through my appreciation of these experiences that drove my early conversations in coaching. One was a genuine interest in what they did and how they did it.

Whenever I looked at these radio presenters I thought, "How do you actually do it?" Literally, I have no idea and couldn't imagine what it's like to be one. So I was genuinely interested in knowing more. With that curiosity I spotted things that they might be doing that could be improved upon. Yet I was really careful in giving feedback because you're dealing with supremely confident individuals and colossal authorities. So all the time, I would go and just be more disarming in my approach and inquire, *"Well, actually, could you have done that any better?"* Whereas previous employers had maybe said to them, *"Oh, I think you could have made that better. I think you could have done that thing better."*

Let me share an example from early on in my career where this approach proved valuable. Very early on in my managerial role in a new station with a very experienced, professional radio presenter, whose first comment to me was, *"Well, what is it you're going to tell me about my job that I don't really know?"* As I took a step back I thought, 'I need to help him see that I'm not a threat because he clearly feels threatened by whatever the bosses have decided to do to bring me down here'. So I was very quiet and all I said to him was, *"I'm not sure there's anything that I can tell you that will make you a better presenter. You know, there might be some stuff, I'm not sure, but what I want to do is understand what makes you good and help you to become great."*

It was being present rather than being prepared in those first few moments. Continuously delivering on my intentions. It opened up a whole avenue of possibilities. He also became one of my biggest advocates in the industry.

At the time, none of what I was doing would be called coaching, because it was literally in the moment. Yet that's how I operate. It's been about letting the person on the other side know, fully convincing them, that I am interested in them. This isn't the same as being able to answer all of their questions. And there is some point in your management life that you do have to take action and decide.

UNDERSTANDING THE CONTEXT AND REALLY CARING ABOUT THE INTENT: MY APPROACH TO COACHING EFFECTIVELY

I think, as coaches, we have a role to take that childhood approach, to say to ourselves, "*Actually, I'm genuinely interested in you, as an individual, in your moment and in your world. So if you talk to me about fishing, and actually, I might not like fishing, but if I show a genuine interest, then perhaps you'll open up to me about everything else.*"

As a coach, you learn from different courses to build rapport and listening, two key skills. Yet how do you do it? You might summarize what the other person has said to demonstrate you've really been listening. But the problem is, as a rule and as adults, you learn all these techniques to show rapport, to show interest. It's a continuous important reminder to every coach, "*I'm not just asking you this because I know it will help build our rapport, I'm asking you this because actually, I'm genuinely interested.*" Otherwise you're just playing the game if you're not careful.

For me, my approach in demonstrating listening and from the feedback I have received from a number of my clients is that when they've met me for the second or third time, they find it really warming to know that I still remember what was said in the first meeting. I take very few notes but I remember loads of detail.

They'd say to me, "*You didn't write any of that down. You didn't take any notes.*"

I'd respond with, "*But you told me when we met that you were doing this and you were involved in that.*"

They would ask, "*How did you know that?*"

And I would honestly say, "*Because I was genuinely interested.*"

Note taking for me is a way of helping remembering ways of genuinely being interested, rather than using your notes to kind of prepare yourself for the moment. It's about,

- OK, so what is it that you've told me before and what is it that you've told me now?
- What's changed?
- What's the addition?

Bringing altogether all that I bring from my experiences has led me to two key elements as being the basics of effective coaching: understanding the context and caring about the intent. I can best demonstrate this with an example.

I was in a meeting one day when one of my senior managers came up to me afterwards and said, "*I noticed in the meeting that you didn't contribute. Can we talk about why that was?"* Now this senior leader is very perceptive and hadn't forgotten to follow up. They said to me later on, *"We had that meeting and you weren't your normal self."* And I said, *"What do you mean by that?"* They responded with, *"Well, normally, you would contribute. But we were in a couple of fairly-heated debates and you just stayed out of it. Why was that?"*

Both the intent and approach they took informed me that they weren't beginning by making assumptions nor thinking there was something wrong with me. Instead, with such an open question with such a disarming tone, allowed me to answer, *"I wasn't prepared to have a fight. It wasn't that important. So I let it go."* They then went onto explain the value I offer, *"But I want you to debate. I want you to contribute."* And from this genuine interest I shared what I needed, *"OK. But then you need to give me something that I care about to contribute. We were having this discussion but I didn't think it was worth the effort."* They then empowered me to intervene in the conversation with, *"But you shouldn't have said that. You should have said, 'Why were you debating this?'"* Following this conversation, I agreed for future meetings that if I thought the topic of conversation wasn't worth debating I would just say it.

Being able to have this type of conversation outside the meeting was a way of demonstrating clear intentions and alignments. And in my example this senior manager and I had contracted with each other. Our intent was to get the best out of me. That was reciprocated with trust. You might call this their coaching approach, and in fact, I find myself doing it now with my team. They know that my intention is always to include them, but I'm also respective of their context - where they're coming from. I think, the whole bit about coaching almost kind of maintains as though that coaching is about correcting some faults in purity or the issues that the coachee has got. I always find that I'm lucky that my coaching journey started from a position of coaching on strengths all the time.

SHARING MY REFLECTIONS OF MY COACHING JOURNEY SO FAR

I was very fortunate that I started coaching from a position of strength. All my clients were good. They know what they're doing. My job is to make them great and exceptional because I deal with quality.

To be perfectly honest, when I first encountered coaching for different kinds of remediation and remedial behaviour, I was astounded. It was a whole new area for me (something I hadn't considered). When I sat in the room and they go, *"Right. I've been sent here for coaching"*, my initial approach is, *"What makes you so good in your job?"* They return, *"Well, because I do this and this."*

It's being prepared not to have your starting point focusing on around what things they have been told to work on. That's starting from almost—well, a no-win situation. And so my first experience of coaching people for improvement when they've been identified as weak in certain areas is always talk about their strengths. When I have someone come to me and say, *"So I've been told by my boss that I'm not very good at presenting. I'm not very good in senior meetings"*, I start by saying, *"So tell me what things you are good at."* That's always my natural starting point. That is where I come from.

My world has come from working with really good people. I'm here to help other people get a good look at what they are really good at. For me it really starts with being genuinely interested in the other, a way of being. My coaching and disarming approach to interactions helps me to achieve what I've shared as being the two key elements for effective coaching: intent and a context that requires those who are party to these coaching conversation to have worked together to build.

The element of context helps with setting the boundaries for having coaching conversations, and in those conversation you can then be implicit in your context. This is because it's in that moment that the recipient needs something from the coach and so the intent of the coaching is generally accepted because previous interactions have been positive. Their desire to come and ask you wouldn't happen if they didn't already think that you are going to add some value.

Question: Through this piece I have shared what's really important for me in understanding the added value my approach to coaching brings. I'm always learning from other people's approaches in the moment. So what elements are key to your practice?

"Becoming a human being, as well as human doing"- How coaching enabled a career transition to new opportunities for me

Chris Paterson

INTRODUCTION

Finding *the good* coach has given me an opportunity to reflect on and share some of my journey to becoming a coach and how coaching has enabled some important differences for me as well as for others.

The main theme is Know Thyself. It is a process of reflecting on this journey as a way of continuing with my coaching – especially of myself!

HOW AWARENESS STARTED FOR ME

I guess I have always been a coach. I've only come to fully appreciate it in the last few years once I had some formal coach training.

By going on my journey of self-discovery, what I've come to learn is that learning, development and growth are some of my most fundamental and core values.

Those have been with me since my school days. I really enjoyed school. I enjoyed university. I enjoyed the acquisition of new information. New ideas and new concepts have always fascinated me.

When I first started work as a trainee accountant, I recall a preference for listening rather than talking in conversations. I would ask friends questions like, "What's stopping you?" This was one of a list of powerful questions that I found in a coaching manual twenty years later!

My awareness of coaching started when I was living and working abroad. I was invited to a one-day 'Introduction to Coaching' course. As a keen sportsman, I thought that business coaching would be a bit like sports coaching (the coach doesn't play on behalf of the player). The distinction between coaching and mentoring and the idea of coaching being about NOT giving advice was totally new to me. I remember enjoying the course and thinking this is something I want to do more of.

TAKING GRADUAL PROGRESSIVE STEPS FORWARD WITH THIS AWARENESS

Sometime after that introduction to coaching, I wanted to set up a Twitter account. The name @ChrisPaterson was already taken. I tried @SmileBeCurious and it was available. Since that moment, it has been a call to action for how I wanted to be, an identity which fits really nicely with being a coach. If I can smile and be curious, then what a lovely way to go about coaching, smiling and being curious.

Starting to practice this coaching at work and championing the development of others through a large team of people who were working for me. In one-to-one conversations, I was more interested in their career aspirations and how they wanted to develop than their day-to-day activities. This provided an opportunity for me to take a coaching approach and practice my skills. I enjoyed helping them and they were pleased that I was taking an interest in them.

What I struggled with was the performance management element of leading a large team. I believe I have a pre-disposition to see the good in others. Some of the feedback I received was that I look at the world through "rose-tinted glasses". I later realised that the ability to hold someone in unconditional positive regard is one of the corner stones of taking a coaching approach. As a coach, I am the sunshine that awakens the brilliance of others so that they can discover it for themselves.

Continuing to build awareness of the coaching process... I then came back to the UK. I had an opportunity to sign up to an internal coaching training course, after which I qualified as an internal coach in a very substantial programme that had been running successfully for a number of years. That took my coaching to a new level. It made it much more of a conscious rather than an unconscious thing and that really started the journey, formally.

Continuing my learning... So I started to notice the difference in my energy levels when I was coaching compared to doing the rest of my day job (leading a Business Unit and team of fifty in sales and marketing). I noticed that a lot of the time I had more energy at the end of a coaching session than at the start. Coaching is something that energizes me, something that's useful to another person and is focused on learning.

So this is really quite a sweet spot for me. It's also an opportunity to be a human being as well as a human doing. It's an opportunity to not just be in front of a computer churning out stuff; with some freedom in terms of where it could happen and when it could happen. So a sense of liberation came from coaching as well.

I decided that I wanted to become an executive coach for my company and met the head of coaching to find out how to get there. There were three things they look for in an executive coach:

1. Coaching competence.

2. Business credibility.

3. Evidence of the journey of self-discovery.

I was told that the experience I had gained from working as a management team member and leader in several countries was plenty in terms of business credibility. I was given some recommendations for how to develop my coaching capability and self-awareness to the level needed. I thought to myself that I was quite self-aware already and so investigated a coaching course. It involved several long weekends. Amazingly I was free on those dates, but I was not able to secure the funding for the course from my manager.

Despondent, I met with the head of coaching again to see if there was a way to get on the course. There was no central funding available, just a reiteration of the advice to pursue the journey of self-discovery by enrolling in the Landmark Forum. This was a tenth of the price of the coaching course and funding was no longer a barrier so I signed up without hesitation. The difference between the person who turned up on the Friday morning at the start of the course and who I was on the Sunday evening was startling as I discovered how little about myself I actually knew.

The weekend had been the most powerful learning experience I had ever had. It changed the way I saw myself and the world. Looking back, this was much more valuable to me that the coaching course I thought I wanted to go on. Over the next six months I completed the rest of the Landmark core curriculum which has helped me to continue the inquiry into who I am and my journey of self-discovery.

Building the practice of coaching... As an internal coach, I have had a steady stream of clients, almost as many as I wanted. Over the last year, I've probably had about ten at a time. I started quite small with one or two, and then realised that the more I coach, the more I enjoyed it. And the more I coached, the better I got at it. It's really gone from there.

CONTINUING TO USE ALL THE LEARNING METHODS ...

Keeping Focus on feedback through Results and Output is really important. I have been very lucky to be able to take advantage of regular supervision and CPD events provided through work. These have helped me grow my coaching muscle.

Every client is also an opportunity for me to learn and develop as a coach. I routinely ask clients for feedback in addition to the evaluation which my company asks them to complete. Through the contracting in the chemistry meeting, I make it very clear that the only reason I do this is to be useful to them. So if it's not working for them, it's not working for me either. That gives them the permission to be in charge and to call the shots.

I have made use of being observed in coaching sessions by a much more experienced coach and they then give me encouragement and pointers for improvement as well.

Sometimes you get those lightbulb moments where the hair stands up on the back of your neck and you really know you're working with something. For me, that's the most rewarding feedback, although I've learnt not to expect that to happen too often.

Another critical element of my development has come from being coached. I have had 3 different coaches over a two-year period and found the experience incredibly valuable on a number of levels. At one level, I was able to watch them coaching me. I made notes of what worked well so that I could use the same with my clients. I was also able to do some important work to help me on my journey including finding and refining my purpose in life (to grow leaders by supporting others to discover for themselves), becoming better at identifying my emotions and making the preparations for a great ending to be able to allow a new beginning as an executive coach.

At the time of writing I have recently left the company where I worked for seventeen years to focus on developing my coaching practice, SmileBeCurious. I have also set up a charity related to coaching young people (more about this in another blog). This would have been inconceivable a few years ago – coaching has transformed me.

CONCLUSIONS

And I think the journey has been as much about me developing as a coach as me developing as an individual, and learning about myself. That has probably been the more powerful element of it in fact. By gaining greater self-awareness, I've been able to develop as a coach.

As a coach, I'm an expert in not knowing. There's something about me being able to share that with clients that makes them okay for them to be vulnerable, to be able to open up and to know that I'm not going to judge them.

You don't need very much training to start coaching, you can set yourself up, get some insurance and off you go. What makes the difference is less about the training or the hours of coaching experience. I believe it comes down to attitude and this journey of self-discovery. It's an absolutely critical component of being a coach which you cannot just sign up for and get from a training course.

'What do I need to do to become a better coach?' Know yourself, know yourself better. And make sure that you're clear about why you do this and what it means to you. The rest will follow.

I really appreciate this opportunity to express and share my story like this. This has been a useful and valuable exercise for me.

Having an 'anthropocene' mindset: fits between coaching and planet, people and prosperity (sustainability)

Geoffrey Ahern

Today's era is called the 'Anthropocene[1]' because humans have an increasingly significant influence on the Earth. The Anthropocene and its 17 UN Sustainable Development Goals ('SDG's) have by now become the general setting for companies' commercial success.

The prospects for worldwide sustainability have reached the more hopeful point, compared to previous widespread denial, of cultural acknowledgement. Even a fund based on prodigious fossil fuel wealth, the Rockefeller Family Fund derived from Standard Oil, is accusing this company's largest direct descendant, ExxonMobil, of trying to deceive policymakers and the public about the realities of climate change[2]. The next (very big) step is effective action.

Yet coaching and sustainability, despite what they can offer each other, are two distinct client services at present. The market for sustainability enabling seems to be being taken up by consultants in packaged silos, with what coaching could add being largely left out.

Alongside this, sustainability itself is in silos:

- Professionals in companies have specific accountabilities.
- NGOs campaign on particular issues.
- Academics publish within outmoded disciplinary divisions and methodological constraints.

---

[1] See for example Purdy, Jedediah. 2015. *After Nature: A Politics for the Anthropocene*. Cambridge: Harvard University Press.
[2] Kaiser, David. and Lee Wasserman. 2016. "The Rockefeller family fund vs. Exxon." In *The New York Review of Books*: 31-35. December 22.

PART 1: Leading edge: Influences on Practitioner's Learning and Development

In this situation, the attempt to make overall sense through linking coaching and sustainability is very important if one believes, as I do, that vision accompanies truly effective action.

What matters even more than the actual sense made by different people is having a culture of big picture sense-making and self-revising discussion about it. This is what the non-didactic approach of coaching individuals encourages.

EXECUTIVE COACHING AND SUSTAINABILITY HAVE BEEN PARALLEL TRACK VOCATIONS FOR ME

As I believe that both coaching and sustainability have significant similarities and where not are complementary, I am motivated to suggest how the mindsets of coaching and sustainability could fit together: the subject of this blog-article.

By 'mindset' I mean underlying and established assumptions about what matters most. Mindsets in sustainability (especially), and to some extent coaching, are often taken for granted. Indeed the outlooks one hardly knows one has have tended to carry the most influence of all. Such in-depth areas may not be easy to pinpoint, but should be examined nevertheless, because there can be no fit between coaching and sustainability services unless, demonstrably, the 'gut feeling' is either mutually right or comes right.

This blog-article outlines sustainability mindsets through five clusters:

1. Sustainability and science.

2. Sustainability and whole population perspectives.

3. Sustainability and the long term.

4. Sustainability and narratives/mythologies.

5. Sustainability and systems thinking.

Within each cluster the fit with coaching is explored. For clusters 1, 2 & 4 the significance seems to be mainly that sustainability and coaching are different but potentially *complementary*. For clusters 3 & 5 there appear to be considerable *similarities*; coaching and sustainability may have more in common than they realise in the face of business-as-usual. Because of these compatibilities, whether through complementary differences or similarities, encounters between coaching and sustainability mindsets could result in combined delivery impacts.

MY VOCATIONAL JOURNEYING TO DATE

About twenty years ago I started the adventure of delivering executive coaching. My only real doubt then was that coaching might not be an entirely liberating influence towards an inclusive prosperity: might it also through effective work with individuals 'psych up' dysfunctional larger-scale operations?

I had promised myself that if this seemed to be unduly the case I would 'listen'. A turning point came eight years ago after a long period of exclusively doing executive coaching, including five years employed by a London consultancy.

Working by this time independently, I began assimilating diverse sustainability perspectives. This arose through sustainability consulting with multinational companies, sometimes alongside wildlife campaigners, helping a business school set up a sustainability-oriented MBA, co-founding a sustainability leadership group and undertaking university sustainability tutoring online to small groups of executives worldwide doing work-based doctorates.

Increasingly, environmental warnings and global inequities had become hard for me to ignore in my corporate work. Furthermore coaching – including my own – had not picked up on the systemic issues underlying the financial crisis.

Also, pushing from the back of my mind to the front, was previous experience from the 1980s. I had published findings then from participant observation and sociological research with an ecologically-oriented global movement. I had been absorbed by matters like social movements, just what kind of knowledge science gives and differences between the major cultural worldviews (indeed the sociological term 'worldview' could be used instead of the more social-psychological perspective of 'mindset' chosen for this context).

During this journeying as an executive coach leaning towards sustainability, a big question I postponed for a long time was how, if at all, coaching and sustainability could come together.

I parked it because answers depended on finding out enough about sustainability first of all; for sustainability as practised in companies was not at all the same as the ecological affinities in the movement I had researched those years back. I knew – and know now – of no one who synthesises executive coaching with a full range of sustainability practitioner issues, but from about three years ago spoke about the possibility. Then I was invited to pilot a twelve-to-fifteen-hour coaching/sustainability course in central London. This took place last summer over six sessions with participants who mixed executive coaching and sustainability expertise.

WHAT MATTERS TO SUSTAINABILITY PRACTITIONERS THE MOST? INTERPRETING MINDSET FITS BETWEEN SUSTAINABILITY AND COACHING

The following mindset interpretations are offered as a starting point for discussion and further developments.

PART 1: Leading edge: Influences on Practitioner's Learning and Development

1. Sustainability and science

Sustainability context. Scientific research is central to the fierce disputes about sustainability's credibility. For example, those who dispute that climate change is mainly human-caused use scientific credentials and these in turn are attacked (rightly or wrongly) for misinterpreting the science. Without scientific backing on issues such as the hypothesis of biodiversity loss or fresh water shortages the case for action disappears. Science is also the basis for validity criticisms of corporate environmental measurement systems such as the Global Reporting Initiative (GRI). The assumption is that we find objectivity through null hypotheses, measurement, statistical analysis etc. Ian McEwen's environmental novel *Solar*, in contrasting science and revelation in a health context, makes an analogous point by asking "Who was going to submit to a vaccine designed by a priest[3]?"

Fit with coaching. Compared to the above, coaching's mindset seems to legitimise its pattern-making with clients through non-scientific means, such as the intuitive fit with one or more axiomatic approaches (Rogerian, psychodynamic, existentialist etc). The fact that statistical reasoning is also actually being deployed may be ignored. For example, in external examining involving coaching MA dissertations I noticed how those who stated that their approach was entirely qualitative not quantitative would often justify reaching conclusion X by stating something quantitative like: "as many as eight out of ten of the interviewees did X!"

Our culture has been described as having an arts/science split. In the recent formative past of the post-modernist cultural climate it was against the flow to make any claims for objectivity. Though coaches quite often bring in the planet through something like Performance Consultants International's[4] "sustainability is at the core of what we do". Such statements rarely seem to be aware of scientific summaries for the public such as the nine planetary boundaries of the Stockholm Resilience Centre.

Impact. The overwhelming impact is ethical. If scientific findings about the likely adverse consequences of business-as-usual to life in the planet are valid, do coaches' ethical guidelines require these threats (for example, by a polluting client company) to be given as much prominence as would be given to a threat to an individual life? In order to start answering this critical question coaching culture needs to consider the nature of science, because so many sustainability issues are to do with probabilities, large numbers of abstract people, the validity of research etc.

What's next? Coaching, through taking science more on board, could mediate by acknowledging how the qualitative and quantitative cannot be entirely separated.

---

[3] McEwen, Ian. 2010. *Solar*. London: Cape.
[4] www.performanceconsultants.com/About Us/Our Values and Vision

Indeed the wisdom of coaching could contribute much to the contextualising of sustainability science. Values are involved in hypothesis formation and in the communication and implementation of findings.

Avoiding subjectivity can be hard even in making sense-based measurements. I recall a scientist telling me how looking at a temperature gauge accurately is no casual matter, that to 'see' a measurement a heightened self-checking state is required. The science validating sustainability, not to be naïve, has to be conceived as taking into account the subjective aspects of our perceptions (i.e. as a subtle realism which is post-Kantian and cognisant of the psychology of perception).

2. SUSTAINABILITY AND WHOLE POPULATION PERSPECTIVES

Sustainability context. Those influenced by the core sustainability science, ecology, tend to think in terms of whole populations, i.e. in collective terms. Thus, in relation to species they focus on overall survival, for example of giraffes throughout Africa.

Fit with coaching. The individualistic basis for human rights espoused by many (though by no means all) contemporary sustainability advocates comes immediately from 'people first' NGO values (such as Oxfam's) and is irrelevant in terms of the science of ecology. Indeed, individual rights are even seen by some ecologists as hindering human survival. In contrast, valuing the individual is the soul of coaching. For coaching, this extends to all people, while some strands in 'ecology' as a social movement prioritise an ethnic, regional or other group. However, coaching's client boundaries, unlike ecology's, are typically fixed around humanity only.

Impact. Professional ecology's 'clients', because they extend beyond human life, are different from coaching's clients. Ecology has very often embraced animals, planetary inclusiveness and, among some spiritually-minded adherents, pantheism (something like Shakespeare's 'sermons in stones'). Indeed dark green environmentalists think that humans should have no ethical privilege, the test of this being that humans should at least sometimes lose out compared to the ecosystem as a whole. Many would extend rights to the planet itself, for example Polly Higgins' campaigns for an international law against ecocide. Questions even arise over whether 'humanoid' artificial intelligence should have ethical standing.

Where those espousing ecology identify first of all with a human population which is ethnic or regional, this is obviously discriminatory. A major example is the 1930s 'Blood and Soil' thinking of Walter Darré, who was Minister of Agriculture in the Third Reich. There is fertile ground also for such intra-human splits today. Thus the author Nilanjana Roy in describing the recent turn towards the right says she has found it hard to stay polite to a childhood friend 'who now expresses hate towards Muslims and Dalits[5]'. Industrially-caused environmental

---

[5] Roy, Nilanjana. 2016. "How to Stay Friends Across the Political Divide." *Financial Times.*

stresses may aggravate pre-existing cultural fault-lines, making it more likely that adjacent peoples will conflict: for example over water control, or as a result of mass immigration to Europe from desertification.

What's next? Here again there's complementary potential. Should coaching be so exclusively oriented to human beings? It has the option of extending the essentialism of seeing humans as intrinsically special to valuing overall relationships. This would include animals, habitat and the planet as a whole. After all, coaches often oppose essentialist absolutes in other situations such as human gender differences.

Coaching should also contribute its identification with individual liberty for all humans. This has its roots primarily in Western culture, as expressed in much of the UN Declaration of Human Rights. Globally this is now in the context of the neo-Confucianism of China, of its large diaspora as in Indonesia and of Islam. In their distinctive ways these cultures, like ecology, tend to be collective in outlook.

3. SUSTAINABILITY AND THE LONG-TERM

Sustainability context. People who think in a scientific, whole population way are likely to add geological time units to those of business-as-usual. Sustainability consultants tend first of all to present their services in terms of alignments with business-as-usual. Introducing sustainability has some useful short-term benefits such as cutting waste and intelligently using regulation. Many other sustainability approaches, such as stakeholder thinking, CR (Corporate Responsibility), creating shared value, society-wide governance by multi-national corporations, are strategically ambiguous: for sustainability protagonists they are Trojan horses, for others they are latently business-as-usual. By the end of the day at least, and probably well before, in order to be credible in terms of ecology, corporate short-termism must be addressed as a sustainability gap.

Fit with coaching. Coaching has much in common. It has to deliver in the here-and-now at the same time as working with behavioural and other patterns which bear on the longer-term. Doing both together successfully is part of the magic of the intervention.

Impact. In the case of both sustainability consultants and executive coaches I have noticed very few if any agitating against immediate profits, and so cutting off the commercial bough on which they are sitting. But both share the need to create long-term thinking in client delivery, though this can be problematic: for example, a coach recently shared the problem of whether the sustainability of oil was on the agenda in his coaching of an oil company board member.

What's next? Acknowledgment of the broad affinity between coaching's and sustainability's long-term approaches could add to the credibility and advance framing of each.

https://www.ft.com/content/2fc36578-ab23-11e6-ba7d-76378e4fef24 Accessed September 10.

PART 1: Leading edge: Influences on Practitioner's Learning and Development

4. SUSTAINABILITY AND NARRATIVES/MYTHOLOGIES

Sustainability context. People tend to justify long-term goals by more than dry science: underlying meanings come into play. Sustainability is certainly no exception!

Sustainability narratives may sometimes be re-combinations of ancient themes. Hence 'mythology', in the old sense of not necessarily untrue, may better describe them than the media-saturated 'narrative' (or the modish term 'imaginary'). In a nutshell for now, the main sustainability narratives/mythologies I am aware of are:

- **Western apocalypse**, which is millennia-old, reconstituted in the immanent form of environmental dread/utopia. This unhelpfully either frightens or hopes excessively, so its cultural construction and psychological projection roots should be exposed.

- **'Back to nature'.** As lived out simplicity (within Schumacher College for example) it provides an essential model. If its unitive assumptions are differentiated it can be made more pertinent to the necessities within which companies and their stakeholders have their being.

- **Geological fatalism.** This is an 'inevitable (so long as it doesn't get educated, North Atlantic me or my family)' approach which agrees with the science behind environmental warnings but extends Darwinian evolution into identifying with the supposed inalterability of business-as-usual. Underlying feelings of despair may be being denied.

- **Eco-modernism.** A 'technology will see us through' identification, eco-modernism is short on roots and so avoids distinguishing between technical fixes and ethical development. But it brings valuable insights into the many-sided nature of 'nature'.

- **A development of consciousness inner path** in which ecological awareness is placed at an advanced 'stage'. This type of vision has cultural antecedents (gnosis, de Chardin for example) which underlie aspects of both some sustainability and some coaching. Its danger is deluded spiritual elitism; its motivational benefits include a sense of salvation through insight.

Fit with coaching. Yet again, there seems to be complementary potential. Coaching's own narratives, though diverse – cognitive, Rogerian, psychodynamic etc – tend to be based within the individual as a unit, or 'in here', and so could bring insight into personal factors (such as projection) influencing the choice of sustainability narratives and mythologies located in a large-scale 'out there'.

Impact. Narratives and mythologies implicit within sustainability often have weak signals but powerful consequences. Where they are dysfunctional or non-integrated they can sabotage the public's perception of the case for sustainability.

What's next? A coaching approach could help these sustainability narratives and mythologies become more conscious, synthesised and constructive. If combined explicitly, they could contribute powerfully towards creating living organisations. In business models selection needs to enhance what matters most to the particular company including its stakeholders: i.e. 'materiality'.

5. SUSTAINABILITY AND SYSTEMS THINKING

Sustainability context. To be effective sustainability professionals need to make recommendations for the future. This means they have to conceive how the planet's many different populations – such as giraffes and humans – interact dynamically over time. This holism in examining factors in their entirety, using transdisciplinary approaches, gives rise to systems thinking. Big system questions of the utmost practical importance are posed in sustainability scenario-building: for example, how companies might avoid plundering nature and instead resiliently pass on equivalent value[6].

The concept of emergence is central to systems thinking, scarily for example in modelling for climate change tipping points. The term 'emergence' salutes the qualitative difference when one state makes a leap into another, as when the mineral world in our evolutionary past somehow gave rise to vegetation. Vegetation 'emerged' because its life makes it qualitatively more than the inertness of minerals even though it is dependent on them for its existence. Imaginative, almost magical, acceptance seems to be how our limited minds can conceive of such qualitative leaps.

Fit with coaching. The process of systems thinking in sustainability has something in common with holistic interpretations offered by coaches. The latter connect different factors together through overarching sense-making.

For example, linking the way a client reacted to me in the here-and-now, what he said about the closed nature of his reports, his description of his teenage son being highly rebellious and what he told me about the authoritarianism of his father, led me, in the role of coach, to make the intuitive leap of hypothesising from these different dimensions (transference, present contexts and the past) that he had a deep-seated need to control. This coaching method of joining together disparate pieces of evidence into greater wholes has analogies with the leap characteristic of 'emergence'. Indeed, systemic thinking is explicitly included in some coaching: for example, the socio-technical approach.

Impact. Recent articles in the *Harvard Business Review*[7], following the usual route from academia to commerce via business schools, have put complex adaptive systems and emergence, difficult though these concepts are, in front

---

[6] Collier, P. 2010. *The Plundered Planet*, London: Penguin.
[7] Reeves, Martin., Simon Levin, and Daichi Ueda. 2016. "The Biology of Corporate Survival." In *Harvard Business Review*. Jan: 47-55. See also other articles in this issue.

of hectic CEOs. Systems thinking enables corporate policy-makers to think about sustainability more effectively, for example to get their heads around probabilities in predictability.

What's next? Again, acknowledgment of these process similarities between coaching and sustainability could, through joining forces, further enable companies to generate greater ecological and social resilience in the face of discontinuous change.

SHOULD COACHING IN THE ANTHROPOCENE LINK WITH SUSTAINABILITY?

Accusations that ExxonMobil deceived the public over climate change were suggested at the start of this blog-article to be emblematic of a new cultural stage of sustainability's acknowledgement. Hypocrisy once uncovered can be seen as the tribute that vice pays to virtue.

Thus ExxonMobil itself is said to have always kept a clear eye on the scientific reality of carbon dioxide causing climate change when making business decisions, regardless of its alleged campaign since about 1990 to confuse policymakers and the public on this very subject[8].

During the past twenty to thirty years there seems to have been a polarisation. On the one hand sustainability has been buttressed by scientific credibility in the minds of educated elites worldwide (indeed without this the Paris Climate Change agreement just over a year ago could not have happened). On the other hand, corporate practice has fallen far short while 'greenwash' (PR sustainability falsehood) has proliferated. Even the most impressively sustainable multinational, Unilever, is constrained by the overall North Atlantic shareholder culture of business-as-usual and short-termism. Hope and cynicism have become increasingly juxtaposed.

Technological fixes alone without mindset change may well help solve many problems. For example, alternative energy developments (as with solar sources) may make ExxonMobil's and other oil company's fossil fuel reserves become 'stranded': i.e. valueless. China is making a huge investment in sustainable technology.

But the dynamic, systemic nature of planet-people-and-prosperity issues such as biodiversity loss, fresh water wars, ocean acidification, immigration from sea level rises, unneighbourly geo-engineering, suggests that mindset change going well beyond compliance with regulation cannot be avoided forever. Coaching skills at least are needed to enable executives to make transformational big picture sense and relate this to their own roles and motivations. Thus coaching as a profession seems likely to become less split off from the overarching ethical precepts of the Anthropocene.

---

[8] See [2].

Meanwhile there is also potential work. Combinations of coaching with sustainability could be needed by the increasing numbers of those corporately accountable for the complexities of sustainability: for example, for harmonising pressures on supply chain costs with social as well as environmental requirements, for going beyond compliance in risk management to a culture of integrity and for inclusive anticipation in sustainability reputation handling.

As a first step, how easy is it for coaches to identify within their practices a relatively painless, cost-free action (however small) which brings their coaching professionally closer to sustainability?

CEOs make good coaches: what motivated me to get into coaching, and how it correlates to my former role and experiences as a CEO

Aubrey Rebello

SHARING MY PROFESSIONAL CAREER JOURNEY, PRIOR TO COACHING

was fortunate to have had leadership roles in a variety of business segments. Among the most challenging was functioning as the CEO of a large Financial Services Company - managing the business while also strategizing and handling a merger. There was a great deal of learning through the merger process, especially in all aspects of HR.

After retirement, I was asked to continue as a full-time adviser. The parent group was forming a new and larger Financial Services Company. I opted to setup the Learning and Development Function. I was given carte blanche to cover employees at all levels from frontline to business heads.

After getting involved with HR and L&D I started thinking, 'After this, what do I do?'

Over my career as a CEO, I noticed it's lonely at the top. You often feel the need to have someone as a sounding board, someone who will question your assumptions without you feeling threatened by it.

That is what made me decide to go into coaching. I felt that I had an advantage coming from business, and having subsequently closely handled HR and L&D work.

INTEGRATING AND EXTENDING RELEVANT EXPERIENCES INTO DEVELOPING MY COACHING PRACTICE

Having experienced what it's like being a business head, I can empathize with and appreciate the issues and concerns that a CEO faces even if our contexts differs. High performing CEOs still may have questions like,

- *"Can I do something better?"*
- *"What is the element of risk in this decision?"*
- *"Am I getting the full picture or is there a blind spot – what am I still missing?"*

Many of these concerns cannot be shared with internal stakeholders. They are typically better handled by an unbiased coach who has time to listen and understand you, and bring in newer/alternative perspectives.

Most coaching assignments that come my way are because of my varied business experience, backed up with my coaching skills.

What I have learnt from my long business experience is the need to be agile, energised, spot opportunities, manage and motivate teams, interact with key stakeholders, especially customers and your own team. You need to do all this under the pressure of delivering good business results and with limited time.

In my coaching practice, I have found that if CEOs can prioritise and manage their time well, they are able to do everything that is required, give good business results and still have a good work life balance. However, they need to develop skills to have shorter business reviews, be better at delegation and monitoring, and escape mail box pressure and information overload.

The CEO therefore needs a coach or mentor, someone who listens and understands:

- You as a person,
- Your role, and
- Business nuances.

Who better to discuss and move forward with than a coach who has also been there?

I also realized that business is heavily dependent on who heads the business, the energy he/she puts into it and the new thinking he/she brings into it. No business is a one person show but the CEO's agility and perceptiveness decides where the business will finally go.

MY PRACTICE IN RELATION TO THE FIELD

Mentoring and coaching is still in its nascent stage in India but it is growing. Indian corporates are starting to see the benefits of coaching. We can expect a 30 percent growth in coach usage year on year for the next three years. Coaching fees for corporates is in the range of USD $250 - 600 an hour. There is however a large untapped market for smaller companies and individuals at fees that may range in USD $100-150 per hour.

From an accreditation standpoint, the course offered by ICF, which I have done, is the most recognised.

Most coaches in India come from the HR domain. Clients in India now feel the need for coaches who have business experience, have faced profit pressures yet are still adequately grounded (not specialised) on the HR side.

These combinations are rare and there is a gap needing to be filled.

CEOs/business heads. This is your opportunity. You could be a mentor/coach to others though you may have sorely missed having one when you needed it the most. More than money, the difference you could make in the client's performance is a reward in itself.

Coaching and living in the paradigm of systematic correspondence

Simon Darnton

This is a story about finding a new way of coaching and a new way of being. When I properly embarked on my journey into coaching, I couldn't have dreamt the direction in which I was going to end up going. I say properly because for years I'd been stuck in a vacillation between head and heart in my career.

Early in my career I trained as a counsellor. Then I moved into the consulting business. In both these worlds there has for a while been a noticeable orientation towards conceptualising psychology and business functions in machine-like, computational and information processing terms. Due to my professional consulting work at the time sitting within the field of knowledge management, my world was steeped in cognitive and technology oriented approaches to knowledge and knowing (including related business processes, systems, culture and change). Despite working as the human advocate in these sometimes large-scale programmes, I was embedded in this way of thinking and operating. It was and still is the mainstream way of the Western world right now.

Then three things happened to me that fundamentally changed things.

1. I became incapacitated by an unusual and complex neuro-otological illness (this is basically a balance disorder)

2. I took up Tai Chi as part of my rehabilitation

3. I decided to embark upon a master's in Psychological Coaching at the Metanoia Institute

1. Balance

Balance disorders are remarkably common yet poorly understood. Standards of both diagnosis and treatment can vary significantly between regions and their hospitals (and which department, because different specialists will view the balance system from very different perspectives). Complex balance conditions are even more poorly addressed. I have the latter.

Even in specialist units where they have high standards of care, the human and psychological ramifications of balance conditions aren't particularly well acknowledged, let alone addressed. What they miss is that our balance is probably the most fundamental mechanism we have for relating to our world. With a balance disorder, the nature of your relationship with your world changes completely. Surprisingly or not, this will typically begin to dismantle your very identity. I've so far only come across one specialist who really understood this. She's a neuroscientist who, while studying balance, acquired a balance disorder herself.

This illness put an end to my previous career for good.

My experience of the rehabilitation process was an interesting one. I was being treated at a leading centre for my particular nuance of balance disorder, headed up by probably the world's leading expert in this field. My experience as a patient was awful; they had no idea how to develop a positive human relationship to support this process. When I was treated, it was invariably in a laboratory room in a dark, unpleasant basement using lots of gadgetry. Despite being told after each session that there was some improvement, as soon as I walked out into the real world of busy London streets, I experienced absolutely no benefit whatsoever (I was told in no uncertain terms that this was my fault, by the way). (I did eventually get moved to another leading hospital where my experience as a patient was much better.)

2. Tai chi

Just a series of slow, fluid, gentle and controlled movements designed to improve health and wellbeing (yes, and great for your balance mechanism).

Yeah, right.

With some teachers this might just be the case, but that's merely the surface. The most frustrating thing about Tai Chi is that with the right teacher it finds a way to get under your skin. It has that strange ability to ask some really compelling questions. Before you know it, you've embarked on a new life-long journey of self-inquiry.

The contract was somehow missing here!

Tai Chi is a highly sophisticated syncretism of lived 'philosophies.' It's also an effective martial art.

Now I even teach Tai Chi while I'm completing a three-year Tai Chi teacher's training course. I'm soon to be teaching four classes a week and I've introduced primary school children to the art. If only I had known... I sigh..

3. METANOIA

I knew about Metanoia from my days in counselling. It has a well-deserved reputation for its training of counsellors and psychotherapists. When I saw it had started a master's in Coaching Psychology I picked up the phone and things just fell into place to get on the programme.

Other people's descriptions of experience really are totally inadequate, however much they might try. I should have looked up the meaning of metanoia in a dictionary, but then I'm not sure I would have believed it.

Metanoia: from the ancient Greek perspective metanoia is a process of transformative change of both heart and mind. I've seen some reference to it being a more mythological dangerous inner journey.

I suppose it depends on how you engage with it, but it was this programme that was to define how I eventually came to coaching. It helped me to define some really important questions, seek my path of inquiry to investigate the questions I felt most passionate about and to do it rigorously within my coaching work.

The question I arrived at became: An inquiry into using the systematic correspondences of five-phase theory in psychological coaching.

It's how I coach with people, but so far it has been rather hidden – my implicit guide. I'm not entirely sure why, other than that I've not had the confidence to openly speak about it. When I have shared it, my experience of reply and engagement from others has been that of resounding silence. That doesn't help to build confidence in one's own path.

THE WORLD OF SYSTEMATIC CORRESPONDENCE

So here goes a journey into the world of systematic correspondence. Please do join me.

So what is this paradigm?

Its roots lie somewhere in ancient China. It is a way of being where one makes sense of the world in terms of relationships. It suffuses Chinese culture even today; it's the way the Chinese think.

Is this paradigm really so different?

I'm right in it, which means I spend a lot of my time trying to convince myself it isn't that different. Then I'm regularly reminded that it is:

> *"The difficulty is to speak Chinese with English... it is because through different strokes [of Chinese characters] something is built, which is not a word, but a symbol, and opens your mind. You must set free your imagination. There is a sort of artistic and aesthetic understanding of things which is necessary to enter the Chinese field of terminology... there is no difference in the Chinese mind between the well-organized political body and the human body of each of us. The Seven Emotions: Psychology and Health in Ancient China, Larre & Rochat de la Vallee (1996, p. 2)*

This paradigm does not readily translate into any individual field of study in the West. It encompasses philosophy, psychology, ontology, epistemology, medicine, sociology, ecology, but does not match or sit within any of them. This is because it is meant to be lived rather than conceptualised.

Yin/Yang theory is probably the most well-known theory that sits within this paradigm. Unfortunately, it also comes with some popular baggage that isn't always helpful. Yin/Yang is a relational and dynamic system of thought where something is only ever Yin or Yang in relation to something else and these relationships wax and wane like the cycles of the moon. Something that is Yin will be Yin or Yang in relation to something else that is also Yin. There will always be some Yang within Yin and vice versa. When something extends all the way into Yang, it will cycle back into Yin as a natural process, and this can be a destructive catastrophic process like floods or bush fires, or one of personal transformation. Whilst Yin/Yang are often assumed to be opposing forces, they are mutually co-operative. So to see Yin as dark or Yang as light, female or male, is not entirely helpful, especially as we in the West tend to hang on to this categorisation in our own dualist ways! In Yin/Yang nothing is considered to be good or bad, better or worse, just simply the nature of things.

> *"Yang does not leave yin; yin does not leave yang. The mutual cooperation and transformation of yin and yang is precisely what makes up the understanding of energy (dong jin)." The Taiji Treatise attributed to Wang Zongyue*

SO HOW ITS IT LIVED, THEN?

Taking five-phase theory, which was the subject of my master's research project, it's origins are very down to earth and practical. Historical references show that it has roots in farming; roots which were developed during the first unification of China where this early form of systems thinking crystallised around 230BC.

In agriculture, it was used as a way to observe the natural patterns of the environment and seasons, to help the sustainable cultivation of crops and tend the land accordingly. It was always about guiding appropriate action in some manner or form. Translating this to martial arts, psychology, medicine, or society at large, it is about how to act or proceed correctly.

The essence of this system is really quite straightforward, or dare I say natural!

> "Water moistens and descends; fire burns and ascends; wood bends and straightens; metal yields and changes; earth receives seeds and gives crops."
> Shujing: Book of Documents[1], Chapter Hong Fan as translated in Rochat de la Vallee (2009, p. 27)

The five-phases; Fire, Earth, Metal, Water, Wood, are 'processes and functions' of the natural world. As microcosms of the natural world, they apply equally as well to humans.

When I started learning all this, it made no real sense to me at all. I was compelled by it, but lost. I reached for books, lots of them, and found an interesting pattern. The western books verged on tomes, spending page upon page in conceptualisations to make sure the phases were explained. The Chinese texts (I read the translated ones) tended to be short and succinct; rather poetic. Remember the quotation above? 'You must set free your imagination, artistic, aesthetic understanding.' I didn't get that then.

Unbeknownst to me, whilst I still had my head stuck in books trying to understand how phenomena might be coherently categorized according to the five-phases, and failing quite miserably, I was embarking on a new phase of rehabilitation. I needed to go for a walk every day. At this point in time, thirty minutes was about my maximum but we had a new baby and he needed his fresh air and outdoor time too. At the back of our house ran a bridleway that meandered through outstandingly gorgeous countryside.

A daily walk along the same path filled me with the dread of impending boredom. A change of perspective was required, so I thought that to alleviate the terror of doing the same thing over and over again, I would pay attention to everything around me. I asked myself whether I could learn how to see if and how things changed every day – what would I notice?

It was one of the most amazing years I've had in my life, not just because of our new son, but because the world around me transformed itself into a fascinating space of continuous movement and change – and I could notice. And while writing this I'm finding a rising wave of nostalgia travel through my senses.

We often make assumptions about what we see and don't in the world, like never seeing a flower open its petals (or closing them for rain), but that's just

---

[1] Confucius. 2009. *Shujing: Book of Documents*, Chapter Hong Fan as translated in Rochat de la Vallee . 27

because we don't slow down enough and pay attention to the flow of what is going on.

At the time, I was still too much of a beginner (and with a less experienced teacher) to know that this is the essence of Tai Chi; to learn how to slow down and pay attention, first within yourself, then to others through observation, and then yourself in relation to others, all in relation to your environment too.

In our world today, slowing down to pay careful attention to ourselves, to what's going on around us, and to follow the flow of things is almost anathema. It was a rather disturbing experience, in me and in my coaching research. Yet paradoxically, it took just this to change the quality of my work and for me to realise just how much time and space there is when you do it.

Principally, this noticing I'd done paved the way to noticing the interconnectedness of everything around me as well. As I was investigating the five-phases, I noticed how they couldn't really be separated or individually classified in their function and it gave me the impetus to begin to intuitively observe, touch and feel their related qualities.

I saw how the sun baked the earth and evaporated water. How water wetted the land to nourish the plants and sometimes flooded the ground. I saw how the roots of trees bound the soil to prevent erosion but if they grew too much they starve the earth of new growth. I saw how earth was something that bound these things together and all through the seasons did these relationships shift and change.

Now I noticed how all these patterns were ever present in the world around me as long as I made the effort to reach out and find them.

To illustrate.

Wood, let's say a tree, can only grow and maintain its health on the basis of a healthy relationship with the sun (Fire), water (Water), essential minerals (Metal), and the support and nutrients provided by the ground (Earth).

Suddenly, five-phase theory began to make some sense to me; the lessons were in movement and change, as well as inter-connectedness. And the world began to change for me.

In the next part of this we're going begin exploring how these qualities might play out in the human microcosm.

To be continued....

Referencing

To be fair on you, it wouldn't be right just to expect you to take my word for all this. Nor would it be particularly honest of me not to acknowledge the shoulders I've used as stepping stones. Because it's not really the way of blogging, rather than disturb the flow of my writing, I've decided to simply provide a list of reading[2] that you may or may not want to take a look at. These represent some of the significant texts I've read, but the knowledge I'm describing in my story doesn't come from them, it comes from the lived experience, they've just helped me to form it. With texts of Chinese origin there are often multiple translations, all of which tend to vary, sometimes significantly so. For example, at the last count I think I have six different translations of the Dao De Jing (or Tao Te Ching), and they're all different.

[2] Ti, Huang. 1995. *The Yellow Emperor's Classic of Medicine*. Translated by Maoshing Ni. Boston: Shambhala. Jarrett, Lonny S. 2004. *Nourishing Destiny: The Inner Tradition of Chinese Medicine*. Stockbridge: Spirit Path Press. LaFargue, Michael. 1992. *The Tao of the Tao Te Ching*. Albany: State University of New York Press. Larre, Claude., and Elisabeth Rochat de la Vallee. 1996. T*he Seven Emotions: Psychology and Health in Ancient China*. King's Lynn: Monkey Press. Mou, Bo. 2009. *History of Chinese Philosophy (Routledge History of World Philosophies)*. Edited by Bo Mou. Abingdon: Routledge. Rochat de la Vallee, Elisabeth. 2009. Wu Xing: *The Five Elements in Chinese Classical Texts*. Monkey Press. Sivin, Nathan. 1990. "Science and Medicine in Chinese History." In *Heritage of China: Contemporary Perspectives on Chinese Civilisation*. Edited by Paul S, Ropp. Berkeley: University of California Press. Unschuld, Paul. 1985. *Medicine in China: A History of Ideas*. Berkeley: University of California Press. Zhang, Yanhua. 2007. *Transforming Emotions with Chinese Medicine*. Albany: State University of New York. For the Taiji Classics see http://www.scheele.org/lee/classics.html

PART 1: Leading edge: Influences on Practitioner's Learning and Development

Back to the future: connecting to core underpinning themes of my practice going forwards

Sue Young

1. INTRODUCTION

A s a new year begins I feel I am on an important threshold. A threshold of endings and beginnings.

It feels a good time to take stock.

What is the direction for my practice going forwards?

I'm going to look backwards to identify key patterns and trends that I aim to use to continuously sharpen and focus on my practice.

1.1 THE WIDER EXTERNAL CONTEXT VERSUS THE MORE IMMEDIATE CONTEXTS

It has been a tumultuous year across the globe – climate change related events, political turmoil, a war-torn Middle East, refugee crisis, Brexit, US elections win by Trump. Massive levels of uncertainty create a difficult time for all organisations whether they be public, private or voluntary.

The consequences of these wider events have their impact on what coaching works with in all the different contexts coaching works in:

- One to one with external or internal specialist coach,

- Peer coaching groups, as part of leadership approach, or

- Relationship management in a range of professional contexts e.g. Professional adviser, healthcare worker.

I currently work in a diverse range of contexts with the core theme of enhancing personal leadership capabilities within an organisational context.

1.2 THE IMMEDIATE CONTEXT OF MY EXPERIENCE, AND SHAPE MY PRACTICE HAS FORMED

To do this review I had to first review the story of my career, re-connecting to key events and influences along the way. I then identified what appeared to me to be underpinning themes of my practice that I share here.

Finally, I review what I am taking forward.

2. THE UNDERPINNING THEMES

I have found shape to my practice through reviewing a number of important themes that I draw from in my practice.

I identify the themes as they work for me, giving some examples of how they are important in my work.

The core themes are:

2.1. An avid interest in how different organisations work in different sectors

2.2. Harnessing personal motivation: The Power of high levels of individual attention

2.3. Connecting People and their learning to the business/organisation context and business strategy

2.4. Creating a safe environment for learning

2.5. Working realistically and openly with the dynamics of Power

2.6. Enhanced self-awareness as a pre-requisite to both enhanced leadership skills and effectiveness as a coach

2.7. The real value of collaborative relationships

2.8. Understanding the nature of learning from our experience

2.1. AN AVID INTEREST IN HOW DIFFERENT ORGANISATIONS WORK IN DIFFERENT SECTORS

Profound initial Experience of employment: My first eight years with ICI Paints Division gave me a first-class experience and insight into the realities of how organisations work – or at least a premium blue-chip complex international business with a strong brand value.

Continuing highlights from self-employment: In my early self-employed history, I developed a depth of understanding of the typical patterns in the development of young businesses and typical challenges and crises, as they evolve.

- **Founders/Authority**: The greatest resource in any young enterprise is the commitment and greatest strengths of its founder(s)/owner(s). The nature of these and associated limitations will be the biggest 'shapers' in the development of that business. I took this away as a key area of learning.

- **The first crisis of growth is bringing in additional people**. Can it maintain the strengths of the culture and upgrade its processes and systems to support the business as it grows? Can the founder(s) release sufficient control to enable others to provide their best contribution to the overall?

- **Stages**: Another major area of learning I have absorbed along the way is familiarization with the typically different stages organisations go through and their impact on the kinds of leadership contribution required at different stages.

- **Culture**: Also the particular flavour of this will vary according to the organisation culture and set of values that are an implicit underpinning of day-to-day work. For example, leadership development priorities in the context of a young entrepreneurial SME will be very different to a government department, that will be different to an international hi-tech aerospace business... and so on.

I have found that these core themes carry through to all forms of organisations.

In my time I have worked with a wide range of clients. This diversity of organisational sector experience helps me quickly tune in to the contexts my clients operate in and helps me establish my credibility sooner in the client relationship.

2.2. HARNESSING PERSONAL MOTIVATION: THE POWER OF HIGH LEVELS OF INDIVIDUAL ATTENTION

From early stages in my career I learned the value of having people more personally involved and connected to what I wanted to achieve.

I have always enjoyed working with different people and striking effective working relationships. I learned that if I understood more about their role and context I would be better able to help them help me! Equally important was for them to get a sense that I recognised and valued their unique contribution.

I started working as an associate of a management development consultancy of which I went on to become a director. Quality of individual attention figured highly in our programme design approach. For example, we always had what we called 'telephone one to ones' prior to a management development programme, to find out more about out about participants' development interests and needs.

In hindsight, this was coaching in that it started building rapport and helped people focus on how they could make best use of the programme in relation to their individual development and business priorities.

Although we made use of theories/models, we preferred to use those that managers could readily relate to, with the emphasis being on things they could take away and start working with Monday morning.

I can see clearly now how much a 'coaching approach' i.e. a high quality of attention to individuals, figured in my development work, long before I formally described myself as a coach.

2.3. CONNECTING PEOPLE AND THEIR LEARNING TO THE BUSINESS/ORGANISATIONAL CONTEXT AND BUSINESS STRATEGY

A major learning point for me through my career is that what seems obvious to me is not always so obvious to others!

Connecting people to overall organisational priorities has always come naturally to me. "What real difference is this intervention aimed at? How does it fit in with the overall direction this organisation is aiming to go in?" In all my consulting and development work I seek this connection.

This draws out probably one of the biggest influences on the nature of my practice, my abiding passion and core area of interest. I retain a strong sense of business strategy with the recognition that, unless the people are fully on board with that, the best formed strategies are going to fall down on implementation.

In coaching managers, part of my questioning is often around the bigger context and influences for their particular role. It is the perspectives that this adds to clients' awareness that adds clarity to their thinking about their priorities, particularly for the longer term.

An associated frequent area of focus is the thinking clients give to how they are enabling their team to 'step up' in terms of their bigger organisational awareness, and how this influences their thinking about priorities, individually and collectively.

2.4. CREATING A SAFE ENVIRONMENT FOR LEARNING

Organisations, when under pressure, or with ineffective leadership, can quickly become unsafe places. People can then easily revert to highly political behaviours, keeping their heads down, being competitive or holding back on information that they feel won't go down well with those in authority.

Of course, coaching is the ultimate 'safe space' where individuals can be helped to explore and find their way forward for themselves. Looking back, creating an environment where people feel they can disclose, explore and be supported has figured in my work, long before I called it coaching.

In training work, we created a non-judgmental, open conversational atmosphere, where colleagues from diverse geographic and expertise backgrounds learned a great deal by exchanging different perspectives. We provided pressurised managers with the 'space' to open themselves up to fresh perspectives and experiences. The challenge came from having to work with others on a range of exercises and business simulations, and giving and receiving feedback. Models and frameworks were selectively used to stimulate fresh insights and perspectives in the group.

Creation of a safe environment is particularly critical in team coaching, where there is the perceived risk of personal conflict with resulting damage to day-to-day working relationships. I always aim to build in to the design individual coaching time, preferably prior to any collective team coaching session. This enables individuals to more openly fully express perceptions, thinking and concerns, which I find helps individuals give of their best in the team meeting.

In conversations with both individuals and the team collectively I am aware of the particular role I play in creating a safe 'holding' space where, with light touch commentary, I 'normalise' the tensions I know that some will be holding. I am always amazed at the quality of self-disclosure that can follow, leading to some high-quality discussion that gets to some real priorities the team needs to address if they are going to achieve their objectives.

2.5. WORKING REALISTICALLY AND OPENLY WITH THE DYNAMICS OF POWER

Over all of this is the overlay of where Power lies and how it gets used, both explicitly and implicitly – an important aspect of organisational culture that any intervention needs to work with, and one that organisational leaders have to work with. It is often the Big Unspoken... Defensiveness is the enemy of learning and ultimately organisational learning and change.

A major discovery on my MSc was in the area of group dynamics where definite tensions and anxieties play out for real – specifically, transference and counter-transference in action.

Particularly over the last ten years or so I have worked more directly in my coaching, both with teams and individuals, with issues around conflict and managing tensions in the workplace.

The focus is always on helping the individual get out of their defensive mindset, exploring different perspectives, seeing for themselves more clearly how they might be contributing and explore how they might change their mindset/ behaviour – or expectations of the situation.

The real edge with any people-development intervention is it helps people work more explicitly and openly with those issues that are in the 'too difficult' box to even want to talk about. In organisations, even today, there can be a huge reluctance to challenge upwards.

In team coaching, the ability to have this open conversation with the team leader is critical to achieving a quality of result. On any team development day, the team leader will pay a major role in the tone they set right at the start, as well as with their behaviour throughout the day.

2.6. Enhanced self awareness as a pre-requisite to both enhanced leadership skills and effectiveness as a coach

What makes people successful is not focusing on their weaknesses, but rather making best use of their strengths; learning to mitigate or manage areas of relative weakness. The most talented people in business, and organisations generally, do not agonise about their weaknesses, but rather are fully connected to and make best use of their strengths.

Following my introduction to Myers Briggs, I have retained a strong inclination to want to include some kinds of psychometrics/inventories in my development work and as part of my coaching toolkit.

As part of my early consulting portfolio I did some search and recruitment work and, as part of this, did comprehensive career diagnosis and personality assessment, as part of getting the best 'match'.

Working with different styles in working relationships has figured in my development work right from early days in my work as a coach and developer.

For me, high levels of self-awareness has to be one of the most important attributes of an effective coach. Unless you are aware of your own personal biases and triggers, how can you possibly be of service to the individual client's needs?

The second area of awareness I would say I've really most honed over the past ten years is my ability to notice my clients' subtle behaviours and my responses more explicitly, and be better able to judge my interventions in the moment.

2.7. The real value of collaborative relationships

I have always been inclined to want to part of something bigger, working to a clear purpose in collaboration with others.

After I left ICI I struggled with the openness and lack of structure I had got used to early on in my career experience. I also missed the easy rapport and shared sense of identity with a team of bright and engaged colleagues. Yet it was a time of adventure and learning. My relationship building skills introduced me to all sorts of opportunities.

- My role in the formation and development of a young consultancy business was a particularly rich period of learning around the management of client contracts and co-facilitating with a range of colleagues, all of who had their particular strengths and preferences. The nature of the client work itself was hugely stimulating, including working as a contract management team in a partnering relationship with the client.

- I also had the experience of working as a board team member and the invaluable learning around juggling director level responsibilities and accountabilities, with client delivery and management. A valuable learning point for me was the deep value to be found in having the more personal, direct conversations required to make the step up in achievements.

The value of teams has continued as a strong theme for me. I have worked both as a leader and as a team member of client teams, and have always found it to be a rewarding process. Professionally, I have enjoyed working as a voluntary team member on a number of projects. These always add to my awareness and thinking about what creates the conditions for collaboration – right back to that quality of attention to individuals!

In my coaching developing more effective collaborative relationships is becoming an increasingly popular theme, either as part of team coaching, or with individuals, as a perceived priority in achieving their leadership goals.

2.8. UNDERSTANDING THE NATURE OF LEARNING FROM OUR EXPERIENCES

A turning point for me in my career was being invited to be part of a small team of three consultants to bid for a 'Self Development Management Programme' for the middle managers of one of the 'Big Four' (then Five) consultancies. We won the contract. The contract director had chosen to withdraw summarily after some internal disagreement. So I had stepped in to take over the client liaison and contract management lead on behalf of the consultancy business.

I see now retrospectively this as the real start of my coaching career – where a core aim of the main programme was to enable people to become more self-managing continuous learners.

After about ten years of design and delivery leadership development programmes, I took time to stand back, and do formal study (master's Degree). My dissertation was on the factors that most affect the self-directed learning of managers in a public sector organisation.

- It was at this time that I first came across the theoretical field of Adult Learning – a set of key principles and features that very much inform coaching (see "Adult Learning – the real leading edge of Coaching" by Sue Young). This was a further powerful affirmation of some key principles I intuitively worked to.

- I studied the theories and research around learning, including transformational learning, where people make shifts in their perceptions, sense making and underlying frame of reference.

I see theories as having their place, but only as additional lenses under which to place and critically review our experience. What additional perspectives might this idea bring, and what are the gaps?

I also have had the good fortune to have worked as part of a coach/facilitator team on a Transformational Leadership programme for the past six years where the golden thread of the two-year programme is the development goals individual managers set for themselves at the start of the programme. Individual learning is supported through a range of applied learning processes, and being tasked with an organisational project.

I've come to a place where I see my business as being about helping experienced professionals to stretch their personal frontiers, learning to trust and truly draw on their full experience, as they lead themselves and others forwards into their future.

- Ultimately, what messages am I picking up from my thoughts and feelings, and additionally in conversation with others?
- What and how am I learning?

Ultimately, if my clients go away with an enhanced ability to reflect on their experience and extend and deepen their thinking, then I see my job is done.

3. CONCLUSIONS

I have really valued this opportunity to consider my practice – in the way the good coach invites.

Even though I hold a lot in my head, quite intuitively, I have rarely taken such a chance to stand back, take such an overview, and see it take such clear shape and form.

This helps me considerably in my confidence, as well as renewing my energy to make sure I really do hold to what I believe is important in the way I work going forward.

My attention now feels it will be even more focused on the detail of each moment as I work; as well as enabling a focus on the bigger picture of where I want to take it going forwards.

I am especially aware that each of the themes I have referred to are still open to further work, for them to become something that is more fully understood. There is still plenty more to learn in each of them!

Question: What are the themes that really stimulate and drive you in what you do? And can we find common areas of interest, even though we might talk about them slightly differently?

PART 1: Leading edge: Influences on Practitioner's Learning and Development

Teasing out the deeper understanding of how coaching works at its best - how teasing, itself, can be productive

Jeremy Ridge

*A**ppropriate* **Teasing consistently** comes up, for me, as important for how coaching can really work at its best. However, it rarely seems to be mentioned, and its particular potential explored, among all the other terms widely used across the field. So it is good to explore this feature of practice for how I believe it can contribute so importantly.

I have in mind how a high level of teasing can often be the sign of a really healthy relationship, such as in a group or team process (e.g. peer coaching). I am often surprised by how readily people resort to teasing as an important way of testing how to relieve tensions that may otherwise go underground, and become highly destructive.

In one form or another, teasing between people even takes place on a considerable everyday scale. Much of comedy relies on it; even marketing and advertising draws on it significantly; even everyday family life often engages in it! For example,

- Times for giving people presents – carefully wrapped – introduces a form of teasing.

- Teasing can be a major feature of negotiation. Making an offer attractive, in order to obtain something important in exchange.

- Even coaching makes attractive promises to people. And then there are all the related books, models and techniques, often equally big in their promises. This is also teasing the reader to believe they are reading all they need to know about how it works.

Teasing, for me, is a way of testing for possible expectations someone may have formed, in a delicate and careful way, for how able another person might be to deal with the possible surprise involved. Learning (as one way of considering what coaching aims to achieve) can often involves surprise because it introduces new things that may not have been fully understood before.

The challenge involved in explaining teasing is often the high levels of subtlety involved in the behaviours that can amount to a form of teasing, e.g. the way people may use all manner of facial expressions and movements, rather than just words, to convey such messages.

Of course, it is important to ensure that teasing is appropriately constructive, rather than its other meanings that are often associated with teasing as being more deliberately aimed to frustrate and even bully.

1. SORTING OUT THE EVERYDAY MEANINGS AND USES OF THE TERM TEASING

In starting to consider this meaning involved in teasing, I am immediately drawn to the range of meanings people can bring to it; such as their experiences of teasing being quite negative. So I start with understanding the meaning that appeals to me in the way the word has come into various uses over time.

The origins of the word in a historical sense can be seen, for example, from the old English use of tæsan[1].

- This involves meanings such as to pull about, pluck, tease, in particular, to gently shred or pull apart for microscopic examination.

- This refers most often to physical materials however, such as woollen thread.

For me, the original meaning in the use of the word teasing is important, which is more about doing something very carefully, lest there be a breakdown in something.

It is even possible to find reported cases where teasing is used overtly and deliberately on an organised social basis, and a clear and important feature of the culture. For example,

> "An Inuit principal of learning that follows a similar teasing pattern is known as issumaksaiyuk, meaning to cause thought. Oftentimes, adults pose questions or hypothetical situations to the children (sometimes dangerous) but in a teasing, playful manner, often dramatizing their responses. These questions raise the child's awareness to issues surrounding their community, as well as give them a sense of agency within the community as a member capable of having an effect and

---

[1] *Webster's New World College Dictionary*. 2010. Cleveland, Ohio: Wiley Publishing, Inc. http://www.yourdictionary.com/tease#uJ7MhBsDdedBHRIJ.99 Accessed September 10.

creating change. Once the child begins to answer the questions reasonably, like an adult, the questions would stop[2]."

After all, our social culture is sometimes something we have to learn about whether we like it or not, that is deemed to be in our best interests to conform to. Teasing can be a form of feedback as to when we have got it right, or not, in gradual steps.

2. LOOKING FURTHER AT THE WAYS TEASING WORKS POSITIVELY BETWEEN PEOPLE IN COACHING

Constructive teasing means identifying something that may be important for someone. Finding those ways to carefully enable the other person to progress towards their learning in a manner that is felt as being in their reasonable grasp is important.

To be effective, coaching has to create conditions across an important range of factors, not just through teasing, by itself.

Teasing is one of the later conditions to introduce – see Carkhuff's detailed and comprehensive framework[3] which laid out a careful and thorough process for first creating a sound foundation for dialogue, and the relationship, before working up to the risks involved in more overt teasing or confrontation. It is important to build the level of established trust and proven goodwill between the people concerned that can insure against the risks sometimes involved in teasing.

Teasing can also be a source for light relief – an important break in the otherwise more serious side of any dialogue. For example, by introducing some humour, through some sort of surprise observation outside of the otherwise more serious process.

Laughing with a tease – in other words seeing, accepting and joining in on the humour involved in a tease is often used by people to signal they are ok with being open to exploring the issues that may be involved.

These short teasing interventions are efficient ways to do some quick testing. Yet there are still times when the space may be best created by the coach more directly. For example, when the coachee refers to having a problem, and the coach offers the surprise perspective that this may be more of an opportunity, rather than a problem, and so taking a much more positive view. Similarly, teasing whether to choose to view the glass as being more half full, rather than half empty.

---

[2] Briggs, J. 1998. *Inuit Morality Play: The Emotional Education of a Three-Year-Old.* New Haven, CT: Yale University Press.

[3] See Carkhuff in Ridge, Jeremy. 2016. Getting trust is the essential outcome that makes coaching possible - and different. *the good coach.* https://the-goodcoach.com/tgcblog/2016/10/3/getting-trust-is-the-essential-outcome-that-makes-coaching-possible-and-different Accessed September 10.

3. LOOKING AT EXAMPLES OF THE BEHAVIOURS THAT CAN BE MORE APPROPRIATE APPROACHES TO TEASING

For me, deeper understanding of how coaching works at its best is to be able to work at a detailed level about the behaviours that make a difference.

Again, the subtlety of the actual behaviours involved still often defies simple illustration. For example, the investment in building trust is not a simple process, and cannot be fully mapped out in a few lines of text, such as it always takes place in a few sentences, or through other behaviours exchanged between people.

Hence, the whole process involved in teasing may often involve very gradual approaches, of which I name three, in testing readiness and reaction about this matter that may be important.

3.1. MORE IMMEDIATE EVIDENCE OF A POSITIVE REACTION TO BEING TEASED

The measure of whether teasing is positive is the reaction evidencing a form of genuine attention to what is raised in a manner that leads to mutual satisfaction.

For example: The coach introduces a perspective that may highlight some challenges to the coachee. Ideally the responses by the coachee looked for are, for example:

> *"I haven't really thought this through, have I…"*

> *"I haven't really tested whether some of these issues are what I have assumed them to be…"*

> *"I am still trying to work out how to test and do something different in these circumstances I have put on the table …."*

3.2. ENCOURAGING THE COACHEE TO TEASE THE IDEA FORWARD BY THEMSELVES

At this level of quality of response, it is possible for the coach to let the coachee tease out their awareness by themselves. It may also become a simple matter of having a factual conversation where the coach can offer his/her perspectives on what might be considered, such as straight forward matter of fact responses…

> *"That's great - keep going…"*

> *"Can we look in more detail at some of the examples of this happening…"*

> *"Can you tell me some more about (something) you just mentioned - what was involved in more detail…"*

3.3. TEASING BASED ON VERY CAREFUL AND SMALL BEHAVIOURS THAT TESTS FOR POSSIBLE REACTIONS

One real feature of teasing is the subtlety that may be important in choosing a behaviour that introduces something of possible surprise.

For example, the hints in nonverbal expressions often used provides the other with options that they may want to raise or ignore... to tease whether the other person is open to being offered a different view:

1. **The hint of a nod!** Someone says something and the reaction may be to nod – but not rise fully to its implications ... or a hesitation – and this will be noticed as something that is part of an overall reaction.

2. **The hint of a smile!** Someone then says something and there is a hint of a smile in the response to it.

3. **The hint of a frown!** Someone then says something and there is this time more of a facial expression – such as a frown, and or a pursing of the lips, a shift in body posture showing some tension.

4. **The suggestion of an offer that may be different in approach**: Someone says something and there is a verbal response which says something like – there may be a different interpretation of what you are describing in order to test interest.

These may be the teasing behaviours that are the precursors to next taking a more direct approach, such as, "You may need to re-think your view about this in order to fully understand and check you have understood why things happened the way they did."

As well as the examples of how teasing behaviour can operate between just two people, there is often greater evidence of teasing being evident, and importantly, when a number of people are involved, such as in teamwork.

4. THE IMPORTANCE OF TEASING IN TEAMWORK AND TEAM COACHING – REMEMBERING THE ESSENTIAL

Remembering the essential basis of teamwork: A team is typically a task where each person involved brings capabilities that are both different and important to what is needed for the overall task to be completed. Teamwork is thus at its best when it starts to enable others to bring the best out of each other. However maintaining an appropriate balance in how each person makes their contribution can be a challenge, and is often a source of tensions that need addressing constructively.

High levels of effective teasing between people in the team are, for me, one of the clearest signs of the highest standard of process in such a collaborative context, as a team. This is when there is an established, accepted, culture (patterns of behaviours) in the group/community that clearly gives permission to this careful testing, and teasing, type of behaviour in the group.

The important role for team coaching is often in taking the lead by introducing these sort of teasing behaviours. High-functioning teams will often quickly take this initiative up themselves. I am often impressed by the naturally learned high skills many have in doing this.

At its best, in these circumstances, everyone realises that challenges can be surprises for some involved, so there is a collective effort to jointly explore and find the right ways to introduce these challenges in a supportive and constructive way. The people who are the focus for these challenges encourage this exploration by openly disclosing their own surprises, thus enabling more matter of fact exploration of the evidence around it.

For example, one person in the team may be seen as behaving in a dogmatic manner because they believe they have special knowledge, or information, relevant to the task – and others may just not see this – and cannot yet understand why the dogmatic person is appearing increasingly dogmatic in their behaviour.

Even at the very start of interaction in a team – seen at its clearest among a team of strangers – is often the sort of start which involves some sort of 'checking in' process that can take place– albeit apparently innocent commentary about something unrelated to the task. Usually there is some banter – attempts at a few comments designed to test the laugh/smile index among those involved.

The team coaching task is then to encourage the sense and importance of this 'non-direct task behaviour' – because for some it can appear off subject and a waste of time.

5. CONCLUSIONS

- **The importance of Teasing in coaching**: Teasing is typically an important indicator, and way to test, and develop readiness in coaching – where readiness is that important ability to process experience, and learning, willingly and effectively. Without readiness, coaching has serious difficulty in working effectively.

- **Teasing as 'easing'**: Progress in a dialogue is about engaging in a manner that others are comfortable with. The comfort may come, first, from positive investment already established, (trust) allowing then more tolerance of risky comments. Otherwise, comments and behaviours that might surprise and disappoint have to be done even much more carefully.

- **The skills of teasing**: Teasing is often very similar to a process of research, carefully testing in small steps to discover what begins to get a positive response. It is about finding the most careful way of testing whether a direction is appropriate. Teasing is a recognition of the importance of small steps in behaviour that can have important impacts. Some themes need to be assessed carefully before going further.

- **Teasing does not have to be always negative**: The importance of leading with teasing along positive themes becomes really important before raising more important but challenging initiatives.

- **It is not simple** to establish simple principles. Interaction between people takes place on such a scale of complexity, along with the risks of how something might be perceived rather than intended, that there can be real risk of negative reactions.

Coaching will always depend on getting some very small behaviours right and then continuing to get them right in lots of small steps. I find that looking through this teasing lens is a useful perspective in continuing to learn about, and share, more of the small things that can really make the important difference.

Question: How aware are you of the subtle sorts of behaviours that you may use in constructive teasing?

PART 2

Cutting Edge: Investigating Patterns from Practitioner Experiences

Coaching Conversations

Isobel Gray

I come alive as Me
in a coaching conversation
As I don't feel I do in other conversations.
Once we have checked in and tested,
building connections between
my and your reality,
We can get down to the business
of creation
Of space, inquiry and fresh perspectives.

Questioning, observing and listening,
Testing, stimulation, probing and sharing feelings;
the quality of silences that support deeper reflection
and fresh insights about ourselves and Life
in all its complexity and richness, for both;
Yet cut to some incisive felt Truth
That would be otherwise lost
in the mists and chaotic currents
of daily organisational life.

Ambitions, plans, opportunities, blockages
Excitements, triumphs, frustrations,
Disappointment, fears,
Impatience, avoidance, trepidation, tension,
Energy ebbs and flows.

Feelings as data about what is really going on
for You,
yet have been pushing away as uncomfortable.
Drawing these out as the richest source of
Intuitive insights and internally held wisdom;
clues to the way through
the morass of 'stuff'.

Seeing clearly the false trails that have been
diverting you from the true way forward
through the tangled undergrowth
to find clear air and space
on the other side.

A unique continuous journey
every time...
All Human Life is here!

CHAPTER 4

LEADERSHIP

Getting trust is the essential outcome that makes coaching possible - and different, why does trust matter?

Jeremy Ridge

I **want to explore** how trust is especially relevant to coaching. How trust makes possible coaching in the first place, and also how coaching is different from many traditional ways of thinking.

It seems to me that trust is what makes living possible – in every sense. We don't set foot outside unless we trust that the path we tread on is not some holographic image hiding a bottomless crevasse. So it is with all of living.

In my coaching practice trust is **the most important result, or outcome, to establish first**, because coaching involves important uncertainties for the Coachee. For example, Coaching is about:

- Enabling someone to find the confidence, and curiosity, to take on further learning – to open up.
- Speaking to opportunities people have, rather than problems.
- Enabling someone to take risks – disclosing to themselves, let alone another person, matters that they have not found the right space to consider elsewhere.

Coaching is also starting to challenge many fundamental structures we have in society. Quite rightly we aim to form structures that recognise and give authority to people who have the best information and ability to make sense of situations and context to know what is best to do.

In Coaching, the customer is king. This is because they have the best knowledge about what matters to them. We are not dealing with remedial issues, e.g. where someone has patterns of behaviour categorised by society as dysfunctional.

There are many treatments that are appropriate for these other, still important, and even urgent, matters.

Coaching is different.

We are approaching people as functional, i.e. able to live normally, and successfully, already, and who are interested in becoming more functional in what they already successfully achieve in life and/or work.

The work of coaching starts with having to build trust. The Coachee must believe that the coach has something to bring to the Coachee's world. The only authority to decide this is the Coachee alone.

This raises some important questions about the sort of process which is appropriate to this. It seems to me there is something in the idea of trust that is central to this process.

EXPLORING WHAT TRUST MEANS

Simple definition of trust: The word is reported as first deriving from old Norse and used in the sense of being strong. Today, a more common definition is simply – **Firm belief in the reliability, truth, or ability of someone or something**[1].

Moving on to more studied definitions: Psychoanalyst Erik Erikson suggested that the development of basic trust is **the first state of psychosocial development** occurring, or failing, during the first two years of life. It is an essential foundation for life. However, Erikson also stressed his work was a tool to think with rather than a factual analysis. Its purpose then is to provide a framework within which development can be considered further, rather than accurate and complete understanding[2].

Psychology sets out to achieve this rigour of complete understanding. However, there is the inclination to see trust as more of the nature of an emotion – not necessarily a rational process. It is a state of perception – expectation – which can bring positive feelings. How it is achieved and why it is sought is still difficult to study/research.

> *"Trust, or lack of it, isn't produced by rational thought process but is processed according to a mental script we may not even know we follow. That is unless we have been in therapy or have come to an understanding of how our childhood experiences have affected us. Even so, we may still not recognize the patterns[3]."*

[1] English Oxford Living Dictionary. 2017. https://en.oxforddictionaries.com/definition/trust Accessed September 10.

[2] McLeod, Saul. 2008 (Updated 2017). "Erik Erikson." In *Simply Psychology*. https://www.simplypsychology.org/Erik-Erikson.html Accessed September 10.

[3] Streep, Peg. 2014. "The Trouble With Trust." In *Psychology Today*. https://www.psychologytoday.com/blog/tech-support/201403/the-trouble-trust Accessed September 10.

This suggests that trust is still somewhat difficult to measure by traditional methods – such as those used by formal Psychology. However, the need and demand for understanding people has seen much work elsewhere. These attempts can also inform us about understanding trust.

OTHER APPROACHES THAT MIGHT INFORM HOW TO GIVE ATTENTION TO WHAT IS INVOLVED IN CREATING TRUST APPROPRIATE TO COACHING

There are many, many, different schools, or approaches, to understanding people in the broader context of their lives.

A useful overview and short summary of how this idea of functional attention to another person has developed, particularly in counselling, which has some important similarities to coaching, is offered as:

- Psychodynamic, refers to the invisible and changeable nature of living. Sometimes we make choices (of feelings); sometimes feelings escalate to become emotions and are dominant, described as:

" ... unconscious (hidden/not admitted or disclosed) – where (early) hidden trauma can lurk throughout life. And hence reference to these hidden drivers of behaviour, such as id ego and superego. As with most things it is easier/more urgent to start with – crisis[4]."

- Humanistic starts from the uniqueness of a person's entity due to their unique perception and experience; whilst also taking a positive view - starting with the opportunity compared with other concerns of starting with the problem.

"Humanistic starts from looking for opportunities rather than the problems a person faces. [Hence coaching's big difference]. Humanistic starts with the search for the interest and capability to learn – when the circumstances fit the equation[5]."

- Behavioural is born out of what (little) can be subjected to schematic research and evidence. This results nevertheless in some important expert lead approaches to important issues.

"Diagnostic frameworks (according to the best known to date) lead to a directive approach – where the expert knows best what is missing or present in achieving (current views about what is) normal standards of behaviour and directs attention from this external framework – ignoring internal frameworks on the assumption that people have very limited internal learning awareness and need direction[6]."

---

[4] Skills You Need. "Approaches to Counselling." SkillsYouNeed.
https://www.skillsyouneed.com/learn/counselling-approaches.html Accessed September 10.
[5] See [4]
[6] See [4]

PART 2: Cutting edge: Investigating patterns from Practitioner Experiences

Each of these perspectives are often seen as three different 'schools' – or separate lenses – by which to help people.

Psychoanalytic and Behavioural schools often create more of a framework of conventional authority for the practitioner to work to. They are also more involved where there is a form of accepted dysfunction. This is because the considered dysfunction enables more authoritative control and direction of the interpersonal process to be exercised.

There may be real value in trusting an external authority. For much of medicine, we have such trust. However, there are also limitations to how all-knowing medicine can be. As well as a need for strict rules – that can be trusted – about straying from what is known. Some approaches may make the issue of trusting the experience another person, as an expert, wants to bring to be quite different from the traditional models of how expertise is based. How to deal with a patient who is the best expert in themselves is such a challenge.

Coaching deals with people who exercise choice about what serves their needs. The contracting process becomes quite different, as the expertise needed can be quite different, which is where establishing trust becomes essential.

TOWARDS A FRAMEWORK THAT INTEGRATES

The framework that has most informed me about how I understand the importance of developing trust, in practice, is best summarised by R Carkhuff[7]. Carkhuff's framework, summarised below, was a work aiming to bring together the various approaches, mentioned earlier, into a more integrative approach. This can also inform the issue of creating trust more appropriate to the circumstances of Coaching.

The framework is still lacking reference to explicit behaviour, which still defies our comprehensive understanding. It is laid out as a progressive pattern, albeit a simplification of principles, that can be different in detail of events, but which still pattern the process overall.

KEY PRINCIPLE

The most important part of the framework is the focus on working from the behaviour of the other person – i.e. not the coach.

- Carkhuff's work uses the term Self-Exploration which is defined as the extent of willingness by the Coachee to engage in sharing personally relevant awareness in the context of the relationship.

---

[7] Carkhuff, Robert. 1969. *Helping and Human Relations* (Vol 1 and 2). New York, NY: Holt, Rhinehart and Winston.

- In effect this is an identification of the process of trust developing. The person concerned builds their confidence in the space and conditions being created for them.

KEY BEHAVIOURS, BY THE COACH, THAT HAVE THE MOST INFLUENCE ON THIS TRUST FACTOR

It's also about the effect of coach behaviours, not the intention. **Observed effects – the verbal and behavioural expressions, by the coach**:

- **Empathy**: Attend to and add to the verbal expressions of the other; as evidenced by the reaction that accepts and builds further their appreciation of where they are.

- **Respect**: Effective at getting across valuing, caring and interest in the other person.

- **Genuineness**: Effective at getting across being fully themselves, with consistency and spontaneity (not rehearsed).

- **Self-disclosure**: Effective at getting across similar levels of intimate sharing appropriate to the increasing levels of disclosure by the other person – compared with the politeness of casual exchanges.

- **Specificity**: Effective at getting across the value of the other person by increasingly identifying what matters in practical terms.

- **Confrontation**: Effective at getting the other person to want to engage effectively with possible discrepancies that arise in the picture presented by the other person.

- **Immediacy**: Effective at getting attention and focus to the immediate and or wider picture of interaction between both parties.

THE NEED TO MATCH THE BEHAVIOURS PROVIDED BY SELF-EXPLORATION

The important skill here is for the Coach to choose behaviours that respond to and match the level of self-exploration offered.

The order of these behaviours normally goes through stages where important psychological contracting/trust building behaviours (facilitative) come before more direct problem solving/learning type behaviours (action oriented).

Empathy, respect and genuineness are considered key facilitative behaviours. These three facilitative behaviours are central to the stage of building trust between the Coach and Coachee.

In my terms, I often practice this as a form of sincere interest and listening – repeatedly – to what the other person is saying. Once I show I understand and accept what is often their initial testing of me, in the initial stages, the Coachee then moves on to deeper levels of self-exploration and expression that starts a more explicit exploration of the agenda that interests them.

I am often surprised by the way the agenda opens up more and more according to the trust that I can establish through these behaviours.

COMPARING AN INTEGRATED FRAMEWORK WITH THESE THREE CONTRASTING APPROACHES

Much of Psychodynamics, and the behavioural approach, rely a lot on the direction of creating the conditions for action. For experts working in these professions, the equivalent of facilitative is the 'diagnosis'. The process then moves into prescribing an expert with derived solutions as the next 'action phase'.

I can certainly appreciate the challenge of dealing with the invisible drivers that the psychodynamic approach attempts to work with. However, there is still too much emphasis on 'negative' drivers in much of the approach.

Elements of the Psychoanalytical approach, such as appreciating drivers that are less visible, and the Behavioural approach, and focusing on real change in behaviour as an outcome are also relevant to Coaching.

Rather than just creating trust, practical outcomes are also essential. However, trust is an essential part of generating concentration and orientation by the Coachee, both being essential to the more action-oriented or problem-solving approach.

Some demonstrable, and effective learning must result – either in the form of sudden insight, or in the form of an action plan for continuing to progressively learn.

The learning involved is often measured by needing to be a visible outcome to others.

However, unless trust is established first, it is unlikely the dialogue will progress to this learning by just carrying out a simple problem-solving conversation.

The trust building process is the feature that I consider the humanistic school emphasis. This emphasis, however, can result in this approach being seen as less concerned with a focus on that end result.

HOW DOES THIS WORK FOR ME IN PRACTICE?

I have found the use of more facilitative behaviours central to the trust building process, important in practice to a wide range of opportunities.

THE CONTEXT OF ORGANISATIONS

In practice, I have found the most important, and valued, opportunities for bringing forward these important conditions for creating trust are best evident in organisations.

Organisations are a classic form of collaborative enterprise. However, the way collaboration is organised does sometimes result in a simplification of the challenges involved.

Providing the standard of facilitative conditions necessary to establish connections that people trust can still be a challenge for those involved. Simpler methods of direction are preferred – even with the risks, and costs, they can bring.

Increasingly, the greatest challenge for leaders, and leadership, is getting people to make a free choice to follow them, rather than rely on knowing the answer the leader wants and exercising various threats to enforce obedience.

Likewise, many other classic methods of bringing learning into organisational behaviour can benefit from a facilitative approach, and can benefit further when combined with the action oriented approach.

A COACHING APPROACH TO TRAINING

Ramamurthy Krishna's blog[8] on *the good coach*, titled "When Training Is Better Done Using A Coaching Approach" explores a theme that I find myself using in practice.

The learning that training is after often requires enabling each person to find their own path to the learning involved. 'One path fits all' is not necessarily the best approach to learning.

TEAM COACHING

Team Coaching is an important example of how the use of a coaching approach can achieve significant results.

This can also result in the extension of the facilitative/coaching approach to what is in effect a form of mediation.

A coaching approach, with a group or team can enable the individuals involved to better understand themselves, and how they may be perceived by others. This can then significantly raise the level of live feedback from all involved. Similar perspectives from different people can then be important validation of feedback; and a practical opportunity to practice adjustment.

PEER GROUP FACILITATION

A growing form of team coaching where the typical structure of authority (as present with teams in organisations) is deliberately neutralised.

---

[8] Krishna, Ramamurthy. 2016. When Training Is Better Done Using a Coaching Approach. *the good coach*. http://the-goodcoach.com/tgcblog/2016/7/19/when-training-is-better-done-using-a-coaching-approach-a-practical-example-of-how-to-use-a-coaching-approach-when-people-still-call-it-training-by-r-ramamurthy-krishna-guest Accessed September 10.

PART 2: Cutting edge: Investigating patterns from Practitioner Experiences

THE 360 APPROACH

At the individual level, use of a 360 approach can also bring important clarity through the use of a more coaching approach – e.g. using a more qualitative approach to generating and interpreting data than a statistical model. Facilitating the expression and interpretation of feedback is important.

THE DEVELOPMENT CENTRE RATHER THAN THE ASSESSMENT CENTRE APPROACH

The same is true of how a development centre for individuals can be powerful when using this approach and the data that is then made available for their personal use. Those involved may then disclose the data to the organisation with more assurance than just the external objectivity of the assessment centre.

INTERNAL COACHING

The growth – albeit cautiously – of Internal Coaching is another example of how a coaching/facilitative/trust building approach can bring significant benefits. The voluntary nature of much Internal Coaching demonstrates an important resource in how people want to contribute in ways that are typically still outside the narrow job description.

CONCLUSIONS AND NEXT STEPS

1. **Trust is an important lens for appreciating how Coaching really can work**: Exploring, and expressing, the way that trust is an important lens for understanding Coaching – through the facilitative approach – has been very helpful, for myself.

   It is important to build awareness of the factors that the ambitions for coaching, held by many people, are more soundly based.

2. **It is important to appreciate what is involved in getting trust to work**: As with many things, what can be complex can be seen as taking too much time and trouble, for some, especially when there are pressures on observable results. Likewise, when you have the skill to do something right, it can take no time at all by comparison.

3. **The evidence I can also observe in fellow practitioners is powerful**: I am always impressed by the levels of – albeit – still intuitive skills that many highly successful fellow practitioners bring to their use of these facilitative, and trust building, practices and skills. The real results that are then achieved when the 'trust contract' is well established are also really appreciated by those involved.

4. **More detailed learning about what is involved in building how trust can add value is still needed**: There is also obviously a lot more to be done to

identify the sorts of behaviours that operate across the dynamic of any dialogue; for example, non-verbal signals are often much more potent and meaningful than verbal signals. Much communication is also often in the form of 'code' more than explicit.

5. **Towards a more integrative approach that appreciates the place of and the importance of building trust**: There is much of value in each and all of the various schools or systems of thought, about what might be involved in Coaching. However, it is important to work more towards the appreciation of how this all works within a bigger, more integrative picture, rather than to promote one particular school as the answer.

My question to you:

- Do you take notice of how trust is developing in dialogue you are having?
- How would you describe what factors you are using to track it?

Having coaching conversations in organisations: focusing on the individual to move beyond stereotypes

Simon Dennis

It's very easy to stereotype and generalize. This becomes more noticeable when you're working in a multicultural, multi-country organisation because you're dealing with people in lots of different countries. Without thinking through what it is you want to actually say, it can be very easy to blurt out, *"Oh, you're Belgian, therefore,"* *"Oh, you're German therefore,"* *"You're American, therefore."*

I attended a recent cross-cultural coach training program in Northern Europe. What fundamentally underpinned the whole programme was to question the relevance of stereotypes when you're dealing with an individual who's there in the room to have a conversation with you.

One of the exercises we carried out early on was to ask all the participants to think through the considerations with cross-cultural coaching. We wrote down all the things you have to think about e.g. technology, speaking slowly, avoiding acronyms etc. And then, a kind of light bulb came on, *"Actually, we don't. What we have to think about is the person in the room."* If the person in the room speaks fluent English and doesn't mind us speaking quickly, and can — what is it you're implying when you speak slowly?

By speaking slowly aren't you just assuming they don't understand you if you speak fast? **More importantly it's about speaking at the pace they can understand.**

And then came, *"How are we going to take this further?"*

It was one line, *"Treat them like an individual."*

The answer was as simple as that. It was literally, 'When you're in the room with them, virtually or physically, just talk to them and listen to them and treat them like an individual, because they might not be anything like anyone else. They won't be like any other person you've ever met.'

EXPLORING FURTHER MY APPROACH TO COACHING IN A CROSS-CULTURAL ENVIRONMENT

I think as coaches, we're lucky.

I think we are lucky in a cross-cultural environment because our natural instinct is to assume less and jump to fewer conclusions (rather than starting at a solution). I'm not going to jump to conclusions about why they're wearing what they are or jump to conclusions about the way they're responding to me, or not. What I am going to do is to ask whether they are struggling to understand what I've said. Are they struggling to pick up the nuances in the question? And asking questions, and in particular direct questions in a non-assuming way, is something that a coach can bring to the situation.

Are you struggling to understand or is there something more to this? It's this idea that as a coach, you've got the freedom and the permission to ask direct questions. For example, when someone appears to be upset by a particular situation or question, it's normal to give them the appropriate space. A coach could also ask if it's something else (and I urge all the coaches to ask the question), "*I noticed that when I asked you that question, you responded in this way. Why was that?*"

Whereas many managers tend to say, "*I noticed that when I said that, you shied away from me. And actually, I know that's typical of where you are from, but I need you to engage.*" That's a huge assumption that the response was simply down to a stereotype. Whereas a coach could just ask the question, "*Why did you respond in that way?*"

Being able to ask that question, and hear their response, is a great transformational piece for cross-cultural organisations. Understanding the difference between making a judgement and stating a fact as part of their training engages their curiosity to ask why. That someone doesn't speak up in a meeting, is just a fact. The judgment is when you think that they're not confident, just because it's assumed that keeping quiet in meetings implies a lack of confidence.

BRINGING 'COACHING CONVERSATIONS' INTO ORGANISATIONS

Sometimes it's necessary to be cautious openly talking about 'coaching' even though it happens all the time all over the organisation. For example, someone might pop over to my desk and start talking about some issues they've got or some challenge. And depending on the topic of conversation, I might say, "*Let's go have a quiet coffee somewhere"* or we might just chat at my desk. I've always got my coaching head ready to engage, and I think that helps because people know that.

What I am conscious of, and there are many others who practice what I do, is that I don't label examples I have shared as coaching either. And then when it comes to our Supervision Group and we're asked, *"So how much coaching have you been doing?"* The response is typically, *"Well, in the formal sense, I've only done maybe 2 or 3 hours since the last time we met. But actually, I'm having maybe five or ten conversations a day, maybe twenty-five a week, which are 'coaching' conversations."* And so we train our managers in having coaching conversations, in having an inquisitive mind.

This also forms part of a tiered view of coaching:

- It starts with coaching conversations (with some very good basic training around coaching and mentoring for all managers),

- Followed by talking to them about what they know about contracting,

- Before moving into the more structured form of coaching.

Thinking back to Ken Blanchard's Situational Leadership, I agree that there are times and places when you have to be directive. You can't do anything but. If someone's put themselves in danger you need to tell them to stop. It's not difficult. It's knowing when to be directive, too. The manager needs to work out the whole platter of stopping points between being directive to asking them one or two pertinent questions that enable them to go away and work on the answer for themselves. It's really managers who are having a range of coaching conversations that are showing an aptitude for extending the world of coaching.

The challenge that then materializes is that we get a lot of managers wanting to switch roles and say, "I'm a coach". Whilst the field works through professionalizing what coaching is it's useful to use the current lens to explore some of the current perceived challenges.

Following 'Coaching Conversations' training is just the beginning towards becoming an 'accredited coach'. There's much more to it, a wealth of training and experiences, especially around some of the basics like boundary setting and contracting. For example, someone may approach you for some advice. You didn't actually give them advice, what you did was to help them explore options for themselves and come up with a resolution.

My response would be that the contract was kind of implicit in the question. However, if they wanted to continue that relationship with that individual, then it's being more explicit and direct to say, "We want to then coach on a formal basis, we would then expect you to contract with them about outcomes and boundaries and all those things."

REFLECTING ON HOW HAVING A MINDSET TO SIMPLY HAVE COACHING CONVERSATIONS CAN BREAK THROUGH STEREOTYPES

There is a whole school of thought around cultural stereotypes, company stereotypes, corporate stereotypes, corporate cultures (Steve Glowinkowski talks a lot about what constitutes corporate culture – and how it can be changed). There is a known bias that senior leaders tend to recruit people who are like themselves subconsciously. Some experts recommend, for a fully functioning organisation to exist and thrive, they require a bit of everything, so recommend using a simple psych assessment like Myers Briggs to test this. From my perspective and experience this isn't necessarily true. What you need to do is treat everyone as individuals and work out what everyone is going to do. Through co-operation you do create culture.

For example, there are companies now like the BBC who recruit, first of all, based on you as a person, your 'fit', not on your skills. When they moved to Salford in the Northwest, their entire online portal was encouraging anyone from the Northwest to apply because they wanted local people. They said, "Go online. Do the tests." All the tests were value-based asking simple things like, what would you do in this situation, if someone comes and tells you that one of their colleagues has been taking drugs in the toilet? How are you going to deal with that situation?

It was testing your approach to value.

At the end of it and depending how you answered they let you know whether you're a good fit, or not, for the BBC. If you are, then you accessed another portal which showed you which roles were currently available where there was a further screening process. Their overall argument is, 'It's much easier to train people in skills because you can retrain as an accountant or a financial controller. But if you haven't got the right set of values, you're going to disrupt their company ethos.'

As I mentioned earlier, having all managers have a coaching conversation mindset as part of the multitude of conversations they have every day is one of the ways we're going to break down stereotypes and they will have an aptitude for extending the world of coaching.

Questions for you:

- How do you have 'coaching conversations' in your organisation?
- Where has it worked best?
- What are some of the contexts where coaching conversations can be a limitation?

PART 2: Cutting edge: Investigating patterns from Practitioner Experiences

Aligning personal values with my coaching approach to deliver impact and value to family managed organizations

Aubrey Rebello

Providing **executive coaching** to any organization requires a sound coaching approach, practice, and an alignment between my personal values (that drive me professionally) and the organization I'm contracted to work with.

For example, if you are not in sync with a family organization's values and the way they want to conduct business then you should decline the offer of work. You could not, for instance offer coaching, or counseling (thinking of an American TV series, the Sopranos) to a mafia family.

STARTING WITH MY VALUES

Values, for me, is everything that should be done ethically.

That is one simple way of putting it: *It should be done in a way that all stakeholders have a share in the benefits: the customers, owners, employees, and business partners.*

1. It is important to have those initial conversations and do your own due diligence before accepting the assignment.

2. It is necessary to check out and confirm whether there is sufficient overlapping values (personally, professionally, family, business) from which a potentially positive relationship will emerge that will result in positive returns for the organization.

VALUES STILL INTACT AND HEALTHY, CONTRACTING FOR COACHING

With the psychological contract in place, it becomes more of the approach to contracting that lays out the process and intention of how the coaching engagement will evolve.

My method to coaching is to let the clients decide (with some help from me) where they want to improve. I ask them to analyze their work life and their personal life, and then decide on three major goals. The goals set are always measurable, stretched, and time bound.

My coaching sessions are normally once a fortnight which translate to approximately twelve sessions over 6 to 8 months to fit in with my clients' busy schedule, especially when travelling is an important part of their role.

Let me share a couple of examples from family managed organizations:

One of my client's, a President of a large company, wanted to reduce his high stress. After discussion, the stretched goal he set for himself was 'Sound sleep seven nights out of seven in the week and blood pressure down to normal'. The goal was achieved, and the change in his work style and personal space was dramatic. The improved business results and family happiness was the icing on the cake.

Another client I was working with was the MD of a large company. He was a visionary. He had built the company from scratch. However, as the business grew, he still remained the focal point for all decisions and the way forward. He was now keen to change this and do it with speed, so as to build a good team and ensure succession.

How does Caesar bequeath his powers?

Easier said than done!

Following our first coaching session, we felt that the best way to do this was to catch the bull by the horns.

We discussed a possible method of engagement. This involved some form of disclosure and in this case it was to share with his team his own weakness.

> *"I don't delegate enough, or I tell you I want a solution and then tell you the solution itself – what I'm actually asking you to do is accept my solutions before you come up with a solution to the problem."*

He called his team for a meeting (which I shadowed). He explained his goal: **'Building a competent team who would be empowered to take most decisions without him'.** He then made disclosures of his perceived weak areas and then asked each of his team members to meet him individually the next day to, *"Tell me two additional things that I need to do differently so that I reach my goal."*

PART 2: Cutting edge: Investigating patterns from Practitioner Experiences

He told them not to be generous because he would know when they were simply humoring him.

The MD opened up and shared his weaknesses. That empowered the team members to give their feedback to 'Caesar' without fear or misgiving.

Such openness from a visionary leader like him had a great emotional impact on the team.

In our subsequent sessions, we discussed the feedback. The client identified three behaviors he needed to change following his turn around with his team. Within six months good leaders emerged, the empowerment and delegation was a success. The 'senators' then started looking into their own shortcomings and began to make changes to be in line with what 'Caesar' had done. This led to a cascading improvement across the 'Empire' (the company).

MANAGING BOUNDARIES WITH PATIENCE

Rivalry, often seen in 'non-owner businesses', can also emerge in family businesses. This ante is raised further because the work and family relationships are intertwined.

The coach can play the role of an independent sounding board, someone whom they can also run some of their internal issues by. The coach becomes that person who will maintain each person's confidence and who will sometimes advise them, who will listen impartially to all members, and then facilitate those discussions and even advise them on how they could proceed.

I reiterate the importance of patience, once one is a sounding board, simply because being patient as the matters unfold is important in convincing the person of the actual situation when they are less emotional. Having the ability to tactfully diffuse the situation is something a family business will appreciate with time. While doing all this you must ensure that bonding and trust is not affected.

Another challenge can fall around 'whose decision will be final', especially when there is a dispute. Then one has to set ground rules for decision making and, where there are differences, whose view will be paramount. It could go by age or it could go by competence. Whatever is acceptable as long as it has been laid out in the beginning; differences can and will appear, but there has to be an acceptable rule for resolution.

Ultimately, families are interested in the overall embedded value that's there in a business, and families understand this value increases when differences reduce and people pull in the same direction.

MY REFLECTIONS

Knowing your own values influences how you behave with your client. That also has influence in the way your clients choose to act on those suggestions/ conversations within their own organization. Managing those boundaries are paramount.

For me, the three things that are required are honesty, building trust, and your own business acumen because if you don't have that then again that's a big issue. Suppose you're only a good listener, you're tactful but you don't have business acumen. Then they don't see any value addition. You would also have difficulty in making business related judgements.

Furthermore, this will all drive the type and quality of relationship you'll have with your client and the stakeholders. Making changes in Caesar's Empire requires humility and openness from Caesar, which something a coach can induce. The opportunities for coaching can be limitless.

Leaders: Coaching the perils of success

Laurent Terseur

A **recurring theme** I have been noticing in my private conversations with leaders over the past few years, is that even those with a great track record and significant success in overcoming perfect storms can experience moments when they look differently at the climate around them as it changes in unexpected ways. In these moments, they can happen to feel for the first time that a shadow is cast on their own ability to operate and lead.

Despite having successfully weathered so many storms, it is no longer obvious to them whether the sun will or will not shine again this time. As fatigue builds-up, what they would normally have seen as a usual test looks like one of a different kind, possibly a bridge too far.

A pattern I observe in these moments, is that the scope of perceived available options reduces as the pain and exhaustion increases, easily narrowing down to a binary and sometimes draining, "Should I stay or should I go?" type dilemma.

Yet, while this surfacing dilemma might look rightly formulated and valid for consideration, I take away from many examples that it can be easy to miss out on more available options or to make an insufficiently informed decision, both to the detriment of the individual's well-being.

I would like to share here some insights from examples of executives who decided to pause and recreate space to think differently when they were feeling trapped in the storm, and how that helped them to get the clouds to tear so that they could see how and where the sun would shine for them again.

1. THE 'NEW BOSS' CHANGE IN THE CLIMATE

I remember an executive who was considering leaving their company after having lost all their drive due to the lack of communication with their new boss.

The first investment they made was to make the time for reflective conversations. Being encouraged to identify their emotions, they could acknowledge they had gradually grown a form of obsession. They better understood what was getting them stuck on "freeze" mode. They then allowed a defined place for these emotions and removed the obsession standing in their way, freeing up a brand-new thinking space in which to review their situation.

A major shift happened.

They realised they were still in charge until proven otherwise. By letting go of the idea of improving their boss, they could focus on doing their job and allow themselves to take initiatives again. Very quickly they were back operating at their best again. It was just as if by looking at the whole wider sky, the dark clouds had just evaporated.

Achieving clarity doesn't always make the clouds vanish though. Instead, clarity can establish the need for substantial decisions.

In another situation I have in mind, an executive was getting increasingly exhausted as they were battling ever stormier elements. By making the time for reflective conversations, they could assess the situation. Being encouraged to take a step back and look at the whole journey, they found out that their phenomenal perseverance and stamina had fuelled their tenacity and resilience so far, but had also blindfolded them. They were not agreeing with the new directions, their sponsors and allies were gone, and they were keeping the behaviours of the new command chain in low esteem. The plan so far had been to stay on the boat and sail those hostile waters until more favourable ones would eventually come back.

What casting the anchor and sheltering in a quiet inlet allowed them to realise, is that it was the course that had changed, not the winds. Persevering against it wouldn't work and might just as well throw the boat against the rocks and harm everyone from crew to captain. It was time to either buy into the new course set by the organisation, or move on and find a new journey they could believe in.

That clarity provided a deep relief.

2. OLD HABITS MEET NEW BUSINESS CLIMATE

In a very large number of situations, leaders keep fighting - they often excel at it. Each challenge is meant to be successfully overcome and quickly followed by the next ones - this is what they do and are used to.

PART 2: Cutting edge: Investigating patterns from Practitioner Experiences

I can think of conversations with executives who had hardwired the behaviour of taking on challenges so deeply that they had lost contact with their own motivation. They were heading straight into the next storm by trained habit, with an unsinkable conviction that after the showers, the sun would be shining... or would it? When those clouds appeared they looked just the same as usual yet created more trouble, this was a real disconnect in their minds.

What they had dropped on their way was the ability to look at the sky not only for its shape, but for what it meant to them and to their organisation.

By holding fire, taking their breath for once, and reflecting on the organisation's purpose and on their own values and drivers, some reconfirmed their engagement with much more clarity, consciously knowing now what gap they needed to fill to be motivated. Other ones could realise they were up for different challenges.

In both cases, it was impressive to see how their levels of energy and well-being rocketed, as they were back in a place where they could make conscious choices.

In those cases, powerful insights kicked in as they reconnected with their values.

3. PERSONAL PRIDE IN PAST SUCCESSES MAKES WAY TO FUTURE OPPORTUNITIES IN A NEW CLIMATE

I think of another leader whose perceived horizon was darkening. As they paused and reflected, they could make sense of what they were seeing. The end of a cycle was also the beginning of a new one. Simply, as they were so proud of what had been built so far, they were emotionally not ready to accept the changes to it. By pausing and reflecting, they could explore all of what they had learned and achieved and then could come to terms with the need to adapt to a changing environment.

The shift was made possible as they acknowledged what they were proud of, so they could let go of it and focus on a new, different sun shining.

4. PERSONAL SUCCESSES MIGRATE TOWARDS COLLABORATIVE SUCCESS TO IMPROVE THE CLIMATE

I also think of another executive who had reached a point where they were seriously considering leaving their organisation. They had been around for long, successfully time leading a high performing division, yet having created for themselves a glass ceiling by inspiring frequently over-competitive relationships across the organisation.

As they paused and reviewed their situation and expectations, taking different perspectives, this executive had an insight on their own values and drivers. That insight dramatically changed their views on the situation. By acknowledging their own important needs for recognition, they could finally make the conscious choices to accept that the top management of the organisation was legitimate in holding a wider agenda than just the one of a star division. A new route appeared, where this executive was happy to play a different game and act more collaboratively, and to consciously address a number of personal beliefs and expectations outside of the organisation that were not relevant to a professional context.

By becoming more aware of how their own ways to contribute to creating the storms, they were in a position to create a much brighter path for themselves.

5. THE EYE IN THE STORM REVEALS ALTERNATIVE ROUTES

Interestingly, this is sometimes when things get quieter that the big dilemma would appear, when least expected. I think of an executive who had been going through the "mother of all storms" for years with an unusual resilience, remaining focused, engaged and even galvanised by the intellectual stimulation and challenge as they were sailing through hurling headwinds. Having been forced to rest for a few weeks, a new opportunity came to them, equally intellectually stimulating but offering a much, much sunnier route.

Whilst no dilemma had surfaced in their mind over those years, it just took an opportunity to chill out, to be more available to observe, notice and make the space for a massive insight that completely changed the course of their journey.

SO WHAT DO WE LEARN FROM THESE STORIES?

I appreciate these fragments of stories would not exhaust the wide array of insights about these moments in a career when the options can appear to be much reduced. Those moments underline one of the real powers of coaching, which is the way it enables one to make choices again.

I would like to single out four common points amongst these examples, which I found enabled those concerned to trigger a different thought process and create a positive shift. They did:

- Invest in a reflective pause, and secure that space they wouldn't find anywhere else.

- Connect to their emotions, to be able to choose their focus and think differently.

- Revisit a multi-faceted reality, looking at all facets, to rebuild a map for themselves.

- Make sense of this reality by confronting it with their own values and motivation drivers.

In my experience, the real shift happens mainly with this last confrontation to what is really true to the individual - the former steps being decisive steps to get to the latter.

Amongst the other areas of my practice, I am quite fascinated by the power that the conversations in this area hold, for considerably reducing levels of distress and restoring more options for leaders and their organisations.

What are your own findings in that space?

How coaching is becoming central to leadership development: Can I still be me if I progress to a more senior management role?

Sue Young

1. INTRODUCTION

I started this two-part series, firstly on my reflections from "Learning To Learn – How Managers Really Learn" where I shared a written piece I produced back in 1999 on what I called then a "developmental approach". I can see many parallels to what I would describe today as a "coaching approach".

In my follow-up post, I see how coaching brings a much sharper focus to just what the developmental approach was aiming to do. In my Practice, this need for a coaching approach – a focus on the individual and what they want to bring to their professional role – is also becoming more important in leadership development.

2. LEADERSHIP DEVELOPMENT: A SHIFT IN EXPECTATIONS PEOPLE NOW HAVE ABOUT TAKING ON LEADERSHIP

There has been a psychological and cultural shift, accelerated over the last decade, as the 'Baby Boomer' generation steps into the most senior leadership roles in the more established and mature organisations with the up and coming X and Y generation bringing, what's perceived to be, a whole new way of seeing their world and their aspirations:

- The up and coming generations are much more questioning;
- They have unprecedented access to information through the internet; and
- They have higher expectations around what they want from their work.

Being in a frustrating unfulfilling experience takes too much of their time – once someone has established a stable earnings base to earn to the level they want, job satisfaction and achievement in their chosen domain becomes more important.

In today's households there are typically two earners with careers to balance and all that goes with managing a family in today's world. Fewer people today than ten years ago are prepared to sacrifice their family and personal time and interests to go up the hierarchical chain in their careers.

I hear more and more capable and experienced managers, with potential to go higher, being more questioning about what they really want.

2.1 TACKLING AMBITION

Ambition is more multi-faceted today. A person's overall lifestyle, of which career is a part, is an important one. If managers look upwards and see senior people putting in excessive hours and exhibiting stress and "not having a life", it can raise fundamental questions.

- Is promotion to a senior level something I really want? I know I don't want what I can see when I look at our senior managers and the stress they are clearly under.

- Also I don't personally value some of the behaviours I see from senior managers - blatant political manoeuvring, micro-management, poor people leadership. There's a Big Question. Can I really be myself and be successful in an organisational senior leadership role here?

- Will I be able to shape my own personal approach to my organisational leadership?

2.2 FINDING MEANINGFUL COUNTERBALANCES TO AMBITION

It's not really surprising then that in these pressurised contexts there is a growth of interest in ideas like 'authentic leadership', resilience and a more 'mindful' approach to leadership.

Gaining a sense of 'I can still be Me' if I progress to senior management is becoming more paramount for people to want to be promoted with an organisation. Or as one client, who was regarded as having high potential for the most senior organisational roles, recently said:

"For the roles to be seen as attractive to me, increasingly it needs to be seen as an opportunity to grow personally. Although it will be challenging, I can see me being able to create my personal leadership approach that makes best use of what I can bring, and in which I can find a challenging stretch that is worthwhile for my growth as a person. I know there will be things that are tough, and there will be frustrations,

but I have a bigger sense of something worthwhile I want to achieve and the confidence to set out on that pathway."

2.3 HOW I AM TAKING ACCOUNT FOR THE SHIFTS IN EXPECTATIONS ACROSS GENERATIONS AS PART OF MY PROFESSIONAL PRACTICE

All of this background has been playing out in the leadership development I have undertaken with both middle and senior managers in organisations. A coaching approach is part of a general move towards a leadership approach that works in a more complex, fast-changing world.

In this context coaching is a means to create more of a shared understanding about what needs to be achieved and how it's going to be achieved.

Traditional top down hierarchical ways of working are being shown to simply not work:

- Essential information to achieving the results is held by a more diverse range of people at different levels, both inside and outside the organisation, and

- There is much uncertainty.

The skills and mindsets of being open minded, inquiry led, good questioning, genuinely listening, relationship building, and being prepared to think more broadly and differently are becoming increasingly important as key leadership attributes.

3. KEY FEATURES OF A COACHING APPROACH IN LEADERSHIP DEVELOPMENT

Programmes I have worked on may contain discrete 'coaching' sessions that fall within the traditional format of private one to one meetings, and there are some that takes a coaching approach overall in that it taps in to the underlying need people have to take charge of their learning, relevant to their individual context and motivations.

I outline here the main features I have worked with on the design and delivery of programmes that I propose are examples of taking a 'coaching approach' to leadership development:

3.1. HIGH QUALITY OF ATTENTION TO THE INDIVIDUAL AND WHERE THEY ARE COMING FROM

A) Engage interests and motivation from the earliest stages of communication

I have seen much information sent out to announce leadership development programmes communicated in a remote, anonymous, top down way. The 'contracting' process for the programme that sets the tone has started way before people turn up for the very first face to face session.

A useful check is always to read through anything before sending it out.

- Can I immediately see what I need to do? – People are busy and will quickly scan for what they need to be doing.

- Can I see quickly how this is relevant to me and how it connects to my priorities and concerns?

- Is it motivational, hooking into my aspirations?

- Does this look important to Board level management, or is it yet another low priority thing from L&D (or at least as far as my boss is concerned).

B) Build in individual preparation to enhance awareness and readiness to get the most from the development process

Features that enhance early individual motivation and interest before people turn up:

1. Use of 360 linked to organisational or external leadership competence frameworks with the opportunity to have an interpretation session with a coach.

2. Similarly use of psychometrics/inventories linked to personality, motivation or some attribute that has been identified as a priority.

3. Endorsement and personal message from a respected Board Level Director, if not the CEO/MD, affirms that the programme is seen as important by the organisation.

4. Individual contact via telephone/teleconferencing before the programme.

5. Personal preparation by way of some cue questions e.g. what do you see as you next 'stretch' priorities for your development that will take you to your next level of capability?

C) Demonstrate high levels of attention to individuals starts with recognising that everyone's different; personality, working style and experience.

Each mix is particular and the nature of the learning process will be unique to the individual. And that is acknowledged explicitly and reflected in the respect, empathy and genuine behaviours shown by the coach/facilitators towards the participants. This demonstrates belief in the individual's experience and potential; the tone and expression of the coaches/facilitators actively shows this. The fact that they're on the programme shows they are already very experienced and highly capable and this is expressed explicitly.

PART 2: Cutting edge: Investigating patterns from Practitioner Experiences

D) An emphasis on 'self-managed learning' as the under-pinning design approach of the programme.

This is characterised by an emphasis on a 'dynamic living' staged process throughout the programme. The individual decides on what they need to learn, and then decides and takes action on the best way of meeting their learning needs.

This self-managed learning process is often extended through the additional elements of learning sets and individual coaching. Also introducing participants to the idea and process of maintaining a learning log to capture progress, experiments and reflections on their experience and testing out new approaches.

Where a programme runs over a longer period of time, individual learning goals become the 'golden thread' throughout the programme. This ensures the individual progress to occur at a more advanced level of learning and achievement. They are not static. They are living. They evolve as the individual evolves their capabilities and motivations.

3.2. An increased emphasis on self and other awareness as central to leadership development - in getting the best out of themselves as well as others

By definition, leaders have to get things done through others. As part of that they have an important role to play in helping others learn and develop in their day to day ways of working.

Understanding patterns in some of the fundamental differences,

- in ways of seeing the world,
- thinking styles,
- working styles,
- being energised and
- relating to others.

Greater awareness of these differences can really add to one's ability to manage one's self and to have more effective working relationships.

Emotional intelligence and taking a more objective 'mindful' approach, being better able to calibrate attention and thinking processes, are also areas for enhancing self-awareness.

A) In leadership the person is the main instrument, and the manager's impact is a highly personal one on their colleagues.

I tend towards a Strengths based approach as one that engages and focuses on that individual's best unique leadership contribution. Weaknesses can often be defined as the flip side of the coin of peoples' strengths. Where behaviour is dysfunctional it is often down to either lack of self-awareness, being blind to the signals from others, or to some flawed defensive mindset, rather than personal fundamental capabilities. Sometimes people may realise that either the role or organisation they're in is not right for them going forward and they need to make a move.

In a group setting, once a conducive open culture has been created, individuals learn from being exposed to differences in action. They then explore these differences with peers in a supportive environment in relation to relationship challenges they are working with back in the workplace.

Today, as previously referred to, people prefer to get more of a sense of the real person in a leadership role. Allowing and encouraging the 'whole person' to more express themselves on the programme, particularly where it is staged over a period of time, can help people feel more comfortable in finding their way to do this in a way that works for them. Feeling able to disclose more, both on personal aspirations and current difficulties and challenges, either as part of a 'checking in' update or in selective programme activities, tends to free up sharing and thinking by individuals in the group.

3.3. THERE IS A STRONG CONNECTION TO THE ORGANISATIONAL AND ROLE CONTEXT, AT DIFFERENT STAGES OF THE PROGRAMME, AND IN DIFFERENT WAYS.

A) Any subject input and group discussions are both connected back to the real context and challenges that people are dealing with.

Any subject matter input is shared with the intention that this is mainly a stimulus, with more time given, to people discussing the implications, sharing and listening to different perspectives from colleagues, sense-making and taking it forward into individual reflection and capturing the key points they are taking away.

B) Visibility from top management and close linkages to the core business.

This starts right from the beginning in terms of how the programme is positioned.

The best and most impactful senior leadership development programmes I have worked on have always involved the attendance of directors or senior managers for more informal and open sessions with participants. This is where they have shared their most important personal learning points from their careers and where there has been open Q&A based conversations. The best of these really open up to a 'view from the bridge' organisational perspectives. They enable senior people to be seen in a more realistic human light – as authentic even! This is a real engaging and motivational experience for managers where there is the opportunity for rare high-quality conversation with Directors in a more informal environment.

C) Contribution from an active and 'organisational savvy' HR/L&D champion.

It's important that any leadership programme is seen to be very effective at making the current business case and speaks from having senior management support. It therefore adds enormous value if the internal organisational champion for the programme has the awareness and coaching capabilities to be able to influence and gain credibility with key senior influencers and sponsors, as well as external providers.

3.4 LEARNING PROCESSES/ELEMENTS IN THE DESIGN OF THE PROGRAMME ITSELF

The following are elements that add to what the individual takes back into their organisational role:

1. **Use of Action Learning or Peer Coaching Groups as part of the design elements mix**. This is where people bring real challenges or issues to a small peer groups. Through listening, asking questions, and offering observations and feedback, the group helps the individual progress their thinking. In other words, the Facilitator/Coach's main role is to hold the space, only intervening to support the process, rather than on content. Managers take a great deal from listening to colleagues' experiences and perspectives. It can be a powerful affirmation and extension to their thinking.

2. **Use of a strategic Work-based Project as a learning vehicle**. This can either be individual or team based. It's where the organisation brings a real organisational strategic issue/project to a small team of participants and they take on a true 'internal consultant' role. The nature of learning that comes from this stretching real experience is very rich, if uncomfortable at times.

3. **Active connection and reporting in to the Line Manager as part of the programme design**. Most programmes these days include the need for the individual to feed back on their development goals and learning from the programme. For example, the most effective approach I have experienced is where there were periodic three-way calls between participant, line manager and programme coach.

4. **Individuals have to source themselves a real mentor as part of the programme**. This is encouraging a more proactive self-managed approach where the individual has to reflect on and decide the best kind of mentor(s) in relation to their objectives e.g. gain exposure/experience of a particular area of work with which they are less familiar, make a connection with a level/area they are particularly interested in, etc.

IN CONCLUSION:

I have found it an interesting process to reflect and write about the different ways I see 'a coaching approach' being part of the leadership development programmes I have recently worked on. To be honest, unless leadership programmes can make use of a 'coaching approach', I am not sure they are fit for purpose in today's world.

What I find interesting is that much of this is not named as 'coaching' by my clients!

So, some questions:

- How do you relate to my description of a coaching approach to leadership development? i.e. high quality of attention to individuals, their context, personal objectives and individual learning needs.

- I'm interested in different aspects of taking a 'coaching approach' in different contexts. Anything you would want to add to my list, from your experience?

Differentiating leaders taking a coaching approach from internal coaches

Doug Montgomery and Laurent Terseur - Making sense of how we define a coaching approach (Part 3)

In our first two blogs of this mini series[1,2] we explored what it took for us as former leaders and managers to expand our existing range of styles by adding a more coaching approach. We shared what we felt were the related benefits and challenges that may be of value to others.

In this third and last piece of the series, we compare and contrast the roles of coaching leaders with the role of the internal coach (and by proxy external coaches who face similar dilemmas).

We define internal coaches here, as individuals who have trained as coaches and enter into contracted coaching assignments with other members of staff within the same organisation and alongside their normal day job.

We observe that internal coaches often start out as leaders or managers who acquire coaching skills to use in their own work. They then decide to take this further with additional training to become internal coaches.

We see both roles delivering important value to the organisation, in different ways, and want to share our insights, drawing from our respective experiences of these two roles in different large organisations. We have identified four key areas defining key differences:

- Agendas
- Consistency of Style
- Systemic implications
- Power in relationships

---

[1] Making sense of how we define a coaching approach from each of our professional experiences
[2] Setting your mind on a coaching approach

PART 2: Cutting edge: Investigating patterns from Practitioner Experiences

AGENDAS

A fundamental difference we see between the two roles relates to their respective agendas and how they impact the boundaries for coaching conversations.

An internal coach spends some of their time coaching other members of staff, from outside their own reporting line and function, with the focus fully on the coachee and their coaching objectives.

We experienced that internal coaching works particularly well in large organisations, where significant organisational separation between coach and coachee is available to allow the internal coach to work outside their personal areas of line responsibility, knowledge and expertise.

We see this organisational distance as desirable and in many organisations insisted upon, as:

- it reduces the temptation for the coach to problem solve and mentor, rather than coach,

- it reduces the likelihood of the coach knowing people in the coachee's story, hence better protecting confidentiality and eliminating potential conflicts of interest,

- it ensures that even if they share an interest in the organisation's success, internal coaches have no direct responsibility for the coachee's projects, objectives or development, allowing them to create and hold a safe space in which the coachee can take responsibility for their actions and choices.

- it provides the coachee a safe environment in which they can speak and explore honestly and openly without fearing possible repercussions.

In our experience, this last point can be a sensitive issue for coaches whose day job stretches across the organisation should reorganisations shorten the distance between coach and coachee. e.g. Doug knows of one internal coach and HR professional, whose responsibilities were changed to work in a division in which several of her former coachees worked.

Similarly, the coaching leader can acquire and use coaching skills to use as a leadership style and encourage the growth and development of their team members, build confidence and find ways of achieving business goals.

However, the team leader using a coaching approach, with direct or indirect reports, has an ongoing interaction with those in their own reporting line and function. They have responsibility for their reports' projects, objectives, performance and development.

Therefore the leader's agenda is structurally more conflicted than that of the internal coach, as:

- they are not in a position to guarantee the absence of implications for the team members, as they have an influence on their performance evaluation, development and compensation, hence they have (and are perceived to have) a vested interest and investment in the individual and situation.

- they are much closer to the action, often being subject matter experts, and having accountability for the overall outcomes puts a greater burden of accountability for progress on them than on an internal coach.

- they are likely to find it more challenging, during coaching, to be non-judgemental and fully allow their team members to be in control of their own thinking about the work and to choose ways of moving forward that are not how the leader would do it.

- they are responsible for assessment and judgement of their team members' performance, whereas an internal coach can keep to a non-judgmental approach at all times.

We have come across examples of all these situations. We hear leaders who want to take up a coaching style express these as fears about the approach. An open conversation about the intention of taking a coaching approach is, in our experience, the starting point for both leader and team member to work out how they get the best out of the style and manage these potential challenges.

CONSISTENCY OF STYLE

The second difference we notice is in the range of styles that leaders and internal coaches are expected to use.

The coaching leader's role, as we have described it in a previous blogs, requires the use of a wide range of styles across the spectrum. This can include 'telling' through 'advising', 'sharing' to 'eliciting', as they adopt the role of teacher, expert, consultant, visionary, manager of plans and resources, mentor or even coach depending on the circumstances.

From our experience, understanding what style is most useful for any given situation is key to engaging in conversations with the appropriate mindset and approach needed to achieve the most useful outcomes.

We see a lot of room to apply the coaching attitudes of trust and curiosity more consistently across all these leadership behaviours and styles. Some coaching questions at the outset of each conversation may help the leader diagnose what style fits best the situation. For example, they could use very simple and open questions with their team members such as; "So what is it you need from me?" Or "What specifically are you stuck with?" to shed light on what the most useful style to adopt would be.

We also learned from our experience that a shift between styles during the same conversation can be appropriate. For instance, starting by setting a clear objective and expectation is part of a manager style. This could switch to a more coaching style to elicit options for how the individual could tackle the task and what actions they will commit to. The conversation could end with a switch back to a manager style when approving resources and arranging times to check in on progress.

The internal coach, on the other hand, has a different relationship with their coachee to that of the leader with their team members. That coaching relationship is usually for a fixed number of sessions over a limited period of time. Within each session, the internal coach can be expected to be consistent in their coaching behaviour and attitude as they remain in their coaching role throughout the relationship. The challenge for the internal coach is not so much to choose an appropriate approach, as to avoid slipping into non-coaching styles, which can cause confusion and undermine the trust the coach claims to have in the coachee's ability to think for themselves.

SYSTEMIC IMPLICATIONS

Our third observation is related to the systemic context in which the leader and internal coach operate.

COLLUSION WITH THE CULTURE

Every organisational system has a culture. This implicit expectation of 'how it is around here', sets the norms of how people behave and what is OK to say and do and what is not OK. As parts of the system, both internal coach and coaching leader are part of the organisation's culture and share in these norms; often unconsciously.

Both coach and leader may therefore fail to challenge the cultural assumption that their respective coachees and team members may be making, i.e. they may be unconsciously in collusion with each other in complying with the culture and miss potentially useful options and opportunities that could add value because they challenge the status quo.

For the leader, there is usually no support to bring these collusions into their awareness. Whereas in effective internal coaching programs, coaches have access to coaching supervision in which they are able to discuss their coaching work with an experienced practitioner. One who may be able to notice and raise awareness of such collusion. An example of such collusion that we have seen is where the coach who gets so caught up in the organisational business in their day job, that they do not recognise the influence of that business on their coachee. Both coach and coachee work under the assumption that being very busy is just the way it is around here, rather than challenging whether that is really true all, or just some, of the time.

Of course, this challenge of noticing collusion extends to internal supervisors, who also need to be aware of their own collusion with the coach with regards to their common system. Since working as independents, and having worked across a number of different organisations across a broader range of services, we can see here an important advantage offered by external supervisors and external executive coaches who are independent of the system. Independents have a more detached view of the system and draw from experiences combined with training in understanding systems and their traps to offer that different perspective.

IMPACT ON RELATIONSHIPS

Organisations are composed of multiple overlapping systems (groups, departments, teams, divisions, offices, etc.). Individuals belong to many of these. The leader and the internal coach will both be influenced by and have influenced the many systems they are part of.

From our experience, the internal coach's work with their coachee:

- has an indirect impact of significant importance on their coachees' systems through the changes and actions their coachees choose to take.

- has a much more marginal impact on their own systems, except for the time they spend away from their normal work and location.

- often provides the coach with satisfaction and fulfilment that energises them for the rest of their work.

- provides the coach with insights across the organisation as they work with people from other parts of the organisation – and are often able to see emerging trends and attitudes change across the system.

In contrast, we observe that leaders taking a coaching approach with members of their team are likely to create a significant and multidimensional impact on their own system:

- by the effect of empowerment, change and action taken by the team members being coached,

- by creating conditions for building trusting relationships within the team, as individuals experience being trusted and asked for their opinions,

- by changing the psychological distances between themselves and different members of their team if they vary the extent of their coaching approach between the various team members. For instance, team members not experiencing for themselves the level of trust placed in their peer, may feel undervalued or excluded from a special relationship. This can adversely affect their relationship with the leader and their peers.

- by multiple coaching leaders across the organisation helping to create a more coaching culture and enabling a more empowered and engaged organisation.

How much coaching leaders are conscious of all or part of the likely impact of their own actions and related perceptions is a key awareness challenge. This should be easier for those internal coaches who switch back to their normal leadership role. At the same time this raises a question about how deeply into beliefs and values leaders should go with members of their team. This takes us into our fourth differentiator between leader and internal coach.

POWER IN THE RELATIONSHIP

Leaders, whether they understand it, like it or admit it, hold an asymmetrical power in relation to those they lead. They make or influence decisions about who does what task or opportunity, who gets rewarded and who gets promoted – or not. So what is the personal and psychological depth to which a leader should seek to coach a member of their team? How do they enhance the level of trust and engagement rather than damage it?

The most common situations in which we observed leaders effectively use a coaching approach include:

- supporting the individual to solve a work problem for themselves.
- supporting others to deliver a tricky task.
- prepare others for a new challenge or new responsibility.
- to build the self-confidence of others in how to think for themselves about a work project or challenge.

This is essentially about business-related content or transactions in which a personal development aspect kicks in as the individual learns that they can think about different options and be creative, and are trusted to offer suggestions and opinions, and to challenge how things are normally done. To use the iceberg metaphor, often used in coaching, much of a leader's coaching approach is on the surface or just below the waterline.

To go deeper under the surface and have a conversation tapping into a team member's fundamental beliefs, values and personal history requires appropriate levels of trust and confidentiality (quite apart from the skills and experience) to safely work at such depth. Such personal information and insight into vulnerability and emotional triggers have the potential to skew an already unbalanced power relationship further in favour of the leader. We are not suggesting that all leaders would take advantage of such a shift. However, being aware of the potential for inadvertent, unintended consequences is important to forewarn for.

Contrasting this with the experienced internal coach, we observe far less asymmetrical power in the relationship with their coachee who is not in their management or organisational line. We acknowledge though, that internal coaches too can still hold or be perceived to be in an unbalanced power relationship by their coachee. The internal coach may be, for instance, in a more senior role than the coachee and therefore be perceived to know more or to hold some influence in the organisation that may be beneficial (or detrimental) to the coachee. Alternatively, the coachee may be more senior and may not trust the coach with relevant but sensitive business information. This can extend to personal information about themselves or other senior executives.

In the organisations we're aware of that have internal coaching programs, the coach training includes significant emphasis on contracting, boundaries and how sensitive personal areas will be handled[3]. They will have looked for obvious conflicts of interest at the chemistry meeting, conflicts that may require an alternative coach to be sought (in some internal coaching programs this is a formal part of the coach – coachee matching process). Less obvious but possible conflicts may have been thought about and discussed by the coach and coachee, such as how the coach will behave, should the coachee's name come up in committees, selection boards, job appointments, etc. that the coach is party to and vice versa.

These explicit coaching agreements create the space in which the internal coach has permission to work with the coachee's beliefs, and is in a position to challenge their thinking, question where these beliefs came from and how they are impacting the future direction the coachee wants to go in. In this way, the experienced internal coach is able to work at a level beneath the iceberg to support the coachee's performance and development in an equal and co-created partnership.

SUMMARY AND QUESTIONS TO THE READER

As we bring this mini-series on leaders taking a coaching approach to a conclusion, we are excited to re-acquaint ourselves with the powerful impact on individuals and organisations that such open and engaging leaders can make. By drawing out the comparison between these coaching leaders and internal coaches, we hope to help organisations and leaders understand the different value these two roles bring.

---

[3] See Hawkins, Peter., and Nick Smith. 2011. *Coaching, Mentoring and Organizational Consultancy; Supervision and Development*: 209-211. London: McGraw Hill Education, OUP.

PART 2: Cutting edge: Investigating patterns from Practitioner Experiences

By considering these four aspects of the roles - agendas, consistency of style, systemic context and power balance in the relationships - we hope that leaders, coaches and those that organise the training and management of coaching programs within organisations will be better armed to develop their internal coaching offerings with greater clarity of each role.

We would be delighted to hear about your own experience as an internal coach or as a leader using coaching approaches, so please add comments?

- What is your perspective on their major differences between the roles?
- What have you noticed about the value added and challenges faced?

Building waves of value working with the client's team - the next contract

KC Char

Every time I act from the edge, waves begin to form.

I believe I do my best work when it is 'on the edge;' as I feel most alive, full of energy and I know the stakes are high. Waves are formed by numerous small droplets that rise and gain momentum before they gloriously spread onto the shore.

When I work with senior teams it's more about orchestrating how the waves need to gain momentum in the same direction. Eventually these waves create positive benefits and results for the client, the team and the organisation overall.

I describe that next stage of how I continue working on the edge whilst,

- Both deepening and strengthening the relationship with the client,
- Understanding and working with the relationships in the team, and
- Adding value in real time.

Through a detailed example, I conscientiously explore how my approach works, step by step, to develop the full potential of the contract.

Writing this blog, I was struck by the importance of getting the relatively small and simple actions right in order to build the wave of the whole process. A process which will have a far-reaching impact in the organisation. Following through on those actions led to pivotal moments which helped me to continually develop the steps that are integral to gaining momentum.

I can broadly describe my approach as follows:

1. Once I gain the client's confidence, I obtain permission to work with their team.

2. I then step into this phase by both observing the team dynamic in a leadership meeting as well as building relationships with the team members one-on-one.

3. My focus is to create an open and constructive dialogue, where they can feel less vulnerable to tell me what they genuinely think and feel.

4. I can thus strengthen my client's understanding of their potential, as well as their needs, and suggest strategies to get the best out of the team.

CONTINUING TO SPREAD COACHING WAVES - MEETINGS WITH THE EXECUTIVE TEAM

This coaching work began after first having a session with the senior executive (as the initial client, the new boss) about how to expand impact within the wider organisation.

After the first session, I agreed with the client that I would be able to add significant value if I

- Got to know the members of the team, and
- See the team dynamics as well as interview them one-on-one.

He agreed. I joined the monthly executive team meeting shortly thereafter. There were more than twenty leaders who represented the businesses and functions at each of these all-day meetings. I share in quite vivid detail my observations of what was happening during the meeting I observed and how I continually made use of the information to advise my client to take the appropriate steps needed to lead the organisation.

THE MORNING SESSION - OBSERVING THE LIMITATIONS OF THE PROCESS

The team members were sitting around a big board room table with the boss (my principal client) seated at the head. I sat towards the end of the table where I could see the boss very well and make notes of the team's dynamics.

The boss asked a few questions to gain understanding and clarity, it seemed. He appeared to have a step back attitude; and even leant backwards in his chair as though looking in from the outside.

It was clear, to me, there were several opportunities for improving the process taking place.

- The current process was very much focused on finding quick immediate solutions; i.e. "How will we deliver the numbers for the quarter? How will we fill the apparent gaps?"

- Some people did other things like read their mails and answer texts on their phones.

- Wider communication about what might have been involved in the matters raised and the broader implications were very limited.

- There was a lack of clarity about whether the topics on the agenda were for information, for discussion or for taking a decision.

- A few of the stronger people with loud voices kept speaking; the remaining 70 percent said nothing.

LUNCH TIME - QUICK WINS ON PROCESS IMPROVEMENT

At lunchtime I caught up with my principal client, the boss, and said, *"Ok, let's take a couple of minutes to the side."* We stepped outside the room where lunch was served and found a quiet spot.

I simply said, *"I'm suggesting a couple of small things for you to keep in mind for the rest of the meeting: You need to be perceived as 'in' the team. You need to shift from 'I' to 'We' and from 'This' organisation to 'Our' organisation. When you speak, use more 'our' and 'we' in your language. And your posture, body language, appears to say that you are not connected to the team – lean forward to show your interest and engagement. You are asking straight questions and gaining clarity which is superb, because they also seem confused on what the 'real' issue is. And it is key to summarize at the end of a topic or get your team secretary to do so. It needs to be clear what was decided, what are the next steps and who is accountable – otherwise nothing will be done, that's my experience."*

At this stage, the client didn't know what to expect from me. I felt that what I was creating added value right there and then. He looked at me intently whilst taking in what I had said, smiled and said, "*Yes, I think you've made some good points. I'll try them.*"

Summing up in a few simple words, here, does not fully capture the fundamentally dramatic shift needed for the boss and the group around the table to start moving toward being a team, taking ownership together for running the business, and moving from 'I' to 'we'.

This was just the start towards making the shift in culture and style evident so that the boss could lead more comfortably by using his strengths. I noted other gaps in what the group needed and what the boss was giving them - especially since they were reluctant to take decisions themselves. The team were used to the previous boss who had a 'command and control' style and who made all the key decisions. It was clear to me that my client had a very empowering style. Hence there were plenty of opportunities to make further use of his strengths.

SESSION AFTER LUNCH - SURFING THE NEXT WAVE OF OPPORTUNITY

The team members noted the changes in the boss' behaviour after we had spoken. Slowly, a couple more of the leaders started talking to me more openly during the break. Some of the doubts and suspicions about what my real agenda might be were starting to be dispelled.

I took the time to seek out and speak with those who were more aloof. They shared their frustrations of how things had changed. They told me that the organisation was in turmoil as a result. When I asked their opinion about the new boss they said, "*There is not much to say because he's only been here for a few weeks.*" I responded with respect and innocently said, "*We make our judgements pretty quickly as to whether someone's effective or not-effective. You also have some views of the way he should lead the company to be successful, so what would those be?*"

My sense is, getting through these little windows at the start is as important as going to speak with them. You can receive a huge amount of data on a one-to-one basis. However, unless you get it right in those first few seconds, it doesn't happen.

END OF DAY - ADDING IMMEDIATE REVIEWS AS A BIG OPPORTUNITY TO IMPROVE THE OVERALL PROCESS

At the end of the whole day, we agreed to debrief. I said to my client, "*We've been sitting for a very long time. Let's take a walk and discuss what happened during the day – we will need to see how to make some sense of it.*" And with that, we both laughed and he said, "*If you can make sense of what happened today, then you are worth every penny of your fees!*" Laughing helped to shift the energy and he continued, "*I am not sure whether to jump off a cliff or try to get my old job back! I did not know what I was getting into – they never tell you the real story in the interview or you wouldn't take the job!*" And we continued to laugh, which really helped to discharge some of the energy pent up in us!

So we went for a walk on the grounds which were pretty large. As we walked the client said, "*For starters, it seems to me that half this group does not belong on this leadership team. And did you notice, there were a few people working on other stuff instead of engaging in the discussions. That infuriates me. I will tell them that if they have more important things to do than run this company, they need not come to my meetings any longer!*"

Once again, I could see where other possible opportunities for coaching were, and some potential improvements, in how the process could work better towards achieving what the client wanted.

It became even clearer from this first period of observation that there was potentially a great deal of additional data that could usefully be brought into what was happening, and not happening, in the team. I thought to myself, *"OK, it's time now to speak to each team member so we can get an idea of where they stand, how they interpret the current situation and their motivation to work with their new boss in a way that could make them all successful."*

MAKING WAVE, AND ADDING VALUE, WITH THE WHOLE TEAM

INTERVIEWING TEAM MEMBERS INDIVIDUALLY TO UNDERSTAND THEIR NEEDS AND MOTIVATION

After my discussion with my client, we initiated a series of one-on-one interviews with all the team members. This also provided an opportunity to discuss the situation prior to the new boss joining the company – what the culture was like and the style of leadership of the previous incumbent, as well as some thoughts and suggestions for the new one. Some were extremely critical of the past leader of the team, who they described as aggressive, bright, a micro- manager who rarely discussed the issues openly, got involved in minute details and, constantly followed up, which left them all exhausted. And now here comes this new boss who's completely the opposite.

It became my job to quantify what was needed to bridge this large gap in order to make him successful. Some of the team were questioning why he had been selected for this position, brought in from outside the company, from a different business, when there were a number of candidates inside. They were really questioning his credibility. This became one of the first areas I worked with my client on to address.

Although at times some team members portrayed themselves as victims, what I appreciated very much was their openness and eagerness to make the company succeed. I assured them that I would not mention their names specifically when I debriefed with their new boss, my client, but that I would summarize their input into specific themes, otherwise what would be the point of speaking to them? I believe they were relieved and appreciated that their voice was being heard. A couple of them were quite surprised that they had been so open with me during the hour interview. One of them said, *"I am not sure why I have told you so much so quickly, for some reason I feel I can trust you to use the information discreetly."*

CONTINUOUSLY AND CAREFULLY BUILDING AND MAINTAINING TRUST

This has again been critical to developing the required foundations to add value – building the contract as we went.

In my own subtle way, I created the conditions to start to relax the other team members and make connections with them. I listened to them and I shared my intent, which was to support the boss, as well as the team, through this transition. They were curious about how things would develop and what opportunities this change could bring.

I work hard on having a non-threatening persona, but still someone to be reckoned with and well capable of being immersed into this context. I recognise there are a few things that I do.

- One is knowing that I know very little about lots of things. I listen deeply, use their words and explore the meaning the words have for them. I ask clear open questions and then probe further, and get them to give me examples.

- I also use my discussions with the team to continually encourage them to come with solutions and not just state the problem. I challenge them to see the issues from different perspectives.

- I also try to meet them where they are and empathize with what they might be feeling.

For example, when the head of one major business area started talking about the issues faced, I could see and feel that she was overwhelmed. Things were going very poorly. Everyone was pointing the finger at this person as there was a problem with the performance of their area of the business which accounted for some of the shortfalls in revenues. When I spoke to her, I could see she was having a very hard time, her shoulders sagged and she looked exhausted. She also had kind, soft eyes that seemed to say, I'm not sure I want to be here at all. I began by smiling and said, "*You know, I've been listening to all the complaints your colleagues made in the meeting, and, my god, you must feel overwhelmed and exhausted!*" She immediately began elaborating on the issues, providing her perspective and appreciated my listening ear.

In these situations, I can empathize well. However, I know that I need to be careful and not to collude with the person. I empathize and then pull back to, "*OK, so what's your responsibility in this? What do you need to do? What can you control and influence? What is one thing the boss can do to support you?*" I saw this was difficult for her as she was so overwhelmed, and she finally said, "*I probably have to leave the company because I don't have the conditions needed to be successful here.*" So I said, "*Here's your opportunity to talk with your new boss, give him your perspective and ask for support.*"

SETTING THE BASIS FOR CONTINUING THIS WORK WITH THE TEAM

Following the series of one-on-one interviews, I wanted to give my client some highlights so he could respond to their feedback and my suggestions. Since we were not able to meet face to face for a couple of weeks, and his agenda was completely full, I suggested we have a call one evening.

I could tell he was tired from all the initial impressions and pressure he felt already. He started with, "*Let me have it then, what did they have to say?*" I said, "*Oh my god, I got an earfull! I need a couple of glasses of wine. And you probably need a scotch... to be able to absorb this!*" "*Oh that good,*" he said with a chuckle. I then went through some of the main themes and how he could constructively address a couple of their key concerns by fine-tuning his style. I was careful to frame this in a way he could receive it because at times he sounded a little confused and frustrated with their comments. I would confirm his reaction and remind him of his goal which was to get the best out of them, until he had the opportunity to make the changes he needed.

However, I had my views on each of them. I first got an understanding of what he thought about them before I divulged my impressions. We developed a frame of reference together in which to share the information. This allowed him to reflect and consider their strengths, what opportunities exist, even as possible disruptors, that make up his team. And what was the best way to work with each of them. That's how we went through the people.

I also made my client aware that there was a lot of fatigue in the organisation. The whole leadership change was adding another layer of uncertainty, as well as disrupting things, and adding to what was already dysfunctional.

Receiving and assessing both the value and usefulness of this information, and connecting to my client's vision, was a key opportunity to get the right contract he wanted to establish with his team right from the start. In addition, I was also developing a better understanding of the complex contracting involved in our work together. I could feel that my client trusted me to do the right thing for him and the organisation. We both wanted to check out and align on the basis of this trust, as we went forwards.

We were developing a rapport and a coded language which we had established (laughter being an important part of it).

The next cycle of the contracting was now complete.

STRENGTHENING, EVEN FURTHER, MY AWARENESS AND CONFIDENCE OF THESE SMALL ACTIONS THAT BUILD WAVES OF VALUE IN TEAMS

Reviewing how I add waves of value to a team, I realized that I have typically responded **quickly with small, short and sharp interventions** that had had an impact; a ripple effect on demonstrating how I worked with the client. I had to continuously find appropriate ways to solicit information from the team, share the information in a way that supports him to adjust to the context, and make better and more constructive decisions to lead.

How I'm strengthening my awareness of these important ways of making this happen:

- It's about managing boundaries with humour.
- It's being visible and seen as working for the boss and their team, with the intent of connecting the dots and helping them see each other's perspectives.
- It's about sharing and delivering their information (without deviation) with a clear intention that it's always about supporting the boss to be better informed for working well in their role.

My approach to coaching hasn't differed with each of the individuals that make up the team, including the boss. Maintaining the boundaries, as part of the contracting with the client, has allowed me to keep my balance and deliver the value I know I can bring to our working relationship. At the same time, I can do the 'right' thing for them in continuing to build the trust which leads to further disclosure... It creates waves.

It's repeatedly appreciating and realising how important it is to get small things just right to create and amplify these ripples!

Question: How do you strengthen your awareness of keeping your attention on the small things whilst in the midst of bigger scale and complex process interventions?

CHAPTER 5

TAKING A COACHING APPROACH IN ORGANISATIONS

How I use a coaching approach at work to build on and add value to how the system works

Simon Dennis

oaching culture is about having the whole organisation operate in a way which is much more people aware, much more perceptive and doesn't just get stuck in the aftermath involved in reporting on the numbers. It's about creating the right conditions to get some real conversations going with the other person. It's about where the other is coming from and what their interests and expectations are. Reporting is one of those areas that I began to experiment with.

We were going through a time where everybody wanted reports and data. Data was king. I was due to attend a customer service review meeting and expected my reports to be challenged. I had the service report in my hand. It was about twenty pages long and it basically showed the customer how we had delivered service over the last month with some year-to-date tracking and trends. I looked around the room. I thought, 'But actually, this reporting doesn't, in any way, reflect what they actually felt - the quality of the service. It is just a set of numbers and data. It's almost like your bank balance, you know, the statement shows you are in the black but, for whatever reason, you don't feel particularly rich or in control'.

It was not quite an epiphany moment, but when they asked for copies of the report to begin the discussion I said, *"I'm actually going to hang on to them for now. Let's just talk about how things are going for you. What went well last month? What didn't work? What's your overall perception of the service we've provided?"* I then started to make some notes, particularly around the service areas that they weren't happy with, but also some of their suggestions for improvement and their future challenges. What followed was essentially a 'coaching' conversation. Lots of open questions, challenging of expectations, "Where could we do better?", "What was the best element of the service?" and "How might we work better together?" It was a genuinely useful and constructive dialogue.

At the end of the meeting, as I was leaving, I put them [the reports] in the bin. And the others said, *"Can we see the service report now?"* I simply replied, *"What's it going to tell you that you don't already know? Those reports are factually correct. Overall last month, we have delivered within the contract boundaries to the levels that we've agreed. But clearly, for whatever reason, that's not the service that you wanted or expected."*

EXPERIMENTING WITH EXPECTATIONS ABOUT REPORTING

There was an expectation on my part. Rather than simply presenting the data, we could have a much more open conversation about the perception of the service. I've seen it work really well because it is not so much just about what happened last month, it's about what are we going to be doing better in the future. The customer's perception is their reality so your report should reflect that as well as the facts!

This motivated me to write a paper on getting people to think about this approach and talk about what they would really be saying in those reports. I want to ask how much we focus on factual data to hide behind versus perception, which may be very different.

Let me share another example. Someone I know was working on a contract in which he was the customer. He received a phone call from the service department who told him that there was an issue, but that everything was back up and running within the service levels in the agreement. They also mentioned that, *"We're planning to do an update - a fix or whatever - with the system at 10 p.m., UK time"* - essentially out of office hours. And the customer just said to them, *"I know it was still within the service level but you still took down five of our largest systems which still caused a lot of trouble. And you can't do the changes at 10 p.m. tonight because that's when America will be online and that's one of our biggest markets."*

This got me thinking again, 'Well, the service report will be accurate, the service department haven't broken any rules. Everything was hunky-dory. They've done the right thing, the fix will be applied out of office hours etc. But at no point would the report reflect the reality that the customer is facing.'

COMPARING EXPECTATIONS ACROSS DIFFERENT INDUSTRIES

It's completely different if you looked at something like the radio industry, where I started my working life. We talked about 'Blackbox' radio - the fact that you can put together a sequence of music that will deliver an audience because you can just program it. It might not have been a big audience but you can deliver it. Essentially creating a radio program to a formula, using standard ingredients (defined mix of music, news, sport etc.), a process if you like.

My boss used to say that the presenter's job was to put the 'sizzle' on the 'sausage'. It's the producer that creates the sausage. I could plan and write a decent breakfast show but if you give me a great presenter to present it, it'd be better than if I presented it.

The challenging bit is ensuring that the talent – the presenter – doesn't break the process but enhances it. In radio you're dealing with egos where if you're not careful they think they are 'bigger' than the process. Then you get anarchy. As a producer you work with the presenter to help them understand that, if you use a process as your baseline, your professionalism will then improve the performance.

In the services industry particularly, that's hugely relevant because there are hundreds of people. Let's take the mobile phone industry. There's lots of mobile phone providers. The only thing that sets them apart is actually the service they provide, so the quality of the service is based on the people that you interact with. When you're delivering people-based services, it's a hugely important thing. It's also interesting when you work in an outsourcing organisation because you can think about companies who outsource. They actually move the same staff from provider to provider. So the assumption is you're just going to get the same service because you have the same people. This is where the other organisation has to say, "Our underlying core...our basic process, is at a level where the same people are going to make it even more enhanced. So you've got to get that bit – the basic process – right."

For a long time, I think we were talking about empowerment. I used to say to our presenters when I was working in radio that, "We want to choose our own music. We want to choose everything we're going to play and put into the show and, basically, we all want to produce our own program. But it's a different skill. Actually, the presenter's skill is in adding to the basic layers created by the producer."

APPLYING THE 80-20 RULE

It's about working with the system, rather than breaking the system. Working within the bounds of it and saying, "We are empowering you but we're empowering you to add value on top of it rather than change the underlying structure," because once you get underlying structure change, that's anarchy. You can't control anarchy. And then you lose.

I used to say on a simple scale when I was delivering laptops as part of my role, "*If you follow a process, you get a laptop from A to B within, let's say, seven days.*" And I said, "*So that's the basic minimum.*" They said, "*That's what we work towards. You all do it. We deliver it. Job done.*" So we have to have something like 75 to 80 percent of business operating at that level, because if everything becomes an exception and you need every laptop in less than seven days, actually, that's a different service. The clients may then say, "*I need to scale up and I need to have a three-day service, not a seven-day service.*" It might take a little while to get to understand it but what we did in the end was recognise, "*Well, OK. So we know that most of the business just operates on a seven-day turnaround, no problem.*" That gave us the capacity that when you do need to create a different level of service, you do need something in three days, we've got the capacity to do a one-off or a five-off exception.

Back to the radio analogy. We would be playing a fairly normal set of music across seven days a week. Then the Rolling Stones will be in town on Monday, so we'd start every hour with a Rolling Stones record. *"That's great. The Rolling Stones are in town. So we're just going to go Rolling Stones mad."* And you can do that but you couldn't do it every single day of the year. You wouldn't sustain your audience. So you have to have the basic platform working to an 80-20 rule so that you've got the ability to flex and be outstanding or exponential at certain times.

I think that's when people get concerned that the process is taking away their empowerment by making them follow a set pattern.

Whereas, if everything was 'emergency' or an exception, we couldn't do it because everyone would be running about like headless chickens. So, for me, that's the message I've captured and I wanted to get to, 'If you get the basics right, you can then coach the individuals to look at how they could make that even better. How could they improve their performance each step of the way?'

And I thought that would make an interesting theme because empowerment can be very strongly informed by a certain kind of coaching approach.

WHAT THIS MEANS FOR ME

What I do is I look for those bits of business that are exceptional and I say, *"What makes them exceptional?"*

Sometimes, it is just the individual. You say, *"That's not replicable."* You can try and capture some of those skills and knowledge but it's not repeatable in that sense. There are some places where you see better performance and think, 'Right, what they've done is they've enhanced that process and they've added an additional template, a specific element or they have an additional meeting or step.' And then you say, *"Well, actually, if it's receiving a benefit, let's cut it into a system for everybody and we all get the benefits."*

Where it is possible to replicate, we have process workshops where we look at a process and we ask, "How can we do this faster, smarter, better?" What we're doing is we're raising that baseline. You're using people's capability to raise the baseline. They might then notice that somebody else had a better outcome than they did following that same process, so the coaching can explore how that came about. "What did they do differently?" "What made it work well for them?"

It's knowing the difference between what is a truly one-off exceptional performance that can't be repeated by just any individual, and then grasping those ones where you can.

Question: How have you found ways to bring a coaching approach to add value to how the system works?

PART 2: Cutting edge: Investigating patterns from Practitioner Experiences

Providing mentoring and coaching in family managed organizations in India

Aubrey Rebello

About 70 percent of businesses in India are family managed, wherein the family is actively involved in the day-to-day affairs of the business. Many of these businesses are companies listed on the stock exchange. The families usually have a controlling stake of 50 to 75 percent.

In the case of such listed companies, government regulations require that independent directors sit on the board. They are expected to protect the interests of minority stakeholders. However, since these directors are appointed by the family, the family is virtually fully in control.

Family managed businesses in India have always been very successful. Some of their key traits include:

- Agility,
- Lean Structure,
- Cost effectiveness, and
- Loyalty.

Even though I work with family managed organizations as a mentor and , and I post my previous executive role in professionally managed companies, this is a totally new and enriching experience for me.

I would like to share what I have learned here.

EXTRA CARE AND AWARENESS ARE REQUIRED IN FAMILY BUSINESSES

Family managed organizations have business challenges like any other business.

Some of the additional challenges peculiar to them are:

- Issues of familial relationships and emotions;
- Personal agendas that may not be overtly shared;
- Individual aspirations, sharing of wealth, succession, and favouritism.

As they say, *family business can fail not because of business but because of family*!

A difference of approach is required when working with these executives in a family business, whether it is between father and son, between siblings, the involvement of their spouses, which is also quite common, to those executives working for public companies.

In my work I have been fortunate to have coached several individuals from different families; acted as a mentor to some, and evolved strategies and ways forward to overcome business challenges, family emotions, succession and wealth distribution issues.

APPROPRIATELY MANAGING MULTIPLE BOUNDARIES WITH ALL THE COMPETING AGENDAS AS THE INDEPENDENT MENTOR AND COACH

The coach first needs to build trust with the main stakeholders. These people, both independently and collectively, have run their businesses for a long time. So the coach must have good business acumen, otherwise they will not be very accepting of the coach.

The four most important skills which the coach needs in various strengths and combinations are:

- Business acumen,
- Listening skills,
- A deep understanding of people, and
- Tact to handle conflicts.

This coaching 'cluster' of skills is typically put to the test when there is a need to build consensus. Sometimes this requires talking separately to individuals and opening lines of communication which may be closed. You have to resolve issues without leaving bad feelings, both because the family is still together and because bad feelings and resentment can easily be multiplied through alternative lines of communication. External professionals, regardless of their attitude to their contemporaries, go back to their own families after work. They are able to get distance. Family owned businesses do not have such distinctions. Family relations and emotions are constant. A bigger factor in the running of the business.

Through mentoring, I provide an independent view to the family that should always be perceived as unbiased, unemotional and an honest arbitration.

This is important because normally what happens, as you get deeply involved into the family and their business operations, there will also be a lot of lobbying by individuals to convince you of their point of view. While you listen to all points of view, it's important to remain neutral. To be someone who is constantly looking at the family interest rather than just the interest of the individual. What I tell them is this, "*I am here to look at your family interest overall so that everyone benefits, and if some individual interest is not taken care of, you have to bear with me, in the interest of promoting and building value for both the family and the business.*"

Doing all this is emotionally quite exhausting as the mentor and coach. It involves tact, sometimes saying unpalatable truths, breaking deadlocks, yet moving forward and still retaining trust.

THE TRUST EQUATION: BUILDING AND RETAINING TRUST

The trust equation is basically made up of two things which I believe clients are looking for,

1. Building trust, and

2. Bringing something to the table, some extra business acumen or perhaps looking at it in a different way, which they had not looked at before.

To achieve this, you first of all need to be very patient. You must understand where they are coming from, but you should also be able to give your opinion, sometimes fearlessly and at some risk. You need to be perceived as a person who, while listening to different views, will not be easily influenced or pressurised by both the situation and the individual who is sitting in front of you.

If you question any assumptions that may be perceived by the receiver as being threatening then it could potentially result in a breakdown in the relationship. If you question them in a non-threatening way however, there tends to be an improvement in the relationship.

Sometimes it is also better to directly ask the family, "*Please tell me if there are any 'no go' areas so that I do not ride into these.*" Of course, such 'no go areas' should not conflict with the coach's ethics. If they do, you would need to disengage. This has not happened to me.

PART 2: Cutting edge: Investigating patterns from Practitioner Experiences

I also tell the family patriarch upfront, "*I will give you my point of view. Sometimes it will be in conflict with yours. You, however, know your business and family far better than me. If you don't accept my suggestion I won't feel bad.*" This reduces pressure on both sides to not be too diplomatic and discussions are more forthright. Surprisingly I find 90 percent of my suggestions accepted anyway.

Eventually you may be treated like a family member because of the things they share with you (which they may not even share with each other).

How you manage and maintain this healthy dynamic will determine Trust, Comfort and the Benefit you bring to the table.

Bringing something to the table

Working in many diverse organizations of various sizes, the coach has to bring business acumen along with the normal mentoring and coaching skills. To take an example, there could be a difference of opinion between family members of how a business should function or the path it should take. It is your views which are sought to help resolve the issue.

In these situations you have to be resourceful, tactful but also frank. It is very important that you make the family members realize that you are a neutral participant and that your advice – based on your business experience and insight – takes into account the overall family benefit.

IN SUMMARY, MY TOP THREE COUNSEL FOR MENTORING AND COACHING FAMILY MANAGED ORGANIZATIONS

1. To be a success as a mentor to family managed business, besides normal coaching skills to work with the individual members, you need to have good business acumen that can only come if you have handled a variety of senior executive roles.

2. You also need to build trust and ensure that individual interests are subservient to the family and business interests.

3. You are 'family' and still 'not family'; independent and unemotional yet always tactful.

How coaching can contribute significantly to mediation

Jeremy Ridge

1. UNDERSTANDING MORE ABOUT HOW COACHING CAN ADD VALUE

Coaching has such a focus on the individual that it is seldom, yet explicitly, seen as something that aims at mediation. However, when the right conditions are created, such as building high levels of trust, coaching can move on to wider uses, such as mediation.

Mediation is about,

- Being in the middle between separate positions, and

- Being able to do something to build connections that may not have been there previously.

The greater depth of understanding coaching can establish with individuals can then be used to enable a better understanding of how to connect positions between different individuals.

Mediation can cover a very wide range of circumstances. However, there are a number of established ways where I find in practice that coaching is often involved in work with people in organisations, that can then lead on to important mediation.

I think it is important to continue to grow the way that effective coaching can contribute to people. This can be in ways that are wider than just a separate set of meetings with just one individual[1].

---

[1] Ridge, J. 2015. Freeiing up our use of coaching! *the good coach. https://the-goodcoach.com/tgcblog/2015/6/25/freeing-up-our-use-of-coaching-contrasting-the-simple-model.html* Accessed September 10.

2. HOW USING COACHING AS AN IMPORTANT PART OF EFFECTIVE MEDIATION IS A NATURAL DEVELOPMENT IN MY PRACTICE

I have found that researching and developing my own coaching practice has driven my understanding of how coaching can deliver across different contexts more broadly. A good example of this is its potential for delivering what can be very powerful mediation.

The understanding, and trust, that a coaching approach can achieve often leads to the coach being able to contribute significantly to enabling individuals to come closer together.

Intervening in the form of mediation can bring important challenges – for example, in the way personal and confidential information arises from the coaching approach., may need to be initiated between the people involved.

This is true even though there are other terms that can seem to mean the same thing: diplomacy, facilitation, negotiation, being an honest broker and even organisation development. **It is the particular power of coaching at its best that makes a particular difference and adds the real momentum to effective mediation.**

However, it is not immediately obvious that these two terms are always well linked. So this is a chance to consider how these links work, in practice, and how they may be more clearly linked.

What I share below is how I've perceived coaching moves from focusing on an individual all the way through to applying a coaching approach/style across an organisation in the context of mediation.

2.1. STARTING FROM A COACHING FOCUS ON THE ONE INDIVIDUAL

The simple, or more currently normal, approach to a coaching contract is where an organisation nominates individuals for coaching as a quite detached and separate exercise.

- The coach never actually meets anyone in the organisation apart from the coachee.
- The immediate boss, and even someone from HR, as stakeholders in that individual's role may be involved directly with the coach and contribute to the agenda for the coaching.

Immediately, coaches will want to ensure that conditions of confidentiality are also clearly set up for the work with the individual concerned.

Likewise, it is important that the individual concerned takes primary responsibility to progress any wider agenda than for a coach to be involved.

However, it is increasingly the pattern where these other stakeholders can also want to have some involvement in the process,

- either with having their own coaching activities, or
- just some informal involvement about how it is going.

Obviously, any involvement needs to be similarly carefully contracted[2].

This also then starts the opportunity for encouraging where functioning between parties concerned to be bettered.

It may be directly part of the agenda even.

This starts to open the potential for ensuring relevant information is clarified and shared between parties. The coach can play an important part in this, either indirectly, or directly as mediation.

2.2. COACHING BASED MEDIATION DURING A 360 INTERVENTION

Another well used method of practice is to use a '360' project.

In broad terms, this is an exercise in gaining feedback from a wide range of the stakeholders to a person's role. This includes people who report in to the person concerned, not just who they report to, and all other colleagues they may need to work with in a less direct reporting relationship.

There are many methods by which the data of a 360 feedback is produced.

There are quantitative – psychometric – models that ask for feedback in terms of an established underlying model for the behaviours and role capabilities typically involved for executives. This can open up the agenda into some previously less articulated areas important to any role. For example,

- A simple quantitative approach is a classic case where the data can just be presented, and left with some general principles of interpretation, or where a more coaching based mediation approach adds much more value.

There is also a more qualitative approach – where stakeholders are interviewed in relation to their observations. These comments are often more closely related to real circumstances; but they are also raised in the language and meanings of the provider, and may be more difficult to understand.

- It involves getting to know the separate parties involved, so as to be able to translate some of the meaning for the other party, which may also lead to a need to have more extensive dialogue between

---

[2] See Flanders, Ian. 2016. "Dispatch From The Internal Coaching Front." *the good coach.* http://the-goodcoach.com/tgcblog/2016/9/21/dispatch-from-the-internal-coaching-front-by-ian-flanders-guest Accessed September 10.

      the parties involved – clarifying expectations, separate from the feedback for example.

I find it is important to include the qualitative option. This frees up the expression of important data. Yet this also requires important work in translating and clarifying what the comments may refer to in the way it is fed back. This then starts the more direct process of mediation.

2.3. GROUP/PEER/TEAM COACHING

This context is often the most direct opportunity for mediation.

Teamwork can be intensive. It can unravel events, making some form of mediation intervention on the basis of the understanding gained from separate coaching dialogues, can also be a challenge in the seconds available.

A good quote about team coaching is reported as,

> *"This can be like working with eight coaching relationships at once.[3]"*

The coach may well be in the same room at the same time with the other eight people when it becomes clear that something has happened that has raised an 'opportunity' for two (or more) of those involved to have a conversation around how some events during the team activity have happened.

This is where a coaching based approach can be brought to bear. It would use the intimate understanding of where the parties involved are coming from (which is often not easily apparent) in order to close the gap that may exist, and enable a constructive understanding between those involved.

This becomes a real challenge for the way contracting has to be achieved and maintained.

- The challenge for the coach in this situation must also avoid breaking any expectation of confidentiality previously established with either party.
- Others will be also watching closely, with regard to their own personal and confidential dialogues with you as the coach as well.
- This is where coaching skills are really tested!

Many coaches understandably prefer to remain in a one-to-one context – only having this intimacy/coaching with one member of the team. They may even make sure they only meet the team member 'outside' of any normal organisational events.

However, I meet increasing numbers of other people in the coaching field who inevitably find they are successfully extending coaching this way.

---

[3] Hicks, Ben. 2010. "Team Coaching: A Literature Review." http://www.employment-studies.co.uk/system/files/resources/files/mp88.pdf Accessed September 10

    PART 2: Cutting edge: Investigating patterns from Practitioner Experiences

2.4. OTHER MORE STRUCTURED FORMS OF LEARNING/TRAINING STYLE INTERVENTIONS

Quite typically, opportunities here may result from initiatives which are not directly labelled as either coaching or mediation. For example, being asked to operate broad leadership development programmes for sets of people from across the organisation.

Other forms of programmes can be also useful, such as principles of effective teamwork or using frameworks around individual differences from psychology (and other psychometrics.) This is often an excellent basis for introducing a great deal of insight into simple gaps that can exist in enabling connection between people (mediation).

It may introduce the theory, along with practical exercises, but then also extend to becoming a more workshop-like style part of the programme involving groups of people conversing about real issues, and not just training examples and issues.

This workshop, as a more open approach, may also directly involve leadership in the organisation that involves the formal leadership, and/or other levels of it elsewhere in the organisation. The opportunities for mediation become much more evident when present in conversations between different people in the organisation.

2.5. LONGER TERM, MORE VARIED AND ORGANISATION WIDE COACHING STYLE INTERVENTIONS

I have found in practice that a programme that may start from small beginnings can also lead to much wider scale activities that involve a wide range of different forms of assistance.

For example, a more structured programme, on principles of teamwork, or leadership, naturally moves to invitations to helping on the practical follow up with individuals on the application of the theory.

It is increasingly normal that attention to the individual, rather than the presentation of the theory, by itself, is a part of such programmes. This is a natural foundation for a coaching approach that can lead on to working on the activities between individuals in various parts of the organisation, i.e. mediation.

This can also be a form of work that is not just one off, but more a continuing relationship with the organisation over years. Once the important conditions of trust have been established, an organisation can be very keen to retain the contribution over time.

3. THE SAFEST PLATFORM FOR HOW COACHING CAN CONTRIBUTE TO MEDIATION – KNOWLEDGE ABOUT THE STUDY OF INDIVIDUAL DIFFERENCES

Mediation between people working together takes place quite naturally and spontaneously in many cases in organisations – where considerable skill is used by many without them ever considering the skills involved as something special. It is often done in a passing moment of conversation, rather than as a formal process.

I have also found in practice that opportunities for mediation are often more informally contracted than formally. As a natural extension, mediation grows out of creating the foundations of what is involved in coaching.

- Mediation only becomes relevant when there is a level of trust established.

- Mediation is a very private matter between those involved.

- Mediation is normally highly informal.

- Mediation is opportunistic rather than planned.

- What is involved as an output in mediation can often be difficult to prove – except to those directly involved.

Trust[4] requires a particular and demanding set of conditions to be in place. It can be difficult to establish; but also the easiest thing to lose.

However, there is the opportunity to establish a degree of tolerance – especially where it is not necessary critical. People always appreciate the difficulties involved in this.

Overall, I find the safest platform is through a focus on individual differences

There are a range of methods available to enable people to identify patterns in people's behaviour. Likewise, there are many frameworks that enable people to consider they may need to appreciate the invisible strengths, and styles, of others i.e. people 'not like them' whom they just don't understand.[5]

As with all these models it is important to not impose the framework, but rather enable people to use them as a means of establishing the framework their experience can form for them. For example:

- An extreme extrovert may have difficulty with an extreme introvert. There are patterns of behaviour that either may prefer that don't easily

---

[4] Ridge, Jeremy. 2016. "Getting Trust is the Essential Outcome Which Makes Coaching Possibility – And Different." *the good coach*. http://the-goodcoach.com/tgcblog/2016/10/3/getting-trust-is-the-essential-outcome-that-makes-coaching-possible-and-different Accessed September 10.
[5] Introduction to Individual Differences. 2001. "Introduction to Individual Differences." http://wilderdom.com/personality/L1-1Introduction.html Accessed September 10.

connect. Translating these technical ideas into practical terms for those involved is a basic principle for how mediation can be applied.

4. LOOKING AT MEDIATION PRACTICE AS IT IS REPORTED CURRENTLY

Mediation is still more often presented as a process most closely used with a need that is a negative crisis, a dispute, and not an opportunity. A lot of the methods of attention toward a person are aligned with a problem. Coaching might struggle to avoid being seen as a remedial treatment only.

Hence, my definition of mediation is more akin to how the word itself originates from the idea of – middle from late Latin mediatus - placed in the middle,

> *"Intervene in (a dispute) to bring about an agreement[6]"*

4.1 WHERE THE CURRENT LEADING EDGE OF THINKING ABOUT MEDIATION IN PRACTICE

Mediation, as with coaching, is:

- Becoming established as a quite distinct and separate activity by itself.

- More often approached primarily as a form of remedial intervention, where there is a crisis because of a breakdown in understanding between parties, and there are potentially important risks and negative consequences involved.

Some useful perspective on current mediation practice is provided by looking at the current positions of various mediation practice communities.

Even sampling some of the communities that are growing their presence, such as in the UK – The Professional Mediators Association[7] (PMA).

The PMA describes themselves as the fastest growing mediation and ADR (alternative dispute resolution) association in the world based in the UK. Their approach is strongly based on the importance of understanding the important technical issue that may be involved in any context. This is equally important in coaching, as well, of course, but often gets less emphasis in current teachings on coaching. On their web site they provide a wide ranging overview of the sorts of knowledge and processes that can be involved in mediation.

There is an important emphasis on how particular circumstances can strongly influence the way the process works.

---

[6] English Oxford Living Dictionary. 2017. https://en.oxforddictionaries.com/definition/mediate Accessed September 10.
[7] PMA. 2017. "Welcome to the Professional Mediators' Association." http://www.professionalmediator.org Accessed September 10.

The emphasis is very much on a transparent and rigorous process of collecting and sharing information, as well as the important matter of attention paid to the element of discussion between those involved as the means for achieving a final agreement between the parties.

High ethical standards (e.g. impartiality) must be established and maintained to ensure the quality of the intervention is maintained

And in the USA, for example, The American Institute of Mediation[8].

In the USA, a more ambitious account is attempted in regard to what mediation involves – especially at the level of interaction with the individuals concerned. They appear to seek understanding of the individuals/parties involved at a deeper level to be more important.

While, again, emphasising the importance of careful process and ethical standards, The American Institute of Mediation also gives indications of further next steps needed, which again emphasises the importance of building their coaching approach. For example, responses mediators in recent training events have given about what they wished they had been taught bring further emphasis on the use of coaching skills as a means of facilitating the quality of the process.

4.2. MEDIATION ALSO SEEMS TO BE GROWING OUT OF PRACTICE - AS IN COACHING

The material from these two examples of growing communities of practice in mediation is important. Mediation is growing from a need that can be met from learning through carefully developed experience, rather than a grand theory based on academic research.

The emphasis on knowledge about the context is important, as well as the understanding of the people involved. There remain similar patterns in the way coaching is still developing.

5. CONCLUSIONS AND FURTHER DEVELOPMENT

1. It has been useful as an exercise to research the connections between coaching and mediation. There are important parallels between coaching and mediation. This means that coaching can be a key part of mediation more explicitly. It is also important to appreciate the wider scope for how a coaching approach can be used.

2. There seems to be scope for making stronger connections between the two fields, of coaching and mediation, although there is little evidence of this being reported at present.

---

[8] Cloke, Kenneth. 2017. "American Institute of Mediation."
http://www.americaninstituteofmediation.com/pg77.cfm Accessed September 10.

3. The use of coaching in the context of organisations, where people are naturally keen to work together more effectively, is an important opportunity where this connection could be better considered.

4. Other practitioners in coaching have also often told me of their work in a manner that is also consistent with extending coaching further. It would be good to encourage more reporting of similar experience and practice.

5. Both coaching and mediation have further progress to make. It could be valuable to see how one might further stimulate development in the other, and vice versa.

For example, mediation requires a high standard of relationship behaviour for it to work. Use in mediation could be an important standard for coaching to set as a standard practice. This would ensure that coaching was operating at its best.

Question: Do you find, in practice, you become involved in what might be called mediation?

Making sense of how we define a coaching approach from each of our professional experiences (Part 1)

Doug Montgomery and Laurent Terseur

We are both passionate about how leaders can change the nature of the conversations within their organisations by using a coaching style to increase engagement and performance. Through our conversations together we realised how each of our individual experiences have influenced and shaped how we perceive a coaching approach and coaching ingredients make a difference when used by leaders. We are still working towards a shared definition of how a coaching approach can best be applied, and realise much work would be required to create and build consensus amongst all practitioners. This is because of all the different experiences and skills integral to this approach.

There's still much to do in our field of coaching. As our way of sharing the learning and congruencies we've developed so far, we've put together a three-part series that provides our respective perspectives of building a common ground with all its nuances and complexities of where both the edges and similarities may exist and overlap. The three themes we began to cover include:

- Our professional experience and journey to adopting a coaching leadership style
- What changes when leaders adopt a coaching style
- How a leadership style can be developed systematically in organisations

OUR INDIVIDUAL JOURNEYS INTO COACHING

Doug Montgomery's story: The value of applying a coaching approach to collectively deliver results for projects and foster individual empowerment and development took a while to develop

My working definition and description

For me a coaching approach is the capability to invite the other person to solve their own problems. I think it starts with trust, empowerment and engagement. It begins with asking pertinent questions and properly listening to the responses. It also involves having a mindset that you actually trust the coachee can solve their problems, rather than telling the coachee what should be done. I think it's important to know what is wanted from the conversation.

A coaching approach is not the same as a formal coaching session, in the sense that a leader taking a coaching approach uses a coaching style as part of their day-to-day conversations with their staff and colleagues. It is not their only style. It is not the best or appropriate style for all conversations. However, it is a style that listens to what the other person has to say and encourages them to think for themselves most effectively.

The starting point for any style of conversation is knowing or finding out what is wanted from the conversation. Those situations where creativity is required, a plan needs to be formulated, or someone is stuck in their thinking, are all examples of opportunities for a coaching approach.

How often have you heard (or taken part in) a conversation, in which the leader explains the goal and its importance, and goes on to tell the individual or team what they will do, step by step, to get there?

The 'How' part opens the way for a coaching approach, with its opportunity to really engage the individual or team by asking them for how they can get there. By me encouraging and trusting their plans and solution, their way of doing it, they become engaged with the problem. They're much more likely to commit to whatever the action is they come up with.

I believe that adopting a coaching approach is a major contributor for managers and leaders to truly engage their staff and to release more of their organisation's potential and free up their own time. That is what a coaching approach is for me, compared to other leadership approaches such as telling, teaching or advising; each of which are useful and necessary, but not sufficient.

My journey to coaching started from organisational leadership

I worked in the pharmaceutical industry for many years. I remember as a young and relatively inexperienced line manager struggling to get the best from myself and from my people. I found myself believing that to deliver results, I needed to know how to do everything. I thought my role was to tell others what to do and how to do it. It felt really important to be seen to know everything. It seemed to be how I would be judged by others. And boy did it make me work long hard hours and make my life challenging and stressful!

I guess I saw leaders as heroic all-knowing figures leading people forward with great confidence. However, I ended up working too hard, making all the decisions and essentially doing everybody else's thinking for them. I wanted them to do it my way because that way I felt in control. I was frightened of getting things wrong, yet unable to stop telling others what to do, even when I was not sure myself. Asking for help seemed like a sign of failure. With the benefit of hindsight, what utter madness that was!

Slowly I learnt to delegate. To ask for help. I learnt how to harness other people's expertise and thinking. In fact, I became so good at using other people's expertise to solve problems that I often ended up leading teams and projects in areas with which I was not familiar. That's when I become involved in the internal coaching program and trained to be an internal coach. That was my first step towards becoming the executive coach, coach supervisor and coach trainer I am today.

My insights from delivering coaching to leaders and managers

As a coach I've also been lucky enough to facilitate workshops for leaders wanting to take a coaching approach into their day-to-day working conversations. For me this has distilled the value of this coaching approach for leaders and their people.

Having met lots of leaders, managers, supervisors and individual contributors during these workshops I now know that the 'telling' and 'advising' style of leadership is pretty much a default setting for most of us. There's a lot of wasted effort going on – leaders taking all the responsibility for the thinking away from the team members.

Let me share an example:

A quality assurance auditor, who came on a coaching approach workshop I ran, shared his experience with me. His job is to audit parts of the business and write reports about failures to comply with standards, protocols.

He contacted me a little while after the course and declared, "*It was amazing. We used to go and deliver an audit report and tell people this is what you need to fix, and it would be a battle and we were not welcome, and it was a horrible job. Since learning how to use this approach, I've delivered the outcomes of the audits and then we sit down and ask... "So what can you do about it?" Just that change of approach from - you must do this - to - here's what you need to achieve and what are your options for achieving that compliance? How can I support you to make sure that you're getting to the right place – is a completely different conversation.*" His approach to his job and his appreciation of his job had changed dramatically.

Another aspect that I learnt through these workshops is that leadership and management are seen primarily as delivering results and that developing people is often seen as a luxury or ignored altogether.

organisations seem to create the impression in the minds of leaders and managers that there's just not enough time for developing people. Typically sending people on a course is seen as development – despite there being no time to embed whatever learning is gained. I am sure that organisations don't do this deliberately, but somehow the message gets distorted in the objective setting and reward systems.

Taking a coaching approach appropriately into the day-to-day conversations actually delivers results while developing people. It's a win-win: it frees up the leader's or manager's time because so much of the thinking and decision making is done by their team members. This allows leaders and managers to get on with their own unique contribution and for the team to get on with theirs.

In a business or work situation, where it's the manager or the leader taking the coaching approach, there is an agenda about what needs to be delivered. Part of that role is to set clear objectives. Yet, I think there also needs to be an agenda about developing people. I want to see how the other person thinks and to develop their thinking skills. I want to get their potential out into the work of the business. It's about a mindset of trusting the people that you're using this approach with. It's about a way of eliciting from them what they can do, rather than the manager telling them what to do and how to do it. So it saves time in the long run. It engages the team and provides, I think, a sure route for empowerment.

LAURENT TERSEUR'S STORY: COACHING INGREDIENTS NECESSARY FOR A COACHING APPROACH TO BE EFFECTIVELY APPLIED IN VARIOUS ORGANISATIONAL SITUATIONS

My working definition and description

I think of a coaching approach as being in service to the other person(s) by stimulating their thinking in a different way than if they were on their own. A coach encourages and challenges the other person(s) to use the resulting insights and take actions that will bring the change they desire.

In a large number of management situations, I believe roles and agendas may make it difficult to apply a full coaching approach. So when it comes to a leadership situation within an organisation, I would rather use the concept of coaching ingredients and break down the coaching approach into its individual components and use each to enhance the traditional leadership recipe by demonstrating a supportive and empowering intention.

For instance, within organisations you generally do not get to choose your manager as you would have free choice in choosing your coach. Yet, coaching someone requires the permission from that person to be coached. I would see this permission as the first ingredient to any coaching approach and an essential condition to make sure any further conversation will be in a safe environment. In practical terms, it starts by securing first the mandate or the permission for such a conversation. It might not always be intuitive for a manager to ask for the *permission* from their report, but there are different ways to bring the degree of empowerment and autonomy that will set a level of coaching that can be used as opposed to more prescriptive conversation modes.

The next ingredient is about giving *predictability and structure*. It's about setting the framework for the conversation, starting by how much time is available and when it's going to happen. Let me share the practical example of a manager asking someone to come in their office. In some instances, it can be perceived as quite a threat to be asked in the manager's office out of the blue. Whereas in the same conditions, if what the discussion will be about and what's going to happen during the discussion is mentioned first, it paves the way for a much more open and constructive conversation.

Another ingredient I see is *showing appreciation*; using encouragements and accentuating the positives. For example, we often see how feedback conversations can be very deflating, whereas with the encouraging coaching ingredient in mind, the picture can be changed by pointing at what's been done well. With their positive contribution being fairly acknowledged, the recipient can open up and be more receptive to the rest of the feedback, as they feel considered.

An additional ingredient is *adding the dimension of stretch* where something new or different will provide a learning or a growth opportunity. What exact level of stretch will be relevant will need to be appreciated from the situation and the context. To be constitutive of a coaching approach, the stretch will still need to be in line with the permission or mandate secured, or will require a new permission.

As mentioned earlier, not all management situations allow for the presence of these coaching ingredients, let alone all of them at the same time. This is why I am cautious with the coaching approach as a whole and in a managerial context.

Having a coaching mindset though, is the next level. There needs to exist trust and respect. I can think of people who are genuinely open to change however they might be imposing change. Perhaps they forget that people around them might not be just as open to change as themselves. It's being mindful of the 'how' that creates the conditions for the change, as well as the ability to foster engagement by building the relevant bridges between competing agendas.

Using coaching ingredients to make change happen will actually bring forward the agenda of the people you coach in the equation, in a relevant way.

My journey to coaching started from personal leadership

I spent over two decades leading teams in highly competitive, international and multicultural, matrix environments. All the way through this career, it has always been deeply important to me to demonstrate that strong performance could be delivered through positive values and collaborative behaviours. This concern initially was intuitive and somewhat unconscious. I became ever increasingly aware of it over the years, investing more time in reflecting on it and experimenting different ways to deliver on it.

I also had the luck to have two distinct and very different experiences in receiving coaching during my career. For my first experience I was imposed a coach I did not chose, in conditions that didn't make me feel safe. As a coach now, I cherish this experience as it gave me the opportunity to experience first-hand how intrusive and unproductive it can feel when ethical fundamentals are not met. For my second experience I enjoyed a wonderful opportunity of development with a coach who earned my trust and provided me with a safe environment in which a high degree of stimulation and challenge made me truly grow. I reflected on my leadership style and on how I could make it more inspiring.

When I became a member of a senior leadership team implementing considerable amounts of change, I dedicated more coaching time to the individuals and teams involved. I then decided to formally train as a coach in order to become both a better leader and to start building my own practice. Investing in my own development resulted at one point in being a senior leader, an external coach, and an internal coach, all at the same time and with all facets of this experience nurturing each other.

Those were great years. They made me passionate about working on the best ways for leaders to inspire and deliver stronger performance by bringing more coaching ingredients to their leadership style and their organisation's culture.

My insights from delivering coaching to leaders and managers

Let me share an example: During my career as a leader, I changed my approach to performance conversations. Appraisal cycles in the organisations I was working for were generally well defined, with clear frameworks and agendas, but eventually I reflected on how I was using this time with my reports and benchmarked it against what I was doing in my young coaching practice.

I found that for these formal conversations to have greater impact on my report's performance and development, I might achieve more by increasing the level of attention paid to their agenda.

To manage that, I brought in three ingredients.

- **Providing some structure and visibility** - I wanted to change the nature of that conversation, introduce permissions and make sure to give my reports the opportunity to work as partners on owning the agenda and defining what a successful conversation would look like.

- **Asking more and telling less** - In the past I would generally speak first. Part of the new structure I offered was to ask them to speak first and share their thoughts on their performance. I would then, where appropriate, reinforce or add my observations - only if needed.

- **Accentuating the positive** - Offering to start first on what they had done well and showing appreciation, then moving on to what they would do differently and providing encouragement.

Taking this approach completely changed the nature of this type of conversation. The biggest impact was that it led to much more open conversations, and so much more in-depth understanding of their expectations and motivation drivers.

The development part of the conversation dramatically changed, as they were much more engaged, enactors of their development and no longer just at the receiving end of the manager's thoughts. And this turned into deeper, more specific and much more motivating insights about how to increase their performance and their future.

OUR REFLECTIONS AND LEARNINGS

In many ways the role of executive coach is freer than that of the leaders and managers that we coach. Both of us are experienced leaders and managers. We have independently learned the value of a coaching approach and the use of coaching ingredients as part of our leadership style. What is emerging from our discussion of how this arose is the realisation that it is important to be able to adopt a variety of styles (teaching, telling, advising, guiding or coaching) and to be aware of what we as leaders are trying to achieve.

That gives us the choice about which style to choose.

The choice depends on the organisational context, the situation, the relationship with and the stage of development of the individual we are working with. When choosing to use the coaching ingredients or a coaching approach our intention is to encourage the other to think for themselves, to engage with the conversation whether it is to problem solve, to receive feedback, to self-assess, or to plan a project or a personal development path. As leaders, we are trusting the other person's ability, expertise and creativity. From this style of leadership, we start to see what they are really capable of, not just that they can follow our instructions. Creating the conditions in which this style is effective is key. It requires both inner awareness and creation of the appropriate environment.

For managers and leaders who are used to taking a predominant directive or command and control style, the coaching ingredients and approach may feel strange as they require one to let go of control. The coach must actually ask others to solve their problems and to do their own thinking. It may feel threatening or even an abdication of hard earned authority and expertise, however, in today's changing complex uncertain commercial world, there are few managers and leaders who have all the answers and experience. Nor do they have the time to do all the thinking. Can leaders afford not to take a more coaching approach into their day-to-day conversations and engage and empower their people? Our experience leads us to believe that the coaching ingredients and coaching approach we have described here are essential leadership skills.

Building companies' sustainability stories:
A role for coaching

Geoffrey Ahern

Mobilising the company's stakeholders on behalf of full sustainability entails the development of their stories about the Anthropocene. The Anthropocene is our era in which we humans have an increasingly significant influence on the Earth.

This article/blog outlines the most common Anthropocene stakeholder stories I am aware of. They vary greatly and can aid or hinder sustainability. I have encountered each one in stakeholder contexts, mostly amongst senior employees. There is a large background literature (for a start, see the references). As I shall describe in the section that follows, these stories are rarely 'pure' but get mixed up. I aim to demonstrate that employees, customers, suppliers and other stakeholders are already acting them out.

In sharing my approach on how to recognise and develop them, I hope that the development of Anthropocene stories can be added to coaching's unique expertise in helping clients build their visions. As coaches at different levels – individual and team – we already do development work by interpreting what's going on through our blends of person-centred, cognitive-behavioural, psychodynamic, existential and other approaches. Anthropocene stories add to these a focus on sustainability.

Development of the stories – the single quotes in the bullets below – seems to me to fall into three groups:

- Relating future 'doom' and 'utopia' – i.e. apocalyptic dreads and hopes – to reason in the present. The challenge is to channel apocalyptic energies constructively now.

- Adding to 'back-to-nature' stories so they can meet organisational realities. The challenge is how glimpses of paradise at the heart of stakeholder back-to-nature personal behaviour and feeling can complement organisational complexities.

- Integrating 'geological fatalism', 'the technological fix' and 'ecology as a development of consciousness' into a good (i.e. sustainable) Anthropocene. This is a challenge: the insight these mindsets bring tends to be isolated.

Multinational and other companies can develop their global operations through the surfacing of their stakeholders' sustainability stories, if only through understanding better how their location varies. For example, research demonstrates that the idea of an apocalypse is deeply embedded in Western but not Asian culture.

This article/blog on companies achieving conscious sustainability competence completes the previous one in *the good coach* (July 19) on getting to conscious incompetence (itself a considerable achievement). My earlier blogs introduced this invited series (January 11) and went on to environmental science's ethical consequences for coaching (March 20) and individual freedom's exclusion from ecology (May 17).

STAKEHOLDER STORIES ABOUT ENVIRONMENTAL SCIENCE

Doing fieldwork as a sociologist of religion (before I became an executive coach), I became very aware of how diffused our individual stories about the world are in practice; my or your take on life is not likely to be conceptually tidy. Worldview influence at the level of the individual is often weakly signalled, latent and overlapping. Frequently occurring diffuseness can combine into powerful patterns at a cultural level (hence the notion of 'ideal-types'), not least when cultural railways carrying ancient stories merge with recent findings from environmental science.

It seems to me that probabilistic environmental science, once downstream of peer-review rigour, usually ceases to be science and becomes story. Thus the scientific accuracy which is necessary for us to secure the future tends to get lost.

I tend to use the term 'story' because it is imaginatively human. 'Mythology' as the word is used now – for originally 'mythos' meant 'story' – might more exactly describe those stories which are deeply embedded, though not 'myth' in the sense of necessarily untrue. I avoid 'narrative' because it has become today's public relations (PR) buzzword, and 'sense-making' because it can belittle rather than respect clients.

Much corporate PR banks on environmental science are being interpreted as unscientific story. If, in contrast, companies embraced the Anthropocene, they could become a positive force for conscious sustainability competence. They already have many techniques in place for stakeholder networking and industry level collaboration.

The story themes follow. Diagnosing the implicit stories…

RELATING FUTURE DOOM AND UTOPIA TO REASON IN THE PRESENT

We should be careful about what we imagine.

Apocalypse has been defined as revelation in which there's a single, final consummation in which the elect will live as a unanimous collectivity on a transformed and purified earth, while the human agents of evil will be physically annihilated or otherwise disposed of[1].

The ancient thought-form of apocalypse is making tracks today in the form of technological utopia and of environmental doom and gloom. This splitting of stories about the world into these two extreme opposites and projecting them into the future makes adverse circumstances bearable, but can too easily degenerate into avoiding taking reasonable responsibility in the present.

Environmental doom

Probabilistic scientific environmental predictions are sombre enough, but in the grip of eco-doom stakeholders add a further, mythological turn. For example, coaching clients may point to China's huge pollution and, feeling overwhelmed and helpless, enter into a 'can't do' attitude. Ironically, this would overlook China's hopeful side, its huge investment in clean technologies and a green future. For example, its panda-shaped solar farm for educating children[2]. Environmental doom collapses the 'we can do' approach we are familiar with into a stunned sense, outside usual historical agency, of inevitable geological disaster. The apocalypse has taken over.

There's a danger, going beyond the salutary need to responsibly know what to avoid environmentally, that in the minds of company stakeholders – consumers, suppliers, employees etc – the capacity to act is paralysed by life imitating the annihilating images of apocalyptic disaster movies, sci-fi, literature and art.

Ecology has been linked to doom in archetypal Western (pre-ecological) works of the imagination, for example:

- Mark Lynas' *Six Degrees* uses Dante's architecture of eternal damnation (his Inferno) as an extended illustration of global warming.

- James Lovelock's *The Revenge of Gaia* (p.146) compares human-caused climate change to the breaking of the ropes of fate in Wagner's *Ring*, the event which in the opera prepares us for the cataclysmic end of the world (*Götterdämmerung*).

---

[1]Cohn, Norman. 2001. *Cosmos, Chaos & the World to Come. The Ancient Roots of Apocalyptic Faith*: 105, 1063, 215. 2nd ed. New Haven: Yale University Press.
[2] http://shanghaiist.com/2017/07/04/panda-solar-farm.php

TECHNOLOGICAL UTOPIA

The California-based Breakthrough Institute imagines a life of abundance achieved through technology. The optimism of 'eco-modernism', going far beyond the 1980s neo-liberalism of Friedrich Hayek and Milton Friedman, envisages a utopia in which the environment will become an extension of mankind. This is through technological progress and acceleration, with the way there often being given a so-called Darwinian justification. For example, high-tech coaching clients might be in the grip of a belief that gene editing has no major eugenic problems. Elect eco-utopian assumptions about progress have taken over.

Eco-modernism even extends to a cybernetic fusion with biology which gives rise to a trans-human consciousness ('singularity'). This software-inspired hubris is supposedly wonderful. It aims to transcend death without paying an all too human existential price.

Order based on fantasy has become unrealistically split off from chaos. A narcissism indicator for this is often that realistic time-scales are replaced by magical thinking: for example, where environmental problems are forecast to be averted through the more efficient use of materials without any consideration of the speed of oncoming climate change. Or, as in the case of the cybernetic rapture of singularity, the environmental crisis may simply be ignored. Or in eco-modernist mythology, as in John's Christian *Revelation* two thousand years ago, salvation may come about through the very struggle with catastrophe[3].

THE 3000-PLUS YEAR TRACKS OF APOCALYPSE IN THE WEST

The formidableness of the apocalyptic thought-form, both doom and utopia, arises because it has been on-going in Western culture (though not Eastern) for 3000-plus years. It has gathered momentum and shaping force – in periods of great change it can be as if its imagery charismatically possesses us, dreams us:

- The long-influential *Revelation* of John at the start of Christianity foretells a new heaven, a new earth. The apocalypse then and later operates through divine intervention, but in the industrial era

[3] For the preceding on apocalypse see: Skrimshire, Stefan. 2010. *Future Ethics. Climate change and apocalyptic imagination*. London: Continuum. Hulme, M. 'Four meanings of climate change', and Buell, F. 'A short history of environmental apocalypse': 21-22, 31; Danowski, Deborah., and Eduardo De Castro. 2017. *The Ends of the World*. Translated by Nunes. Cambridge: Polity; Jonas, Hans. 1984. *The Imperative of Responsibility. In Search of an Ethics for the Technological Age*: 62-63. Chicago: University of Chicago Press; Macfarlane, Robert. 2016. "Generation Anthropocene. How humans have altered the planet forever." *The Guardian* 02.04.16; Ridley, Matt. 2015. *The Evolution of Everything. How Ideas Emerge*. New York: Harper Collins; Desrochers, Pierre. 2010. "The environmental responsibility of business is to increase its profits (by creating value within the bounds of private property rights)." In *Industrial and Corporate Change* 19 (1): 161-204; Pellizzoni, Luigi. 2011. "Governing through disorder: neoliberal environmental governance and social theory." In *Global Environmental Change* 21: 795-803; Arnaldi, S. 2012. "The end of history and the search for perfection. Conflicting teleologies of transhumanism and (neo)liberal democracy." In *Neoliberalism and Technoscience: Critical Assessments*. Edited by Luigi Pellizzoni and Marja Ylonen. Ashgate Publishing.

PART 2: Cutting edge: Investigating patterns from Practitioner Experiences

apocalyptic mythology was also brought down to earth to manifest through history itself: in Marxism as a final withering away of the state; in Nazism as the Thousand Year Reich.

- The apocalyptic thought-form was ancient even at the time of John. It became accessible through a branch of Judaism, through the influence on it of the dualist Persian Zoroastrian religion, and through the building up to these by developments in Near Eastern combat mythology[4].

LIBERATION FROM THE DYNAMICS OF APOCALYPSE

Thus apocalypse splits good and bad and projects both into the future. John's *Revelation* speaks of "things which must shortly come to pass" (King James translation), and Ray Kurzweil's singularity has a similar time-scale. The splitting of present reality and projection into the future have been explained as a reaction to stress – under the persecutory Seleucid Greek and Roman empires; or through the destabilising environmental predictions of the Anthropocene.

Liberation from apocalypse would integrate these splits and projections into the present situation. Coaches are well-placed to enable this.

Beneficial influences of the apocalypse, for example, its sophisticated sense of time, can be retained while its imaginative grip on stakeholders is loosened, making more energy available for corporate sustainability 'can-do':

- Emerson, a founder of environmentalism, himself understood that the veil of the apocalypse can be taken off in the here-and-now: indeed, 'apocalypse' originally meant uncovering.

- The transcendent ending of doom/utopia can be understood (among other interpretations) as a human drama occurring in every moment of experience.

Liberation from the apocalyptic stories of some employees and other stakeholders would enable multinational companies to connect more fully with non-apocalyptic others. As a largely Western construct, apocalypse is alien to many in China and elsewhere in Asia: it differs from reasoned focus on the present in quasi-Confucian and post-Buddhist cultures[5].

---

[4] See Cohn, Norman. 2001. cited in 1 above; Hall, John. 2009. *Apocalypse. From Antiquity to the Empire of Modernity*. Cambridge: Polity.
[5] Hodder, A. 1989. *Emerson's Rhetoric of Revelation. Nature, the Reader and the Apocalypse Within*: 24.33.71. London: Pennsylvania University Press; Skrimshire, Stefan. (2010), "Eternal return of apocalypse". In *Future Ethics. Climate change and apocalyptic imagination*: 223. London: Continuum: Boyce, Mary. 1979. *Zoroastrians. Their Religious Beliefs and Practices*: 84. London: Routledge and Kegan Paul.

PART 2: Cutting edge: Investigating patterns from Practitioner Experiences

ADDING TO 'BACK-TO-NATURE' STORIES SO THEY CAN MEET ORGANISATIONAL REALITIES

Many stakeholders, including coaching clients, are personally motivated to go back to nature: for example through hiking, white water rafting, keeping pets, gardening, yoga. Back-to-nature stories have become clichés in advertising: for example, linking the precision of new cars to mountain roads through rugged landscapes or using images of baby-eyed mammals like seals (not flies!). In urban conditions there are back-to-nature yearnings.

Companies will need to expose stakeholder back-to-nature energies to practicalities in order to harness them to sustainability innovation. Critically important issues include:

- Responsible restraint of innovation, i.e. the 'precautionary principle', needing to consider the risks of not going ahead as well as those of doing so (for example, nuclear power in relation to global warming).

- There not being enough Earth for organic farming alone to feed the vast human population.

- Restoration of wilderness having no easily identifiable point in time.

The genie of technology being already largely out of the bottle, mankind's future might depend on new corporate ground-rules for when the stopper should be pulled out no further, or even to put the genie back. This could involve a reformed capitalism with processes for agreeing slow down, acceleration, sufficiency or even re-enchantment.

A more sophisticated back-to-nature seemingly appeals to some coaches and people developers. For example, in calling for a metamorphosis supported by ground-breaking scientific discoveries as well as by tapping into ancient wisdom cultures[6]. Back-to-nature's pantheism and mysticism – such as Spinozian and Goethean science from the West, non-dualist Vedanta and Jainism from the East – need to deploy sufficient differentiation to be capable of influencing companies and politics. Otherwise the unity of everything can justify anything, as with the Charles Manson murders.

The hold of the back-to-nature story is partly explicable by its shaping in the era of early industrialisation. The Romantics recast Eden: Jean-Jacques Rousseau imagined his noble savage, and against the backdrop of new, grimy factories nature became sublime[7].

---

[6] Hutchins, Giles. 2015. "The next stage of organizational evolution." *Triple Pundit*. www.triplepundit.com/2015/05next-stage-organizational-evolution. (Broken link) Wednesday May 20th.
[7] Kumar, Satish. 2013. *Soil, Soul, Society. A New Trinity for Our Time*. Lewes: Leaping Hare Press; Armand, Jean-Louis. 2012. "The bringing together of technology, sustainability and ethics." In *Sustainability Science* 7 (2): 113-116; Pellizzoni, L. and M. Ylonen. 2008. "Responsibility in uncertain times: an institutional perspective on precaution." In *Global Environmental Politics* 8 (3): 51-73; Attia, Peter. 2013. "Mega-sized concerns from the nano-sized world: The intersection of nano- and environmental ethics', In *Science & Engineering Ethics* 19: 1007-1016.

INTEGRATING 'GEOLOGICAL FATALISM', 'THE TECHNOLOGICAL FIX' AND 'ECOLOGY AS A DEVELOPMENT OF CONSCIOUSNESS' INTO A SUSTAINABLE ANTHROPOCENE

I suggest below that further insightful stakeholder stories, which I shall outline, could be taken out of their isolation and integrated into the big picture of a good (I.e. sustainable) Anthropocene:

GEOLOGICAL FATALISM

In Werner Herzog's (2007) Antarctica documentary *Encounters at the Edge of the World*, participants explain the current dominance of mankind as just another evolutionary bloom in which ecological mishap is to be expected. The Earth will survive, humans are insignificant; in the light of the Earth sciences, to understand this is merely to discover what has been there all along.

Such a 'geological fatalism' fails to make sufficient connection between human causation of the Anthropocene and human responsibility. No difference is perceived between human-caused extinctions today and natural processes in earlier extinctions. Educated, maybe poetically expressed, doom is somehow thought to get one off the hook of having to act. Geological fatalist employees are often clients of coaching.

Geological fatalism's Sadean vision of the cruelty of nature contrasts with back-to-nature's tendency to rosy sentiment. If they are related to each other there's potential for a more satisfying vision.

The technological fix

Reliance on technological fixes to solve environmental problems need not be utopian. It is often pragmatic, a one-dimensional decoupling of human development from natural resource use through intensifying farming, forestry, house-building, solar and wind energy storage, planning for asteroid mining etc. Sadly, clients motivated by technological fix stories often do not see that sustainability solutions also involve morally considerable subjects with whole life engagement[8].

Ecology as a development of consciousness

A development of consciousness approach involving ecological agency, or responsibility transcending biological determinism, is a strand in much environmental thinking. Examples: the emergence of the shamanic personality through the development of consciousness; 'ecosophy', that is a personal worldview guiding decisions involving oneself and nature; eco-therapy; the earth awakening[9].

---

[8] Matthews, Freya. 2011. "Towards a deeper philosophy of biomimicry." In *Organisation & Environment* 24 (4): 364-387.
[9] Berry, Thomas. 1988. *The Dream of the Earth*. San Francisco: Sierra Club Books; Naess, Arne. 1989. *Ecology, Community and Lifestyle. Outline of an Ecosophy*. Cambridge: Cambridge University Press; Jordan, Martin. 2009. "Back to Nature." In *Therapy Today* April: 26-28; Russell, Peter. 1982. *The Awakening Earth*, London: Arcana.

The downside is that where spiritually aware clients talk about developmental stages, other corporate stakeholders may sense elitism. It is difficult to rank human development on an ascending scale without implying that some people are more valuable than others.

On the upside, consciousness is essential for achieving sustainability. Its development is, for some, an overall story capable of integrating apocalypse into the present, differentiating back-to-nature and adding responsibility to geological fatalism etc.

TOWARDS EACH COMPANY MAKING ITS OWN ANTHROPOCENE STORY

To summarise, collective motivation coming from the diversity of stakeholders is necessary for the company to be fully sustainable. Anthropocene stories of different kinds are already latently present. Through engaging with and integrating them each company has an opportunity to consciously shape its own. This will be around what is most material to its industrial, social and geographical context, crafting its particular microcosm of the planetary whole through continual dialogue.

Existing models include consumer concerns about the ethics of food production being addressed through consultation[10]. Unilever's Sustainable Living Plan[11] speaks of integrating sustainability into its brands, marketing and innovation, and of changing behaviour. Coaching may be uniquely well-placed to take the further step of motivational vision-building through enabling the surfacing of stakeholders' sustainability stories.

Regional types of Anthropocene culture already seem to be emerging. Research in Northern European, post-Protestant cultures has linked environmental leadership to evolutionary, developmental, spiritual-unitive perspectives, including positive views about human potential, an emphasis on the internalisation of authority and an integration of multiple modes of knowing[12].

As we have seen, stakeholders' Anthropocene stories sometimes border on experiencing the sacred. In integrating its own story, the company is likely to create a pragmatic platform which is acceptable to the pluralism of both revealed religions and secular outlooks.

I wonder if what I have attempted to say here relates to the experience of other coaches.

---

[10] Korthals, Michiel. 2008. "Ethical rooms for maneuver and their prospects vis-à-vis the current ethical food policies in Europe." In *Journal of Agricultural and Environmental Ethics* 21 (3): 249-273.
[11] See https://www.unilever.co.uk/sustainable-living/
[12] Hedlund-de Witt, Annick. 2014. "The integrative worldview and its potential for sustainable societies: A qualitative exploration of the views and values of environmental leaders." In *Worldviews, Culture, Religion* 18 (3): 191-229.

Learning to Learn - how managers really learn

Sue Young

INTRODUCTION

As part of our regular Summer review in the quieter time of August, I have been reviewing some of my older business and professional papers. One of the more poignant items I discovered was an article I wrote in 1999. Well, it's been a powerful discovery and re-connection process to some fundamental principles that still inform my approach in my work with individuals, teams and groups. What I then described as a 'developmental approach' I now call a 'coaching approach'.

I recall at the time I was between client projects so was able to turn my attention to writing for use with clients and as part of our suite of marketing materials. I wrote some 'Thought Papers' at the time describing my practice approach to client training and development work. I am struck by the strength of alignment to current principles that underpin my work today.

At that point in time I was one of four founders and Directors of a thriving consultancy business that specialised in bespoke development and training programmes for large international organisations. As part of our mix of interventions we worked with groups, teams and individuals. We called the latter one-to-ones then. The coaching bodies that existed were in very early stages and not generally well known. Coaching was seen mainly in the corporate market, either as a high-status perk at Board level, or remedial. In some organisations, it is still perceived this way!

In my development work then, I drew on my organisational experience, alongside several of the well-established theories - Maslow on motivation, Transactional Analysis, Learning Styles and a number of psychometrics like FIRO and Myers

Briggs, as well as various theories around management and leadership. I had read around the field of learning and related in particular to the humanistic school of thinking – the likes of Carl Rogers, Maslow, Carkhuff and Roger Harrison.

It was still early days for concepts such as Emotional Intelligence and use of Competencies. I hadn't yet embarked on my Master's in the field of individual, group and organisational learning, so had not yet discovered the formal fields of adult learning and group dynamics. Some of the latter patterns of behaviours I could intuitively see playing out in the various roles I had held. In ICI, as an external consultant and in my development work with groups and teams.

It is interesting now to see how my intuitively held beliefs from my direct experience that I can now see align so closely with the underpinning key principles of adult learning[1]. Today (as always) learning is inextricably linked to how people think, feel and relate to others. Particularly in an ever changing, complex world. It is this reality, unique to the individual's context, that coaching works with more directly than other formal learning activities.

The paper that follows is an exploration of my perspectives and thinking at that point in time. The underpinning fundamentals of my practice approach have remained pretty constant, although how I put these into practice has evolved considerably as I have gained in my diversity of experience.

THE ORIGINAL PAPER (1999): HOW MANAGERS REALLY LEARN

Training And Development Will Not Be Seen as Relevant to Success in Business until It Addresses the Issues of How Managers Really Learn, Especially in Today's Complex Business Environment.

Much is written these days about the Learning organisation. This is as much a function of how individual managers learn as the information systems and processes that companies put in place to enable transfer of knowledge. Training and development you would think therefore should therefore be moving centre stage. Not so.

Most formal training and development activities are not generally regarded by line management as contributing to their career progression or longer-term success.

Most training is seen as having a temporary effect at best. "Don't worry, he's obviously just been on a training course; he'll soon be back to normal," is a typical comment when someone returns from a training course.

Understandably, most managers are unaware of how they learn. They don't stop to think about it. They just get on with it and if something is not working,

---

[1] See Young, Sue. 2015. "Adult Learning – The Real Leading Edge of Coaching." *the good coach*. http://the-goodcoach.com/tgcblog/2015/7/21/adult-learning-the-real-leading-edge-of-coaching-by-sue-youn.html. Accessed September 9.

give up and try something else. Managers are usually focused on more immediate practical business priorities rather than taking time out to reflect on how they have developed, what works for them, what doesn't and why.

WHERE TRAINING HAS TRADITIONALLY COME FROM

Traditional training either aims at:

- Simple tasks that can be isolated and are narrow in focus, for example writing or presentation skills, or

- Acquiring and applying specific knowledge i.e. where there is a heavy emphasis on content or subject matter.

While valuable for certain requirements the limitations of this approach are where the nature of the learning is more complex.

Yet traditional training approaches have proved not to be of great help with the following typical learning needs managers in organisations face today:

- What is required of me in this fast-changing organisation where the job description I had a year ago doesn't seem that relevant?

- How do I develop more general business awareness and then apply it to my situation?

- I know my approach as a manager works for me in 80 percent of situations but I know it doesn't some of the time, and what should I do about it?

- How do I deal with the wide range of different people I have to work through, often of very different nationalities and cultural backgrounds?

- How do I influence the many people I depend on for my results but over whom I do not have direct authority?

RECENT DEVELOPMENTS...

Have recognised the need to find different ways to deal with today's demands on people in business.

For example, recent years have seen the advent of the 'change programme', along with a programme of courses rolled out through the organisation, focusing on communicating a strong 'vision' of the direction the business needs to go in and what is required.

Cascading from the top, where these programmes tend to fall down is if people at all levels do not have the opportunity to think it through for themselves and take responsibility for applying it to their part of the business. At worst, if they are not followed through on a long-term basis, these programmes can in fact do damage to the credibility of the company's leadership and can be cynically written off as "yet another initiative."

'Competencies' have become increasingly widely used, both for business strategy and to provide performance benchmarks for individuals, against which the individuals can receive specific feedback on their performance. This was, again, a step forwards in providing a framework to link individual learning needs to the needs of the business. However, managers can be understandably sceptical of an approach that, if too rigidly applied, can oversimplify the complexity of the real world.

Daniel Golenz's concept of Emotional Intelligence, or EQ, brings an additional dimension to competencies. It promises to bring rigour to the assessment and development of areas that most people intuitively have always recognised as being central to success. Qualities such as the ability to take a longer-term view, to manage conflict constructively, to be realistically aware of one's own strengths and weaknesses, have always been known to be important to personal effectiveness. Golenz promotes that these qualities can be learnt, thus bringing a potentially powerful tool to training and development in business.

IMPACT OF TODAY'S NEEDS ON APPROACHES TO TRAINING

Helping people to cope with the increasing complexities they face in learning to operate in their role is a challenge for business and HR specialists.

An analogy is that of learning to drive. You can break this down into its different components, yet this does not ultimately reflect the range of awareness and skills involved in driving a vehicle. It is unlikely we would say someone is a good driver immediately after they have passed their test.

One criteria of good driving might be a high level of anticipation or awareness of the infinite range of possible events you may need to react to and need to know how to react to in different ways and under different circumstances. We often call this 'road sense'. The challenge facing organisations is how to help managers develop 'role sense', how they can operate more effectively in their role in the business.

TOWARDS DEFINING 'DEVELOPMENT'

The dictionary defines development as "to come or bring to a later or more advanced or expanded stage; grow or cause to grow gradually".

A crucial aspect of development is that it is a step-by step-process. We cannot get to an end point without going through the stages en route. One stage builds on the previous stage.

Development is a process which takes place instinctively and intuitively and which embraces a complex, interrelating series of factors which all operate at the same time.

The extent to which we are able to learn and develop is a function of our awareness of this range of factors. This awareness comes either from ourselves or our environment.

For any training to be effective, it has to take account of these fundamental principles of how people learn – a developmental approach.

A DEVELOPMENTAL APPROACH TO TRAINING

Rather than rigidly separating training and development, as some can do, a developmental approach to training is to design and run training events which inherently build in fundamental developmental principles:

1. **The importance of motivating the 'learner'**. If managers cannot see the relevance of a training programme or how it will help them, they are not going to be motivated to learn. Too often companies do not give sufficient attention to this and managers can attend courses because they've been told to go with no expectation that it will be useful. At worst they can be hostile, at best not ready to take responsibility for their learning.

2. **Awareness as a pre-requisite to learning**. When people don't even know there is a problem, let alone what it is, they are not ready to consider or take in new information or perspectives.

3. **People already know a great deal more than they think they know**. When given the right environment and space, people have a lot of wisdom about what works and what doesn't. The learning issue is about opening up that awareness and then developing the ability to apply it.

4. **Learning has to be seen as relevant both by the individual and the business**. It cannot take place in a vacuum. This means starting with understanding the needs of the business and how this relates to what is required of people in their roles. One of the tutor's roles is to help people interpret and make sense of what is happening in their organisation as it impacts on their role. This puts a responsibility on training and development professionals to really understand what is going on in the business in order to judge what is needed and then to help managers with their learning needs in that context.

5. **People have to develop objective self-awareness** of their own strengths and weaknesses in order to learn how to extend their capabilities in more demanding business situations. That is, to be able

to see themselves as they are generally seen by others. It requires a balanced acceptance of oneself and how one is. It also requires the judgement to be able to manage oneself and be able to flex behaviour according to the demands of the situation.

6. **You can't tell people what to do, you have to help them see what to do.** This is partly creating an environment where their own natural awareness can be accelerated, and partly providing frameworks and experiences which help people make sense of it for themselves.

7. **Learning and awareness take place stage by stage**. If people have not yet developed a certain level of awareness about themselves or their environment, anything they are told will miss the mark. This is because they will not be able to relate to it from their experience. You have to start where people are in their experience and awareness and build on that.

8. **Learning can be an emotional experience** and there can be blockages to learning which have to first be overcome. For example, the fear of failure can be a major blockage to learning for some. For some senior managers who have developed a style where they have established themselves as the authority on most issues, public acknowledgement that they do not have all the answers can be difficult. For this reason, as HR professionals readily recognise, some senior managers are 'untrainable'.

9. **Individuals have to take charge of their own learning**. Part of the objective of any programme should be to build a foundation of awareness and confidence which enables individuals to do be more capable of managing their continuing development. There is another factor which is operating in business which leads to this as a prerequisite.

    In today's organisations where no one person has all the answers and there is more freedom needed for individuals to scope the answers for themselves, the ability of people to be self-directed and not wait to be told is essential. A developmental approach is directed towards helping people take more charge of this.

10. **Learning is unique for each individual**. Critical to a developmental approach is the recognition of the need for a high quality of attention to individual needs. Any group development and training activities should have built into them the opportunity for individuals to make personal sense of their experience. This places particular demands on the design of development programmes and places particular demands on the tutors.

IN CONCLUSION

In designing and developing training and development programmes, HR professionals need to bear in mind the fundamental principles of how people learn.

Too often a great deal of money is spent on programmes which are then imposed without taking sufficient account of the way people operate, thereby not achieving the training objectives, either for the individual or the organisation.

It comes back to the old adage. "You can lead a horse to water but you can't make it drink". With people this will always be the case, but at least by taking more of a developmental approach you can greatly increase the likelihood of real learning taking place.

SOME QUESTIONS TO LEAVE YOU WITH:

- What were you doing fifteen years ago, and retrospectively what role did 'a coaching approach' play in your work, (from yourself, or colleagues) even if you didn't call it that?

- What have been the career experiences and theories that have most influenced your personal coaching approach?

- How does my description of the core principles I named at that time as forming part of a 'developmental approach' fit (or not) with your personal coaching approach?

When training is best done using a coaching approach

R. Ramamurthy Krishna

would like to take the opportunity to consider the fit between training and coaching in organisations, and how this fits into my practice:

- Is training different from coaching?
- Is coaching just a way of doing training?
- What are the differences between coaching and training?
- Can coaching be used as an approach to training?

I would like to look in some detail at one project I undertook recently, as I believe it illustrates some of these issues very clearly.

1. SOME OF THE DIFFERENCES ALONG THE TRAINING VERSUS COACHING CONTINUUM

There are many combinations, as well as variations, as to how some learning/behaviour change programme can be constructed and delivered. It may be over simplifying to use the 'PowerPoint presentation' as the typical feature of one end of the training approach – where training is an expert-led activity.

You know when you're on expert-led training when:

- Communication is one way.
- The trainer creates themselves as 'the expert' on the subject at hand.
- The expert presents instructions about what has to be learned.

- The learning takes place using the expert language about what is involved.
- The expert is also the judge about whether something has been learned.

A coaching approach, however, can be very different because:

- Communication is open to all.
- The participants themselves bring with them important expertise.
- The expert has to be a facilitator or coach in order for the individuals in the group to be able to take the lead in the agenda.
- The participants' own terms are more in evidence in the discussion.
- The participants are the important judges of the outcomes.

2. AN EXAMPLE OF AN APPROACH TO USING A COACHING APPROACH IN TRAINING

I shall talk through a recent project that helps to illustrate some of these differences. It is a project that helps to show this 'coaching approach', albeit done under the general heading of training.

WE WERE ASKED TO CARRY OUT A 'TRAINING' PROGRAMME:

The project began with the central client administration contracting with me a training programme to be delivered to a group of staff. However, I was confident that the client would give me a wide scope in how I went about the project. I had worked for them before, and the results I have achieved to date have given them confidence in my approach. However, they are still more comfortable using terms such as 'training'– with all its implications!

HOW THE TRAINING TASK WAS DEFINED FOR US:

This is a project for a group of about twenty people – all in a particular function for a global organisation, all working in the same function, but in different units of the organisation locally. The head of the department had requested me to intervene and see how this group could work better together. Though they worked separately in their units, they also needed to work together for the department.

The words 'work better together' are quite open, without suggesting what the detail needed to be about.

Similarly, the task was set as an event where I and a colleague, and twenty participants, all arrived at a central location and its training rooms for a two-day programme.

EXPECTATIONS ABOUT THE WAY THE PROGRAMME WOULD WORK AT THE BEGINNING:

The participants, as usual, were clearly expecting some PowerPoint style presentation to start the programme. The people who had announced that this programme would take place, with bold enthusiasm, had also said something about neuroscience, et cetera.

The parties present were expecting some images of the brain and that I was going to talk a lot about the brain, etc., etc. This was their expectation, and what they were expecting to encounter.

To counter this expectation, I started the discussion by basically saying that I had nothing to offer them. That they should decide what it is that they wanted to take back with them.

"Very ambiguous; a very ambiguous opening."

REALITY CLASHES WITH EXPECTATIONS:

They were just not thinking what to do and what to ask. One of them said, *"Please tell me what is there in the menu card."* (A typical detailed programme outline.)

So I explained to them that the menu card was huge and gave them a few examples of what was possible in the menu card, and over and above the menu card. Instead I told them that we were looking to talk about what they knew, and I said, *"We are going to work on something collectively."*

At that point, I actually posed them a question, *"Guys, you all have about twenty years' experience plus, and you're saying that you've reached this point knowing nothing, right?"* I continued by asking, *"What is it that I can teach you? There is nothing new that I can add. I would prefer to pick up on what you already know and then put it into a frame that we can work on, and give you an insight which would add more value to them, and value to you."*

And that was the point/moment they opened up. They then started talking about what they wanted to learn. They then ended up talking about communication. They talked about the aspects of communication that they didn't like, such as being belittled, the lack of respect, and the lack of confidentiality and how people formed a coalition, etc., etc.

As they were talking I just noted down their words and added them to the flip chart. I asked them how they would like the next two days to go. They said that they wanted to look at some ideas for working on all of these things. They wanted to have some fun and bring in some crazy ideas.

They wanted to have fun, and they wanted to learn as well.

And so, we wrote the word 'fun' on the whiteboard.

PART 2: Cutting edge: Investigating patterns from Practitioner Experiences

We agreed that, "*The next two days, will be fun.*" But also at the end of the programme, they needed to define an acronym for FUN. There would be a lot of learning, but what they would take back with them was FUN, with a very different meaning. We said, "*Let's start by looking at what that acronym might be.*"

They talked about 'freedom unlimited' and moved on to talk about, 'friendship united', etc., etc. We picked up on them all and we collectively confirmed that, "*This is to be the theme for the next two days, right?*"

I reiterated to them that this would indeed be what they were going to be working on. The theme being 'fun' and that we were going to each bring our own knowledge, and that all of us would put it together and convert it into a lot of fun-based learning.

They responded positively.

And then I said, "*There will be a lot of questions that we will form—we will go through a process of dialoguing. I will ask some questions and you in turn will ask me questions back; that's how we'll exchange ideas. And we'll continually keep records of what we learn, and then move at the end of day two towards fun.*"

The entire group in the room was already bubbling with excitement. The group was geared up because they felt respected. They felt a tremendous amount of autonomy and that there was a real conversation going on. They knew that this was going to be more than just a fruitless exercise—we had our written agenda. I, as well as they, were just clearer on how we were going to work together which had really come about through our contracting stage. For the remaining time there would be learning. What was learned would then be converted into knowledge and then given back to them.

4. WORKING THROUGH THE REAL AGENDA...

They talked about communication and various aspects of communication. They mentioned what they liked or didn't like, such as being belittled, their dislike for being powered down, the need for transparency and the need for trust etc.

Then we asked them to start talking about examples of how that would work.

It was at this point that we said, "*Let's hold on for a minute. You guys all know each other.*"

They responded by saying, "*Yes, we know of each other. But some of us do not know each other.*"

I said, "*Okay. Now that such issues are coming out, it's important for those people who do not know each other well to pair up and sit together for the next two days and start dialoguing with us. Therefore, an informal team will now take place.*"

We moved them together and asked them to continue with their dialogue. As they pressed on with their dialogue, they were talking with each other and were raising those aspects of communication that they didn't like. Things that caused them to feel slightly humiliated and that they were not a part of the team etc.

We captured what they wanted to focus on with regard to communication. It was not planned, but it just so happened that my colleague wrote all their negatives with a red whiteboard marker and everything that they wanted to take back in green.

My colleague said, "*Can you look at this now and see the dangers in red and the positives might be those written in green?*"

I then expanded on my colleague's sharing, "*Look at what has been captured through listening to your dialogues. Some are written in red, and the other things that you seem to need to learn are in green. What does that tell you?*"

They walked around and said, "*Red looks like danger and green looks something that we want to learn.*"

And so, we introduced the concept of red and green. "*Okay. For the next two days, we are not bothered about whether it is a threat or a reward. We don't want to use any terminology. For your understanding, we'll use the red system and the green system. We'll continue to develop with red and green; red and green because that came from you.*"

Now, everyone there understood the concept of threat and reward very clearly, and they took that with them.

INTRODUCING EMAILS!

We then exposed them to a small activity. We asked them to look at the communication which they we're having: to look at the e-mail they read, and the conversations that they were currently having. How many of them were loaded with red, and how many of them were loaded with green? **They were very clear that many of the communications, especially those via e-mail, were loaded with red**.

We then asked them to reflect on this, "*What each of you rated as red, can you also understand that it is not red on the e-mail? It is only red internally to you creating your own internal emotions to raise. If you want, I can talk very, very basics about how the brain works etc. But that is not what I'm interested in. We could even throw in all the types of brain parts and tell you how they work, but even that's not important. What's important to realize is that all this red is affecting our health, which is far more important. And that is what we should be selfish about.*"

This began to make a lot of sense to them. The more questions I asked the more examples started to come from them.

5. CHECKING HOW OUR COACHING APPROACH TO TRAINING WORKED

We asked them at one point to simply write on a sticky note how they felt the workshop was going. And they responded with, "*Really nice,*" and more of them wrote, "*Very interactive.*" One person even wrote that, "*We know we have nothing to give, but we're picking up from your knowledge, and we are building on it highly-interactively.*"

The trust level from facilitating that point of view, and the level of acceptance from them, that we can learn something here, was shared by another participant, "*I don't need to feel threatened that there's going to be a new training-based concept that was set up as part of the expectation. This was extremely hard for us, though it was not stated, and that was the unstated part, which really gave us that power to continue doing.*"

They were really very surprised that there wasn't any PowerPoint available. That I was not following a typical training structure, but instead building on the things that were coming from the floor as they came up and putting them into the frame, which was extremely well-received.

We also followed through on the outputs in various ways as a way of ensuring that this session started to change the way the organisation worked. We continued to get similarly positive comments as well as very highly motivated and confident feedback about how they were doing things differently, and were much better as a result.

6. CONCLUSIONS

1. It is interesting to see how in an international organisation there is a balance between processes that are generally common in organisations, as well as an emphasis on the processes that can have an important local focus. The emphasis here was on respect and self-esteem. They became strong themes, and support, when investigating what was going on with regard to communication among the group.

2. The real challenge is the confidence and skill the leader can bring to 'letting go' and knowing how to stimulate other participants into sharing and building appropriate leadership. It is still more difficult to consider what this involves – which is why this exercise can be so useful.

3. Coaching language is very different from merely teaching people basic facts about neuroscience. Neuroscience doesn't tell us exactly what to do with the immediate people in the room, from moment to moment. There are also plenty of other models around in coaching. But again, I still feel that we were working and choosing behaviours that make a difference, and which are still so 'intuitive' that we need to work hard to express exactly how they work.

CHAPTER 6

BOUNDARIES, CONTRACTS AND CONTRACTING

The importance of detailed understanding of the context, and having ready access around an organisation, in helping to appreciate the circumstances and boundaries inherent in any coaching intervention

Ian Flanders - Dispatch from the [Internal Coaching] Front

HOW COACHING INTERVENTIONS CAN START – OPPORTUNISTICALLY

Last week I found myself sat opposite a colleague being asked whether I had any spare coaching capacity at the moment. I responded that I had, and asked what they had in mind. It transpired that they were looking for a coach for a relatively newly appointed senior manager.

But after this promising start, things began to get complicated!

This area of the business had seen significant change; a new leader, consolidation of roles and head-count reduction. The 'potential' coachee had come through these changes that, on paper at least, made them the obvious deputy and possible successor to the leader.

But as I listened to the background of the situation, it became clear that consideration of 'deputy' or 'successor' had not been part of that decision-making process. The newly appointed leader did not, and had never seen, the subject of our conversation as his successor and clearly saw another member of his team as their 'deputy'.

And I sensed that there was a growing concern that an awful lot of eggs might have been placed in the wrong basket.

THE IMPORTANCE OF CLARIFYING EXPECTATIONS FROM COACHING THAT ARE BOTH CLEAR AND RELEVANT

Thinking that the 'issue' was all out on the table, I asked "*So what are you looking to me to do?*" It now emerged that there was one more twist in the tale.

Concerned about what they were sensing, and knowing that the annual review was approaching, the leader sought feedback from a number of the report's colleagues and stakeholders. Without further ado, the leader laid the feedback out in front of their report in all its glory.

It was in relaying this tale, and the reaction it provoked, that the leader alarmed their HR manager, who was speaking to me now.

The HR Manager had recognised that raw feedback, delivered without explanation or support, could be extremely damaging and that a coach was a possible better approach to helping someone process feedback productively.

Now, we were able to get down to a sensible conversation about what an internal coach could contribute to this situation, but also what the limitations of any intervention would be.

ESTABLISHING 'SAFE SPACE' IS FUNDAMENTAL TO A COACHING INTERVENTION

Coaching in organisations has largely shaken off the stigma of being a remedial intervention and, as a result, gained broad credibility with potential coachees.

I stressed that I could not, and would not want, to 'fix' this coachee. For me any such attempt would both compromise my role as a coach and blur unacceptably the responsibility boundary between coach and line manager. Nor would I report on the coachee to their line manager, or the business, for the same reasons.

The role that slowly emerged as we continued talking was to position oneself/get alongside the coachee in order to help them to understand the situation they now found themselves in.

It would require that a 'safe-space' be created:

- Fashioned from trust, within which the coachee could unpack the feedback given to them,
- Take time to digest it, and
- Decide what they would do as a result.

I stressed therefore that the work between coach and coachee would be confidential. In truth this is the way I always work, but I state it to the coaching sponsor every time, as an inviolable law.

CONTRACTING FOR THE POTENTIAL SCOPE OF THE POSSIBLE AGENDA IN COACHING

It struck me as we were talking that the possibility must exist that the subject of our conversation might decide to leave the business, and indeed that this might be one of the desired outcomes.

When I shared this reflection, it was clear that with the sudden loss of the 'basket' in this way risked the business equivalent of an awful lot of scrambled eggs.

This prompted me to state the possibility that the insight gained by the coachee through the coaching process might have the effect of hastening a decision of this nature, especially if the coachee came to realise that it was in their best interests.

This outcome statement was acknowledged as true.

Realizing both the circumstances and boundaries, I agreed with the HR colleague that they would talk to the leader and set out the basis for my possible involvement.

This basis was:

1. We agreed that the 'option' of working with me as a coach should be offered, not forced upon the potential coachee.
2. I also asked for a meeting with the leader before any approach was made to their subordinate, to make clear to them the basis upon which I would act.

REFLECTING ON THE CONVERSATION I AM STRUCK BY TWO THINGS

One is recognising those important forces that may be relevant for the internal coach to intervene on.

The business and the business' agents have objectives that must be delivered:

*   Fix them or change them;
*   Prevent a management vacuum;
*   Maintain credibility.

The coachee, if that is what they become, will want help. Someone to hold at bay the anxieties pressing in on them whilst they try to make sense of the situation they find themselves in. I also had to reflect on whether there might be consequences for me, as coach:

*   Will I, my career, my future, be impacted by the outcome of this situation?

- Can, should, the coach be responsible for the 'outcome' under such circumstances?

My second reflection is that the person who was the subject in this coaching conversation may not be the only person who would benefit from coaching.

Being able to think through the needs and consequences of a business reorganisation, and, being able to deliver difficult messages to your subordinates without destabilising the team are leadership competencies. It seems clear that for some the importance of these skills has to be learnt the hard way.

The [internal coaching] front line is a challenging place to work!

So ... What experiences do you have about internal coaching?

What did I leave unsaid? Coaching reflections from the well of unease

Alan Robertson

EXTRACTING LEARNING FROM 'VAGUE' CASES

C was one of the coaching cases which left me with a vague sense of unease. I've come to realise that this can be a reliable indication of a lesson to be learned. But I also know that you have to subject that vague sense to some hard scrutiny to extract the learning from it.

So what does some tough retrospection have to offer in this case?

I find myself reflecting on the questions:

- *What did I leave unsaid?*
- *What did I not say to this coachee that I now wish I'd said?*

READING THE CLUES AND SIGNALS DURING CONTRACTING

Here are the bones of the story. 'C' is big and loud. His personality is as colourful as the shirts that he wears, a stab of individuality in the rather reserved corporate culture in which he was then working. At the time of our coaching work together he was in a sales role, distributing complex products across a diverse set of relatively small country markets in Europe and the Middle East. While he had a share of some administrative support, he was essentially a solo operator, expected to nurture and pursue opportunities to grow his fragmented but emerging market. It's a lonely role, but he was an energetic individual and responded to the challenge by throwing his considerable energy at it.

His coaching was made at his own request. The HR department agreed to it, and one of his immediate managers. (He has two in this matrix organisation.) After meetings with C and this manager to explore the purpose of his coaching,

I drafted three objectives, which they and HR approved. The aim was to build his internal brand, profile and reputation. More specifically,

- It was to develop his capabilities to influence without having positional power,

- To win greater recognition from more senior stakeholders in the firm, and

- To present his business plans in a highly professional way.

In retrospect it now seemed obvious that C was an outlier in that organisation.

"He needs to learn how to present his proposals in a way that will secure acceptance in this culture," his manager says. This was a clue in itself.

The fact that he was speaking of C in the third person while he sat with us in the same room at the time is another.

C's lurid shirt is a third.

Being comfortable with being an organisational outsider myself – I have worked as an independent for twenty-five years now – something that I used to know has drifted off into my peripheral awareness. In memory I know that one has to have network, connection and acceptability to be influential and effective in a corporate context. In practice I have lost sight of just how important this is.

I missed the clues in this case.

Consequently I failed C.

I failed to do one of the things which an experienced coach should expect to be doing: **catching weak signals and amplifying them to bring them to the coachee's attention and hold them there.**

This is not about telling the coachee what things mean. It's about making sure that clues and their possible significance are made loud enough and clear enough and for long enough to receive the coachee's consideration.

FOLLOWING THROUGH ON THE 'AGREED' COACHING OBJECTIVES

At one level it seems all too clear what C needs to do to tackle his coaching objectives.

Like many 'sales' people he over-relies on one voice. He advocates. He pushes his case. And he pushes it to a fault, not perhaps with external clients, but certainly internally, arguing for support and more resources to pursue the business opportunities that he sees in his territory. *"It feels like everything is a battle right now,"* he tells me. But advocacy is a battling voice, so it's not surprising if it makes discussions feel like battles.

I asked him what feedback he has been given in the past about himself. "I've been told that I need to become more neutral and listen more." So we work on developing these capabilities. We do it by,

- Increasing his use of articulation,

- Explanation through clear, factual exposition, and

- His use of inquiry, asking questions to engage shareholders in his thinking by way of their own interests and concerns.

I wanted him to learn how to lead and participate in a process of joint opportunity-spotting and problem-solving rather than trying always to talk people into submission and agreement.

TESTING THE REAL VALUE OF COACHING

C is characteristically energetic about learning and applying these new voices. He embarks on producing two major pieces of written work simultaneously.

- One is his business plan and the rationale behind it.

- The other is an innovative paper on a new way of calculating client value and allocating resources.

The business plan eventually runs to well over a hundred pages. It takes him several months to research, consider and write. In the meantime he starts to trail a draft of his much shorter paper on how to value clients with a few selected individuals in his division. He is able to have some informal discussions with two or three senior people. His initiative and ideas are well received by them.

Unfortunately in the process he misses an important window in the annual business planning cycle. This, at least, is not because I have failed to say something. I've already reinforced his managers' message that the business plan should be his priority.

C however is insistent that he is not prepared to sacrifice quality for speed. He's determined to produce the most rigorous, innovative and persuasive business plan his managers have ever seen. When it is finally complete, one of his colleagues describes it as the most impressive piece of work of its kind that he has ever seen. But C's two managers are unimpressed and will not put it forward for further consideration. They tell him bluntly, "*You've delivered it too late.*"

This rejection is a defining moment for C.

PIECING TOGETHER THE MISSING CLUES, RETROSPECTIVELY

During the interim review of our coaching the two of them talk at each other for half an hour, without either yielding ground on their points of view. One of his managers – the one who took part in the pre-coaching conversation –

concedes that there is good work in it. But he keeps returning to the point that C has failed to meet the budgeting window. C argues that a good plan takes time to research and should be considered when it's ready, whenever that is.

Afterwards I asked C if he realised what voice he has been using. "*Advocating,*" he admits. "*but...*" and promptly does more, as he proceeds to justify himself and his behaviour. It's another moment when, as his coach, I need to be the amplifier of the signal. What I should have said is that he had gone well beyond advocacy into preaching and that he'd got the reaction and the resistance which was all he could reasonably expect from all that relentless pushing.

Instead I asked him how he proposed to speak to his other manager. "*I'm going to ask him what he thinks of the content of my plan and for his answers to the questions I've put forward in it.*" This sounds more promising, but that meeting – when it comes – turns out no better.

His manager refuses to read the document. Apparently, he merely glanced at the Executive Summary, made no further reference to it and then proceeded to tell C what his plan should be.

"*So then what did you do?*" I ask.

"*We ended up in an argument,*" C replies, with evident frustration. This is where I should have pointed out to C just how strongly his dominant advocacy voice still had him in his grip.

For his own development he might perhaps have been better served by being confronted with that feedback than with help in thinking through alternative strategies for engaging this second manager. Because, as it turned out, the second manager can never be engaged. He remains fixed in a position in which he will not examine or discuss the very substantial analysis or logic behind C's plan, while at the same time both rejecting its conclusions and saying that C must decide what he does next.

It is a powerful illustration of how quickly meetings become unproductive if the participants talk at each other rather than entering into a conversation.

In the meantime the first manager, the closest person C had to a sponsor, abruptly left the firm. In so doing he left C effectively isolated and after a further painful six months C too left the business. It was an unhappy ending to the story.

EXTRACTING MY LEARNINGS AFTER SOME TOUGH RETROSPECTION

We'd like all our coaching assignments to end well. Of course, it's naïve to define coaching success simply in terms of meeting the objectives originally set, when the real issues to be tackled often only emerge during the process.

Equally, it's simplistic to expect success to take the form of propelling the coachee's career onward and upward, however gratifying that might be for a coach's self-regard. These are heroic fantasies with the coach playing the part of the white knight.

In reality, each of the stakeholders in the process has to be entitled to a personal view of whether, to what extent and in what ways a coaching intervention has succeeded or failed.

- C's first manager, in this case, actually declared himself satisfied with the coaching. "*I can see that he's developed. He's using voices that he didn't previously have. It's a more mature way of presenting a case.*"

- The second manager never gave a view. He was never invested in the coaching, perhaps – for whatever reason we can only speculate – never even committed to developing a working relationship with C.

- C himself was positively pleased with his coaching. "*I've learned to value myself more.*" And he acted on that self-belief. He left to become self-employed and to pursue his own business.

But just as the coachee and the sponsors are entitled to judge the process and outcomes of coaching, so is the coach. And in this case I recognise now that I missed some moments and some clues that I could have caught and held up for all of us to think about more deeply at the time.

Part of the coach's distinctive role as a transitory partner is to say things that might not be said by others whose candour is potentially compromised, whether by the need to preserve an ongoing relationship or by vested interest or by the blindness born of familiarity.

So what, in hindsight, do I wish I'd said to C?

I wish I'd pointed out that working for yourself can be a hard context in which to apply insights about yourself. Self-employment certainly provides freedom of expression and action and a correspondingly broad vista of learning opportunities. But it is also a context in which it is all too easy to remain stuck in one's existing tendencies, preferences and habits. I could have joined the dots connecting my observation of C's tendency to fall back into advocacy, a voice centred in self, and his intention to move into a context centred in self-employment. There was a potentially valuable insight to be shared, if only I had noticed it at the time.

But months before that, during the time we were coaching together, I could have been saying, "*Where's your manager on this?*" "*Why did he use that expression about learning to present your business case in a way that will secure acceptance in this culture?*" "*Where's your other manager?*" "*And where are they now?"* If I'd been more attentive to the need to keep asking those questions, I might have served C sooner and better.

I TAKE TWO PARTICULAR LEARNING POINTS AWAY FROM THIS CASE

The first is the value of repeatedly asking yourself, "What am I not saying here?"

That's an explicit question that I am now bringing into my practice, a question to keep in mind not only during the coaching session itself but also in reflecting between sessions. It's a hard question. It needs thought.

It also directs attention towards the second learning point, which is to keep puzzling over the story. That leads you where you need to keep going. Back towards details that you might have overlooked, the fragments of information that didn't fit into the model or mental framework that you were working with at the time. The weak signals that need to be amplified before they can be accurately heard. The clues that reveal the deeper problems.

It's a reminder that good coaches direct inquiry and challenge not simply at their coaches but also at themselves.

The Coaching Contract - What's in a name?

Lynne Hindmarch

Most professions have jargon, only fully understood by the initiated. The coaching profession has jargon too, but has the added misfortune of having two words widely used within the profession which have a rather different meaning elsewhere. One of these is 'supervision' (which has been much debated and I won't dwell on here), and the other is 'the contract' (or 'contracting').

I have a problem with the use of both the terms 'contract' and 'contracting' (but I'll simplify things by focusing just on the word contract in this piece) and I decided to use this blog as a way of exploring my difficulty with the term by reflecting and writing about it. In that sense, I am using the blog as part of my reflective practice. I am also interested in other people's views on the word, if they too have issues with it, and how they address them.

THE IMPORTANCE OF THE PROCESS OF CONTRACTING

I am acutely aware of the importance of the process of contracting in working with a client. Indeed, when I trained in supervision some years ago, there was a strong emphasis during the course on establishing the contract. Both as a supervisor and as a coach, and in teaching the importance of the coach/client contract to our supervisees. There was a good reason for this: often difficulties between supervisors and coaches, and between coaches and clients, arise because of lack of clarity in an inadequate contract.

In my own supervision practice I have seen a number of problems that have developed because the coach and client have not fully developed the contract between them. Often this is to do with boundary issues, when the coach confuses the client (and sometimes themselves) by moving between a coaching approach, a consultancy approach or a counselling approach. Therefore, I can immediately sense some tension, between my dislike of the term, and the value of the process.

So, what lies behind my problem with the term?

WHAT DO WE REALLY UNDERSTAND ABOUT 'THE CONTRACT' AND 'CONTRACTING'?

When coaches talk to other coaches about 'the contract' and 'contracting' we understand, within the context of the profession, what we mean. Our clients, however, don't, and it is easy to forget that they don't.

How contract is generally defined

The Oxford Dictionary defines a contract as:

> "*A written or spoken agreement, especially one concerning employment, sales, or tenancy, that is intended to be enforceable by law.*"

A further definition is:

> "*An arrangement for someone to be killed by a hired assassin.*"

Hmmm. Perhaps it really is time to review the term.

For me the word 'contract' grates with how the values underlying my coaching practice. This takes a broadly humanistic approach, drawing on Carl Rogers assumptions that for people to grow and develop they need an environment that provides them with genuineness (openness and self-disclosure), acceptance (being seen with unconditional positive regard) and empathy (being listened to and understood). Although I run my coaching practice as a business, and of course recognise and work with the commercial realities of my clients' organisational lives, when I'm coaching the more 'hard-nosed' aspects of my business are definitely in the background.

The difficulty I have with the first definition (let's skip over the Mafia-inspired definition) is the commercial and legal connotations associated with it which feel at odds with my approach to coaching. I considered possible alternatives as part of my practice, such as the word 'agreement'. The term 'agreement' can also have legal and commercial associations, but it has a broader meaning, such as: "*an arrangement as to a course of action: eg reached an agreement as to how to achieve their goal.*" (Merriam-Webster Dictionary.)

How contract is currently described in coaching

At this stage I decided to explore what various coaching books had to say about contracting. Interestingly a few of them made no mention of the process. However, a number did, especially those which focus on coaching supervision. Nevertheless, none of the books I looked at mentioned outright any difficulty with the term. In fact, some suggest that the practical discussion around fees and cancellation arrangements can be the start of build up a trusting and empathetic relationship with the client!

Some of the coaching texts I read avoided the term 'contract' altogether by referring to it as 'the working alliance', for example. This discussion might cover sharing information about each other, explaining the coach's approach, training, experience and describing the ethical framework the coach works within. The benefits of this approach are that it gives the coach the opportunity to begin to develop trust, empathy, respect and genuineness.

PUSHING THE AWARENESS OF, AND UNDERSTANDING, OF THE CONTRACT AND CONTRACTING PROCESS

Thinking about this further, I wondered if the contracting process could be split into two parts.

- Stage One, the Contract.
- Stage Two, the Agreement.

Stage One, the Contract, as a formal arrangement between the client and the coach (or indeed between the coach and the sponsor or organisation) which may include the more commercial aspects of the coaching arrangement. This may include:

- The number of sessions,
- The length,
- The fee,
- Missed sessions payment,
- Who is going to be involved,
- Confidentiality,
- Where the sessions will be held etc.

I would describe these as the 'pay and rations' aspects of the coaching programme, where I would find the use of the term contract quite appropriate, containing as it does both commercial and potentially legal obligations, with less likelihood of changes being made. Hawkins and Smith[1] refer to these as the 'practicalities' of the contract.

This would then be followed by Stage Two, the Agreement. This is a conversation I have with the client once the coaching sessions start. It may have been explored a little in the initial pre-programme discussions, but it is

[1]Hawkins, Peter., and Nick Smith. 2006. *Coaching, Mentoring and Organizational Consultancy: Supervision and Development*. Maidenhead, Berks: McGraw-Hill.

PART 2: Cutting edge: Investigating patterns from Practitioner Experiences

the focus of the early part of the first coaching session. The agreement is a more fluid arrangement, where the process can be revisited and changed if both parties agree. Indeed, in coaching and supervision I encourage revisiting the agreement to see if it needs updating or revising. How often one revisits it depends on the individual coach, but I tend to touch on it lightly at least every other session. It might simply be, "How do you feel about how we are working together? Is there anything that you might want to change?". It gives the client the opportunity to raise any questions and share what is working well for them and what might need changing.

Having reached this juncture in my reflection, I decided it would be useful to explore further what might be contained in Stage Two, the Agreement.

BUILDING IN COMPLEXITIES THROUGH AN AGREEMENT: MESHING VARIOUS FRAMEWORKS OF AGREEMENT TO MEET MY PRACTICE

1. Some authors, such as Katherine Tulpa[2] describes the agreement as,

- Covering the psychological contract,

- Defining outcomes, and

- Setting realistic expectations, to create an optimum learning experience. (I liked the emphasis on learning here.)

Tulpa suggests that it is useful to explain in advance the purpose of the contracting session, perhaps by sending a draft learning agreement beforehand. This may include aims, business goals, potential development areas, desired outcomes and previous feedback.

In my practice, I take this a stage further I would also ask if the client has had any contact with the helping professions before. This can establish early on if the client has had any therapy or counselling, is on any medication for illnesses such as depression, or has had coaching before. This initial session may include a meeting between coach, client, boss or sponsor.

2. In their book, Whitworth et al[3] provide a number of intake forms and checklists, including a model coaching agreement. This may be somewhat too process driven for some, but provides a number of useful frameworks for modifying; for instance, questions the coach might ask the client in the first session. They also suggest different forms of agreement depending on whether working with individual client or corporate client.

---

[2] Tulpa, Katherine. 2006. "Coaching Within Organizations." In *Excellence in Coaching*: 26-43. Edited by Passmore, J. London: Kogan Page.
[3] Whitworth, Laura., Karen Kimsey-House, Henry Kimsey-House and Philip Sandal. 1998. *Coactive Coaching*. CA: P Palo Alto.

3. O'Neill[4] describes contracting (developing an agreement) as "in many ways... the most important phase" which reinforces my own view of its position. For her it is about building a relationship and establishing credibility.

- It gives the client the opportunity to ask: Can this coach help me?
- It also gives the coach the chance to ask: Is this client open to feedback?

O'Neill suggests starting to coach right away to give the client a flavour of the work. (I have done this in the past during the initial 'chemistry' meeting with a client. I found that in doing so I covered so much ground with the client that she said she didn't need any further coaching. This wasn't quite what I planned.) Her chapter goes into much more detail on how the relationship develops, what questions may be going through the client's head, as well as the coach testing the client's willingness to focus on their own behaviour and the contribution they might be making to their problems. O'Neill also includes goal setting and establishing measurable goals.

4. Flaherty[5] describes (in what he calls the enrolment process) the importance of the coach and client making explicit what they are committed to accomplishing in the coaching programme. He emphasises the joint nature of this - the commitment of one member is not sufficient. He also raises what barriers there may be to a successful coaching programme, such as work commitments, an unsupportive boss or outcomes that may be only temporarily important.

This is in line with my own approach to the agreement process when working with a client. We draft it together, typically working under four broad headings:

1. The purpose of the coaching programme (such as providing a safe and confidential space to discuss their developmental goals);

2. Practical issues (such as building the coaching sessions into their working day;

3. Professional issues (such as confidentiality); and

4. Psychological issues (such as delivering feedback).

It is explicitly stated that the agreement is likely to evolve during the work we do together.

REFLECTING ON MY CONTRACT-AGREEMENT APPROACH

1. The exploration I have made in this blog of the term 'contracting' has been a useful way to reflect on my own difficulties with the term. Used simply in its narrow and more popularly understood definition, I saw it as giving a formal and misleading tone to what coaching actually is about, which is much more inclusive.

---

[4] O'Neill, Mary Beth. 2000. *Executive Coaching with Backbone and Heart*: 91-11, San Francisco CA: Jossey-Bass.
[5] Flaherty, James. 1999. *Coaching: Evoking Excellence in Others*. MA: Elsevier Burlington

2. Taking the time to review and understand how others have reported or described what the contract/contracting involved from various coaching texts has enabled me to think about splitting the process into two components, the formal Contract, and the more fluid Agreement, which I find more attuned to how I work as a coach.

3. It has also helped me revisit my approach to the process and more consciously think about what I cover, particularly during the conversation around the agreement, as part of how I manage the intake with new and existing clients.

Setting your mind on a coaching approach

Doug Montgomery and Laurent Terseur -Making sense of how we define a coaching approach (Part 2)

In our first piece "Making sense of how we define a coaching approach from each of our professional experiences" and as part of our mini-series, we explored each of our respective journeys toward adopting a coaching style in past leadership roles within large organisations. Since stepping out from existing structures and becoming independent executive coaches, we became even more aware and certain of a coaching approach. We believe it integral to being an effective leader and manager.

By encouraging leaders and managers to invest in their coaching approach in day to day conversations, we are inviting them to increase their options for how they inspire and lead. Drawing from our experiences, which involved several exploratory conversations, we singled out two elements that we think are needed in order to grow and embed a more coaching style:

1. A change of mindset
2. A change of psychological contract.

1. A CHANGE OF MINDSET

We believe that leaders taking a coaching approach are setting a clear intention to encourage and stimulate individuals and teams to take more responsibility for solving problems, being creative and making an effective contribution. In other words, a genuine and tangible way to walk the empowerment talk!

From our 'on-going' experiences a shift in mindset is required to convert a leadership style to an approach more like coaching. The behaviours we've observed that demonstrates this change is occurring include,

- noticeably telling a lot less,

- noticeably listening a lot more,

- and asking more questions that draw out people's ideas and thinking.

We describe this as a 'coaching mindset'; a trusting, non-judgemental and clear intention to be present with the other and curious about what they have to say.

1.1. A TRUSTING MINDSET

In each of our experiences, we both believe that the first choice to be made by leaders, who want to engage in an approach more coaching-like, is choosing to trust their colleagues' experience, skills, creativity and capabilities.

This may seem a given. Yet we see many leaders struggling with this. Just as we too confess that in our time we did not always trust individuals in our teams to be able to do a great job, or rather, we did not trust them to do it our way!

Table 1: We share here some common examples of trust-breaking assumptions and offer related questions that challenge these assumptions and open up a more trusting mindset.

Examples of Assumptions	Possible self-challenging questions
They don't have all the skills or knowledge that I have!	What skills and knowledge do they already have? What am I underestimating about them?
They are not going to do it my way!	What is the outcome we want here? How many different ways could that outcome be achieved?
They don't see all implications/the larger picture and they might create trouble with some stakeholders!	What have I explained to them about expectations and boundaries? What are they responsible for and when do I expect them to call for help?
They always ask for our advice or instructions rather than think for themselves!	How have I encouraged and contributed to this behaviour? How do I want them to behave from now on?
This one is a bridge too far for them!	What are the gaps we need to fill for them to be up to the task?
It's quicker to just tell them what to do rather than coach them!	What will be the long term benefit for both of us as they are encouraged and trusted to think for themselves?
I will feel vulnerable if they think I don't have the answers!	It's ok for me not to have all answers. So how can I be a great catalyst tapping into all available potential and resources so the reaction happens and produces all its effects. Even if I have an answer, what do they think, and what might I learn from them?

PART 2: Cutting edge: Investigating patterns from Practitioner Experiences

During our time as leaders, and Doug's experience teaching coaching skills to leaders, we have come across many assumptions that can get in the way of trusting colleagues. We've collected these assumptions and share some of the most common examples we've come across in Table 1 .

However, we learned that when these assumptions are gently probed, they can often be replaced by a more positive, trusting mindset. Trusting others to come up with solutions and actions is then likely to see them buy-in to the actions and be more motivated to drive them through. Trusting leaders are then rewarded with freed up time and the confidence to trust their reports again next time.

1.2. Non-judgemental mindset

Another useful mindset change we think is needed to support a coaching approach, is to become less critical and more curious about what others think and what can be learned from the experience. This means suspending judgment, letting go of the 'my solution is best' habit, and instead encouraging the other person to offer possible solutions and use their own resources. We both experienced and observed how much:

- A sure way to stifle someone's willingness to offer ideas is to critique them as they make them. It is demoralising to be asked for ideas and have them rejected before you've finished offering them.

- A fear of harsh judgement and blame drive protectionist behaviours, playing safe, and hiding of failures - not what most organisations really need in challenging times.

Our learning over time has been that by exploring ideas, by being open to learning from both successful or less successful experiences, i.e. by being kinder to others (and to ourselves!), leaders with a more coaching style can craft conversations. These conversations can be more reflective. They can focus on growth and the opportunities to improve performance.

1.3. A clear intention

The third mindset change we'd encourage leaders to adopt is to become more aware of their intention.

We observed (including our own experiences) that those who succeed in unlocking performance through asking rather than telling conversations are the ones,

- who have grown a sound awareness of both the situation,

- their feelings about it and

- how it fits into the bigger context.

In other words, they have a clear intention on what they want to achieve and what style will best suit that intention. This increasing awareness then helps

PART 2: Cutting edge: Investigating patterns from Practitioner Experiences

them to focus on the key outcomes from a task or situation rather than having their attention immediately being absorbed by the problem and finding a solution. It's making sure that the desired future outcome was clarified with their reports. It's helping them secure a shared understanding of what good looks like. It's also leaving space for them to come up with options for getting there, selecting appropriate actions and taking away both the plan and the motivation to deliver it.

An example: One of Doug's team (let's call them Sam) came asking for advice on how to present a potentially contentious idea to the divisional leadership team (LT). Instead of simply offering a judgement of whether this was wise, or how Doug would go about this (a default setting for many of us), he decided that this was an opportunity to use the coaching approach.

Doug asked what the desired outcome of presenting the idea to the leadership team was. This resulted in a silence as Sam thought about what he wanted to achieve and what success would look like. It became apparent that the likelihood of the idea being adopted was slim at this stage and that the purpose was to begin a longer discussion about a new technology. It was also an opportunity for Sam to raise his profile by being in front of the LT.

Once that was established, further questions about options that could serve these outcomes were asked. A plan of engaging individual LT members about the idea and the technology before the meeting was devised. It also emerged that it may be premature to present to the meeting and that the conversation could be started in the individual meetings with each LT member. The thinking and options came from Sam, who took the one-to-one LT engagement on with energy and commitment. Although the idea was not adopted, his profile as one who thinks ahead grew amongst the LT.

Sharing the intention and desired outcomes in a way that helps their reports understand and open up to coaching style conversations brings us to the second useful change; a change in contract.

2. A CHANGE OF CONTRACT

Leaders and managers with such a trusting, non-judgemental mindset and clear intention are much more inclined to invite their reports and colleagues to take more responsibility for their contribution to the conversation.

We have noticed that when a conversation tips more toward a coaching style, it involves a different nature of relationship with a higher degree of engagement from their colleagues. In our experience, the more willing these colleagues are to take ownership for their part in the conversation, the more open and powerful will be their reflection and their contribution. And, especially when it is about sensitive areas such as their behaviour or performance, the safer and the more efficient will be the conversation. If they feel forced into such a conversation they may feel threatened. They may be inclined to withdraw, with potential counter-productive impact on the relationship.

From our experience, some leaders and managers intuitively get this change in the nature of the relationship and create the safe conditions for it to happen – often unconsciously. Yet it is unusual for people used to setting the tone and pace of conversations with their colleagues to consciously review the nature and levels of expectations and permissions underpinning their relationships in the work place.

We believe reviewing these hidden, psychological contracts in the workplace can shed useful light here.

2.1. AWARENESS OF EXPLICIT AND IMPLICIT CONTRACTS

Examples of explicit contract: Employees have a written work contract with their employer agreeing on the terms of their relationships. Further formal pieces of contracting such as policies and procedures etc. add-up to form a body of explicit contracts of terms conditions and rules.

Examples of implicit/psychological contracts: There is a set of unwritten, and often unspoken, contracts, between for instance an employee and their manager.

Each employee will have their own unique set of expectations and desires of how they expect to be treated and what they are expected to do, which may/may not be visible to their manager. Similarly, each leader and manager will have unspoken and unwritten expectations and assumptions about their role and what their staff and bosses expect of them. That leader or manager will also have expectations of their staff, their boss, the organisation, etc.

Over years of promoting more coaching style conversations as leaders, we've heard many barriers and assumptions arising from these unspoken, unshared personal psychological contracts (some of which we shared in Table 1). Likewise, assumptions exist that can raise very similar barriers too at reports level; such as "it's up to the boss to tell us what to do."

It is important for leaders to grasp the subtleties that exist around these psychological contracts. They are important. They are complex contracts because they are interwoven, numerous, bespoke and unconscious.

2.2. AWARENESS OF THEIR IMPORTANCE

We believe that over time these implicit expectations have a life on their own and get hardwired as relationships become embedded. In concrete terms, individuals get used to their respective roles and styles and most often expect them to stay unchanged!

We found that more often than not, these implicit psychological contracts are subconscious on both sides and therefore have never been actually agreed with the other party. These 'secret' contracts can work well and may never surface. However, they may also be breached when the status quo changes, resulting in great upset when one or more expectation is not fulfilled and confusion for the one who inadvertently broke an agreement they did not even know existed!

We noticed for instance that such a breach in the unspoken agreement may occur, when a leader decides to change from always telling to adopt a coaching style without checking the expectations held by themselves and their team. Starting to ask for ideas when the team has been used to a command and tell mode may bring a level of uncertainty which may even come across as a threat if more context is not provided.

By contrast, bringing to the surface the fact that they're trying something new, and sharing their intentions in doing so, they give their counterparts the time and the opportunity to create a new and explicit contract on how they work together.

In our experience, leaders who consciously decide to make changes to their usual style achieve less disruption. They also create a much greater positive impact by sharing with their team their intention to support their learning and development. It empowers the team by adopting a new approach to their conversations.

2.3. AWARENESS OF THE COMPLEX 'LAYER CAKE' OF CONTRACTS

Recognising the importance of implicit contracts, we have further formed an opinion that leaders and managers willing to invite their colleagues to join them in less directive conversations need to sharpen their sensors and grow a sound awareness of where they operate in the complex 'layer-cake' of explicit and implicit contracts.

We share below in Table 2 some examples of this complexity as we observed them.

From what we have observed, a great deal of progress is obtained by those leaders who,

1. Have grown the habit of being conscious of what they are trying to achieve and also being attentive to all the signals from their colleagues and the broader environment.

2. At minimum apply the individual coaching skills of listening deeply, asking open questions and being present to their colleagues – all skills not requiring overt permission and relevant to enhance all leadership styles.

Table 2: Examples of complex layer-cake of contracts

Examples of situations	Examples of Challenges	Examples of Implications
Nature of the leaders' agenda	Unlike a coach, who focuses exclusively on the coachee's agenda, a manager has a primary agenda for delivering an expected level of performance by their team.	It is important for a manager to be mindful at all times of the boundaries, to be in position to secure the right agreement with their counterparts so they feel safe and willing to explore.
	Whilst the conversation can be non-directive to a certain point, ultimately it belongs to a bigger agenda.	People might not otherwise know whether it is a safe place to say what they really think, nor easily trust there is a genuine intention to hear what they think.
Factors outside the reach of the involved manager and report	An employee may have been accumulating frustration with the broader organisation.	This could spread to their expectation of their manager and have a detrimental effect on their unconscious psychological contracts in place with the manager, since the manager is associated with the organisation's agenda.
Levels of permission	Within the same team: Some members may feel comfortable with a more coaching style as they have been exposed to it from early days, and, finding it working well, have formed the relevant implicit agreements.	Each relation ship leaves a higher or lower level of permission to experiment with a new style. Some relationships have scope for leaders try out a number of new things as they have already established such agreement.
	Whereas other team members previously used to a different style might be cautious with the new one, possibly associated with other (adverse) changes.	Some require a more formal recontracting, to allow everyone to understand the intentions and implications behind the changed style, so that they can adjust their choices about how much responsibility they accept for thinking, solving and being creative.

3. IN CONCLUSION

Setting your mind on having a more coaching approach as a leader and manager has encouraged us to reflect upon our own individual experiences and observations, and build some form of consensus between us on what's been most important in how we've demonstrated and tried to role model this in each of our approaches. In this dialogue, we have come to the current conclusion that there needs to be clarity of mindset, contract and intention if one wants to change the nature of conversations to a more coaching approach.

Choosing to adopt a more 'coaching' mindset requires a deeper awareness of the individuals who will be impacted by the change. It's in effect altered the 'complex layer-cake of contracts' which have to be managed just as carefully as managing the change that's happening to the leader who's making the change.

The most useful questions that we learned to use on ourselves; "*What is my intention here? What am I trying to achieve? What is the nature of conversations I need to have? What is my mindset as I approach this conversation?*"

Even though we used to work in different industries and contexts, growing a greater awareness of our default styles has helped both of us become more effective in using these styles appropriately and contribute to creating a greater sense of trust and a greater engagement in others workplace.

Team members working with more coaching-orientated leaders are then more likely to feel empowered to take more ownership and responsibility for their own thinking. Both successes and challenges are treated as learning opportunities, making them feel more able and supported to take calculated risks without fear of failure and blame.

Questions:

- What have you changed in order to take a more coaching approach into your leadership style?
- What have you noticed encourages other to take up a coaching style in their leadership?

[Internal] Coach/Client relationships, inside and outside the coaching bubble; far more complex than just a question of definition

Ian Flanders - Dispatch from the [Internal Coaching] Front

I recently took the decision to stop working with a coachee. On the face of it, letting go of a client may be part of any coach's practice. For me as an internal coach however, it was something that had consequences on a number of levels.

BEYOND DEFINITIONS

The relationship of coachee to internal coach, outside the coaching relationship itself, is an interesting one. It often arises in relation to definition. An internal coach is described as someone who works with clients from their own organisation, but who do not work in the same 'chain of command'. However, almost in the same breath it seems, managers-as-coaches are talked of; being defined as someone who manages their team in a coaching 'style'. Clearly the client bases for these two 'coaches' are based upon completely different premises. But, as Ronnie Corbet would say at this point, I digress.

THE ORIGINAL AGREEMENT

I started working with Chris two years ago. My 'day-job' was in one function within the organisation, whilst he was a leader in another, unconnected function. Our teams interacted, as did we, but neither of us felt that our 'day-job' was a barrier to a coaching relationship.

The coaching agenda that Chris initially defined centred on his team.

- He wanted to explore options to change the structure, skillset and strategy of the team, in order to better support the needs of the business.

- Later, he introduced to our coaching sessions the topic of his own future career direction.

Having worked together within a coaching relationship for eighteen months my job role was expanded. As a result my leadership responsibility was expanded to include the function in which Chris was (and is) a senior manager; suddenly we were in the same 'chain of command'. He did not report directly to me. His boss, my direct report, sat between us, but to complicate things further his new boss was not the person who had initiated his coaching journey. We were three colleagues, interconnected, but the nature of each connection, and the lens it created through which my coaching relationship with Chris was visible, was unique to each of us.

RE-CONTRACTING FOR COACHING

For Chris it appeared that his main concern relating to this structural change was the potential loss of a 'thinking partner'. He valued the coaching sessions, using them as part of his process to design and implement the changes he believed necessary to move his team's performance forward. He was happy to carry on as before. Chris' boss appeared caught in a dilemma; supportive of coaching, indeed a coachee himself, and reluctant to challenge their new boss (me), but, very concerned at being out of the loop on the redesign of a key area of their function.

At this point I took the initiative to say that I felt it inappropriate to continue the coaching relationship with Chris.

However, this proved not to be the end of the story. Chris approached me to ask for specific coaching support to help him think through his future. He stated that he wanted to go back into the safe space that he and I had created to explore how he was feeling and think through how he wanted to move forward. I expressed my concern that I did not want to, as coach, come between Chris and his boss. He said that he understood this, but felt that the nature of his objective in restarting our coaching relationship would not create a conflict of interest. I agreed with him that any future collaboration should be with the full knowledge of his boss.

When I discussed Chris' request with his boss it became clear they recognised that the significant organisational changes Chris has experienced were having a significant impact on him, and that support to think through the implications and to decide how to move forward was in the interests of both Chris and the organisation. It was clear from our discussion that Chris' boss trusted me to respect the boundary between coach and line manager; I agreed to meet Chris again as his coach.

THIS DECISION PROVED TO BE A MISTAKE

Both Chris' boss and I respected the coach-coachee-manager boundaries, but Chris did not. When we met, Chris chose to use the time to question an organisational design decision that his boss, with my agreement, was implementing. He had been briefed on the proposed changes by his boss, but it became clear to me that, reflecting on the changes, he now had a number of personal concerns. He attempted to use the coaching session to reopen the decision and recruit me to his side.

I stopped the coaching session and became the function leader. I experienced intense feelings of disappointment, but also anger, and I am sure that both these emotions were visible at the end of the meeting.

REFLECTING ON MY TRAINING, WHAT I'VE LEARNT FROM MY EXPERIENCES

During my initial training to become a coach I instinctively felt that, for me, it would be inappropriate to coach someone who was 'connected' to me in the organisation. I know that I am not alone in this belief.

But this is now the second time that I have been drawn into this situation.

I reflect that, for me, there is a need to consider not just whether I can respect and maintain the boundaries in such a relationship, but also need to take a realistic, hard-headed view of whether the other parties to the coaching relationship can do the same. I need to be mindful that my 'ego' will always assure me that any internal relationship complication can be handled, and recall, with humility, the personal evidence that proves this is not the case.

How actual practice informs appreciation of the complex challenges in effective team coaching

Sue Young

INTRODUCTION

I am increasingly asked to do more team coaching, in addition to one-to-one coaching just by itself. I felt it would be an interesting time to take stock of my approach and review the underpinning principles/values I practice in my team coaching.

- In particular, working with the subtleties of how much communication in teams can be unspoken, directly.

- As well as covering such a range of different agendas, all at once!

I have also noticed that this is becoming a more general theme emerging in the field of coaching. Many terms such as action learning, peer groups etc. are already popular practices. I am especially interested in how team coaching can operate at the level more towards the scale of organisation development, involving a scale of issue involved, which can have wide implications around the organisation.

1. THE NATURAL OPPORTUNITY FOR ORGANISATIONAL TEAM COACHING, ALONG WITH MORE DYNAMIC CHALLENGES

For me, coaching **organisational leadership teams** is the most challenging form of coaching. This form of team coaching combines:

- The high quality individual attention of one to one coaching, with

- The highly dynamic, and open, interactive nature of working with a group of highly capable individuals on challenges that requires the coach to make judgement calls 'on the hoof'.

Being involved in this type of coaching has **a scale of potential impact**. Working with leadership teams, the whole system with its established dynamics and culture, lives in the room.

I believe this form of coaching is a central part of organisation development for real.

The potential value of a team-coaching intervention lies in the likelihood of real organisational impact for this group of people both individually, and collectively. It will also have a major impact on the health and functioning of the whole organisation.

I am going to review my approach here through a series of overview headline principles, along with some case illustrations. I hope in further blogs to explore some of the particular issues involved, in more detail. I have also taken the opportunity to review some of the writings in the field.

2. A SAMPLE OF CURRENT, AND POPULAR, DEFINITIONS OF TEAM COACHING

A number of labels are thrown around in relation to working with teams – team building, team facilitation, team development – and now, team coaching. In a similar fashion, there have been a number of attempts to define team coaching. Here are some examples:

2.1. **Clutterbuck (2007)**[1] defines team coaching as "helping the team improve performance and the processes by which performance is achieved, through reflection and dialogue."

He introduces the term "performance" as task deliverables and also acknowledges attention to processes or ways of working. While at a general level, this all applies, it does not reflect the organisational context that I see as such a fundamental underpinning of team coaching within organisations.

2.2. **Kets de Vries**[2] (2005) "Leadership team coaching is defined as leadership coaching in a group setting with the intention to establish a foundation of trust, develop the capacity to constructively resolve conflict and build accountability amongst its members in order to achieve better results for the organisation."

De Vries brings in more organisation context through use of terms such as "leadership", "constructively resolve conflict", "accountability" and "results for the organisation".

What is missing from this for me is the interaction between the individual and the team, and how coaching addresses this.

---

[1] Clutterbuck D. 2007. *Coaching the Team at Work*, Nicholas Brearley, London .
[2] Kets de Vries, M F R. 2005. "Leadership group coaching in action: The Zen of creating high performance teams". In *Academy of Management*.

2.3. **Hawkins**[3] (2014) thought the title "systemic team coaching" to be more applicable to leadership teams in organisational settings, which he went on to define in more detail as follows:

> *"Systemic team coaching is a process by which a team coach works with a whole team, both when they are together and when they are apart, in order to help them improve both their collective performance and how they work together, and also how they develop their collective leadership to more effectively engage with all their key stakeholder groups to jointly transform the wider business."*

I see this incorporating more explicitly the wider relational scope for team coaching, emphasising the individual more when he incorporates "when they are apart."

In general terms, this definition holds. However, in terms of my personal practice where it misses is on the quality of individual attention involved. At the end of the day if team coaching is going to have sustainable impact then it's down to what each team member takes back into their part of the organisation.

Each of these attempts at definition still leaves me with a sense that more is needed. In my experience (and needs more attention) the reality of contracting and working as a team coach is highly variable, dynamic and responsive, and in line with the priorities and readiness of the client(s).

The client is usually the team leader, formally, to start with, and then the team itself in a broader organisational context:

- Both in relation to the more tangible nature of the organisational task,
- And the more intangible and usually unspoken aspects of the organisational culture.

While in general terms the general definitions hold well, they do not bring to life for me the organisational and people complexities involved.

3. BRINGING TEAM COACHING TO LIFE, FOR ME

So what are the features of how team coaching works, for me?

I have had a number of different team leadership and team member roles and have worked as a consultant and coach with management teams in private and public sectors, both in the UK and internationally.

Each principle has intuitively come to me but all have been deeply embedded through my career. I run through a set of 12 key principles that's guided my approach, as headlines with a few comments.

---

[3] Hawkins, Peter .2014. *Leadership Team Coaching; Developing Collective Transformational Leadership* Ed. 2. Kogan Page.

1. Are we a Team – what is our collective purpose?

2. The role of the team coach is an enabling one.

3. High quality of attention to individuals and their personal needs and contribution in their role.

4. The Team Leader as a crucial element, both enabler and blocker.

5. Working with differences more explicitly.

6. The need for continuous contracting on several fronts.

7. Creating a climate of greater openness.

8. Bringing in external stakeholder perspectives.

9. Bringing in the big unspoken issues and hidden agendas.

10. Integrating personal feedback as part of the individual and collective learning process.

11. Designing in sustainability with team coaching interventions.

12. The essential value of an external professional sounding board/supervision in team coaching.

While I draw from formal knowledge across a multidisciplinary field of theory, the most important ways I have learned are from my experience of working with teams - discussions with colleagues and clients, both on the job and in review afterwards. I see it as a continuous learning process, and this is a useful focus for me in checking out how it works, for me.

1. ARE WE A TEAM - WHAT IS OUR COLLECTIVE PURPOSE?

In my experience, even the most capable and senior management teams struggle with (or even ignore) this one.

Developing an effective leadership team requires focused investment of time and energy to establish common ground and a common team agenda to which everyone contributes.

In complex organisations, an individual's area is a demanding and complex task. The senior team is often geographically dispersed. In the day to day pace and thrust of organisational life individuals are often struggling with what they have on their plates - how are they going to cope with additional time/task commitment? Even time at team meetings becomes a reporting ritual that adds little value and is just something to be got through.

Much of the team coaching assignment is often around this; helping a team develop its own collective vision and common sense of purpose and strategy in relation to the bigger organisational context. This thinking then informs individual focus and thinking. For example, what information do I hold from my area that the whole team needs to be aware of as it has an impact on our overall strategy?

Strategy is a living thing that needs to be kept under continuous periodic review, rather than something formally committed to paper then set aside while we get back to the real day-to-day business.

2. The role of the team coach is an enabling one

I see team coaching as an enabling role, rather than coming up with the solution. The fundamental judgement calls about what to take forward in the organisation remain with the team. This links to the objectives for the coaching - around creating the conditions to enable the kinds of conversation needed to help the team find its own way forward.

Of course, the team coach is making the judgement call in collaboration with the client, around when to do what, in what sequence and identifying the kinds of stimulus or support needed. This, together with their credibility and the relationship they build with the team, are what they bring.

The role of team coach is multifaceted – coach, mediator, facilitator, process provider, providing selective inputs around relevant frameworks, models, tools and ideas, observer, feedback giver and sometimes just to listen.

3. High quality of attention to individuals and their personal needs and contributions in their role

One of my aims is to help enable that individual to bring the best of themselves and their knowledge/experience into the team. I always aim, where possible, to build in confidential individual sessions.

Interestingly I tend not to name these sessions as 'coaching' as often that term is perceived as being remedial, implying some deficit, and can set up defensive barriers that would get in the way.

The purpose of these individual sessions is to provide confidential space where team members can express and develop their thinking about how they see the team's objectives and their contribution to that.

I usually aim to produce a compilation of anonymised answers to a few common cue questions around how they see a 'bigger picture' strategic perspective on the team's Task, Processes and Key Relationships. For example, how do they see priorities for the overall team, the main opportunities and challenges, and the scope they perceive for greater collaboration that would add greatest value to overall team objectives?

Often this very thinking process in itself is individually developmental in encouraging senior managers to take a more 'whole-organisational' and longer-term strategic perspective

That then naturally leads into what they see as their current and potential contribution to the Department/Unit/Whole-organisation overall objectives. It is also an exploration of their leadership approach, engaging their people in the overall direction. How are they helping their managers to develop and contribute to bigger organisational goals?

In my experience, they often relish the luxury of that 'space' held by somebody else to think and reflect more than they would naturally otherwise do.

Of course, the credibility, tone and style set by the coach is critical. Do they trust and respect the coach as a person sufficiently to be open to genuine exploration in order to self-disclose? Do they believe their coach's abilities to understand the nature of the business and leadership challenges they face?

4. THE TEAM LEADERS AS A CRUCIAL ELEMENT, BOTH ENABLER AND BLOCKER

The tone and climate in a hierarchical world set by the team leader is critical. It must especially be right if people are going to open up to express whatever they really think, particularly if it is a different perspective or feedback that could be perceived as negative or difficult. They need to have the confidence that they will not be 'punished' or get a negative response.

Usually the team leader leads/holds the formal contract. Even if the 'paper' contract is formally held elsewhere, e.g. by HR, then people will be looking to the formal leader's response.

In my team coaching there are always individual sessions with the team leader. I find usually they discount the inhibiting effect their formal position may be having on people's willingness to share what they really think.

The team leader can make a uniquely valuable contribution if they model the kinds of behaviour required to build trust and encourage collaborative ways of working. This often requires them to know how to be more open and self-disclosing with each of the individuals and the group as a collective.

5. WORKING WITH DIFFERENCES MORE EXPLICITLY

In my experience, the best teams comprise individuals with very different and complementary strengths. I find selective use of psychometrics and profiling tools help people make more sense of differences; some of them look at personality styles, others ways of working and ways of seeing the world.

- Instruments like Belbin's Team Roles I particularly like in a team context as it is simple and people can relate easily to the needs of a team and to the different contributions required.

- The Strengths Deployment Inventory is another that I like with its specific focus on strengths and different motivators and its ability to visualise a team and its dynamics around behaviour linked to personal values

Every coach has their preferred instruments. For me they are catalysts to helping people talk about personal differences in a way that is less threatening. It also provides fresh thinking about practical ways to improve working relationships.

6. THE NEED FOR CONTINUOUS CONTRACTING ON SEVERAL FRONTS

Clear contracting is important in individual coaching. In team coaching managing boundaries through clear contracting is core to the on-going team coaching process.

At the outset, there is the need to contract, formally, with the commissioning client, most often the team leader. They usually have a clear picture of the felt need. In my experience, this is often the symptom of a bigger need. There is also the need to contract – albeit less formally – with every individual team member, particularly around confidentiality. Unless individuals trust me not to feed back to the boss, that severely limits what the coaching is able to achieve.

7. CREATING A CLIMATE OF GREATER OPENNESS

The coach has to demonstrate this, as well as facilitate it in others, to start with, but if trust is built right from the start, the 'mature' others, usually, quickly pick up on the lead in contributing as more open and ready team members pick up and start to build.

In my experience, people feel the benefits it yields are more real and open conversations. For example, the fact that everyone holds valuable information and perspectives that have useful contributions toward the way forward. Some hold information from the 'front line' with feedback and real perspectives from end users. These are often the source of fresh insights and innovative thinking. This kind of front line input is the lifeblood of keeping a strategy a living item under continuous review in order to enhance abilities to respond more quickly.

8. BRINGING IN EXTERNAL STAKEHOLDER PERSPECTIVES

Senior teams get caught up in being over-focused on day-to-day tasks and firefighting and internal matters. It's very easy to become distant from end users and the eternal realities that services and products need to work with.

9. Bringing in the Big Unspoken Issues and Hidden Agendas

It's very typical for there to be areas in leadership teams that never quite get on to the agenda for attention, let alone discussion.

These 'unspoken' issues are usually at the heart of team coaching. They are in the too-difficult pending tray due to the different hidden agendas of individuals.

There are different flavours of unspoken. Some examples I have experienced are:

- Issues where there is unresolved conflict. Nobody wants to offend and risk making it worse. The result is that people diplomatically avoid the subject and the tension lurks beneath the surface.

- Issues that are complex that carry a high degree of risk and uncertainty– they are in the too-difficult box and people do not want to risk failure.

- Fear of losing power or control leads to people being cautious and holding back – "I do not want to upset the apple cart". It means retaining a sense of control.

- People in the team that are perceived as difficult. This may be personal style and/or they may be raising or representing difficult issues that others are avoiding. At worst that individual may become the scapegoat. Particularly if they have a strong style that can be used as a deflector "XX is so assertive/aggressive...", by deflecting attention away from the issue they want to avoid.

10. Integrating Personal Feedback as Part of the Individual and Collective Learning Process

I do this in a number of ways. In team sessions I offer selective observations, particularly on things I see happening – either behaviours I see or process issues e.g. "I'm noticing a falloff in energy around this issue"

I also introduce feedback processes as part of our way of working. For example, asking at the end of a session what people have found of greatest value and what they would want more/less of/differently at our next meeting. In this I am seeking to introduce them to approaches they can continue to use as part of their normal way of working, ensuring they are extracting explicitly key learning points from their team exchanges.

Finally, I introduce personal feedback between team members to encourage greater openness and building of rapport and comfort around this deeper level of collective learning.

11. Designing in Sustainability with Team Coaching Interventions

I define sustainability as demonstrating and working with approaches and ways of managing themselves that will enable the team to better manage their working processes and relationships going forwards. Approaches that will enhance their effectiveness as a working team.

I believe it is important to develop team members' capabilities to take these ways of working down into their teams and staff.

12. THE ESSENTIAL VALUE OF AN EXTERNAL PROFESSIONAL SOUNDING BOARD/SUPERVISION IN TEAM COACHING

Finally, in a very demanding and complex area of work as team coaching I find it essential to have a number of sources of coaching supervision:

- Self-supervision – writing this piece has stimulated higher levels of awareness and reflection than might otherwise have taken place. It's a rich learning process in its own right.

- Supervisory conversations with my formal peer supervisor(s) and trusted colleagues.

4. SOME CASES THAT BRING TEAM COACHING TO LIFE, FOR ME

I outline briefly here the sorts of cases that, for me, help to show how these principles can apply – in different ways, and to different extents. Team coaching is more complex and 'messy' than the text books would have us believe! The examples I share are intended as 'snapshots' to illustrate the diversity of needs that team coaching can involve.

CASE 1: THE TEAM THAT WAS HAVING ISSUES ENGAGING WITH THE WIDER ORGANISATIONAL TEAM AND EXTERNAL STAKEHOLDERS

A series of customer service errors had received much negative publicity for this organisation. A formal review and report had come out with a key recommendation being to develop more collaborative ways of working across the technical expertise and functional silos. My brief was to work with the SMT on this overall objective.

As I had individual conversations with team members and observed their quarterly SMT Review Meeting, it became clear that there was a strong focus on immediate task focus with absence of attention to external parties and absence of real intelligence from customer and users.

The challenge became more one of working with the senior team on:

- Considering the impact of decisions and actions in their area on other areas, as well as what they needed from other areas.

- Developing more external focus, developing closer relationships with key external stakeholders.

- How they shared information and market intelligence with each other.

- Holding a longer-term perspective on the whole business so that each SMT member felt able to take on board and pass on to their area.

- How they were going to engage their managers.

It took some time, and process, inside the senior team to get a constructive, collective focus on these more external facing opportunities. This was in addition to building a more open dialogue process which brought in the diversity of perspectives required for better quality thinking and decisions, compared to the typical more internal short-term task focus in their meetings.

Energy in the team coaching, on an Away Day, was focused on exposing the team to hearing first-hand end users' experiences, and hearing from leaders facing similar issues in completely differently sectors. The stimulus from this was then brought in to their team idea generation. This opened up discussions on how they could practically adjust day-to-day ways of working to bring in greater end user focus and responsiveness to external stakeholders. There was a generation of fresh thinking and approaches. The idea was also to generate excitement, motivation, even to have an enjoyable experience and to stimulate change in the largely internally focused agenda at SMT meetings.

Part of the coaching also involved working with senior team members on getting their own separate teams engaged through review of day-to-day ways of working and involving them to generate new thinking about improvements.

Case 2: The team dealing with challenges of physical distance and unfamiliarity with each other's roles

This group was called together to form a project team, and their outcomes would have important contributions to make to the strategic opportunities the organisation was facing. This was a very large and complex internationally spread organisation.

The members of the group had considerable challenges in becoming a team! Their current everyday management roles were very demanding and they were geographically dispersed.

Practical ways of slowly building the attitudes and skills needed to work as a highly integrated team took time, and a lot of learning about each other, let alone the task given to them.

I had individual coaching sessions with them as well as four team sessions over the course of a year.

I used Tuckman (forming, storming, norming, performing) Myers Briggs (MBTI) and the Belbin framework to raise awareness of the typical stages teams go through and used the Belbin and MBTI instruments to raise awareness of different styles in the team. I got them thinking about how they could make best use of them in how they worked. This accelerated their abilities and brought greater focus on process and relationship aspects of managing their internal client.

As they developed their cohesion and the project got well underway, my role evolved to observing and asking occasional questions, encouraging them to review their way of working, both within the team and with their internal client, and provide feedback to each other. By the end of the year they were truly self-managing.

The project helped what was a highly structured and hierarchical organisation learn and build confidence in the idea of building project teams to drive and pilot innovation. This became a major strategic benefit, in itself, apart from what the team eventually achieved.

One of the team members (on the basis of the personal credibility they achieved) was invited to continue on a part-time basis to extend the project into exploring how it could be more embedded into an on-going change organisation-wide initiative.

CASE 3: A TEAM OF COACHES - LAYING OUT STANDARDS FOR EXECUTIVE TEAM COACHING FOR A PROFESSIONAL ACCREDITATION BODY

There is nothing quite like working with a group of experts on a subject! I was a team member, rather than holding a separate role from others. However, of course, as team coaching experts we were all facilitating the team!

Again, the biggest challenge involved was about the range of practice models involved in each team member's highly successful team coaching practice. Integrating these approaches, as well as integrating any standard framework to encompass others approaches not directly involved became one of the longest, and most informative projects, about team coaching I have enjoyed.

5. CONCLUSIONS AND NEXT STEPS

This has been a powerful exercise for me in reviewing all the files of experience I hold about my team coaching practice.

A major area that stands out for me in this review is just **how much the team coach's role is concerned with drawing out and normalising the "unspoken" issues and tensions around them**. Helping the team navigate and discover ways to manage the more difficult conversations and identify and realise the true opportunities they have.

It has also made me aware of just how much more there is to some of these projects than could be explained, simply. I could write a book about each of these cases; and even then I suspect there would still be so much left unsaid about what and why the team coaching worked as well as it did.

In doing this overview it has raised my level of interest in exploring some of these themes in more depth. I'd be really interested to hear about others approaches and their key learning points about the multi-faceted and challenging area of team coaching.

Doing edge work creates waves of value for the client, and the organisation

KC Char

WHAT DOES IT MEAN TO WORK ON THE EDGE?

To work on the edge:

- I have to be fully present, take every detail into account and make quick, sharp decisions.

- I feel fully alive and become acutely aware of what I am doing and saying, and the impact.

- I have to interpret the meaning of what my client and other stakeholders are communicating to me in words, expressions and tone.

When I visualize what I mean by edge work, I think of skiing in the Alps along a narrow pathway where I have to ensure I stay on track. Lots of skiers (of various levels of expertise) are around me, some racing past me, others following right behind almost touching my skis. The edge feels dangerously close, beyond which is a drop of thousands of feet. Not being a very good skier, this is both a frightening and exhilarating experience. This is how I often feel when working with my clients.

I do this edge work with CEO's and senior executives usually over a one-year period - a minimum amount of time for the benefits to be experienced. Some of my assignments last over three years. When I became aware, some eight to ten years ago, that this is the work I wanted to do, I began declining other assignments that did not challenge me to stay on my toes!

COACHING ON THE EDGE

I believe I do my best work when it is 'on the edge' as I feel alive, full of energy and I know the stakes are high. I would like to explore in future posts what this edge work entails for my practice, and describe how it can create value for both the client and multiple stake holders in the organisation.

In this first case, I describe how I worked on the edge from the first face to face meeting. A detailed example that explores my approach to contracting, it follows a 'chemistry' session to on-board a senior business head who was joining the organisation. As part of their visit and orientation program, a meeting was arranged with me.

IT ALL STARTED WITH A DELAY

On arrival, I was asked to sit in a bare conference room to await this leader. After about 20 minutes an assistant came in and said, "I just heard that your meeting is going to start two hours later. I suppose it is best you wait here? I can bring you some coffee?" I wondered what the reason was for the delay, but unfortunately the assistant had no further information.

Whilst I was waiting I made two flip charts: [1] the first hundred days written down with the key focus areas and [2] the critical deliverables for success of a senior executive. It was part of my preparation of what I'd imagined, from other executives I had coached at this level, would be on their mind. I wrote the following:

- Assume operational leadership,
- Take charge of the team,
- Align with key stakeholders,
- Engage with the culture, and
- Build strategic priorities.

I had used these criteria successfully with other leaders. It seemed to align with typical thinking of what was important for success in the first one hundred days.

THE INITIAL FEW SECONDS OF MEETING

Finally the executive arrived, very self-assured with an open gaze and half smile, and said, *"Oh I'm really sorry, my plane was delayed; and on top of it there were no shower facilities in the arrival lounge at the airport – I had counted on that after an overnight flight!"* I raised my eyebrows and half smiled too in response. *"So I had to go to my hotel to shower and get ready."* With that smile and twinkle in the eye, it made me feel a sense of lightness of let's not take all of this so seriously!

He then rolled his eyes and continued, *"and it took another half hour at the hotel to get my clothes ironed."* I was a bit surprised at the level of transparency with the details of the delay, so early on in our meeting, and I found myself smiling back and making a quick connection to this person I had just met. It seemed to be a mutual feeling as it resulted with "*I'll cancel the first meeting after yours so that we will have at least two hours to speak and see what may come out of our discussion around coaching.*"

Perhaps, in this moment, I was a source of 'lack of pressure' and I had the sense that he had become curious about what coaching could offer him. I felt relaxed and my initial impressions were, "*Wow, very self-assured even though he is brand new to this organisation.*"

THE FIRST WAVE OF VALUE: TELLING THE CLIENT WHAT I THINK THEY NEEDED

I began with a coaching question that had proven useful with most clients, "*Well okay, now that we have two hours together, what would you like to get out of it that will make a difference for you?*" Instead, looking straight back at me, he quickly fired back with, "*I've travelled for ten hours and I'm not sure I want to get asked many questions – you are the expert who has done this before, so what do you want me to get out of this time?*"

I laughed, which is usually my way of gaining some time to think. I quickly processed what I knew so far since meeting, he is being straight and transparent, not playing the social game or following my rules. Rather than following a format of what's normally worked I responded in kind, "*Ok! From my side, I would like to explore how we may possibly work together and the value it can give you.*" And this was met with a smile, "*that sounds like a great result for two hours.*"

And so I started by inquiring whether any personality assessments or 360s had previously been carried out. This reached its conclusion when the potential client said, "*Well, I don't really put much weight on personality assessments – I have not seen the value. I've taken a number of them and I do have some 360s. The most important thing for me right now, is how I will get started in my new position and hit the ground running.*"

Great! I was now able to share my flip charts then and what he could focus on in the first one hundred days. The response was positive, "*Wow! Those are great areas of focus – very pragmatic, which I like.*" I could tell he had begun thinking and relating to his own experience. He began speaking about each of the criteria for success and as I explained what was behind each, he put his own context to it and began to take a few notes. He then said, "*Can you send this to me?*" I immediately said, "*Sure, I'm happy to send this to you and adapt it based on our discussion.*" And then he shared more explicitly how he worked which confirmed some of my initial impressions, "*I like things simple and straight forward; not too many models that consultants keep throwing around.*"

At this point, the conversation shifted into understanding further how leaning into the edge I was offering would work for him. *"How does this coaching work? What am I going to get out of it besides talking to you and getting your advice?"* I was about to respond with something like, it's going to be up to you what you get out of it, which I know is also true, however, I made up my mind and stepped up with, *"Well, that could be one part of it. Often people in very senior positions do not have anyone they can really talk to inside the organisation, so being able to discuss the undiscussables and having a thought partner is very useful. In addition, from my experience and what clients have told me, getting real time feedback and suggestions can be invaluable."* He responded in kind, *"As I mentioned I'm a very pragmatic person, so I like to know what the outcomes would be."* Here was the word 'pragmatic' again and I made a mental note of coming back to it to understand the meaning of this word and how it translated into his leadership style.

Meanwhile, I shared a couple of examples of specific outcomes that other clients had benefited from by working with me. It was through sharing this information and how he was responding, I said to myself, *"I really have my potential client listening now!"* and followed up with, *"I have done several on-boarding assignments with leaders taking on key positions. Did you know that about 40 percent of senior executives who change jobs or get promoted fail in the first eighteen months?"* I smiled as I said this, raising my eyebrows slightly, and he laughed! Again, looking directly at me he said, half smiling, *"Oh so you're going to ensure that I make it past the eighteen months? Is that the ultimate goal?"* I said, *"Well besides making it – thriving and succeeding is what you want, right? Well it could be. But I'm not in charge of that. You are!"*

THE SECOND WAVE OF VALUE: TRUST EVOLVES IN UNUSUAL WAYS

Another shift occurred in our relationship, when he told me something that they had not shared with anyone yet in this new company, a personal situation that was going to make it even more challenging, than what would be usual for all senior executives, relocating their families to a new country.

Again, I was surprised by this transparency and openness, and in order to reassure him I said in a serious tone, *"The basis of our relationship, if we decide to work together, is trust. So I want you to know that you can trust me."* Reflecting back on this moment, this is where I made a slight blunder because it was met with a rather serious look and response, *"Oh I don't work along the basis of trusting someone who tells me to trust them. I will trust you to start out with, however, if you break that trust for whatever reason, then I will not trust you again."* I wondered about that and decided not to say more on that subject. Yet I appreciated that he was going to be direct with me, and was clearly setting his expectations.

At this point, we still had no 'formal' contract and there was about half an hour remaining. In that hour and half, we had built sufficient mutual respect and trust that he wanted to admit something to me, "*I have not had (one important organisational function) report to me in previous positions. I would prefer to know in more depth about some of the work they do, enough to ask the right questions and challenge them when necessary. Since I need to get up to speed quickly, would you know somebody who could help me?*" I said, "*Let me think about this. I could see you having a couple of sessions with someone who has this expertise, and whom you could ask any question to, so that you feel more comfortable and competent in your new context.*"

I gave him an example of another executive whom I'd worked with who had been in a similar role and position. Every time he went into a meeting with people in that important organisation function, all the technical experts involved would smirk at his lack of knowledge of the sophisticated work they believed they were doing. What he did was to engage two experts from outside the company to come and tutor him for couple of months, so he felt comfortable discussing and asking the key questions. I said, "*This is quite normal, there are usually some gaps when one takes on a new role with a huge scope. Identifying these ahead of time and speeding up the learning curve is a great strategy.*"

In my way I normalized the situation without bringing any judgement to it. This allowed him to express that actually it was just something that needed to be learnt. In turn it allowed him , I think, to see me as a great resource.

ADDING FUTURE WAVES OF VALUE: GETTING INTO THE ORGANISATION PROVIDES BIG OPPORTUNITIES TOO

We'd explored quite a few important points when he started to share with me that he really wanted to know what the new organisation and executive team were actually like. At this point, he had no idea. When he said that, I thought this is good, because now I can do what I do best which is to get into the organisation and talk to the people. That's the only way I can support him to get on board quickly.

AT THE EDGE: PUTTING THE CONTRACT IN PLACE

The moment had arrived where we started to seriously negotiate what my role as coach could be. It started with a suggestion of attending an offsite strategy meeting and facilitating that. I was now confident enough to suggest something else. What was offered wasn't something that would help him make the most important use of my time and strengths and give him the added value he deserved. So I countered with, "*I can facilitate your strategy meeting. However, what I had in mind was to meet your team one on one to get an understanding of their context and what they need from you as the leader.*" He hesitated a few seconds and then said, "*Yes, let's think about how we might do this so it can be useful.*"

We finally reached the end of our conversation. In the normal way of ending such a session we shook hands, and left on a positive note, *"This is great. Really nice meeting you. Thank you. Get back to me on a couple of those points that we discussed."*

I did.

I didn't hear from him for several days and took a bold step to put a contract together. I sent the executive concerned a contract for six months and I roughly calculated I would spend about two days a month working with him. The contract contained the typical fees per day, and other relevant charges and, with the covering email, sent it through to him with the next steps. In the contract, I wrote, based on our first discussion, these are the areas we will focus on: your first hundred days with a few bullets (after weighing up what's really required). And followed with, *"Anything else that you want to speak about within this package?"*

It was met with a simple response of, and awareness of my previous work with the organisation, *"Send it to the appropriate person for processing."* I took it as given that this was the approval and contacted his assistant to ensure that it would be taken through the formalities of obtaining a purchase order etc. The assistant and I established a rapport as we communicated on this and she turned out to be a key stakeholder because what followed was the challenge of getting our sessions scheduled onto his packed agenda. So I decided a different tactic. This is where many coaches stumble, I believe.

I called the assistant again— and because we had established some rapport, she explained how busy this new executive was and how difficult it was to get on his agenda. I said, *"You know what, this coaching is really important for him in the first six months to be successful in this new role. So please make some time on the agenda."* I made some executive decisions on dates together, and found out when the key meetings for the executive were and we scheduled six half-day sessions at his office.

After our second session, the assistant shared with me the waves of value I was bringing. *"I can see that he needs you – there are just too many things happening and getting on board to lead this complex organisation is not easy. However, after he sees you he seems a lot calmer and focused! You're important for his well-being."*

We were now off!

REFLECTING ON THE WAVES OF VALUE FROM WORKING ON THE EDGE

Taking the time to reflect on how I add waves of value really starts with knowing that I work best when my coaching is on the edge. Breaking down what that edge is has helped me to realise the number of edges I am working with both psychologically, and physically, to create the necessary conditions for that first meeting.

PART 2: Cutting edge: Investigating patterns from Practitioner Experiences

- What mattered most when working with this client was those initial few seconds where we quickly processed a lot of verbal and non-verbal behaviours and made a choice of how we each responded, which provided the gateway into having a longer conversation that lasted two hours.

- In every moment of our conversation the contracting process was happening, and this typically occurred when I had found the appropriate content for the conversation that resulted in him leaning into my edge. It is this connection that leads to the waves of value that I can bring to our working relationship. I can see this in the way that people offer and add detail that allows them to disclose something that is personal and important to them.

- By continually finding and creating the right conditions in that initial meeting – where some approaches may work for some and not for others – it was my job to prove that I was able to 'add value'. Knowing where my real strengths lie, and when the right conditions and relationship had been created with the client, I was able to confidently share and articulate the relevance and value of these strengths to them.

It can inevitably always feel like being on the edge - of uncertainty as making a difference, and creating those waves of positive difference involves doing things – differently. Yet, I realise how important it is to get small things just right to create these effects – often it's the small ripples that build!

Question: How do you know when you're working at your edge and making waves of value in that first meeting that leads to results?

CHAPTER 7

INTUITION

Challenge, Trust and Intuition in the Coaching Relationship

Luis San Martin

"THROWING THE BALL BACK"

This is a very personal article about coaching. As such, you will find personal reflections and several personal confessions. Let me start with a confession: I am a tennis player. As far as I know from my personal experience and from seeing other players, it is a chronic condition. So far there's nothing I can do about it. Like with any chronic condition, you may as well get used to living with it and try to enjoy it as much as you can.

Now let me tell you about another tennis player: Tim Gallwey. The very first time that I heard about his seminal book *The Inner Game of Tennis*[1] I was in London. I had been selected for one of those leadership training programs multinational companies send you to – Thomson Reuters in my case. One of the trainers mentioned the inner game theory and the book. As soon as I heard the title I was alert and interested. I wanted to know more. That day, I went into a bookshop in Piccadilly street, bought a copy and read it as the tennis player I was.

Reading the *Inner Game of Tennis* left an impression in me, lasting even until I became a coach years later. In 2012, The Association for Coaching interviewed Tim Gallwey. Again, the interview left a lasting impression – if you haven't seen this interview before you can watch it on youtube[2].

I totally recommend it.

In this interview, Mr Gallwey summed up his vision of coaching, reviewing key insights in the development of coaching as a discipline. He explained how important it was for him to realise that coaching was about putting the focus

---

[1] Gallwey, Timothy. 1986. *The Inner Game of Tennis*. PAN Books.
[2] https://www.youtube.com/watch?v=q8Xov1NgXgQ

on the coachee learning, rather than on the coach teaching. He also described the coaching conversation as one where, and I quote, *"the coach has to keep throwing the ball back, the leadership ball back to the coachee, so that he is taking responsibility and accountability for the choices that he's making. He's thinking for himself, she's thinking for herself."*

CHALLENGE IN THE COACHING RELATIONSHIP

I believe that Tim Gallwey is really serious when he talks about "throwing the ball back". There's no bigger challenge for any tennis player. As coaches, we don't dispute that challenge is essential to coaching. The more important question to be asked is how each of us do it. How much, how deep and even when to challenge is something we all probably have different ideas about.

As individual members of the coaching community, we all share a set of competencies and training without which we couldn't do our work. Furthermore, we would probably agree on the key elements we must find in any definition of coaching. However, most certainly, all of us put coaching into practice in a very personal way and have a different idea of what challenge is. And thank God for that.

At the end of the day, coaching is – or should be – a very personal thing.

You are who you are as a coach. For me, it is much like a musician performing classical music. Classical musicians share the same set of skills, they have the same formal training needed to read a very complex score where they will find, with impressive detail, everything they need to perform. Every trained musician can read the same music score written by, for instance, Mozart, Beethoven or Chopin. However, when they sit to play the same score on the piano, not every performer will sound quite the same. Their music will not touch you in the same way. They bring their personality, passion, years of training and the mood they are in when actually performing and it all becomes part of the music.

The same can be said of coaches putting coaching into practice. Each one of us interprets challenge in their own way. For me, and based in my experience, the right challenge is determined by a triangle formed by three things:

1. Trust in the coachee,
2. Trust in my intuition, and
3. Being present and working with what is in the moment.

1. TRUST IN THE COACHEE

"Don't forget the essence. Don't forget that what we're dealing with is a human being, that has great potential and is somewhat handicapped by their interferences and that's a delicate job. (...) Learning is an inherit capability within people and you don't have to put it into people, you

have to encourage it and bring out and that's the privilege of a coach"
Tim Gallwey - An Association for Coaching Interview

I suppose, the very first thing you have to do if you want to be trusted (and deliver on this privilege of a coach) is trust yourself. It is very difficult to expect that your coachee trusts you if he or she doesn't feel trusted by you. People pick up on those things.

Establishing trust is one of the foundations of the coaching relationship. It is important, among other things, because you never know where you are going to go in the coaching process or how your coachee will respond to or resolve a challenge. This is a fascinating reality. One that, as a coach, I enjoy.

My coaching experience has taught me to acknowledge that the client 'knows', even if they think they don't know, and that eventually they will have the ability to self-regulate. This could be presented as a gestaltic approach to coaching, of course. Clarkson[3] words it as follows:

> *"Gestaltits assume that people know at some level what is good for them. (...) The counsellor uses himself or herself actively and authentically in the encounter with the other person. It is more a way of being and doing than a set of techniques or a prescribed formula for counseling. Gestalt is characterized by a willingness on the part of the counselor to be active, present as a person and interventionist in the counseling relationship. This is based on the assumption that treating the client as a human being with intelligence, responsibility and active choices at any moment in time is most likely to invite the client into autonomy, self-healing and integration."*

I must say that in my experience this has always been true. So it is more than a theoretical stand point. Trusting that the client 'knows' is, for me, essential. As coaches we work with the coachee's responsibility and awareness, yet:

- It is the coachee who makes his or her own choices.

- He or she will live with the consequences of those decisions, and

- If the coaching process is done in a conscious way, no matter what the outcome, the coachee will have strengthened his or her ability to learn and self-regulate.

- They will also have the personal structure to rise to future challenges.

There is something to be said about when to throw the challenge. As coaches we will often clearly see what the challenge is but choose to develop the relationship further before we face the client with it. A stronger relationship or a more confident client could determine the success of the process. It is not uncommon to face this dilemma at the very early stages of the process, even in chemistry meetings.

---

[3] Clarkson, P. 1989. *Gestalt Counselling in Action.* Series Editor Windy Dryden.

Experience has shown me that it's best to wait, develop the relationship and make sure that a number of things are in place before throwing the ball.

2. TRUST IN MY INTUITION

It was pretty late in life that I found out that I am an 'N'. I guess that when this happened I started to take my intuition more seriously. Since then, I feel that I have come a long way but I am still learning to 'use' my intuition. Before that, I knew I was intuitive but I didn't take it as seriously as I do now.

According to Jung, Intuition is a mental process that individuals tend to favour when gathering information or drawing conclusions about issues. Obviously, being an "N" conditions all my experience of intuition and I couldn't speak about it as an "S". Intuitive people know but they don't know how they know. Intuition (as Sensation) is considered by Jung an irrational (non rational) function because it is often reflexive or involuntary, rather than conscious or deliberate[4] . Talking about intuition though is not as easy as talking about logic or reason, because there is part of intuition that will always remain 'hidden'.

Intuition connects, in a way, the conscious and the unconscious. The unconscious plays an all-important role in determining our behaviour, performance, decisions or our capacity to think[5]. No matter how hard we try or how many frameworks we develop, coaching is not an exact science. It never will be. The unconscious must be recognized in both coach and client and attended to. As coaches, we have to learn to let ourselves go with it and flow with it.

How do you do that? It's something,

- You learn as you go,
- You learn to relate to your intuition,
- You learn to trust yourself with it.

It's a process of discovery.

From my coaching experiences, there is a moment in the coaching conversation when I know I have to throw the challenge. It emerges clearly. The coaching relationship has been sufficiently tested, by now I know that my coachee "can take it" but I still wonder if it's best to wait, gather some more information. If I should present it crudely as I see it or maybe I should dress it a bit... In those moments, I've always trusted my intuition to decide when and how deep to challenge. So far, I have not regretted it.

I remember this one occasion in which, after the session, I thought I shouldn't have gone so deep, but presenting the challenge was very clear to me during the session and it went very naturally. I wondered for days whether I had overdone it. I only

---

[4] Ewen, Robert. 1993. *An Introduction to Theories of Personality*. Psychology Press.
[5] Bion, Wilfred Ruprecht. 1970. *Attention and Interpretation*. Tavistock Publications.

knew I'd done it right when the results became apparent in the coachee. She was at the time having a really hard time facing this reality that I presented to her. However this challenge meant a huge turning point for her, life changing. She was very grateful about how much this process gave her, clearly exceeding the objectives we had set. I am always amazed when I remember how that happened.

3. BEING PRESENT

As Liz Hall[6] reminds us, at least two of the main professional coaching bodies, The Association for Coaching (AC) and the International Coaching Federation (ICF), include presence as a core competency. Furthermore, she discusses that there is very little in the coaching literature about how to develop a presence and defends that, and I quote,

> *"Mindfulness is perfectly suited in the development of presence, helping (the coach) to meet requirements such as (...) to be present and flexible during the coaching process, dancing in the moment; access their own intuition and trust one's inner knowing – going with the gut, be open to not knowing and take risks, and to demonstrate confidence in working with strong emotions, being able to self-manage and not be overpowered or enmeshed by client's emotions".*

Being mindful is the opposite of being on autopilot. It is the result of maintaining a meditation practice. In meditation we train being present, in the moment, on the dot.

- We train focus and know clarity.

- We pay attention with intention and notice when our attention has shifted.

Chogyan Trüngpa[7] one of the greatest Tibetan meditation Masters writes about it in a very eloquent way:

> *"In the process of losing your awareness, you regain it because of the process of losing it. Slipping, in itself, corrects itself. It happens automatically. You begin to feel highly skilled, highly trained."*

It is important to say that we can train attention, focus, clarity, awareness and being present. The training is the daily meditation practice and the results just come as a consequence of maintaining that practice.

A daily meditation practice prepares us, certainly is key for me, to be in an optimal state in the coaching conversation. Free flowing to recognize what is and how to work with it to better serve the client.

We could again quote Chogyan Trungpa[8] when he says,

---

[6] Hall, Liz. 2014. *Mastery in Coaching, A Completely Psychological Toolkit For Advanced Coaching.* Edited by Jonathan Passmore. Kogan Page.
[7] Trüngpa, Chogyam. 1984. *The Sacred Path of the Warrior.* Shambhala Dragon Editions.
[8] ditto

"First, you must trust in yourself. (...) At that point your discipline becomes delightful rather than being an ordeal or great demand. When you ride a horse, balance comes, not from freezing your legs to the saddle, but from learning to float with the movement of the horse as you ride. Each step is a dance, the rider's dance as well as the dance of the horse. (...) You have to relax with yourself in order to fully realize that discipline is simply the expression of your basic goodness. You have to appreciate yourself, respect yourself, and let go of any doubt and embarrassment".

As coaches being present allows us,

- To recognize what is and work with it,

- To accept it without judgment,

- To let go of our assumptions and mental constructs,

- To genuinely trust in our abilities and those of our coachee.

We have to acknowledge that we cannot see things as they are but as we are and that the same is true of our client. Being present will help us to 'see things' in a more mindful and 'objective' way and our client will be the great beneficiary of it.

CONCLUSION

It is very clear that presenting a challenge is essential to coaching. How this challenge is presented depends on a number of things that are not as easy to grasp. It is not possible to present a formula resulting in the perfect challenge. Rather, a good challenge depends on a set of competencies that the coach brings and also, largely, on a great deal of personal qualities. For me, the decision of how and when to challenge depends basically on three things: trust in the coachee, trust in my intuition and, thirdly, my being present.

Major coaching models such as The Inner Game, Gestalt or Mindfulness share evidence of the importance of personal qualities in the coach rather than a set of techniques or a prescribed formula. They also supply ways to develop those personal qualities and help and encourage the coach:

- To have his or her own *way of being and doing,*

- *To trust the coachee,*

- To trust *their own intuition and inner knowing,*

- *To be present as a person and interventionist,*

- To 'dance in the moment',

- *To be open to not knowing and take risks, and*

- *To demonstrate confidence.*

PART 2: Cutting edge: Investigating patterns from Practitioner Experiences

Using Intuition wisely? That's quite a journey

Claire Sheldon

DO YOU USE INTUITION IN YOUR COACHING PRACTICE?

Me too! But it's only in the last few years that I've started unpicking what that actually means. And the truth is... Well it's tricky to articulate. It's difficult to make sense of the slippery, elusive, hard-to-put–your-finger-on phenomenon that is intuition in coaching.

- I could write about the empirical evidence (a plethora for other professions, but limited – so limited – for coaching);

- I could point to the practitioner literature (contradictory – and mostly supporting the assertion that 'successful coaches are highly intuitive[1]');

- I could reference my own research.

But talk to any coach and it's the stories that resonate...

AND BEFORE THIS STORY, SOME CLARITY ABOUT TERMS

There's a lot of disagreement about 'the what' and 'the how' of intuition. And there are some touch points.

It's not instinct – that's an evolutionary imperative. It's not insight – that's a 'eureka' moment providing a logical path between a problem and its solution.

For me, intuition is the outcome of our intuiting, a link between our non-conscious and external stimuli, the fizz, anxiety or inner smile that signals knowing-without-knowing-how.

---

[1] Skiffington, Suzanne., and Perry Zeus. 2000. *Behavioural coaching: How to build sustainable personal and organisational strength.* Sydney: McGraw-Hill.

PART 2: Cutting edge: Investigating patterns from Practitioner Experiences

- It's System 1 – fast, preverbal and automatic), as opposed to System 2 – time intensive, conscious and effortful[2,3].

- It has most value in complex, fluid environments where there's no right or wrong answer, and where vast amounts of disparate data need to be processed and acted on quickly[4] (Klein, 2003).

Bells should be ringing here.

Because that describes every coaching conversation, every coaching relationship I've been part of. And I suspect the same is true for you. I also suspect that your experience of working with your intuition will, in some way, mirror mine.

WHAT I LABEL 'INTUITION' IS CRITICAL TO MY PRACTICE

It's at the heart of some of my most exuberant, exciting and insightful sessions. I know too that my 'intuition' isn't always right. I can confuse it with my values, prejudices and beliefs. It can be out of kilter, jolting the rhythm of a session or spiking the coaching relationship. When a client revealed that 'very small opinions of yours rocked me', I realised my clients might be buying into my interventions because I was the coach. Not a skillful intuitive. I know that putting an intuition on hold can be hugely productive, but also that ignoring my intuition has resulted in some of my most difficult and bruising coaching transactions.

SO WHAT DIFFERENTIATES THE SUCCESS FROM THE CAR CRASH?

I believe it's what happens in that full-of-potential moment between noticing and acting on an intuition. In that moment,

- I might choose to stay put, keeping my intuition
  (or interpretation of it) to myself...

- I might choose to enter the territory, sharing my intuition
  (or interpretation of it) with my client...

- Or I might make an intervention that is more or less elegant and effective.

In this blog, I want to share a story about getting it right, an intervention that appeared to fly in the face of reason, yet hit the transformational mark...

MY STORY

I'm with a client. Let's call him Tim. We're in a central London café. He's a delight to work with. Committed, enthusiastic, self-aware. A lot happens in the space between our sessions. Today he's played his blinder. He's alluded to his extreme and debilitating performance anxiety in previous sessions. A presentation – particularly

---

[2] Kahneman, Daniel. 2011. *Thinking, fast and slow*. London: Penguin Books.
[3] Evans, Jonathan. 2008. "Dual processing accounts of reasoning, judgement and social cognition." In *Annual Review of Psychology* 59: 255-278.
[4] Klein, Gary. 2003. Intuition at work. New York: Currency Doubleday.

PART 2: Cutting edge: Investigating patterns from Practitioner Experiences

to senior people – has him stuttering, tumbling over his words, turning crimson. And in the lead up he becomes increasingly anxious, unable to sleep or to focus on his work. Not only is his response debilitating. It's exhausting and potentially career limiting. He has an important gig coming up and wants, more than anything, to manage his nerves. I listen as he takes me through his strategies. He's ticked every managing anxiety box, done every course, read every book, googled every dry-mouthed symptom. He can tell me about the time when, fresh faced and innocent, he'd speak up in class without a care. He's covered the ground. Then re-trodden it.

Nothing's shifted.

I'm feeling stuck and helpless when something catches my attention: "If only I could get through the introduction..." I'm tentative: "*How about we try that right now?*" He's game.

We do a short breathing exercise to help Tim centre and prepare himself. "*Stand up,*" I say. It's a ludicrous request. The café's quiet. While perfect for a coaching conversation it felt inappropriate and exposing for introductory declamations. So why my suggestion, "*Let's go outside*"? I'm not sure where it came from, but it felt right. And I knew Tim would push back if the experiment felt too extreme – we'd developed sufficient respect and rapport. Stepping out into the noise and bustle of the pedestrianised street I had no idea where the work was heading but felt confident we were on the right track. At my suggestion Tim stood in the middle of the road, introducing himself and his presentation to anyone and no-one.

We graded the experiment. He made his introduction louder and clearer as I stepped further and further away. Tourists and off-duty beauticians didn't give him a second look. Taking things up a notch, he emulated the fear inducing 'walk up' until walk, eye contact and body language were pitch perfect. The introduction easy and natural. He smiled, nodded, confirmed, "*I'm enjoying it – it feels different. I've got it!*" My initial response was to step back inside for Tim to reflect on his learning. Something stopped me. "*Let's go for a walk,*" I said. As we wove through Soho, Tim talked me through his plans for the weeks, days and hours before the presentation, nailing his preparation, how he'd get support from colleagues, his self-support...

The result? We parted outside the café agreeing to a call before the big day, a call that Tim didn't need. Here's his emailed narrative:

> "*Feeling much more relaxed and calm about it all, dare I say almost looking forward to it.*"
> "*Feeling perfectly fine about it now...*"
> "*Practiced a few times now with various different people. One final run through.*"
> And finally – "*Smashed it...*"

REFLECTING ON 'MY INTUITION'

Subsequent conversations confirmed that the session had been transformational. Something big had shifted for Tim. So what happened in that session? What possessed me to make this potentially shame-inducing intervention with this particular client? I've no idea what triggered the idea – that's the nature of intuition. But I can unravel what I'd done to prepare the ground for responding so confidently to my intuition and can pinpoint what I did in the moment too.

My research leads me to believe there are four preconditions for effectively accessing and using intuition. Two of these, Trust and Permission, are co-created with the client. Expertise and Maturing as a coach are still about the coach in relationship, specifically about their personal development.

- **Trust**: My relationship with Tim had evolved over time. He'd worked with me on an extended leadership development programme as well as being a coaching client. In our first and subsequent sessions, levels of self-exposure led me to believe we'd built rapport and trust quickly and effectively.

- **Permission**: In our contracting session, I'd positioned somatic and intuitive data as valuable adjuncts to the rational and obvious, seeking Tim's permission to share, explore and enquire. He'd experienced this happening in both group and one-to-one settings. And he'd reported a slow build in confidence, and that he valued the space to speak, to be challenged and to be heard.

- **Expertise**: Expertise is an enabler. Attending to the mechanics of the coaching session it gave rational System 2 the space to notice my intuitive message. And in that moment it contributed two things. It helped me choose whether or not to share my intuition with the client. And it supported me in sharing my intuitive prompts in ways that added value and opened up the coaching. Expertise does not guarantee that I'll notice an intuition or notice it well – personal distractions or environmental issues may get in the way. I might still misjudge an intuition or get my timing wrong.

  Which bring us to...

- **Maturing as a coach**: Maturing as a coach influences how I understand and use intuition. While closely linked to Expertise it is both subtly different and more complex. Maturing as a coach means balancing gut and reason, paying close attention to an intuition when it enters my consciousness. I need to make detached and nuanced judgements about both its value and what I'll do with it. And I can only do that if I recognize when personal 'noise' impairs my intuitive judgment.

PART 2: Cutting edge: Investigating patterns from Practitioner Experiences

The self-imposed moment of slowing down and re-centring as I took James through the breathing exercise bought both of us value! It helped me move from 'what am I going to do here?' to 'trust the moment'. From this place I was more courageous, better able to tolerate not-knowing. Crucially, this meant I attended to the strength of my intuitive imperative. I initiated an intervention that felt edgy, even a little dangerous, but calculated, relevant, right. Five minutes earlier I might have self-censored and succumbed to System 2's pleas to play it safe.

Is this the end of the story? Yes and no. In the busy, anonymous street I was in familiar coaching territory – supporting a client as they step into their power. Tim grew taller, more expansive, came more sharply into focus. I can rationalise the second intuitive nudge that then took us walking the streets. I was unwilling to return to the place where we'd started, I was embedding James' plans and intentions kinaesthetically as well as orally, but that wasn't it. I was on an intuitive roll and my gut said it would work.

And that's the thing.

My research provides me with a model and preconditions for working elegantly and effectively with intuition. But the real prize is learning to use intuition wisely and with confidence. And that's quite a journey...

Question: How do you use intuition in your practice?

Intuition as a Leadership Asset

Larissa Conte

ntuition is one of the most frequent and mysterious topics I explore with my coaching clients.

It inspires curiosity, intrigue, skepticism, judgement, and profound personal growth, as we work together to develop their intuition as a powerful asset. In this article, I share how I help leaders develop their intuition as a key capability by exploring:

- What intuition is and how it relates to intellect,
- How to develop intuitive capacities, and
- How to leverage intuition for more effective leadership.

DISTINGUISHING INTELLECT AND INTUITION

Though U.S. culture, and even our dictionaries, can conflate intellect and intelligence, **I regard intellect and intuition as two core forms of human intelligence.** Intelligence derives from the Latin *intelligere*, meaning to understand, comprehend, or perceive (and it has its own wide-ranging set of definitions). In this frame, I see intellect and intuition as two distinct ways that humans understand and make sense of the world around us. Here's what 'intellect' and 'intuition' mean to me:

- **Intellect is a way of knowing that sources from thinking.** It relies on the powers of the mind (logic, reasoning and analysis), explores structural coherence/incoherence, and seeks to answer "How can I understand my experience and the world through ideas and reasoning?"

- **Intuition is a way of knowing that sources from feeling.** It relies on our sensing abilities (feeling energy and emotions in self, others,

PART 2: Cutting edge: Investigating patterns from Practitioner Experiences

> relationships, and the larger living fabric), explores stylistic coherence/incoherence, and seeks to answer, "What's the information in what I'm feeling?"

It's easy to understand why intellect and intelligence are often equated as meaning the same thing if your worldview positions logical reasoning as the only way to understand life. In the U.S., we rely on intellect as our primary means of understanding—still strongly imprinted upon by the Cartesian legacy from the seventeenth century of "I think, therefore I am"—with our whole educational system designed around successive layers of intellectual development and little-to-no dedication to intuitive development. However, feelings are rich with information, and I believe each of us has a deep intelligence that sources from feeling.

Though the following content is often attributed to Albert Einstein, Bob Samples interpreted Einstein's perspective on intuition and the rational mind while also asserting his own view:

> "Albert Einstein called the intuitive or metaphoric mind a sacred gift. He added that the rational mind was a faithful servant. It is paradoxical that in the context of modern life we have begun to worship the servant and defile the divine."

People often discount intuition on the basis of being less rigorous or trustworthy than intellect, but my current hypothesis is that both intuition and intellect can be biased by our worldviews or experiences. Namely, both of these forms of intelligence are valuable ways to understand ourselves and the world, but neither is a foolproof route to truth.

One of the primary values of intuitive intelligence is self-understanding— knowing what you want and the lessons you have to learn from your desires.

Intuition often first comes up with my clients because they want to have a deeper connection to their true desires and authentic self.

> "I want a new job. I'm miserable where I am. But I don't even know what I'm best at or what would be most fulfilling for me to pursue next."

> "I don't like the way I've been leading. I feel like I've been being my idea of who a leader has to be—not my true self. But I'm scared that if I start being myself, people won't accept me and my business will fall apart."

> "I don't feel good about this deal. It looks right on paper, but there's something that feels really wrong about it and I don't know what to do."

It comes up because they want to feel a sense of integrity in their decision-making, rather than making decisions based on rationalizations. But because we're so habituated to the belief that intellect is the only form of intelligence, we often push aside what feels most aligned with our truth because we believe that will be the likeliest route to success or because we crave social acceptance. The continual act of ignoring our inner listening or denying what we hear erodes our intuitive abilities. That's why listening is foundational to living our truth, as I wrote about in my prior article, and is a critical first step in intuitive development.

Intellect and intuition are great teammates in the process of Wayfinding. At the most basic level, intuition tells us our Yes and our No. It is not our ideas about why Yes or No—it's just the pure feeling. Once we know our feelings about something, then we can inquire into the underlying information behind the feeling, and chart the best course forward. In my experience, I often use intuition to perceive a feeling and any available information in that feeling. Then I use my intellect to understand the call or information in the feeling, track patterns, and assess how to best act on that feeling. I rely deeply on both my intellect and intuition and constantly interweave them in my day-to-day choices.

PRACTICES FOR BUILDING INTUITION

Here are several of the core practices I use with clients, and for myself, to help develop intuitive capacity:

- First, you have to give yourself permission—without this, you can't even engage the territory.
- Then you need to deepen your listening to understand how your Yes and No register for deeper fluency in how you sense things.
- With these two skills in place, you can explore skills like:
- Listening to right timing
    - Finding balance, and
    - Honing your intuition with others.

GIVING YOURSELF PERMISSION

Starting with permission might seem like an obvious or unnecessary step, but it's the most important one because we so deeply stigmatize intuition in the U.S. Establishing permission and legitimizing intuition with my clients starts with some form of role modeling and disclosure about my experiences with intuition. This is integral to how I coach and, in turn, helps my clients recall times in their lives when their intuition communicated valuable information. In my experience, giving permission takes an initial effort. It needs to be revisited again and again as you build your intuitive capabilities because you're learning to trust the muscle. Often you want it to perform at the level of your intellectual development, but need to give it time to strengthen and take shape.

As one of the women in the Intuitive Leadership Circle I ran with Laura Griffiths said:

"I started this journey with an intent to be more like myself, which is the exact opposite of everything I've ever done in my life. I've learned I can go against the norms of thinking with my head, leading with my ego, and that from that place, something magical can happen, but it actually takes serious intention to be authentic. I've gotten the permission to feel here. This is the only forum where I feel I've had that permission in my life. Or rather the only one where I've given it to myself and taken it."

DEEPENING YOUR LISTENING

Next, I create practices for clients to listen for their Yes and No and how to act on this information, as I detailed in my prior article. I have people start with listening for their Yes and No, and how it registers in their sensing. This is because if we can't hear and foster what's aligned in our own life, then we won't be able to do this effectively in the more complex systems of our teams and businesses.

This skill often takes a few weeks to initially develop because we're so habituated to denial behaviors like rushing around, being busy, filling our lives with distraction, and not paying attention to our bodies. When you don't hear the information your body is sending you and you keep carrying on in extended denial, the small signals of necessary change build up a pressure system that arrives with a bigger impact. It's like the Earth's plates that build up pressure when try to move past each other without the mini slippages and tiny earthquakes to relieve the gradual build-up. That's how we get the big earthquakes in our lives—a divorce, a coronary, failure of your business, etc. So it behooves us to listen and react to the small, early signals.

Most people have a clear sensing vocabulary for Yes and No that are quite distinct, and I have them begin with getting fluent in those feelings. Then I have them notice what helps or prevents them from hearing their Yes or No, in addition to where they act on this information in their lives, where they don't, and why. After that, I usually have them take actions to come into alignment with their truth and to listen for more complex information beyond just Yes and No.

LISTENING TO RIGHT TIMING

Once you've gained clarity about whether you're a Yes or No to something and that it's best to take action on the information, that doesn't mean it's currently the right time to act, because you need to listen inwardly to yourself and outwardly to your context. **Listening to right timing is the practice of sensing how your internal needs align with your external conditions**. Just because you might want something to happen and feel ready to do it, your environment, the people you're interacting with, the systems you're in, etc., might not be open to it for any given reason and you have to sense what's appropriate when.

In the example of a colleague I was advising, she was designing a large event and wanted to get the invitations out before the end of last year. She said, "I feel the like the invitations want to be sent right now." I paused because it was the second week of December and I didn't think anyone wants an invitation for an event several months into the New Year just before the holidays. I asked, "Do the invitations want to be sent right now, or do YOU want them to be sent so you can have them off your plate even though it might not be the best timing for the invitees?" After she sat with it, she realized it was her own internal pressure communicating to her and not the right time for the recipients.

FINDING BALANCE

Balance isn't an idea. It's a feeling. It's a constantly changing one at that. It requires consciously creating tension between seemingly paradoxical attributes or feelings.

When we crave balance in our lives, like work-life balance, we need to be able to sense and foster fulfillment in multiple areas of our life that have contrasting natures. The focus and performance we bring to our work are quite different than the spaciousness and renewal of personal time. Often we struggle at balance because we're used to applying one life strategy in all circumstances, like high-performance and being constantly on, while being weak in the attributes that balance our habitual mode and/or have difficulty holding multiple awarenesses and shifting gears between modes of being.

The act of finding balance has a great deal to do with structure and space (or surrender) in a way that's similar to building a fire.

- If your kindling bundle is jammed full of sticks, there's too much wood and not enough air, so the fire isn't going to catch when you try to light it. It's just suffocated and constricted. This is akin to when we apply too much structure, force, or will to a situation, closing down the necessary space for creative ignition.

- On the other hand, if you only have three sticks spread way apart, there's not enough density of fuel (structure) and the fire won't light. Much like when we go into total surrender without any clarity of listening or intention, we get blown to and fro by the winds of life and lack the container for aligned, creative emergence to occur.

The sweet spot lies in what I call focused receptivity—listening with both intent and openness of mind. It's having a clear curiosity about something without attachment to how things will unfold. It's a practice that relies on astute listening, continual feeling, and dynamic evolution.

HONING YOUR INTUITION WITH OTHERS

Because intuition is about feeling emotions and energy—essentially perceiving style in the invisible realm—one of the main ways to hone your intuition is by developing your ability to verbalize the subtleties you feel and to check those feelings against others' perceptions. Like any discipline, the practice of putting language to distinctions is a powerful way to advance your intuition. And because what you're talking about has no physical form, I find it incredibly helpful to develop distinctions through shared observation and discussion with others. One way I do this with clients and colleagues is to share our perceptions of how something feels (a piece of art, a person, a bird, the environment we're in, etc.) or to ask clarifying questions about how they feel about an event in their life to evoke greater precision.

Just as a beginning naturalist may first start by recognizing plants and then learn what distinguishes ferns from shrubs and annual flowering plants, so too do my clients start with perceiving something that feels 'good' and then move on to being able to distinguish feelings like buoyant from content, inspired, or enamored. The invisible landscape often has more than one type of feeling occurring, much like natural ecosystems, so it's helpful to develop your species recognition of different feelings and energies, so you can more effectively map complexities and relationships.

LEADING FROM INTUITION AND INTELLECT

Once my clients have baseline comfort with their new intuitive skills in their personal lives, we then explore how to apply intuition at work. **Intuition is a powerful leadership tool because it enhances one's ability to sense alignment, misalignment, and the need for change in systems.** Specifically, intuition can improve your abilities to:

- Sense (im)balance, trajectory, and the main impacting forces on a system at any scale—from the individual to team, department, organization, the wider community, the market, etc.

- Feel friction or obstruction points, have early sensing of needed changes to prevent systemic weakness, and anticipate systems crash at any level.

    - A frequent example of this, which causes great energetic drain in teams, is interpersonal friction and what's not being said.

- Effectively steward energy, resources, and pacing across those scales.

- Generate creative aspects of work, like coming up with new ideas and strategies or feeling if a concept is clear enough for experimentation or execution.

Applying intuition in any one of these ways can then be combined with intellectual investigation or execution to reveal a clearer path forward for growth.

Due to the social stigma around intuition, the biggest challenge for people is often not sensing, but rather, communicating information from their intuition to an intellectually-oriented person or group in a way that lands. I recommend starting with small-scale intuitions first and building from there, as is wise on any developmental journey. Here are some guidelines for choosing if and how to best communicate your intuition at work:

First, locate where the feeling is coming from and assess whether it's appropriate to communicate.

- *Is it partially or wholly a trigger or aspect of your ego?*
  If so, there's personal work for you to do to resolve your sense of charge.

- *Are you accurately sensing something going on in your team, another person, or a relationship?*
  In this case, it may be wise to communicate.

Next, assess how to best communicate.

- *Can this information be received or do you have to share it to honor your own sense of integrity?*
    - It's always ideal for such information to be received, but sometimes we see things that a system or power structure is in forceful denial about that we have to give voice to for our own integrity.
    - If No to both of these questions, consider whether or not it's best to share.

- *What is the best timing and forum to share?*
    - Use your intuition and your intellect to determine whether the immediate moment or another setting in the future is most appropriate. The skill of listening to right timing is key here.

- *Who is the best audience and what do they care about?*
    - As with any effective communication, it's important to connect the information you want to relay with your audience's needs and concerns. If you don't, it likely won't land.

- How can you best share the information you're perceiving?
    - Some options include asking a question to direct group awareness toward what you're sensing and stating how you're feeling. For example. "We feel stuck to me. Does anyone have an idea of the best way to move forward?"

The more you practice sensing at work, combining your intuition and intellect, and communicating your intuition to others, the easier your will find it is to flex your intuition as a reliable leadership asset.

My question to you: How can you develop your intuition for more effective leadership?

PART 2: Cutting edge: Investigating patterns from Practitioner Experiences

Don't risk just trusting your Intuition - get to know it!

Jeremy Ridge

1. THE IMPORTANCE OF INTUITION TO COACHING PRACTICE

For me, Intuition is a term that has real value for referring to our most important asset – our big bank of stored experience and potential knowledge that we have acquired throughout life's experiences.

Unfortunately, we still don't quite understand how it works – exactly.

Likewise, for me, Intuition is central to coaching:

- It is the process that enables us to operate at the speed needed in the behaviours that enable the coaching relationship to work.

- It is a useful lens for looking at what the coaching task is about – helping someone else find the space and process to get to know themselves better. This often means enabling the coachee to understand what appears intuitively for them.

- It is a powerful source of learning, about coaching itself, about the way to show up in any coaching process – what happened, and how/why exactly, and what can be learned from it – i.e. researching yourself as a coach.

I want to focus here on the last one of these three areas, above.

INTUITION IS ALSO SOMETHING THAT STILL DRAWS LITTLE ATTENTION

In a world where being 'evidence based' always requires producing evidence that enables others to travel the same path of experience, where reproducible knowledge is a result of established scientific methods in the social sciences and humanities, understanding and acknowledging intuition is still primitive.

Consequently, this often limits research to what current scientific method can measure.

And we still seem to lack a methodology for evidencing intuition. So, I thought I'd share my 'on-going' research on how I consider intuition works for me in relation to coaching.

After all, intuition is not necessarily always fully right. The experiences that have produced it may not have been representative of what is involved in a new situation. And it can be tempting to want to believe something rather than still test it!

To date, there have been several pieces shared on the good coach in which each of the coaching practitioners have, in their own way, acknowledged and tackled this conundrum about intuition. For example,

- Luis San Martin (4.10.2017) celebrates being intuitive as a means for accessing the unconscious, but also leaves the exploration of this because there is part of intuition, *"that will always remain hidden"*.

- Claire Sheldon (5.2.2017) similarly tackles intuition directly. Intuition is all about knowing-without-knowing-how; but then also goes on to warn how *"I know too that my intuition isn't always right. I can confuse it with my values, prejudices and beliefs."* Claire then goes on to explore how to get intuition right. In coaching, this hinged on establishing what Claire refers to as trust in the relationship, and then permission, as a basis for being able to bring her intuition into it.

Intuition keeps on coming up as important to coaching, yet still difficult to tie down and this is what I want to report on.

2. WHAT CAN BE LEARNED FROM OTHER WIDER VIEWS ABOUT THE IDEA OF INTUITION

As always, there are the shoulders of others to stand on in considering most matters.

A Wikipedia summary[1] is quite comprehensive about the origin, definition and core meaning of the term. The word intuition is described here, in the way it was originally used to mean to consider, in its original sense of careful attention. This is a meaning that attracts me (for "Attention!" is what really makes coaching work... or not!).

There are also a range of other meanings in how others use the meaning of intuition. For example, something that is best left as utterly invisible, and so intangible, that it defies explanation. Therefore it is not to be taken too seriously. You might even just plain ignore it!

---

[1] https://en.wikipedia.org/wiki/Intuition

There are a lot of people who say things like trust your gut instinct... of course I can take these words as useful metaphors. I am not sure the gut is where experience gets processed and I am not convinced instinct is the same as intuition either!

For me intuition is something important by itself.

For me, intuition is like compressed knowledge – stored like a zip file for efficiency and space saving – which we can use even without opening it up to see how it arrived at what it knows. But it is also important to check it out, to open up the file.

I see a useful differentiation between the different approaches to this intuition idea. I have summarised, below the typical range of these views into three different levels:

    2.1. The tightly closed view.
    2.2. The 'reflective' perspective – open but limited in ways to get to know it.
    2.3. How to get to know it – sorting out the evidence trails of experience.

2.1. THE TIGHTLY CLOSED VIEW

At one level, intuition is viewed as irrelevant to knowledge. For example, some comments I overheard recently were:

> *"Like so many other words grappling with explanations for human behaviour, intuition is beautifully vague and open to all sorts of interpretation. It simply gets used in the sense of 'gut feeling', contrasting it with considered, rational decision making."*

Reference to this term 'gut feeling' is a common way of linking intuition to being some form of visceral/body like sensation. There is no brain involved in it.

This viewpoint is often very dismissive as being something not worth paying attention to as it is, by definition, almost impossible to understand. It is some sort of random act that is unprovable, unpredictable and also unreliable.

2.2. THE 'REFLECTIVE' PERSPECTIVE

I have also come across progressively higher and higher levels of appreciation – where there are attempts to try and engage with this tough idea. For example, Cholle[2] shares his expert view about Intuition, and how it's used for in *Psychology Today* as follows:

> *"... Instinct and Intuition, as I define it, is this:*
>
> - *Instinct is our innate inclination toward a particular behaviour (as opposed to a learned response). (There is still a question about what is not a learned response. Is breathing learned or instinct, for example.)*

---

[2] Cholle, Francis. 2011. "What Is Intuition, And How Do We Use It?" In *Psychology Today*. https://www.psychologytoday.com/blog/the-intuitive-compass/201108/what-is-intuition-and-how-do-we-use-it# Accessed September 11.

- *A gut feeling—or a hunch—is a sensation that appears quickly in consciousness (noticeable enough to be acted on if one chooses to) without us being fully aware of the underlying reasons for its occurrence.*

- *Intuition is a process that gives us the ability to know something directly without analytic reasoning, bridging the gap between the conscious and nonconscious parts of our mind, and also between instinct and reason.[3]"*

So, here, intuition is more than just visceral – and shows up as some sort of consciousness – ironically linked to something referred to as non-conscious. At least in the sense that it is difficult to see/observe it in the sense/way that much of knowledge currently needs to be seen, for example through a form of analytical reasoning.

The author then goes further:

> *"... studies now show that only 20 percent of the brain's gray matter is dedicated to conscious thoughts, while 80 percent is dedicated to nonconscious thoughts."*

And then,

> *"... But let's not stop there. Here are three ways to listen to that internal voice and allow its guidance into your everyday life:*

1. *Keep a journal. Writing your thoughts and feelings down on paper— even if you "think" you have little to say—helps the nonconscious mind open up.*

2. *Turn off your Inner Critic. Listen without judgment. Allow the inner dialogues to happen without fear or ridicule.*

3. *Find a Solitary Place. A place where you can allow emotions to flow freely..."*

This approach would appear to reflect the preoccupation in the current coaching world with the term Reflection as some method of creating a space to simply capture this intuition, but without being very specific about how that space can always produce results.

2.3. HOW TO GET TO KNOW INTUITION – SORTING OUT THE EVIDENCE TRAILS

The next level that's bringing closer together how intuition works, whilst still at a very high level (particularly when it relates to the brain), is through the retrospective linking and sorting out of relevant evidence trails that lead to intuitive reactions. A piece of work reported by Hodgkinson et al[4] (2008) reports

---

[3] ditto

[4] University of Leeds. 2008. "Go With Your Gut – Intuition Is More Than Just a Hunch." In *Science Daily*. https://www.sciencedaily.com/releases/2008/03/080305144210.htm Accessed September 10.

an important example of the way that intuition can be researched and produce the more tangible understanding of how it works:

"... intuition is the result of the way our brains store, process and retrieve information on a subconscious level and so is a real psychological phenomenon which needs further study to help us harness its potential. Yet science has historically ridiculed the concept of intuition, putting it in the same box as parapsy-chology, phrenology and other 'pseudoscientific' practices. Intuition is the brain drawing on past experiences and external cues to make a decision – but one that happens so fast the reaction is at a non-conscious level. All we're aware of is a general feeling that something is right or wrong."

The article cites the recorded case of a Formula One driver who braked sharply when nearing a hairpin bend without knowing why – and as a result avoided hitting a pile-up of cars on the track ahead, undoubtedly saving his life.

"... The driver couldn't explain why he felt he should stop, but the urge was much stronger than his desire to win the race. The driver underwent forensic analysis afterwards, where he was shown a video to mentally re-live the event. In hindsight he realised that the crowd, which would have normally been cheering him on, wasn't looking at him coming up to the bend but was looking the other way in a static, frozen way. That was the cue. He didn't consciously process this, but he knew something was wrong and stopped in time."

The article is less informative about the exact process of forensic analysis. However, this does at least suggest forming greater awareness about intuition, and how it works, is possible.

The perspective provided by these three samples, summarises, for me, the views available about intuition and provides some useful understanding about my own perspective. The tightly closed view may need more than mere evidence to open it up, ironically. If people have locked themselves into a limited form of evidence it leaves them with a substantial learning curve in order to access intuition for themselves. Reflection (and associated terms such as 'reflexivity') suggest some openness to the idea, but reflection by itself, about just yourself even, can risk effectively living in a vacuum, and risks being unhelpful. There needs to be something that informs reflection. And that is often what can be missing.

3. RESEARCHING ONE'S OWN INTUITION: MY STOP THE CLOCK APPROACH!

Rather like in coaching, itself, I have found that the way to make progress with Intuition is often a matter for what works for each individual, rather than taking one approach that will work for everybody.

PART 2: Cutting edge: Investigating patterns from Practitioner Experiences

I even took research seriously when I completed a Doctorate on the way to make sense of everything that flows from intuition in Coaching[5]. Even then, this research had to be kept simple, to fit the academic agenda.

3.1. HOW I UNDERSTAND MY WAY OF RESEARCHING MY INTUITION

The simplest description about what works for me, is best described as I see it as taking time to 'stop the clock!'

Experience is about reactions and responses. And these build over time. I barely think consciously about 'crossing the road'. It happens automatically – from the intuitive accumulation of doing it many times.

However, with some of the areas of life's experience it is important to understand just where I have got to, which involves having a context, and how I got there.

- 'Stopping the clock' is my way of being able to find the time to investigate experience.

- 'Stopping the clock' means I am able to choose to not have to carry on with events as they happen.

- Then, the process is about taking the trouble and effort to re-wind and re-play just what event is linked with what in any set of experiences around a particular theme.

- And then, unravelling these chains of events and interactions between them.

'Stopping the clock' is simply about events and the re-call of them – with the major event being just one's own reaction, yet also linking the reactions between separate people.

Considering the intuition involved in saying "Hello": *For example, even saying hello to someone happens so fast that processing all the data available in a second or two is less than feasible in a reproducible way. You can hardly say 'stop the clock', I want to consider the infinite range of word and body (and clothes!) and other context configurations that are appropriate; as well as look in the manual for the appropriate interpretation and response in the circumstances. This is also assuming I have obtained the objective perception about what the other person has produced as initiating my assumption that hello is appropriate... maybe one day!*

All of this information flashes through the cognitive channels with scant ('cognitive') awareness, and results in a choice, and then action – in half a second .... And then there is the next event etc. etc. etc.

---

[5] Ridge, Jeremy. 1975. *The Development and Operation of the Effective Interpersonal Relationship Skills relevant to Career Development Problems from Staff Assessment at an Industrial Research Laboratory* – PhD. The University of Aston. (Available to download https://www.the-goodcoach.academy/)

'Stopping the clock' can only realistically happen afterwards. So many processes are taking place, and I have learned to build conscious awareness about them. This has to be done without all the data that may be relevant. This might include the full data about what caused the reactions in response to my saying hello. Another big intangible is also information about the context that has already created expectations even before saying hello etc. There is also the added complexity that perception of the hello moment has probably not been perfect, on either side.

I have worked hard to build the ability to zoom in on events, in detail, as I recall them. I have learned to run them in slow motion, quite visually. I can separate the events down to the wide range that happens in a second, as well as zooming in on the micro behaviour of the extent to which a frown was forming or a smile flickering.

This all depends on where my 'attention camera' was focused. There is still plenty I don't focus on, or hold in the film memory. So I have to hold, and build, my attention with practice. The trick is to replay/stop/repeat the play/use slow motion i.e. 'stopping the clock' and investigate a small sample.

3.2. Unpacking the intuitive processes involved in the hello process of 'settling down' or 'checking in' before a meeting starts

My equivalent of the racing driver story is how forensic analysis can be used to unpack compressed events that just happen as an intuitive process in the hello process at the start of a meeting. This is a normal part of team coaching.

This set of events is often described by participants as some sort of simple settling down process, or checking in, even before the meeting proper starts. Yet, this is where the real exchanges. Contracting is the going on that often amounts to the real meeting itself.

An example: Using video replay of events and playback of meetings in team coaching.

The task:

Creating a short (30 to 40 minutes) one off, neutral, task for a small sub group to go off and work on – which is recorded and then reviewed with both this group, and the rest of the team.

A neutral task refers to a task where there is no natural, technical, authority for what is involved.

The review process, afterwards, enables that opportunity to stop the clock, review the footage frame by frame, capturing the details of events and their effects on others.

The review often focusses on key questions such as,

- **When did the meeting actually start?** Settling down to the work space (e.g. arrange of seating around the table) involved and other initial banter is not seen as part of the meeting proper – until someone typically suggests "shall we begin?"

- **How best to enable the awareness that participants can typically bring to the interpretation of events apparently unrelated to the task, and rarely ever discussed as part of the meeting proper,** such as where people sit – such as in the centre of the work space, or at the edges, or corners.

- **Creating conditions where participants can disclose and share constructively the more often disguised and hidden personal agendas.**

During the detailed review afterwards, the earlier review often results in the conclusion that the meeting was over before it started!

Formally writing up this whole process, and illustrating the evidence, is quite a task, of course. Even several minutes of settling down, when viewed frame by frame, and person by person, amounts to a bulk of evidencing that is not common in my experience of research into these sorts of matters. But I am often amazed at how observant and articulate people can be about these invisible and rarely stated causes behind what happens.

The importance of this shared degree of insight and understanding gives me confidence in how the invisible processes often referred to as intuitive can be unravelled.

4. CONCLUSIONS

Putting words to this phenomenon of Intuition has been helpful to me.

1. It helps to sharpen the focus I use, to make the best use of my intuition and the need to keep on engaging and doing it – like keeping physical muscles healthy and strong.

2. It has also helped me to map the gap that can exist between those who are avowedly just not interested in learning and managing this amazing resource of intuition. There are still many resources we have not made the best use of yet – but at least we have learned the earth is best not seen as flat.

3. It also helps me in connecting to others who are excited by the idea but who are still developing their perspectives on how best to engage with intuition.

As Steve Jobs commented, "... *intuition is more powerful than intellect!*[6]"

---

[6] Kismatandkarma. 2013. "Power of Intuition: What Steve Jobs Learned in India." *Kismatandkarma.* https://kismatandkarma.wordpress.com/2013/12/01/power-of-intuition-what-steve-jobs-learned-in-india/ Accessed September 11.

CHAPTER 8

QUALITIES OF ATTENTION

The Value of Quality Attention to 'Individual Differences'

Sue Young

My intent is to explore practical use of individual differences in coaching and how I apply this in my personal coaching approach.

A coaching approach works from the particular foundation of understanding that people have built for themselves. This sort of understanding may still be some way from the concepts about individual differences formed in such fields as Psychometrics. In a practical discipline such as coaching, the nature of individual differences for most people is where we only get to know ourselves through interaction with others.

- How otherwise do we get a sense of ourselves?
- What do we have to compare and contrast with?

There is value in these more formal frameworks of individual differences. However, a coaching approach needs to work from the other person's frame of reference, rather than impose an expert type solution. I want to explore how this balance is best achieved.

The context for my coaching is mainly working with middle and senior managers in organisations. organisations are sometimes like a separate world, with their own cultures and processes. Working in them can require very particular forms of behaviour. However, in my experience, organisations are still in the early stages of learning to work with the reality that people are importantly different in their aspirations, strengths, style preferences, values and motivation – despite the attempts to impose 'the system'.

In the organisational process of coordinating resources towards a collective purpose, attention to individual differences can be lacking. In that context, quality of attention to the individuals involved can help close the gap.

I believe this is one of the reasons for the growing popularity of coaching.

1. AN APPROACH TO BRINGING INDIVIDUAL DIFFERENCES INTO COACHING

The relationship between coach and client is the vehicle for the learning process. The individual client is unique. Unique in the ways they perceive their world, learning style, working style, the way they talk, personality, values, beliefs and life experience. This is an essential focus for a coaching approach.

Hence in my coaching practice, it's how I give that the Quality of attention to the individual. For example, that is the differentiator as an approach to manager development is different compared to other approaches. This is the added value. Individuals are unique, yet there are patterns around some of the differences. Making sense of some of these patterns can be highly relevant to coaching.

There are two important aspects to this that come into my coaching:

1. Working with differences in the coaching relationship – style differences between coach and client.

2. The client working with differences in key working relationships and issues around those differences that come into the coaching agenda.

1.1. APPRECIATING THE WAY WE LEARN ABOUT IMPORTANT PATTERNS OF INDIVIDUAL DIFFERENCES

Individual Differences is a vast field of formal, academic, research. It is like another world where we attempt to scientifically identify and measure our differences.

When helping managers become more aware and able to articulate their preferred style of operating, and recognise its potential implications, I often make use of inventories and psychometrics. I tend to use those that clients will be most able to easily relate to and find most relevant and helpful.

I find this particularly useful in early stages of a coaching assignment. It provides a framework and language around differences that can help the client make sense of some of the patterns and how they relate these to their experience.

In using these I am aware of the need to focus on explaining their meaning in a clean way, not ladened with my own personal bias and preferences, so I am enabling the client to explore for themselves, seeing if it adds fresh insights and draw their own interpretations and conclusions.

I am also wary of making sweeping generalised judgments. I must stay mindful that the science is necessarily limited, at present.

Ultimately it is down to the client to make their own sense of the information they have gathered from their day to day experiences. Coaching conversations can help this process – drawing out meaning in relation to the unique context of that individual.

This day to day experience often comes from one's awareness of self and awareness of others.

1.2. AWARENESS OF SELF

Awareness of self is a precursor to awareness of others, which would be our ability to give another person quality attention. It is only through being with others that we gain a sense of ourselves in the first place. Indeed, who we are is partly determined by our experience of others, particularly in early formative years. It is a lifelong learning experience. To be able to truly respect, empathise and yet challenge the thinking of the client we need to come 'clean' to that interaction.

What I mean by 'clean' is not being contaminated by blindness to our own personal needs, motivations and personal biases. If we don't hold this awareness we can tend towards lines of questioning and intervention that is more about us and our needs and preferences, rather than those of our clients. We need to be able to notice our feelings. Only so that we introduce them when and as appropriate. So we can pay closer attention to the client, particularly toward their needs, both explicit and implicit.

1.3. AWARENESS OF OTHERS

I define an awareness of others as seeing the world through another's eyes.

Sometimes I've come away from several coaching sessions in a day feeling a sense of how different I've been with different clients. This is an 'in the moment' response to them as I'm experiencing them.

This is central to the coaching process of researching their awareness of differences.

I need to hold back, to begin with, on introducing other research and models.

This is what coaching is all about, after all. We start by working with the client's world of learning as a priority rather than naively imposing a different world as the solution. Especially true where the solution may not be as simple as some models like to suggest.

2. GETTING THE BALANCE BETWEEN FORMAL, AND INFORMAL, METHODS FOR APPRECIATING INDIVIDUAL DIFFERENCES

I have found that some formal models make more sense to some people than others. It is always important, first, to enable the other person to bring out their own ideas about their experiences of these differences. This can be done through getting them to speak about their own self, and their awareness of others, as far as they can. This may or may not lead to the use of more formal instruments.

2.1. USE OF PSYCHOLOGICAL BASED QUESTIONNAIRES/INVENTORIES WITH CLIENTS

This enables fresh perspectives on self, particularly in working with others most effectively. In my experience it is the typical patterns in personal style/ways of operating that some of the psychological/psychometric instruments generate, leading to fresh insights. I find such inventories, at their best and well used, can be both affirming and clarifying for people. They can bring articulation and cohesion to aspects of themselves that they kind of intuitively knew, but throw into sharp relief some of the core patterns of how they operate. I find this can help refine their thinking about how they want to develop themselves going forwards and the areas they want to pay particular attention to.

For example, when I took one of my client teams through the Myers Briggs instrument, using experiential exercises to bring the style dichotomies to life, one of the managers had a breakthrough in insight in how to relate to her staff. She went on to trying different things out in her leadership role, which added enormously to her style range and impact.

In the early stages of coaching assignments where the client is scoping and broadening their thinking, taking stock, both in terms of where they are, and where they want to go is a typical approach I take.

The focus of my coaching in early stages tends to be on data gathering for the client from various sources – 360 competence based feedback instruments and selected psychometrics and inventories. I select these in discussion with the client, typically at a first scoping meeting where terms of reference for the assignment become finalised. This selection arises naturally from the issues and needs that emerge in that first meeting.

These concepts sometimes are best used to work from where the client has reached in expanding their perspective and understanding of differences. It is not a matter of always using formal instruments or terminology, either.

In 360 feedback, I find that clients often find the richest data to be the open comments, rather than any formal structure and terminology in an instrument that measures capabilities. It really brings the strengths to life in more individual and real terms. Everyone's attention tends to be drawn towards the more negative 'things that they could do to improve'.

Formal models (even in 360 frameworks) can appear too black or white, or extreme and over simple, against a person's characteristics and preferred patterns of behaviour. So I find it important, for example, to introduce such concepts that our 'weaknesses' are the flip side of our strengths. Our greatest strengths are also the foundation of our weaknesses – either when we misread the situation and use our strengths inappropriately, or we over-do our strengths. The most successful people succeed by making best use of their strengths, rather than being perfectly rounded, or being required to focus on their weaknesses.

2.2. EXAMPLES OF HOW INFORMALLY I PICK UP INDIVIDUAL DIFFERENCES

From the very earliest stages of contact I am observing and absorbing a wide range of data about the person, for example:

- **Their level of engagement and motivation**, noticing any changes in relation to themes/subjects.
- **The way they talk** – fast, slow, considered, calm, measured, enthusiastic, emphatic, monotone, variety in tone, etc.
- **The language they use** – is it positive and active or more passive, abstract, general or lots of descriptive detail.
- **Their appearance and style in how they look** – e.g. low key, smart, fashionable, stylish, casual.
- **The way they think** – are they fast thinkers or slower, more considered, reflective.
- **How self aware are they in how they talk,** or are they caught up in the detail of what they are saying, and
- **Do they reveal** in what they say the nature and quality of their attention to people in their way of working?
- **Hints of working style** of a person from what they pay attention to and areas they do not attend to e.g. balance of attention to the Big Picture and ideas and the practicalities around implementation.
- **Are they extraverted** i.e. stimulated by interaction and variety or are they energised by their own ideas and thinking?
- **Are they structured and planned** in their approach or flexible and open?
- **Any sense of their personal values** and how they see their careers as part of their life balance.

- **Clues on potential longer-term issues** from what they are saying, ready to play back to affirm and highlight areas for potential attention in the coaching conversation.

- **Energy** – noticing where they are energised and where their energy seems low in the conversation.

- **What is absent** in what they spontaneously talk about.

During all of this I am actively picking up on opportunities to develop the relationship and rapport. I do this through reflecting a few things back which I judge as sounding potentially central to this person. I tune in to the person and am always looking to help them become more explicitly aware of their strengths, what they stand for and what they uniquely bring to their context. After all, this is what leadership is all about!

3. SOME CASE EXAMPLE

3.1. THE CLIENT WRESTLING WITH HER SENSE OF BEING SEEN AS 'NOT VERY DYNAMIC!'

The client, herself, was low key in appearance and style. My first impressions were that she was quite withdrawn – she didn't put herself out there. She came across in a way that I saw as highly intellectual and bright. She had no experience of coaching and I identified the need to warm her up and put her at ease.

I noticed early on she started defining herself as "not very dynamic". On asking what she meant by that she muttered, "*Not showing a lot in terms of initiative. I'm not into strategy and 'blue sky thinking'...I want to be achieving defined tasks...*"

Yet, with encouragement, empathy, and playing back the meaning I was taking from what she said, I built trust to the point of her being increasingly more personally disclosing.

As I listened I found her to be a highly capable people manager within a highly technical environment. She had a balanced and mature judgment. She had achieved a great deal. Yet I judged, with her quiet and low key but proactive problem-solving approach, she could be easily underestimated. That her strengths could easily be invisible to others, particularly where they were strongly extroverted. It became clear that she was very good at managing a team and getting the best from people in a very under-stated way.

I picked up very quickly on a lot of information about her within a short period of time. I was focused on observing and being quite minimalist in my interventions, creating a lot of space, affirming and encouraging her to tell her story more fully. The outcome was she found the space to step back, get in touch with her underlying feelings of anger and frustration at how she was overlooked. Once she felt able to express that, she was able to connect to her natural quality of thinking and came up with some good fresh insights and ideas on practical steps.

I did not consider it relevant to introduce formal psychometric profiling, as the client was arriving at the perspectives through their own efforts.

3.2. THE CLIENT WHO HAD BEEN TOLD THEY WERE TOO 'FLIPPANT'

This person could not have been more different; outgoing, personable, humorous, obviously ambitious, quick and bright. The pace of conversation was a lot faster. I had his 360 and Myers Briggs reports. From both his ratings and the comments he was clearly highly regarded, both personally and professionally. His Myers Briggs showed him to be highly extrovert, flexible and spontaneous in style.

His body language looked bored. I judged I needed to quickly capture his attention. I asked him to tell me his career story to date. It became clear that he was very good at reading people and prided himself on his ability to 'win around' difficult senior characters. In fact he particularly enjoyed this challenge.

Picking up on key elements of his story it became apparent that the comments in his 360 that most 'got' to him were about him coming across at times as 'flippant'. I gave him my feedback on the basis of my observations of some of his behaviour I had seen in our meeting – humorous throwaway comments and a relaxed style that could be taken as 'flippant'. This is particularly true of those who are more traditional in their style and approach, as I knew some of the hierarchical culture could be. He was also younger than the norm in his role and at a senior level. He sat up. I'd caught his attention! He then disclosed that when he was feeling particularly frustrated by being blocked, having tried all sorts of ways to win people over, there were a few occasions he had reverted to deliberate "rebellious child" behaviour.

We went on to have a lively exploration with a great deal of humour and teasing banter around how his natural open and collegiate style was a contrast to the traditional culture. In fact some could even find that personally threatening. In general that freshness of perspective and lack of inhibition with the most senior people in the organisation had served him well. We then went on in our subsequent conversations to explore ways he could tweak his style to add to his 'gravitas', without losing his natural style.

3.3. THE LEADER DEALING WITH OTHERS WHO 'SIMPLY DIDN'T GET IT'

A client was about to embark on a big change programme with the division he was leading. In our first meeting he told me about his challenging objectives, his strategic priorities, and the resistance he was expecting from people who he saw as being 'stuck' in their ways of working they had always worked to. The main thing he wanted from his coaching was really to have a regular tracking and review 'check in' with some thinking time in a hectic day to day pace.

I could sense from my experience of him why he was experiencing his people to be 'stuck'. He spoke quickly over a broad range of subjects and was highly conceptual and focused on achieving ambitious targets in his style. I could easily see how he could easily lose people in terms of their understanding. I could see this as potentially a major factor in his leadership effectiveness and he seemed oblivious to this.

In our third session I felt we had built sufficient trust and credibility for the value of our coaching sessions that I chose to move on the opportunity of the impact his kind of behaviour was having on me.

> "I'm becoming aware of disconnecting. You are covering a lot of rich and diverse information so fast it is becoming a bit of a blur and I feel I'm losing track. From what you have previously said about some of your people 'simply not getting it' I'm just wondering if they are having a similar experience."

There was a pause of silence. Then a roar of laughter from him. We went on then to have a productive conversation about individual differences and how others with more concrete and practical immediate problem-solving styles might really struggle to understand him. Then there may be a reluctance to question or stop him due to the felt risk of looking stupid and wanting to impress the new boss.

He was sufficiently keen to develop his leadership approach to be open to the feedback and motivated to experiment with small tweaks he could relatively easily make with some more conscious attention.

Once again, I realised that my own awareness of individual differences was helping my coaching approach, but did not require reverting to more formal profiling.

4. IN CONCLUSION...

The idea of individual differences is central to the whole of coaching. Along with the vast field of formal research available, and all the models and methods for assessing these differences.

To date, this has been a very useful exercise in strengthening my own awareness and reflections in a number of very important processes in my coaching practice. For example,

- I can see clearly how I intuitively adjust my coaching approach to the style of the individual.

- I move towards them to help them respond naturally and free up their thinking. It also helps build client trust in the coaching process in a way that enables me to better challenge and stretch their thinking.

- I adapt my language and approach to theirs rather than impose my own.

However, how all of this background understanding gets implemented is really important – lest it undermine how coaching really works.

Appreciating the other world of the individual comes first and foremost, despite the understanding that can be well represented and summarised by some of these models. Yet this more formal information needs to be integrated with other more informal data. This includes observations and testing out and inquiring collaboratively with the client.

This exercise has merely started to open up the understanding of the complex formulas for combining these two areas – how the formal research and frameworks need to be considered in the context of the individual in front of me.

Each individual is different, from some simple pattern, after all.

Has my coachee got what it takes? Have I?

Alan Robertson

This is a case about creating the conditions for engagement.

'H' approached coaching reluctantly.

Actually, that's a massive under-statement. He had already cancelled twice before he finally turned up for his re-scheduled session. Even then he didn't come straight into the room. He stood in the open doorway, filling it with his physical presence. He was well over six feet tall. He glowered at me.

"You'll never get close to me," he announced.

It's the best opening line I've ever heard in coaching. This promised to be interesting.

"Good morning," I replied brightly. *"Would you like to come in?"*

"You don't catch me like that," he retorted, not moving.

There was a pause while I wondered what to do. They say you should work with what's in the room, but we hadn't even got that far yet.

I couldn't think of anything else, so I said, *"Well, I'm about to have a coffee. You're very welcome to join me."* I got to my feet and turned away towards the coffee flask that my client had provided. When I turned back, H was sitting at the table. He'd chosen a seat directly opposite mine with the table between us.

It's natural to be apprehensive about coaching, about receiving feedback, or even about the suggestion that you might need these things. I could understand that H might be reluctant. It was his extreme way of expressing it that was intriguing.

He was unusually open about being closed; most people would probably do more to mask their resistance with some pretence of participation.

Coaching had been his boss' idea. He wanted it for himself and had decided that the whole of his senior team should have some. H was one of the functional Directors in the team. He was also the least enthusiastic member of the senior management team about the Managing Director's insistence that they should each have an individual coaching session and then a half-day team development workshop together.

"*I've told him I think this is a complete waste of time and money,*" H told me matter-of-factly, as he stirred the coffee I'd brought to the table for him.

"*Your colleagues generally seem to have found their one-to-one sessions valuable,*" I countered. "*At least that's what they said at the end of their sessions. Of course, it may be they were just being polite.*"

"HUH." His grunt was dismissive, whether of my comment or his colleagues wasn't clear, but at least he was still in the room.

TACITLY NEGOTIATING OUR RAPPORT

I pressed on. I thanked him for making the time to complete the psychometric battery that I was using to provide a source of potential insights for the coaching and the teamwork. I didn't mention that it had been a pain in the butt, having to chase him repeatedly to get him to complete it. I glanced again at his scores: several markers of high dominance, low scores on many, although not all, of the working-with-others dimensions, low openness, a tendency to distrust others. That was all congruent, I thought, with the combative display that he had put on in the doorway.

Other indicators offered more of a prospect that we would be able to have a conversation. He had a constellation of high scores suggesting an outgoing personality: extraverted, interested in influencing others and an activist learning style. He also had high creative interest and yet a low score on ingenuity. I could ask him how that unusual combination played out in practice. But I chose an easier starting place.

"*The problem with any psychometrics,*" I explained, sliding his score sheet across the table so that he could see and have it for himself, "*is that they can only provide clues and indications. They don't give you answers as such. So we need to figure out what they might signify in your particular case, and then we need to decide which, if any, of these results are relevant and important. And we need to do all that before we can even start to discuss what you might do with them.*"

It's an explanation I've given hundreds, or even thousands, of times. It's one form of the speech that I'd expect any thoughtful user of psychometrics to employ. It puts the owner of the psychometric profile in the pilot's seat. It acknowledges that the psychologist is only the co-pilot, a collaborator rather than a judge, an expert resource made available to the person who is centre stage. I regard it as an essential step when using diagnostics in coaching, because coaching cannot be done without conversation, and conversation cannot be done without at least some willingness, on both parts, to open up.

I couldn't call H a coachee at this stage. All that had happened up to this point was that he'd thrown a couple of provocative remarks ahead of him into the room, rather like stun grenades, and I'd poured us coffee and offered some introductory explanation in exchange. At some level he'd heard enough to feel ready to join in. So when I invited him to talk, not about himself or his personality, but to give me some context by telling me about his job and the sort of demands it made, he promptly did so, freely and energetically.

It was a turning point in the conversation, but the real pivots were still to come.

GETTING TO KNOW THE REAL PERSON SITTING IN FRONT OF YOU FROM ALL THE AVAILABLE CLUES

I listened to him. He spoke well. He was lucid and informative. He drew on a wide vocabulary and used it to communicate precisely but at the same time fluidly and easily. I started to ask more questions. He developed and elaborated what he was saying. More strikingly, he showed that he could readily infer where my lines of inquiry were heading, anticipating questions and answering them proactively. He clearly had a quick mind.

As he was doing this, I was staring at the reasoning scores in his psychometric profile. They looked upside down, not because I was sitting on the wrong side of the table but because they reported both his abstract and verbal reasoning abilities to be at the low end of the scale. They didn't fit with what I was hearing.

I interrupted his flow.

"I've got a puzzle, and I need you to help me make sense of it. I'm listening to you talk. You talk well and it sounds as if you think well too. You're clearly more capable than your scores on these reasoning tests would suggest. So, help me, please. What are these low scores about?"

Experience had already taught me that while it's very hard to get a high score on a reasoning test by accident, it's very easy to get a low one. Perhaps his activist approach had caused him to rush into the questionnaires without reading the instructions carefully, or maybe he'd become bored or distracted while doing them, or possibly he hadn't even attempted to answer them, for fear of doing badly, preferring the sanctuary offered by declaring the whole process a waste of time. I wasn't, however, prepared for what happened next. There was a long pause. He moved his chair round the table so that he was sitting close beside me. He lowered his voice and he said, very quietly...

"*I'm Dyslexic.*"

My reaction was immediate, spontaneous and hopefully made up with compassion what it lacked in deliberation.

"*Good grief! How do you cope with that?*"

His answer threw light on the comments that his Managing Director had previously shared with me. H was very good at his job with clients. His subordinates worshipped him. They thought he was a wonderful, involving manager. His difficulties were with his fellow directors, who found him prickly and difficult, especially in senior management team meetings, where he tended to be short, belligerent and obstructive.

This made a lot more sense when H confided how he dealt with his dyslexia. Talking was not a problem. It was one of his strengths. But things became very difficult for him, if a paper or a slide presentation was put forward without having been circulated beforehand. In that situation he struggled to pick up the details or to keep up with the discussion. He hated that. He felt it made him look slow and as if he had nothing to offer. His coping strategy was to raise objections, refuse to agree to anything on the spot, insist on taking issues away to think about them more deeply. Outside the meeting what he actually did was to share the documents in confidence with selected members of his own team. "*Read this carefully,*" he'd say. "*Then talk me through it, give me your views and we'll have a discussion about it.*" His subordinates relished the trust that he was placing in them. For his part, H got his briefings in a form that worked for him – the spoken word rather than the written.

"*Have you ever thought about sharing the fact that you're dyslexic with your senior team colleagues?*" I ventured.

He looked at me as if, far from being usefully thought-provoking, I was probably insane.

"*You don't understand,*" he said. "*They would destroy me. You've got no idea what it's like to be from a minority background ethnically, educationally and socially, sitting in a room full of guys who've all been to posh universities.*"

I pointed out that he was making an assumption, that he might be worrying unduly, that personal development entailed taking some risks, but he remained unconvinced.

We talked about other things instead. He was most interested in how he could develop his ingenuity. He was attracted to open-minded environments and enjoyed the company of creative people. He wondered if he could learn some creative techniques. I talked him through a couple and recommended some audio tapes.

Our one and only coaching conversation ended much more convivially and positively than it had begun. Even so, I didn't feel that I'd been as much help to him as I would have wished. Instinctively I gave him one final provocation as he again stood in the doorway, this time on his way out.

"*By the way,*" I asked, returning directly to his opening remark from two hours earlier, "*how close did I get?*"

He stalked wordlessly back into the room and towered over me. He was several inches taller than me and I was beginning to question the wisdom or usefulness of my inquiry. He leaned down and spoke very softly into my ear.

"*Only my wife knows me as well as you do!*"

Then he grinned, turned on his heel and left the room.

THE REAL RESULTS – MY COACHEE HAS GOT WHAT IT TAKES!

The real turning point in H's case came, not in our coaching session, but two weeks later, when the whole senior management team had gathered to discuss how they might use the work I'd been doing with them. I'd set the usual ground rule in place beforehand; the individual alone could decide whether, when and how much of their psychometric profile and their coaching session to share. H arrived at the very last moment. I'd almost concluded he wasn't going to turn up at all. He looked fierce and unapproachable. He offered no words of greeting.

The Managing Director called the group together and everyone except H sat down. As the MD started to introduce the session, H interrupted him.

"*Just before we start, there's something I want to say...*"

I braced myself for the announcement that this whole thing was a waste of time and we should all go and do some real work instead. But what he actually said was...

"*I'd just like you all to know that I'm dyslexic.*"

It was a breath-taking disclosure and the reflex reaction from his six colleagues was equally wonderful.

"*Goodness!*" they gasped. (There were some unprintable variations in the exact phrase used). "*How on earth do you cope with that,*" they chorused.

This was the real turning point for H, for his interactions with his fellow directors and for the improved trust, openness and quality that characterised subsequent meetings.

And the credit belongs to H and to him alone. I'd assumed he didn't have it in him.

The conclusions I draw from this case are simply stated, but I think profoundly important to keep in mind. It takes courage to be a successful coachee, coupled with a willingness to experience vulnerability. And if these are qualities of a good coachee, they also need to be qualities in a good coach.

The Gift of Feedback

Lisa Haydon

WHAT IS OUR OPPORTUNITY AS COACHES TO LEAD BY EXAMPLE AND TO GIVE FEEDBACK NOT ONLY TO OUR CLIENTS BUT OTHERS AROUND US?

recently became a certified executive coach. While I had always considered myself a coach, the investment in the certification gave me a methodology and new skills to be a great coach. The journey to my accreditation included working with a number of new coaching clients.

As I progress along my learning journey, one aspect that continues to surprise me is the immediate feedback clients want to give about a coaching session or their work with me. These recent feedback experiences have created a refocus on and awareness of the value of feedback.

Change in the business world is constant. Whether strategy, objectives, technology, teams, culture, process, skills, accreditation, or engagement styles, our work environments are in a constant state of change. This means that professionals also must always be in a constant state of change.

While self-management is ideal, and often the expected course of action, self-management in isolation does not create the top performing professionals or outcomes.

Feedback has become more important to our work worlds, to staying current and to being successful.

GROWING UP WITH FEEDBACK

We have grown up with feedback, from childhood through to careers as seasoned professionals. Companies have organisational structures that support feedback. Performance management systems are in place for feedback. To round out our ability to give feedback, we receive training on how to deliver it.

While the skills, expectations, and processes are all in place, do we really use feedback, both positive and constructive, with the regularity and the impact that we could?

In the early days of our careers, we receive feedback regularly. As you progress through your career, feedback becomes the scheduled performance review plus a sporadic discussion. The more senior you are, the less feedback you get.

In my experience, the most frequently provided feedback has been constructive and development orientated. What is the power and potential of adding more positive, reinforcing, and supportive feedback to our discussions? My coaching clients have shown me how that looks and feels.

DOING MORE TO EMBED FEEDBACK

What can we do to embed feedback into our coaching work and everyday engagements? Here are a couple few ideas of to consider:

- Leverage your growth mindset
- Use your coach(ing) approach
- Optimize the power and impact of language
- Make it real-time
- Don't over-assess giving feedback, just do it
- Establish the leading practice for others to follow
- Be generous in your feedback

IMPARTING FEEDBACK

The feedback from my clients has been invaluable, energizing, and confidence building. Their feedback was not delivered by way of an approach or a methodology but from their heart. It wasn't thought about; it was immediate. The feedback they gave was real, and it conveyed exactly how they felt. As a receiver, I was surprised, elated, energized, affirmed, supported, and connected.

- What is our opportunity as coaches to lead by example and to give feedback of value not only to our clients but others around us?

- How can we consistently impart a feedback mindset to our clients, coaching colleagues, our network and be an advocate for real-time feedback at all stages of professional development?

I became a coach to help business leaders develop, learn, and realize goals. While I had expected to be the one to support my clients, they have also supported me in becoming a better coach. My clients have given me the gift of their feedback, and now I am very motivated to share the feedback experience with others.

Beyond Personality Assessments: Anxiety - Resilience And Confidence

Lynne Hindmarch

I have chosen **Anxiety** to write about because it often has a major impact on other aspects of a person's behaviour. Anxiety is a complex area. Difficult to define. Broadly one could describe it as a person's capacity to deal with stress and pressure.

In discussing Anxiety, I will focus on the two areas which emerge most frequently in my coaching conversations: **Resilience and Self-Confidence**.

There are a number of important factors that the psychometrician needs to take into account during feedback when addressing the anxiety scores.

- Firstly, are the scores representing state or trait? That is, the person's score may be reflecting what they are currently experiencing in their life (state), or the score may be indicating more stable and enduring aspects of the individual's personality (trait).

- An important part of the feedback is to establish this with the client. A question such as 'How do you see yourself typically in terms of dealing with stress and pressure?', or 'To what extent is your current life situation affecting your score?' can verify the person's habitual anxiety level.

- One also needs to bear in mind that when a person takes a personality assessment, whether it is for development purposes, such as coaching, or for selection purposes, they are often in a process of transition, which in itself can increase an individual's anxiety level.

REMINDER: As in my earlier blogs, I am focusing on extremes of behaviour, which fall at the upper or lower limits on the normal distribution curve. These are the aspects of behaviour where we are likely to be most consistent and may be associated with strengths. Being less inclined to flex our style may cause us difficulties in certain situations.

RESILIENCE

I start with Resilience. This is a particularly important trait because of the effect it can have on many other aspects of an individual's personality.

BEHAVIOURAL CHARACTERISTICS OF HIGHLY RESILIENT INDIVIDUALS

I think of Resilience as the 'bounce-back factor' - how quickly a person recovers from a setback. Someone who is highly resilient is likely to cope with pressure better than most people.

- They are emotionally stable, that is, they experience fewer ups and downs in mood than most people.

- They have a positive outlook - 'glass half-full' people.

- They are calm in a crisis, and their calmness can help calm other people.

- Their calm manner means that negative emotions are less likely to affect them, and they can think clearly and consider how to tackle the crisis without being overcome by panic.

For example, watching the 2016 Olympics in Rio, you can see how emotionally stable many of the top athletes are; the triple gold medal winning British cyclist Jason Kenny perhaps being the epitome of this.

It is clear that the highly resilient individual has a number of very desirable characteristics in the workplace. This becomes even more apparent at senior levels in organisations, when coping with increasingly frequent crises and pressure becomes even more necessary. There are however, aspects of Resilience which the individual needs to be aware of, and this mainly relates to the impact of their behaviour on others. For instance,

- Coping so well with pressure themselves, the resilient individual may expect others to react in a similar way, and unwittingly put them under more pressure than they are comfortable with.

- The resilient person's capacity to stay calm in a crisis can appear as disengaged, lacking urgency or not caring by others who may be reacting more emotionally to the emergency.

- Finally, their tendency to have a positive outlook may mean that they don't allow for potential drawbacks and delays when assessing, for example, how long a project may take to complete.

In coaching, the highly resilient person is likely to deal with tough feedback without becoming overly emotional. They are more inclined to consider what they can do to address the issue than feeling depressed.

CASE STUDY OF A HIGHLY RESILIENT INDIVIDUAL

The client case: Susie was an IT Director in a learning and development company. She was responsible for a major project: setting up a new on-line learning system. Susie had been sent for coaching because the company felt that she wasn't taking the position seriously enough. There had been a couple of incidents when the timetable slipped and had caused problems in other parts of the business.

Feedback following a personality assessment: Feedback with Susie covered the advantages of her calm manner and ability to cope and put things into perspective. It is always important to obtain a client's 'back story', and gentle exploration revealed that she had experienced a major tragedy in her life some years earlier. This had provided a 'benchmark' for later negative events. Compared to what she had already gone through, nothing else could be that bad. This had given her the resilience to cope effectively with negative experiences in her life. She was better than most at putting setbacks into perspective.

Coaching to move forwards: Our coaching focused on the impact Susie's high resilience was having on how she was perceived and how her team experienced her. Susie took her position and responsibilities very seriously; her team knew how hard she worked and were grateful for her ability to take crises in her stride. However, Susie's bosses were less involved in the day to day management of the project and interpreted her calmness as a lack of understanding of the seriousness of the project.

Discussing with Susie a way of addressing this, Susie commented, "*What am I supposed to do? Running around like a headless chicken is not me, and in any case would be counterproductive.*" She decided to be more proactive in the way she communicated with both her managers and her team. She kept in closer touch with her managers to update them on progress and to also express any concerns verbally as they weren't being picked up from her body language. She also learned to listen more, meeting with her team members on an individual basis, so they felt free to share their worries and how they were coping with the pressure. This also gave her the opportunity to learn about possible setbacks, to avoid slippage on the progress of the project.

BEHAVIOURAL CHARACTERISTICS OF INDIVIDUALS WITH LOW RESILIENCE

A person who is low on resilience is more likely to experience significant changes in mood.

- They may experience more highs and lows than most people, and managing their emotional state may take a lot of their attention and energy.

PART 2: Cutting edge: Investigating patterns from Practitioner Experiences

- They may feel passionate about their work which may be expressed in an emotional and excitable way. This can be motivating for others, but they may equally become disheartened.

- Their tendency to feel things intensely may mean that they lose control of their emotions in conflict. They may lose their temper.

- They may more quickly experience stress and feel the effects of pressure.

Low resilience may also affect how other traits are expressed. For example, if they are also spontaneous and enthusiastic they may be inclined to act impulsively and take risks.

When I first began feeding back personality assessments, I was concerned at the reaction I would get from clients where a Resilience score was low. What I quickly realised was that the client already knew that they were not coping well; after all, they had answered the questions! The positive aspect of this was that it often gave them the opportunity to talk about the issues that were troubling them, their current coping strategies and what was going on in their lives that may be affecting their current score. The feedback session can sometimes provide a release.

So when working with a client with low Resilience, the coach needs to be particularly sensitive to the client's emotional state. It is a good example of where the coach needs to be very clear about their boundaries, and the areas where they can and cannot work with the client. Supervision can be vital here. It is possible that further help may be needed from a specialist source: a visit to the GP, counsellor or therapist. Clients low on resilience can get depressed, so this is something to look for. Taking setbacks to heart, they may benefit more from small steps in goal-setting, so they experience success, which will help them stay motivated.

CASE STUDY OF AN INDIVIDUAL WITH LOW RESILIENCE

The client case: Tony was a Team Leader with a technology company. Highly intelligent, he was valued by the company for his knowledge and expertise. The company was keen to promote him and he was equally keen to move up. However, on two occasions he had been promoted to the next level up, and twice he had been demoted during the trial period because he could not cope with the role. Unsurprisingly, this had left him feeling low and dispirited. The coaching was intended to help him prepare better for promotion.

Feedback following a personality assessment: During feedback, Tony was able to open up about his feelings when we discussed his low score on Resilience. Checking out how typical the score was of him, he shared that he had always been prone to low moods, but the current situation had exacerbated it. Talking about his feelings in a safe environment had already made him feel better.

Coaching to move forwards: Coaching Tony, it was important to help him realise that he didn't need to feel governed by his emotional states; it was possible to make changes, particularly in the way he reacted to situations. One area of exploration was the metaphors he was using to describe his situation: feeling like he was on a slippery slope, like a helpless child or in a ditch with steep sides so he was unable to climb out. Helping Tony reframe the loss of control he was describing with more positive and proactive metaphors was one way he could begin to move forward.

We also worked on small steps he could take ('low-hanging fruit') to help him begin to feel successful. He identified people around him whom he trusted and could support him in his endeavours. Further work included helping him develop coping strategies to learn to manage his moods, particularly anger, such as breathing techniques and anchoring.

An interesting footnote. Tony was on a restricted coaching programme, only six sessions. By the end of the programme, we had made some progress but still had some way to go. I caught up with him about a year later. He said that the coaching had been a valuable watershed for him and helped him to recognise that he needed to do further work on himself. He had had a period of therapy and was now in a much more positive and stable mindset. The results of coaching are not always immediate or predictable.

SELF-CONFIDENCE

Feedback can provide a framework for discussing areas that the client may find hard to talk about and which may have been masked during previous coaching sessions. This is particularly true of self-confidence, as low self-confidence can be hidden behind high social confidence - that is, feeling comfortable in social situations. The socially confident individual can be misinterpreted as being confident in their abilities when in fact the two characteristics are quite different.

Let us start by looking at a person who has a high level of self-confidence.

BEHAVIOURAL CHARACTERISTICS OF A HIGHLY SELF-CONFIDENT INDIVIDUAL

- The confident client will focus on the positive aspects of themselves, not the negative.

- They will be comfortable taking on new challenges, even if they take them out of their comfort zone.

- They can instil confidence in others, particularly in situations where there is a lot of change or uncertainty.

- They believe they can sort out problems.

- Their self-confidence can help them rise through an organisation's hierarchy.

However, a high level of self-confidence does not necessarily equate with a high level of ability. It can lead to over-confidence, arrogance and complacency. For example, a confident individual may maintain their self-confidence by blaming others or the situation for any failure, thus avoiding responsibility for any part they may have had in contributing to the problem.

If other characteristics are present, such as a high level of social confidence (comfort in social situations), a lively style (quick acting) and dominance, this person may be a risk-taker and not see the drawbacks to decisions they make. Their self-confidence may also mean that they are less likely to listen to other viewpoints. Yet, if a self-assured person is also more modest, less dominant and more people oriented, this can mitigate some of the overbearing characteristics of the highly confident person. Though there may still be frustrations around believing that one is right but not being able to assert it.

From a coaching perspective, the highly confident person may be harder to coach, as they don't take on board negative feedback. Their high level of self-confidence means that they may not recognise that they have development needs. This is illustrated by two examples below.

TWO CASE STUDIES OF HIGHLY SELF-CONFIDENT INDIVIDUALS

Client case [1]: William was a senior executive in a consultancy where he was heavily involved in developing new businesses at which he was very successful. Coaching was suggested to William because of his bullying behaviour to subordinates.

Feedback following a personality assessment: William's assessment indicated that he was particularly confident and sure of himself. He was also socially confident, which meant he came across as lively and quick to engage. His profile also showed that he was somewhat detached, having little interest in other people and their lives, lacking in both empathy and compassion.

During our feedback, we discussed the advantages of his style in selling (which is basically what he is doing), in that he was task focused and effective at building relationships with clients. In discussing the drawbacks to his style, he accepted the effect his behaviour was having on others, but was not inclined to change it. He justified it by referring to external factors such as the highly pressured nature of the work, the hours he put in and the low ability levels of the people around him. His stance was: *"The company likes the money I generate but not the way I do it."*

His value system placed money and the amount he earned above his relationships with people (unless they were useful to him). He was not motivated to change. Although he was interested intellectually in the psychometric feedback and discussed his behavioural style with enthusiasm, it didn't create any desire in him to do anything about it.

Coaching to move forwards: The coaching focused on the triggers for William's angry outbursts, managing his behaviour differently and exploring alternative leadership styles. However, after a few sessions he began to change or cancel coaching sessions at short notice. Eventually he decided that coaching wasn't right for him and having the honesty to say that whilst we could have interesting conversations about his style... nothing was likely to change. I was disappointed but not surprised.

Client case [2]: Max came for coaching as part of his preparation for a partnership position. The company placed a lot of importance on emotional intelligence and felt that Max had developmental needs in this area. Max's strong self-confidence meant he was fairly dismissive of the feedback initially, but was keen to 'go through the motions' so he could become a partner. He was a somewhat shy and reserved person, and careful about how much he disclosed to other people.

Coaching to move forwards: At first Max viewed the coaching as a 'tick box' activity, but his desire to achieve partnership provided the motivation for him to stick at it. One area we worked on was the effect his lack of openness was having on his ability to build effective relationships. As an initial step I encouraged him to ask clients and colleagues a few simple questions, and disclose something about himself, as a first step to building closer relationships. To his surprise he discovered that a colleague he had worked with for some time was a keen rock climber, which was also one of Max's passions. Before long, they were planning a rock-climbing weekend.

Max's high level of self-confidence meant that he was unlikely to become a champion for personal growth and development, but he was motivated by a desire to change his behaviour if it served his self-interest.

BEHAVIOURAL CHARACTERISTICS OF AN INDIVIDUAL WITH LOW SELF-CONFIDENCE

- A person who is low on self-confidence is more likely to doubt their abilities, despite clear and objective evidence that they are perfectly capable.

- Their overwhelming characteristic is that they worry: about their performance, their self-appraisal may be negative, they may be sensitive to criticism and look at remarks in a negative way.

- They may take responsibility for mistakes even when they weren't at fault.

- This means that they work very hard to avoid criticism and blame.

In this respect they may be driven by fear of failure, which can be such a strong motivator that clients may be reluctant to give it up, as they see it as an important part of their success.

CASE STUDY OF AN INDIVIDUAL WITH LOW SELF-CONFIDENCE

The client case: Tina was a senior executive in a retail business. She had asked for coaching as she was feeling inadequate in the new position she had recently taken on.

In our first meeting in her office, Tina explained how she often felt she wasn't up to the job. I looked around her office. On every wall there were certificates and awards of excellence, clear evidence of how good she was at her job. On the filing cabinet was a bottle of champagne - a recent thank you for an exceptional piece of work. However, these things didn't alter Tina's feelings of low self-confidence. It was easy for her to dismiss the success as the hard work of her team, or just luck. Although Tina had done very well despite her feelings of inadequacy, it was likely to hold her back from further progression.

Feedback following a personality assessment: Feedback with Tina showed her that her view of her abilities was unrealistic. She was exceptionally hard on herself. The assessment revealed that she also had a tendency towards perfectionism, which meant that she had exceptionally high standards. Her work was consistently good. She gave 100 percent of herself to her job. However, the combination of high standards and low self-confidence can lead to fear of failure. Fear can be a very strong motivator, but is often accompanied by high anxiety. This meant that Tina was taking on too much herself and not delegating sufficiently. Her work-life balance was very poor.

Coaching to move forwards: There were a number of areas to address. Where low self-confidence was an issue, we worked on the way she processed information about herself. One of the key differences between a person with low self-confidence and high self-confidence is the information about themselves they pay attention to. A person with high self-confidence notices information that confirms their view of themselves as being able and competent; anything that contradicts that view tends to be filtered out. A person with low self-confidence, on the other hand, does the opposite. They are more inclined to notice what they interpret as criticism or failure, and filter out the positives.

The coaching helped Tina refocus her attention on the positive messages that were coming her way. They allowed her to reframe her habitual tendency to take comments as criticisms.

FINALLY...

Assessment of a person's anxiety level and the subsequent feedback can provide a platform for starting to address their issues. Exploring resilience with the client, and how it manifests itself in their behaviours, is a useful approach as a coaching intervention. An exploration of resilience simultaneously diagnoses their levels of self-confidence. This could include discussing the difficulty that a high level of self-confidence in a client presents to the coach, touching on how self-doubt can be both a driver (fear of failure) and an inhibitor (feelings of inadequacy). An appropriate strategic intervention for some awareness and learning to take place.

Helping a coachee to recognise that how they traverse the change curve impacts those travelling with them, especially if they are the 'guide'

Ian Flanders - Dispatch from the [Internal Coaching] Front

I've just read Lynne Hindmarch's piece in this blog on resilience. I was particularly struck by her assertion that highly resilient people may, without realising, impact those around them by:

- Expecting those around them to be able to react to stressful situations in the same way as they do, but in doing so actually increase the stress level those around them feel.

- Appearing disengaged or uncaring by seeming calm and unaffected when others feel anything but!

It chimed with, and made me reflect again, upon a coaching session I'd had earlier in the week with a senior manager who was having to confront some difficult feedback from their team.

ANXIETY, STRESS, RESILIENCE WERE NOT WORDS THAT FEATURED IN OUR COACHING SESSION AT ALL

Instead, the coachee talked about having taken on responsibility for all the customers in their business unit; previously the customers were split between two teams. As a result the number of people he was now responsible for had increased significantly. The handover process from the colleague who had previously held responsibility for the other team was now his boss.

Six months on, the new boss had sought feedback on each of his reports from stakeholders, including their subordinates. The feedback the coachee received was a tale of two teams: old and new.

For the old team everything was basically ok. For the new team however, their boss was "uninterested", "indifferent", "lazy?" When they were able to talk to their new boss they were often cut-off half way through as their boss grew "impatient". Immediately following this feedback, the coachee had driven for several hours to a business meeting. Though initially "shocked and upset" by the unexpected feedback, by the time he arrived at his destination had absorbed the feedback, rationalised it and decided on a plan of action to address the issues: Resilience in action!

In this initial session we started to explore the differences between my client and the boss; the previous leader of the other team, that now formed one half of the coachee's enlarged team. The coachee identified that the other manager had involved himself in the detail of what the team were working on, often having discussions with people on a daily basis. For the coachee this was overly intrusive, didn't demonstrate trust in people to do their job, and was not appropriate for a senior manager. As we explored this difference in styles the coachee reflected that the change in structure, resulting in a change in manager for half of the new, enlarged team, was significant. However, for the coachee, "as a strong T" (MBTI), change was something to be got on with.

By their own reckoning the coachee, from hearing shocking and challenging feedback, had traversed the change curve, end to end, in about three hours. The punch had rocked him back on his heels, but he had stayed upright and was back in the fight! Resilience in action.

REFLECTING ON THIS SESSION

With the benefit of Lynne's piece for company, it seems clear that she was describing exactly what I was seeing. It is clear that I need to help the coachee to explore how different people travel along the change curve, and what role they can play in supporting these travellers. But, I also need to help him to see how his own journey, in this case a sprint, also impacts the journey of others, who, are looking to their new leader for support and guidance. For these people it appears that their guide had run off along the trail and abandoned them!

My other reflection is that my coachee genuinely believes that his approach empowers his team, demonstrates trust and gives them space to grow. For him, the 'old' half of the team is proof that this approach works and is appreciated. However, I need to help him to see that for the 'new' half of the team the potential benefits of their new leader's approach are lost.

This is because their leader, in striding out resiliently along the new [change] trail, is not bringing the 'new' team with them. It is clear that the benefits of change need to be sold to some people, which is ironic given the team's day-job! I noted after our session that my job would be to "slow [him] down, and make him explore his own and other people's feelings and perspectives more." I will now add to this that I need to get the coachee to recognise their role as a change 'guide', and the need to ensure that, as a guide, they do not lose any of the party they are responsible for getting safely to the end of the change curve by setting too fast a pace.

PART 3

Opportunities at the Competitive Edge: Branding, Professional Development and Societal Needs

Busy going nowhere

Isobel Gray

I have a never-ending to-do list
Get inspired,
Start things,
Get diverted
Then lose the plot
What was I doing?

Various attempts to
get organised;
Organiser software
Excel spreadsheets
Timelines, reference manuals
Organise space
Diary and planners
Virtual and paper-based
Self-help books.

I struggle to maintain
a balance
between the minutiae
of day to day Life management
and taking strategic time
on the big important issues
like what are my goals
longer term?
What am I avoiding?

Nothing has worked
on a sustainable basis
What is the common factor?
ME.
I get disheartened
Demotivated
Self esteem plummets

I don't get to the important things;
Usually in snatched times
on themes of long term interest,
conversations, keeping in touch

I'm becoming a flitting, busy little bee
Going nowhere fast!

CHAPTER 9

BRANDING AND PROFESSIONAL DEVELOPMENT

Devising the best business brand for coaching practice

Lisa Haydon

"A brand is not just a logo, it's the overall experience you give to customers and audience. Your brand expresses the value you provide. It's you!" Amy Locurto

I chose the profession of coaching because I want to help others and am passionate about making a difference. I believe I bring experience, insights, and training to my work. I and my fellow coaches want to be the best for our clients and to do great work. organisations and professionals who have worked with coaches can attest to the impact coaching has had on them. Coaching is a viable and growing professional services business that bears proven impact to executives and businesses.

Consumers of professional services easily pay for lawyers, accountants and consultants. Yet I find the conversation of paying for coaching isn't always the same negotiation. The price, or deemed value, can be wide-ranging. Is this fact a result of the coach or the client? Coaches can be uncomfortable determining their value and being definitive in what their financial value is. The market will tell us if there's a business model so I attribute this challenge to the mindset of coaches.

THE AWKWARDNESS OF COACHING FEES

As a recently launched full-time coach, I am now focused on making my coaching services a business. For years I've done coaching for free and saw it as part of my personal brand. Now coaching is my profession. It is how I earn my living. I have comfortably negotiated a coaching engagement as a client, but now as the coach negotiating the fees, I spend time considering how to package and price the fees for the client. I cringe slightly as I send a proposed contract that includes a fee. Why does the fees part of the coaching contract continue to feel uncomfortable?

DEFINING COACHING VALUE

Early in my coaching career, I was introduced to a successful coach with similar professional experience as mine. We had a great introductory conversation and promised to stay in touch. She closed our conversation with, "When you start pricing your services, call me for a discussion." And I did. She asked me what I saw my coaching value as and what that should be worth. She challenged me on that definition of value for one of my areas of specialization, business development coaching. Her words stick with me in every pricing conversation, and it still hasn't begun to feel any easier. I've spent years setting and negotiating pricing for services, yet when I set pricing for myself, there's a discomfort. Without the business advice of my fellow coach, I may likely have undervalued my services.

ADOPTING YOUR BUSINESS MINDSET

Coaches are watching the adoption of coaching and the profession's growth with keen interest (check out: "An Insider's Guide to Coaching & Leadership Development"). We are professional practitioners that have skills and experience that the market needs and wants. We are in the business of helping. We do add value and value comes with a cost. I believe our opportunity is to reconcile the helping part of our business and the business part of coaching services. Both the helping services and the business model must co-exist.

Chris Guillebeau's book, *The $100 Startup*, outlines the concept of creating your business well. One of the elements he positions is the concept of finding and leveraging convergence. Convergence represents the intersection of your passion and what others care about. Your business is in the intersecting space of these two business fundamentals. Know what your convergence is, define it as your business and price your services accordingly.

As I grow my business and leverage my professional business development expertise, my business becomes more defined. Despite all my experience, business acumen and learnings, there's that little voice in my head that continues to analyse whether I've got the fee for service right. As I work on my own coaching business development, ensuring a business mindset is a critical success factor. Below I've captured key things I believe need to exist to have a successful coaching business. At the heart of a coach's success is the mindset of seeing the delivery of their coaching services as a viable and vibrant business.

THE BUSINESS MINDSET

Here's my take on the core elements to be aware of, and master, for a successful business mindset and coaching business:

- Clearly define your products and services.
- Establish trust and credibility to provide your services.

- Maintain and invest in professional branding.

- Define your business differentiators well.

- Understand why clients buy your services.

- Know your addressable market, i.e. geography and target client.

- Develop a business plan.

- Set financial goals, review them and make them a priority.

- Have a business advisor. This person may or may not be a coach, and, should they be a coach they must have a successful coaching business.

- Know client needs, know your value and know the fees the market will bear.

- Stay attuned to client and market trends.

- Most importantly, have confidence in all of the above.

The coach I met many months ago who began to influence my own mindset on the business of coaching recommended the book, *The Prosperous Coach*. This book appeals to my business mindset and aligns with how I need to look at the business of coaching. My now go-to reference coaching business book continues to shape how I think about my coaching business and how I make it a business.

BEING A GROWTH MINDSET CEO

Many of us operate as 'solopreneurs,' and it's our personal brand that bears a high correlation to our coaching success. As the CEO for a high growth business, what can and do you need to do to capture your business' full potential? Invest time in your business and your business strategy. Take time to consider what the potential is for you in a profession that is entering into growth and set the action plan for building a highly successful coaching practice.

Dancing with resistance

Robbie Swale

This is a piece written for and about coaching, covering the incredibly powerful topic of Resistance. Resistance is a part of almost all the work I do with clients, and for me personally almost all the work I do to build my business.

--

The first year of anything is an incredibly rich learning opportunity.

When I reflect now on my first year as a coach, there are so many lessons I learnt. But above all - above the importance of working with great coaches who have my back, above having a supportive community around me, above learning more and more about business development and enrolling clients - was the importance of dancing with my Resistance.

I'm struck, day by day, that my work stands on the shoulders of so many giants. I have a vision board with pictures of many of them. One of the huge privileges of the modern world is the easy access to the books, videos, podcasts and blogs of so many people of great wisdom. And on the topic of Resistance, I feel particularly privileged.

For my birthday, not long before I first started training as a coach, but before I knew I was going to train, my brother gave me two books. Those books have had a huge impact on my coaching and my coaching business, dealing as they do with the ever-present challenge of our Resistance.

WHAT IS RESISTANCE?

Steven Pressfield, as my brother, Ewan Townhead, a writer and coach, poetically puts in his own writing on the subject, is St George in the battle with the dragon of Resistance. In his book, *The War of Art*, Pressfield dissects and exposes Resistance in all its glory, including – near the beginning – these wonderful sentences:

There's a secret that real writers know that wannabe writers don't and the secret is this: it's not the writing part that's hard. What's hard is sitting down to write.

- 'What keeps us from sitting down is Resistance.'

And:

- 'Most of us have two lives. The life we live, and the unlived life within us. Between the two stands Resistance.'

Resistance is everything that stops you taking those steps towards the life you really want to live. It's the little instinct that takes you to Facebook instead of the work you know you should be doing; it's what leaves the gym membership unused, the paint set in the cupboard and the guitar unplayed; it's what keeps the idea for a new business in your head and not out in the world. It's those words, which you tell yourself, which can stop you doing pretty much anything: "I'm not ready."

I'm getting some Resistance right now, as I write this piece. Here's what it's saying "Have you planned this piece enough? Is it really going to be useful to other coaches? Are you sure it's not just a vanity exercise for you? Shouldn't you change it more so it gets you more clients? You aren't going to finish it before you need to leave for your meeting, so you might as well stop now." You see, Resistance is devious. It knows exactly what to say and do to get you to stop. It will tie you in knots to prevent you from taking the steps you need to take, the steps towards the unlived life within you.

RESISTANCE FOR COACHES

In *The War of Art* there is a list of Resistance's Greatest Hits (you can read it on Steven Pressfield's website in an excerpt from the book). It reads like a list of topics that I, and I believe other coaches, are faced with from our clients in every session. But it also reads like a list of the challenges that are faced by coaches themselves: 'the pursuit of a calling', 'the launching of any entrepreneurial venture or enterprise', 'any program of spiritual enhancement', 'education of every kind', 'an enterprise or endeavor whose aim is to help others', 'the taking of any principled stand'. These are all on the list, and from my experience apply to any coach starting their practice. And the chapter ends with this quote:

"In other words, any act which disdains short-term gratification in favor of long-term growth, health or integrity. Or, expressed another way, any act that derives from our higher nature instead of our lower. Any act of these types will elicit Resistance."

Whether you like it or not, Resistance is on my journey with me, and will be with you, too, on your journey to the unlived life you want.

PART 3: Opportunities at the competitive edge

SO WHAT CAN WE DO ABOUT IT?

AWARENESS

The first step is awareness. I regularly share the online excerpt from the War of Art with clients as a way to bring the language of Resistance into our sessions: this gets it out in the open, it names it. Resistance is there, or at least it is if you are trying to do any of the things on Pressfield's list (and pretty much all clients and all coaches are). As marketing guru, general font of wisdom and big Pressfield fan Seth Godin says (his book, The Icarus Deception, was the second book Ewan gave me), Resistance will always be there. As Seth puts beautifully, if you can't get rid of it, you just have to learn to dance with it.

DANCING WITH RESISTANCE

You may be thinking – perhaps this is your Resistance – 'If it's not going away and it's trying to stop me getting the things I deeply want, then surely everything is hopeless.' Luckily, everything is not hopeless. More Pressfield:

> *"Rule of thumb: The more important a call or action is to our soul's evolution, the more Resistance we will feel towards pursuing it."*

You can use your Resistance, your fear, as Seth Godin also says, as a compass. You can follow it to what you really want. And if you're feeling it maybe it's doing its self-doubt bit, 'Am I really a writer?' 'Am I really a coach?' you're on the right track. So, how does the dance go?

As any professional dancer knows, it starts with discipline, with practice. Pressfield calls this 'turning pro'. We already know how to be a professional, we've all done it at some point or other. It's how we behaved in the jobs we didn't like, the ones which weren't our calling or our heart's desire. We turned up, whatever, and we stayed all day. We don't take it too lightly, but we don't take it too seriously. We get better at it. We have a sense of humour. We accept payment.

Most importantly, any dance involves steps. In the dance with Resistance, these are small steps, but – as with dancing – at some point you have to start. Here's one last beautiful quote from Steven Pressfield:

> *"Our inspiration is always there, but it's at the moment when we commit to something and make the start that we let inspiration in."*

It feels impossible: procrastinating all day, scared, miserable. And yet. And yet. Finally taking that step, no matter how small, you get that feeling. Everyone reading will recognise it. If you're a coach, it's the little buzz of sending the scary email requesting a referral, or updating your LinkedIn profile to say 'coach' for the first time or actually approaching the building where you will meet your first paid client. If you aren't, you'll know it from submitting an application for the job you want, emailing the person you want to have coffee with to talk about something that's important to you. Getting the paint set out of the cupboard and finally putting brush to canvas.

That's inspiration. But it's not done. Another step needs to be taken. It can be as small as you like, as long as you take it. And after that, take another. And another.

RESISTANCE FOR COACHES AND MY TIPS FOR DANCING WITH IT...

Here is the voice of Resistance, speaking to Robbie the Coach, and to the lovely and wonderful coaches I know.

> *"I haven't done enough coaching to work with clients."*

> *"I need to finish my website before I start talking to people about my coaching."*

> *"I need to learn more about coaching before I'm ready to charge."*

> *"Who would pay me to coach them? I've only coached people for free so far."*

> *"I'm not ready to talk about my coaching business until I've worked out my niche."*

> *"I can't coach this person, what do I know about their work?"*

> *"No one will ever pay me for this. It's rude to even ask."*

> *"I'm not worth this."*

> *"It will never work."*

> *"I'm really scared."*

Read them back, look for the ones that resonate with you or the ones which you've heard people you know say. Or the similar sentences that your Resistance is saying to you. Look out for the language of Resistance, words like 'enough', 'not ready', 'when it's finished', 'more'.

We all have that voice. Coaching, for most people, is a calling and a dream. It is getting paid to work with people, making a difference, using all those skills which you took for granted but you have found out are special in you. Changing lives and changing your life. As a calling and a dream it is so vulnerable to Resistance.

Here are my top three tips to help guide you through the minefield of Resistance as you grow your coaching business. There are plenty more, and I'd love to hear from anyone who has great tips, or great struggles with Resistance.

1. Become aware of Resistance. Maybe this article is all you need. Maybe you also need to read my brother's blog, or the pages on Steven Pressfield's website or maybe you need to buy yourself *The War of Art* and *The Icarus*

Deception (or get a family member to give them to you for a forthcoming birthday). Whatever it takes, make sure you're aware. Make sure you're looking for it.

2. Get a coach. When you're talking about coaching to people, it's almost certain you say something like "The thing that sets it apart from mentoring, and counselling, and therapy, is that it's always forward looking." And in that forward momentum is the next small step, which lets the inspiration in.

   Whoever your coach is, they will help you take those steps. In those steps you will start to beat Resistance. I've been lucky to work with two amazing coaches, Mike Toller and Joel Monk, and both have guided me wonderfully through my Resistance.

3. Launch early. Nothing is ever ready. Ever. Steve Chandler and Rich Litvin say, in their awesome book, *The Prosperous Coach*: "Don't wait for 100% readiness. It will never come. When you are 80% ready, go for it." But 80 percent is too much.

   Launch as soon as you can. You can tweak your website tomorrow if you see a problem, or add another page next week, but get it online today. You can tweak your invitation email next time you send it, but send it to someone today. You can coach your next client after you've been on that training course, but you can make a difference to this client right now. And if you aren't, you're not just damaging yourself and your business, you're not helping everyone you could be helping. You can do it. And once you take those steps, maybe the website doesn't need proof reading a fourteenth time. Maybe the email doesn't need to be perfected again. Maybe you will change the life of this person, right here, right now.

Go on. Start. Go out there. Take some steps. Change some lives.

What's the magic age or years of experience you need, before you can be an excellent executive coach?

Lilian Abrams

Everyone has their own unique path to becoming an executive coach.

I personally came to executive coaching only after completing graduate psychology and business degrees. I then spent more than another decade actively performing a wide variety of organizational development (OD) and leadership development (LD) work.

I do know that other coaches have had quite different paths, however. I have also been asked by people in their twenties about becoming an executive coach, as well as by therapist friends and career-switchers. This has led me to wonder whether or not one could serve as an effective as an executive coach without certain characteristics, including at least a decade of in-the-trenches, organizational experience.

I am typically loath to deny anyone their desire to try to do anything new, or well, at any age. However, I do wonder if this is always realistic. As a very thoughtful, long-experienced coach and coach supervisor remarked to me, "One just can't skip developmental stages, can one?" She was referring to people maturing as an executive coach.

By this comment, she was suggesting that there are developmental stages for a coach, accompanied by specific knowledge, which one requires time and active experience to acquire. This makes intuitive sense: A talented tennis player at thirteen years old is not at the same level of skill and performance that they are, say, five or more years later, after many additional hours of practice, experience and coaching.

That said, maturity in and of itself is likely not necessarily dependent on age. In a discussion on evaluating coach proficiency, and matching coaches to clients, another experienced coach recently commented, in a week-long, online conference/discussion event hosted from the UK that "the stage of development of and perceived maturity (not age) of the coach is considered to be an important element of the matching (of coach to client.)" This makes sense, along with the idea that the capabilities of any individuals should be judged individually.

Nevertheless, going with an assumption about normal maturity, and proceeding with the more likely scenario that experience helps develop it, what kinds of exposure, over time and experience, does one need to have to be successful as an executive coach?

(For our purposes, I will define 'success' as "the accomplishment of an aim or purpose.[1]" I will also posit that the aim or purpose for an executive coach is to "partner with clients in a thought-provoking and creative process that inspires them to maximize their personal and professional potential, which is particularly important in today's uncertain and complex environment," as per the ICF definition of coaching. Finally, APECS[2] notes that "executive coaching differs from other forms of coaching in that it is primarily concerned with the development of the executive in the context of the needs of their organization." APECS further defines 'Executive' as a person who has a level of leadership responsibility (financial/operational/people) and/or responsibility for policy formulation and/or who makes a significant business critical individual contribution to the organization."

THREE CATEGORIES OF CHARACTERISTICS INVALUABLE FOR AN EXECUTIVE COACH

From my experiences and conversations with peers and suppliers, I have broadly grouped what I perceive to be a mature and successful coach into three categories: Business/organizational knowledge, psychological knowledge, and personal qualities, both internal towards oneself and outwards towards others. I added this last, practical category of personal qualities, because if this function is not managed effectively, an external coach will not be able to practice or grow their service offering with clients. (And while internal coaching is a growing practice, at present the majority of coaches seem to be external.) And the stories I have heard, and tell below, bear this addition out:

I. BUSINESS/ORGANIZATIONAL EXPERIENCE

- **Business experience** – At a minimum, knowing how a business works from a functional perspective. Potentially, even greater depth is gained by those who have themselves have served as executives in an organization. In addition to being valuable for context, language, and relationship-building

---

[1] Googled definition of success, Accessed 1-1-17
[2] https://www.apecs.org/

with organizational clients, demonstrating this quality hastens the building of trust and respect needed for a healthy coaching partnership.

- **Organizational savvy/knowledge** – This refers to having a good understanding of the informal structure and dynamics of a business: the operations of politics, ambitions, resources, the culture, and all that informally is needed to for people to get things done effectively, inside an organization. This will give you material to draw on, and to help guide organizational clients towards their own solutions.

II. PSYCHOLOGICAL KNOWLEDGE

- **Psychological knowledge** – At least possessing some breadth of valid knowledge concerning core, hopefully well-researched psychological theories and models, especially those that are often at play in interactions between human beings in a social/organizational context.

- **Being 'psychologically-minded'** – Being willing and able to look beneath the surface of human interactions, including one's own, to understand the dynamics in action. This includes being willing to work with one's own and others' thoughts, feelings, and behaviors, and help guide their movement in a particular direction.

III. PERSONAL QUALITIES

- **Self-reflective and development-oriented** – This is 'walking the talk' of coaching. Is one just as willing and able to look at one's own behavior, beliefs, motivations, emotions, thought-patterns, etc., as we'd hope our most motivated clients are? And are we as willing and effective at instituting changes to develop, in whichever ways we deem best, through that examination? Finally, are we as coaches demonstrating the willingness and ability to regularly find and utilize the same kind of space we offer as a service to our clients, for ourselves, through coach supervision and/or other methods of self-reflection? Do we apply what we learn to improve our coaching practice? And how do you know you have applied it successfully?

- **Creates and maintains a safe, accepting, and trustworthy relationship with others** – To create the right space for our clients to share what is most important to them, we need to be able to show and support, at all times, words, actions, and attitudes that consistently convey respect for the client and their safety in all regards. We need to let them know, sincerely, that whatever they say will be accepted as normal by the coach (within ethical and practical limits.) We need to lead them to feel they can trust their coach to support them with sincere caring, good attention, and constant respect. This includes but goes beyond the limits of confidentiality and other ethical expectations, which are delineated early on and continually expected between coach and client.

- **Formal training and qualifications** – This can be either, or a combination of, academic training and professional coursework. A graduate degree is common and often expected, at the master's level, preferably in a relevant field like Psychology or Business. Many hiring organizations also prefer or require accreditation from a professional association such as APECS, ICF, EMCC, or others.

- **Entrepreneurial** – External executive coaches often function as sole practitioners, and/or contractors to and/or of others. In order to provide the service we do, we must make ourselves "find-able" and "hire-able", to those who could benefit from it. We must be willing and able to create and manage running our own practice and business, including successfully executing the business functions of marketing, sales, branding, accounting, purchasing, legal, and any and all other functions needed to successfully run a business (just like our clients).

Please note that these are a few items in an initial attempt to start articulating what might ideally contribute to the development of an excellent executive coach. Others' thoughts, additions, challenges, and suggestions are welcome, to clarify and refine this list.

CHECKING OUT MY CRITERIA WITH THE MARKET

Various professional executive coaching associations, coaching firms, and client organizations reflect these criteria in terms of who they hire as executive coaches. For example, despite fifteen years of coaching experience, one pharmaceutical firm did not even want to talk to me about possibly coaching their executives until after I had attained PCC accreditation from the ICF. As an organization dedicated purely to executive coaching, APECS's accreditation criteria require at least five years of practice, with a significant percent of one's work consisting exclusively of stand-alone executive coaching engagements. For accreditation, APECS also expects an executive coach to demonstrate organizational, business, psychological and ethical knowledge, as well as detailing specifics of a coach's commitment to regular learning and self-reflection practices, including supervision.

COACHING FIRMS CAN BE EVEN MORE STRINGENT IN SOME OF THEIR CRITERIA

I spoke with the heads of two global executive coaching organizations and asked them about their hiring criteria for their coaches. One, which I'll call Org. A, requires an advanced degree and at least seven years of executive coaching experience at the mid-to-upper levels of executives from commercial businesses. They do not accept coaching experiences from non-profit or governmental settings, citing the differences in the organizational knowledge and practices that coaches would require for their main client base. They also require that their coaches have been independent and self-supporting for at least five, and preferably seven or more years, with coaching experience in at least 20 different client companies. (This is in part where my Entrepreneurial criterion comes from, above.)

Org. B, on the other hand, said that their main criteria include, will the client hire them? As this leader said, a CEO will hire someone who they feel can help them, in their business context, asking "What can this person teach me that I don't already know?" While this leader said it's not the coach's age, per se, that leads the CEO to answer that question "yes" and hire Org. B's coaches, it's also unlikely for a coach in their 20s to have the context to help senior leaders. Org. B's main criteria for coaches are, does this coach have the experience, skills, background, and presentation to get hired by our clients? They would like to see at least two years of coaching experience, and a "reasonable" client list, as well as a commitment to staying independent.

I then asked both of these leaders for examples of a coach's personal qualities, which I thought might be helpful in narrowing down what is essentially needed. Org. A cited judgment, maturity (there is that word again), and the flexibility and adaptability to go where the client might want to go in a session. Other "obvious" personal qualities were said to be high quality coaching, analytical, intuitive, caring, curious, and able to push-back on clients. This organization avoids those who offer consulting rather than coaching, and coaches that are "uninspiring", "wooden", "lacking a spark of learning", and/or "who don't draw you into a relationship with them." As an exemplary story of a coach-fail, they told me a story of an interview with a coach who wanted to work for them. Immediately after being invited to sit down for the interview, this coach pulled out a nail file and started filing their nails. This was not an example of maturity, good judgment, or much of anything else desirable in their eyes.

Org. B had some similar examples to give. In their experience of interviewing coaches, the most common lack was 'sufficient external experience' in coaching individual leaders. One coach-candidate had graduated from an Ivy League institution, had a decade of coaching and of personal leadership experience as an executive, and over thirty years of business experience. Yet, as they probed deeper in the interview, this individual was not able to convince the interviewers that they could win or execute an executive coaching assignment on their own. Similarly, another potential candidate had similar years of business and coaching experience, a relevant PhD, PCC accreditation... but had mostly done internal coaching or with small business owners, and on the topic of career change as opposed to broader leadership issues. This coach-candidate also wasn't taken on for the reason that they were not convincing to interviewers, that a client-leader would hire them.

Granted, these are perspectives from the leaders of only two coaching organizations. However, there seems to be a rough convergence of personal and professional factors between them, on what makes for an effective practicing executive coach.

WHAT DOES THIS MEAN, AND WHERE TO GO NEXT?

The opportunity to speak with others and share from my own learning and experience about the characteristics that might be required for a good, and even successful, executive coach is only the start of a very important question to me. Each of the above categories might be refined or changed, since they are based on a small number of people's experiences and points of views. For example, greater light could be shed on what 'maturity' might mean, and look like, for each unique coach, in terms of their actual behaviors and actions. Also, how might maturity be pragmatically identified and evaluated, regardless of the age of the person?

As above, it can mean and look like something different for each person, and can vary by context. People might now "know it when they see it", yet verbalizing/describing what it is and how it is embodied at a rigorous level requires the coach or those hiring coaches to be aware and able to express what this means and looks like clearly, and variously, for their audiences. More importantly, the validation of the items, and the varying specific impact of different levels of these qualities, remain to be described more concretely as well as conceptually.

Furthermore, the third category 'Personal Qualities' is a recognition of what I and others bring to our professional experience and for the broader market. Without a doubt, it's important to have a good understanding of commercial practices, since that provides a real indication of how relevant these services are with the current market needs. How do I and others know that we are maturing in our practice, and that our maturity is continually having the same positive, reproducible impact on each of our clients that we'd like to have?

Doubtless, it's important to check with others on the standards being set for what makes an excellent executive coach. There's still much to investigate and discuss! I am interested in hearing how 1) you might add to the list of initial criteria I've articulated, and/or 2) how you articulate for yourself what makes you a good coach. I look forward to our conversation!

Thanks to all those who have contributed, directly or indirectly, to this piece, including: Yvonne Thackray, Heads of Org.'s A and B, Fiona Adamson, Margaret Bishop, Bath Consultancy Group, Michael Frisch, Jeremy Ridge, Chris Smith, Nick Smith, Denise Wright, and many other colleagues, in APECS and elsewhere.

Managing time for enhanced business results

Aubrey Rebello

A**s a former** CEO and based on my experience of mentoring several CEOs, I have observed one overwhelming need for success. That need is Time.

Most CEOs carry with them business specific skills. For success CEOs also need to focus on the following:

- Their Customers.

- Sustainable Resource Creation.

- Attentively Outward Looking for opportunities, threats, trends etc.

- Networking and leveraging all stakeholder engagement.

However, to do all this the CEO needs to have Time.

Most CEOs put in long hours. They get trapped into hectic schedules. They end up exhausted and bogged down into managing the business.

Most CEOs are not masters of their time. They are slaves to activities required to 'Manage the Business', rather than 'Lead the Business'.

From my experience a large proportion of my engagements with CEOs, whether through mentoring and/or coaching, has been working on goals which are unique to each individual, but are in essence targeted toward 'Better Time Management' – so as to get enhanced Business Results along with improved 'Work Life Balance'.

HOW DO WE CHANGE THE SCENARIO?

I find the best way is to make the CEO more aware of how he spends his time.

One intervention that I have found useful is to have the CEO maintain a detailed log of his week activities, both work related and personal for all seven days of the week. Those who have maintained the log find the analysis revealing.

- Most of their time is spent in meetings, reviews, emails, telephone calls, crises and travel.

- Not much time is spent on planning, preventive activities, resource building, scanning for opportunities, networking, meeting customers etc.

SOME WAYS TO SAVE TIME WHICH HAVE WORKED FOR MY CLIENTS

Typically, what I work on with CEOs with time management is making them aware of how to redress a healthy balance of managing and leading their business within working hours, and how to rebalance that quality of time out of hours for their personal and family well-being. Having been through similar experiences, I share with them (and remind them) of how I ultimately reduced my time on activities that expended a lot of energy and time with minimal positive output that may be applicable in their role.

I share some of those quick wins, though it takes longer in practice to embed and become part of their group/team culture.

Meetings and Reviews – Reduce where possible. Most internal meetings fall into three to four categories. Create a template for each type of meeting and have everyone prepare as per template. Modify template going forward. Unnecessary 'chatter' will reduce. Meetings will be shorter and more productive. Have a morning walk around and meet your key managers. 'Talk and walk management' can work wonders. Some meetings could be 'Standing Meetings'. Absence of chair comfort would help ensure shorter meetings.

Emails: In this digital age CEOs end up with 150 to 250 mails a day. Most of them internal. One easy way to reduce this is to lay a guideline that mails should be sent for only two reasons:

- To Seek Approval in case it is not within the delegated powers.

- To Inform in case a CEO has indicated he needs to be kept updated or the information is so critical for business that it cannot wait to be told through normal MIS or Review meetings.

I have found this reduces the emails by about 70 percent. If it does not, then it indicates the CEO needs to delegate more and needs to reduce his follow-up to only critical activities.

Also an email should not intrude on other activities. Have two to three slots to read and answer mails. Your mind is programmed to read and answer mails and therefore more productive.

Outgoing Calls: Have fixed time slots and make most calls in one go. Your mind is in call mode and all calls will be more productive.

External Travel: Better Planning can be 'combined with other work or reduction.' Travel and airport wait time can be used to read long reports, make calls, think and plan.

The above disciplines have reduced time spent on activities required to manage the business by almost half for most of my clients.

'To Do' List

Another good practice is to have a daily 'To Do' list. Most CEOs have this in place. However, a normal 'To Do' list often lacks a long-term focus. I have encouraged my clients to lay down Long Term Business and Personal Goals which are specific and measurable e.g. for a new product Launch, entering new geography, acquiring another business, an overdue family vacation etc.

Based on these long-term goals I have asked my CEO clients to make a three month (current month and next two months) rolling action plan. Why three months? Looking forward in some detail for three months is doable and the action plan can therefore be more specific.

Founded on the three-month rolling plan, a comprehensive detailed plan can be made at the beginning of the month. This is then broken up into a weekly plan. A daily 'To Do' list is generated from the weekly plan. A 'To Do' list made on this basis ensures that along with routine matters the actions necessary for long-term goals are in place. This also provides some free time for unanticipated events. With greater planning, foresight and suitable preventive measures, the unanticipated events should reduce.

Such a 'To Do' list shifts focus from the non-avoidable daily grind to strategic actions more suited to achieve long-term goals. Most of my clients who have followed this discipline find dramatic improvement in their productivity, speed of response and business results.

As their daily 'To Do' list is in line with their own forward thinking and long-term goals, every day actions bring more meaning and energy to the CEO, who will be less prone to feeling tired at the end of the day. This also means that the CEO ends up having free time and feels more relaxed.

WHAT THIS MEANS?

Being relaxed and not hassled is not a luxury but a prerequisite for CEOs. This ensures time for good peaceful thinking, planning, building resource, being outward looking, meeting customers and networking.

Not being in the thick of action at all times; CEOs can then observe trends, opportunities and threats more incisively which brings value to their business.

Now with time on their hands, CEOs end up doing everything required to 'Lead the Business' and not just 'Manage Business'.

The end result? 'Enhanced Business Results with a Better Work Life Balance'. It's a Win-Win Situation.

How have you captured the CEOs attention to focus on time?

Unique ladders of sustainability

Geoffrey Ahern

The ultimate step of transforming business into conscious sustainability competence is the Holy Grail of 'Anthropocene': i.e. our era in which humans have an increasingly significant influence on the Earth. Yet, as sustainability gathers pace, much of business-as-usual seems to be moving in the opposite direction by becoming increasingly split off from value. Voters see with dismay how remuneration committees are in the pockets of boards, emissions tests are fraudulent, insurance sales spurious and so on.

Given this stand-off, much ostensible company sustainability is hollow. There's a diversity of sustainability complexity with overlapping, confusing acronyms (GRI, CR, CSR, TBL, ISO14001 and so on). Analysing it for rhetoric may seem like a gunfight at the OK Corral shoot-out, but the resulting overview assists those servicing leaders for good, like coaches.

From my experience of working with, and observing, sustainability leadership, I suggest here that each organisation has its unique ladder of awareness as it climbs towards sustainability. Commonly found rungs include:

- **'Greenwash'** – i.e. false but fair-seeming sustainability claims: though deceptive, greenwash at least admits the legitimacy of sustainability. In time may become a hostage to fortune.

- **Alignments between business-as-usual and sustainability** (e.g. cutting out waste); alignments are easy win-win.

- **Strategic ambiguity**: formulas like 'creating shared value' ('CSV') often fake cohesion between opposed business-as-usual and sustainability interests, yet yoke them together enough to avoid overt conflict.

- **The dark side**: sustainability can be abused because it muddies the waters of accountability. Despite this the shareholder-only mindset is being transcended.

- **Making sustainability an indispensable part of the company's policy and strategy**. This long step towards full conscious incompetence requires new eyes to acknowledge the emptiness of the company's sustainability to date.

Great sustainability leadership, my focus, provides new vision supportively at the right corporate moment, freeing organisations to move further ahead on the journey from unconscious to conscious incompetence. Because true sustainability values are close to those of coaching and other responsible business services, providing know-how about how these values are being obfuscated could be a professional opportunity as the Anthropocene gathers pace.

What would it take for companies to make the further step still (the Holy Grail) of moving from full conscious incompetence towards conscious competence? I suggest that conscious competence would entail the mobilisation of a critical mass of stakeholders, broadly defined. In relation to this, in the article/blog to come in this invited series, I explore sustainability stories. The present blog follows on from the previous ones on individual freedom's exclusion from ecology (the good coach, May 18), and on the ethical consequences for coaching of environmental science (March 20).

Rungs on the ladder of awareness.

Experience points to the uniqueness of each company's sustainability challenge, though of course there are also common sectoral, national and transnational factors. Thus the hierarchy of awareness suggested by the 'rungs' that follow here is illustrative only – each company needs to find its own special way.

FALSE BUT FAIR-SEEMING GREENWASH

Hollow sustainability manifests especially in greenwash. For example, incorrect natural fibre claims in clothing; 'clean coal'; and 'environmentally responsible' bottled water[1]. Greenwashing is, of course, so common because of end-user pressures, like those for cheap clothing with rapid fashion turnarounds. As a result, external costs (such as pollution) by emerging market suppliers may not be followed up through the supply chain.

Yet greenwash is an advance from being unabashedly unsustainable because its pretension to new-found virtue is vulnerable to exposure as bogus. Completely unconscious incompetence, in contrast, ignores sustainability altogether.

---

[1]Knufken, Drea. 2010. *The Top 25 Greenwashed Products In America*. Business Pundit. www.businesspundit.com/the-top-25-greenwashed-products-in-america Accessed September 11.

ALIGNMENTS BETWEEN BUSINESS-AS-USUAL AND SUSTAINABILITY

Alignments between short-term profits and sustainability create real sustainability outcomes (unlike greenwash). However, they are only partial solutions which do not go beyond compliance; thus no company can ignore enforceable regulation or reputation loss and cutting out waste is a profits win-win.

Sustainability gains often accompany technologically-driven change:

- Innovation in corporate products can produce major sustainability efficiencies; thus storing solar energy could turn fossil fuels into stranded assets.

- Sustainable innovations in markets can sell recent inventions; for example, the high volume of Africa's low margin consumers transacting business through mobile phones (this is thought to save energy use overall).

Sustainability vision aligned with commercial motivation may seem to go beyond the basics of legal compliance by combining the two in a single name like 'Eco-Advantage', but does not change corporate culture by itself. To the extent that sustainability thinking is cordoned off into corporate niches – which may be deliberately held in readiness for landscape or other transformational market change – it is skin-deep[2].

THE FAKE SUSTAINABILITY OF STRATEGIC AMBIGUITY

Strategic ambiguity can be an advance from alignment because it brings in a wide-ranging sustainability vision – maybe by combining environmental and people issues – and purports to integrate it creatively with business-as-usual. Under the surface however, strategic ambiguity is a 'structural fudge'.

Structural fudge is often necessary for internal coherence given the closeness of the unsustainable, business-as-usual starting point. How far coaches or people developers delve behind such strategic ambiguity may depend on the sustainability maturity of the corporation and individual client (in much the same way coaches make or withhold psychological interpretations depending on the extent of client self-knowledge). Strategic ambiguity about sustainability may represent a split between (or cognitive dissonance within) stakeholders, employees, executives etc[3].

[2] Schaltegger, Stefan., Erik Hansen., and Florian Ludeke-Freund. 2015. "Business models for sustainability: Origins, present research, and future avenues." In *Organization and Environment* 29: 1-8 (1); Esty, Daniel., and Andrew Winston. 2009. *Green to Gold. How smart companies use environmental strategy to innovate, create value, and build competitive advantage*. Hoboken NJ: John Wiley.;Geels, Frank., and Johan Schot. 2007. "Typology of sociotechnical transition pathways." In *Research Policy* 36: 399-417.
[3]Wexler, Mark. 2009. "Strategic ambiguity in emergent coalitions: the triple bottom line." In *Corporate Communications: An International Journal* 14 (1): 62-77.

Within the following much-vaunted, overlapping contexts there is frequent strategic ambiguity about sustainability:

- **Stakeholders**. This term, which arose in the 1980s, recognises that the social and environmental effect of companies extends beyond shareholders to employees, customers, the supply chain, those affected by pollution, the public in general. Yet companies traditionally owe the highest standard of care (a 'fiduciary' duty) to their shareholders only.

There is a fudge problem in our new Anthropocene circumstances, in which we all need to take responsibility together for the care of the planet, because the solution of extending the same duty of care to all affected stakeholders is held to be too radical. Instead there have been equivocations, for example the influential advocacy about twenty-five years ago that already-existing common morality would suffice and could be brought more fully into profit maximisation (the financial crisis of 2008 has shown up such complacency[4]!)

- **Creating shared value** ('CSV'). This is about redefining the purpose of the corporation in terms of a claimed higher form of capitalism. CSV is said to focus on the interdependence of business and society, to reconceive products and markets, to redefine productivity in the value chain, and to build supportive industry clusters and create pre-competitive frameworks. But it has been criticised for underlying greenwashing, ignoring social need, giving a purely efficiency-oriented answer to the normative issue of sustainability and for not questioning the sanctity of corporate self-interest.

    CSV can be a stepping stone from business-as-usual towards conscious sustainability incompetence; for instance Nestlé, which has been much criticised for non-sustainability, orients itself in terms of creating shared value[5].

- **Corporate Social Responsibility** (CSR). 'Davos', a media-saturated word, creates widespread ambivalence. We all know that CEOs of multinationals ritually converge on the World Economic Forum in this posh Swiss resort to talk (among other matters) about commerce's unintended consequences, like poverty and global warming. Lamentably, says the founder, Klaus Schwab, a great many business leaders are not

---

[4] Goodpaster, Kenneth. 1991. "Business ethics and stakeholder analysis." In *Business Ethics Quarterly* 1 (1): 53-73; Ghoshal, Sumantra. 2005. "Bad management theories are destroying good management practices." In *Academy of Management Learning and Education* 491: 75-91.
[5] Porter, M. and Kramer, M. 2011 and 2006. "Creating Shared Value." And "Strategy and society: the link between competitive advantage and corporate societal responsibility." In *Harvard Business Review*, Jan-Feb: 63-77, and in Harvard Business Review 84 (12): 78-92; Crane, Andrew., Guido Palazzo, and Laura Spence. 2014. "Contesting the value of creating shared value." In *California Management Review* 56 (2): 130-153. ; www.nestle.com/csv.

engaged. Thus 'Davos' is an ambiguous facade. Yet its air-miles are justified in that CEOs through their very attendance are legitimating corporate social responsibility, including the big idea that companies themselves are global citizens with duties[6].

- **Collaborating interorganisationally**. Umbrella bodies like the Forest Stewardship Council comprise stakeholder groups for environmental, social and economically viable management of the world's resources. Though they are rooted in business-as-usual, these inter-corporate platforms also stake out a moral legitimacy which goes beyond narrow self-interest and which has the potential to emerge into society-wide governance[7].

DARK SIDE ABUSE OF SUSTAINABILITY

The possibility of employee abuse of power increases once the traditional tightly drawn focus on shareholder interests is loosened and coordinating the interests of a wide range of stakeholders takes over.

At its most obvious, the dark side of self-interested executive behaviour ends up in financial corruption, as in the case of Enron in 2001. Less obviously, the dark (or grey?) side occurs when employee self-interest fails to rise to the sustainability occasion. Thus companies fall short in opportunities for multi-stakeholder conversations between businesses, governments and citizens: for example, for securing whole system, catchment-level approaches to improving water quality; or for making living wages precompetitive; or for ensuring that one sustainability goal is not undermined by another[8].

MAKING SUSTAINABILITY AN INDISPENSABLE PART OF THE COMPANY'S POLICY AND STRATEGY

The sham of strategic ambiguity needs to be transcended for the sake of achieving full conscious incompetence. Acknowledging – at the right moment – the company's sustainability performance as incompetent can thus be highly meaningful, a major employee achievement. Unilever's sustainability vision and Marks and Spencer's green Plan A lead the field because they define big gaps between full sustainability and current practice.

[6] Schwab, Klaus. 2008. "Global corporate citizenship: Working with governments and civil society." In *Foreign Affairs* 87 (1): 107-118.

[7] Scherer, Andreas. and Palazzo, Guido. 2010. "The new political role of business in a globalized world: A review of a new perspective on CSR and its implications for the firm, governance and democracy." In *Journal of Management Studies* 48 (4): 899-931; Brammer, Stephen., Gregory Jackson, and Dirk Matten. 2012. "Corporate societal responsibility and institutional theory: new perspectives on private governance." In *Socio-Economic Review* 10: 3-28.

[8] Cennamo, Carmelo., Pascual Berrone. And Luis R. Gomez-Majia. 2009. "Does stakeholder management have a dark side?" In *Journal of Business Ethics* 89 (4): 491-507; and Walker, P. 2017. "Peace, justice and corporate strategy." In *The Environmentalist* (May): 26-28.

- 'Sustainable development' has long been (since its origins in the Brundt-land Report 1987) strategically ambiguous. It has a noble destination, the achievement of combined intra- and inter-generational environmental justice, but has not got on the right road because it has yoked the incompatible horses of environmental justice and profits together as equals. This has been accompanied by a tradition of research with a dismal – and inconclusively answered – question: whether sustainability leads to increased profits (assuming it does not, continued pollution is still not an option given risks like global warming). Today, there are hopeful signs that research is moving on from this backwards-facing question to a new stage of acknowledging tensions and paradoxes[9].

Once enough sustainability infrastructure is in place, the gaps between strategic ambiguity and full sustainability may be addressed:

- Sustainability can reduce profits, at least in the short-term, for example by adding to the costs of engaging with stakeholders when drilling for gas.

- Sustainability has to negotiate commercial landscapes which lock in market failure: for example there have been systemic reasons for the UK's refrigeration industry's continued use of HFCs even though they are 7,000 times more atmospherically toxic than carbon dioxide.

- Sustainability encourages imitation of best industry practice – but this can reduce competitive advantage for individual companies.

- The more sustainability meets obligations to future generations by lowering discount rates, the more it adds to present costs.

Thus corporate sustainability – through greenwash, alignments, strategic ambiguity, the dark side – is often hollow, and the beneath-the-radar corporate chat which says so rumbles the rhetoric.

Getting to the stage of corporately acknowledging this vacant sustainability space opens up the opportunity to mobilise such folk wisdom credibly. Coaching, particularly team coaching, could be invaluable for this.

DEVELOPING STAKEHOLDER RELATIONSHIPS

After fully acknowledging sustainability incompetence, what then for leadership? How can capitalist multinational companies advance towards the end stage of conscious sustainability competence? This sustainable state will

---

[9] Gao, J. and P. Bansal. 2013. "Instrumental and integrative logics in business sustainability." In *Journal of Business Ethics* 112: 241-255; Van der Byl, C. and Natalie Slawinski. 2015. "Embracing tensions in corporate sustainability: A review of research from win-wins and trade-offs to paradoxes and beyond." In *Organization and Environment* 28 (1): 54-79; Hahn, T., J. Pinkse., and L. Preuss. 2015. "Tensions in corporate sustainability: Towards an integrative framework." In *Journal of Business Ethics* 127: 297-316.

pay the price of ceaseless wakefulness because unconscious competence, the model for a sustainable pre-scientific society, is too dangerous for our technologically dynamic Anthropocene era.

As the company, perhaps assisted by coaches, climbs the ladder of awareness towards sustainability, the leadership problem increasingly becomes focused on the outside: market failure, landscape lock-in and investors' pursuit of immediate profits above all else. These factors explain the vagueness of later stages in models for big companies to achieve sustainability: examples can't be found!

Moving towards conscious sustainability competence requires much more than a living company: i.e. a human community that keeps awareness of its identity alive through being sensitive to the surrounding world and testing new ideas while being financially prudent.

- No longer in the West is there a Protestant ethic – though there may be an Islamic one – which can legitimise the social welfare legacies of businesses. In the profits culture of late capitalism quoted companies are acutely vulnerable to venture capitalism and asset-stripping, as in US Kraft's takeover of UK Cadburys in 2010.

Yet systemic change towards sustainability is occurring. It makes itself felt through the influence of myriads of internal/external connections involving employees, contractors, competitors, consumers, suppliers, governments and other stakeholders:

- Out of the blue, as when a board member is questioned about melting icecaps by a grandchild being shaped by the nursery school curriculum (today's 'what did you do during the War, Daddy?' question).

- Predictably, as in employment – companies like Nestlé need to recruit the ablest from environmentally concerned up-and-coming generations.

In an overall context of incremental change towards sustainability, the company may yet sometimes have to react by leaping, or otherwise risk losing the initiative:

- Businesses may face a sustainability priority paradox in which they have to genuinely prioritise sustainability in order to survive commercially. For e.g. when BP ceased to be 'Beyond Petroleum', BP risked its position in the non-fossil fuel long-term of sustainable energy. The sustainability priority paradox resembles alignment, but in reverse because sustainability is no longer subordinate to profits.

- Otherwise businesses moving towards the green economy seems to be incremental (unlike Marxism's previous great challenge to capitalism through all-or-nothing political revolution). Full sustainability challenges existing business-as-usual with gradual but radical reform through separating development from the absurdities of GDP-defined growth, and through advocating convergence and per capita GDP contraction in the most flagrantly resource-consuming world economies.

Furthering the tendency for companies to develop their stakeholder relationships is surely a crucial part of the leadership answer once sustainability incompetence is fully acknowledged. The next article/blog examines motivating stakeholder stories, narratives and mythologies which have not yet been considered in the sustainability discussion[10].

Over many years I've seen how indispensable coaching can be for personal and group vision-formation. I wonder how this experience can best be brought into the development of companies' sustainability visions.

---

[10] De Geuss, Arie. 1997. 'The living company." In *Harvard Business Review* 75 (Mar-Apr): 52-59; Santana, Adele. 2012. "Three elements of stakeholder legitimacy." In *Journal of Business Ethics* 105 (2): 257-265.

Being paid to learn

Aubrey Rebello

LEARNING THROUGH COACHING

As a coach, I encounter talented clients from diverse backgrounds. At the end of each coaching session I become a 'richer' person in both my learning and monetary.

I have been lucky to have had a diversity of clients: college principals, priests, owners of family-managed listed companies and leaders in Indian and multinational corporates. I have also had a rare experience of coaching in parallel, a chairman and MD of a company and his son, who was a director in the company. Each of these interactions has given me new insight.

WHEN YOU'RE WORKING AS A BUSINESS LEADER, YOU ARE ALSO LEARNING.

This learning is however through interactions with a relatively less diverse diaspora: your team, colleagues, customers, competitors, social and professional circles.

As a coach you get to observe and interact with a wider variety of people from diverse businesses and professions. These people open up to you. A friend or even a spouse would not open up in the same way as a client opens up to you during a coaching journey.

This 'opening up' I would say enriches me. Hopefully it enriches my fellow coaches in ways you may not achieve from interactions in normal professional, business or social circles.

As a coach you are making the client take certain actions in order for him to reach his goals. The client learns 100 percent from his actions and for me, as the coach, I also learn from at least 30 to 40 percent of the process.

It is said that during coaching the client goes through two journeys:

1. The Goal (specific and measurable) journey which is very obvious; and

2. An Emotional journey which makes each of them a changed and improved person.

While guiding the client to his goals the coach is also a partner in the journey. The coach therefore also goes through an emotional journey and comes off as a changed and improved person.

It is a mutual enrichment for which the client pays and hence my refrain "Why am I getting paid when I am learning?"

APPLYING LEARNING'S IN COACHING AND CROSS UTILISATION

Having had the opportunity to work with diverse individuals across multitude of sectors and organizations, I would say several of the issues faced are common across clients and organizations.

There is therefore an opportunity for cross-utilization of learning to my other assignments. Many of the lessons I have received from one client session can be many times gainfully used to help another client. In a way, a coach becomes a catalyst for skill sharing.

Summarising from my four years of coaching practice, I have identified 8 key factors that have helped me be successful in business and cross-utilize the learning I take from each assignment; this is what I bring, these experiences and insights, into those conversations:

1. Agility

2. Customer Focus

3. Team Engagement and Goal Alignment

4. Behavioural Issues

5. Time Management: A Leader is free and available and not bogged down

6. Anticipating Pattern in so called "Unforeseen Events": With 80 percent of unexpected events occurring this show a pattern in which the Client, being in the midst of so many actions, frequently fails/misses to notice this.

7. Managing and Leveraging different stakeholders

8. Business Specific Skills

PART 3: Opportunities at the competitive edge

RELOOKING AT MY COACHING JOURNEY

Believe me, we as Coaches also have a journey of improvement to take. Whilst helping our clients to enhance their capabilities, coaches can also look at their clients as a mirror and correct their own deficiencies. Luckily, we are paid by our client on this journey.

When I relook at my career and life, I sometimes feel that if I had taken a break from being a CEO, worked as a coach for a few years and then returned to managing business, I could have been an even better CEO.

Would some of you business leaders take a sabbatical and try this out? Alas it's too late in the day for me.

WHAT NEXT

I am being paid to learn. I am continuously learning about patterns of behaviours and events because I am able to work with a diverse range of individuals in a wide variety of sectors which I wasn't able to work with previously in my role as a CEO. I hope to continue sharing my learning experiences in future posts.

Having worked as a coach for four years and with the lessons I have taken from client interactions, I believe I would have been a better CEO today.

Would you consider taking a break and becoming a coach, as part of your own personal and professional learning and development?

What if there was a guarantee that you will perform even better when you return to your original work role?

Making sense of how supervision fits into coaching

Jeremy Ridge

1. SUPERVISION IS A GOOD IDEA, BUT HOW DOES IT WORK IN COACHING?

Supervision suggests you can have someone looking over your shoulder. Someone with all the answers. Someone who can guide you in what to do and not to do. It is also pretty much the meaning in established professions which then monitors the use in practice of an agreed set of measurable standards and processes have been tried and tested for always delivering desired results.

However, the complexities of coaching theory, previously illustrated in my blog-article[1], "How we can define coaching – 'Do it for Yourself' (DIY)" on coaching definitions challenges this ideal of always knowing what to do and not to do in coaching.

SO WHAT EXACTLY DOES SUPERVISION SUPERVISE?

Some of the challenges for supervision are:

- The supervisor may not be present.

- They may not know the context.

- They may not have all the answers about what should be done – as there are so many models of coaching.

My practice in working towards having a positive effect on other people, often referred to under this 'coaching' banner, has always been about looking for ways to 'check what I am doing is working properly'.

---

[1] Ridge, Jeremy. 2015. "How We Can Define Coaching – 'Do It For Yourself.'" *the good coach*. http://the-goodcoach.com/tgcblog/2015/12/11/how-we-can-define-coaching-do-it-for-yourself-diy-by-jeremy-ridge Accessed September 11.

Some of the circumstances for getting it right also requires very careful navigation, lest surprises and inappropriate actions may start to work negatively, and with potentially serious consequences.

So it is useful to take stock of how this works for me. It's a sort of self-supervision exercise! Although I also need to know how to make the best of possible mechanisms of supervision, as they are often promoted in the field.

I also refer to experience and practice from providing supervision to other coaches, when they like to formally call it supervision, as well as through more informal practice of similar processes.

At the end of the day, it would seem to be more about whatever works for each coach, in their kind of practice and for the kind of person they are; for how they consider it is best to check themselves out in the circumstances – with appropriate others.

2. CURRENT THINKING

So let's start with, how supervision is supposed to work for coaching.

2.1. A GENERAL DEFINITION

"The action or process of watching and directing what someone does or how something is done: the action or process of supervising someone or something[2]"

2.2. HOW SUPERVISION IS USED IN OTHER CONTEXTS

Academia

In **academia**, supervision is the aiding and guiding of a postgraduate research student, **graduate** student, or undergraduate student, in their research project; offering both moral support and scientific insight and guidance. The supervisor is often a senior scientist or scholar, and in some countries called **doctoral advisor**.

Business

In **business**, supervision is overseeing the work of staff. The person performing supervision could lack a formal title or carry the title **supervisor** or **manager**, where the latter has wider authority.

Society

In **society**, supervision could be performed by the state or corporate entities to monitor and control its **citizens**. Public entities often do supervision of different activities in the nation, such as **bank supervision[3]**.

---

[2] http://www.merriam-webster.com/dictionary/supervision
[3] https://en.wikipedia.org/wiki/Supervision

This begins to show up some of the current complications about how supervision is seen, and not seen, to work in the coaching field. For example,

1. Coaching is not a remedial exercise, and

2. It often works across many different contexts, and

3. Draws from many different areas of knowledge and learning.

Mature 'professional' bodies normally have a form of best practice/required practice guidelines that are quite stipulative and based on agreed research. It is why they are worthy of the term professional. This is where any practitioner malpractice that may bring the profession into disrepute may lead to professional registration being curtailed, and even removed/barred from continuing to professional practice in the marketplace.

This makes a process of 'checking' important. Especially in those professions where it typically involves a one-to-one situation and there is risk of bias or where the client/patient is vulnerable. It is a good standard for coaching to also work towards embracing.

2.3. MY EXPERIENCE OF HOW SUPERVISION IS BEING USED IN COACHING

One conclusion I've drawn thus far from all my interactions in this field and that drives this enquiry for me is the current dilemma in the idea that 'a supervisor' is:

- *the* total solution, in coaching, and

- that they are readily available with all of the answers that any coach needs, for every situation.

Another dilemma is 'who sets the agenda' for supervision. If coaching is a 'reflective and developmental exercise' and the coach sets the agenda, then supervision actually often seems more like 'coaching the coach' than supervising the coach.

I would expect in a field promoting coaching that we would be seeing a clear practice of coaches getting coaching after all!

2.4. SOME CURRENT PERSPECTIVES ON SUPERVISION IN COACHING

Hawkins and Smith[4] (2008) put forward a useful framework (adapted, here for the purpose of this blog-article), that compares the functions of supervision in coaching with other, related, one-to-one helping professions.

---

[4] Hawkins, Peter., and Nick Smith. 2011. *Coaching, Mentoring and Organizational Consultancy: Supervision and Development.* Maidenhead, Berks: McGraw-Hill.

Extending 'The Functions of Supervision' to include its professional orientation (Adapted from 'The Functions of Supervision'[5])

	Hawkins & Smith	Proctor	Kadushin
Professional Orientation	Coaching	Counselling	Social Work
	Developmental	Formative	Educative
Function	Resourcing	Restorative	Supportive
	Qualitative	Normative	Managerial

Hawkins and Smith also describe how the function of the supervisor is to ensure a 'quality of work' that is 'appropriate'. Less detail or information is shared around what contexts this mark of 'quality' could be tested against.

So Hawkins and Smith introduce this term 'qualitative' into their framework, which again implies coaching is still developing some tested, validated and agreed framework, that may be more readily found in other professional areas more easily than in coaching. For example, the reference to the term 'normative', by Proctor, and 'Managerial' by Kadushin, as applied in the field of counselling and social work respectively, implies a clear reference to external standards.

This implies coaching is still a more open field of work, with implications that coaching supervision needs to be more open in approach.

2.5. RECENT THINKING IS ALSO BEGINNING TO APPRECIATE A VARIETY OF WAYS MAY WORK BETTER FOR SUPERVISION

A recent paper presented by Gilbert, Lucas and Turner[6] at the Fourth International Supervision Conference 2014, emphasises supervision in Coaching as primarily reflective practice.

Again, I am not sure I can see the logic of why supervision doesn't refer to this as the opportunity for 'coaching' rather than for 'supervision!' - especially when working in the field of coaching.

Similar to other authors in the field, there is less mention of context here. However, it does emphasise the variety of ways in which 'supervision style' reflection can happen.

Similarly there is much less of any emphasis on any 'context' of required standards for the variety of ways that supervision can be practiced:

1. Paid for one-to-one supervision.

---

[5] ditto
[6] Gilbert, S., Lucas, M., and Turner E. June 2014. 4th International Supervision Conference. http://business.brookes.ac.uk/commercial/work/iccms/coaching-supervision-conference/2014/

2. Paid for group supervision.

3. A peer supervision chain.

4. Co-coaching – e.g. in triads.

5. 'Mindfulness' practice/meditation.

6. Other one-to-one supervision (timely rather than periodical).

7. Reflective journaling.

8. Action learning sets.

9. Other group supervision

10. 'Something else'

It further suggests that supervision in coaching may still be on an emerging path, as much as coaching itself.

This certainly seems to tally with my practice experience – where there is a great deal of diversity in the ways I 'check myself out!'

3. HOW DOES MY PRACTICE SIT IN THESE FRAMEWORKS?

As shared above, the current definitions for supervision are too simple for my practice. I tend to revert to my own definition of supervision's aims; 'checking out what I am doing is appropriate, and suitably contracted for' guided by the following:

3.1. DIRECT CONTACT WITH THE DATA OF WHAT IS GOING ON

For me, what matters is who will have the best data/information about the circumstances – not just the best theory.

For example, the most valuable supervision I can get is the live shared data from the 'team' (of coaches) I often work with. This is in contrast with the 'separate' supervision, which like today's simple coaching model, requires the coach, and supervision, to be in a detached space. The team knows more of the context, as well as a greater appreciation of how my contribution may be working.

3.2. THE DIVERSITY OF PRACTICE - 'A COACHING APPROACH'

It is different for each of the different ways that coaching is carried out. I refer back to my good coach blog 'Freeing up our use of coaching! ... contrasting the simple model of coaching with a more 'open' model for coaching[7], and the wide range of other ways coaching can be carried out – now often referred to as through 'a Coaching Approach'.

---

[7] Ridge, J. 2015. Freeing up our use of coaching! *the good coach*. https://the-goodcoach.com/tgcblog/2015/6/25/freeing-up-our-use-of-coaching-contrasting-the-simple-model.html Accessed September 10.

3.3. THE NATURE AND PRACTICE OF CONTRACTING

This can range from being very formal and very detailed – almost 'legalistic' through to highly informal and highly emergent – where the nature of the agenda depends on the way the dialogue and relationship takes shape.

If the client is to work in the way that suits them, there are requirements to contract in some manner that takes their preferences into account.

Hence contracting may not be a simple process that starts at the beginning and is never reviewed again.

Even the subtleties of 'ethics' can vary from person to person, organisation to organisation, as well as in time and circumstances.

3.4. LEARNING ABOUT THE RIGOUR INVOLVED IN UNDERSTANDING WHAT IS GOING ON IN COACHING

I still see how much coaching capability, and learning about what is involved, still comes more from everyday life/work and coaching client experience than it does from the considerable diversity of text books in the field.

I have found it is most important to establish a frame of reference for my own practice that enables me to check out, for myself, as a priority, what is appropriate.

The dynamism of the chemistry between two people is substantial. Arguably still more complex than measuring brain waves. It still seems to be in the 'invisible' zone as even a subject to talk about, let alone study.

This is more than just 'informal' – rather it may just be invisible for many people.

It can take time though to establish a common language, ways for referring to the events of coaching, especially during supervision as an exercise.

4. EXAMPLES OF HOW THIS WORKS IN PRACTICE FOR ME

4.1. RESEARCH INTO MYSELF:

This is an important starting point; a never-ending journey (and still a subject of some need for further work in the field generally).

One important example, here - as mentioned in an earlier good coach blog "Smiling and Laughter really matter in coaching[8]" - was how I found I was particularly interested in such things as 'humour' as a particular route into understanding and appreciating how to interpret events with people.

It remains an important source of how I supervise myself – in being able to find how to create conditions that raises a genuine smile as an important indicator of approval.

[8] Ridge, Jeremy. 2015. "Smiling and Laughter Really Matter in Coaching." *the good coach*. http://the-goodcoach.com/tgcblog/2015/7/27/smiling-and-laughter-really-matter-in-coaching-by-jeremy-rid.html Accessed September 11.

4.2. RESEARCH INTO - RESEARCH

Where are our frontiers of understanding about getting the best out of people up to, and going to?

Academic standards of rigour provide an important basis for checking out whether interpretations are evidence based.

This standard of rigour is another important component of bringing supervision into my practice.

4.3. THE CLIENT - OR COACHEES THEMSELVES

They are a primary source of information about how things are going.

There are always the important conditions of confidentiality, and basic principles of engagement (including exceptions to confidentiality, such as any matter that is not considered appropriate in the context), to be established.

In executive coaching, the client may well be multiple, and more complex. This is an area that always needs care.

Normally, coachee reactions and feedback are both essential for knowing how things are going and necessary for how to work further towards an appropriate direction.

4.4. IMMEDIATE COLLEAGUES

This may arise from working with other coaches in for example, a 'team coaching' context where the other colleagues are directly involved in the process – either at the same time or in the same context. This provides the possibility of important feedback and information about how practice is working drawn from direct observations.

4.5. 'WIDER' COLLEAGUES IN THE FIELD, GENERALLY

This may be from keeping up to date with the field more widely. Or it may be more of a personal network of dialogues with colleagues where we have similar interests, but do not work directly together.

4.6 FAMILY AND FRIENDS

This is still somewhat radical to suggest, but the people who know me best, and who have the well-practised skills of knowing how to reach me, are often found in places which are less than formally expected.

Of course, no details of actual contracts are ever disclosed. However, the intimacy of awareness and practice in knowing how to reach me for who I am is power enough.

All these sources of information provide a continuing stream of data that enables all-important processes of checking how things are working.

5. MY LEARNING AND CONCLUSIONS, SO FAR

I have found it useful to review, here, how the main stated reason for supervision in coaching may well be achieved through a range of other mechanisms then the more rigid processes or frameworks sometimes promoted in the field.

1. I have yet to find how individual supervisors in coaching are 'appointed' – let alone also 'supervised'.

    This does not deny the value of development that many coaches can enjoy. So why isn't this called coaching then?

2. My experience of the reality of coaching practice brings many others into the formula for checking out whether what is required is being achieved, other than a more detached single person with the 'authority' of being the supervisor with all the answers.

3. I find it is important to always hold that the coaching work involves starting from a position of considerable lack of information – e.g. about the coachee, and what their development circumstances actually are, and how they are perceived by the various stakeholders who can be involved.

    So a 'cautious and step-by-step approach' that continuously checks with those involved is essential.

    Further this needs to be done 'informally', and even sometimes intuitively, lest the process of checking out becomes too dominant, stagnant and costly.

4. Executive coaching typically provides contact with people who are naturally inclined towards greater rigour concerning results and outcomes.

    This can even extend to work with people in leadership positions who can be better versed in appreciating even small changes in learning than many can seem to be able to report in the coaching field.

5. This also opens up the issue that many people have skills and practices in their work that are not labelled as coaching, but on close examination are indeed very highly effective in the same way as coaching can be. Again, I see how their use of 'supervision' for this is measured by the results they (and others) are looking for in the context.

6. Finally, supervision emphasises to me something that has to be managed by the coach in a manner that is appropriate to them. An important test is often simply for any coach to enquire how they are doing this.

My Question To You: "How Well Can You Articulate Your Own Ways Of 'Checking Yourself Out'?"

PART 3: Opportunities at the competitive edge

Pursuing professionalism and rigor in coaching: The usefulness of peer coaching for personal and professional development

Yvonne Thackray and Larissa Conte

C oaching as we understand it today is part of an evolutionary process in elevating human potential. As societies continue to realize that each individual has greater potential to live beyond their limitations, coaching has tapped into that growing awareness. Coaching has filled the gap left by the decline of lifelong structured developmental experiences like guilds, formal mentoring and initiations. At the same time, rapid commercialization of coaching has resulted in a proliferation of practitioners without clear standards of practice—reminiscent of the Wild West. This poses challenges to coaches and clients alike. It has also led to a continual reinvention of terms for coaching without actually making sense of what coaching is and how it can make a difference alongside all other approaches that support a similar agenda. Self-appointed professional bodies and related institutions started with good intentions, yet seem to be disconnected from actual market needs. Without clear guidelines of what is a legally defined 'professional' coach, it leaves clients exposed and demands coaches self-direct their own learning whilst checking and comparing how their approach is developing with respected peers.

Working independently as practitioners, the challenges and opportunities coaches face are often quite a lonely affair. There is no set organizational system we need to follow, and so we usually author our own growth paths to the best of our ability. We often want to improve our coaching skills and behaviours (e.g. rigor of practice, clarity of approach, what we aim to deliver, etc.), as well as our business skills (the type of clients we want to attract, pricing, agreements, etc.). Quickly scanning the broader field of coaching, the majority of the available 'trainings' and 'supervision' seem to focus either more on business development or personal development, less so on both 'personal and professional' (PP) development. The obvious challenges of designing and engaging in one's own PP learning curricula were the main impetus for us—Yvonne and Larissa—to develop a collaborative relationship of reflection and writing as peers in the coaching space.

What we mean by peer coaching:

1. Amongst peers, we share coaching conversations to further articulate our triangulated thoughts about the practice of coaching.

2. More broadly, we belong to many different peer coaching relationships/ groups.

In our peer-coaching relationship with each other, we've decided to report on our learning. Some of this learning is sourced from other peer coaching relationships or groups we also participate in.

HOW OUR COLLABORATIVE PROCESS EMERGED

Larissa was introduced via a mutual acquaintance in London to Yvonne, who's the founder and one of Leadership Team members at *the good coach*. We quickly fell into a routine of meeting over Zoom for ninety minutes every 3-4 weeks (often with a 12-hour time difference) inspired by our mutual interests, shared curiosities and reciprocal coaching that satisfied each of our PP agendas and *the good coach*'s agenda. We decided that we could benefit from each other's individual learning and explore the finer points of coaching together. This resulted in our agreement to appropriately share and discuss, through periodically reporting on *the good coach*, our experiences of coaching in how we practice — how enriching that might be!

This naturally led us to disclose more about ourselves to really begin to get to know each other, including our foibles. Managing what we would then disclose from our conversations, we've contractually agreed with each other to share what we deemed to be relevant and pertinent to each article.

With the current information and understanding we each have of our practice to date, we share what we consider to have been important shifts in how we practice. It means our sharing can be considered to be still quite broad and high-level (macro level) as we're still in the early stages of recounting events[1]. Yet, it's still a useful starting point that provides us with relevant evidence to systematically build toward a more common understanding and draws on our respective, diverse experiences as practitioners. We appreciate that while we are able to consider similarities, there are inherent risks in declaring patterns because they can minimize the complexities and personal differences we've each overcome to get to where we are now. We're still learning from each other about our collaboration. We're beginning to map our surface

---

[1] Examples of micro level events - talking at the behaviour level of individual differences (see for example posts by KC Char, Sue Young, Jeremy Ridge, Larissa Conte, Alan Robertson).

features representing distinct edges or common typologies of our coaching in the hopes it may help serve others on their unique paths.

Our expectations are that each of our articles deepens our PP knowledge bank and adds value to the field overall. We both do not feel that what we're offering is the 'final solution', but rather a 'snapshot' of what's been most relevant to date from our ongoing experiential learning and what's been of most value in our practices.

Key insights

This article is primarily about how we've used the insights gained from peer-coaching conversations to shape our practices. For our first co-written piece we:

- Offer some signposts and hard-earned knowledge to those just starting out as independent coaches.
- Give more perspectives (data) for established coaches to consider when mentoring or supervising rising coaches.

COMMONALITIES IN OUR COACHING PATHS

After sifting through our abbreviated autobiographical journeys into coaching we became aware that the sum of each of our experiences to date had resulted in quite similar perspectives that, in turn, shaped our approach to practice. We were both struck by how driven we are by our personal motivations to make coaching part of our professional services. We wanted to learn how we can continuously improve our coaching skills as part of our continuing PP development. Here are some common patterns we found:

- **Our learning paths have primarily been intuitively led, rather than explicitly structured.** Despite all the coaching models and coaching psychological theories that focus on growth and development, it's very hard to map that knowledge directly onto each person's growth as a coach. Instead, it's very specific to each individual. Our learning and development as coaches has had to move beyond over-reliant or evangelical adherence to any given model. Even acknowledging the partial nature of every model can be challenging. Rather, we engage with our practices as part of our PP with a great amount of critical thinking and inquiry from a wide range of disciplines.
- **We both created and continually shape our careers by listening to our passions and following our innate curiosities.** This is a riskier choice compared to some of our peers whereby organizations have typically invested in their career pathways for their professional technical role (i.e. graduate training programs offered by organizations through to leadership training for managers). Without a specific framework that manages progression,

we each had to develop our own continuing PP framework that more accurately reflected our different challenges in pursuing what we wanted to achieve. This demanded a greater learning curve of understanding our role, developing the self and creating our own entrepreneurial role in an open market.

- **We've partnered with others to close our gap of understanding and develop our strengths.** The greatest and most direct professional feedback we've received about who we are and what we're doing is through intimate relationships. Learning from each of our many experiences, it's a combination of both personal reflections and peer conversations (you might even call it coaching), particularly with those peers who are invested in us, and invested in building a relationship on a shared agenda.

- **Putting ourselves in different organizational contexts informs our ongoing PP development**. We've both followed a path that's taken us through diverse professional settings as employees and consultants, which has afforded us exposure to a wide variety of organisational cultural patterns. Recognizing pattern similarities (e.g. reading and deciphering contexts, personalities, systems, and cultures) gave us the opportunity to present alternative perspectives and appropriate interventions with a more coaching approach regardless of the role we held. It's important to note that our learnings here resulted as much from our successes as from our mistakes. The mistakes helped us hone our understanding of where we could grow and recognise our limitations as coaches.

Learning and development has played a central role in both our personal and professional lives. At this point in our careers, it's now more about continually developing the right balance of matching our experiences with understanding how we practice in order to have longevity, credibility and respect in each of our respective markets. Making the right choices in our self-directed career development can be a circuitous route. It requires conscious effort to know what the real learning is from each experience that matches reality, rather than our own personal worldview. Integrating those learned experiences deepens our development of understanding of who we are and how we can more efficiently and effectively coach the needs of our clients in their context.

MAPPING 6 KEY SHIFTS THAT SIMILARLY INFLUENCED OUR INDIVIDUAL PRACTICES

The following elements are what we consider, so far, to have been the key shifts that made a positive difference in how we each practice.

1. Confidence.
2. Target client/Ideal audience/Knowing our market.

PART 3: Opportunities at the competitive edge

3. Valuing and selling our services.

4. Legitimacy and validation.

5. Exploring ethical boundaries and professionalism.

6. Partnering.

While this list is neither exclusive, nor comprehensive, we offer these insights surfaced from our discussion of our growth as coaches.

1. CONFIDENCE

Working Description/Definition(s): A feeling of self-assurance arising from understanding how one's coaching skills and behaviours are repeatedly having the desired, beneficial effects with each client.

Having confidence in delivering coaching and being able to talk with confidence about how we coach has been an important area of growth and development as practitioners. We feel this comes from experience, and also from realising that we were doing a lot of informal coaching before we formalised our practices, rather than believing a lot of the rhetoric[2]. One professional aspect of coaching is being able to talk more concisely about what it is we do and how we do it in a way that's consistent with each of our clients. This not only translates into confidence in our ability to communicate about our practice, but also our ability to communicate with people in many different life stages and contexts, to enable both of us to mutually assess fit in the coaching relationship. When we're with the client, this translates into how well we understand the client's context and their desire engage us to achieve their agenda because they have decided to trust us.

LC: "*Thinking back on my lifecycle as a coach, I was first paid five years ago. Prior to that point, I'd constantly been coaching people since 2005, but not paid for it. As I looked at different coaching bodies and their accreditation, what I needed to do was the math. I looked at the many hours in my life spent coaching, which added up to over 10,000 hours of coaching - and that was the first main way in which I gained confidence in my experience and abilities.*

"*There have been many iterations and evolutions on my coaching path, and for me, the first main step in building my confidence was about bridging the gap between coaching as a passion and coaching as a craft/career. What's currently available in terms of roadmaps for creating a coaching practice don't seem very helpful. Something that's missing for me, and what helps motivate our work together, is to first get to know myself and the consciousness inside my own body. How do I listen?*

---

[2] Example would be how the ICF has changed its requirements (and other bodies ensuing) that coaching doesn't count until you've completed a certified coach training course. For example see https://the-goodcoach.com/tgcblog/2015/9/2/culture-driven-from-the-centre-comparing-two-coaching-bodies.html, and https://the-goodcoach.com/tgcblog/2017/2/28/making-sense-of-what-i-do-how-my-coaching-practice-is-taking-shape-by-yvonne-thackray.

How do I learn and create alignment in my own life? What are my gifts in the process of being in continual learning and growth? What have I learned and embodied that I can use to uniquely contribute to others on their path? By learning how to be coached and coach oneself on the developmental journey, that's a big part of where I found my positioning and niche in coaching. To know that I had experience gave others value. I could locate myself in the field of coaching was all crucial for me."

YT: *"In a similar fashion looking back at my coaching career, I was first paid seven years ago. I'd literally came off an overseas coach training program, and when I returned to Hong Kong someone recommended me to coach the CEO of a multinational luxury goods conglomerate. This was my first paid coaching client. It was also the first time I had to engage with business development, sales and delivering on the coaching agenda. I closed after our first meeting, and my rate was what we'd call average for mature coaches. I was hired with no questions asked and was paid in full for the whole coaching package upfront. I started building up my portfolio of clients, checking out different rates, and the immediate questions that kept popping up for me were,*

- *How many sessions does a client really **need**? and*

- *What is it that I'm doing that keeps bringing people back to me as a coach? For example, one client had to travel an almost three hours round trip for a ninety-minute conversation.*

I realised in a short period of time I couldn't follow a framework that was conflated with the norm by approved training schools and bodies because it simply didn't work for my practice. It was useful to trial and test out their framework, and I also quickly realised that you can't force people to follow a set template. And so my motto, since then, has always been to allow the client to self-direct their own learning and to follow that rather than having a tight structure at the start. This is really a negotiating process between myself and the client. The client wants to know what technical expertise I'll be bringing to the conversation. Once they have the evidence they need they'll need to know that I'm working with them from a seemingly robust knowledge base and that there is a shift in the growing relationship where they can confidently continue to take the lead supported with my style of coaching. Recognising early on that that this is a consistent pattern of how I practice, has helped me appreciate who I work better with - confident and humble, mature and independent, autonomous lifelong learners - with confidence. Saying that, there are times when it is useful to introduce a light structure!"

2. TARGET CLIENT/IDEAL AUDIENCE/KNOWING OUR MARKET
Working Description/Definition(s): A specific description of the clients (individual and groups) that each coaching practitioner's approach works optimally alongside with and shares a mutual agenda.

Economic situations can dictate who we work with as clients, and sometimes coaches, need to work with clients out of economic necessity rather than deep alignment—especially when they are first starting out. However, at different stages of our coaching career, we start to filter out and identify those clients who we are most suited to work with rather than working with anyone and everyone. Typically, those who we are better at working with help us in deepening our learning and understanding of what's working, and more importantly why it's working. It's both motivating and validates more often than not why we are working hard in this field.

LC: *"This is one of the hardest questions to answer in coaching. I think the reason for this is that people want to get paid, particularly when starting out. This tension can result in a Jack-of-all-trades pitch as a coach—willing and claiming to be able to do virtually anything the client needs, even though you may not be the best option for all the work. This challenge came up for me as someone with a great variety and depth of tools in my toolkit. An early, hard learning I had on this front was about the coaching/therapy line when a client with clinical depression came to me via a referral. I shared my reservations and caveats about my abilities and she chose to engage, despite the known limitations. Though we worked together for a while, it became clear that I was unable to adequately serve her. This was a powerful lesson and a case of learning about my boundaries by crossing them.*

As I've defined and redefined my target audience over the years, I first asked myself 'What can I do really well and offer as a point of value to my clients?' Since then, as I've gained more experience, it's not just a question of what I can do, but what I most want to be doing. So really assessing my capacity not only in terms of ability, but passion for the work. Now I seek clients who've cultivated a sense of self-awareness and want help shedding unhelpful patterns to embody a more authentic expression of who they are in their lives and work. Today I position myself as a rites of passage coach. I seek clients with big hearts, bright minds, passion for serving the greater good, desire to transform and the courage to do the inner work."

YT: *"Rigor has, in its various forms and ways, played an important role in my journey. For me, demonstrating rigor suggests a level of competence that has been accumulated from their experiences and from a variety of resources. There is a sense of clarity, honesty and wisdom that emerges from that space of working through the various challenges of producing rigorous work.*

And so, embarking on my own practice whilst (unconsciously) applying this principle to myself and others, I quickly realised that I didn't have the capacity nor passion to be a coach that fits everyone and everything. I became weary. Through my sampling I began taking a more cautious approach that then allowed me to quickly become aware of those individuals who I work best with. I quickly recognised that I have a tendency to work with individuals who've started their self-awareness journey with certain abilities/curiosities, rather than those on the cusp of embarking, and quite independent individuals who know their own mind and quite happy to share what they think. They know what they want. They often lead our conversations.

It also became clear that my expertise was operating in a specific context - the field of coaching - and this led to the good coach project. What becomes challenging when I do engage in conversations with many peers about their target market is that it typically spirals down to a comparison of client. One which focuses on rates and marketing opportunities, rather than how they add value with clients in their specific contexts and situations in which it's most appropriate to pass clients onto other coaches who better fit their client's changing needs."

3. VALUING AND SELLING OUR SERVICES

Working Description/Definition(s): Exchanging currencies for services provided that mutually meets and satisfies their market.

Selling our services has probably been the most pressing issue when working as an independent coach. The reality is that coaching (in the purist sense) accounts for 20-30 percent[3] of our overall business but our coaching approach informs 100 percent of our practice. It's okay to take a blended approach - whether that's coaching and training, coaching and facilitation, coaching and consulting, or some multiple combination. If money and rates are constantly the key focus in building and maintaining a practice, then burnout is likely and precipitated with a swift decision that an independent practice isn't the right pathway. In coaching, this is where being 'agile' and having a 'plan' to consistently test our approach is of most value.

For us, it's understanding these commercial pressures and distilling that question down to how to brand and sell our services with integrity. From a slightly different lens, Yvonne began to inquire about this through her master's in Anthropology and came across people studying about 'commoditizing oneself'. People are very uncomfortable with selling coaching because it seems as if there's nothing being tangibly exchanged. The reality is coaches, in general, haven't yet developed the language set or have that level of confidence to talk about the value at that level in their context. As coaches, we are quite unpractised talking about our practice, i.e. what we're *really* doing when we're coaching. This ultimately led to the beginnings of *the good coach*.

Without following a conventional career pathway, Larissa and Yvonne had to learn very quickly the nature of the value proposition that we bring across all of our coaching clients. Similarities of approaches include,

1. **Understanding client context is critical**; counter to the commonly-held myth in coaching that you don't need to know the client's context. It's in understanding the specifics that we can best leverage our general experiences in a way that's relevant to each unique client.

---

[3] This finding is similar to the survey findings carried out in "Building towards an Anthropology of Coaching: Constructing Identity." Yvonne Thackray (2014)

To do this we need to excel at assessing and tracking our client's realities.

2. **Listening intently to what they do and don't say** to reflect on their behavioural patterns and empathize with their experiences. This helps clients feel acknowledged and trust that you get them.

3. **Asking the right questions and offering informed opinions** that open up new perspectives. Mature clients want to work with coaches who can help them access another way of seeing their situation. Someone who can share insights based on experience and equip them to make better decisions.

4. **Creating space for reflection and learning.** When the clients believe that we're here to work on their agenda, an emergent learning space is created that needs to be continually maintained. This allows the client to work through their challenges to make cognizant sense of how they can better deal with the unknown.

5. **Reminding them to celebrate their successes**. High-achievers commonly go from one challenge to the next without taking time to acknowledge and celebrate their accomplishments. We create a space for pause and recognition not only for what they've done in each phase of their journey, but who they've become in the process.

In addition to the above, we each hold a deeper awareness and curiosity of how more subtle and nuanced behaviours add to the value of what we provide:

- **Tone and body language**: Different styles of tone and embodiment continually occur across contexts and clients. In order to appropriately convey understanding and connection, we listen and respond to what tone best matches each moment. Speaking with a softer tone and using informal gestures might be called for, whilst in other circumstances, a more assertive, strategic tone is needed. How it'll be received depends on the intention and the level of readiness of the client to want to engage in their own learning. In one example, Yvonne became more aware of how her tones shift whilst doing a test run with a coaching partner who mirrored that Yvonne was talking in a therapeutic voice that might have been inappropriate for the corporation context, but perhaps not for the individual. If we're doing our work well as a coach we're typically following the language pattern, structure, meaning and tone of our clients.

  In addition, we also need to be aware of our own personal styles of communicating and how others might react to it. When Yvonne first met Larissa, she felt Larissa spoke with confidence and gravitas whilst using a deeper tone that naturally commands attention and authority along with a hint of playfulness to connect and make space for reciprocation. Larissa experienced Yvonne as having a precision of mind that is deeply intellectually curious and committed to intellectual rigor while also having significant emotional intelligence and light heartedness.

- **Boundaries**: Coaching can often be experienced and presented as simply having a conversation with someone who's a good listener, typically likened to a compassionate friend. This is just one of many boundaries to be managed. It's important to understand and share how these honed skills are not something that should be freely given away in today's capitalist economy. For example, Larissa shared that part of her early journey was constantly having coaching conversations in social settings. "*I needed to stop doing this because I realized I was giving my skills away, and why would people pay for it if they could reliably get it for free? It'd be like if a doctor was freely treating everyone they encountered in social gatherings. I needed to get clear on how I show up in my various friendships—who I reciprocally receive love and coaching support from—and how I show up in my more extended community relationships where I have clearer coaching boundaries. This took the shape of general agreements with myself and clear, active listening to what I do or don't want to give in each situation.*"

4. Legitimacy and Validation

Working Description/Definition(s): Receiving external and independent feedback that one's practice meets expectations of what's considered to be both professional and ethical within and across organizations.

Legitimacy is always an interesting question in coaching because anyone can call themselves a coach. Are you legitimate through certifications, tenure, clientele, reviews, affiliations, trainings, personal experience in your area of coaching, notable accomplishments, content creation and/or social media following etc? There are so many ways people render legitimacy in our field and coaching credentials are often meaningless on their own.

The only current way of showing legitimacy and validation for our coaching is through the people who are willing to engage our services. Prior titles, short-term marketing and access to one or many accreditations can get a coach in the door, but they don't guarantee delivering an appropriate standard of coaching that would be consistent across the field and, specifically, to the needs and contexts of that client. Because of the murky nature of legitimacy in the coaching industry, we've each found our own way to validate our work in our respective markets.

LC: "*In 2012, I started my first coaching business, Lionhearted. By this time, I'd already spent 10,000 hours coaching people—Malcolm Gladwell's cited number for achieving mastery in a field—and had very strong reviews. But I was having a hard time selling myself in a traditional business context as I switched to working with corporations from non-profits. I kept receiving the feedback that I had the skills, but needed brand recognition to legitimize myself in the business community.*

At the surface level, people wanted to see what companies my clients hailed from as a signal. That I was at a certain caliber and had reliable experience. But the conversation about brand helped me understand the wider implications of creating my own brand—telling the story of my full background and skills not only as someone who could provide impactful, relevant coaching services, but as someone who could also run a business and create an enjoyable customer experience."

YT: "*My biggest concern early on was responsibility. Not responsible for the other person, but a sense of responsibility of delivering something of value that can be construed as being professional. This line of questioning personally and professionally had a knock-on effect on my confidence and legitimacy to practice. To manage this, I began investigating, researching and comparing how different training schools and professional bodies worked on validation (legitimacy) whether through mentoring or accreditation. Spending a few years of elapsed time sorting through this is not an easy question to answer. For example, even the European Mentoring and Coaching Council (primarily European based self-certification professional body) (June 19 2017) is having challenges publishing a Wikipedia page because of the "lack of independent sources.*

Working through the evolutions of my own practice ("Making Sense Of What I Do, How My Coaching Practice Is Taking Shape") and re-orientating the good coach into a collaborative project has helped me to understand how my approach is legitimized by my clients (coaching practitioners), and in turn how my clients are being validated by their clients, and how we each fit into the field of coaching. Another way of saying this, is to understand how to both legitimize and validate my practice. It's helped me to develop more overtly and explicitly what my niche is in coaching, and importantly continue to align with my motivations and passions."

5. Exploring ethical boundaries and professionalism

Working Description/Definition(s): This is an opportunity for practitioners to clarify their code of conduct (coaching approach), including personal and organizational behaviours, values, and their guiding principles of coaching.

We've each found alternative ways to independently validate our practices. Knowing how we're doing amongst peers and colleagues in the coaching space is one way of more formally assessing the relative position of our practice. We've each crossed a number of thresholds where we recognised that we hadn't made any *massive* mistakes nor did we do any active harm. We've checked this out from the feedback we received which often required us to see beyond our personal emotions to acknowledge and realise how our behaviours impacted our clients.

One area we explored was coaching situations that resulted in limiting client engagement.

- **Coaching impact in complex systems**
  There's a large area of coaching focused on tactical or technical training supported by clear rules to meet a specific organizational need. This approach contrasts with coaching people in modes of thinking and practicing dynamic decision-making based on principles. This latter approach is more fitting for supporting people in complex systems, since simple rules often don't equip people to make situationally-appropriate decisions.

  From Larissa's experiences and observations, *"Being invited to participate in these systems as an outside party can position the 'objective/non-biased' practitioner as an 'expert'. For some coaches, this can be his/her own mini-pulpit. If coaches present their perspectives as truths—rather than disclosing their own bias and take responsibility for it—that's one way coaches can abuse their power. Ultimately this posture inhibits dialogue and ignores the deep well of personal and institutional wisdom within each individual".*

  Given this, it's important to recognize and honour the level of power and responsibility you hold as a coach, respectfully and with humility.

- **Coaching impact at the individual level**
  It's often very easy for coaches to suggest that the coaching didn't have the intended outcome because the client wasn't engaged or ready. There are situations where this is true. However, asking coaches to explain the reasons for this outcome can be very challenging, particularly when they've missed the behavioural cues.

  Yvonne shares a particular experience where this became the case, *"I remember working as an associate and meeting with a client, a Chinese woman who held a senior management position in a multinational tech organization. I was there to give some feedback after they took a leadership assessment. In that first meeting, as soon as she looked at me, she both directly and indirectly questioned why I was there. I didn't represent her ideal. Furthermore, she hadn't had an opportunity to choose. Thrown into the situation to have to prove why you're the right person rather than sharing how my technical skills would be of benefit to her was something I was inexperienced at doing. It was simpler and much easier to rationalise and suggest that the person wasn't ready for coaching, but the reality was I wasn't ready. And passing 'the ball back' to the recipient to ask what they think of their results sometimes isn't the answer to building that rapport!"* Again, this is an ethical inquiry into professionalism that's about honouring the client's agenda rather than the coach's.

6. Partnering

Working Description/Definition(s): Working with other individuals where shared interests are openly discussed and mutual benefits can be achieved through a shared agenda that leverages each other's complementary strengths. This can behaviourally be seen by the high degree of trust, support, humour[4], laughter and teasing[5] that represent the quality of the partnership.

It's been interesting to learn through our individual pathways that we've always been looking for partners to work with interdependently. Starting a private practice is, for a want of a better word, awful! It's good from the aspect of having control over what we do, however, we also lose that value of working in groups and teams where we can brainstorm, test ideas and create a more powerful outcome through the creativity of group process. Finding the right partner(s) to work with is a bit like dating and has required each of us to go through a number of evolutions of asking what we're looking for that lets our shared agenda live prosperously.

LC: *"In my first coaching business, I hardly pursued partnership at all. I assumed I had to do it all alone and didn't know how to structure my business or working patterns to effectively leverage partnership. By comparison, I've designed Wayfinding to include a guild-style partnership model where I work on experiments across different facets of my offerings with colleagues, while also keeping some work solo. I think this approach emerged because I didn't want to co-found a venture with anyone (that felt like a marriage that I'm not ready for at this point) but I love getting to work and be in creative, supportive relationship with others.*

After ten or more years of partnering with people, I've gotten quite clear on what I look for and what I avoid in professional partnerships. For me, it always starts with the person—would I want to spend a lot of time with this person? Do we have a shared sense of values and purpose? Can we laugh together? Are we committed to each other's learning journeys and growing our relationship through this collaboration and do we each recognize that doing so is as much the work as

---

[4] See Ridge, Jeremy. 2015. "Smiling and Laughter Really Matter in Coaching." the good coach. http://the-goodcoach.com/tgcblog/2015/7/27/smiling-and-laughter-really-matter-in-coaching-by-jeremy-rid.html Accessed September 11.
[5] See Ridge, Jeremy. 2017. "Teasing Out The Deeper Understanding Of How Coaching Works At Its Best – How Teasing, Itself, Can Be Productive." the good coach. https://the-goodcoach.com/tgcblog/2017/6/6/teasing-out-the-deeper-understanding-of-how-coaching-works-at-its-best-how-teasing-itself-can-be-productive-by-jeremy-ridge Accessed September 11.

whatever we make together? If I can't say an enthusiastic 'yes' to all of these, then I don't even consider the partnership.

Then I consider our skill sets—do we have comparable levels of professional excellence and aspiration, while also bringing diverse enough expertise to the table that we can each learn from the other? Are we both oriented to a dynamic/responsive way of working that relies strongly on balancing real-time listening, planning and execution?

Then we explore the space for collaboration—what is a discrete experiment we want to commit to exploring with each other? And what's the clear sense of value that each of us would contribute and gain from the partnership and experiment? The experimental frame is critical for me in partnership because it allows us to date as partners—to focus on a specific project and time to get to know each other and then evaluate afterwards if we'd like to try another experiment. I have no assumptions that anything's going to go on forever. I think it's important to keep listening and to design checkpoints in the partnership. In all my partnerships, I want to keep exploring and growing together—just loving each other as human beings, really—as long as it's mutually beneficial."

YT: *"Developing partnerships at tgc has always been core, but my understanding of how partnerships needed to be structured to support how the vision changed over time. I knew I was searching for independent and experienced individuals who had an opinion about their practice and coaching, interested in the bigger picture, and were invested in making a difference that would eventually benefit everyone than a few through a much fairer and transparent process. In different rounds of finding these partners, I realised that it was not that simple to find someone who was interested in all of these aspects. They do exist! It just takes time to find the opportunity to make something happen. Individuals who are similarly passionate about the vision and chose to engage and commit their energies, and strengths, to this inquiry and platform is how our core team and community emerged."*

OUR COLLECTIVE LEARNINGS

Coaching is one of the potential professions where your personal identity is as important as your professional role. Coaching is demanding because, not only do you have to understand yourself, you also need to know how what you're delivering impacts your client and your credibility. It's also a challenging profession because of the distributed, undefined nature of the field.

For us, the biggest value we've both received as we went through this the process was the opportunity to articulate what we've learned through our coaching career so far. Identifying some common patterns and finding common everyday words that closely represented our work constantly gave us deeper insights and clarity of how others might perceive how we practice.

PART 3: Opportunities at the competitive edge

This is what we think is missing for practitioners in their PP learning—a personalised, structured approach that continuously helps them to understand their learning styles, their clients and how their coaching approach can be measured through delivery with rigor and professionalism. Hopefully, by sharing our 6 key shifts, which made a positive difference in how we each practice, this will motivate others to begin mapping out their own self-directed learning curriculum, independently or with another peer.

Question: How are you pursuing professionalism and rigor in your coaching practice?

CHAPTER 10

CONNECTING COACHING TO SOCIETAL NEEDS

How coaching is becoming an essential basis for much bigger scale interventions

Sue Young

Post-Brexit, the themes In this blog are just as, if not more relevant, for people carrying out coaching who take it as an approach to life, part of something bigger. I Include In this the role and intrinsic value of a 'coaching approach' In organizations, as a way of operating.

I was inspired at the time of writing (Dec 2015) by the positive role 'coaching behaviours' played in the achievement of reaching the Paris Climate Change agreement – e.g. off-line conversations where individuals were actively encouraged to fully express their concerns and were genuinely listened to. The traditionally power-disadvantaged countries were effectively led in getting their collective act together and getting their Voice heard. The result of all the hard work was achieving a real consensus[1].

I am struck now by the contrast of the negative style of communication in the very recent Brexit campaign, resulting in fear, closed minds, defensiveness and lack of demonstrated respect for other perspectives. The negative impact on the aftermath has been a sense of polarisation, disorientation and massive uncertainty across the entire UK population, leading to an unprecedented post-war political crisis.

A salutary reminder of the role of core coaching attributes of respect, empathy and openness leading to the real listening that is essential to achieving consensus.

I watched the final speeches from the Paris Climate Change Conference and was struck by the scale of the task and achievement. 195 countries and their representatives, the national interests, the translators, the negotiators all

---

[1] See the story of how final agreement at the Conference was reached on https://www.theguardian.com/environment/2015/dec/13/paris-climate-deal-cop-diplomacy-developing-united-nations

coming to an agreement. There was such a strong sense of personal and individual connection having been made.

Where coaching involves special and careful use of essential behaviours

I was also struck by the different style and attention to personal relationships conventionally untypical of such large scale international conferences. For example:

- A real sense of handling and working with individual differences.

- A great deal of attention being given to ensure that the voices of the traditionally weakest were heard.

- An explicit recognition that the nature of circumstances and challenges involved are very diverse.

- That there was clear demonstrated respect, empathy and trust amongst the players at the end.

The urgent non–negotiable imperative of climate change and increasing demand from democratic nations is driving the use of behaviours (most of which are taking place in individual conversations in 'safer' space behind the scenes) that we very much associate with coaching – mutual respect, active listening, helping others articulate their perspective and rapport building between individuals with different interests and perspectives.

Seeing the scope for these special behaviours

I see strong parallels between such large scale world events and in the 'coaching approach' at use in organisations. This goes way beyond the traditional coaching format of confidential one to one sessions which may be contracted for in particular contexts such as in the executive, sport and health fields.

Coaching behaviours can be a natural choice

They have always been there as part of the mix of people in a society. The diplomat, the local 'wise' woman or man, who is regarded as source of wise counsel, the local priest or vicar as a source of confidential 'space'. The difference today is the explicit attention to this form of interaction as an organisational behaviour, operating not only with individuals, but teams and, increasingly, as a key part of some organisational cultures.

Getting these quality behaviours into organisations is still a challenge; coaching has been increasing hugely in popularity in recent years[1]. Coaching skills and a coaching mind set are becoming increasingly regarded as an important part of leadership and management. The awareness is there, but the readiness, by

1 See blogs in the good coach

individuals and organisations to make the adjustments required is still a major issue occupying the growing number of organisations seeking to integrate more of a coaching approach as part of their culture.

EXAMPLES OF HOW THEY ARE BEGINNING TO BECOME A FUNDAMENTAL PART OF WIDER ORGANISATION INTERVENTIONS

So what is driving this wider attention to the subject of coaching and the use of such behaviours? Wide reference is made in writing and research to the impact of such factors as the pace of change, greater global connectivity, increased uncertainty and volatility. There is a greater requirement for managers to quickly learn, and to be able to do this collaboratively with a wider and more interdependent, complex range of stakeholders. All of this at a relentless pace. As a coaching practitioner and facilitator, I hear about and work first hand with how this plays out in organisations on the ground.

For example:

- **High potential manger development:** Coaching is increasingly part of the mix of interventions used on high potentials and middle to senior leadership development programmes.

- **Leadership development:** Coaching is often part of the core subject matter on leadership development programmes, where it is increasingly regarded as a core leadership capability.

- **Internal coaches:** The training of internal coaches has grown in organisations as more businesses see the value of having dedicated internal coaching resources. Most people in organisations take this on as a part–time role, in addition to their mainstream role. A few organisations, such as the major professional firms, have sufficient enough demand that they now seek to add value through use of a dedicated team of internal coaches.

- **Coaching skills programmes:** Increased availability of dedicated coaching skills programmes made available to people at all management levels.

- **Action learning or peer learning groups:** I see an increase in use of 'action learning' or 'peer learning' groups where the aim for that small group (typically six to eight in size) is to support each other in their learning goals and act as co–coaches. The emphasised role of the group is to help each other to think. They seek to only bring to an individual's slot what that individual wants. The facilitator/ supervisor's role is to ensure that space is held. Intervention on the process only happens when, for example, there is a rush in enthusiasm for group members to impose their solutions. Although it is not always called that,

PART 3: Opportunities at the competitive edge

undoubtedly these kinds of learning groups use and model their own coaching approach.

- **Organisational learning interventions:** Increasingly, I am involved in work related organisational learning interventions that take a coaching approach. Team coaching would be one such, where the emphasis is on working with both the team collectively and individually on progressing organisational priorities e.g. developing strategies and key relationships and their ways of working to be more aligned whilst collectively developing their agenda as a team. These projects tend to be highly dynamic and responsive as they need to work closely with the messiness of the realities of how the individual, team and the organisation works – and particularly where it doesn't work!

- **Organisational change interventions:** I am noticing a rise in increasingly organisational change interventions where there is an emphasis on use of coaching approaches as a core part of the overall organisational direction and strategy.

To give an example of this:

A regional healthcare group in the National Health Services (NHS) I am working with is piloting an intervention aimed at individuals on the front line in a range of professional healthcare roles. The goal is to better equip and enable these individuals, encouraging them to experiment with ways to extend their use of coaching approaches. These includes both with fellow healthcare professionals and to increase the use of health coaching approaches with patients.

Seventy percent of national and local healthcare spending is taken up on medication and health professionals' time supporting people with long–term chronic health conditions. These are usually not immediately life threatening, but they are situations where successful outcomes, both for the individual and for the wider NHS system in terms of effectiveness, depend on the individual's capabilities and motivation to self–manage a health regime that suits the individual's life circumstances as much as possible.

This is a dramatic culture shift from the traditional 'expert' led medical model. There are an increasing number of service businesses deploying a coaching approach as part of their service delivery, where a high degree of individual attention is part of the proposition or where close interdependent relationships in the supply chain are vital to delivery.

So what are these still elusive coaching 'qualities' that all of these example interventions illustrate and represent as a direction in the future for coaching?

There is a multitude of definitions of coaching[1]. All of these focus in on the nature and qualities of the coaching process.

I would see the following as underpinning wider themes that define an organisational–wide 'coaching approach' moving into the future:

- **Recognising it is a process of continuous learning, not a simple formula approach**: the recognition that there are no 'quick fix' solutions; an iterative evolving approach is required as on–going learning, both individually and collectively, is going to be crucial to organisational and business success.

- **Attention to creating a learning environment:** where the design and testing of new approaches is seen as critical and individuals are actively encouraged to experiment; there is no failure but what matters is the learning we're taking forward from this experience.

- **Actively seeking to engage individuals, in a manner appropriate to each individual's needs**: gaining the value of their knowledge and experience, as core to any change initiative or programme. The leaders' and managers' ability to do this well is regarded and assessed as a major performance measure.

- **The ability, motivation and courage to put wider organisational priorities before a narrow more self–interested priority**: coaching capabilities and values of staying open, genuinely respecting and valuing differences, building rapport and good questioning and active listening are the skills underpinning this fundamental orientation.

- **Use of feedback:** e.g. 360, team reviews, as a way of working being widely used.

- Learning is regarded as synonymous with change.

- **Coaching support is available in a range of formats suited to the range of context requirements:** regarded as an integral part of organisational development, learning and business strategy, needing to be tailored to the circumstances, stage of development and resulting needs of the organisation.

We should recognise where and how this is happening – spontaneously.

In writing this, it's emerging in a way that could sound idealistic. I contend that all these elements are presently in place in different mixes in different places. There is currently a clear direction present for those with eyes to see it, if they raise their outlook to a larger perspective. It requires those of us involved in

---

1 See Ridge, Jeremy. 2015. "How We Can Define Coaching – 'Do It For Yourself.'" the good coach. http://the-goodcoach.com/tgcblog/2015/12/11/how-we-can-define-coaching-do-it-for-yourself-diy-by-jeremy-ridge Accessed September 11.

coaching, in all its different manifestations, to see what we are already doing as part of something bigger.

For example, I am reminded of the mind set power embedded in Steve Jobs' comment to John Sculley. At the time Jobs was trying to entice Sculley to leave his high–profile, comfortably–successful role in Pepsi to join Apple, then a small fringe player in the computing world.

> "Do you want to sell sugared water all your life, or do you want to change the world?"

All of us in coaching choose to have our own vision of how we see the future of coaching and take this into our practice whether we be leaders, managers, independent coaches, organisational coaches, or even just do coaching as part of what we do.

Achieving the potential coaching has to offer happens in millions of events and interactions already. Bringing these individual voices together into professional and organisational communities in a way that raises the dialogue to this larger perspective will massively add to the speed of embracing all that a coaching approach is capable of achieving. I see 'the good coach' (mentioned above) as potentially one of these communities, representing what experienced coach practitioners can bring to the table to build these differences into a bigger whole.

Integrating coaching ethics for the anthropocene: 'gut feel' and 'on principle' coaching approaches to sustainability

Geoffrey Ahern

As part of a small team, about two years ago I explored some British coaches' actions to sustainability science. I did so again in London last summer, while piloting a twelve to fifteen hours sustainability course with participants who mixed executive coaching and sustainability expertise. There seems to be ambivalence towards sustainability in our novel 'Anthropocene' era in which humans have an increasingly significant influence on the Earth.

In the team we concluded that the coaches we encountered (not representatively selected) were concerned that:

- Introducing sustainability into the agenda would hijack the coaching process.
- They would fall into the trap of being prescriptive.
- Different considerations apply at organizational and corporate levels compared to what we do to be sustainable individually.

These reservations link in with the wider experience of seasoned environmental campaigners. They have found it difficult to connect the science behind Earth research to everyday gut felt. This seems to be because the science is highly specialised and drily expressed. It is involved with likelihoods and not certainties (probabilities which are put into abstract numbers not painted in vivid pictures). Yet the impact of the scientists' findings is overwhelmingly ethical and of the utmost importance for long-term human survival given that behavioural principles about preserving the planet follow urgently from them.

COACHING IN THE LIGHT OF SUSTAINABILITY SCIENCE

Over the past eight years I have had parallel occupational tracks: both executive coaching and sustainability (consulting, 'one planet' MBA co-creation, co-founding a sustainability group, university teaching of sustainability). Now I am asking whether there is a basis for greater collaboration between coaching and sustainability.

This blog-article looks at how the principles following from sustainability science findings can be further integrated with coaches' gut feel. It draws on the distinction between 'gut feel' (including intuitive wisdom) and 'on principle' approaches in contemporary Western ethical theory.

- I summarise sustainability science and its fit with coaching.

- Then I consider the further integration of sustainability science principles into coaching ethics in terms of advance framing, permission from task and having finance as sustainability's ultimate language.

THE 'GUT-FEEL'/'ON PRINCIPLE' CONTRAST IN RELATION TO SUSTAINABILITY SCIENCE

In many life and death situations, gut felt ethics integrate well with 'on principle' ones[1]. But it seems that preserving the planet is different because of the nerdish nature of science:

- Recently US President Donald Trump was, via visual media, in-your-face to billions when displaying his signature for the reviving of the tar-sands Keystone XL oil pipeline[2]. His 'gut feel' truth-is-what-I-say-it-is style is charismatic. In comparison the truth-maze (or validity) issues of peer-reviewed scientific publications on the greenhouse-intensive nature of tar-sands oil are intellectual and complicated.

It's challenging to internalise the abstract principles implicit in probabilities from Earth research on outcomes relating to the biosphere, climate change, fresh water shortages and so on:

- The gut feel of coaches, unlike Donald Trump's, may well be generally favourable to sustainability.

- But this often seems to be without having an accurate overview of the science.

---

[1] See for example Poon, Joanna. and Mike Hoxley. 2010. "Use of moral theory to analyse the ethical codes of built environment professional organisations..." In *International Journal of Law in the Built Environment*, 2 (3): 260-275.
[2] Holland, Steve. and Valerie Volcovici. 2017. "Trump clears way for controversial oil pipelines." Reuters. www.reuters.com/article/us-usa-trup-pipeline-idUSKBN1582oN Accessed September 12.

- Yet the risk management specifics of environmental science's probability predictions for billions already and about to be born have a very big impact on mankind's ethics, including coaching ones.

SUSTAINABILITY CONTEXT

How can laypeople including coaches get an overview of sustainability science which is as valid as possible? The answer is – by clicking the mouse a few times, so long as you know where to go.

A very useful, inclusive planetary model comes from Stockholm University (the Stockholm Resilience Centre). It makes informed estimates to identify a safe space for humanity and life[1].

- Out of the nine interacting boundaries constructed, biosphere integrity and climate change are considered to be at the core. Biosphere integrity, given that species are becoming extinct at a rate 100-1000 more than what could be considered natural, is currently estimated to be high risk, whereas climate change is still in the zone of uncertainty (increasing risk).

Tipping points from one state into another cannot be predicted and outside the safe zones are increasingly likely.

The Intergovernmental Panel on Climate Change's ('IPCC's') 2013-14 Report[2] is also authoritative. Vast resources have gone into this risk analysis. The report assessed more than 30,000 scientific papers and had more than 830 core authors and 2000 expert reviewers from over 80 countries. Its summarising text was approved line by line by one-hundred-and-ninety-four countries[3].

- It is 95-100 percent likely that human influence has been the dominant cause of observed global warming since the mid-twentieth century, and without major behavioural change global temperature increase by the end of the 21st century is 66-100 percent more likely than not to exceed 2° C (RCP4.5, 6.0).

All this is at the planetary level – so what does it have to do with coaching in companies? Stakeholder pressure and governmental regulation increasingly involve companies in sustainability measurement and implementation processes. Coaching can help with the buy-in to and application of environmental systems such as TNS, GRI and ISO14001 and with jogging alongside sustainability role holders belonging to bodies like IEMA.

---

[1] Go to http://www.stockholmresilience.org/research/planetary-boundaries.html
[2] See http://www.ipcc.ch/report/ar5/wg1/
[3] Scott, Daniel., Michael Hall and Stefan Gössling. 2016. "A review of the IPCC Fifth Assessment and implications for tourism sector climate resilience and decarbonization." In *Journal of Sustainable Tourism* 24 (1): 10.

What matters here is focusing on the things that count, not the things that can be counted[1]. For example, in one project to draw up an environmental proposal for the board, after having waited until near the end of the deadline for a key technical report, it was not helpful to receive rows of figures which lacked any meaningful context-setting!

FINDING THE FIT WITH COACHING

Coaching's main emphasis, whether relating to individuals or groups, is on inner worlds or on being 'in here'. This empathic quality contrasts with the 'out there' quantification from sustainability science's measurement of the sense-world and its numerical procedures like the formation of null hypotheses, predictions of experimental results etc.

Coaches find validation through supervision, CPD or MAs to apply axiomatic systems of thought: Rogerian, psychodymamic, cognitive and so on. The validity of sustainability science is established through observation-based peer-review.

These two different ways of being link to the 'gut feel'/'on principle' sustainability ethics distinction made earlier. How can they fit together? First, what is meant by 'science' needs to be clarified and the differences acknowledged:

- The big difference between experimenting in the natural world and being systematic in the humanities/arts can be masked because in the English-speaking world the same word 'science' is used to describe both, unlike in German which has two different words (Naturwissen-schaften and Geisteswissenschaften). Some 'gut feelers' may think that coaching is already applying science and so there's no pressing need to think about validity as applied in specialisms such as climate science and ecology. Closer to home, though, their practice might be different: if their child's life was threatened by illness most would surely use science-based medicine rather than faith healing if they had to choose between the two.

The above assumes that the world is knowable objectively:

- In a post-modern cosmos all may seem to flow with no chance of deriving any non-subjective, sense-based knowledge through the trickery of our perceptions (though coaches may support sustainability on other grounds such as moral or aesthetic ones). Probably some coaches would on philosophical grounds reject the very possibility of objective scientific research on the environment; if so, of course, it's consistent for them to ignore it.

---

[1] Vanclay, Frank. 2004. "The triple bottom line and impact assessment: How do TBL, EIA, SEA and EMS relate to each other?" In *Journal of Environmental Assessment Policy and Management*, 6 (3):266.

'Gut feel' and 'on principle' ethics can fit further together through coaches becoming aware of the many opportunities to bring environmental research closer to their practices. The impossibility as a layperson of understanding specialist publications need not prevent the application of critical principles more generally.

I recall not having the specialist background to continue reading the research of a scientist[1] of vouched-for integrity and standing who disputed global warming. Even so, we laypeople are often in a position to make risk assessments: for example, we can be shrewd when it comes to discovering whether or not the great majority of climate specialists support the hypothesis of global warming. We can be in a position to make informed judgements about matters adjacent to science. This includes the disinformation allegations (relating to carbon emissions) made against Exxon[2]. After being present at a climate debate (under Chatham House confidentiality rules) between a prominent politician who denies climate change and a professor of climate mathematics, I had no doubt as to which of the two's arguments came across as more considerable.

Many coaches have a science background, some even in sustainability science, or are keen science followers. Maybe there's enough of a mix in coaching culture for science-derived 'on principle' approaches to sustainability to interact beneficially with gut feel ones.

INTEGRATING SUSTAINABILITY SCIENCE'S ETHICAL IMPACT WHEN COACHING IN COMPANIES

Taking responsibility is at the heart of sustainability science's impact. The impact for coaching is affected by what mix practitioners have of the two main ethical stances, gut feel and principled, in typical corporate contexts. Denying one or the other does not make sense given their strong roots.

- In terms of recent Western ethical theory, gut felt approaches link in with the strong post-World-War-II revival of Aristotelian practical wisdom (phronesis), with emotivism, and also, in using challenging interaction to move presenting client problems on creatively, with existentialism.

- Modern 'on principle' ethics include developments from both Kant's treating others always as an end and never as a means only and, alternatively, from Bentham's and Mill's utilitarianism involving happiness consequences where everyone's happiness counts the same.

These standpoints need to come together in practice.

---

[1] Taylor, Peter. 2009. *Chill. A reassessment of global warming theory*. Forest Row: Clairview.
[2] 'See for example Ward, B (2006), Email to Esso UK Ltd, Policy Communication, The Royal Society, and reference 2 in my first the good coach blog (Jan 11 2017).

ADVANCE FRAMING TO THE CLIENT: 'ON PRINCIPLE' AND 'GUT FEEL' ETHICAL APPRAOCHES

It makes precautionary sense for coaches to explicitly frame sustainability in advance of the coaching. Indeed last year the converse was necessary for me: because my website frames me as involved with sustainability, where the client's presenting situation had nothing to do with the subject, I made it clear beforehand that I did not anticipate bringing it up and did not do so. But what is the ethical situation if there has been no prior explicit mention of 'sustainability' (or a synonym), but just the usual general mention of the ethical boundary of the coaching being something like not doing harm to others? Ethical codes for coaches and others stress that doing harm ('non-maleficence') should be avoided and that where possible good should be done ('beneficence').

From the 'on principle' point of view we should be as responsibly alert about the planet as we are about business-as-usual. For example, that we should be as concerned about client carbon emissions as we are about safety breaches on an oilrig. This is because mainstream environmental science demonstrates overwhelmingly that without sustainability there is a huge risk to life globally.

When coming from the gut feel point of view the coaching focus is more likely to be immediately local:

- Unlike the planet in some future time, the oilrig is here-and-now.

- Unlike billions of people including the unborn, you can see the employees and subcontractors on the rig and form images of their actual children.

- Unlike the complicated percentage certainty ranges given for global risk scenarios, you can be more-or-less sure that without adequate health and safety the oilrig will lose lives.

  "When one dies it is a tragedy; when a million die, it is a statistic', as has been said by one expert on impact." Joseph Stalin

Thus there is a dilemma over whether interpretation should be from the 'on principle' or the 'gut-feel' point of view or, as suggested here, a mix of both. Assumptions reflecting circular thinking do not get us out of the dilemma:

- For example, coaches say that coaching starts from the client's agenda and that to bring sustainability up is to steer it covertly: it's to pretend to be a coach while presenting as a sustainability consultant. The reasoning behind this is circular if there's exclusively a gut-feel interpretation of what constitutes the client agenda and no 'on principle' thinking blended in. Given humanity's survival on the planet is at stake, preventing harm to others through sustainability could on principle be seen as belonging to the presenting agenda.

The objection above about starting from the client's agenda can also ignore how the coaching process steers the client covertly. Its advance framing to the client is not absolute, for if the felt experience of the journey influenced by the coach really could be entirely disclosed beforehand (and of course it can't), the added value of journeying would be done in advance, thus pre-delivering the coaching at the framing stage. Given that inevitably there's a lack of full prior disclosure about the processes of the coaching to come, it is questionable whether prior disclosure to the client about bringing up the awesome subject of our survival on Earth must be fuller than this.

There may also be an assumption that needs to be challenged. This is that the coaching process itself is, to a considerable extent, an exception to the prior disclosure rules. It may be deeply felt that coaching happens in all cultures and so implicitly that we all know about it. Therefore its processes do not require the same degree of advance explanation to the client as is required for external agendas like sustainability. But coaching as practised today is not culturally universal. I remember how as recently as three decades ago an unusual London consultant was said to have broken new client delivery ground by doing a lot of paid, externally supplied 'mentoring' as it was termed; later this was re-labelled as the (then new-fangled) 'coaching'. The 'universal' belief about coaching ignores how much contemporary Western culture has shaped and framed it into particularity.

INTERPRETING PERMISSION FROM TASK TO BRING UP SUSTAINABILITY IN COACHING

As each client is unique, permission to bring up sustainability through following the client's personal discourse cannot easily be typecast. Business roles are more readily put into categories. They seem to vary in the degree of permission they can be deemed to give to the coach to raise the subject of sustainability.

In the case of sustainability specialist clients, the permission from task is likely to be strong.

Permission may also be present when coaching board members: i.e. where the buck stops. At this level and in this context, a utilitarian kind of 'on principle' approach might be particularly appropriate given the prominence of sustainability legislation based on the planetary rules we should adopt in the best interests of the maximum number.

Does permission from task apply widely to all multinational and other corporate executives? Principle-based ethicists might see task as giving sufficient permission because sustainability is prescribed by the seventeen Sustainable Development Goals (SDGs) of the UN and, where material, is likely to be specified in formal job descriptions.

What about gut feel ones? Given corporate goals of profitability through effectiveness, the SDGs are likely to be lip-service only so, for gutfeel coaching approaches, bringing up sustainability science without pre-contractual framing may seem like false pretences. Such lip-service is itself a dilemma for gut felt coaching ethics because it raises questions about freedom and choice.

- If SDGs are formally stated to be part of the job when this is not so in practice, there may be a hypocritical and perhaps illegal workplace practice with which the coaching complies. The business-as-usual context may be screening out the possibility of sustainability arising in a gut feel way from the client's drama. Thus there may not be the freedom or authenticity for Aristotelian wisdom or other non-principle-based ethics to apply[1].

The unsatisfactory situation above may be behind many of the calls for business ethics to be based on the 'on principle' approach of treating sustainability as an end in itself and not just as a means for profiting more effectively over time.

AN IMPLEMENTATION TWIST FOR COACHES: THE ORGANIZATIONAL LANGUAGE OF SUSTAINABILITY LINKS IN WITH THAT OF FINANCE

Financial language is extended to include sustainability. This is not restricted to companies. Even a trustee-owned park seeks funding through monetarising its carbon sequestration and its contributions to reducing health, education and well-being budgets, to lowering emissions through installing cycle paths etc.

Sustainability science's quantification of the planet – also of people in the aggregate, as in totalling numbers of refugees – matches that of accountancy. The single bottom line of conventional accounting is extended to the 'triple bottom line' (or 'TBL') of abstract calculations involving planet, people and prosperity (to some greens this is an abhorrent slipping into the skin of a materialist dragon).

It is vital that sustainability values are separately asserted so that they are intrinsically valuable and not reduced as ends in themselves through association with finance. This is obviously the case where sustainability cannot be even approximately quantified in monetary terms (for instance, biodiversity is invaluable). Despite the real dangers, unless sustainability is also given some financial expression it is difficult to see how emissions, pollution etc. can be checked in time. For a long time already the single bottom line of traditional accounting has included qualitative factors such as 'good will' which, by using conventions, provide a focus whereby the underlying realities can be probed.

---

[1] See also MacIntyre, Alasdair. 2007. *After Virtue*: 25-27. Indiana: University of Notre Dame Press. Translated by Howard V. Hong and Edna H. Hong. New Jersey: Princeton University Press.

Expressing sustainability ethics in terms of money gives rise to the distinctive post-industrial state of being (as Goethe put it) both Dives and Lazarus at the same time. Contemporary ambivalence of this sort is something that coaches help clients integrate.

WHAT'S NEXT?

Comparing (as above) the characteristics of gut-feel and principle-based ethics in different corporate situations is a high level integrative process. Though sustainability ethics should not be legitimised through financial considerations alone, money is also a necessary lowest common factor attempt at integration.

Monetarising sustainability is probably the quickest route for the norms of planetary survival to be internalised by commerce, the immediate decision-maker on our planetary fate. New norms including legal sanctions have grown from financial accounting; definitions of behaviour related to fraud and greed have developed and become more differentiated. Money itself started as an abstraction from barter but is now seen as real, a matter for strong feelings. It is as buyers that we have the biggest influence on the Anthropocene. Let's hope for everyone's sake that through accountancy the abstract ethical principles derived from sustainability science will also become internalised and so 'gut feel' in time.

I wonder what most coaches think is the proper relationship between human survival on Earth and coaching ethics.

Brexit: in the wake of the UK referendum, how important and valuable is coaching now?

Yvonne Thackray

Whether for better or worse, all our futures have changed after Brexit. We are waiting to see what the consequences will be as the details start to come through. This is democracy.

Many will be grappling with what this means and how it may impact on their jobs, roles, relationships with each other (colleagues and families) and the future. What is perceived by one side as being simple with many opportunities, others perceive as complex and unnecessary risk taking, especially when there currently lacks any strategy or plan on how to move forward for all of society. These are real issues and challenges that will dominate many of the conversations in the coming days, weeks and months.

While reported analysis is typically focused on the broader categories such as education, age, geographical location, salary, employment status, no one has really addressed the individual responses and reasons of why this is happening. And this is what we do as coaching practitioners, this is our 'bread and butter'. It's important we are also equally equipped to handle, both personally and professionally, what's shared in these conversations.

We think we really do have a role, a mandate even from society, to support individuals, peers and groups to find and share their voice and to be listened to and heard in a way that offers fair opportunities for individuals to continually reach and grow their potential.

At **the good coach**, we'd like to ask you what your thoughts are and let us listen to what you want to say. Using these responses we will write a fair and reflective blog-article that shares our voices, thoughts and suggestions over the next week, month or even few months, sharing with readers (ours and yours), coaches, practitioners working in organizations, leaders and generally interested individuals.

WHAT WE KNOW SO FAR

the good coach, and many of us who participate in the community, are still in shock. We're still processing the results of the UK referendum after finding out early on Friday morning that the UK was leaving the EU, and are now waiting for Article 50 to be triggered, or if it will be invoked at all.

Events even in the initial few days following Brexit:

- Been voted out of the EU (with Remain strong in cities) - "a dramatic demonstration of democracy that highlights the great divide in Britain and consequences in EU as all are operating in unchartered waters". It shows the divide between political class, education and generation.

- Lost a Prime Minister, and there is a Tory campaign going on to find his replacement which may lead to an early general election. A vacuum in leadership and direction, even a workable strategy, from the Leave campaigners because they never really thought their campaign would succeed. There is disarray within the Labour Party and the First Minister of Scotland is looking for independence.

- A civil service, which has perhaps twelve senior members, who have the skills to negotiate bilateral agreements and more, who need to go onto training courses, or find other places to implement the unknown strategy/course to be set by the next PM. This also includes increased workload, which was formally carried out in the EU, with decreased human resources.

- Financial services are quietly implementing their contingency plans to move to other locations because they know that their clients do not want to be exposed to the uncertainty and risk that now exists in the UK, which is definitely an opportunity for others. This will have knock-on effects for everyone whether it's around less public spending or higher taxes because they are dependent on the EU passport.

- All sides of the debate completely misread the sentiments of the British public for how they would be using this vote to be more vocal around the discontent towards the British government with the #regrexit i.e. whilst voting to Leave they thought they'd still remain. What promises will be kept; how EU funding can really be maintained; what is the role of the expert; and how do you 'heal' the tensions that are visible between perceived immigrants, immigrants and locals?

PART 3: Opportunities at the competitive edge

WHAT DOES THIS MEAN FOR OUR FUTURE – HOW UNCERTAINTY WILL HIT EVERYONE – ESPECIALLY BUSINESSES, CAREERS AND JOBS

The future has been changed. Something that we never thought would occur in our lifetime has. We're wondering what the consequences will really be. The government, at least, had enough foresight in 1997 and granted operational independence over monetary policy to the Bank of England. We're all grappling in different ways with the loss of control that we thought we had, the principles that we believe in, which also fundamentally underpin coaching. This referendum has really questioned our resolve towards coaching... what does this mean for coaching?

Tomorrow when people walk into work in the morning, how are they, or even you, going to manage their anxiety with respect to their work, identity, family and future? Especially as we all work internationally.

What we've heard already and has been put forward:

- Where will work go in the financial services, and who's going to mobilise and become that country's immigrant if they want to keep their role?

- Real concerns for job security in the Civil Service whose role was to translate relevant EU law into British law, as well the immense changes for the Civil Service itself.

- Concerns for small business owners and white-collar workers in various size organizations – with the lack of investment in businesses there is higher job insecurity.

- Personal security and heightened anxiety of Brexit-related racial abuse.

- Immense pressure on a reduced Civil Service which is expected to start negotiations even though there is a significant gap in delivery and that expected professionalism to just be able to get on with the mandate.

- Working with the younger generation who think that the older generation has taken away their choice of future, whilst the older generation see their decision as in their best interest of the country, having lived through those forty years and seeing that it hasn't worked for them.

A scenario we can see is coaching with high potentials, who typically fall into the younger generation age bracket. How might an older executive coach who is perceived to have voted to Leave affect the coaching relationship?

the good coach aims to be a living platform for independent views and contributions about how coaching can make important contributions to our lives. There is a real need, or opportunity, for this in the changes that are taking place in life, society and communities around the world. Brexit shows the importance and challenges involved in bringing views together more than ever...

And so we sent out a survey to ask what the good coach readers – coaches, practitioners working in organizations, generally interested individuals, leaders – thought about the following:

1. Do you think the Referendum will have an impact on your practice? Why?

2. What advice/coaching do you want to give other professionals going through this uncertainty?

3. What advice would you give to other coaching practitioners who will be working with their clients through this uncertainty?

Even those who may not be impacted directly as they are not living in the UK and EU chose to share. This is because as coaches we are always working with professionals who work through uncertainty and unchartered waters.

OVER 70 PERCENT OF TGC READERS WERE EITHER 'WORRIED' OR 'SAD' FOLLOWING "BREXIT MEANS BREXIT"

We received many response and views from all around the world including UK, France, Hong Kong, Germany, Netherlands, South Africa, United States.

Over 25 percent of the good coach readers responded through surveys, one-on-one and peer conversations (both face to face and virtually), via email, and even a few readers/practitioners have followed up by writing their own post and even one of them making it a family affair.

Many our readers represent professionals working in a range of industries at different levels, as a permanent member of staff, or as consultants to a range of organizations. Over 70 percent who responded to the survey were personally 'worried' or 'sad' following the results, and those who were observing from outside of the UK had some very wise words to share about democratic voting,

> "We need to do what we can to foster belief in democracy whilst at the same time making sure that undemocratic forces do not highjack the system. But simply not liking the result of a democratic election is not a good enough answer. I would encourage - and do encourage - everyone to go vote..."

> "I would strongly push for minimizing the 'they are all racists and uneducated dumbos' reflexes and start a debate on the root cause of the issue - the unhealthiness of our system in general, where people, like most of my clients, are on the winning straight (albeit believing that they are also losing out) whilst the people in the north, the areas where there was a strong out vote, are indeed and have been for many years suffering from actually having been left behind."

PART 3: Opportunities at the competitive edge

"We (Netherlands) are interdependent. Although the system has failed, it is not wise to wish for the past. This result causes a scar, a separation between the old and the young, between so much more..."

WHAT THE GOOD COACH HAS LEARNT FROM OUR READERS: OUR TOP 3 LEARNING AND REFLECTIONS

1. With a shrinking economy, there could be less work available because coaching isn't seen as a high priority within organizations. Some do see opportunities to provide more specific services especially around strategic and operational coaching, and potentially collaborating with trusted peers to deliver these new deliveries to work alongside the new business cycles.

2. Overall there is a strong sense of how each practitioner is offering a glimpse of their coaching approach to support their clients, individuals and/or teams, rather than offering a simple model of coaching to handle complex issues.

3. A strong learning mindset is unequivocal amongst all who responded. They've all responded with the opportunities and potential that coaching can provide themselves, their peers and clients to make sense of all the information and chart an even more meaningful direction that's absorbing the changing landscapes.

A sample of responses following our survey:

WHAT DO YOU THINK THE IMPACT ON YOUR PRACTICE MIGHT BE?

Overwhelmingly over 90 percent were concerned or very concerned about the impact, and this is what some of them had to say,

"Less work; delays to projects."

"The impact is likely to be economic - less work."

"A cut in discretionary budgets will mean fewer contracts. Money is more likely to be spent on relocation, redundancy, consulting..."

"The search for and roots of the causes of why this has happened coincide with the search for and roots of why this coaching thing matters. This was more a protest vote about something still hidden (not what it is said to be a protest about.) Such as people lacking the wherewithal, and support, to become something that matters for themselves compared to how they now perceive others. Previous generations were happier with their small 'lot' in life. But now... ambitions and expectations are growing. Sounds like what coaching is about, doesn't it?"

PART 3: Opportunities at the competitive edge

"There may be the need to support more clients in resilience and courage in order to take more risks as they navigate an uncertain future. I hope to be able to work with such people and companies and allow them to find /re-find their strengths and direction."

"I do a lot of work for the civil service. I can see potential see more demand for confidential role support in being to safely talk about concerns and take some time to think. That's the situation now - the mind boggles about the pressures for the civil service. Mind you I worked for a department when Gove was put in charge and showed complete insensitivity to people's interests and needs. On the other hand, I can see organizations diverting resources from learning initiatives as a freeze on non-essentials takes place. I see overall the uncertainties facing organizations having a definite short term negative impact. Longer term, who knows?"

"I am in France so perhaps some expats will come back. For sure main brokers who are in the UK will see their global or UE assignments decrease and there will be less work coming our way from there."

"The pound devaluing will impact my GBP income, bank charges will go up, the economic unrest in the UK will probably mean fewer international programmes being driven from the UK, UK coaches might even look more outside the UK for work..."

"I'm practicing in HK but there is quite a mood shock and uncertainty here. There has been an impact on the need raised by clients on how to manage their work, projects and career in the increasing uncertainty and the irrational voters."

WHAT WOULD YOU SHARE WITH YOUR CLIENTS WHO ARE GOING THROUGH THIS UNCERTAINTY?

"The impact of Brexit is a vivid example of complex change; I'm likely to draw on it in conversations around change."

"Insights from complexity science."

"Call a coach! Talk things through. Crises often provide more intense relationships - use that. Move to the level above tribal differences - be a unifier."

"Think opportunities, not problems... become more comfortable with your abilities to learn and progress. Realise how this will be the real difference between people, going forwards."

"I would share that it is a natural reaction to feel uncertain and different emotions at this time. What's important is to focus on how to harness these energies in a positive and clear direction to find our own resilience and courage. It is critical to support our own people and keep optimistic about what we together can achieve."

PART 3: Opportunities at the competitive edge

"Depends on the client. If I had a reasonable relationship I'd be prepared to be more self-disclosing. I'd seek to stimulate multiple perspectives, risk assessment and a 'glass as half full' perspective options. It would be so dependent on the context. If the client wanted to more fully release negative feelings, I'd create that safe space that helped them fully express fears and concerns. I'd also generally feel able to share my perspectives and the evidence supporting those, while being open to and respecting different perspectives."

"Although it is still not easy for me, I have seen many comments like "OK what do we do now?" and "what type of opportunity to change the model do we have here"?"

"First and foremost - take a breath - this is democracy! Second, I would listen to their fears and help them see where self-efficacy might lie for now. Third, if it does not lead to war directly - which it won't - it might have less real effect on my clients - who tend to be all rather well off than they fear. We have lived through economic recessions before."

"Know yourself, your core value and competence. This is like the compass helping you to chart your course in the midst of a thunderstorm. Be more sensitive to the changes in the external environment though... something that seems distant can have an immediate impact to you."

WHAT WOULD YOU SHARE WITH OUR PEERS WHO ARE GOING THROUGH THIS UNCERTAINTY?

"Have you ever asked a question which has been as powerful as the leave/remain question has been in surfacing previously ignored or suppressed differences? If so, what was it?"

"This is an opportunity for growth."

"Although this may affect chemistry (prospects might explicitly ask your opinions; the young might regard elders with suspicion) once you're coaching, just coach. It's not about us."

"Review and reflect what is it you want to achieve through coaching"

"This event could really bring forward the momentum we are building for the value to be added through the value to be brought for people through coaching. However, it will become much more important to present this value, in a manner that is really meaningful, and more incisive, which also means to the audience and even each individual, not some general statement which just coaches believe in."

"Here is an opportunity for us to walk the talk! If we are feeling uncertain due to the 'interesting times' then we must reflect on our own emotional

responses, to learn from them and to turn them into something positive with which to support others from a deeper state of empathy and clarity."

"With peers, I'd be more open about my real perspectives and challenges for coaching in particular - typical patterns with clients, any trends/patterns I saw emerging. I'd also be open to hearing others experiences. With trusted peers, I would be more disclosing about my thoughts and feelings and be more open to exploring options and potential opportunities"

"To pay attention to this, thinking and translating how this would impact on their client base. This would be a good context to bring into the next session the ability to anticipate what the client would pop up for help for and be prepared to have the right coaching."

WHAT NEXT?

Reading what our readers have shared, I'd like to put forward an idea, even a hypothesis, *"Coaching is intrinsically linked to societal development and has happened as part of, rather than an exception to, the evolutionary development of any societies."*

Each relative stage of development has been slow and painful to achieve some form of stability. What has evolved from each of those stages is an aspiration that everyone can reach their potential. Yet this is not the norm. Neither is it something to be expected from the social rules which each individual lives by. It's more an exception. This raises another question, how were a select group of individuals reaching their potential before there were even coaching practitioners?

Obviously, we're using an example that's currently happened in the UK, but I'm certain that our peers and readers will have similar examples in their nation they can quickly refer to especially when expressed like this,

> *"One of the most important ideas to emerge from micro-economics - or at least, the one with the most consequences for democratic politics - is 'loss aversion'. People hate to have things taken away from them. But whole swathes of the UK have spent the last decades feeling that things are being taken away from them: their jobs, their sense that they are heard, their understanding of how the world works and their places in it. The gaps in our society have just grown too big[1]."*
>
> - *John Lanchester (Brexit Blues, London Review of Books)*

And it's those gaps that we think coaching can help to bridge, or even narrow.

This event, as we shared in our first post, informs us that:

---

[1] Lanchester, John. 2016. "Brexit Blues." London Review of Books [Online] 38 15: 3-6. https://www.lrb.co.uk/v38/n15/john-lanchester/brexit-blues Accessed September 12.

"We really do have a mandate from society to support individuals, peers and groups to find and share their voice and to be listened to. To be heard in a way that offers fair opportunities for individuals to continually reach and grow their potential."

After all, this is what we do in coaching.

And as one of our readers pointed out, "This event could really bring forward the momentum we are building for the value to be added through the value to be brought for people through coaching. However, it will become much more important to present this value, in a manner that is really meaningful, and more incisive, which also means to the audience and even each individual, not some general statement which just coaches believe in."

We agree.

The comments shared by our readers, even in this short and impromptu survey, has given us indicators that our approach is relevant. It is working towards answering this 'value add' of coaching by publishing practitioners' blog-articles that share personal and professional experience of coaching. Importantly, they provide (self) evidence and articulation of how they do what they do in their market.

We recognise that as coaching practitioners, we all do coaching and have our own coaching approach, yet the way we do it and how we achieve our experiences in coaching is unique to each of us, which also makes it very hard to replicate.

It is this sort of information shared as blog-articles that are helpful because it brings the voice and experiences of practitioners, in their own words. Explicitly being able to talk about what it is that they do and how they engage, and discovering all the different sets of language of how this is done, will begin to build that practitioner knowledge base. Having access to this knowledge base and its following analysis, whilst limited at the start, shall provide more rigour and objectivity for delivering those coaching conversations. Conversations that may then be considered of having professional standards that the market and society accept as both enhancing and protecting an individual's freedom.

For *the good coach*, the result of the referendum has provided both clarity and evidence that coaching is a long-term endeavour. There are many opportunities and places for us all to practice, and to recognise (rather than compete with) all the informal and formal ways coaching is being applied. And that starts with understanding how we, as the role models, are able to reproduce the conditions and behaviours that always ensure, at least 99.999 percent of the time, similar positive results.

So what does the Brexit vote mean for executive coaches?

Doug Montgomery

was inspired by a question raised by *the good coach* about the impact of coaching following the Brexit vote. I've been doing quite a few hours of coaching with a number of different clients following Brexit who have raised their concerns and I generalise below.

QUICK UPDATE OF THE SITUATION

The EU referendum result has created a considerable uncertainty across the country, in the markets, for businesses considering investments, for exchange rates, for EU citizens working in the UK and UK citizens working in EU countries.

- What did the Leave campaign actually mean when they encouraged us to take control of our borders?
- What will our access to the Single Market cost?

Some banks have already declared that they will move UK jobs into Europe. There are mixed messages about what the economy is doing. Sterling exchange rates have shifted significantly, favouring exporters and disadvantageous for importers. David Cameron has resigned as PM and been replaced by Theresa May, Nigel Farage has stepped down as UKIP leader (again), Boris is Foreign Secretary, Michael Gove has been sacked, and Jeremy Corbyn is under pressure from the Parliamentary Labour Party and in a leadership election with Owen Smith. The Scots are unhappy with exiting the EU and making independence noises again. Who knows what the future holds for the UK?

WHAT IS OUR ROLE AS COACHES AMIDST THIS UNCERTAINTY?

My coaching style sits at the non-directive end of the coaching spectrum. That means, I do not see it as my job to tell my clients what they should be thinking. I do not tell them how to interpret their personal and business circumstances. I don't even tell them what decisions they should be making. What I do is bring lots of support, empathy and encouragement, questions and observations, and an ability to create a space in the uncertainty in which they can pause and think. This may seem like a luxury in the busy-ness, pressure and current urgency (perhaps this is even our new normal). As an old boss of mine once said – when you face a major challenge, I want to see you thinking before you act!

I have noticed that in corporations today, it is easy to be operating like a 'human doing', consumed by the task list and with too many emails to answer, rather than as Human Beings. One way to reconnect with ourselves as human beings is to find space to pause and to think. As coaches we can model, through our presence, pace and calmness, that thinking space in which there is no one driving the agenda other than our client. This might be the only meeting in which they are not being advised or told what to do.

WHAT ARE THE IMPLICATIONS FOR EXECUTIVE COACHES WORKING WITH LEADERS IN THE UK AND HOW WE WORK WITH OUR CLIENTS?

As a coach we may work with professionals who sit on both sides of the Referendum vote. Regardless of the result, though, there is a parallel playing out with some of our clients and the desire of both Remain and Leave campaigns to create apparent certainty; a sense of certainty of the future that tends to:

- Create a partial world view that is certain – either black or white, and encourages the gathering of the evidence to support that view and dismissal of contrary evidence. Unfortunately, this can limit the options and possibilities that are really available to us.

- Seek that sense of control. When we experience a loss of control we can feel threatened and that triggers our limbic flight, fight or freeze response which shuts down our thinking capacity.

I have spoken with clients and sponsors since the vote who are worried about losing EU employees and fearing a skill shortage. They are also holding off making investments and are seeing their sector freeze in the face of the uncertainty.

In reflecting on what my clients have shared, and the work we have done in coaching, three things come to mind:

- Goals and Their Importance

- Circles of Control and Influence
- Possibilities and Options

GOALS AND THEIR IMPORTANCE

The first thing that I am reminded of is the importance of clear goals and desired outcomes. We have re-established the clarity of what my client wants from their coaching. Often in times of great change and uncertainty, as we face now both professionally and personally following Brexit, it is difficult to remain clear about what we want and why it is important. It is easy to be distracted by the unknowns while trying to make sense of what has just happened. It was necessary to spend time on re-creating a clear and specific vision of what outcome my client wanted to create. This re-establishes the platform on which the coaching session and the assignment is built.

Key learning: Enquiring about what makes this outcome important starts to uncover the motivation and commitment to it. This well-formed outcome should be positively stated and within their control. Giving them an outcome that when it is achieved, is actually what they want. By reconnecting with what the client really wants, times of uncertainty and chaos can reveal opportunities thrown up by the new circumstances.

CIRCLES OF CONTROL AND INFLUENCE AND CONCERN

One of my clients came into the session clearly agitated and upset. He proceeded to vent his anger and frustration with both Remain and Leave side's ineptitude, lying, incompetence, cowardice, ignorance, etc. etc. He then bemoaned the uncertainty and how powerless he felt in the face of not knowing what the immediate and long-term future holds.

Once he had run out of steam and regained his cool, we started to explore what he did know and what is in his control and influence. This idea, first introduced by Stephen Covey in 7 Habits of Effective Leaders and adapted since, helped me to help my client separate the things that concern him into three categories;

- the things we have control over,
- the things we can influence, and
- the things that concern us, yet which are outside of our control and influence.

I have used this analysis to help clients recognise where they are currently placing their attention, and decide where it is most useful for their energy and attention to be focused instead. I have noticed that this allows them to let go of the desire to control everything, especially those things that are outside their control, and begin to accept that things happen even if they don't want them to. It allowed them to start making contingency plans and to spend their time and energy more productively. This helps them to step out of the potential roles of Victim (feeling and acting helpless) or Persecutor (blaming others) within the Drama Triangle (Karpman), and instead to step into Choy's Winner's triangle by choosing an appropriate response and regaining their own power within the situation. This was re-empowering and re-focussing for my Brexit client.

Key learning 1: What is in our control? We can control our choices of response to the new circumstances, to the emotions that they are evoking in us. We can control our thinking and importantly our mindset. Being able to access an "I'm OK, You're OK" mindset (from transactional analysis Life Positions) can help us to be at our best in any given situation, and invites others to join us in that mindset.

Key learning 2: What can we influence? We can influence more that we may imagine. How our team responds to the referendum outcomes through the example we set in our behaviour and words and body language. How our business prepares for the various scenarios that may play out. The way we share our perspectives with colleagues and friends.

Key learning 3: What is concerning us yet not in our control or influence? These are the things that can consume a lot of energy and attention, in a very unhelpful way if we let them. It is easy to create a feeling of helplessness ("I'm not OK, You're not OK") when our attention is focused on these items rather than on the things we can control and influence. It may be more useful to keep an eye on these areas of concern to monitor how they are changing and evolving so that we can adapt those things in our control and influence to respond to the changing circumstances.

POSSIBILITIES AND OPTIONS

The third approach I've applied arose from a need for certainty and the potential dilemma that that created for another client. This client asked for my support in making a choice between two unattractive options. She could go ahead, at great risk, with a planned project which had already had considerable time and effort invested in it or cancel the project in the light of the uncertainty and risk losing the potential benefits. It was important to her to choose one of these unattractive options.

Dilemmas are interesting beasts. They appear as clear choices between two clear options. However, often the simplicity of the dilemma duality is hiding other possible options.

So, when I heard my client describing the situation in such black or white terms and struggling to choose, I invited her to pause and take a few moments to explore what other possibilities exist. Starting with rechecking the overall outcome purpose and expected benefits from the project, we then brainstormed possible ways forward. Early on we included the craziest idea she could think of, which I find often unleashes creativity, and put judgement to one side while ideas came forth. After a short time, she had several viable options to choose from.

She made a plan to slow the project overall and to press ahead where she had sufficient data and confidence to generate enough benefit for the investment. She also came up with how she would communicate this to her stakeholders.

Key learning 1: Recognise the limiting duality of a dilemma.

Key learning 2: Invite exploration of other possible options that lie between the extremes being described.

Key learning 3: What limiting assumptions are being made that is reducing the situation to black or white – what is hiding in the shades of grey? (Nancy Kline offers a way to challenge limiting assumptions in her book *More Time to Think*.)

As coaches, I believe that one of our roles is to create a calm space for our clients to pause from the busy-ness of business and to think clearly, to shift gear from Human Doing back to Human Being.

In all three reflections I have shared above, what strikes me most is that the opportunity to stop and spend some quality thinking time with a coach who is really present, supportive and challenging without judgement is common to them all. That small oasis of time to step out of the hustle and bustle of task-focused business, full of distractions and demands on attention, is missing for most executives today. It is not surprising that mindfulness is a popular buzzword in the workplace. I could see my clients visibly slow down, pause for thought during our sessions, reconnect to themselves and disconnect from the Human Doing they spend so much time as.

SO, WHAT DOES THE BREXIT VOTE MEAN FOR US EXECUTIVE COACHES?

I suspect, that like our clients, it means facing not knowing how things will work out. Not having the answers and experiencing all the feeling of vulnerability that not knowing evokes in us. What will we do in the face of those feelings of uncertainty and perhaps even fear? We could try to create a sense of apparent knowing and certainty. Or we can walk beside our clients, sharing the journey into the unknown together, sharing the not knowing, and trusting that the client will, with our support, listening and questioning, find a way forward. With respect to what we do as coaches, is Brexit really any different from any other fast changing situation our executive clients face?

Pillars for coaching in socially-turbulent times

Larissa Conte

2016 was a tumultuous year across all fronts—politically, ecologically, socially, economically—and 2017 is poised to be similarly ripe with turbulence and great change. In this global and social context,

- What is the role of coaching and the contribution of our field?
- How can we support individuals and teams to grow into their potential and be agents of change, while also taking steps in our work to affect larger, positive social change?

Following the U.S. election of Donald Trump as president, I shared a rich conversation with the good coach's incisive and wonderful, Yvonne Thackray, about these questions and my approach to showing up now as a coach. In general, I believe we're here, as coaches, to hold space, create clarity, and offer practices for our clients to grow into their greatest selves. So how does our practice shift or evolve to meet these times?

I call upon the following pillars for myself and with my clients to more effectively navigate and positively contribute in these times. Interestingly, the core principles are the same for both coach and client.

1. Prioritize your foundation of self-care.
2. Make space to process what's going on.
3. Learn about change, uncertainty, and fear to better surf the waves.
4. Be curious about your biases and blindspots.
5. Take a stand for what you believe in.

6. Find your leverage points, prioritize, and act.

In addition to outlining dynamics or approaches for each pillar below, I share illustrative stories from my experience applying these pillars to more closely align my coaching practice with a socially-relevant business model for these times.

1. PRIORITIZE YOUR FOUNDATIONS OF SELF-CARE

The night of the U.S. presidential election, I went to bed prior to the winner being announced because the outcome, while not final, seemed clear and I was exhausted. I'd been holding space for great anxiety amongst my U.S. and international clients in the days leading up to the election and had very intense feelings of my own. I knew if I was going to be of help to anyone the next day or the rest of the week, I'd need to connect to my foundation and resources, amongst which sleep is primary.

The same was true for my clients in the days after the election. I realized this as every single one of them expressed energetic turmoil and emotional exhaustion. I encouraged them to prioritize sleep, minimize media consumption until they could feel centered, and created a visualization for them that served as an antidote to the internal tornado they were experiencing.

Why? **I strongly believe in self-care as the foundation for effective change, since it directly influences our health, growth, and leadership.** If we aren't taking care of ourselves, we can't possibly show up well for others. That's why I champion self-care and inner listening from the outset of each client relationship, and hold it as critical to my own business success. Whether in times of calm or great change, our self-care routines are the foundation that ground and nourish us. They act as both anchors and wellsprings, and we need routines on all levels—physical, emotional, mental, spiritual—that fill our well and allow us to show up. When the seas of life are stormy, self-care helps create an inner calm from which we can meet and best navigate the outer storm.

On a deeper level, the practice of self-care and the listening that's required to create alignment in our own beings allows us to have deft skill at perceiving misalignments and key leverage points in systems. We need this skill as coaches, of course, but all of us need this at this time as our systems—social, political, ecological, etc.—are evolving to address the different friction points and misalignments that are threatening the health of our systems as a whole.

To me, it seems that if we are to make great strides collectively, we must make individual strides toward internal alignment. We do this by no longer choosing to abuse ourselves or ignoring what we most need.

2. MAKE SPACE TO PROCESS WHAT'S GOING ON

After going to bed on November 8, I woke up in the middle night, heard that Donald Trump had won, and went outside to sit under the stars. Being inside felt too small to hold all that I was feeling. It happened to be a clear night in San Francisco, and I sat on the roof for two and a half hours bearing witness to the massive emotions roaring through my heart. I not only felt myself, but the city, the country, the upset and tensions in the human collective, Life and the Earth, the arc of history, the mystery . . . It was a lot to feel.

The heart, I'd recently learned through personal experiences, is an organ of sensation rather than an organ of action. Much like a riverbed, the heart is meant to let the river of emotions flow through the act of feeling. And so I sat there feeling everything—tension and all—knowing that (1) I wouldn't be able to be of significant service until I'd tended to my own feelings and (2) clarity on what to do or how to take action would arise in the ebb of the emotional tide.

Living at this time brings up so many feelings. The constant stream of stories about war, injustice, cruelty, death, innovation, art, brilliance, survival, triumph, etc. are coming faster than humanity has ever had access to. Often, faster than we can digest and incorporate in our beings. This can be profoundly overwhelming. Sometimes we don't want to feel because opening up to all of this—truly letting it in—can feel like we're going to drown. The feelings are so strong. The downside of choosing to be numb, though, is that the feelings accumulate and are more difficult to access and release, the longer we let them stagnate.

That's why we, as coaches, can play such an important role for our clients by regularly giving them a space to pause, feel, and process how they're being affected by larger events. We can also ask them, "How else are you making space to process in your life?" since we are not always available for them.

We also need to prioritize such space for ourselves, whether it's with our own coaches, therapists, colleagues, friends, or family. I make this space for myself through regular one-to-one check-ins with colleagues and friends, and am beginning to convene a regular circle for colleagues to feel and process together in this New Year.

I've also been asking myself, "How can I hold space for wider circles of society in meaningful ways?"

3. LEARN ABOUT CHANGE, UNCERTAINTY, AND FEAR TO BETTER SURF THE WAVES

As I sat under the stars that evening, I could feel fear in the big field and its impulse to rise up in me. But I've experienced the damaging effects of allowing fear in my consciousness and body, so I held an acute awareness to not let it take root. Instead I watched the impulse and breathed through it, opening back up into the feeling, into my center, and into not knowing what the future holds.

While the exact details of each new event or moment of change differ, there are underlying patterns and principles that, when understood, make navigating change and the mystery much easier. Here are some of the patterns I've experienced humans having in relationship to change, uncertainty, and fear.

- **Change makes us present to the uncertainty and mystery of life, and always poses a great opportunity to grow and learn as we encounter new circumstances**. It shakes up the illusion that we are in control and have any idea what is going on. This can be exciting and ripe territory to grow, but it can also be uncomfortable, destabilizing, and generate an impulse to latch onto something concrete. Interestingly, fear often fills this role.

- **Fear distracts us from feeling our feelings or being present to the bigness of the mystery** because it focuses in on a very specific point and just ping-pongs around the field of our awareness. Fear is a very, very small aperture and the payoff we get from it is that we don't have to look at the big picture. We don't have to look at or feel the complexity, intensity, or the overwhelming, crushing reality that we have no idea what's going to happen. There's something in humans that really can't stand not knowing, so we have a strong incentive to distract from the reality of the mystery. But the cost is that fear delays the digestion of feelings. It clouds our vision. It cripples our creativity. In my own experience, fear also palpably poisons the health of my body.

It's a subtle position to find the place of realistic honesty about the state of things, not be naive about where certain aspects of the tide may go, and also hold an optimistic and committed perspective for the greater good. Ultimately, I believe in the possibility that we can find our way forward together. I shared these perspectives on change, fear, and mystery with my clients the next day and in the weeks after as relevant. They felt empowered by knowing why we give into fear and how we can reorient our awareness to a creative, grounded place.

4. BE CURIOUS ABOUT YOUR BIASES AND BLINDSPOTS

As coaches, we're trained to dance with the fact that each person has a subjective (aka limited) experience of reality, we each adopt unique behaviors and biases based on our beliefs about reality, and we each carry blindspots about ourselves and the nature of things. Basically, we make a living from helping people see their limiting beliefs and blindspots and learning to grow beyond them based on our own life experience.

I think we have a great responsibility as coaches to own our own biases and limitations, and how they impact those we serve. To see the ways we're limited in what we can offer and the ways in which we are divisive, judgemental, adversarial, uneducated, or closed. It's tough work, but feels utterly necessary if we are to be effective guides in helping others examine and live beyond their shadows.

In addition to leaning more into helping my clients examine their blind spots and limiting beliefs about the collective, I've been more curious about how to leverage these skills more broadly for society and ever more deeply in my own self-examination. Especially as societal events arise, I've been asking myself:

1.   Who do I think I am? What's my concept of myself as a participant in the collective?

2.   How am I racist, classist, gender normative, xenophobic, etc.? How do I other or separate from people?

3.   How am I using my skills and privilege, and for whom?

4.   How is my self-concept or my commitment to human thriving as a coach mis/aligned with my other beliefs and behaviors?

5.   What's required for me to own, feel, learn, and do, so I can be a more effective agent of healing?

I believe that so much of the work right now is about,

- Recognizing where and how we're fractured,
- Listening into those divides and shadows with curiosity,
- Asking what's required to evolve to more life-supportive patterns, and
- Understanding the interrelatedness between the individual and collective levels.

It's brutally uncomfortable to delve into this territory yet it's required for evolution. It's also part of the gift we as coaches can contribute—holding space to encounter and learn from personal shadows and our collective shadows.

5. TAKE A STAND FOR WHAT YOU BELIEVE IN

After some sleep, my night vigil, and grounding the morning after the election, I knew I was in a place to give to others on a day when many in the country and around the world had heavy hearts. On that day, at that time, emotional support felt like the most critical thing to give. I wanted to give people a sense of love and fellowship in an immediate way, especially those who had been most targeted by Donald Trump's slurs and threats and those who've already been in the long fight for civil rights who were feeling exhausted looking at the road ahead.

Living in San Francisco's Castro neighbourhood—one of the first gay neighbourhoods in the U.S.—I was inspired to run down to the morning commute trains wearing a t-shirt I made that said "Free Hugs." I stood there for two and a half hours offering everyone who walked by a hug. About half of the people ignored me or acknowledged me and politely declined. But the other half either softly stepped into the offer or walked directly to me through the crowd. Each hug differed in its tone—some hopeful and light with a laugh saying, "I totally need a hug today," while others collapsed into my arms with sobs and the heaviness of grief. Some were brief and guarded, while others stretched into a deep embrace. Some said, "We're going to be OK," and others lamented in great despair. A gorgeous spectrum of people—gay, straight, Black, Latino, Asian, White, women, men, disabled, mostly adults, and one baby.

Feeling all these hearts, meeting all these hearts as I hugged each person was a profoundly moving experience. Each heart, whatever it held in it was beautiful and I could feel the strength, goodness, love and beauty that connects us all. All told, I hugged about 175 people and shared the story with my online community, which cascaded its own wave of impact.

One of the great gifts of our feelings is that they reveal to us our values and inspirations. When we are so moved internally, it can cause us to act externally. These times we live in ask for each of us to stand for what we believe in. As a coach, as one who stands for the potential of each individual, I stand for the potential of all individuals, all of life. So I am communicating this ever more clearly in my practice and how I choose the business I take, in addition to the actions I take in my personal life.

6. FIND YOUR LEVERAGE POINTS, PRIORITZE, AND ACT

Ultimately, we have limited energy. There's only so much we can do to affect change. On top of that, the current arc of change seems to be more akin to a marathon than a sprint, so being strategic with our energy and focus is key. Given this, how does one prioritize which actions to take?

I asked myself this question a few days after the election, focusing on how to best leverage my networks and involvement with them, since collective intelligence seems crucial to address these never-before-encountered challenges on our plate. These four guiding principles seemed key for my strategic action:

1. Leverage your strengths.
2. Connect with allies working in the same space to fortify best practices.
3. Connect with allies working in different spaces to cross-pollinate efforts and teach each other.
4. Choose one to three networks/circles to invest in.

Then I identified six main circles that connect to my gifts and passions and narrowed down to the following three:

- Coaches and healers.
- Cross-sector change makers who share a common community connection.
- Heart-centered business allies.

Issue the invitation to potential circle members or in convening these circles. The next steps I outlined were:

1. Accept another's invitation.
2. Agree on the purpose of the circle.
3. Get clear on how involved each person wants to be and in what role.
4. Start prototyping and experimenting together to see what's possible.
5. Evolve from there.

With my clients, many of them experienced a swirling of indecision about what to do after the election and where to direct their energy. I helped them focus and prioritize with the following questions:

- Based on your skills and your position in life, what can you do to be the most effective lever for the change you wish to see?
- What are your strengths that you can lean into to really leverage? Yes, we all need to grow right now, and it's also a time to use your strengths.

PART 3: Opportunities at the competitive edge

WHAT'S NEXT? GETTING INVOLVED ACROSS SCALES

Many of our opportunities for learning right now seem to be about how we take care of the self while being a contributing participant in the collective. This doesn't mean subsuming the self into the collective, but rather holding awareness and a sense of accountability for our individual bodies and beings, as well as the collective body. We get to learn how health and thriving on different levels interrelate.

There are massive imbalances in our social and ecological body right now with so many points to intervene. It's as if we've had a shared quadruple bypass globally. Now we get to look at where the blockages exist and try to create the connections that lead to greater flourishing. The complexity of challenges before us are beyond any one person's capacity to solve, so we must work together to find a way that isn't yet clear.

Yes, turbulence is intense and can be exhausting and full of loss. But it is also ripe with creative opportunity and movement that emerges into the space created by the shedding. May we each use our best skills and listening to discover a way forward that works for the whole.

Questions:

- How do we do that?
- How can we not be adversarial whilst at the same time not being be naïve?
- How can we learn from everyone's perspectives and ask what none of us have considered yet?

PART 4

Moving Forward, What Next?

CHAPTER 11

PRACTITIONER RESEARCH

Time for a paradigm shift in coaching - my call for a turn towards autoethnography

Margaret Chapman-Clarke

t is 7.15 pm on a Monday evening. I am sitting overlooking Scarborough's North Bay. There are four mature gentlemen in evening dress, complete with bow ties posing for a photograph with the castle ruins and the sea as the background. I don't see that often in this part of town. Most people dress in shorts, t-shirts and flip flops, with children carrying buckets and spades. It is sunny. The sea is calm. I have been reflecting on what I might write to succinctly capture the peaks and troughs of coaching (past, present and emerging future).

So I start with my story, looking back at my key contributions to the field and the journey that led to my 'discovering' autoethnography.

I am living between two 'centres'. This one, Scarborough, is what I call 'centre two.' It is where I am at my most creative. Centre one, is York. This is where I get embroiled in 'the stuff of everyday life' and my professional work as a psychologist. Both centres allow me to do what is most important to me and my practice – I research, write, speak, design and lead mindfulness and compassion seminars and coach.

Scarborough is also the place for storing my papers and back copies of journals, and where, it seems my story is located. Here I have books and files from those early days of coaching and its rise as a phenomenon.

I have a quick look through my papers and I am surprised at how extensive it is. 2004 stands out as a particularly significant year, so that's where I will begin.

MY KEY HIGHLIGHTS FROM 2004

1. It is the year that I and fifteen psychologist peers proposed the establishment of the Special Group in Coaching Psychology within the British Psychological Society.

2. It is the year in which I designed the UK's first Psychology of Coaching programme for the Chartered Institute of Personnel and Development (CIPD).

3. It is the year the CIPD drew together a number of experts in the field, who helped publish the first Buyer's Guide to Coaching and Coaching Services. The desire of these early 'movers and shakers' was to produce a response to challenge what was perceived as the 'wild west of coaching'.

4. The newly emerging coaching bodies were forming and making tentative steps towards collaboration, also with the intention of wanting to do something about the 'cowboys.'

5. The CIPD launched a new professional magazine Coaching at Work and I joined the editorial board.

6. Meanwhile, a number of key players who had been proponents of mentoring for two decades were asking what was new about coaching, and therapists described coaching as the 'new kid on the block'.

7. I was calling for an evidence-informed approach in coaching in a BPS journal, the Selection and Development Review.

8. I spoke in Sydney Australia, as the only British speaker at the first international conference on evidence-based coaching sharing my work in emotional intelligence and team coaching.

The coach is dead: long live, the accredited coach!

As I look at these key highlights from 2004, I wonder what really is new!

I am reminded of a key text by the American psychologist Tim Hall, who wrote in 1996, that the 'career is dead, long live the career.' He was commenting on the media hype that was heralding the death of the traditional, hierarchical career; which, from my research at the time, if it is dead now, it was very much alive and well in the minds of the Building Society managers I interviewed. However, a critical aspect of that study, I recall now, and which still remains the driving force behind my work are the managers who said respectively that 'all development needs support' and 'everyone needs someone to help them to develop at work'.

Back then, my recommendation was, to quote the title of a book by, one of those early movers and shakers, the late Eric Parsloe "everyone needs a mentor". Now it is as if 'everyone needs a coach' provided it is an 'accredited coach.' There was no need for the Berkeley Consulting Group to worry; coaching has not been assigned to the executive fad graveyard!

COACHING HAS BEEN SAVED FROM THE 'EXECUTIVE FAD GRAVEYARD[1]'

It's 2017. We have come a long way since Stratford Sherman and Alyssa Freas wrote their piece for Harvard Business Review entitled the "Wild West of Coaching[2]" ! Professional bodies are now global and set their own standards for membership. They collaborate. The Institute of Leadership and Management (ILM) are at the forefront of accrediting, what Tony Grant calls the third generation of workplace coaches, managers who coach.

Such is the foothold of coaching today, that in a blog entry for People Management on July 25 2017, Jane Simms presents this skill as a given:

"Jonny Gifford, the senior adviser for organizational behaviour at the CIPD, asserts that: "...we need to see a similar shift in attitude towards conflict resolution as we did to coaching a decade ago. "Mediation-type skills need to be a core part of what it takes to be a good line manager, just as coaching skills now are[3]. "

A maturing field, at what cost?

So how did we get here and what have been the costs and benefits?

In the March 2017 issue of Coaching at Work, I was asked what I had observed since those heady days of the 'wild west' and the time when everyone called themselves a coach (usually after a weekend course!). I noted how the field had matured, and it was now at a stage, where like so many emerging professions, it was looking to gain credibility; seeking standardisation and a need for potential members to demonstrate evidence against competences.

Yet in this drive for standardization and these calls for mastery we are at the risk of being reductionist. We are at risk of closing down innovation and creativity.

I noted a word of caution.

These competency frameworks are fast taking on a life of their own and in our desire to be seen as a legitimate profession, rather than an area of practice, we risk losing something really quite precious if we do not get back to recognising what is the essence of coaching. Which is, providing a special dedicated space where two people engage in a dialogue.

---

[1] Berkley Consulting Group. 2004. *Saving Executive Coaching from the Fad Graveyard.* http://www.berkeleyconsulting.com/Leadership/Saving%20Executive%20Coaching%20from%2 othe%20Exec%20Graveyard.pdf
[2] Sherman, Stratford and Freas, Alyssa. 2004. "The Wild West of Executive Coaching". In *Harvard Business Review.* https://hbr.org/2004/11/the-wild-west-of-executive-coaching
[3] Simms, jane. 2017. "There's more than one way to solve a problem". In *People Management.* CIPD. http://www2.cipd.co.uk/pm/peoplemanagement/b/weblog/archive/2017/07/25/there-s-more-than-one-way-to-solve-a-dispute.aspx

454 | TRANSLATING Coaching Codes of Practice

This is often, certainly in my work, an existential meeting where these individuals connect, each bringing their own story, one helping another to create a new story with which to navigate their world.

AUTOETHNOGRAPHY: AN ANTIDOTE IN A POST-TRUTH AGE

A decade on from when I started sharing my story, I continued with my practitioner-based research, looking for that elusive evidence-informed approach that captures the essence of coaching. I discovered autoethnography.

In 2015, I called for peers to turn towards autoethnography[4]. This is an approach which calls for an inclusion of the self and our experiences in practicing and writing about coaching. This means making explicit what underpins your, my and our worldviews as coaches and making transparent the how of what we do, not hiding behind techniques or calls for mastery. It is to know ourselves first, or as Jackee Holder put it in her keynote at this year's Coaching at Work conference; "to know our story".

Autoethnography speaks to the current zeitgeist in which members of *the good coach* community are at the forefront; this is the move towards narrative and creative approaches in coaching. It is illustrative of a broader trend, which is about healing the split between our cognitive and embodied ways of knowing and being, a split which Richard Strozzi-Heckler suggests has for too long plagued coaching[5].

CRITICAL REFLEXIVITY, HUMANISING PRACTICE

Writing that speaks to an 'autoethnographic turn' in coaching requires that we make explicit what informs our practitioner and authorial voice; our story. This means being critically self-reflexive, what in autoethnographic work is described as 'being vulnerable with a purpose'. In an age of post-truth, relative truth and even 'downright mad opinion' we need to get back to what it means to be engaged in a conversation with another human being, who is struggling, as we too struggle.

The narratives such as those that appear in this book; the two previous texts and those that appear regularly on *the good coach* blog 'tell it like it is.' They are autoethnographies, stories that are lived and are told with integrity, passion and a genuine desire to reveal experiences of what it is to be a coach, and to be coached. To quote one of my clients it is "a magical space" and what another speaks, metaphorically, of a place to "tune her violin".

No two autoethnographies are the same. In the same way that each of our client's stories are not the same. My 'take' on autoethnography, is shaped by my research exploring coaches' experiences of mindfulness training through

---

[4] Chapman-Clarke, Margaret. 2015. Coaching for Compassionate Resilience Through Creative Methods in Hall, L. *Coaching in Times of Crisis and Transformation*
[5] Strozzi-Heckler, Richard. 2014. *The Art of Somatic Coaching: Embodying Skilful Action, Wisdom and Compassion*

PART 4: Moving forward, what next?

poetry. It is an 'integrative, mindful and transpersonal' approach that puts the human back into our scholarship and practice in coaching.

WHY I CALL FOR 'AUTOETHNOGRAPHIC WRITING'

At a recent conference, Emeritus Professor of Coaching and Mentoring Bob Garvey asserted that it was still psychology that dominated the field. Psychology sadly all too often seeks to reduce human experience to variables that can be manipulated and measured, and however approximate, statistical significance assures us that we can hold a degree of certainty at what we are looking at provides us with 'proof' that it works. It is however approximate. Again, I urge a note of caution, as the sociologist Nikolas Rose reminds us, *"psychologists are the unacknowledged legislators of mankind[6] "* – so let's hold these psychological theories, models and tools with a light touch!

Unlike the positivist science that drives psychology in autoethnographic work 'our secrets are disclosed and histories made known.' At the start of this piece I shared with you my experience in the present moment; this gives you a glimpse of my story. And in the spirit of 'being vulnerable with a purpose' my hope is that through my words I connect with what is both specific and at the same time universal. This is beautifully captured in one of the 'vox-participare' (participant-voiced) poems from my mindfulness-in-coaching research. It is written by Lesley. She is an executive coach aged sixty-eight, who has survived and lives with a particularly virulent form of cancer[7].

THE YIN AND YANG OF LIFE

So much loss of hope for a full, energetic vibrant post-work phase countered by so much generation of hope for nourishing health, joy, humour and laughter. The hope for life never wanes. I am loving every second of every change within every day. There is still only one real dread – that of over forty years, to lose the life of my children, of our children and now them for theirs. All else is face-able, however unwanted.

What will it be like for those I love when my physical presence is no longer? Tears may shed but their lives will go on so well without my presence, my touchability. How will I be recalled to mind? What will trigger that recollection? What further thoughts and feelings will be nourished by that interaction of memory of me? I can never know, cannot control or shape that – their memory and its attachments will be theirs – all theirs and so unique – and I will never know. But I do know I will be loved, am loved now and what more can I hope to live with?

---

[6]Rose, N. 1999. *Governing the Soul: Shaping of the Private Self*
[7]Chapman-Clarke, Margaret. 2016. Discovering Autoethnography as a research genre, methodology and method: The Yin and Yang of Life, In *the Transpersonal Psychology Review*. 18 (2)
http://shop.bps.org.uk/publications/transpersonal-psychology-review-vol-18-no-2-autumn-2016.html

Knowing... can be so fleeting, here one moment so strongly and then fade, be lost, gone. Does it return in a different way on another day? It is my own – where does it come from? I feel no God, see no God and hear no God; I know I am alone within my life and how I make it. What makes me make it the way it is? I have no answers but love the questions. I sit here, holding my pen, eyes half closed listening to my life breathe gently. How can I break these moments of still, peaceful wonderment to share who and how I am?

When Lesley revisited this poem she talked of how important it is to embrace vulnerability, before our strengths can be regained and nourished. As Art Bochner writes, this is the power of autoethnography writing which is, like coaching, an existential calling.

Authenticity really does make a difference

Sally East

was interested to take up this invitation by *the good coach*, and have a go at a personal blog type short piece that was meaningful to me, as well as being of practical value for others interested in helping people.

'Authenticity' as a really important aspect to my Practice.

One very important lens I use to understand, and practice coaching is through the idea of 'Authenticity'.

Part of presenting the subject of Psychology to people has to begin with some 'authentic' use of definition. Building on some really useful work from others in a similar vein – when they were searching for their 'authenticity', I start with Kierkegaard[1] who describes authenticity as a 'way of being'.

The flip side of this, of course, is being 'inauthentic'. Heidegger[2] believed/said that in reality we live in constant tension between being authentic and inauthentic. Seeing it as a continuum thus shapes my thinking and my introspection of my 'self'. It is where I am at one with myself? at any given time with any given 'hat' on.

AUTHENTICITY STARTS WITH ME, THEN!

So this is about me. It is about my take on the authenticity of me. It is about relating to others in order to help others – my personal sharing, and especially to help us all share, that I hope will contribute towards what we understand about what each one of us does that works.

---

[1] Kierkegaard, Soren. 1846. *Concluding unscientific postscript: Kierkegaard's writings* Vol 12.1.
[2] Heidegger, Martin. 1962. *Being and Time.* Translated by J. Macquarie and E. Robinson. San Francisco, CA: Harper.

PART 4: Moving forward, what next?

What does authenticity mean for me and my 'self' in relation to the world around me? I guess my thoughts are towards a somewhat existential perspective. I live according to my values and lead what I define as a purposeful life.

I immediately think of Cooley's concept of the 'looking glass self' which states that a person's self grows out of their social interactions with others[3]. That view of ourselves comes from the contemplation of personal qualities and impressions of how others perceive us.

My perception of myself then leads on to how I believe I have values relating to concern for others, including also a sense of ethics, and integrity. All very laudable I hear you say, but how does that translate?

A SUMMARY OF HOW MY JOURNEY HAS WORKED FOR ME

I left school at eighteen and only knew that I wanted to work in education, with people, specifically in Psychology, with some element of research.

This led me to a few years in a library which I thoroughly enjoyed. To quote a colleague 'people are my kind of library.'

I then embarked on a part time Psychology degree with the Open University. Here I really started to find my authentic self, intellectually and personally, with many questions being answered for me.

I went into teaching after further academic study completing a PGCE, where I found out more about myself as I lived on campus for the year as a 'proper' student. I also learnt that as a teacher (professional identity/'hat') it is important to be yourself in the classroom and not adopt a false 'teacher' persona. I worked on this from day one.

I then ventured into a study programme/MSc in Organisational Psychology, thinking of expanding my Further Education job and my Psychology offering. Following this experience, my work involved more direct contact with people and more overt learning. I worked with my alma mater the Open University in a variety of roles, including a project working with young people in Widening Participation, running events. I looked at identity – 'who am I' – loosely exploring one's authentic self.

Within the Widening Participation project I found myself drawn towards bridging the generation gap, specifically in order to know where these students, whose average age was seventeen, were coming from. I felt in our meetings that we were equal.

This has become a major area of my continued practice now. The question is how?

THAT WORD 'CAREER!'

To be authentic I need to do things that are meaningful and resonate with other people. I need to find a key to their door to look at what skills and interests they

---

[3] Cooley, Charles Horton. 1922. *Human Nature and the Social Order*. New York: Charles Scribner's Sons.

can use, above all in a practical way. This is still very widely addressed through the 'door' of the term 'Career'.

This means finding a common language with them, whoever they may be. I have always had an affinity (I think!) with young people within my career in teaching and lecturing. I have been using a career assessment tool with clients of all ages, but mostly young people, for 10 years in career coaching across schools. I am very used to unpacking psych' speak!

I have also been told I am somewhat ageless!

For example, I had a conversation with a client only yesterday who was 'half my age' and had been in teaching for a year. They were looking to 'get out' but they were concerned they might be 'too old' for a new career. Taking time to look at one's inner strengths, skills and ability as well as, most importantly, personality (which may often be sidelined in careers discussions) is imperative and, on reflection, is what I did.

KEY ELEMENTS OF AUTHENTICITY - OVERT/COVERT DISCLOSURE? IS THERE A HIDDEN AGENDA?

I would like to take this chance to explore further what really makes a difference as to how to get authenticity to really work: for me, anyway!

The issue of how much one should disclose with a client is very important. I will really only disclose anything if I feel it will help move the client on. For example, with a recent client I shared that I also worked in teaching. Showing that I had 'on the ground' knowledge of their situation resonated with them.

I try to present my 'true self' to create relationships based on trust. This encourages the client to do the same. By sharing information, where appropriate, I can demonstrate that I trust my client and that there is an implicit (as well as explicit) psychological safety. I try to help the client to unpack themselves and their wants and needs in terms of the workplace and how they fit within it.

I always try to put them at their ease and find out about them as people (without being intrusive) before we go through the results of their profiling diagnostics. I have clear goals that I want them to get to. My service is giving them what they want and contracting (don't understand this word within this context) with boundaries.

Importantly, I want to share my affinity with others; it has been said that I have an almost 'throw away' style of 'how are you doing?' when I first meet clients which enables clients to relax into the interview.

SELF REGULATION

Self-regulation is an integral element to my practice. It has always fascinated me in both a physical and psychological way.

PART 4: Moving forward, what next?

A simple model is always to start with 'physical self-regulation'. I have remained about the same size and shape all my adult life and am no paragon of virtue when it comes to eating, drinking and exercising. I have a genetic make-up that helps; but I really do everything in moderation generally and seem to have a body that knows when it has had enough.

Extending this into my practice, I help others to see how they can help to regulate themselves and how they can make choices about their behaviours and choose the goals that work for them in order to be authentic with themselves.

This is important, as Harter[4] argues, as people who report being true to themselves (i.e. regulate themselves) usually experience higher self-esteem, more positivity and more hope for the future. This suggests more resilience through bad times and better psychological well-being; and higher self-esteem and life satisfaction[5]. Self-efficacy is also really important making people feel as good as they can be realistically.

CHALLENGES AND CONGRUENCE

The biggest challenge I face is when I do not feel congruent with a piece of work that I am asked to do.

I was recently asked to work in an educational environment in which I did not feel socially comfortable. There was incongruence between my values and that of the establishment, and some long-running beliefs underlying this (yes, I will own it!) prejudice. I try to think that it will be an experience: as I say to my clients when they are thinking about work experience, "All experience is good experience even if it turns out to be bad experience."

HOW DOES THIS WORK IN THE REAL WORLD? A FEW TIPS

I've shared my approach: let me translate how I make it work:

1. I always arrive in an open way either face to face or via Skype, asking people about themselves in a non-intrusive way and seeking background information including non-verbal communication which might help me. Often it's what they don't say as much as what they do!

2. I try to raise the energy level to raise the client's awareness of themselves by smiling a lot and creating an environment where they feel I have a genuine interest in them as a person overall.

3. I sometimes communicate vulnerability (where appropriate) overtly or covertly sharing an experience or just saying 'sometimes I feel like that too.'

[4] Harter, Susan. 2002. "Authenticity." *Handbook of Positive Psychology*: 382-394. Edited by C.R. Snyder and S Lopez. Oxford, UK: Oxford University Press.
[5] Kernis M.H. and Goldman B.M. 2005. "From thought and experience to behaviour and interpersonal relationships: A multicomponent conceptualisation of authenticity." In *On building defending and regulating the self: A psychological perspective*: 31-52. Edited by A. Tesser, J.V. Wood and D.A Stael. New York: Psychological Press.

4. I try to imagine where they are, what their surroundings might be the physical situation.

5. I keep focused on the structure so we don't just have a very congruent chat but a grounded discussion on the facts of the report.

6. Always establish a common language and frame of reference with the client from the start and ensure that I am being as in their 'world' as possible.

EPILOGUE

A lot of my work relies on the perceived 'efficacy' of Psychology, and its research background, which provides useful tools that enable people to make sense of their learning and experience.

But, of course it is the way the tools are used that really makes an important difference, which is why I also have this interest in how this whole idea of Coaching is growing.

It is great to have had this chance to reflect and report on my own journey and practice.

And now... A couple of questions for you to consider:

*   Do you ever consider this idea of authenticity?
*   How do you make sense of it for yourself?

How writing about my practice with *the good coach* is a valuable approach to practitioner research

Sue Young

1. WHY "PRACTITIONER RESEARCH?"

'm definitely not an Academic. Rather I'm a Practitioner. So how can I hold a practitioner researcher stance? Because I'm drawn to it. It conveys greater objectivity, rigour and independence in thinking.

My last piece was about sharpened articulation and confidence around what I stand for in my coaching practice since writing with *the good coach (tgc)*. My writing has progressively helped me pull together the various strands of experience, knowledge, values and beliefs that underpin my coaching into a more felt sense of coherence about what I bring as a coach; what I do and what I don't do.

When I started this writing I deliberately kept it open rather than being overly planful, and have been led by my natural emerging attention and energy. I have enjoyed this process of writing as a way of getting in touch even more effectively with my own experience. I have explored my underlying assumptions and thinking – which is what I get from approaching it as research.

However I recognise that, satisfying as this is, my writing has had other unanticipated outcomes and benefits:

- **In my coaching I notice I am becoming more confident, responsive and flexible in adjusting my approach moment by moment.** I do this in response to closer observations of the client at a more subtle level, with light touch monitoring and an adjustment approach throughout the session. Where I feel uncomfortable or have picked up discomfort from the client, I have taken this as a signal and sought to be more immediately open with the client about my observations. It feels more relaxed and natural.

- **I'm more actively open to the information coming from the client** and, although I come with information from previous meetings and have contingency options in mind, I focus on being open to what the client brings – I make no assumptions.

- **Since writing I also find myself more actively reflecting after coaching sessions.** I feel I am becoming more reflective and conscious in the way I operate. My self-supervision reflections, note taking and subsequent supervision conversations with colleagues are richer.

Having heard the term bandied around, is this what 'Practitioner Research' means?

2. A BIGGER CONTEXT FOR MY INTEREST IN PRACTITIONER RESEARCH BEYOND MY PERSONAL PRACTICE

I have now been involved in writing for *the good coach* (tgc) over a period of about twenty months. In this time I have introduced new bloggers to *the good coach*. I have also learning to helped these newcomers both find what they stand for in the unique context of their coaching practice and a true expression for their selves.

I have also worked with the 'blogitorial' team, both getting support as an author, and in developing tgc's collective experience and articulated approach, in supporting and guiding our contributing authors, as much or as little required. I am involved in and contribute to tgc operational team's continuing dialogue and thinking about the vision and continuing development of tgc and its various publishing and research ventures.

As I have engaged in conversation with more coaches in their different contexts, I have become more and more enthused about the potential innovation in the field of coaching that tgc brings. In particular the expression of people's coaching approach, core values and beliefs, resulting in a more active review of their coaching practice, both in a personal and in a bigger context.

Confidence is growing amongst tgc authors to share the moment by moment dilemmas, judgement calls and reflections on their experiences and what they might have done differently. Sometimes it's more of an exploration of an underpinning theme in the context they work in, that they wish to explore; for example this blog/article I am writing now, a personal inquiry into the theme of Practitioner Research, and how that relates to my practice – past, present and into the future.

3. A NEED FOR WRITING ABOUT COACHING THAT MORE REFLECTS THE REALITIES OF PRACTICE

It's difficult, as an experienced coach, to find any books or writings on coaching that explore the realities of the coaching experience. As a colleague recently said to me, *"In coaching books there's currently a lot of theory written about for its own sake – it's a bit sterile. Most of the writing about coaching is bland and too detached from the day to day realities of coaching in organisations."*

Having attended several university coaching conferences recently with the theme of 'practitioner research', I was initially excited at the prospect to touch base with the 'thought leadership' in the coaching world. Particularly on the subject of research in coaching and what that means. I'd already become tired with the dominance of the one-way presentation format of most of the professional conferences in our field. I still like to keep abreast of developments and themes emerging in the market so I do 'check in' periodically.

I discovered that I had misunderstood the purpose of these more academic conferences. The purpose was obviously to showcase students master's and doctorate dissertation research. There's nothing wrong with that per se. The format was primarily one of presentation with space for questions. I sensed it was the academic constraints... a method led focus and a formal one-way presentation format. It forced an over generalised approach that did not allow for sharing or exploring of the more detailed and complex realities that day to day practice would explore.

In summary, there's little evidence of any real widespread sharing of practitioner experiences out there, which should be the foundation of practitioner research. What is the link between Practice and Research and how is that relevant for our work as Coaches working with organisations? What is the definition of Practitioner Research anyway?

4. WHAT DO THE WRITINGS IN THE FIELD SAY ABOUT PRACTITIONER RESEARCH APPROACHES?

DEFINING THE TERRITORY...

Rather than throwing that label around glibly, I thought it worth surveying the field of theory and writings around the themes of 'Practitioner' and 'Research' by outlining my understanding of the map.

The simplest of these seemed to be the term 'Practitioner'. According to 'dictionary.com' but very similar elsewhere, the definition was given as follows:

1. A person engaged in the practice of a profession, occupation, etc. e.g. a medical practitioner.

2. A person who practices something specified.

3. Christian Science. A person authorized to practice healing.

Translating this into our context, a practitioner is essentially someone whose main occupation can be specified. Out of interest, in the writings around it is associated most often with the established professions (legal, medical, teaching) or the public services.

Moving to examine the meaning of the word 'Research' it becomes more diversified. The meaning of the word derives from the medieval French word 'resercher' or to go about seeking. In the Oxford English Dictionary it provides the following definition:

"A careful study of a subject, especially in order to discover new facts or information about it".

Beyond this very generalised definition there are several different approaches / philosophies to research that can be broadly divided in two main overall categories – Quantitative and Qualitative Research. The first of these aims, to quantify research outcomes to make them directly measurable, tends to be more 'fact' focused. The Qualitative Research approach is more concerned to understand participants' subjective perspectives and perceptions.

While helping to 'bound' the territory these definitions still don't help me come up with a more meaningful definition of 'Practitioner Research' in the coaching, or professional, context.

DELVING A BIT DEEPER... LEARNING AS AN EXPERIENCED PRACTITIONER IT'S ABOUT RIGOR

Donald Schön[1], was an author and researcher who was interested in how professions operate. In particular he looked at the link between thinking and action. He made a valuable contribution through his introduction of the concepts of 'reflection-in-action' and 'reflection-on-action'.

"The former is sometimes described as 'thinking on our feet'. It involves looking to our experiences, connecting with our feelings, and attending to our theories in use. It entails building new understandings to inform our actions in the situation that is unfolding.

The practitioner allows himself to experience surprise, puzzlement, or confusion in a situation, which he finds uncertain or unique. He reflects on the phenomenon before him, and on the prior understandings, which have been implicit in his behaviour. He carries out an experiment, which serves to generate both a new understanding of the phenomenon and a change in the situation.

... The act of reflecting-on-action enables us to spend time exploring why we acted as we did, what was happening in a group and so on. In so doing we develop sets of questions and ideas about our activities and practice."

Schön also raised the professional practitioner's *"dilemma of rigor versus relevance"*.

---

[1] Schön, Donald. 1983. *The Reflective Practitioner: How Professionals Think In Action.* Basic Books.

I like this idea of research as it introduces the idea of rigor – a form of checking oneself out. It's a form of self-supervision. Many experienced and capable coaches operate intuitively and learning and adjustment takes place moment by moment implicitly. I believe it's only by reflecting back more consciously can that learning be fully integrated and applied going forward.

IT'S BEING A CHANGE AGENT

Research was a core strand in my master's (University of Surrey, MSc Change Agent Skills and Strategies – CASS). The terms 'Action Inquiry', 'Action Research', 'Participatory Research', 'Practitioner Inquiry', 'Co-operative Inquiry', along with 'Self-reflective Inquiry' were terms we explored.

As 'change agents' working with organisations these forms of modern research approaches seemed to more accurately recognise the more participative context and the more complex and interrelated factors involved. Learning personally and collectively is also an inherent part of these kinds of research approach.

While there are differences in emphasis, depending on their roots, there seem to be some key principles they have in common:

- *The research focus is 'with' rather than 'to'; it is inclusive and participatory.*

- *The research is action orientated. Lewin[2] believed that the motivation to change was strongly related to action: If people are active in decisions affecting them, they are more likely to adopt new ways.*

- *It can include first, second and third person research. That is research on my own action, aimed at primarily personal change; research on my group/team, aimed primarily at improving the group; and research primarily aimed at theoretical generalisation or large-scale change.*

I see some links to coaching in these principles. Third person comes through in that my coaching will usually try to help my clients think about larger organisational/external realities that may need to be taken into account in the issues they are seeking to address.

There is importance in the insight around how a collaborative, iterative process and the emergent group consensus can achieve more. Particularly in more complex contexts, rather than necessarily strong, over simple, initial goal orientation.

Orme and Shemmins[3] believe that various practitioner research approaches and models *"demonstrate that 'research mindedness' goes beyond a critical, practice-led reflection and understanding of existing research and moves into the ability to use research skills within practice - to become 'reflective practitioner researchers'."*

---

[2] Lewin, Kurt. 2013. "Lewin's field theory". *Kurt Lewin.* http://www.kurt-lewin.com/field-theory.shtml
[3] Orme, Joan. and David Shemmings. 2010. *Developing Research Based Social Work Practice*: 174. Palgrave.

A precise definition of 'Practitioner Research' is very dependent on the particular professional and organisational context it is defined within. This would include its explicit and implicit cultural values, purposes and beliefs. Whatever the research approach, the essence is that of observing, capturing experiences and feelings as valid data.

For me it requires an advanced level of capabilities in terms of being able to step outside and take a more objective stance. One that seeks to be open and receptive to seeing multiple perspectives.

IT'S ABOUT CONTINUOUS LEARNING

Practitioner research would appear to be a continuous learning process. Learning theories linked to the idea of Practitioner Research, theories that resonated with me when I first came across them a few years ago, was the concept of single-loop, double-loop and triple loop learning originally developed by Argyris and Schön[4] in the 1960s.

- In Single-Loop learning organisational members establish rigid strategies, policies and procedures. They spend their time detecting and correcting deviations from the 'rules'. Little or no time is spent on investigating the reasons for the divergence.

- In double-loop learning members of the organisation are able to reflect on whether the 'rules' themselves should be changed, not only on whether deviations have occurred and how to correct them. This kind of learning involves more "thinking outside the box," creativity and critical thinking.

- Finally, in triple-loop learning participants would reflect on the 'rules' themselves – do these rules still serve us or has our environment and situation changed. Do we need to review our ways of working and how we learn? Both individually and collectively, more fundamentally.

It strikes me that these theories are at the heart of the territory I work with – coaching leaders at all levels in organisations. They help my clients step back and see for themselves that multiple perspectives are the only path to sustainable learning and change.

They also bring out as a key dynamic in people interactions the distinction between 'espoused theory' and 'theory in action'; the difference between what people say and what they do. This theory puts forward that, by understanding more explicitly their intuitively held 'map of the world", individuals can raise' their levels of self-awareness. They can be more conscious of their choices, firstly in their thinking and subsequently in their actions.

---

[4] Argyris, Chris., and Schön, Donald. 1974. *Theory in Practice: Increasing Professional Effectiveness.* San Francisco: Jossey-Bass.

Both Schön and Argyris appear to be taking the natural learning process of practitioners working in an organisational context more into account.

For me, this draws out the real potential value to the practitioner of adopting more of a 'practitioner research' mindset. This involves cultivating higher levels of objective Self-Awareness, awareness of the Client, and the context in which the prior two elements are placed.

In summary, I started to search for where Practitioner Research is explicitly taking place. It is still a relatively young concept (the past 25 years or so) so it is not widespread. Interestingly the sectors where Practitioner Research or Inquiry approaches are more explicitly used include Social Services, Education, Community initiatives and professions where a 'helping relationship' can be core to their work.

5. SO WHAT IS MY INTERPRETATION AND USE OF 'PRACTITIONER RESEARCH PRINCIPLES IN MY PRACTICE

- **The process of writing about my coaching practice is an on-going practitioner research process.** I've incrementally developed and built on. It's an awareness. A 'mindset' you hold. For example going into a recent coach "chemistry" session – what data am I picking up about the client – both individual and contextual. What would build rapport with this style of individual with their expressed interests? What assumptions am I at risk of making? Am I the right person for them? Being open to the possibility I may not be. Noticing their behaviour, body language, expression and the direction and level of their energy. What about their attention in the conversation? Being sure to follow that and where (selectively) may I want to intervene, and with what intent?

  As part of raising my awareness, and over the past several months, I have redoubled my interest in capturing reflective and research minded notes immediately after my sessions. I find this process helps me more critically examine and retain key points I want to take forwards. Writing, and then reviewing, the words that give meaning to my experience provides a sharper opportunity to consider and research than other forms of reflection can bring.

- **The focus for practitioner research for me always operates at three levels –** considering factors / influences at different levels; Self as Coach, Other (Client) and the Context (such as the organisational stakeholders and the wider System or social domain). In my day to day coaching practice these three lenses allow me to notice what the client brings in from their bigger context unprompted and what they don't.

  At all levels of management and leadership both individual and organisational learning are inextricably linked. For example, an over controlling manager I was coaching recently came to his own personal realisation, through the coaching process, that he was actually holding back the potential contribution of team members. He acknowledged how that was having a negative impact on the performance of the team.

- **It is an incremental developmental and action orientated learning process.** Energy and attention evolve as you evolve and grow as a practitioner. I've adopted a 'go with the flow' approach, trusting myself at any point of time in terms of themes and whatever issues are drawing my attention at that point in time. It's a continuous learning and adjustment process.

- **Writing blog/articles integrates and embeds current themes coming out in my practice and approach.** The writing process stimulates more active reflection, observation, highlights fresh perspectives. It helps me make sense of and integrate my evolving experience into new thinking and action. I find writing personally engaging because it helps me make more explicit to myself what I think. It draws on my experiences and reflections to develop new insights. I also find this to be true when I have stimulating and perspective extending conversations with others. Writing, even if only personal notes, helps me integrate and take those insights forward in more tangible form.

- **I actively encourage my clients to adopt a more curious approach to observing themselves and others and situations,** drawing on their observations and experiences more explicitly. Typical outcomes from my clients are deeper awareness, reflection, clarity and confidence in direction. So, in my coaching with managers and leaders, I see part of my overall goal is to help them become "research practitioners", i.e. more naturally seeking multiple perspectives drawing on different sources of data to inform their choices.

For example, I was recently coaching a senior manager who had taken on the lead in coordinating a Change programme following organisational re-structuring. Our conversations helped him step back and see there were some gaps in his knowledge of some key stakeholders' agendas and aims. There were a couple of more remote but key players that had not come onto his radar, but he realised they certainly had the power to stop things happening if they were so motivated. Before our conversation he had not identified the need to get more closely alongside them to understand where they were coming from, and what levers he could best seek to pull on to influence their thinking.

- **Peer exchange, in my experience, under the right conditions, extends and enriches insights.** It provides additional insight from listening to others' experiences and ideas. However, the right conditions need to be created in the group for peer exchange to work. Building trust is fundamental. Building rapport around objectives, individual and collective, is really important. This includes having respect for differences and genuine interest in others' perspectives. Once trust in the group and the process has been established,

PART 4: Moving forward, what next?

self-disclosure and openness of sharing perspectives grow. This leads to producing deeper and higher quality data on experience and perspective, the real foundations of practitioner research.

6. CONCLUSIONS

In conclusion, being a more effective Practitioner Researcher overlaps with what I already do with my clients. It encourages greater ability to step back and see multiple perspectives, it extends their perspectives on the options available to them and it allows them to think both more creatively and critically.

The relational context of coaching is all about holding an open inquiry towards one's Self as an important part of adopting a 'researcher' mindset. All of this is core to learning, which is core to what coaching is all about.

It has been important to link the idea of writing to the idea of researching. Both these words can have many meanings, but it helps to clarify what they can mean for me, in my practice.

It has also been valuable to research what others in the wider community have considered, which can help me continuously develop my practice.

I also see it is a 'mindset' thing. To be a true practitioner researcher we have to approach our clients with an open mind. If we are too locked into our preconceptions and a planned approach, then we're at risk of not creating the environment that enables our clients to fully explore and express what they need to as part of their personal learning journey.

Also retaining the objectivity and rigour that a "research" mindset requires will enable us to better examine the data in front of us, including our own observations and feelings – all data that better enables us to see more clearly what is going on with the client. Certainly, writing with tgc about my practice helps me do this.

In conclusion I see myself as a Practitioner Researcher, albeit a continuously learning one!

Do see yourself as a Coach Practitioner Researcher, and what does that look like for you in your context?

Listening is foundational to living your truth

Larissa Conte

Listening is one of the most fundamental skills in a coach's toolkit. I've found that few things have advanced my coaching practice (and life) as much as continually refining my listening skills. While this may seem obvious or rudimentary, I've been blown away by the layers of subtlety that exist in the realm of listening. In my growth, I've learned to listen more deeply to myself, my clients, our shared space, the larger field, and how all of these realities interact.

In this article, I explore how deeper listening to our own truth can advance our ability to serve clients more effectively and share:

- how my understanding and capacity to listen have evolved,
- some approaches I use to cultivate refined listening, and
- the impact that deeper listening has had on my practice.

FIRST, WHAT IS LISTENING?

I view listening as **receptivity to the field of information moving in each moment**.

In the case of listening to another person, it is a posture of openness that takes in all of what they are expressing. This is regardless of how conscious the person is of what they're transmitting or how much I may or may not understand about what they're communicating. It's as much about openness to sound, tone, body language, emotion, and energy as it is about listening to the words they speak. Listening is a multi-level sensing experience that creates room for the other person to fully be where they are.

In this way, listening is 'holding space'. It's creating a loving, receptive, non-judgmental space for another to experience and reveal their truth. I've found that the more I invest in the quality of my listening, the more easily and readily others share their deepest truths with me in a comfortable way because they can sense the space I'm holding for them. More often than not , people initiate sharing deeply-held truths very quickly with me in personal and professional settings, which they then reflect they wouldn't normally share. I've seen this pattern increase in my life in correlation with my growing ability to listen and hold greater space for others. And all of this has sourced from advancing my inner listening.

Inner listening, or listening inwardly to myself, is receptivity to the fullness of what I'm experiencing. Beyond just my thoughts, it includes my body sensations, emotions, energy, mental images and intuition. To me, listening is a deeply musical act—it's the sensing of harmony and disharmony. It's also a lot about feeling. As I've expanded my ability to perceive what alignment and misalignment feel like in my body and how to recognize my own truths and false beliefs, I'm more effective at helping others do the same. I attribute this both to the pattern recognition I've gained through doing my own work, as well as gaining refinement in the internal tuning fork of my listening. I've gained somatic (body-based) imprinting of what harmony and disharmony feel like, and how to uncover the pathways that help move energy and emotion. But it took me repeated, sharp wake up calls to listen to the inner knowing my body was communicating because there were so many reasons I didn't want to listen to my truth.

WHAT GETS IN THE WAY OF LISTENING

In order to listen, we have to have the awareness to slow down, open up, and feel. All of these attributes go against the rhythms of modern, industrialized culture. We move at breakneck speed, are habituated to constantly push, to feel disconnected from each other and our bodies more often than not, and regard thinking as the only or most important form of human intelligence.

All of these patterns were firmly operating in me when my dad died. I was 22. His death was like a lightning bolt that shocked me into expansive listening and evaluation. I realized I was pushing my body too hard in my drive to 'achieve' the status quo path of success, which suddenly seemed absurd, knowing in a visceral way that I'd never incorporated before that I could die any moment. I'd already begun to question some of the above cultural assumptions though my master's work having experienced the havoc I was wreaking on my body as a hyper-driven student-athlete. Thankfully, my dad's death had the silver lining of firmly launching me onto the path of listening to and following my truth.

It isn't only these cultural habits and personal narratives that get in the way of our listening. We're also internally motivated to avoid listening, because listening can result in us being uncomfortable with what surfaces—especially when listening to ourselves. In addition to potentially being uncomfortable with what we hear, listening brings forward the pesky element of accountability. As one of my clients said, "*The trouble with listening to myself is that the I actually have do something about what I hear.*" Oh, yes, that. We all have a part of ourselves that wants to exist in denial and avoidance because then we don't have to be uncomfortable, don't have to do the work to examine the falsehoods in our story, and don't have to figure out how to grow and create alignment in our lives.

I believe that the drive to avoid our deepest patterns is profound, and often unconscious; hence, why we're in business as coaches. This part of us that denies and wants to keep things in the shadows of our consciousness is not a stand for our greatest self. That's why it's important to recognize the payoff we get from denial, so we can use it as fuel and motivation to courageously listen to what's true within us.

OVERCOMING THE URGE TO PUSH AND LEARNING TO LISTEN MORE DEEPLY

When I was twenty-nine, I had another lightning bolt moment that catalyzed layers of listening in me that I never thought possible. I had a near-fatal accident that Western medicine helped me survive through interventional surgery, but had little guidance in regard to recovery. By listening to my body for 6 years about how to uncover my healing path, I gained an advanced immersive training in inner listening. **I listened to my truth as if my life depended on it, because it did**. I did so by listening to and navigating by my Yes and my No. By this, I mean the inner knowing that exists in my body, our bodies about how to create alignment.

My dear colleague and collaborator, Laura Griffiths, who's worked for over 10 years as a coach and bodyworker, describes our inner knowing in the following way: "*Our body knows how to heal a cut. In the same way, we have this other 'knowing' in our beings that knows how to generate alignment and health. We know when we're hungry or thirsty. We also know when we're uncomfortable emotionally or when we're passionate about something. All these little signals direct us as to how we can create greater alignment in ourselves.*" Along with examples from my personal journey, this is how I explain that **listening is foundational to living your truth**.

I believe that, as coaches, we're only as good at listening for mis/alignment in others as we are at listening to it in ourselves. Which is why it's critical that we continually commit to living our truth. It brings authenticity to our practices and personal lives. It equips us to train clients to live in alignment with their own beings. We help them learn that by not simply operating on Pushing Autopilot all the time or falsely thinking that endless doing will produce success, we can come out of depletion, step into true listening, and apply the correct measures to flourish in our lives.

PART 4: Moving forward, what next?

With almost every single client, I begin by helping them connect to their inner knowing through listening. I start by asking people to close their eyes and then posing easy Yes/No questions in our session about thirst, hunger, comfort in their current body position, etc. (Having one's eyes closed helps people start to develop their listening because they're not distracted by external visual information). I usually end with a question that doesn't have a Yes/No answer to help them realize they can hear valuable information beyond Yes and No. I'll ask them, "*What's the most nourishing thing you could do for yourself this evening?*" They always get clear information and then are at choice about whether they want to choose that course of action or not. Following that session, I give them awareness practices to help them get curious and start tracking their own patterns:

- How do your Yes and No show up in your body? What do they feel like?
- Notice where in your life you act on your Yes and No and where you don't.

This assignment is the doorway to greater awareness. People will come back with observations like,

"Wow! I literally don't ever listen to myself."

"I actively go against my listening every single time I get an indicator to take care of myself."

"Every time I feel uncomfortable in a conflict and I disagree, I don't say anything. I don't know why…"

These observations generate curiosity, which is the path to more awareness, because once we get curious we want to know more. That's the great thing about humans. And clients notice me noticing them wanting to become aware, which also motivates them.

From all my personal experience and experience training others in inner listening, I've seen humans experience a Yes in their bodies as a feeling with qualities like opening, brightness, warmth, expansion, softening, happiness, while the No can feel constricting, dark, tight, small, tense, hard, blah, or downright terrifying. Despite these patterns, I always ask clients to notice what their Yes and No feel like first, because I don't want to assume how information registers in their being. In general, people from industrialized cultures need help to learn how to not sprint and how to develop their inner listening muscle memory.

This information is quiet, especially at first—unless we ignore something important for long enough that it arises through an explosive expression that's built up great pressure through long-standing denial. Having experienced various explosive information moments and having almost died, I often implore clients to listen so they don't have to get a violent awakening to listen to their truth. But because the impulse to avoid listening can run so deeply in all of us, sometimes this is what's required. Sometimes we need the shock of a lightning bolt moment to be motivated to listen.

WHAT I LISTEN FOR IN MYSELF AND IN MY CLIENTS

Even before I meet with clients, **I need to be clear on my invitation as a coach**—What's my Yes? What's the work I'm best equipped to do and most passionate about doing? And how do I keep this invitation current in my external branding and storytelling as I evolve?

These days most clients come to me with a conscious or unconscious desire to do deep soul work as it relates to their leadership. As I've shifted my internal intent in that direction, I have very few clients who come to me for just strategic thought partnership, though I can do that. I hold a bigger space for my clients now and it starts with me knowing my Yes first, so that when they show up, I can be present and fully available to every aspect of them.

ASSESSING FIT

In my practice, I can generally assess someone's intent for seeking coaching and whether I'd be a good fit for them in about a half an hour. Having listened to myself, I know how I'm best equipped and most want to support people, and what's required from them and our chemistry to engage in that way. Here are some of the indicators I listen for in our first conversation:

- **Alignment of context and style.**
  Both people need a clear sense of each other's context to understand the transformation the client is seeking and whether I, as a coach, feel equipped to help foster that process. The client also needs to get a clear sense of my style to know whether they resonate, since skills alone don't determine fit. Some examples of style, as you think about your own, include: inquisitive, humorous, logical, intuitive, dynamic, structured, etc.

- **Ability to trust and be vulnerable.**
  My hunch is that initial trust sources from a client's sensing of our listening, skills, and style. I pay attention to how comfortable the client can be with me in bringing their vulnerability forward. The aim is to surface the heart of why the client is seeking help in 15-20 minutes. As I said before, this can often look like people unintentionally sharing deep, dark secrets in our first or second conversation, and without the verbal prodding to go there. Since my style is to dive into what's deeply real with clients to spur root cause transformation, I seek clients who are open to deep vulnerability and seeking the space to open in that way.

- **Do you want to be fixed? Because I'm not here to fix you**.
  I'm here to be my client's companion on their growth path. I offer reflection and pattern recognition in a territory that's familiar to me. But the client is

the only one who can discover what they need and choose the required changes. I don't have the power to do that, nor do I purport to have authority over their being in that way. It's not how I work, and I'm also highly skeptical of practitioners who stand in this posture.

- **Coachability.**
  This could be a whole post and has already been explored by other coaches here on tgc, but I have a few thoughts. If I sense a client has a very strong commitment in their ego to being right, broken, obstinate, or closed, I personally don't proceed in the relationship. This is a subjective assessment, but I need to sense a fertile opening within them to considering the possibilities that (1) They don't see everything (2) They can change their current state and (3) They want to do the work. Otherwise, it's not in alignment with the type of practice and work I'm seeking. So, I think we each need to define what coachability means and doesn't mean for ourselves.

IN THE COACHING FLOW

Once I've established my fit with a client and we're engaged in coaching, there are a whole host of things I listen for during sessions to guide my practice.

Some Core Things I Listen For In Myself:

- **My energy level**
  If I'm mentally foggy or scattered before a session, I try to prioritize gathering myself for several minutes before encountering the client. If I'm feeling deeply exhausted or unwell, I'm usually incapable of holding quality space and deep listening for another. Despite my best efforts, sometimes I'm just not in a space to serve. In this case, I'll share transparently with my client and ask if they'd prefer to postpone our call.

- **My ego**
  I always keep one eye out for any desire I may have to be right, have 'the fix', look good, focus on myself rather than the client, or choose from business motivations rather than true service, since no amount of self-awareness eliminates the ego (in my experience). And my ego doesn't give a damn about other people.

- **Body mirroring/empathic experiencing of the other's state or emotions**
  As I've deepened listening to my Yes and No, I've come to hear/feel other people's Yes and No, their energy, and their body reactions in my own body. I listen for these and if something's occurring that doesn't feel like mine (like a clenching in my throat or a knot in my stomach), I'll ask the client to check that I'm tuning into their experience, since where we store emotions or memories in the body is crucial information.

- **Triggers or blind spots of my own**
  This is rarer than in my early coaching days, but I do pay attention for when a client brings something up that triggers me or that I'm unaware of in myself. These are usually indicated by a strong energy in me that's not consistent with the client, so I take note to investigate in my solo work afterwards, rather than let that energy influence the coaching session.

Some Core Elements I Listen For In Clients

- **Story and self-limiting beliefs**
  This is a no-brainer for coaches, but I'll say I listen for whether someone's telling a story that's life-affirming and open to possibility, or one that's life-diminishing and limited. It may be a whole self-defeating story or a fragment thought embedded in a larger narrative. Regardless, I'm always hunting these with my listening.

- **Body language**
  People communicate so much through their body—their posture, facial expressions, gesticulations and where they rest their hands. For example, when a client is constantly holding or massaging the back of their neck, they're usually holding a lot of stress, so I'll ask about it or pause our conversation and help them relax.

- **The energy behind the words that people say**
  On the obvious level, we can listen to someone's level of excitement how lit up or not they are through their tone of voice. More subtly, I experience a silent type of music that happens when people speak, where a word or phrase may have a lot of energy behind it even though their tone of voice doesn't change. To me that signals information, like a signpost, so I'll ask them about it and the associated thought or feeling behind it, because it's usually a thread that will help us find the way forward.

- **Engagement on the journey**
  I can feel if someone is in. They are telling the story that they want wholeness, they are ready to do the work, to love and accept themselves, to integrate all the parts of who they are. When they show me their cracks and vulnerabilities, in return I help fill the cracks with gold. The cracks are the gold. That's where the gold lies. So it's in that notion of the cracks, the way I feel their awareness of the cracks, help clients feel into them, and perform inner alchemy that I support people's yearning for wholeness.

THE PRACTICE OF LISTENING AS WAYFINDING: REFLECTIONS AND WHERE NEXT

Listening and responding to what I hear real-time is key to my style as a coach, which is why I call my practice Wayfinding. We find the way together through focused receptivity to what's occurring in each moment. By doing this together, my clients learn how to do this on their own. I love that. Ultimately because I want them to outgrow me. So it's key in my practice, to get ever clearer on the types of people who'd best receive the unfolding approach to transformation that I'm equipped to offer.

I learned years ago that when I have very structured ideas of plans and programs for coaching, they get dashed on the rocks. What I'm best at is accompanying someone in the mystery of their unfolding, of life's unfolding, with what patterns I do know. That's my way. It's what is authentic to me. It requires me to feel myself and my clients continually in real-time to find the leverage points for them. I see this as my gift, and as our gift as coaches. **To me, coaching is feeling people, falling in love with their true selves, and mirroring who they really are back to them, so they can grow into that self.** That's my job. I get to fall in love with tons of people, with their whole selves. It feels like the luckiest job on the planet! Which is my truth. And when I'm in my truth, people feel safer with me and can have a more honest assessment of their own Yes and No.

I think it's critical in selling ourselves as coaches to not only tell clients what we'll work on with them, but to let them know how we'll dance with them. It's the style thread I mentioned above. How do you want to dance? Some people really like a ton of structure and they want a program that reflects that-e.g. they want to know how long they're going to be engaged in coaching, they want to know what other people have received from doing it, etc. And if that's your style as a coach, great. To the best of our abilities, we need to put forward a clear invitation of how we're going to hold the space for clients and dance with them to help them decide if we're best for them.

Thus for me, coaching is a fluid, unfolding, real-time exploration of someone's life and the avenues that they want you to accompany them on. And they should always have the authority to step away when they feel done. Sometimes though, business motivations can sully that choosing and that granting of authority, because the coach, who's also a business operator, can operate from scarcity. For me, as the coach, it's critical to have very little ego about it and bow and say, "Thank you, good luck," with humility and that listening. That practice of listening is also why I don't offer extended coaching program packages. I make my clients assess themselves every month so they have to hear whether they want to keep working with me. It's a mechanism to build their inner listening.

In the bigger perspective of listening, I think it comes back to understanding the social relevance of our work. It involves looking at the context of what's happening for humanity right now, and asking how we connect our individual offerings and developments to where both the pressure points in society, as well as the flowering edges are. I see the practice and art of listening as being critical on the individual, organizational and social levels. By listening we can foster our best growth together. The more we can role model and train people in it through our practices, the better.

My question to you: How do you go about listening for living your truth?

Giving a shape to coaching practice - my identity and my 'home' for work!

Jeremy Ridge

People often refer to having a 'coaching practice', but my curiosity is frequently aroused by what this practice may mean at a practical, and meaningful, level.

I think Bill Green has put together a useful perspective on the term Practice. He writes: "*It is a term that circulates incessantly, and seems constantly and sometimes even compulsively in use, without always meaning much at all. Rather, it seems to float across the surface of our conversations and our debates, never really thematised and indeed basically unproblematised, a "stop-word" par excellence[1].*"

So – what is practice for me?

My Practice seems quite like a reflection of me. It is something like an identity. As well as being something like how I choose to live – as evidenced by the 'home' I live in. The detail and shape of how we set up our domestic home is always unique – just like the detail of each Coach's practice.

Practice seems to be an idea that has emerged from the evolution of speciality services. It is often linked to being professional. However, the term professional can be used very differently. Some people refer to being professional because they earn their living by providing these services. Others refer to professional because they go further and are a member of a professional community which identifies shape and substance (types of relevant knowledge) and the boundaries of practice, as well as accountability.

Shape, for me, is like a map which identifies substance and boundaries between different elements - such as land and sea. Though there is still a considerable

---

[1] Green, Bill. 2009. *Understanding and Researching Professional Practice.* Edited by Bill Green. Sense Publishers.

diversity in views about the substance of Coaching, when someone talk about a coaching practice suggests that there is some form of recognisable shape.

There are indeed established shapes in other professional practices; for example, in the medical profession. One easy form of shape, for me, arises in the stages of evolution of my Coaching Practice. This also builds further on previous blog/articles for *the good coach*[2] .

PART 1. PREPARING THE GROUND FOR SHAPING COACHING PRACTICE

Even starting with simple ideas such as shape still raises some other questions. For example, the sort of substance and boundaries involved in approaching creating a meaningful picture of Practice. Five themes come to mind from my experience of how we are making more sense of Coaching.

1.1 THE SOURCES OF KNOWLEDGE REQUIRED

Knowledge is traditionally assumed to be understanding that is reasonably stable and reliable. Definition is agreed and meaningful.

Conventional science leads the way in this. Albeit limited to whatever methods are available, which can then limit the knowledge. Statistical significance is still a form of value judgement, as with probability estimates, for example.

Another example, the current approach to much research in coaching may not best be the simple extension of many current practices in fields like psychology, economics or other social sciences because of the changed boundary conditions and the nature of the knowledge involved.

It seems to me that the greatest knowledge about how coaching works lives in the heads of practitioners. This experience is a form of knowledge. It has evidence of achieving results for the practitioner (and others they are working with), and is therefore pragmatic and may be contrasted to traditional approaches to evidence in academic journals (or books).

In Coaching, Practitioners seem to operate from a book (of knowledge) they have learned personally, of their own that becomes the Home they operate from. This still doesn't yet get well researched or reported on.

In effect, as Yvonne Thackray[3] concluded from her formal research of Constructing [Coach's] identity:

---

[2] See Ridge, Jeremy. 2016. "Using a Research Approach to Learn From Coaching Experience." *the good coach*. https://the-goodcoach.com/tgcblog/2016/4/21/using-a-research-approach-to-learn-from-coaching-experience-my-learning-about-coaching-readiness-as-an-example-by-jeremy-ridge Accessed September 12.
[3] Thackray, Yvonne, 2014. *Building Towards an Anthropology of Coaching: Constructing Identity -* MSc. University College London. (Available to download https://www.the-goodcoach.academy/)

"A coach's identity is sutured (as in the medical use of the term) from a plurality of identities and periods in their life history, becomes more closely aligned with the self".

1.2 THE NATURE OF IDENTITY

Many forms of identity still seem to be adopted from social contexts; (e.g. I am told I am English!). These can be expectations for living up to the identity I am expected to conform to. Increasingly however, people are making choices, still in context, that are more personally derived and unique to them. These choices are the formation of their identity and can be seen to be more internally driven than externally derived.

This choice of a more personally derived identity can then become an important basis for Practice. It is the reality of how a particular person creates patterns/shapes in their living. In Coaching, one unique person meets another unique person and a unique exchange happens between them. Events, when described at a general level, might have similarities between different people. But the approach to dealing them will be unique... And that's the real essence and importance of coaching... creating the conditions for those involved to get to them.

This makes using conventional scientific approaches very difficult to apply to what is always unique as events, rather than reliably common!

1.3 EXPERIENCES IS THE RESEARCH THAT MATTERS MOST

Application of knowledge to a practical context; (e.g. the term technology – in the sense of inventing useful things or to solve practical problems) ideally requires perfect knowledge of the context. However, context is frequently too complex to reduce to a simple framework.

Continuous learning through trial and error, through experience, is the reality – even with mature professional practice models (see Table 1). For example, Kahn even goes so far as to suggest that real mastery in mature professions, such as Medicine, is also based on intuition, not just knowledge. This is due to the complexity of contexts, in practice, and that intuition is still something mainly learned through experience.

1.4 COACHING KNOWLEDGE (THE HOW) AND COACHING OPERATIONS (THE WHAT)

There is an important relationship between Coaching Knowledge and Coaching Operations. I am always conscious of marketing what I do in an operational way which,

- makes sense to what the user/buyer is looking for through the lenses of the words they use; and
- is often involved as 'the what' as an 'output'/ results focus, e.g. improving leadership development.

PART 4: Moving forward, what next?

Level of Performance	Attributes of Performer (looking at overall performance encompassing simple tasks, routine and non-routine complex tasks)
Incompetent	Unable to perform
Novice	Rules (protocol)-based performance. Unable to deal with complexity Task seen in isolation
Advanced beginner	Guidelines-based performance Able to achieve partial resolution of complex tasks Task seen as a series of steps
Competent	Performane not solely based on rules and guidelines but also on experience Able to deal with complexity with analysis and planning Task seen as one construct
Proficient	Performance mostly based on experience. Able to perform on acceptable standards routine Able to deal with complexity Related options also seen beyond given task
Expert	Performance based on experience and intuition In complex situations moves easily between analytical and intuitive solutions All options related to the given task are considered Achieve excellent performance
Master	Performance becomes a reflex in most common situations Sets new standards of performance Mostly deals with complex situations intuitively Has a unique vision of what may be possible related to the given task

Table 1. Attributes of levels of performance in the context of healthcare – modified from professional standards for conservation[4]

How to get to operational output has to be derived from the Knowledge about how to stimulate the coachee, as a person, in the Coaching situation, often separate and distinct from the knowledge of the market.

The knowledge that drives a coaching conversation is not always present in the conversation itself. For example, empathy is an important function in coaching, but the term is rarely used in the coaching dialogue itself. You do it,

---

[4]Kahn, Kamran, and Ramachandran. 2012. "Conceptual framework for performance assessment: Competency, competence and performance in the context of assessments in healthcare – Deciphering the terminology." In *Medical Teacher* 34 11.

not talk about it! The knowledge involved is often still poorly reported and may be invisible in its real form even to the Coach involved.

A meaningful picture of Coaching Practice has to cover this Knowledge Base – not just the Operational or Business Model.

1.5 PATTERNS IN COACHING PRACTICE ALWAYS CONTINUE TO DEVELOP

There is some assumption that knowledge is stable. However, even in medicine, as knowledge grows, so a practice also has to continuously evolve – hence the requirement for formal continued professional development of many professional bodies.

This reality is even more the case with Coaching. Each new person I work with adds immensely to my appreciation, and knowledge about how others live.

Overall, it still seems there are few conventions for reporting on the full detail of practice. I want to make a start. The most immediate way for this seems to me to start with more of an overview of important features of my Practice and how it has developed – through what can seem to me to be stages.

PART 2. STAGES IN MY COACHING PRACTICE

The choice for my level of description, here, hinges on more of a macro (and longitudinal study of self), than a micro view (of individual events). Within each pattern of each stage there are many other stages and patterns!

The stages I have identified are:

2.1 Building Knowledge during the Early learning focus

2.2 Making contemporary sense of the early learning Knowledge base

2.3 Researching the context - organisations and opportunities

2.4 Realisation of the Practice in particular operational terms - commercial

2.5 Scaling Practice to other operational areas – coaching communities

2.1 BUILDING KNOWLEDGE DURING THE EARLY LEARNING FOCUS

Main influence on Practice: Collecting raw data on multiple similarities and differences between myself and other people.

My start was very formative. To be honest, I can still remember a lot about childhood and the experiences of gradually building my knowledge through noticing similarities and differences with other people. I can also remember the building of my own patterns of behaviour and their consequences. This was the personal knowledge base I was starting to build. Even in childhood choice happens.

The learning that emerged has been central to forming my approach to coaching that emerged.

Summary of outcomes:

1. **Detached curiosity**. For me, curiosity is a major 'emotional' type driver. In the sense of a strong internal driving force that influences much of my life. It involves the study of my reactions, compared to how others react to the same circumstances – even how circumstances are perceived differently!

2. **Follow the system.** Society has set up a range of opportunities/channels for those who want to enquire in the early stages of life – one universal structure everyone was expected to pass through is the education system. This became my fascination. Friends settled down. My curiosity took me on and on through its various stages.

3. **Not finding a place in the system**. I passed exam after exam, but was still searching for how my identity fitted the social context. This stage was completed with a first academic degree in economics. This syllabus still did not enable me to settle on a clear direction, however.

2.2 MAKING THE CONTEMPORARY SENSE OF THE EARLY LEARNING KNOWLEDGE BASE

Main influence on Practice: Enabled me to establish a clearer foundation and focus for what I could bring to (coaching) practice from other established bases.

I had a lot of data, but I was still searching to make sense of it in the wider social context. I was still looking for a direction. It was time to appreciate how people choose a direction more formally!

I was fortunate (or made a choice without realising it!) to have ended up at a university that was interested more in practical knowledge than mere academic knowledge. I was invited to combine disciplines, to extend my interests by combining Economics and Psychology, because Economics was seen to be part of a wider whole of the social sciences. In particular, reference to Psychology enabled an appreciation of the major field of Individual Differences in organisational settings. This added important perspectives on the basics of knowledge available in the wider field.

I started with a Master's degree, in Applied Psychology. This enabled a first work at adding Knowledge to a practical context[5] and then ventured to a cross disciplinary Doctoral study[6] .

---

[5] Ridge, Jeremy. 1970. *The Role of Experience in Management Decision Making* - MSc in Applied Psychology. The University of Aston. (Available to download https://www.the-goodcoach.academy/)
[6] Ridge, Jeremy. 1975. *The Development and Operation of the Effective Interpersonal Relationship Skills relevant to Career Development Problems from Staff Assessment at an Industrial Research Laboratory –* PhD. The University of Aston. (Available to download https://www.the-goodcoach.academy/)

Summary of outcomes:

1. **Links to current Knowledge**: This enabled me to get at the current frontiers of where knowledge about the wider social sciences was up to.

2. **Rigorous Study and progressive testing of the use of my Knowledge** as both formal and learned (in a Doctorate) in a practical, operational context.

3. **Forming an articulate (to me anyway) basis for the knowledge** – Both personal as well as formal as a basis for my Practice.

2.3 RESEARCHING THE CONTEXT - ORGANISATIONS AND OPPORTUNITIES

Main influence on Practice: This entailed a focus on a particular context – the knowledge for how to approach the structures and language often involved in organisations on a wider basis (moving beyond the start provided from my Doctoral research). Which would let me both test and refine my strengths in practice.

The ultimate achievement involved in practice is the positive reaction created by circumstances I can create. The complexity of the context often involves important learning about the context, as you become involved (a form of careful research). This also hinges on the positive readiness of other people who might be involved to be attracted to opportunities rather than being unable to progress with where they had got to with the opportunities – hence why Coaching is attractive, rather than the more clinical, problem oriented approaches.

Summary of outcomes:

1. **Finding how others in the field go about similar activities in application**: In effect trying out various routes to contracting to add value (e.g. through commercial approaches). Employment in a role following my initial research/expanding to different organisations (such as management consultancy) and/or work at established business schools.

2. **Test and build methods for my preferred way to go about it**: I found that my learning about the foundations of practice added to what was being done by others. As well as learning where other approaches worked best compared to my own emerging preferred approaches.

3. **Researching how practice partnerships were important in providing more powerful approaches**: E.g. Working as a Practice Team, in team coaching, where my persona and knowledge could work well with some people, while other colleagues' personas were also more appropriate to others. It enabled an effective team approach.

2.4 REALISATION OF THE PRACTICE IN PARTICULAR OPERATIONAL TERMS - COMMERCIAL

Main influence on Practice: Once the learning about the context is tested and proved, my approach can be put to use – completing a cycle/cycles of combining Knowledge and Context knowledge from experience, to different operational contexts that met market demands.

This lead to the implementation of a more market oriented programme. I may present the product in a way that the client wants to hear. However, to me, I am still doing what I do no matter what it is called!

Summary of outcomes:

1. **Identifying, setting up and marketing set products based on Coaching**. For example, a particular approach to a Development Centre (compared to traditional Assessment Centres), which is similar to coaching, is enabling participants to lead and appreciate their own perspectives in/amongst a mix of colleagues/peers. It is possible to also add, where relevant, structures from other sources e.g. individual differences to increase awareness. Forming a coaching relationship with each participant separately and then integratively with others involved (e.g. in team-working).

2. **Forming and scaling up** teams to enable delivery of formally structured products based on Coaching e.g. Running programmes of Development Centres across large sections of organisations.

3. **Scaling of organisational interventions**: Seeing how formal structure for intervention created many other less formal opportunities for making contributions. Ones which required essential Coaching skills[7].

2.5 SCALING PRACTICE TO OTHER OPERATIONAL AREAS - COACHING COMMUNITIES

Main influence on Practice: My curiosity and experience of working with what others also bring took me forward to more Knowledge and other operational contexts. This created connections to others involved in similar operations of establishing a general practice of coaching.

This involved getting further appreciation of how others worked in the field and how the idea of community was evolving. There are still a wide range of forms of communities with Coaching in their title and focus. Likewise, the real challenge is the appreciation of the realities of practice that individual Practitioners really use – in practice. It is still a challenge to fit this all together.

---

[7] See *"How Coaching can contribute significantly to Mediation"* by Jeremy Ridge

Summary of outcomes:

1. **Researching a sample of various relevant communities.** I had joined as a member a range of bodies – even establishing myself as a 'Chartered Psychologist'. I took on a series of roles across different bodies as they clearly had different positions in the field which provided some mapping of the issues involved in getting greater connectedness between them.

   For example: Executive roles in a sample of relevant membership/aspiring professional bodies linked to getting the best out of people through particular attention in relationship behaviour: The ABP (Association of Business Psychologists), BPS SGCP (British Psychological Society Special Group in Coaching Psychology) and APECS (Association for Executive Coaching and Supervision). In some cases I was a founder member (ABP and APECS). Even with the BPS SGCP it was still in very early years.

2. **Testing various initiatives within these communities.** Executive roles can be primarily administrative, rather than leadership based. There were still opportunities for leadership through launching a range of project, and initiatives within these bodies. For example, with the approach to accreditation used in APECS.

3. **Scaling this understanding into my Practice in what I saw were priority areas - *the good coach*!** *the good coach* provides a clean opportunity to re-cast the approach to appreciating the realities of Coaching Practice, and create a different form of system for its clarification.

PART 3. CONCLUSIONS AND NEXT STEPS

I stated in Part 1, above, that this exercise was a start. And Part 2 lays down some foundations and consistent patterns about the identity or shape of the home that is my practice in Coaching.

Practitioner Research: Practice never stops learning and developing. It is the very nature of human life. It is a form of research. There is also the need to appreciate the context for any learning. It cannot take place in a vacuum. Research into one's practice, as practitioner research, can cover a wide subject area.

Identity, and my home, as well as my practice is a summation of my experience – It reflects its limitations, as well as its extent. It creates a shape, along with boundaries, that helps both myself and others become more aware of where we each stand and operate.

Coaching embraces a considerable complexity of what can be involved. I have found the opportunity of *the good coach* a good opportunity to try some sampling

PART 4: Moving forward, what next?

of bits of this complexity, and it has been valuable to have this opportunity to approach a next level of overall perspective. This is by no means final, however!

The intuition referred to in Kahn's table, above, is also, I believe something that can be researched and understood more explicitly for what it is and what it involves. This piece has helped give that a more overt shape. There is still more intuition to explore! For example:

- **The bigger picture perspective used here**. This is more like the current shape of the continents in the global picture! A lot more detail could be added to the level of shape chosen here. However it is also possible to get lost in the detail – not seeing the wood for the trees. This perspective, here, gives me a more connected view than the hectic pace of every day Practice can sometimes demand.

- **The Evidence base involved in this perspective**: What matters in this approach to reporting is the sense making it offers to me. I have plenty of detailed evidence in mind. It is another matter altogether to produce this in the still early forms available of formal evidence presentation. I'm mindful that the level of evidence presented here lacks some standards required in research elsewhere. However, research, in the more academic sense, can also lack the methodologies for creating practical meaning.

- **Finding the elusive Patterns of Practice can still be difficult for some**. I am aware how difficult it can be for many in the Coaching field to find patterns in their Practice. This does not mean they are not there. Rather it can be difficult to see the wood from the trees. This exercise has been useful to demonstrate some ways it may be possible.

- **Knowledge versus the Operational aspects of Practice**: The distinction between Knowledge and Operational aspects of Practice are a critical feature. The approach developed during the Doctoral Research, establishing confidence about the nature of the essential [personal] Knowledge Base, was designed well enough to enable a longer-term basis for Practice that has worked throughout.

- **The opportunities for establishing this idea of Community of Practice in Coaching:** I have found *the good coach* a very useful way of focusing on some of the current dilemmas for establishing Coaching to be as effective as it can be. It is more than reporting the wider picture of what others are doing – in practice. It is the way I believe we can extend what we are personally doing. A real approach to researching oneself with a degree of rigour that becomes instinctively more attractive to others when they see the chance to better meet the real person – or the real Coach!

Question: Can you see the value of sharing more of how you practice at a level of detail that speaks to your identity?

PART 4: Moving forward, what next?

Why should anyone be coached by me?

Alan Robertson

he good coach invited me to think more broadly and explicitly about how I coach and where that approach comes from. That's what *the good coach* is about. Though it would make this article a bit longer, I have some debts to acknowledge and that takes a bit of space and explanation.

New acquaintances can be disturbing. There was a time when I'd have kept them at arm's length for that reason, but these days – somewhat to my own surprise, but probably because I'm conscious that time is running out – I find that's part of their attraction. I've become more of a networker. People who work in the same domain can be particularly unsettling. Not so much when they introduce you to a new idea or author or approach, but when they say something that jolts your own thinking.

The editors (blogitors) of *the good coach* did so recently. They were reviewing my last blog. They liked it, I'm pleased to say, and they published it, but they all had a similar comment about it, *"I could infer how you managed to shift the conditions from one of resistance to opportunity. Perhaps in another blog you might share in more detail how you did that[1]."* A similar suggestion had been made about my earlier blogs.

More details about how I did it? Hmm... Even supposing that I could articulate an answer to that question, and perhaps if I turned my mind to it I could, I wondered if it would be an honest answer. At the time, in that particular coaching session that I had been describing, I wasn't using a piece of conscious technique. I was improvising. I was reacting to what was happening in the interaction in the moment.

I don't want to retro-fit explanations when I reflect on past coaching assignments. I'm not sure how much help that would be, either to me or to anyone else finding themselves in the fleeting moment of a similar situation

---

[1] Sue Young, The Good Coach, personal email correspondence.

in the future. But I'm also unsure whether that is a brutally honest response to the blogitors' invitation or simply an evasive one, so I'm going to endeavour to answer their question. How do I do it? What is my approach to coaching and where does it come from?

I have no formal qualification in coaching. That's quite a risky admission these days, when clients seem to be increasingly keen to screen prospective coaches on the basis of their formal qualifications. But I don't have one, and with 40 years' experience of working with people, I don't feel inclined to spend any time I might have left in acquiring one. I'll take my chance on personal referrals continuing to provide opportunities to coach.

In the absence of a particular school, course or qualification, I have no ready headline to describe my way of coaching. In any case I have something close to abhorrence toward being technique-driven or to subjecting people to pre-defined procedures. I find it de-humanising whenever I'm 'processed' and I try not to do it to others. It's the coachee as a unique individual who has to be the centre of attention, not whatever might be in the coach's rattle bag[2].

I take the view that the coachee is already in motion. It's my responsibility to catch up with them and their story, with where they're trying to go and how they're trying to get there, as they see it[3]. If I can do that, then there's some prospect that I might become a useful travelling companion for them for a while. I'm Dr Watson to their Sherlock Holmes. I endeavour to be helpful, but the coachee is the central character and the one who ultimately has to figure things out.

My approach to coaching is largely intuitive. Until I started blogging about it (and until those provocative blogitors started encouraging me to think about it even more explicitly), I hadn't realised just how much I rely on intuition. But what does that mean? I'd like to think that intuition is the mark of a quick, agile and penetrating mind, but we've already established that's Holmes' department and what we're trying to nurture in the coachee. I'm not sure you need it to be a good coach, although I'm sure it helps.

What I can't claim is that my mind feels invariably quick, agile and penetrating when I coach. On the contrary, much like the well-meaning but often slightly bewildered Dr Watson, I spend much of the time gradually uncovering things that might or might not be relevant, discussing them with the coachee, wondering what they might mean, and how they might be pieced together into something that the coachee is willing to take away and try and then to come back prepared to talk about until, between you, you've either made some progress with the coachee's issues or recognised that you can't.

---

[2] The Rattle Bag is the title of an anthology of personally inspiring poems compiled by the two great poets, Ted Hughes and Seamus Heaney
[3] I got the image of the coach having to catch up with the journey that the coachee is already on from James Flaherty's book, 'Coaching: evoking excellence in others', Butterworth-Heinemann, 1999

It's a puzzling process, literally and metaphorically. It's not tidy. It's iterative.

So I'm an intuitive (Myers Briggs INFJ, if anyone's interested). I've just done what intuitives do. I came up with an imaginative notion and pursued it to see where it might lead. I do that a lot when I coach. It's a way of opening up possibilities for the coachee to explore, a way of enabling them to step outside their existing pattern of thinking (often a source of stuckness) and consider their issues in a new light. However they are sensing and experiencing their reality, I'm confident that I can generate some alternative ways of looking at it. I don't expect these perspectives to provide or to be the answers, but rather to unlock and stimulate the coachee's way of thinking about and tackling their challenges.

I aim to generate a fresh sense of possibilities for thought and action.

But I can hear the blogitors in my mind's ear, "All right, Alan, but how do you actually do that?"

By talking. So let me squeeze one more insight out of Holmes and Watson and why I like them so much as an analogy for the coaching relationship. The two of them do a lot of talking. That's how they figure stuff out. And beyond the talking there's a world of action where the drama plays out to its conclusion. That's true for coaching too. But the talking is pivotal.

The point is that the sense of possibilities is not generated by me personally but by the conversation. The possibilities emerge spontaneously from the conversation that I'm having with the coachee, in the moment, as we're talking.

I have a particular fascination with talk. This might seem strange for an MBTI introvert and may deserve a blog of its own, but the more immediate point to explore here is the question of where I learned to use talk in the way that I do. There's no doubt in my mind that the way I talk is central to the way I coach.

I'm also inclined to believe that much of what we call intuition is actually past experience which has been very thoroughly assimilated into general principles about how to think and how to behave. Principles which have become automatic and function below the level of conscious awareness. So here, I think, I'm probing back in time to see how my way of talking was born from experience.

It started round the Robertson dining table when I was young. We talked a lot at meal times. My wife tells me it astonished her when she first came for a meal. In her family people ate at mealtimes. In mine we ate and talked. It's a miracle that we didn't all choke to death and my grown-up children still worry that I might. At my Father's table we reported on our day. We told stories and jokes. We quizzed each other and teased each other. We laughed a lot. It was a formative experience. It gave me the habit of listening to other people and enjoying what they have to say, of expecting and respecting differences of view and opinion. It taught me how to relate. It also showed me a way of getting over taking myself too seriously – an important lesson, because I've always been prone to that – and fortunately a lesson in which my own family continue to give me remedial classes.

My next lessons in how to hold productive conversations came at Oxford. I had the good fortune to be there as a history undergraduate and the even greater good fortune to be taught by two outstanding tutors, Harry Pitt and James Campbell. Sadly they're both dead now, but their teaching lives on in the way I coach.

At its best an Oxford tutorial is extraordinarily like a coaching session. Once a week two students, or sometimes in specialist subjects only one, have a dedicated hour with their don, the subject matter expert. The student brings the essay, his or her attempt to make sense of a question, reads it to the tutor and then engages in a deeper discussion of the topic. The student attempts to get to grips with the subject and with whatever other questions and issues arise.

One of the things you very quickly learn from studying history is that, as the saying goes, *'there is no such thing as history; there are only historians.'* There is no single, objective truth, only perspectives and interpretations, any of which can be maintained with great passion and commitment by its holder. It's a valuable lesson to take into working with people and life more generally.

Tutorials with Harry Pitt were lively affairs. Sixteen years before he started tutoring me he'd been fighting in the Battle of Normandy. He retained a young tank commander's relish for swivelling his aim towards the weakest part of your argument. It could have been learning by humiliation, but Harry ensured that it never felt like that. He engaged with you with great gusto, good humour and respect for your opinion, however strongly he held his own. "*Yes, but what do you make of this...*" "*I don't personally agree with you on that and here's why...*"

Harry treated you like an intelligent equal even when you clearly weren't and it was massively encouraging. You worked hard for Harry because you wanted to deserve the good opinion that he already seemed to have of you.

Tutorials with James Campbell were altogether more daunting. You worked hard for him because you didn't want to sound or feel idiotic as you presented your thinking and waited for his response.

James' capacity to listen and absorb what you were saying was phenomenal. Sometimes he would sit still while you were talking, but more commonly he was busy. Stoking, lighting and re-lighting his pipe, going over to his bookshelves to look something up, or fussing over his cats, all of which were named after Anglo-Saxon kings and queens. (I once had six kittens clambering over me while I was trying to read an essay). When you finished he'd say, "*Let me see if I've understood.*" "*What you seem to be saying is...*" He would then provide a detailed and lucid summary that was usually more articulate and finessed than the original. Then, because he generally started on a positive note, he'd say, "*Yes. That's quite good.*"There would be a pause. "*But...*" And he would then proceed to suggest various ways in which your analysis and conclusions might be questioned, re-examined and improved. The breadth and depth of his own scholarship was awe-inspiring, but he never used it to dominate his pupils. His intention always was to provoke you to push your own thinking harder and further. That's the development that he was looking to nurture and encourage from one week to the next.

I try to emulate my own tutors when I coach. Outside the formalities of tutorials both Harry and James were very personable, approachable, witty and entertaining. I used to lunch with James once a year during the last decade of his life and he never stopped being intensely interested in what you were doing and how you were thinking about what you were doing. He and Harry were wonderful role models for how to conduct conversations to enable others to think for themselves.

Trade union shop stewards were the next test and development for the talking skills that I use today. I became the Industrial Relations Manager in a heavily-unionised factory in a major international industry, at the unusually young age of twenty-seven. For nearly 2 years I'd witnessed my predecessor battling with the shop stewards. The relationships were terrible. The discussions, not only between management and unions but also among the different unions, were combative, distrustful, painfully protracted and too often unproductive.

I came into the job with a clear sense that my priority was to create more trust in the relationships and that the only way to do that was through a different way of talking. I remember announcing, in my first meeting in the chair, "*Industrial Relations in this factory are now under new management. There will be no more empty promises. And there will be no empty threats. I will do what I say I will do.*"Seeing it in print nearly 40 years later, it all sounds rather muscular and over-dramatic, and of course the shop stewards thought it was just another piece of empty managerial rhetoric. Time and experience showed them that I was prepared to stand by what I had said. They could trust that.

What I was calling for was plain speaking on both sides. I was also making the point that we don't just talk for the sake of talking; as far as I was (and still am) concerned the purpose of talking is to surface and resolve problems, to move things forward. The trade unions came to appreciate the immediacy, authenticity and value of that. Over a period of years the posturing and rhetorical displays gradually disappeared. Negotiations which had previously taken months came to be resolved first in weeks and then in days. We still had grievances, disputes, disagreements and occasional strikes, but we sorted them out.

The other lesson that industrial relations taught me was that what I had to say was only ever part of the process. Moving things forward is a collaborative activity. What the other party says and how they say it, the quality of how you listen to those things, how you choose to respond, and the nature of the dialogue that emerges from the interaction of all these different variables: these are all parts of what makes talk productive.

So I'd like to acknowledge the people who taught me how to listen when I was a young man, and an industrial relations manager, and, initially at least, over-endowed with self-assurance. Some of these people were my managers. Some were people who worked for me. Others were people I had to interview; some I hired and some I had to fire. I learned most from the shop stewards with whom I worked over a period of years, co-creating a new way of working together that contributed to us winning major industry awards on a regular basis and an enviable reputation for the quality of our industrial relations.

Thank you:

Joe, doggedly diligent as the convenor, probably the hardest job in industrial relations;

Angus, who'd stepped down but never ceased to counsel all sides to think clearly and act with moderation;

Jimmy, the radical who both charmed and was charmed by Margaret Thatcher when she visited the factory;

wee Geordie, who always folded his cap and sat on it to keep it warm when he came to meetings and earned respect by giving it;

big Hughie with the piratical grin and the missing teeth who always got straight to the point;

Jimmy who felt he hadn't done his job if he didn't start by making a demand that he knew you'd reject because you both understood that it was unreasonable;

Pearl who pushed her colleagues at least as hard as she pushed management and always towards making agreements;

Bobbie, the most open-minded, rational and productive of negotiators;

Tom, who understood the value of maintaining room to manoeuvre;

Jack and Tommy, the double-act whose anger over injustice was a force which served us all well.

I can still see your faces. I can still hear your voices. I can hear the different ways you spoke and spoke for others. I can still remember specifics from many of the high stakes conversations that we had. It wasn't your job to teach me. You set out to represent your people. What I learned from you was not just how to listen, but more importantly to appreciate how very different individuals can be, even when they are all ostensibly of a type or in the same role. You taught me how it takes time and patience, and the open-minded exchange of questions and views, to hear each other's uniqueness and individuality.

Auld Acquaintance is not forgot.

Now I'm going to close this piece as I started it, with reference to another relatively new acquaintance. The day before yesterday she too disturbed my equilibrium through something she said[4].She was telling me how she uses that phrase 'Why should anyone be led by you?' to encourage leaders that she is coaching to think deep and hard about what they bring to being a leader[5]. It prompted me to think that as a coach I have a similar responsibility to be able to answer the corresponding question, 'Why should you be coached by me?'

And that, it seems to me, is perhaps the question that *the good coach* is inviting us all to address, the question that I have been endeavouring to answer in this blog.

Of course, it is for the coachee to decide whether the answer feels satisfactory, but speaking for myself – and I can't claim to do any more than that – it has felt useful to set out a more clearly articulated answer for myself and for my prospective coachees to consider.

---

[4] Credit and thanks for this unexpected provocation go to Gwen Stirling of Seeds of Transformation.
[5] Goffee, Robert., and Gareth Jones. 2000. "Why should anyone be led by you?' In *Harvard Business review*.

PART 4: Moving forward, what next?

Making sense of what I do, how my coaching practice is taking shape

Yvonne Thackray

My coaching practice has evolved over time to focus on working directly with coaching practitioners:

1. Who are engaged in continually building and developing their own personal knowledge base that's integral to their business practice by understanding what it is they're delivering to their clients (with a level of certainty), and

2. Who are interested in contributing their personal knowledge to a growing body of practitioner knowledge in the field of coaching for their communities, and society, more generally.

MY ASSUMPTIONS AND OUTLINE OF AN APPROACH

To make sense of what I do and how it's evolved, I have developed my understanding by inverting the best practices used to report on research (commonly used across all disciplines) which can be described as follows,

- Making sense of the outcomes from my practice (the impact), which

- Draws upon my own experiences as a practitioner (the results/data), and

- Checking out my experiences, and influences, with others (literature and/or peer review), that leads to

- Understanding how I've gone about doing what I do (the methodology), to then

- Making adjustments/refinements within my practice and see whether the outcomes are aligned with those changes, and then the cycle begins again.

I'm still in the early stages of this process. This is because the frameworks available in our field are insufficient and inadequate (compared to other established disciplines and professions). Any information that is currently available rests on very narrowly defined boundaries and conditions, which has been extrapolated beyond its useful limits as a form of explanation. Information which could then work across a multitude of contexts and scenarios. In my opinion, there is still so much to learn, experience and understand. As a field, we're still developing a language. We have not yet agreed to definitions that get to a level of understanding and detail of what's really happening and which consistently deliver robust results.

Importantly, it's the practitioner who has continuously found ways to deliver their approach to coaching to their market (which even academics/researchers have difficulties accessing), and have a business that's ultimately being validated by its longevity in the market. They are the real researchers.

My practice revolves around understanding how they realize their practice by helping them share their experiences, their patterns of behaviours, and their approaches in their natural language. The impact of my approach can be seen by both the quantity and quality (see criteria) of blog-articles published on *the good coach* (a repository) that respects individual differences (diversity) in such an inclusive field.

For me, this is what practitioner research is and should represent. Eventually these reports (blog-articles shared from practitioner experiences) can then help inform and build consensus towards best-practice (standards), even principles (ethics), which have been proven to work across a multitude of situations and contexts (profession) and better supports practitioners professionally. This is the desired future... Meanwhile, let me share how I want to contribute to this.

MAKING SENSE OF HOW I HAVE BEEN SHAPING MY PRACTICE

Without a familiar and recognisable structure, it can be challenging to see what my practice is. Especially when it is generally interpreted to mean how I practice my business rather than how I practice coaching. Both are important because they are strongly linked; they represent the necessary cycles of understanding between the market opportunities for the service provided (the impact) and the robustness of the service delivered (the how) that can then lead to further market opportunities.

How I shape my practice, the way I'm using it here, can currently be described as working at two levels. At the external level, it's more around how observers see what it is I am doing which has some recognisable outlines that forms a shape that make sense to them. The other internal level is more personal. It is how I access data, process it and then make decisions. What I have learnt so far is how my coaching is being shaped through the decisions I made as part of my business practice (that included many peer conversations) which is beginning to be recognised by others.

What I share next are my top three drivers that have consistently been shaping my practice:

1. **A conscious choice was made early on in my practice to choose to work with clients with whom I could deliver my best services to and not to be a one-size fits all type of practitioner**. I realised quickly on, at the beginning of my practice which I call the testing phase, that I work better with independent, mature healthy individuals who are already mapping out their journey to live a more successful and fulfilling life, however they choose to define and measure it. I also understood my limitations. I wouldn't be able to work with everyone on anything because not everything would be fulfilling or make the best use of my strengths.

2. **I have a personal preference to continue my learning whilst working with clients, which helps me to continuously engage in my research enquiry around the field for coaching.** My clients have also decided for themselves how my coaching approach will help them to support them in the myriad ways they go about creating their future. This may never be fully articulated, more an implicit awareness and understanding, yet quality partnerships are being developed. Partnerships in which all parties involved are receiving value from realising this potential in different ways and with growing confidence and clarity.

3. **My practice has also been driven around my curiosity for understanding how the standards purported in coaching haven't evolved or developed since the inception of self-appointed bodies and their related training schools**. There is a real gap between what I understood to be a professional used in other functional disciplines like engineering, law, medicine, compared to how it's currently being used in coaching.

   Being a professional invokes degrees of trustworthiness that any 'registered practitioner' will deliver the best practice to their clients packaged in the works contracted for ethically. They should regularly demonstrate, evidence and self-report to agreed standards and criteria in their accumulated working experience. Periodic training and relevant academic education is also important in order to maintain a recognised standing in society for the profession the coach represents.

   These standards and criteria have been extracted from the current body of knowledge from which other professions rely on and confidently refer to. They do so having been rigorously tested and proven in various scenarios and contexts to consistent results.

PART 4: Moving forward, what next?

In coaching it seems that 'being a professional' refers more to the business models used to meet populist market trends. This is because we lack a coherent and robust body of knowledge. One which any practitioner's practice can both build upon and contribute to that meets a fundamentally growing societal need in the market place.

ASSESSING THE WIDER COACHING MARKET AS PART OF MY PRACTICE

My interest in the field and market, and how I choose to practice, has stemmed from one simple yet open-ended question, 'What is coaching?' It seemed natural that the first port of call to find answers to my questions was by attending institutions that were deemed to be reputable in delivering the requisite programmes. The added bonus being that after completing their program work would be available (once you have worked out your niche).

I attended a handful of institutions in different parts of the world in the hope of finding the answer. It was quite an initial investment that I thankfully recouped through alternative means. Over and over in my investigations, each of the coaching organisations (training schools, academic institutions and conference providers) provided a general description of coaching that fitted the skills training model they were delivering. That model is fundamental to all the different stages of individual development in how to use it. Furthermore it can easily be adapted to various market opportunities because it operates at a level of generality.

A useful (and seemingly expensive) starting point to understand where the market is reported to be, is that coaching is the sum of your experiences of using proprietary coaching models!

More recently, in some of the latest publications, such as 'The Sage Handbook of Coaching[1]' – the proposed 'Go-To Academic Resource' – the editors shared some of their opinions in their Introduction of where they see the field heading,

> "... the demand for coaching services may continue to be strong for a very long time to come, albeit perhaps with more individualistic, industrialised societies where traditional social structures are less evident. Whatever the case, the ability of practitioners to deliver valued services will rest upon the existence of a rich and texted knowledge base that can provide good and relevant guidance for practitioners." (pg 4)

> "... it should be noted that this book is nor primarily focused on advancing the professionalization of coaching. Rather its primary aim is to stimulate the development of the knowledge base for coaching, thereby making a contribution to further establishing coaching as an applied discipline. As

---

[1] Bachkirova, Tatiana., Gordon Spence and David Drake. 2017. *The SAGE Handbook of Coaching.* SAGE Publications. Ltd. https://us.sagepub.com/en-us/nam/the-sage-handbook-of-coaching/book245418#description Accessed September 12.

such, this Handbook requires no unified definition of coaching, irrespective of how desirable that might be in principle [it provides readers (usually practitioners) with an early indication of the author's view on the fundamental question: What is coaching?]" (pg 5)

"...the intention of this Handbook is to provide graduate students, scholars, and researchers with a premier point of contact with the current theoretical and empirical knowledge base [through the use of rigorous scientific methods] along with many of the established and emerging debates in the scholarly literature." (pg 1)

"Despite the explicit academic orientation of this book (concerned with mapping the field and critiquing the knowledge base), many authors seemed to be naturally orientated towards addressing the needs of practitioners, through recommendations for practice, rather than stimulating the creation of knowledge through thoughtful analysis of the literature and recommendations for future research." (pg 18)

"Until a reasonable way of conceptualising coaching is proposed, the onus will continue to fall to researchers to provide clear descriptions of the coaching intervention they study, in order for their findings to be comparable to others." (pg 7)

The conclusions shared so far didn't satisfy my curiosity. They do however provide a map, a vision even, of where these experts see the field moving towards. Also, my list of questions kept growing and seemed to be outpacing the information that was being shared. The questions I'm currently holding are more focused on how coaching is really being addressed in the market. For example,

- **I realised that I am better working with certain individuals at different stages of their learning and development than with everyone.** Why isn't this addressed in any of the training or published media? How does andragogy and the stages of development fit in with coaching? How do you know when to pass clients onto other coaches who would be better suited working with them? How do coaches talk more confidently about what it is they are doing? How do you appreciate individual differences and learn to access the client's world through their use of language to explain what it means in their everyday context?

- **Accepting my services is one of the many contributions that is part of the clients' schema.** Is there a bias/overconfidence in how significant the coach's contribution has been to the client in reaching their solution? When is it appropriate to be using ROI? How are those contributions really being measured? How do coaches more accurately talk about their contributions? How much do coaches understand regarding their clients' real intentions for coaching? How often are coaches recontracting? Does age matter? How do coaches talk about the quality of coaching they deliver as the sum total of all their learnt experiences to date?

- **It's my responsibility to create and sustain the conditions for building the trust and rapport at the level of the client's readiness, the real contracting.** How is this really being measured? How aware is the coach of their behaviours and reactions to what's been shared and impacts on how the client responds? How do we assess the level of readiness of the client to participate in coaching? How reliable are chemistry meetings? How much should be disclosed as part of creating the conditions for engagement? How much working knowledge of the client's context is important in getting access to them? What are the real 'power' dynamics in any coaching conversation? How do you decipher and select the right phrases and words to unlock further meaning behind the client's context? How do you make those connections that are most meaningful in their context that lets the client know that you're listening?

The real knowledge, a term that itself needs to be debated in our field, should be and contribute to a two-way street to learning and development. It should inspire dialogue, critical thinking and meaningful action which impact and influence an individual's confidence, maturity and independence to practice coaching. Nevertheless, there are different developmental stages to learning. Hence each of these organisations do fulfil a service for different segments of society.

Overall, it would seem that the key contributors have reached a plateau in terms of their real contributions to the field and in their carving out of what authority, or guidance, should lie in ensuring practitioners deliver good practice. For example, I have had to look elsewhere for answers and I completed a Master's in Social Anthropology to investigate coaching identity.

HOW MY COACHING PRACTICE IS TAKING SHAPE

I've developed and grown my specialism (or niche if you prefer) in, and around, coaching. The real knowledge lies with the real experts, the practitioners,

- who are doing it day in day out (regardless of whether they call it coaching or not),
- in their chosen practice to supports others, and themselves,
- to be better at what it is they want to continue achieving even more confidently whether in their professional and/or personal lives.

It's quite radical, and still a long way to go for it to be acknowledged as the norm, for individuals to request PROFESSIONAL help that focuses on improving the quality of life - living to our potential both personally and professionally. In addition, having access to considered written material, that is readily available to those who are interested in or curious about what coaching is, is limited with the current politicking in our field.

My role as a coach is to help access those experiences (whether through conversations, writing or in combination) and help make them more readily available. Hence the nature and the shape of my practice, where my target audience (as the lingo goes) is mature practitioners of coaching. Ones who can recognise the benefits of honestly reporting on their experiences and sharing their learning for both themselves and with other stakeholders, including, but not limited to, other practitioners, peers, communities, the coaching field, curious individuals and society itself.

Mutual benefits are being shared through this contract, and what I have learnt so far coaching coaches, or applying my coaching approach working with practitioners, include:

1. **Understanding further the contexts and cognitive patterns of each practitioner.** Each of the practitioners I work with have their own unique styles and ways of operating in their practice. It is important that I do not make assumptions of what it is they are saying, that may or may not match their actions or behaviour, without any clear reference points or facts. Otherwise, this results in inferring what's being said rather than understanding what is actually being shared in their context.

    That is why when I participate in any conversation, verbally or as part of the writing process, I feel fortunate to be a part of their learning process because they are sharing their cognitive patterns of how they make sense of what it is they are doing within their practice. My approach to coaching, in both cases, begins with [1] appreciating their level of readiness and [2] where they want to take the conversation/theme that supports them in their practice.

    These are some of my indicators for what I perceive to be of maturity and independence exhibited within a coaching practitioner. They have decided what they want to focus on and carry through onto paper that explains in various detail, and breadth, their practice. With every iteration of working with each practitioner, there is measured growth and development. This is observed in the number of ways. Each practitioner then uses their blog-articles as part of their business development.

PART 4: Moving forward, what next?

2. **Delivering my actions with care and consideration to build both respect and trust.** Once I begin to grasp their language and meaning making that they are sharing through their words and approach to structuring, I begin to hypothesise further their motivations and intention. What it is they are looking to share in their latest piece. I begin to ask more succinct and hopefully poignant questions (whilst also sharing where I've come from to make such a question) that helps them to consider and clarify that what they have said is actually what it is they are wanting to share.

3. **Appreciating different topics of interest, commitments and their motivation to find ways to continue their learning and development.** No one practice is the same because we are each working at different leading edges. Spending the time to talk and write about what is currently most important to them in their practice, and that they then continue to share in those pieces on a more regular basis informs me that this approach to coaching is working for them.

   This is really an important part of, the ongoing contracting I have with them. Importantly, they are continuing to find novel ways to challenge themselves in how they want to talk about their experiences and share their learnings from their practice, and that I can continue to add value too. After all, coaching is a two-way street.

4. **Learning from others - mapping out the diversity.** Having this opportunity to both work and learn from others has allowed me to continue my broader research topic of 'what is coaching?' I am just one practitioner amongst many, and I'm certain that I'll never have the same exact experiences as others, but situations might occur where similarities may emerge and so we can learn from others. I have also expanded on my own vocabulary. It also allows for a more collective voice to be shared, as evidenced in various publications, that begins to extend in detail and expand in scope a more inclusive and sophisticated mapping of diverse coaching practices.

WHERE NEXT?

As I shared and outlined at the start of my piece, I am still at the beginning of understanding what my coaching practice is really about. I am more comfortable and focussed in exploring, and comparing, in more detail the first three parts (impact, results, literature & peer review) in making sense of how my practice is forming its shape against other known parameters.

I'm continually dipping in and out of building, deepening and, even in many cases acknowledging, those awareness's and learning how to talk about it more explicitly as part of my practice.

Reflecting on where next,

- **I am still developing my explanations of what it is I am doing in my practice, and what I've shared here are really the outlines and key themes of my practice which can be expanded on, for sure, more considerably.** I have written elsewhere some pieces on these themes as part of my learning and development, and only now starting to integrate those thoughts of how it influences my approach to practice.

- **I'd probably say that what I've shared is still quite general i.e. it doesn't have that specificity that allows others to reproduce what it is that I'm doing in their own way.** As I shared earlier, I currently have simple metrics that informs me that what I am doing currently works, and I feel that it is through collaboration with peers that I'll be able to begin to become more explicit in what I'm doing.

- **I'll still continue reading, and learning from others how their thoughts and explanations compare to my experiences.** This is how I learn and adapt what has worked for others and bring it into my approach because it lends itself to my practice. Working with peers, whether in a team and/or as individuals, will continue to help me better articulate my methodology which in turns help me better serve my clients.

I appreciate that what I've shared will make sense to some, more than others, and for sure this is just one of the many ways to talk about the shape of our practice. I've covered some core principles and key learnings that mark the foundation of my practice, and how it's perceived to be recognisable in a normal market place. Furthermore, I continue to enjoy recognising how my identity is intertwined with what I do in coaching, and how important it is to acknowledge those biases as part of my sharing (rather than leaving them out).

I'm curious, "How would you begin describing the shape of your practice?"

PART 4: Moving forward, what next?

Epilogue
Coaching Conference
Laci Ritas

Right this is going to be
Really interesting;
The theme of
Practitioner Research.
It's good to see
This theme be so
Up front...

Arriving...
The women smooth
Around; smiling,
Exchanging pleasantries
Well groomed, contemporary
Mainly of a certain age.
Confidently in charge.
This is their ground.
Fewer men,
Again of a certain age
Not so smart casual;
The uniform of the
Academic and liberated
Professional man -
Casual trousers, open shirt
And jumper...
Style Jeremy Corbyn-ish

About 70 people
In the large room
Setting the scene.
Session introducer
Waxing on about the excitement -
How this was so innovative...

In to the keynote speaker
To set the tone for the day;
Declared himself proudly
As somewhat of
a revolutionary.
The coaching bodies

PART 4: Moving forward, what next?

Both come across as
Positively oppressive.
Then proceeded to
Tell us about his
Vast in depth knowledge
And opinions...!

For coaching
The importance of critical thinking
And challenge.
The approach of the bodies;
Competencies based -
Reductionist to over-simple -
Is barking up the wrong tree.
Then proceeds to eruditely
Draw on a lot of theories
From Aristotle onwards
And jargon words,
Just to demonstrate
How the current models
Fall short.
Professionalism is obviously
A dirty word meaning
'You must do
This, That and the Other..'

His rigour - he knows what
He's talking about.
There's lots of nodding
In the room.

Says the context
Is crucial to coaching
That's never acknowledged.
A highly relevant point,
Yet never expands.
Awaiting his pointers to the future
They never come...
The Emperor in his new Clothes
Parading before us.

PART 4: Moving forward, what next?

When somebody observes
"There is certainly narrowness
In current interpretations
Of that word 'professionalisation',
But isn't it a real issue
That coaching needs to address
In perhaps a different interpretation
Of what it means?"
He ducks and weaves,
Saying something feeble
Like he finds that
He draws on very
different things in
Coaching sessions...

Then in to a series
Of speaker led sessions...
Practitioners doing
research projects
As part of Doctorate projects
And how they've
Gone on to
Turn it to commercial advantage.
Or academics talking
About themes; hiding
Behind general language,
And jargon and
Personal pet theories.
No real interest in
Sharing experience
and gaining insight
into perspectives
other than their own.

All frameworks and models;
No real practitioner experience
Of researching their own practice.
No real definition of terms.
Where is the client's Voice?

PART 4: Moving forward, what next?

Where is the practitioners
True Voice about the realities
Of day to day practice?

No space in sessions
Given to real
Exchange and discussion
About Practice.
Academics and students
Talking on and on;
No real discourse,
or practitioner research
even!

Is this really the
Leading Edge of
Coaching practitioner research?!
The individual practitioner
Or their client
is nowhere.
And they call this a
Coaching Conference?!

I wonder
Was the real purpose
To showcase,
To sell more
professional doctorates?

PART 4: Moving forward, what next?

Laci Ritas's poem, 'Coaching conferences' sums up succinctly where the academic field is currently. This informs us that there is still a lot to do; wonderful opportunities for the field of practitioners to engage in through their experiences and research. *the good coach* approach reflects, and represents, this intention and opportunity. We're not in a rush because we appreciate that this is a long term project. We're more interested in finding those patterns that may eventually lead to similarities that have evolved from the realities of the diverse practice that already exists.

We hope that after reading our third book - whether it's in your private space sitting in your favourite seat, or as part of a discussion group with peers as part of an in-house exploration or with a group of like-minded individuals, or simply with others around you – it has motivated you to start sharing your own experiences as a form of practitioner research through blogging.

As you've witnessed there isn't one way to do this, and so tailor your blogs to begin with what's most important to you right now in your practice, and begin exploring how you like to make sense of your coaching approach. And then, enjoy sharing your leading edges and personal knowledge bases with the wider community with the support of *the good coach*. To begin stimulating some ideas check out the Blogger's Guidelines that is available to read both on the website: http://the-goodcoach.com/the-guidelines and towards the end of Translating Coaching Codes of Practice, or even connect with one of the blogitors at *the good coach* (email: blogs@the-goodcoach.com) to begin a conversation about what you'd like to take as your first step.

What we do know is this – the real knowledge lives where everyday practitioner practices. We just have to keep finding ways to get to it. Share with us how we can do it better.

CONTRIBUTOR'S BIOGRAPHY

Organized alphabetically

Alan Robertson is Director of Business Cognition Ltd, co-creator of VoicePrint and a senior visiting teaching fellow at both Cranfield University and the Cass Business School in London. Scottish by birth, upbringing and temperament, Alan's working life is committed to helping individuals be simultaneously independent-minded and collaborative, capable of thinking for themselves and working effectively with others. He loves to make a useful difference for people.

Email: alan@businesscognition.co.uk
Website: https://letstalk.voiceprint.global
Linkedin: https://www.linkedin.com/in/alan-robertson-11010414/
—----------

Aubrey Rebello brings to the table over 40 years of rich & varied Corporate Experience as CEO, Director, and Business Head with Tatas & Bayer. He has strategised and managed a major merger, was CEO of a large NBFC, and Profit Centre Head of a large Business. In all his assignments he has rapidly scaled up revenues & profits. In many areas he has also built up Structures & Processes from scratch. Post retirement Aubrey continues as an Advisor to a Tata Company. Aubrey is also an Executive Coach to several Indian and Foreign Corporates. He is also an expert in Family managed Businesses serving as a Business Consultant and Mentor to Business Families. Having had Leadership Roles in different work Areas & Industries. Aubrey's expertise is in Financial Services, Automobile Industry, Mergers & Integration, Materials Management, and Learning & Development. He is also a Certified Executive Coach - International Coach Federation & NEWS Switzerland. He has several hundred hours of coaching experience at the MD & CXO levels.

Email: aubrey_rebello@rediffmail.com
Linkedin: https://www.linkedin.com/in/aubrey-rebello-b166404a

Aurora Aritao is an organizational leadership consultant and executive coach who believes in the value of developing reflective and effective change agents in organizations. She brings 15 years of corporate experience in tech product marketing, leading cross-cultural teams while defining, launching and growing award-winning technology solutions for companies like Optus (AU) the Vodafone Group (Global) and Microsoft (HK). Her training in clinical organizational psychology at INSEAD (EMCCC) reflects her passion for deeply understanding organizational behavior and the interrelationship between personality, leadership style, culture, and organizational decision-making. Aurora also facilitates leadership training for the NeuroLeadership Institute and AchieveForum.

Email: aurora.aritao@insead.edu
LinkedIn: https://hk.linkedin.com/in/auroraaritao
Website: the-goodcoach.com

—----------

Chris Paterson is a husband, father, executive coach and founder of a charity. Coaching has changed his life for the better and through coaching he has discovered his purpose in life is to grow leaders by supporting others to discover for themselves. After 20 years working for large multinationals, he has set up his own coaching and facilitation business, SmileBeCurious Ltd. The fact that being a coach allows Chris to learn about himself and the world whilst being useful for others is a wonderful sweetspot. Chris has a fascination for the application of coaching techniques in all walks of life.

Email: smilebecurious@gmail.com
Website: http://associationforcoaching.site-ym.com/members/?id=49244240
Linkedin: https://uk.linkedin.com/in/smilebecurious

—----------

Claire Sheldon has over 20 years' experience as an executive coach and facilitator. Having labelled herself 'an intuitive coach', her curiosity about what that might mean triggered an MA dissertation. Her research breaks new ground, clarifying how coaches talk about and use their intuition. She uses her model, Working at the Boundary, to support her work as a coach – and to help coaches and supervisors draw on their own intuition with elegance and wisdom.

Email: claire@thetallhouse.co.uk
Website: www.tallhouseconsulting.co.uk

Dino Laudato has 20+ years' experience of delivering business critical services and leading large teams with global reach and presence at GSK. He has extensive experience of living and operating in the diverse cultures of the Middle East, Continental Europe, the UK and USA. For the past 5 years, he has worked as an internal coach in GSK helping individuals and high-performing teams to achieve their business needs and performance improvements. Coaching is a way of enhancing leadership capabilities creating high performing and resilient teams by providing a space to think. This ignites his passion for watching people to develop into the best leaders they can be.

Email: dino.laudato@awareness-coaching.com
Website: http://www.awareness-coaching.com/

—----------

Doug Montgomery (PhD, APECS Executive Coach, ICF PCC) is an executive coach and coach supervisor, coach training facilitator, mentor coach and ILM coaching and mentoring tutor. Doug developed his leadership skills in increasingly senior roles over 28 years in pharmaceutical R&D at GlaxoSmithKline. Doug's coach training started while at GSK and led to becoming a Director of Coaching at GSK's Coaching Centre of Excellence. He left GSK to set up Elmbank Coaching and fulfil his passion for coaching and supporting the personal and professional development of leaders, sportsmen and fellow coaches.

Email: doug@elmbank-coaching.co.uk
Website: www.elmbank-coaching.co.uk
Linkedin: Doug Montgomery

—----------

Geoffrey Ahern is experienced in executive coaching and sustainability. APECS accredited and working independently for the past decade, he has been a Fellow of the Centre for Leadership Studies, University of Exeter and before that was employed for five years as an executive coach by Coutts Consulting Group. After 2008 he carried out multinational corporate consultation on sustainability in association with the World Wildlife Fund/IUCN and became an Honorary Lecturer in sustainability at the University of Liverpool's Management School. He has published widely including a second edition of the book of his PhD (LSE 1981) on an ecologically-oriented global movement.

Email: geoffrey@geoffreyahernconsulting.com.
Website: geoffreyahernconsulting.com

Ian Flanders (a pseudonym, to protect the colleagues he coaches) is a senior manager and internal coach in a European manufacturing organisation. He is also a PhD student, researching how internal coaches experience their role.

———----------

Isobel Gray is an OD Consultant and Executive Coach. She writes poetry in her spare time. "I started writing poetry about 5 years ago. My first poem was a spontaneous outpouring of thoughts and feelings the day we chose to have our beloved cat put to sleep when the vet discovered that she had advanced stages of cancer. And it grew from there, so she left me a very special legacy. I write poems on a range of themes - nature, people, and Life, including organisational life, which my work provides very privileged access to. I find it an earthing and liberating form of creative expression.

Email: isobeligray@gmail.com
Website: https://the-goodcoach.com/the-bloggers#/isobel-gray/

———----------

Jeremy Ridge (Dr.) (BSc Econ, MSc Applied Psychology, PhD) has been in practice through a number of stages in providing attention to people and their development. Jeremy began with research into Organisational Behaviour (PhD); and then developed a Business / Practice designing and leading 'Development Centres' as a key mechanism for organisational change and development, with a range of large international organisations. This work naturally lead to a wider interest in the field. Jeremy has also worked with a number of professional bodies in executive positions, for example Chair of APECS (Association of Executive Coaching and Supervision).

Email: jeremyridge@mac.com
Website: https://the-goodcoach.com/the-bloggers#/jeremy-ridge/

———----------

Julian Danobetia

Email: julian@downthecorridor.com
Website: www.downthecorridor.com

Katy Tuncer is the APECS accredited Executive Coach and former McKinsey consultant who founded Horizon37. Her services include: Individual and Team Coaching, Strategy-led Facilitation, Leadership Training Courses, Workshops and Seminars. Katy has devoted her career, since joining The British Army 20 years ago, to discovering and examining what works in leadership. Her experience spans McKinsey, small professional services firms, the Metropolitan Police, tech start-ups and community movements. She has led transformations in hugely diverse organisations – as an executive, a board member, an advisor and a founder. She has innovated, failed, succeeded, and challenged convention in leadership. And she has bolstered her personal learning through her role as a trusted coach to senior leaders – sharing and analysing their unique leadership journeys. Katy works out what each client needs to perform outstandingly, and to achieve sustainable satisfaction in their work. In periods of new challenge she bring practical, tailored and business-led leadership.

Email: info@horizon37.co.uk
Website: www.horizon37.co.uk
Linkedin: www.linkedin.com/in/katytuncer

—----------

K C Char has held leadership positions in international organizations for many years. For the last 15 years, KC has applied this experience to advise, consult and coach senior leaders and their teams. KC's work draws from this rich experience, challenging clients to stretch themselves and find their edge, and effectively lead their people to perform at their best.

—----------

Larissa Conte is a leadership coach, rites of passage guide, and org transformation designer through her business, Wayfinding. She specializes in facilitating transformation and alignment across scales to foster power that serves. With deep experience in the energetics and mechanics of transformation, Larissa helps clients develop inner listening, shed what no longer serves, and navigate from their center, so they can more skillfully steward creative energy in their life and companies. Her work weaves 10+ years of experience in the diverse fields of leadership coaching, organizational culture consulting, ecosystems science, ceremony design, and holistic healing. She's worked with hundreds of leaders across startups and the Fortune 100, and is based in San Francisco.

Email: larissa@wayfinding.io
Website: wayfinding.io
Linkedin: www.linkedin.com/in/larissaconte/

Laurent Terseur is a former senior executive with a genuine care for people and over two decades senior experience in multi-cultural, highly competitive corporate environments, first as a group treasurer in pharmaceuticals and manufacturing, then in sales and leadership roles in the corporate and investment banking divisions of Deutsche Bank, JP Morgan and Barclays. Laurent is an APECS Accredited Executive Coach and an ICF Professional Certified Coach. He coaches individuals and teams, English as well as French native speakers. His practice integrates insights from cognitive neurosciences and systemic coaching, and is informed by his track record in building highly collaborative and effective teams, his business acumen, and his multi-faceted understanding of matrix organisations.

Email: laurent.terseur@gmail.com
Website: https://the-goodcoach.com/the-bloggers#/laurent-terseur/
Linkedin: www.linkedin.com/in/ltecd

—----------

Lilian Abrams (Ph.D., MBA, PCC) is an organizational psychologist with over 20 years of Fortune 50 consulting experience, in all manner of organization and leadership development areas as well as applied research. She is a highly experienced, accredited, senior executive coach (ICF, APECS), and is now in progress towards receiving Coach Supervision accreditation from the EMCC. She works with leaders of all types, and most often with leaders of multi-cultural, high-achieving/potential, women, and/or technical backgrounds (e.g., Finance, R&D, IT, Engineering, etc.) Client organizations include ADP, BASF, BMS, HSBC, Invesco, KPMG, MetLife, MOMA, Warby-Parker, Sanofi, Times Mirror, New York Presbyterian/Weill/Cornell/ Columbia Hospital, UTC, Unilever, and the US FAA, and others. As Board Member and Education Chair for New Jersey Organization Development (NJOD) Learning Community, she facilitated mutual learning to bridge the gap between academia and practice. Lilian has taught graduate-level leadership and research methods topics at numerous universities over the past two decades, and continues to teach, publish, and serve, always seeking to learn and bring the right learning to the right people at the right time.

Email: labrams@abramsandassociatesllc.com
Website: www.abramsandassociatesllc.com
LinkedIn profile: Dr. Lilian Abrams

Lisa W. Haydon is a Certified Executive Coach and the owner of Pivotal Coaching. Through Pivotal Coaching, she focuses on enabling companies and professionals to realize growth, transformation and strategic goals. Key areas of client services include leadership development and business development coaching. The Pivotal Coaching relationship incorporates programs, methodology and outcome measurements that guide targeted development for growth and results. Lisa brings to her work with clients nearly 30-years' corporate experience in coaching, leadership, strategy, teaming, clients, change, revenue growth, and helping people succeed.

Email: lisahaydon@pivotalcoachingservices.com
Website: https://www.pivotalcoachingservices.com/
Linkedin: https://www.linkedin.com/in/lisahaydon/
———-------—

Liz Hill-Smith is an APECS certified executive coach and organisational leadership and change consultant. She creates the mental space for her clients to open new perspectives, flourish and succeed. Having been a specialist in leadership, change, organisation development and strategic thinking for over 20 years, Liz is passionate about enabling leaders to develop empowering and transformative mindsets, often using constellations based approaches to create transformations in thinking and insight.

———----------

Dr. **Lucille Maddalena** is an Executive Coach, Leadership Trainer, and Consultant in Organization Development. Best known for her work supporting Senior Executives during career and business transitions, she guides the alignment of team goals with expectations by bridging interpersonal communication with practical business management. As a key part of global leadership initiatives, she has created coaching models for clients, functioning as Master Coach to identify and manage Leadership Coaches at regional sites. She has guided over 6,000 corporate executives at Fortune 100 firms to successfully advance in their careers during times of organization change. She holds a Doctorate in Education with an interdisciplinary major in Human Communications and Labor Education. Working with Senior Leaders and their teams she is recognized for her commitment to build engagement and trust within all levels of the organization.

Email:lucille@mtmcoach.com
Website: www.mtmcoach.com

Luis San Martin is Founding Chair of the Association for Coaching in Spain and sits on the editorial advisory board of The International Journal for Mindfulness & Compassion at Work. He brings an exceptional business experience to his work as executive coach and organisational development consultant which includes CEO responsibilities in multinational companies in several countries. His business career background spans more than 20 years in the UK, Spain and South America working for companies such as McGraw-Hill, Thomson Reuters and Grupo Santillana (PRISA Group). He works internationally and is passionate about working with people as he believes that everyone can continue developing themselves beyond their own expectations. Luis is bilingual in English and Spanish and works in both languages.

Email: luis@thecoachingquality.com
Website: www.thecoachingquality.com
Linkedin - https://www.linkedin.com/in/luis-san-martin-81818741/

—----------

Lynne Hindmarch (MSc, MA, APECS) is a business psychologist who works as an executive coach and coaching supervisor. Her practice also includes team building, career counselling and assessment for selection. She has over 25 years' experience of psychometric profiling, and is qualified in a wide range of assessments, which she uses to help clients increase their self-awareness. She has published papers, articles and book chapters on a range of subjects including self-doubt, self-efficacy, coaching and power and the use of psychometrics in coaching. Her background is in counselling, higher education, training and development in organisations, and consultancy. She is Co-Chair of The Psychometrics Forum.

Email: lhindmarch@obc.org.uk
Website: www.obc.org.uk
Linkedin: www.linkedin.com/in/lynne-hindmarch-76a60b7/?ppe=1

Margaret Chapman-Clarke (CPsychol, AFBPsS, CSci) is a psychologist, mindfulness researcher, writer and gestalt coach and first to call for a turn to autoethnography; which she describes as 'an integrative, mindful and transpersonal approach that puts the human back into our scholarship and practice in coaching.' Described as a 'true pioneer' in coaching, Margaret has worked with the All Party Parliamentary Group on 'Making the business case for mindfulness; spoken nationally and internationally on emotional intelligence, positive psychology, resilience and published the first evidence-based text on mindfulness in the workplace (Kogan Page, 2016). She has a particular interest in reflexive, creative and expressive writing in coaching and for wellbeing.

Email: mc@eicoaching.co.uk
LinkedIn: www.linkedin.com/in/margaret-chapman-clarke

—----------

Peter Young (BSc Biology, MA Psychological Coaching) has been independently coaching, training and facilitating in organisations since 2001. His long-standing passion has been to help organisations to perform at their best and to be great places for human beings! He's to be found in environments that span city law firms, start-ups, and global not-for-profits. Prior to becoming a coach he had a career in the book publishing industry, culminating in the role of Operations Director on the board of Lion Publishing plc.

Email: peter@bladonleadership.com
Website: www.bladonleadership.com
Linkedin: www.linkedin.com/in/peterjohnyoung

—----------

Petra Macdougald is internal Cross Divisional Lead Coach in Euroclear Bank, Brussels. She provides individual, team and group coaching at all levels of the company and is also responsible for the internal Job+ coach programme, the training of new coaches as well as supporting leadership development programmes. Her business career of 30 years in the finance industry prior to her full time coaching appointment mainly focused on roles relating to relationship management and strategy and included managing and developing teams. Petra's passion for personal development increased over the years in line with her involvement in people management. This interest led her to become involved in coaching and in 2012 she became an accredited business coach. Petra is an active member of the Belgian Internal Coaching Network and a Member of the Association for Coaching.

Email: petra.macdougald@euroclear.com

R Ramamurthy Krishna brings 30 years of multi industry, multinational culture experience. A Global Professional in Human Resources, A Professional Certified Coach from International Coach federation. He is the only Indian to be admitted to Association of Professional Executive Coaching and Supervision, United Kingdom. Krishna bring a rare flavour of neuroscience to leadership having been certified by Neuroleadership institute, Australia. An active blogger, author and speaker. He is also one of the few persons in Chennai to run his own Executive Coaching School. He held senior leadership position in Human resources in Multi National Organisation and presently engages himself as Practicing Cognitive Transformationsist and Perspective Partner with Potential Genesis HR Services LLP.

Email: rrk@potentialgenesis.com
Website: www.potentialgenesis.com

——----------

Robbie Swale. I am a career and leadership coach. I work with clients to help them to find their path and be extraordinary as they walk it. I have led a varied career in the private, public and charity sectors, including five years of working in arts and culture, as a venue manager and then subsequently in training, career and leadership development. Alongside my coaching work - for my coaching business and for other organisations like Coachingpartner and the Coaching School - I write a regular blog on LinkedIn and occasional longer posts.

Email: robbie@robbieswalecoaching.com
Website: www.robbieswalecoaching.com
Linkedin: https://www.linkedin.com/in/robbieswale/

——----------

Rosemary Harper is the Joint Managing Partner at Keary Harper LLP. She has coached for 23 years at board and executive level in the UK and internationally. She has led major coaching interventions, and coached many management teams, and has accrued well over 10,000 hours of face to face coaching. Her business background includes becoming the first female director at BAe Systems. Rosemary is an Accredited individual and team coach with APECS.

Email: rosemary@kearyharper.co.uk
Website: http://www.kearyharper.co.uk/

Sally East. I am currently working as a freelance career coach predominantly for an organisation that provides assessments and coaching for young people in schools to help them to make decisions relating to A levels, Further and Higher Education, and careers. I also work with adults looking for career transitions. The test that I use looks at aptitudes, interests and personality, and helps individuals to gain an insight into these relating to the work environment. My background of teaching in pre and post compulsory education within a largely widening participation environment enables me to help individuals explore their skills, interests and their own personality, and to maximise this within their career choices.

Email: sallyeast@ntlworld.com
Linkedin: https://uk.linkedin.com/in/sally-east-b4a22749

——----------

Simon Darnton works with leaders, entrepreneurs and executives who want to explore important questions, develop themselves or their organisations, and improve performance. He draws on a unique blend of business, psychology, and extreme sports experience, working in collaboration with clients to effectively navigate their personal and professional challenges. He holds an MA in Psychological Coaching. He also teaches Tai Chi Chuan.

Email: info@simondarnton.com
Website: www.simondarnton.com

——----------

Simon Dennis has over 20 years' experience of service delivery and continuous improvement in a variety of roles and industry sectors. He trained as a coach and coach supervisor and, as Head of Coaching at Fujitsu UK & Ireland, he established a Coaching Community utilizing internal and external coaches to meet the business need for performance improvement and provided a basis for establishing a coaching competency for the organisation. He has continued as a coaching ambassador for Fujitsu, presenting at conferences and contributing to publications and professional bodies in order to promote the use of coaching for performance and particularly internal coaching as a valid and valued approach. He is married with two daughters and lives in Manchester, North-West England.

Email: simon_dennis@sky.com
Linkedin: https://www.linkedin.com/in/simon-dennis-b81a2a3/

Sue Young, (MSc CMC IC, MAC, APECS) has worked for over 25 years in the UK and Europe with senior and middle levels of management as an OD Consultant, Executive Coach and Leadership Team Coach in a range of private, public sector and not-for-profit organisations. She enables greater leadership at all levels in an organisation, engaging people in organisational and cultural change. She has developed specialisms in working with High Potential individuals and groups from traditionally social disadvantaged backgrounds, helping them realise their leadership potential, and in developing coaching skills and attributes for Health professionals, and organisations' specialist internal coaches.

Email: sue.young@innovapartnership.co.uk
Website: www.innovapartnership.co.uk

———----------

Yvonne Thackray's field of specialism is coaching - a mega multidisciplinary subject - that works across many disciplines and hierarchical levels. She is a practicing coach, researcher, author, blogger, the snipper whapper and editor. Yvonne has almost a decade of experience in coaching coaches and other international clients across various industries and levels. She founded the good coach and currently serves as one of its Directors to ensure that the good coach's approach is in-line with best practices for achieving real independence and building a representative practitioner knowledge base. #sharingthevoicesofcoaching

Email: yvonne@the-goodcoach.com
Website: www.the-goodcoach.com
Linkedin: YvonneThackray

GUIDELINES TO BLOGGING

We see blogging as a form of practitioner research, and a meaningful approach to personal and professional development in coaching.

Encouraging coaches to blog about their practice takes on and expands on, how blogs are currently being shared. We hope that after reading the blogs, this has inspired you to share too.

Sharing your coaching experience is a courageous act in itself. Writing expends more energy because it requires conscious thinking and sense making of what is actually happening during the process of coaching.

Importantly, blogs are individual expressions that start with one's own word in order to bring out the ambition of being the best each coach can be.

Reach out to us and let us know what you would like to blog about, or even send your blog to the blogitoral team, who will be your first point of contact (email: blogs@the-goodcoach.com).

- We will read your blogs carefully and with respect, and offer any 'light' touch support that you might require (which may be none or a little) before we all agree to publish.

- We may also suggest edits for clarity as part of the publishing process.

- We have no set rules for blog length - it's open to you to write as much (~2000 words) or as little (~500 words) as you wish.

- Once we've published your blog, you'll be informed when someone posts a comment.

- We moderate all the comments as they come in, but if you're ever worried about this, just contact us.

TIPS for writing a blog

- **Context:** Coaching is a big subject ... still developing ... and everyone does it from their own way – which is why we need to recognise this and appreciate it more

- **Sharing our knowledge:** Blogging here is about sharing your own experiences, and practice, in doing coaching

- **Share your knowledge:** We invite you to share your experience of how you live it, and make sense of it

So ....

1. What headline(s) do you want to talk about?
Be guided to something you feel positive and strongly about what you have been doing – in what coaching is about as you see it. (Remember a lot of people are finding they have been doing what is now called coaching for quite a time, or they just see it called something else!) And where you would feel good to have had a go at explaining it in ways others could appreciate.

2. Why do you think that matters?
This isn't a race or a comparison exercise. It's about you and what is important to you. That is what matters – in whatever aspect it comes to you. This is about talking about yourself – not others!

3. What part(s) of your experience and practice were this headline involved in?
Be detailed and expansive about how you saw what was going on, how you were involved, and how you saw things working, as well as reports from the others involved. At the same time, please be general/impersonal about the actual examples. We don't need to know the content details – for reasons of confidentiality – about the practice you are talking about.

4. Linking to the wider languages/disciplines
Making sense may involve expressing yourself, in your own words, and also offering some linkages to some of the current popular words you have come across to use in referring to what you are talking about. We are still building common language/agreed terms and there is still important diversity in how people feel it is best to refer to this multifaceted area of coaching practice.

5. What are some possible further steps/questions that could be useful for others to consider for themselves in what you have been talking about
Blogs are short summaries – not long detailed research reports, so there is a license to say more and say it more freely. We are celebrating your experiences in a blog, rather than fitting in with what someone else says was the right thing to do. It's about what you believe works for you in working with coaching with others.

FINALLY...

- **Have fun whilst you write** – start anywhere and just write, and if there is an image/video clip/quote that helps make your point add it. There is always time to go back and edit. For now, just go with the flow of writing.

- **Be comfortable with your style** – it's not about conformity, it's about diversity and the freedom to express your experiences of coaching in your own style and approach.

- **More than just writing** – explore all the creative ways that you'd like to share your knowledge whether as a passage of writing, a paragraph of text with some bullet points, or as a poem. Enjoy the experience, and you're readers will too.

- **We've got you** – if you don't feel like your blog reads well, whether it's around the flow of the blog or being grammatically correct, don't worry. We are here to provide that 'light' touch and support.

OUR POSITION AROUND COPYRIGHT

Following the UK Copyright Law (who are members of the Berne Convention for the Protection of Literary and Artistic Works) any leading practitioner (author) who publishes their blog through the good coach (automatically) owns the copyright of their specific piece of work. The author, to their best of their abilities, has checked that any referenced materials are fair use, appropriately referenced, fact-checked, and where necessary sought the necessary permission for use.

Under the Creative Commons Attribution 4.0 International license the author (licensors) gives the good coach permission to distribute, remix, tweak and build upon your work, even commercially, as long as the good coach credits you for the original creation.

BIBLIOGRAPHY & REFERENCES

Albrecht, G.A. and C. Brooke, D. H. Bennett and S. T. Garnett. 2013. "The Ethics of Assisted Colonization in the Age of Anthropogenic Climate Change." In *Journal of Agricultural and Environmental Ethics* 26: 831.

Armand, Jean-Louis. 2012. "The bringing together of technology, sustainability and ethics." In *Sustainability Science* 7 (2): 113-116.

Arnaldi, S. 2012. "The end of history and the search for perfection. Conflicting teleologies of transhumanism and (neo)liberal democracy." In *Neoliberalism and Technoscience: Critical Assessments*. Edited by Luigi Pellizzoni and Marja Ylonen. Ashgate Publishing.

Argyris, Chris., and Schön, Donald. 1974. *Theory in Practice: Increasing Professional Effectiveness*. San Francisco: Jossey-Bass.

Attia, Peter. 2013. "Mega-sized concerns from the nano-sized world: The intersection of nano- and environmental ethics", In *Science & Engineering Ethics* 19: 1007-1016.

Bachkirova, Tatiana, Gordon Spence and David Drake. 2017. *The SAGE Handbook of Coaching*. SAGE Publications. Ltd. https://us.sagepub.com/en-us/nam/the-sage-handbook-of-coaching/book245418#description Accessed September 12.

Bandura, Albert. 1997. "Self-efficacy: Toward a Unifying Theory of Behavioural Change." In *Psychological Review* 84: 191-215.

Bandura, Albert. 1994. "Self-Efficacy." In *Encyclopaedia of Human Behaviour* 4: 71-81. New York: Academic Press.

Banerjee, Subhabrata. 2007. *Corporate Social Responsibility - The Good, the Bad and the Ugly*. Cheltenham: Elgar Press.

Bauer, Talya, and Berrin Erdogan. 2012. "Chapter 3 - Understanding People at Work: Individual Differences and Perceptions." In *An Introduction to Organizational Behaviour*. https://2012books.lardbucket.org/books/an-introduction-to-organizational-behavior-v1.1/s07-understanding-people-at-work-i.html Accessed September 11.

Bernstein, Nicholai. 1996. *Dexterity and Its Development (Resources for Ecological Psychology)*. Edited by Turvey. Mahwah, NJ: Lawrence Erlbaum Associates, Inc.

Berry, Thomas. 1988. *The Dream of the Earth*. San Francisco, CA: Sierra Club Books.

Bion, Wilfred Ruprecht. 1970. *Attention and Interpretation*. Tavistock Publications.

Blanchard, Ken. 2007. *Situational Leadership II: The Integrating Concept in Leadership at a Higher Level*. FT Prentice Hall.

Boyce, Mary. 1979. *Zoroastrians. Their Religious Beliefs and Practices*: 84. London: Routledge and Kegan Paul.

Brammer, Stephen, Gregory Jackson, and Dirk Matten. 2012. "Corporate societal responsibility and institutional theory: new perspectives on private governance." In *Socio-Economic Review* 10: 3-28.

Bramwell, Anna. 1989. *Ecology in the 20th Century. A History*. New Haven, Yale.

Briggs, J. 1998. *Inuit Morality Play: The Emotional Education of a Three-Year-Old*. New Haven, CT: Yale University Press.

Buell, Frederick. 2010. 'A short history of environmental apocalypse'. *Future ethics: climate change and apocalyptic imagination*. Edited by Skrimshire,S. Continuum Press: London.

Carkhuff, Robert. 1969. *Helping and Human Relations (Vol 1 and 2)*. New York, NY: Holt, Rhinehart and Winston.

Cennamo, Carmelo, Pascual Berrone, and Luis R. Gomez-Majia. 2009. "Does stakeholder management have a dark side?" In *Journal of Business Ethics* 89 (4): 491-507.

Chan, Benedict. 2015. "Animal Ethics, International Animal Protection and Confucianism." In *Global Policy* 692: 172-175.

Chan, Gary. 2008. "The Relevance and Values of Confucianism in Contemporary Business Ethics." In *Journal of Business Ethics* 77: 347-360.

Chandler, Steve and Rich Litvin. 2013. *The Prosperous Coach: Increase Income and Impact for You and Your Clients*. Maurice Bassett.

Chapman-Clarke, Margaret. 2015. "Coaching for Compassionate Resilience Through Creative Methods" in Hall, L. Coaching in *Times of Crisis and Transformation*.

Chapman-Clarke, Margaret. 2016. "Discovering Autoethnography as a research genre, methodology and method: The Yin and Yang of Life", In *the Transpersonal Psychology Review*. 18 (2) http://shop.bps.org.uk/publications/transpersonal-psychology-review-vol-18-no-2-autumn-2016.html.

Chemero, Anthony. 2010. "An Outline of a Theory of Affordances." In *Ecological Psychology* 15 (2): 181-195.

Clardy, Alan. 2005. "Andragogy: Adult Learning and Education at its Best?" *ERIC*. http://eric.ed.gov/?id=ED492132. Accessed September 4.

Clarkson, Petruska. 1989. *Gestalt Counselling in Action*. Series Editor Windy Dryden.

Clutterbuck, David. 2007. *Coaching the Team at Work*. London:Nicholas Brearley.

Cohn, Norman. 2001. *Cosmos, Chaos & the World to Come. The Ancient Roots of Apocalyptic Faith*: 105, 1063, 215. 2nd ed. New Haven: Yale University Press.

Collier, Paul. 2010. *The Plundered Planet*. London: Penguin.

Collins English Dictionary – Complete and Unabridged. 2014. 12th Edition. HarperCollins.

Cooley, Charles Horton. 1922. *Human Nature and the Social Order*. New York: Charles Scribner's Sons.

Cramer, Phebe. 2000. "Defense mechanisms in psychology today: Further processes for adaptation". In *American Psychologist*, 55 (6): 637-646.

Crane, Andrew, Guido Palazzo, and Laura Spence. 2014. "Contesting the value of creating shared value." In *California Management Review* 56 (2): 130-153. http://www.dirkmatten.com/Papers/C/Crane%20et%20al%202014%20in%20CMR.pdf Accessed September 11.

Curry, Patrick. 2011. *Ecological Ethics. An Introduction*. Cambridge: Polity Press.

Danowski, Deborah and Eduardo De Castro. 2017. *The Ends of the World*. Translated by Nunes. Cambridge: Polity.

Davary, Bahar. 2012. "Islam and Ecology: Southeast Asia, Adat and the Essence of Keramat." In *ASIA Network Exchange*. 20 (1): 12-22.

De Geuss, Arie. 1997. 'The living company." In *Harvard Business Review* 75 (Mar-Apr): 52-59.

Desrochers, Pierre. 2010. "The environmental responsibility of business is to increase its profits (by creating value within the bounds of private property rights)." In *Industrial and Corporate Change* 19 (1): 161-204.

Drees, Willem. 2013. "Islam and Biomedical Ethics". In *Zygon*, 48 3: 733-744.

Dyer, Gwynne. 2010. *Climate Wars: The Fight for Survival as the World Overheats*. Oxford: Oneworld: 183.

English Oxford Living Dictionary. 2017. https://en.oxforddictionaries.com/definition/trust Accessed September 10.

Esty, Daniel, and Andrew Winston. 2009. *Green to Gold. How smart companies use environmental strategy to innovate, create value, and build competitive advantage*. Hoboken NJ: John Wiley.

Evans, Jonathan. 2008. "Dual processing accounts of reasoning, judgement and social cognition." In *Annual Review of Psychology* 59: 255-278.

Ewen, Robert. 1993. *An Introduction to Theories of Personality*. Psychology Press.

Fiedler, F. 1978. "The Contingency Model and the Dynamics of the Leadership Process." In *Advances in Experimental Social Psychology* 11: 59-112.

Flaherty, James. 1999. *Coaching: Evoking Excellence in Others*. MA: Elsevier Burlington.

French, John and Bertram Raven. 1959. The Bases of Social Power. In D. Cartwright and A. Zander. *Group dynamics*. New York: Harper & Row.

Gallwey, Timothy. 1986. *The Inner Game of Tennis*. PAN Books.

Gao, J. and P. Bansal. 2013. "Instrumental and integrative logics in business sustainability." In *Journal of Business Ethics* 112: 241-255.

Geels, Frank and Johan Schot. 2007. "Typology of sociotechnical transition pathways." In *Research Policy* 36: 399-417.

Ghoshal, Sumantra. 2005. "Bad management theories are destroying good management practices." In *Academy of Management Learning and Education* 491: 75-91.

Gibson, James. 1979. *The Ecological Approach to Visual Perception*. Boston: Houghton Mifflin.

Gilbert, S., and M. Lucas and E. Turner. June 2014. 4th International Supervision Conference. http://business.brookes.ac.uk/commercial/work/iccms/coaching-supervision-conference/2014/.

Gigerenzer, Gerd. 2008. *Gut Feelings: The Intelligence of the Unconscious*. Penguin Books.

Gladwell, Malcolm. 2005. *Blink*. Penguin.

Godin, Seth. 2012. *The Icarus Deception: How High Will You Fly?* Portfolio Penguin.

Goffee, Robert and Gareth Jones. 2000. "Why should anyone be led by you?' In *Harvard Business review*.

Goodpaster, Kenneth. 1991. "Business ethics and stakeholder analysis." In *Business Ethics Quarterly* 1 (1): 53-73.

Green, Bill. 2009. *Understanding and Researching Professional Practice*. Edited by Bill Green. Sense Publishers.

Guillebeau, Chris. 2012. *The $100 Startup*. Currency.

Hahn, T., J. Pinkse. and L. Preuss. 2015. "Tensions in corporate sustainability: Towards an integrative framework." In *Journal of Business Ethics* 127: 297-316.

Hall, John. 2009. *Apocalypse. From Antiquity to the Empire of Modernity*. Cambridge: Polity.

Hall, Liz. 2014. "Mindful coaching." *Mastery in Coaching, A Completely Psychological Toolkit For Advanced Coaching*. Edited by Jonathan Passmore. Kogan Page.

Haq, S. Nomanul. 2001. "Islam and Ecology: Toward Retrieval and Reconstruction." In *Daedalus* 130 4: 141-177.

Harter, Susan. 2002. "Authenticity." *Handbook of Positive Psychology*: 382-394. Edited by C.R. Snyder and S Lopez. Oxford, UK: Oxford University Press.

Hawkins Peter. 2014. *Leadership Team Coaching, Developing Collective Transformational Leadership* Ed 2. Kogan Page.

Hawkins, Peter, and Nick Smith. 2011. *Coaching, Mentoring and Organizational Consultancy: Supervision and Development.* Maidenhead, Berks: McGraw-Hill.

Hedlund-de Witt, Annick. 2014. "The integrative worldview and its potential for sustainable societies: A qualitative exploration of the views and values of environmental leaders." In *Worldviews, Culture, Religion* 18 (3): 191-229.

Heft, Harry. 2001. *Ecological Psychology in Context: James Gibson, Roger Barker, and the Legacy of William James's Radical Empiricism (Resources for Ecological Psychology).* Mahwah, NJ: Lawrence Erlbaum Associates, Inc.

Heidegger, Martin. 1962. *Being and Time.* Translated by J. Macquarie and E. Robinson. San Francisco, CA: Harper.

Hodder, A. 1989. *Emerson's Rhetoric of Revelation. Nature, the Reader and the Apocalypse Within*: 24.33.71. London: Pennsylvania University Press.

Hulme, M. 2010."Four meanings of climate change", *Future ethics: climate change and apocalyptic imagination.* Edited by Skrimshire,S. Continuum Press: London.

Jarrett, Lonny S. 2004. *Nourishing Destiny: The Inner Tradition of Chinese Medicine.* Stockbridge: Spirit Path Press.

Jonas, Hans. 1984. The Imperative of Responsibility. In *Search of an Ethics for the Technological Age*: 62-63. Chicago: University of Chicago Press.

Jordan, Martin. 2009. "Back to Nature." *Therapy Today* April: 26-28; Russell, Peter. 1982. The Awakening Earth, London: Arcana.

Jung, Hwa. 2013. "A Prolegomenon to Transversal Geophilosophy." In *Environmental Philosophy* 10 1: 83-112.

Kahn, Kamran, and S. Ramachandran. 2012. "Conceptual framework for performance assessment: Competency, competence and performance in the context of assessments in healthcare – Deciphering the terminology." In *Medical Teacher* 34 11.

Kahneman, Daniel. 2011. *Thinking, fast and slow.* London: Penguin Books.

Kaiser, David and Lee Wasserman. 2016. "The Rockefeller family fund vs. Exxon." In *The New York Review of Books*: 31-35. December 22.

Kaplan, Robert and Robert Kaiser 2003. "Developing Versatile Leadership." In *MITS Loan Management Review* 44 4: 19-26.

Keidel, Robert. 1995. *Seeing Organizational Patterns: A New Theory & Language of Organizational Design.* San Francisco: Berrett-Koehler.

Kernis M.H. and B.M. Goldman . 2005. "From thought and experience to behaviour and interpersonal relationships: A multicomponent conceptualisation of authenticity." In *On building defending and regulating the self: A psychological perspective*: 31-52. Edited by A. Tesser, J.V. Wood and D.A Stael. New York: Psychological Press.

Kets de Vries, M. F. R., E. Florent-Treacy and K. Korotov. 2013. "Psychodynamic Issues in Organizational Leadership". In The Wiley-Blackwell *Handbook of the Psychology of Leadership, Change and Organizational Development*, New Jersey.

Kets de Vries, M. F. R. 2005. "Leadership group coaching in action: The Zen of creating high performance teams". In *Academy of Management.*

Kierkegaard, Soren. 1846. *Concluding unscientific postscript: Kierkegaard's writings* Vol 12.1.

MacIntyre, Alasdair. 2007. *After Virtue*: 25-27. Indiana: University of Notre Dame Press. Translated by Howard V. Hong and Edna H. Hong. New Jersey: Princeton University Press.

Kilmann, Thomas. 2007. *Conflict Mode Instrument.* Mountain View, CA: CPP, Inc.

Kleeberg, Bernhard. 2007. "God-nature Progressing: Natural Theology in German monism." In *Science in Context* 20 3: 547.

Klein, Gary. 2003. *Intuition at work*. New York: Currency Doubleday.

Knowles, Malcolm. 1984. *Andragogy in Action*. San Francisco: Jossey-Bass.

Korthals, Michiel. 2008. "Ethical rooms for maneuver and their prospects vis-à-vis the current ethical food policies in Europe." In *Journal of Agricultural and Environmental Ethics* 21 (3): 249-273.

Kumar, Satish. 2013. *Soil, Soul, Society. A New Trinity for Our Time*. Lewes: Leaping Hare Press.

LaFargue, Michael. 1992. *The Tao of the Tao Te Ching*. Albany: State University of New York Press.

Larre, Claude. and Elisabeth Rochat de la Vallee. 1996. *The Seven Emotions: Psychology and Health in Ancient China*. King's Lynn: Monkey Press.

Lo, Y. 2001. "The Land Ethic and Callicot's Ethical System (1980-2001: An Overview and Critique." *Inquiry* 44 3: 334.

Lowcarbonworks, Bath. 2009. Centre for Action Research in Professional Practice (CARRP), Insider Voices, Human Dimensions of Low Carbon Technology. University of Bath conference 14/7/09.

Matthews, Freya. 2011. "Towards a deeper philosophy of biomimicry." *Organisation & Environment* 24 (4): 364-387.

McEwen, Ian. 2010. *Solar*. London: Cape.

Mebratu, Desta. 1998. "Sustainability and Sustainable Development: Historical and Conceptual Review." In *Environmental Impact Assessment Review* 18 6: 493-520.

Mou, Bo. 2009. *History of Chinese Philosophy (Routledge History of World Philosophies)*. Edited by Bo Mou. Abingdon: Routledge.

Nair, Chandran. 2011. *Consumptionics. Asia's Role in Reshaping Capitalism and Saving the Planet*. Oxford: Infinite Ideas.

Nuyen, Anh. 2008. "Ecological Education: What Resources are there in Confucian Ethics?" In *Environmental Education Research* 14(2): 187-197.

O'Neill, Mary Beth. 2000. *Executive Coaching with Backbone and Heart*: 91-11, San Francisco CA: Jossey-Bass.

Orme, Joan and David Shemmings. 2010. *Developing Research Based Social Work Practice*: 174. Palgrave.

Page, Kogan. 2012. "Psychometrics in Coaching." In *Using Psychological and Psychometric Tools for Development*. Edited by Jonathon Passmore. Kogan Page.

Pellizzoni, L. 2011. "Governing through disorder: neoliberal environmental governance and social theory." *Global Environmental Change* 21: 795-803.

Pellizzoni, L. and M. Ylonen. 2008. "Responsibility in uncertain times: an institutional perspective on precaution." *Global Environmental Politics* 8 (3): 51-73.

Pfister, Lauren. 2007. "Environmental Ethics and Some Probing Questions for Traditional Chinese Philosophy." In *Journal of Chinese Philosophy* 34: 101-123.

Poon, Joanna and Mike Hoxley. 2010. "Use of moral theory to analyse the ethical codes of built environment professional organisations..." In *International Journal of Law in the Built Environment*, 2 (3): 260-275.

Porter, M. and Kramer, M. 2011 and 2006. "Creating Shared Value." And "Strategy and society: the link between competitive advantage and corporate societal responsibility." In *Harvard Business Review*, Jan-Feb: 63-77, and in Harvard Business Review 84 (12): 78-92.

Pressfield, Steven. 2012. *The War of Art: Break Through the Blocks and Win Your Inner Creative Battles*. Edited by Shawn Coyne. Black Irish Entertainment LLC.

Purdy, Jedediah. 2015. *After Nature: A Politics for the Anthropocene.* Cambridge: Harvard University Press.

Reed, Edward. 1996. *Encountering the World.* New York: Oxford University Press.

Rees, Martin. 2003. *Our Final Century. Will Civilisation Survive the Twenty-First Century?* London: Random House.

Reeves, Martin, Simon Levin and Daichi Ueda. 2016. "The Biology of Corporate Survival." *Harvard Business Review.* Jan: 47-55.

Revans, Reginald. 1984. *Action Learning: Back to Square One, in The Sequence of Managerial Achievement.* Bradford: MCB University Press.

Ridge, Jeremy. 1970. *The Role of Experience in Management Decision Making* - MSc in Applied Psychology. The University of Aston. (Available to download https://www.the-goodcoach.academy/).

Ridge, Jeremy. 1975. *The Development and Operation of the Effective Interpersonal Relationship Skills relevant to Career Development Problems from Staff Assessment at an Industrial Research Laboratory* – PhD. The University of Aston. (Available to download https://www.the-goodcoach.academy/).

Ridley, Matt. 2015. *The Evolution of Everything.* How Ideas Emerge. New York: Harper Collins.

Rochat de la Vallee, Elisabeth. 2009. Wu Xing: *The Five Elements in Chinese Classical Texts.* Monkey Press.

Rose, N. 1999. *Governing the Soul: Shaping of the Private Self.* Free Association Books.

Santana, Adele. 2012. "Three elements of stakeholder legitimacy." In *Journal of Business Ethics* 105 (2): 257-265.

Schaltegger, Stefan., Erik Hansen., and Florian Ludeke-Freund. 2015. "Business models for sustainability: Origins, present research, and future avenues." In *Organization and Environment* 29: 1-8 (1).

Scharmer, Otto. 2009. *Theory U: Leading from the Future as it Emerges.* Berrett-Koehler Publishers.

Scherer, Andreas. and Palazzo, Guido. 2010. "The new political role of business in a globalized world: A review of a new perspective on CSR and its implications for the firm, governance and democracy." In *Journal of Management Studies* 48 (4): 899-931.

Schön, Donald. 1983. *The Reflective Practitioner: How Professionals Think In Action.* Basic Books.

Scott, Daniel, Michael Hall and Stefan Gössling. 2016. "A review of the IPCC Fifth Assessment and implications for tourism sector climate resilience and decarbonization." *Journal of Sustainable Tourism* 24 (1): 10.

Sivin, Nathan. 1990. "Science and Medicine in Chinese History." In *Heritage of China: Contemporary Perspectives on Chinese Civilisation.* Edited by Paul S, Ropp. Berkeley: University of California Press.

Skiffington, Suzanne., and Perry Zeus. 2000. *Behavioural coaching: How to build sustainable personal and organisational strength.* Sydney: McGraw-Hill.

Skrimshire, Stefan. 2010. *Future Ethics. Climate change and apocalyptic imagination.* London: Continuum.

Smith, K. 2008. "How Immigration May Affect Environmental Stability." In *Scientific American.*

Soundararajan, Vivek., and Brown, Jill. 2016. "Voluntary Governance Mechanisms in Global Supply Chains: Beyond CSR to a Stakeholder Utility Perspective." In *Journal of Business Ethics* 134: 95-96.

Stein, Guido. 2010. *Managing People and Organisations: Peter Drucker's Legacy.* Emerald Group Publishing Limited.

Strozzi-Heckler, Richard. 2014. *The Art of Somatic Coaching: Embodying Skilful Action, Wisdom and Compassion.* North Atlantic Books.

Sylvan, Richard, and David Bennett. 1994. *The Greening of Ethics. From Human Chauvinism to Deep-green Theory.* Cambridge: White Horse Press: 91,137.

Taylor, Peter. 2009. *Chill. A reassessment of global warming theory.* Forest Row: Clairview.

Thackray, Yvonne, 2014. *Building Towards an Anthropology of Coaching: Constructing Identity-* MSc. University College London. (Available to download https://www.the-goodcoach.academy/).

Ti, Huang. 1995. *The Yellow Emperor's Classic of Medicine*. Translated by Maoshing Ni. Boston: Shambhala.

Trüngpa, Chogyam. 1984. *The Sacred Path of the Warrior*. Shambhala Dragon Editions.

Tulpa, Katherine. 2006. "Coaching Within Organizations." In *Excellence in Coaching*: 26-43. Edited by Passmore, J. London: Kogan Page.

Unschuld, Paul. 1985. *Medicine in China: A History of Ideas*. Berkeley: University of California Press.

Vanclay, Frank. 2004. "The triple bottom line and impact assessment: How do TBL, EIA, SEA and EMS relate to each other?" In *Journal of Environmental Assessment Policy and Management*, 6 (3):266.

Van der Byl, C. and Natalie Slawinski. 2015. "Embracing tensions in corporate sustainability: A review of research from win-wins and trade-offs to paradoxes and beyond." In *Organization and Environment* 28 (1): 54-79.

Walker, P. 2017. "Peace, justice and corporate strategy." In *The Environmentalist* (May): 26-28.

Webster's New World College Dictionary. 2010. Cleveland, Ohio: Wiley Publishing, Inc. http://www.yourdictionary.com/tease#uJ7MhBsDdedBHRIJ.99 Accessed September 10.

Wexler, Mark. 2009. "Strategic ambiguity in emergent coalitions: the triple bottom line." In *Corporate Communications: An International Journal* 14 (1): 62-77.

Whitmore, John. 2001. *Coaching for Performance*. London: Nicholas Brealey.

Whitworth, Laura, Karen Kimsey-House, Henry Kimsey-House and Philip Sandal. 1998. *Coactive Coaching*. CA: P Palo Alto.

Winnicott, D.W., 1960. "The Theory of the Parent-Infant Relationship." In *The International Journal of Psychodynamics* 41: 585-595.

Wong, Pak-Hang. 2015. "Confucian Environmental Ethics, Climate Engineering, and the 'Playing God' Argument." In *Zygon* 50 1: 28-41.

Vygotsky, Lev. 1978. "Readings on the Development of Children." In *Mind in Society: The Development of Higher Psychological Processes*, 79-91. Harvard Cambridge, MA: University Press.

Young, Sue. 2007. *An Inquiry into the conditions that stimulate greater self-direction in learning in organisations*, – MSc. The University of Surrey. (Available to download https://www.the-goodcoach.academy/).

Zhang, Yanhua. 2007. *Transforming Emotions with Chinese Medicine*. Albany: State University of New York.

ONLINE REFERENCES

Berkley Consulting Group. 2004. *"Saving Executive Coaching from the Fad Graveyard."* Berkeley Consulting.http://www.berkeleyconsulting.com/Leadership/Saving%20Executive%20Coaching%20from%20the%20Exec%20Graveyard.pdf

Bizcom_coach. 2015. "What is Feedback?" *Business Communication.* http://bizcommunicationcoach.com/what-is-feedback-definition-of-feedback-in-communication/ Accessed September 9.

Bregman, P. 2017. Podcasts. http://peterbregman.com/podcast/alexis-stenfors-a-barometerof-fear/#.WZj2ExQo57Y

Buettner, Dan. 2008. "What is your Ikigai? How to Live to be 100+." *TED Talks.* https://www.ted.com/talks/dan_buettner_how_to_live_to_be_100 Accessed September 9.

Cholle, Francis. 2011. "What Is Intuition, And How Do We Use It?" *Psychology Today.* https://www.psychologytoday.com/blog/the-intuitive-compass/201108/what-is-intuition-and-how-do-we-use-it# Accessed September 11.

Cloke, Kenneth. 2017. *American Institute of Mediation.* http://www.americaninstituteofmediation.com/pg77.cfm Accessed September 10.

Consultants, Performance. 2017. *Our Values and Vision* https://www.performanceconsultants.com/values-vision

Darnton, Simon. 2001-2016. Inside the Minds of Motorcycle Racers. Simon Darnton. http://www.simondarnton.com/inside-the-minds-of-motorcycle-racers

Dreifus, Claudia. 2007. "Through Analysis, Gut Reaction Gains Credibility." *The New York Times.* http://www.nytimes.com/2007/08/28/science/28conv.html?_r=0 Accessed on September 9.

Flanders, Ian. 2016. "Dispatch From The Internal Coaching Front." *the good coach.* http://the-goodcoach.com/tgcblog/2016/9/21/dispatch-from-the-internal-coaching-front-by-ian-flanders-guest Accessed September 10.

Hefferman, M. 2017. "Silicon Valley is developing a trust deficit" *Financial Times.*

Hicks, Ben. 2010. "Team Coaching: A Literature Review." http://www.employment-studies.co.uk/system/files/resources/files/mp88.pdf Accessed September 10.

Hindmarch, Lynne. 2016. "Beyond Personality Assessments: What The Coach Can Learn About Patterns Of Behaviour And Their Implications: Anxiety (Part 1)" *the good coach.* https://the-goodcoach.com/tgcblog/2016/8/28/beyond-personality-assessments-what-the-coach-can-learn-about-patterns-of-behaviour-and-their-implications-anxiety-part-1-by-lynne-hindmarch Accessed September 10.

Holland, Steve. and Valerie Volcovici. 2017. "Trump clears way for controversial oil pipelines." *Reuters.* www.reuters.com/article/us-usa-trup-pipeline-idUSKBN15820N Accessed September 12.

Hutchins, Giles. 2015. "The next stage of organizational evolution." *Triple Pundit.* www.triplepundit.com/2015/05next-stage-organizational-evolution. (Broken link) Wednesday May 20th

Introduction to Individual Differences. 2001. "Introduction to Individual Differences." http://wilderdom.com/personality/L1-1Introduction.html Accessed September 10.

Kismatandkarma. 2013. "Power of Intuition: What Steve Jobs Learned in India." *Kismatandkarma*. https://kismatandkarma.wordpress.com/2013/12/01/power-of-intuition-what-steve-jobs-learned-in-india/ Accessed September 11.

Knufken, Drea. 2010. "The Top 25 Greenwashed Products In America". *Business Pundit*. www.businesspundit.com/the-top-25-greenwashed-products-in-america Accessed September 11.

Krishna, Ramamurthy. 2016. When Training Is Better Done Using a Coaching Approach. *the good coach*.https://the-goodcoach.com/tgcblog/2016/7/19/when-training-is-better-done-using-a-coaching-approach-a-practical-example-of-how-to-use-a-coaching-approach-when-people-still-call-it-training-by-r-ramamurthy-krishna-guest Accessed September 10.

Lanchester, John. 2016. "Brexit Blues." *London Review of Books* [Online] 38 15: 3-6. https://www.lrb.co.uk/v38/n15/john-lanchester/brexit-blues Accessed September 12.

Lewin, Kurt. 2013. "Lewin's field theory". *Kurt Lewin*. http://www.kurt-lewin.com/field-theory.shtml

Macfarlane, Robert. 2016. "Generation Anthropocene. How humans have altered the planet forever." *The Guardian* 02.04.16

Maddalena, Lucille. 2015. "Critical Assumptions in Coaching." *the good coach*. http://the-goodcoach.com/tgcblog/2016/3/7/critical-assumptions-in-coaching-by-lucille-maddalena-edd-guest. Accessed September 4.

Maddalena, Lucille. 2013. "On By – Taking the Risk." *Mtm Coach*. http://www.mtmcoach.com/on-by-taking-the-risk/ Accessed September 9.

McLeod, Saul. 2008 (Updated 2017). "Erik Erikson." *Simply Psychology*. https://www.simplypsychology.org/Erik-Erikson.html Accessed September 10.

Merriam-Webster. http://www.merriam-webster.com/dictionary/

Namka, Lynne. 2008. "Defense Mechanisms That Affect Relationships." https://byregion.byregion.net/articles-healers/Defense_Mechanisms.html. Accessed September 9.

PMA. 2017. "Welcome to the Professional Mediators' Association." http://www.professionalmediator.org Accessed September 10.

Ridge, Jeremy. 2017. "Teasing Out The Deeper Understanding Of How Coaching Works At Its Best – How Teasing, Itself, Can Be Productive." *the good coach*. https://the-goodcoach.com/tgcblog/2017/6/6/teasing-out-the-deeper-understanding-of-how-coaching-works-at-its-best-how-teasing-itself-can-be-productive-by-jeremy-ridge Accessed September 11.

Ridge, Jeremy. 2016. "Getting Trust is the Essential Outcome Which Makes Coaching Possibility – And Different." *the good coach*. http://the-goodcoach.com/tgcblog/2016/10/3/getting-trust-is-the-essential-outcome-that-makes-coaching-possible-and-different Accessed September 10.

Ridge, Jeremy. 2016. "Using a Research Approach to Learn From Coaching Experience." *the good coach*. https://the-goodcoach.com/tgcblog/2016/4/21/using-a-research-approach-to-learn-from-coaching-experience-my-learning-about-coaching-readiness-as-an-example-by-jeremy-ridge Accessed September 12.

Ridge, Jeremy. 2016. "Attention! What Really Makes Coaching Work." *the good coach*. https://the-goodcoach.com/tgcblog/2016/2/19/attention-what-really-makes-coaching-work-or-not-by-jeremy-ridge#sthash.kMIE3Dat.dpuf Accessed September 9.

Ridge, Jeremy. 2015. "How We Can Define Coaching – 'Do It For Yourself.'" *the good coach*. http://the-goodcoach.com/tgcblog/2015/12/11/how-we-can-define-coaching-do-it-for-yourself-diy-by-jeremy-ridge Accessed September 11.

Ridge, Jeremy. 2015. "Smiling and Laughter Really Matter in Coaching." *the good coach*. http://the-goodcoach.com/tgcblog/2015/7/27/smiling-and-laughter-really-matter-in-coaching-by-jeremy-rid.html Accessed September 11.

Ridge, Jeremy. 2015. Freeing up our use of coaching! *the good coach*. https://the-goodcoach.com/tgcblog/2015/6/25/freeing-up-our-use-of-coaching-contrasting-the-simple-model.html Accessed September 10.

Roy, Nilanjana. 2016. "How to Stay Friends Across the Political Divide." *Financial Time*s. https://www.ft.com/content/2fc36578-ab23-11e6-ba7d-76378e4fef24 Accessed September 10.

Shanghaiist. 2017. "China is building a super adorable solar farm that's shaped like a panda." *Shanghaiist*. http://shanghaiist.com/2017/07/04/panda-solar-farm.php

Sherman, Stratford and Alyssa Freas. 2004. "The Wild West of Executive Coaching". In *Harvard Business Review*. https://hbr.org/2004/11/the-wild-west-of-executive-coaching

Simms, Jane. 2017. "There's more than one way to solve a problem". In *People Management*. CIPD. http://www2.cipd.co.uk/pm/peoplemanagement/b/weblog/archive/2017/07/25/there-s-more-than-one-way-to-solve-a-dispute.aspx

Skills You Need. "Approaches to Counselling." *SkillsYouNeed*. https://www.skillsyouneed.com/learn/counselling-approaches.html Accessed September 10.

Streep, Peg. 2014. "The Trouble With Trust." *Psychology Today*. https://www.psychologytoday.com/blog/tech-support/201403/the-trouble-trust Accessed September 10.

For the Taiji Classics see http://www.scheele.org/lee/classics.html

Thackray, Yvonne. 2015. "Making Sense Of What I Do, How My Coaching Practice Is Taking Shape." *the good coach*. https://the-goodcoach.com/tgcblog/2017/2/28/making-sense-of-what-i-do-how-my-coaching-practice-is-taking-shape-by-yvonne-thackray Accessed September 12.

Thackray, Yvonne. 2015. "Culture Driven From The Centre: Comparing Two Coaching Bodies." *the good coach*. https://the-goodcoach.com/tgcblog/2015/9/2/culture-driven-from-the-centre-comparing-two-coaching-bodies.html. Accessed September 12.

Young, Sue. 2015. "Adult Learning – The Real Leading Edge of Coaching." *the good coach*. http://the-goodcoach.com/tgcblog/2015/7/21/adult-learning-the-real-leading-edge-of-coaching-by-sue-youn.html. Accessed September 9.

Unilever. 2017. *Sustainabile Living*. https://www.unilever.co.uk/sustainable-living/

University of Leeds. 2008. "Go With Your Gut – Intuition Is More Than Just a Hunch." *Science Daily*. https://www.sciencedaily.com/releases/2008/03/080305144210.htm Accessed September 10.

Wikipedia. https://en.wikipedia.org/

NOTES

NOTES

NOTES

www.ingramcontent.com/pod-product-compliance
Lightning Source LLC
Chambersburg PA
CBHW050452190326

41458CB00005B/1257